Practitioner Series

T0237883

Springer
London
Berlin
Heidelberg
New York
Hong Kong
Milan
Paris
Santa Clara
Singapore
Tokyo

Other titles in this series:

John Hunt

Java for Practitioners

An Introduction and Reference to Java and Object Orientation

Springer

John Hunt, BSc, PhD, MBCS, CEng
Department of Computer Science, University of Wales, Aberystwyth, Dyfed,
Wales, SY23 3DB

JayDee Technology, PO Box 153, Chippenham, SN14 8UT

ISBN-13:978-1-85233-093-4 Springer-Verlag London Berlin Heidelberg

British Library Cataloguing in Publication Data
Hunt, John
    Java for practitioners : an introduction and reference to
    Java and object orientation. - (Practitioner series)
    1.Java (Computer program language) 2. Object-oriented
    methods (Computer science)
    I.Title
    005.7'12'62
    ISBN-13:978-1-85233-093-4
Library of Congress Cataloging-in-Publication Data
Hunt, John, 1964-
    Java for practitioners : an introduction and reference to Java and
    object orientation / John Hunt.
        p.   cm. -- (Practitioner series)
    Includes index.
    ISBN-13:978-1-85233-093-4   e-ISBN-13:978-1-4471-0843-6
    DOI:10.1007/978-1-4471-0843-6

        1. Java (Computer program language)   I. Title.   II. Series:
    Practitioner series (Springer-Verlag)
    QA76.73.J38H865   1999
    005.13'3--dc21   98-49617

Apart from any fair dealing for the purposes of research or private study, or criticism or review, as permitted under the Copyright, Designs and Patents Act 1988, this publication may only be reproduced, stored or transmitted, in any form or by any means, with the prior permission in writing of the publishers, or in the case of reprographic reproduction in accordance with the terms of licences issued by the Copyright Licensing Agency. Enquiries concerning reproduction outside those terms should be sent to the publishers.

© Springer-Verlag London Limited 1999

The use of registered names, trademarks etc. in this publication does not imply, even in the absence of a specific statement, that such names are exempt from the relevant laws and regulations and therefore free for general use.

The publisher makes no representation, express or implied, with regard to the accuracy of the information contained in this book and cannot accept any legal responsibility or liability for any errors or omissions that may be made.

Typesetting: Ian Kingston Editorial Services, Nottingham UK

34/3830-543210 Printed on acid-free paper

Dedication

For Denise, Always

Contents

Preface

The aim of this book is to provide current practitioners with an introduction not only to Java, but also to the object-oriented model upon which Java is based. This is essential, as it is not possible to move from languages such as C and Pascal to Java without also moving to object orientation. This is indeed the problem with many Java books: they teach you only the language, and mostly ignore object orientation (or at best devote a single chapter to this). In many ways it is object orientation which is harder to learn (the Java syntax is relatively small and straightforward). It was because of this that I was motivated to write an earlier book aimed at those wishing to learn Java and object orientation. However, that book did not deal with the many issues in the Java platform which real-world developers must be familiar with. Thus the current work builds on the format of that book, but is divided into five parts.

Part 1 is entitled "Java and Object Orientation". It introduces both the Java language and object orientation. It leads the reader by the hand through both these (sometimes complex) subjects.

Part 2 is a "Developers' Handbook". It deals with many of the aspects of the Java platform (which includes the Java language, the Java Virtual Machine and the Java class libraries) that you will need to deal with in real systems. Each chapter in this section can be read in isolation as and when needed. It acts like a reference, but unlike many reference texts, it introduces any theoretical issues associated with a particular topic before providing a detailed description of how to handle the specific technique in Java, illustrating this by example and including further references.

Part 3 is entitled the "Java Art and Style". The chapters in this part tell you how to use best practice to write the most effective Java programs, how to ensure your Java programs are reliable and how to maximize the performance of your Java programs. It includes a Java exam for those of you who are interested in taking Sun's Java Programmer Certification examination.

Part 4 deals with "Object-Oriented Design", which is essential for the construction of well-formed Java programs. This part of the book presents an extended worked example which covers all the aspects of an object-oriented design. The design process described is based on the Object Modeling Technique, but uses the Unified Modeling Language notation.

The final part of the book looks to the future of the Java platform.

Content Summary

Part 1: Java and Object Orientation

Chapter 1: Introduction to Object Orientation
This chapter introduces the range of concepts and ideas which make up object technology. It presents the background that led to the acceptance of object orientation as a mainstream technology and discusses the pedigree of the Java language.

Chapter 2: Elements of Object Orientation
This chapter provides a more formal definition of the terminology introduced in Chapter 1. It also considers the advantages and disadvantages of an object-oriented approach compared with more traditional procedural approaches.

Chapter 3: Why Object Orientation?
This chapter presents the motivation behind the object-oriented (OO) model and compares and contrasts simple implementations in languages such as C and Pascal with how they would be achieved in an OO language (such as Java).

Chapter 4: Constructing an Object-Oriented System
A typical problem for many people when being introduced to a new approach is that they understand the terminology and the concepts, but not how to use them. This chapter aims to alleviate this problem by presenting a detailed worked example of the way in which an object-oriented system may be designed and constructed. It does so without reference to any particular language, so that language issues do not confuse the discussion.

Chapter 5: A Brief History of Time, the Universe and Java
This chapter provides some background on the history of Java and the development environments which are available to support it (such as the Sun Java Development Kit). It also considers some of the tools that you will encounter.

Chapter 6: Java 2 Platform: Java's Third Age?
This chapter considers the Java 2 Platform (previously known as Sun's Java Development Kit 1.2). This release introduces many new features which will be critical to Java's success in the commercial world.

Chapter 7: Basic Java
This chapter introduces the Java syntax and examines the structure of a basic Java application.

Chapter 8: Java Building Blocks
This chapter considers classes, instances, methods and variables, as well as interface specifications in Java. These are the basic building blocks of any object-oriented program, and in particular of a Java program.

Chapter 9: Java Constructs
This chapter presents further details of the Java language, including numbers, operators, variables and message passing. This chapter also looks at the `String`, `Integer` and `Character` classes.

Chapter 10: Control and Iteration
This chapter introduces control and iteration in Java. That is, it looks at `for` loops, `while` loops, `do` loops and control statements such as `if` and `switch`.

Chapter 11: The `Person` *Class*
This chapter presents you with a detailed worked example of software development in Java. This example presents a very simple class definition which uses only those concepts which have been introduced at this stage. The intention is to illustrate how the constructs and language elements can be combined in a real (if simple) application.

Chapter 12: Classes, Inheritance and Abstraction
This chapter considers how you should use inheritance, abstraction and classes in Java. It considers the role of classes and when to create subclasses and define abstract classes.

Chapter 13: Encapsulation and Polymorphism
This chapter considers how to achieve encapsulation in Java. It considers how the visibility of methods and variables can be modified. It presents packages and how they are defined and used. It also discusses issues associated with the polymorphic appearance of Java.

Chapter 14: Data Structures
This chapter discusses the Java classes which are used to construct data structures. These classes include `Array`, `Vector` and `Hashtable`.

Chapter 15: The Collection API
New in the Java 2 Platform are an extended set of data structure classes known collectively as the Collection classes. This chapter describes these classes in detail and considers when they should be used.

Chapter 16: An Object-Oriented Organizer
This chapter presents a detailed example application constructed using the `Vector` class. The application is an electronic personal organizer that contains an address book, a diary (or appointments section) and a section for notes. The remainder of this chapter describes one way of implementing such an organizer. At the end of this chapter is a programming exercise.

Part 2: Java Developers' Handbook

Chapter 17: Graphic Programming Using the Abstract Window Toolkit
The Abstract Window Toolkit (AWT) is a platform-independent set of classes for constructing graphical interfaces. This chapter looks at how to construct windows and generate graphics.

Chapter 18: User Interface Programming
This chapter considers the Java Delegation Event Model and the range of GUI construction classes in the AWT.

Chapter 19: Managing Component Layout
This chapter introduces the layout managers provided with the AWT. These objects control how components are laid out within an interface in a portable and useful manner.

Chapter 20: Putting the Swing into Java
This chapter introduces the Swing set of graphical components. It also describes how to move AWT-based interfaces to Swing-based interfaces.

Chapter 21: Swing Data Model Case Study
This chapter looks at the JTree Swing component as an example of a component which possesses a complex data model. To illustrate this, a simple class hierarchy viewer is presented.

Chapter 22: Observers and Observables
The Observer interface and Observable class are used to implement the Java dependency mechanism. This mechanism allows one or more objects to be informed about changes in the state of an object, without that object knowing anything about the first set of objects. It is particularly important in the construction of reusable object-oriented graphical user interfaces.

Chapter 23: A GUI Case Study
This chapter describes a detailed worked example of how to construct a user interface for the organizer application developed earlier in the book.

Chapter 24: Combining Graphics and GUI Components
This chapter brings together the graphic elements of Swing described in Chapter 20 with the user interface components described in previous chapters.

Chapter 25: Applets and the Internet
This chapter examines the facilities in Java for programming for the Internet. It introduces applets and URLs.

Chapter 26: Concurrency
This chapter describes the concurrency mechanism of Java. That is, it describes the way in which Java implements lightweight threads.

Chapter 27: Exception Handling
In Java, exceptions are objects (just like almost everything else). Thus, to throw an exception you must first make an instance of an exception class. This chapter considers exceptions and how to create, throw and handle them. It also discusses defining new exceptions by creating subclasses.

Chapter 28: Streams and Files
This chapter discusses one of the most common class hierarchies in Java, the Stream classes. The Stream classes are used (among other things) for accessing files.

Chapter 29: Serialization
This chapter explains how objects can be stored to file and restored from file using serialization. This provides a very basic persistent object system for Java.

Chapter 30: Sockets in Java
This chapter describes how sockets are implemented in Java.

Chapter 31: Java and Remote Method Invocation
Remote Method Invocation (or RMI) is one way of implementing distributed systems in Java. RMI is a very simple and effective. This chapter explains how RMI works as well as presenting a detailed worked example illustrating this.

Chapter 32: Servlets: Serving Java up on the Web
The power of Java can be applied to server side software as well as to client side software. This chapter tells you how servlets are written, what they are used for and how they interact with browser requests.

Chapter 33: Java Database Connectivity
JDBC (or the Java Database Connectivity API) is the method provided in Java to integrate relational databases with Java programs. This chapter explains how it works and how you should use it. A detailed example is provided.

Chapter 34: JavaBeans Software Components
This chapter introduces Java's component model, referred to as JavaBeans.

Chapter 35: Java Native Interface
The Java Native Interface (or JNI) provides a means for C programs and Java to be interfaced. This allows legacy systems to be easily and simply integrated into a Java program.

Chapter 36: Byte Code Protection
This chapter considers how the byte codes (or .class file) generated by the Java compiler can be protected from decompilation.

Chapter 37: Java, IDL and Object Request Brokers
This chapter considers Java's interface to the OMG IDL interface definition language for use with CORBA-compliant ORBs.

Chapter 38: Inner Classes and Reflection
This chapter looks at when, where and how you should use inner classes. It also introduces the reflection API, which allows flexible and highly reusable software to be written.

Part 3: Java Art and Style

Chapter 39: Java Style Guidelines
This chapter aims to promote readable, understandable, concise and efficient Java code.

Chapter 40: Common Java Bugs and Programmer Errors
This chapter looks at the types of bugs which can be introduced in Java programs and highlights some of the weaker areas of the Java language and implementation.

Chapter 41: Reliable Java Systems
This chapter considers the approaches which should be adopted to maximize the reliability of a Java program.

Chapter 42: Performance Optimization
Performance in Java systems is often cited as a problem. Therefore this chapter looks at how you can optimize your Java program.

Chapter 43: Java Self-Test Examination
This chapter presented a Java self-test examination which follows a similar format to that of Sun's Java Programmer Certification examination. This allows you to determine how well you know Java.

Part 4: Object-Oriented Design

Chapter 44: Object-Oriented Analysis and Design
This chapter introduces the concepts of object-oriented analysis and design. It reviews a number of the more popular techniques, such as OOA, OMT, Objectory and Booch. It also briefly considers the unification of the OMT and Booch notations.

Chapter 45: OMT and UML
This is a very brief chapter outlining the design method to be used for the remainder of this part of the book.

Chapter 46: Use Case Analysis
This chapter introduces the Use Case Analysis step of the design process being followed. It also introduces the case study used throughout this section of the book.

Chapter 47: The Analysis Phase: Object Modelling
This chapter describes the OMT analysis phase, which is concerned with producing a precise, concise, understandable and correct representation of the real world.

Chapter 48: The Analysis Phase: Dynamic Modelling
This chapter describes the dynamic modelling step of the analysis phase. The dynamic model describes the behaviour of the application and the objects which comprise that application.

Chapter 49: Functional Modelling and Operations
This chapter presents two ways of documenting a functional model of your system and considers how this functional model should be generated. It also addresses the association of operations to classes.

Chapter 50: The Design and Implementation Phases
This chapter considers the final two phases in the OMT design process. These are the design and implementation phases.

Part 5: The Future

Chapter 51: The Future for Java
This chapter brings together the many threads in this book and considers the future of object-oriented systems.

Typographical Conventions

In this book, the standard typeface is Minion. However, source code is set in Courier (for example, a = 2 + 3;). A bold font indicates Java keywords, for example:

```
public class Address extends Object {...}
```

Source Code

All source code examples are available on the Web at:

```
http://www.springer.co.uk/comp/support/
```

Trademarks

HotJava, HotJava Views, JavaChips, picoJava, microJava, UltraJava, JavaOS, JDBC, Java, Java Development Kit, Solaris, SPARC, SunOS and Sunsoft are trademarks of Sun Microsystems, Inc. VisualBasic, Visual C++, DOS, MS-DOS, Microsoft Windows and Windows 95 are registered trademarks of Microsoft Corporation. Apple is a registered trademark of Apple Computer, Inc. Café and VisualCafé are trademarks of Symantec Corporation. UNIX is a registered trademark of AT&T. The X Window System is a trademark of the Massachusetts Institute of Technology. All other brand names are trademarks of their respective holders.

Acknowledgements

I would like to thank Alex McManus (my co-author on *Key Java: Advanced Tips and Techniques*, also from Springer-Verlag) for many useful discussions on subjects presented in this book. His insightful questions and comments are always useful. Thanks should also go to those students who have unknowingly tested the design elements of this book and to Tim Huckvale for many useful and detailed comments. As always I would also like to thank my wife Denise for her patience with me during the book writing process.

Part 1

Java and Object Orientation

1 *Introduction to Object Orientation*

1.1 Introduction

This book is intended as an introduction to object orientation for software engineers and others who are actively involved in the software industry. It assumes familiarity with standard computing concepts such as stacks and memory allocation, and with a procedural language, such as C. From this background, it provides a practical introduction to object technology using Java, one of the newest and best pure object-oriented languages available.

This book introduces a variety of concepts through practical experience with an object-oriented language. It also tries to take you beyond the level of the language syntax to the philosophy and practice of object-oriented development.

In the remainder of this chapter, we will consider the various programming paradigms that have preceded object orientation. We will then examine the primary concepts of object orientation and consider how they enable object orientation to be achieved.

1.2 Programming Paradigms

Software construction is still more of an art than a science. Despite the best efforts of many software engineers, software systems are still delivered late, over budget and not up to the requirements of the user. This situation has been with us for many years. Indeed, the first conference to raise awareness of this problem was the NATO Software Engineering Conference of 1968, which coined the term *software crisis*. Since then a variety of programming paradigms have either been developed explicitly to deal with this issue or have been applied to it.

A programming paradigm embodies a particular philosophy. These philosophies usually represent an insight which sets a new type of best practice. For a programming language to support a particular paradigm, it must not just allow adoption of the paradigm (you can use object-oriented programming techniques in assembler, but would you want to?), it must actively support implementations based on the paradigm. This usually means that the language must support constructs which make development using that paradigm straightforward.

The major programming paradigms which have appeared in computer science can be summarized as follows:

- *Functional* Lisp is the classic example of a functional language, although by no means the only one (ML is a very widely used functional language). These languages place an emphasis on applying a function (often recursively) to a set of one or more data items. The function then returns a value – the result of evaluating the function. If the function changes data items, this is a side effect. There is limited support for algorithmic solutions which rely on repetition via iteration. The functional approach turned out to be an extremely useful way of implementing complex systems for early AI researchers.

- *Procedural* Pascal and C exemplify procedural languages, which attempt to move to a higher level than the earlier assembler languages. The emphasis is on algorithmic solutions and procedures which operate on data items. They are extremely effective, but software developers still encounter difficulties. This is partly due to the increased complexity of the systems being developed, but also because, although high-level procedural languages remove the possibility of certain types of error and increase productivity, developers can still cause problems for themselves. For example, the interfaces between different parts of the system may be incompatible, and this may not become obvious until integration or system testing.

- *Modular* In languages such as Modula 2 and Ada, a module hides its data from users. The users of the module can only access the data through defined interfaces. These interfaces are "published" so that users know the definitions of the available interfaces and can check that they are using the correct versions.

- *Object-oriented* This is the most recent "commercial" programming paradigm. The object-oriented approach can be seen as taking modularization a step further. Not only do you have explicit modules (in this case, objects), but these objects can inherit features from one another. We can of course ask "why another programming paradigm?". The answer to this lies partly in the failure of many software development projects to keep to budget, remain within time-scales and give the users what they want. Of course, it should not be assumed that object orientation is the answer to all these problems; it is just another tool available to software developers.

This book attempts to introduce the object-oriented programming paradigm through the medium of an object-oriented programming language. It assumes that the majority of readers have a background in at least one procedural language (preferably a C-like language), and compares and contrasts the facilities provided by an object-oriented language with a procedural language.

Object orientation, even though it is quite different in many ways from the procedural approach, has developed from it. You should therefore not throw away all that you have learnt using other approaches. Many of the good practices in other languages are still good practices in an object-oriented language. However, there are new practices to learn, as well as new syntax, but remember that it is much more than a process of learning a new syntax – you have a new philosophy to learn.

1.3 Revolution Versus Evolution

In almost every area of scientific endeavour there are periods of evolution followed by periods of revolution and then evolution again. That is, some idea or theory is held to be "accepted" (not necessarily true, but at least accepted). The theory is refined by successive experiments, discoveries etc. Then the theory is challenged by a new theory. This new theory is typically held by a small set of extremely fervent believers. It is often derided by those who are staunch supporters of the existing theory. As time continues, either this new theory is proved wrong and disappears, or more and more people are drawn to the new theory until the old theory has very few supporters.

There are many examples of this phenomenon in science: for example, the Copernican theory of the Earth rotating around the Sun, Einstein's theory of relativity and Darwin's theory of evolution. Men such as Darwin and those who led him to his discoveries were revolutionaries: they went against the current belief of the times and introduced a new set of theories. These theories were initially derided, but have since become generally accepted. Indeed, Darwin's theories are now being refined further. For example, Darwin believed in a mechanism for the fertilization of an egg derived from an old Greek theory (pangenesis). Every organ and tissue was assumed to produce granules which combined to make up the sex cells. Of course, we now believe this to be wrong and it was Darwin's own cousin, Francis Galton, who helped to disprove the pangenesis theory. It is unlikely that we will enter a new revolutionary phase which will overturn the theory of evolution; however, Einstein's theory of relativity is already being challenged.

Programming paradigms provide another example of this cycle. The move from low-level to high-level programming was a revolution (and you can still find people who will insist that low-level machine code programming is best). Object orientation is another revolution, which is still happening. Over the past ten years object orientation has become much more widely accepted, and you will find many organizations, both suppliers and users of software, giving it lip service. However, you will also find many in the computer industry who are far from convinced. A senior colleague of mine once told me that he believed that object orientation was severely over-hyped (which it may be) and that he really could not see the benefits it offered. I hope that this book will convince him (and others) that object orientation has a great deal to offer.

It is likely that something will come along to challenge object-oriented programming, just as it challenges procedural programming, as the appropriate software development approach. It is also likely that a difficult and painful battle will ensue, with software suppliers entering and leaving the market. Many suppliers will argue that their system always supported approach X anyway, while others will attempt to graft the concepts of approach X onto their system. When this will happen or what the new approach will be is difficult to predict, but it will happen. Until then, object orientation will be a significant force within the computer industry.

1.4 Why Learn a New Programming Paradigm?

The transition from a procedural viewpoint to an object-oriented viewpoint is not always an easy one. This begs the question "why bother?". As you are reading this book you must at least be partly convinced that it is a good idea. This could be because you have noticed the number of job advertisements offering employment for those with object-oriented skills. However, that aside, why should you bother learning a new programming paradigm?

I hope that some of the reasons will become clear during your reading of this book. It is worth considering at least some of the issues at this point.

1.4.1 Software Industry Blues

There is still no silver bullet for the problems in the software industry. Object-oriented technology does not remove the problems of constructing complex software systems, it just makes some of the pitfalls harder to fall into and simplifies traditionally difficult problems. However, difficulties in software development are almost inevitable; many of them arise due to the inescapable intangibility of software, and not necessarily all by accident or poor development methods.

We should not, however, just throw up our hands and say "well if that's the case, it's not my fault". Many of the problems which beset our industry relate to some deficiency in how programmers build software today. For example, if a software development project runs late, then merely adding more people to it is likely to make matters worse rather than get the project back on schedule.

Object technology is not the first attempt at addressing these issues. However, past attempts have met with mixed success for a number of reasons, some of which we consider below.

Modularity of Code

Traditional procedural systems typically relied on the fact that not only would the data they were using not change its type, for example, but the way in which they obtained that data would not alter. Invariably, the function (or functions) that used the data also directly obtained the data. This meant that if the way in which data was accessed had to change, all the functions which used that data had to be rewritten. If you have attended any sort of software engineering course, you will say that what was required was another function which obtained the data (it thus acted as an intermediary). This function could then be used in many different places. However, such application-specific functions tend not to get used in "real-world" systems for several reasons:

- *Small subroutines are too much effort.* Although many people talk about reusable code, they often mean relatively large code units. Small functions of one, two or three lines tend to be defined by a single programmer and are rarely shared among a development team, let alone several development teams.

- *Having too many subroutines leads to too little reuse.* The larger the number of subroutines available, the less likely that they are reused. It is very difficult to search through a code library of small subroutines trying to find one which does what you want. It is often much quicker to write it yourself!

- *It may not be obvious that a function is reusable.* If you are a programmer working on one part of a system, it may not be obvious that the function you are writing is of generic use. If a function is small then it is not identified by the designer as being a useful reusable component.

Ability to Package Software

Another issue is the way in which programming languages package up software for reuse. Many systems assume that the software should be partitioned into modules which are then integrated at compile time. Such fixed compile-time integration can be good for some types of problem, but in many cases it is too inflexible. For example, while this approach can ensure that the modules being reused are compatible, developers may not know until run time which modules they wish to use, and therefore some form of run-time binding is necessary.

UNIX pipes and filters are examples of software systems which can be bound at run time. They act as "glue", allowing the developer to link two or more programs in sequence together. However, in this case there is absolutely no error protection. It is quite possible to link two incompatible systems together.

What would be really useful would be a combination of these features. That is, the ability to specify either compile-time or run-time binding. In either case, there should be some form of error checking to ensure that you are integrating compatible modules. An important criterion is to avoid the need for extensive recompilation when, for example, just one line is altered. Finally, such a system should, by definition, enforce encapsulation and make packaging of the software effortless.

Flexibility of Code

In early procedural languages, for example C or Pascal, there was little or no flexibility. More recent procedural languages have introduced some flexibility, but need extensive specification to achieve it. The result is internal flexibility at the cost of interface overheads, for example in Ada. Object technology allows code flexibility (and data flexibility) with little overhead.

1.4.2 The Advantages Claimed for Object Orientation

There are a range of benefits which can be identified for object-oriented programming languages. Not all of these are unique to object-oriented technology, but that does not matter; we are talking about the good things about object orientation here:

- *Increased code reuse* Languages such as Java encourage reuse. Every time you specify that one class inherits from another (which you do all the time in Java), you are involved in reuse. In time, most developers actively look to see where they can restructure classes to improve the potential for reuse. As long as this is not taken too far, it is an extremely healthy thing to do.

- *Data protection for little effort* The encapsulation facilities provided as part of the language protect your data from unscrupulous users. Unlike languages such as Ada, you do not have to write reams of specification in order to achieve this protection.

- *Easier integration with encapsulation* As users of an object cannot access the internals of the object, they must go via specified interfaces. As these interfaces can be published in advance of the object being implemented, others can develop to those interfaces knowing that they will be available when the object is implemented.

- *Easier maintenance with encapsulation* This point is really a variation on the last one. As users of an object must use the specified interfaces, as long as the external behaviour of these objects remains the same, the internals of the object can be completely changed. For example, an object can store an item of data in a flat file, read it from a sensor or obtain it from a database; external users of the object need never know.

- *Simplified code with polymorphism* With polymorphism, you do not need to worry about exactly what type of object is available at run time as long as it responds to the message (request for a method to be executed) you send it. This means that it is a great deal easier to write reusable, compact code than in many other languages.

- *More intuitive programming* It has been argued that object orientation is a more intuitive programming paradigm than other approaches, such as the procedural approach. This is because we tend to perceive the world in terms of objects. We see dials, windows, switches, fuel pumps and automated teller machines (ATMs). These objects respond to our use in specific ways when we interact with them. For example, an ATM requires a card, a PIN etc., in a particular sequence. Of course, those of us who have programmed before bring with us a lot of baggage, including preconceptions of what a program should be like and how you develop it. I hope that this book is about to turn all that on its head for a while, before putting everything back together again.

1.4.3 What Are the Problems and Pitfalls of Object Orientation?

No programming language is without its own set of problems and pitfalls. Indeed, part of the skill in becoming fluent in a new programming language is learning what the problems are and how to avoid them. In this section, we concentrate on the criticisms usually levelled at object orientation.

Lots of Confusing Terminology

This is a fair comment. Object orientation is littered with new terms and definitions for what appears to have been defined quite acceptably in other languages. Back in the early 1970s, when Smalltalk, one of the very first object-oriented programming languages, was being researched, many of the terms we now take for granted were already quite well established. However, Smalltalk introduced many of its own terms, which have remained in object-oriented languages to this day. It would be reasonable to assume that even if the inventors of the language liked their own terminology, early users would have tried to get it changed; but they didn't.

One possible answer is that in the past (that is, during the early and mid-1980s) object-oriented languages, such as Smalltalk, tended to be the preserve of academic and research institutions. (Indeed, I was introduced to my first object-oriented language while working on a research project at a British university during 1986–87.) It is often the case that academics enjoy the mystique that a language with

Table 1.1 Approximate equivalent terms

Procedural term	Object-oriented term
procedure	method
procedure call	message
non-temporary data	instance variable
record and procedures	object

terminology all of its own can create. By now, it is so well established in the object-oriented culture that newcomers just have to adapt.

The important point to remember is that the concepts are actually very simple, although the practice can be harder. To illustrate this, consider Table 1.1, which attempts to illustrate the parallels between object-oriented terminology and procedural terminology.

These approximations should not be taken too literally as they are intended only to help you visualize what each of the terms means. I hope that, by the end of the book, you gain your own understanding of their meaning.

Yet Another Programming Paradigm to Master

In general, people tend to like the things they are used to. This is why many people buy the same make of car again and again (even when it gives them trouble). It is also why computer scientists refuse to move to a new word processor, editor, operating system or hardware. Over the years, I have had many "discussions" with people over the use of LaTeX versus Word versus WordPerfect, the merits of Emacs versus vi, of UNIX versus Mac, or of Windows versus DOS. In most cases, the issues raised and points made indicate that those involved in the discussions (including me) are biased, have their own "hobby horse" to promote and do not understand fully the other approach.

Object orientation both benefits and suffers from this phenomenon. There are those who hold it up almost like a religion and those who cast it aside because it is so different from what they are used to. Many justify this latter approach by pointing out that procedural programming has been around for quite a while now and many systems are successfully developed using it. This is a reasonable statement and one which promotes the *status quo*. However, the fact that object orientation is a new software paradigm, quite different from the procedural paradigm, should not be a reason for rejecting it.

Object orientation explicitly encourages encapsulation (information hiding), promotes code reuse and enables polymorphism. Most procedural languages have attempted to present these advantages as well; however, they have failed to do so in such a coherent and concise manner. Ada, for example, is not only a large cumbersome language, it requires an extensive specification to be written to enable two packages to work together. Any error in these specifications and the system does not compile (even if there are no errors or incompatibilities in the code). Ada95 has introduced the concept of objects and classes, although, for most object technology practitioners, the way in which it has done this is both counterintuitive and unwieldy.

Many Object-Oriented Environments Are Inefficient

Historically, object-oriented development environments have been inefficient, processor-intensive and memory-hungry. Such environments tended to be designed for use on powerful workstations or minicomputers. Examples of such environments include Lisp Flavors (which even required specialist hardware, e.g. the Symbolics Lisp machine), Self and Smalltalk-80 (the forerunner of VisualWorks, a commercial Smalltalk development environment). These machines were expensive, sometimes non-standard and aimed at the research community.

With the advent of the PC, attempts were made to rectify this situation. For example, Smalltalk/V was designed specifically to run on the PC and the first version of Smalltalk that I used was on a 286 PC. The current versions of Java products, such as Symantec's VisualCafé and Borland's JBuilder, are now extremely efficient and optimized for use on PC platforms. Indeed, Sun's Java Development Kit (JDK) is available on UNIX, Solaris, Windows 95/98/NT and Mac OS.

Although 16 Mbyte of RAM is advisable on many of these systems, any 486 machine or above provides ample performance. The issue of additional RAM is not large; RAM can be purchased at reasonable rates and many industry pundits predict that 128 MByte (and more) will soon become the industry standard. Indeed, systems are now emerging which assume that a user has access to larger amounts of memory; for example, Microsoft's J++ requires a minimum of 24 MByte to run the debugger.

C++ and object-oriented versions of Pascal (such as Delphi) are no more memory- or processor-intensive than any non-object-oriented language. However, it is worth noting that these languages do not offer the same level of support for the programmer as, for example, Java and Smalltalk. In particular, they do not provide automatic memory management and garbage collection.

Java Environments Are not Suitable for Serious Development

Many object-oriented languages are interpreted, for example, Eiffel, Smalltalk, Objective-C and Java. If you intend to construct large applications in such languages you want to be sure that the performance of the resulting application is acceptable. In addition, for real-world applications you also wish to know that the facilities provided by the language, and any support environments, are up to the task.

We shall first consider the issue of compilation time. At present, all Java compilers produce an intermediate representation called byte codes, rather than a machine executable form. These byte codes are then interpreted by the Java Virtual Machine. The compiler available with Sun's JDK is relatively slow (and certainly slower than compiling comparable programs with Delphi or Visual Basic). However, vendors such as Symantec and Microsoft have developed Java compilers which are much faster (up to twice as fast).

The next issue is performance. The Java interpreter provided with the JDK is not particularly fast and is certainly a lot slower than a comparable C++ program. For applications of any size, this is a serious problem. What are really required are native code compilers for Java. Although some are being developed, these are not currently commercially available. However, companies such as Symantec and Microsoft have produced Just-In-Time (JIT) compilers which compile a piece of code once and then cache it. This means that any code which is executed repeatedly is converted into native machine code only once, resulting in a significant improvement in performance. Although there is still a run-time overhead, it is almost certainly faster than the standard Java interpreter, and some estimates suggest up to a 20-fold improvement.

The next issue is the application development facilities provided by the language. These can greatly affect the development time and the reliability and maintainability of a system.

For example, Smalltalk is a dynamically typed language, which has significant implications for large software development. However, the designers of the Java language took into account many of the problems which programmers have to deal with when developing large applications. In particular, they considered the problems associated with C++ programs (such as memory leaks) which can be extremely difficult to identify and debug. They added features to Java to remove the potential for introducing such bugs (for example, dynamic memory allocation and garbage collection). The Java language developers also considered the compilation of source code and dependencies between source code files. They provide an automatic compilation facility (achieving the same goal as a manually defined make file) to simplify application construction.

Finally, in the real world consideration must be given to issues such as portability (both to current hardware and to future hardware), distribution (as the move towards network computing grows, the network is the computer!) and evolution of the language (as new features are required). Once again, the Java language designers have considered these issues, and Java is "architecture neutral". It assumes nothing about the hardware on which it executes. The designers also made significant attempts to specify rigorously parts of the Java language which might be affected by different platforms. Thus the size of an integer in bytes is explicitly defined and the language explicitly incorporates facilities for dealing with TCP/IP protocols, URLs etc., allowing it to be seamlessly integrated with the Web. Packages and objects also allow new facilities to be added without significantly affecting existing ones.

1.5 Pedigree of Object-Oriented Languages

In the horse or dog breeding world, the pedigree of an animal can be determined by considering its ancestry. While you cannot determine how good a language is by looking at its predecessors, you can certainly get a feel for the influences which have led to the features it possesses. The current set of commercial object-oriented languages have all been influenced to a greater or lesser extent by existing languages. Figure 1.1 illustrates some of the relationships between the various languages.

Figure 1.1 only partially illustrates the family relationships as, for example, Ada95 should have a link from Smalltalk (or possibly C++). However, it attempts to illustrate the most direct influences evident in the various languages. The diagram is also ordered in roughly chronological order. That is, the further down the diagram a language appears, the more recent it is. This means, for example, that Smalltalk predates C++, and that Java is the most recent object-oriented language. Notice that

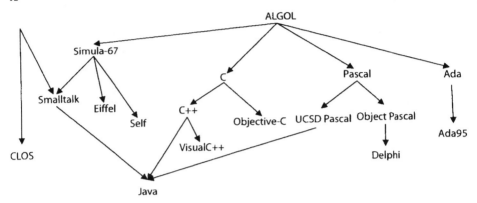

Figure 1.1 Partial Java family tree.

Lisp, ALGOL, C, Pascal and Ada are not object-oriented, and that Simula is, at most, object-based.

The extent to which a language can be considered to be a *pure* object-oriented language (i.e. one which adheres to object-oriented concepts consistently) as opposed to a *hybrid* object-oriented language (i.e. one in which object-oriented concepts lie alongside traditional programming approaches) tends to depend on its background.

A pure object-oriented language supports only the concept of objects. Any program is made up solely of interacting objects which exchange information with each other and request operations or data from each other. This approach tends to be followed by those languages which most directly inherit features from Simula (C++ is a notable exception). Simula was designed as a language for discrete event simulation. However, it was influenced by many of the features from ALGOL 60 and was effectively the first language to use the concepts which we now describe as object-oriented. For example, it introduced the concepts of class, inheritance and polymorphism.

The language which inherits most directly from Simula is Smalltalk. This means that its ALGOL heritage is there for all to see in the form of structured programming constructs (although the syntax may, at first, seem a little bizarre). It is a pure object-oriented language in that the only concepts supported by the language are object-oriented. It also inherits from Lisp (if not syntax, then certainly the philosophy). This means that not only does it not include strong typing, it also provides dynamic memory management and automatic garbage collection. This has both benefits and drawbacks, which we will discuss at a later stage. In contrast, Eiffel, another pure object-oriented language, attempts to introduce best software engineering practice, rather than the far less formal approach of Lisp. Self is a recent, pure object-oriented language which is still at the research stage.

Many language designers have taken the *hybrid* approach. That is, object-oriented constructs have either been grafted onto, or intermixed with, the existing language (for example, C++). In some cases, the idea has been to enable a developer to take advantage of object orientation when it appears appropriate. In other situations, it has eased the transition from one approach to another. The result has often been less than satisfactory. Not only does it mean that many software developers have moved to their new object-oriented language believing that it is just a matter of learning the new syntax (which it is not), they have written procedural programs in which objects are limited to holding data, believing that this is sufficient (which it is not). It is really only safe to move to a hybrid language once you have learnt about object technology using a pure object-oriented language.

1.6 Fundamentals of Object Orientation

The object-oriented programmer's view of traditional procedural programming is of procedures wildly attacking data, which is defenceless and has no control over what the procedures do to it (the rape and pillage style of programming). In contrast, object-oriented programming is viewed as polite and well-behaved data objects passing messages to one another, each data object deciding for itself whether to accept the message and how to interpret what it means.

The basic idea is that an object-oriented system is a set of interacting objects which are organized into classes. Figure 1.2 illustrates a simplified cruise control system from a car. It shows the objects in the system, the links between the objects and the direction in which information flows along these links. The object-oriented implementation of this system would mirror this diagram exactly. That is, there would be an object representing each box; between the boxes, there would be links allowing one object to request a service from, or provide information to, another. For example, the cruise control electronic control unit (ECU) might request the current speed from the speed sensor. It would then use this information when asking the throttle to adjust its position. Notice that we do not talk about functions or procedures which access information from data structures and then call other functions and procedures. There is no concept such as the ECU data structure and the ECU main program. This can be a difficult change of emphasis for some people, and we shall try to illustrate it further below.

The aim of object-oriented programming is to shift the focus of attention from *procedures that do things to data* to *data which is asked to do things*. The task is not to define the procedures which manipulate data, but to define data objects, their attributes and the way in which they may be examined or changed. Data objects (and procedures) can communicate with other data objects only through narrow, well-defined channels.

1.7 The Basic Principles of Object Orientation

- *Encapsulation or data hiding* Encapsulation is the process of hiding all the details of an object that do not contribute to its essential characteristics. Essentially, it means that what is inside the class is hidden; only the external interfaces can be

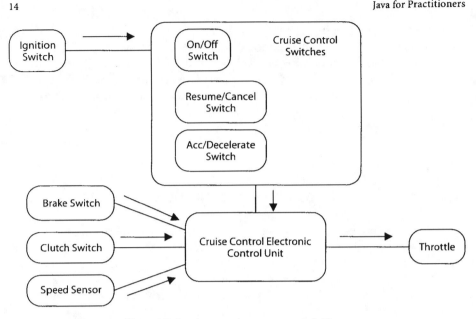

Figure 1.2 A cruise control system as a set of objects.

seen by other objects. The user of an object should never need to look inside the box!

● *Inheritance* Objects may have similar (but not identical) properties. One way of managing (classifying) such properties is to have a hierarchy of of classes. A class inherits from its immediate parent class and from classes above the parent (see the hierarchy in Figure 1.4). The inheritance mechanism permits common characteristics of an object to be defined once but used in many places. Any change is thus localized.

　　If we define a concept *animal* and a concept *dog*, we do not have to specify all the things which a dog has in common with other animals. Instead, we inherit them by saying that dog is a **subclass** of animal. This feature is unique to object-oriented languages; it promotes (and achieves) huge amounts of reuse.

● *Abstraction* An abstraction denotes the essential characteristics of an object that distinguish it from all other kinds of object and thus provides crisply defined conceptual boundaries, relative to the perspective of the viewer. That is, it states how a particular object differs from all others.

● *Polymorphism* This is the ability to send the same message to different instances which appear to perform the same function. However, the way in which the message is handled depends on the class of which the instance is an example.

　　An interesting question to ask is: "How do languages such as Ada, C and Lisp relate to the four concepts above?". An obvious issue is related to inheritance. That is, if we define a concept animal and we then define a concept dog, we do not have to specify all the things which a dog has in common with other animals. Instead, we inherit them by saying that a dog is a **subclass** of animal. This feature is unique to object-oriented languages; it promotes (and achieves) huge amounts of reuse. The next four sections expand on each of these basic principles in more detail.

1.8 Encapsulation

Encapsulation or data hiding has been a major feature of a number of programming languages; Modula 2 and Ada both provide extensive encapsulation features. But what exactly is encapsulation? Essentially, it is the concept of hiding the data behind a software "wall". Those outside the wall cannot get direct access to the data. Instead, they must ask intermediaries (usually the owners of the data) to provide them with the data.

The advantage of encapsulation is that the user of the data does not need to know how, where, or in what form the owner of the data stores that data. This means that if the owner changes the way in which the data is stored, the user of the data need not be affected. The user still asks the owner for the data; it is the data owner that changes how the request is fulfilled.

Different programming languages implement encapsulation in different ways. For example, Ada enables encapsulation using packages which possess both data and procedures. It also specifies a set of interfaces which publish those operations that the package wishes to make available to users of the package. These interfaces may implement some operations or provide access to data held within the package.

Object-oriented languages provide encapsulation facilities which present the user of an object with a set of external interfaces. These interfaces specify the requests to which the object will respond (or, in the terminology of object orientation, the requests which the object will understand). These interfaces not only avoid the need for the caller to understand the internal details of the implementation, they actually prevent the user from obtaining that information. Users of an object cannot directly access the data held by an object, as it is not visible to them. In other words, a program that calls this facility can treat it as a black box; the program knows what the facility's external interfaces guarantee to do, and that is all it needs to know.

It is worth pointing out a difference between the object-oriented approach and the package approach used in Ada. In general, a package is a large unit of code providing a wide range of facilities with a large number of data structures (for example, the Text IO package). In an object-oriented language, the encapsulation is provided at the object level. While objects may well be as large and as complex as the typical Ada package, they are often much smaller. In languages such as Smalltalk and Java, where everything is an object, the smallest data and code units also naturally benefit from encapsulation. You can attempt to introduce the same level of encapsulation in Ada, but it is not natural to the language.

Figure 1.3 illustrates the way in which encapsulation works within an object-oriented language. It shows that anything outside the object can only gain access to the data the object holds through specific interfaces (the black squares). In turn, these interfaces trigger procedures which are internal to the object. These procedures may then access the data directly, use a second procedure as an intermediary or call an interface to another object.

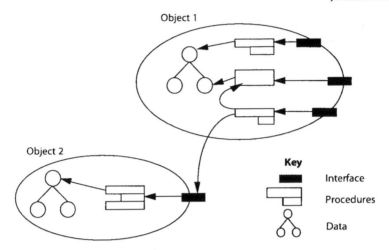

Figure 1.3 Object structure and interaction.

1.9 Inheritance

A class is an example of a particular type of thing (for example, *mammal* is a class of *animal*). In the object-oriented world, a class is a definition of the characteristics of that thing. Thus, in the case of mammals, we might define that they have fur, are warm blooded and produce live young. Animals such as dogs and cats are then instances of the class mammal. This is all quite obvious and should not present a conceptual problem for anyone. However, in most object-oriented languages (Self is an exception) the concept of the class is tightly linked to the concept of inheritance.

Inheritance allows us to state that one class is similar to another class but with a specified set of differences. Another way of putting it is that we can define all the things which are common about a class of things, and then define what is special about each subgrouping within a subclass.

For example, if we have a class defining all the common traits of mammals, we can define how particular categories of mammals differ. The duck-billed platypus is a quite extraordinary mammal which differs from other mammals in a number of important ways. However, we do not want to define all the things which it has in common with other mammals. Not only is this extra work, but we then have two places in which we have to maintain this information. We can therefore state that a duck-billed platypus is a class of mammal that does not produce live young. Classes allow us to do this.

An example which is rather closer to home for most computer scientists is illustrated in Figure 1.4. For this example, we assume that we have been given the job of designing and implementing an administration system for a small software house that produces payroll, pensions and other financial systems. This system needs to record both permanent and temporary employees of the company. For temporary employees, we need to record their department, the length of their contract, when they started and additional information which differs depending on whether they

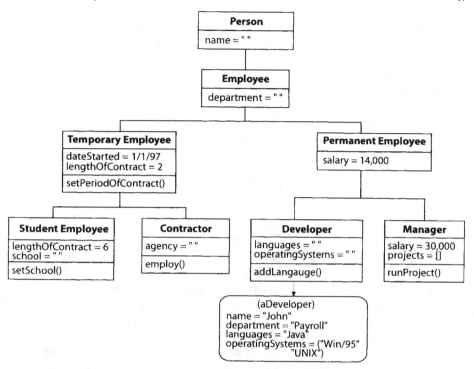

Figure 1.4 An example of inheritance.

are contractors or students on an industrial placement. For permanent employees, we need to record their department, their salary, the languages and operating systems with which they are familiar, and whether they are a manager. In the case of managers, we might also want to record the projects that they run.

Figure 1.4 illustrates a class hierarchy diagram for this application. It shows the classes we have defined and from where they inherit their information.

- *Inheritance versus instantiation* Stating that one class is a specialized version of a more generic class is different from saying that something is an example of a class of things. In the first case, we might say that developer is one category of employee and manager is another. Neither of these categories can be used to identify an individual. They are, in effect, templates for examples of those categories. In the second case, we say that "John" is an example of a developer (just as "Chris", "Myra" and "Denise" may also be examples of developers). "John" is therefore an instance of a particular class (or category) of things known as developers. It is important to get the concept of specializing a class with a subclass clear in your mind. It is all too easy to confuse an instance of a class with a subclass.

- *Inheritance of common information* We place common concepts together in a single class. For example, all people have a name and all employees have a nominated department (whether they are permanent or temporary). All temporary employees have a start date, whether they are contractors or students. In turn, all classes below Employee inherit the concept of a department. This means that not only do all Managers and Developers have a department, but "John" has a department, which in this case is "Payroll".

- *Abstract classes* Figure 1.4 defines a number of classes of which we have no intention of making an example: Employee, Permanent Employee and Temporary Employee. These are termed abstract classes and are intended as placeholders for common features rather than as templates for a particular category of things. This is quite acceptable and is common practice in most object-oriented programs.

- *Inheritance of defaults* Just because we have stated that Permanent Employees earn a default salary of £14,000 a year does not mean that all types of employee have that default. In the diagram, Managers have a default of £30,000, illustrating that a class can overwrite the defaults defined in one of its parents.

- *Single and multiple inheritance* In Figure 1.4, we have only illustrated single inheritance. That is, a class inherits from only one other class. This is the case in many object-oriented programming languages, such as Java and Smalltalk. However, other languages such as C++ and Eiffel allow multiple inheritance. In multiple inheritance, you can bring together the characteristics of two classes to define a third class. For example, you may have two classes, Toy and Car, which can be used to create a third class Toy-Car. Multiple inheritance is a controversial subject which is still being debated. Those who think it is useful fail to see why other languages do not include it, and vice versa. Java does not include multiple inheritance.

1.10 Abstraction

Abstraction is much more than just the ability to define categories of things which can hold common features of other categories of things (for example, Temporary Employee is an abstract class of Contractor and Student Employee). It is a way of specifying what is particular about a group of classes of things. Often this means defining the interface for an object, the data that such an object holds and part of the functionality of that object.

For example, we might define a class DataBuffer which is the abstract class for things that hold data and return them on request. It may define how the data is held and that operators such as put() and get() are provided to add data to, and remove it from, the DataBuffer. The implementation of these operators may be left to those implementing a subclass of DataBuffer.

The class DataBuffer might be used to implement a stack or a queue. Stack could implement get() as *return the most recent data item added* while Queue could implement it as *return the oldest data item held*. In either case, a user of the class knows that put() and get() are available and work in the appropriate manner.

In some languages, abstraction is related to protection. For example, in C++ and and Java, you can state whether a subclass can overwrite data or procedures (and indeed whether it has to overwrite them). In Smalltalk, the developer cannot state that a procedure cannot be overwritten, but can state that a procedure (or method) is a subclass responsibility (that is, a subclass which implements the procedure in order to provide a functioning class).

Abstraction is also associated with the ability to define abstract data types (ADTs). In object-oriented terms these are classes (or groups of classes) which provide behaviour that acts as the infrastructure for a particular class of data type (for example, DataBuffer provides a stack or a queue). However, it is worth pointing out that ADTs are more commonly associated with procedural languages such as Ada. This is because the concepts in object orientation essentially supersede ADTs. That is, not only do they encompass all the elements of ADTs, they extend them by introducing inheritance.

1.11 Polymorphism

Polymorphism is a strange sounding word, derived from Greek,[1] for a relatively simple concept. It is essentially the ability to request that the same operation be performed by a wide range of different types of things. How the request is processed depends on the thing that receives the request. The programmer need not worry about how the request is handled, only that it is. Effectively, this means that you can ask many different things to perform the same action. For example, you might ask a range of objects to provide a printable string describing themselves. If you ask an instance of the Manager class, a compiler object or a database object to return such a string, you use the same interface call (toString, in Java).

The name "polymorphism" is unfortunate and often leads to confusion. It makes the whole process sound rather grander than it actually is. There are two types of polymorphism used in programming languages: overloading and overriding. The difference in name relates to the mechanism that resolves what code to execute.

1.11.1 Overloading Operators

Overloading occurs when procedures have the same name but apply to different data types. The compiler can determine which operator to use at compile time and can use the correct version.

Ada uses exactly this type of overloading. For example, you can define a new version of the + operator for a new data type. When a programmer uses +, the compiler uses the types associated with the operator to determine which version of + to use.

In C, although the same function, printf, is used to print any type of value, it is not a polymorphic function. The user must specify the correct format options to ensure that a value is printed correctly.

---

1 *Polymorphos* means "having many forms".

1.11.2 Overriding Operators

Overriding occurs when a procedure is defined in a class (for example, Temporary Employee) and also in one of its subclasses (for example, Student Employee). It means that instances of Temporary Employee and Student Employee can each respond to requests for this procedure (assuming it has not been made private to the class). For example, let us assume that we define the procedure toString in these classes. The pseudocode definition of this in Temporary Employee might be:

```
toString() {
    return "I am a temporary employee"
}
```

In Student Employee, it might be defined as:

```
toString() {
    return "I am a student employee"
}
```

The procedure in Student Employee replaces the version in Temporary Employee for all instances of Student Employee. If we ask an instance of Student Employee for the result of toString, we get the string "I am a student employee". If you are confused, think of it this way:

> If you ask an object to perform some operation, then, to determine which version of the procedure is run, look in the class used to create the instance. If the procedure is not defined there, look in the class's parent. Keep doing this until you find a procedure which implements the operation requested. This is the version which is used.

In languages such as Java the choice of which version of the procedure to execute is not determined at compile time, because the compiler would have to be able to determine the type of object and then find the appropriate version of the procedure. Instead, the procedure is chosen at run time. The technical term for this process of identifying the procedure at run time rather than compile time is called "late binding".

1.12 Summary

In this chapter you have been introduced to the background and history of object orientation. You have explored the main concepts which underpin object orientation and have encountered some of the (sometimes arcane) terminology used. There is a great deal of new information in this chapter which can, at times, appear to make obsolete all that you already know.

The object-oriented view of the world can be daunting for a programmer who is used to a more procedural view of the world. To adjust to this new view of the world is hard (and some never do). Others fail to see the difference between an object-oriented programming language and a language such as Ada (we refer here to the pre-Ada95 version). However, object orientation will become second nature to many once they have worked with object-oriented systems for a while. The key thing is to try things out as you go along and, if possible, have someone around who understands a bit about object orientation – they can often illuminate and simplify an otherwise gloomy network of tunnels.

1.13 Further Reading

There are a great many books available on object orientation. Some of the best known include Booch (1994), Budd (1991), Wirfs-Brock *et al.* (1990) and Cox and Novobilski (1991). An excellent book aimed at managers and senior programmers who want to learn how to apply object-oriented technology successfully to their projects is Booch (1996). Another good book in a similar style is Yourdon (1994).

Other books which may be of interest to those attempting to convince themselves or others that object technology can actually work are Harmon and Taylor (1993), Love (1993) and Meyer and Nerson (1993).

Other places to find useful references are the *Journal of Object-oriented Programming* (SIGS Publications, ISSN 0896-8438) and the OOPSLA conferences. The OOPSLA conferences are annual worldwide conferences on Object-oriented Programming: Systems, Languages and Applications. References for the proceedings of some recent conferences are listed at the back of this book. There are also references for the proceedings of the European Conference on Object-oriented Programming (ECOOP).

For further reading on the software crisis and approaches aimed at solving it see Brooks (1987) and Cox (1990). For a discussion of the nature of scientific discovery, refinement and revolution see Kuhn (1962).

Booch, G. (1994). *Object-Oriented Analysis and Design with Applications*, 2nd edn. Benjamin Cummings, Redwood City, CA.

Booch, G. (1996). *Object Solutions: Managing the Object-Oriented Project*. Addison-Wesley, Menlo Park, CA.

Brooks, F. (1987). No silver bullet: essence and accidents of software engineering. *IEEE Computer*, April.

Budd, T. (1991). *An Introduction to Object Oriented Programming*. Addison–Wesley. Reading, MA.

Cox, B. J. (1990). There *is* a silver bullet. *BYTE*, October, pp. 209–18.

Cox, B. J. and Novobilski, A. (1991). *Object-Oriented Programming: An Evolutionary Approach*, 2nd edn. Addison-Wesley, Reading, MA.

Harmon, P. and Taylor, D. (1993). *Objects in Action: Commercial Applications of Object-Oriented Technologies*. Addison-Wesley, Reading MA.

Kuhn, T. (1962). *The Structure of Scientific Revolutions*. The University of Chicago Press, Chicago, IL.

Love, T. (1993). *Object Lessons: Lessons Learned in Object-Oriented Development Projects*. SIGS Books, New York.

Meyer, B. and Nerson, J. (1993). *Object-Oriented Applications*. Prentice Hall, Englewood Cliffs NJ.

Wirfs-Brock, R., Wilkerson, B. and Wiener, L. (1990). *Designing Object Oriented Software*. Prentice Hall, Englewood Cliffs, NJ.

Yourdon, E. (1994). *Object-Oriented Systems Design*. Prentice Hall, Englewood Cliffs, NJ.

2 Elements of Object Orientation

2.1 Introduction

This chapter is intended to reinforce what you have already learnt. It concisely defines the terminology introduced in the last chapter and attempts to clarify issues associated with hierarchies. It also discusses some of the perceived strengths and weaknesses of the object-oriented approach and offers some guidance on the approach to take in learning about objects.

2.2 Terminology

- *Class* A class defines a combination of data and procedures that operate on that data. Instances of other classes can only access that data or those procedures through specified interfaces. A class acts as a template when creating new instances. A class does not hold any data but it specifies the data that is held in the instance. The relationship between a class, its superclass and any subclasses is illustrated in Figure 2.1.

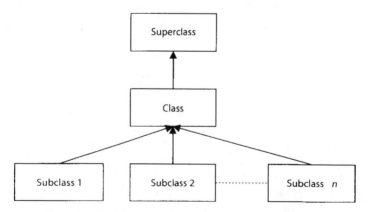

Figure 2.1 The relationship between class, superclass and subclass.

- *Subclass* A subclass is a class which inherits from another class. For example, in Chapter 1, Student Employee is a subclass of Temporary Employee. Subclasses are, of course, classes in their own right. Any class can have any number of subclasses.

- *Superclass* A superclass is the parent of a class. It is the class from which the current class inherits. For example, in Chapter 1, Temporary Employee is the superclass of Student Employee. In Java, a class can have only one superclass.
- *Instance or object* An instance is an example of a class. All instances of a class possess the same data variables but contain their own data. Each instance of a class responds to the same set of messages.
- *Instance variable* This is the special name given to the data which is held by an object. The "state" of an object at any particular moment relates to the current values held by its instance variables. (In Java, there are also class-side variables, referred to as static variables, but these will be discussed later). Figure 2.2 illustrates a definition for a class in pseudocode. It includes some instance variable definitions: fuel, mileage and name.

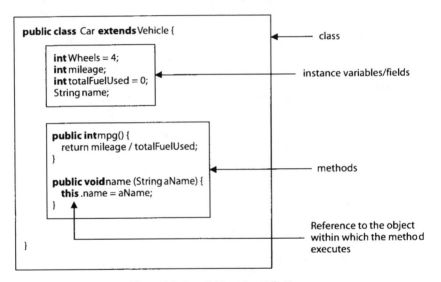

Figure 2.2 A partial Java class definition.

- *Method* A method is a procedure defined within an object. In early versions of Smalltalk, a method was used to get an object to do something or return something. It has since become more widely used; languages such as CLOS and Java also use the term. Two methods are defined in Figure 2.2: one calculates the miles per gallon, while the other sets the name of the car object.
- *Message* One object sends a message to another object requesting some operation or data. The idea is that objects are polite, well-behaved entities which carry out functions by sending messages to each other. A message may be considered akin to a procedure call in other languages.
- *this* The special (pseudo) variable, **this**, is a reference to the object within which a method is executing (see Figure 2.2). It enables messages to be sent to the current object as allowing requests for instance variables.
- *Single or multiple inheritance* Single and multiple inheritance refer to the number of superclasses from which a class can inherit. Java is a single inheritance

system, in which a class can only inherit from one class. C++ is a multiple inheritance system in which a class can inherit from one or more classes.

2.3 Types of Hierarchy

In most object-oriented systems there are two types of hierarchy; one refers to inheritance (whether single or multiple) and the other refers to instantiation. The inheritance hierarchy (or *extends* hierarchy) has already been described. It is the way in which an object inherits features from a superclass.

The instantiation hierarchy relates to instances rather than classes and is important during the execution of the object. There are two types of instance hierarchy: one indicates a *part-of* relationship, while the other relates to a using relationship (it is referred to as an *is-a* relationship).

The difference between an *is-a* relationship and a *part-of* relationship is often confusing for new programmers (and sometimes for those who are experienced in one language but are new to object-oriented programming languages, such as Java). Figure 2.3 illustrates that a student *is-a* type of person, whereas an engine is *part-of* a car. It does not make sense to say that a student is *part-of* a person or that an engine *is-a* type of car!

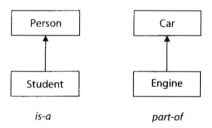

Figure 2.3 *is-a* does not equal *part-of*.

In Java, *extends* relationships are generally implemented by the subclassing mechanism. It is possible to build up large and complex class hierarchies which express these *extends* relationships. These classes express the concept of inheritance, allowing one class to inherit features from another. The total set of features is then used to create an instance of a class. In contrast, *part-of* relationships tend to be implemented using instance variables in Java.

However, *is-a* relationships and classes are not exactly the same thing. For example, if you wish to construct a semantic network consisting of explicit *is-a* relationships between instances you will have to construct such a network manually. The aim of such a structure is to represent knowledge and the relationships between elements of that knowledge, and not to construct instances. The construction of such a network is outside the scope of the subclassing mechanism, as it relates to links between objects and not links between subclasses and parent classes and would therefore be inappropriate.

If John is an instance of a class Person, it would be perfectly (semantically) correct to say that John *is-a* Person. However, here we are obviously talking about

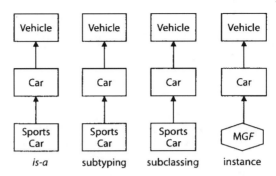

Figure 2.4 Satisfying four relationships.

the relationship between an instance and a class rather than a subclass and its parent class.

A further confusion can occur for those encountering Java after becoming familiar with a strongly typed language. These people might at first assume that a subclass and a subtype are essentially the same. However, they are not the same, although they are very similar. The problem with classes, types and *is-a* relationships is that on the surface they appear to capture the same sorts of concept. In Figure 2.4, the diagrams all capture some aspect of the use of the phrase *is-a*. However, they are all intended to capture a different relationship.

The confusion is due to the fact that in modern English we tend to overuse the term *is-a*. We can distinguish between the different types of relationship by being more precise about our definitions in terms of a programming language, such as Java. Table 2.1 defines the relationships illustrated in Figure 2.4.

To illustrate this point, consider Figure 2.5, which illustrates the differences between the first three categories.

The first diagram illustrates the potential relationships between a set of classes that define the behaviour of different categories of vehicle. The second diagram presents the subtype relationships between the categories. The third diagram illustrates a straight specialization set of relationships. Notice that although *estate car* is a specialization of *car with hatch*, its implementation (the subclassing hierarchy) indicates that it does not share any of its implementation with the *car with hatch* class. It is worth noting that type relationships are specifications, while classes (and subclasses) are implementations of behaviour.

Table 2.1 Types of *is-a* relationship.

Specialization	One thing is a special case of another
Type	One type can be used interchangeably with another type (substitutability relationship)
Subclassing or inheritance	An implementation mechanism for sharing code and representations
Instantiation	One thing is an example of a particular category (class) of things

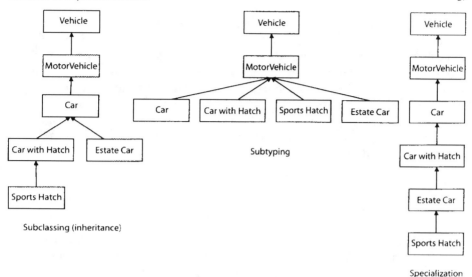

Figure 2.5 Distinguishing between relationships.

2.4 The Move to Object Technology

At present you are still acclimatizing to object orientation. It is extremely important that from now on you do your utmost to immerse yourself in object orientation, object technology and Java. This is because when you first encounter a new language or paradigm, it is all too easy to say that it is not good because you cannot do what you could in some other language or paradigm. We are all subject to the "better the devil you know than the devil you don't" syndrome. If you embrace object orientation, warts and all, at least for the present, you will gain most.

In addition, it is a fact of life that most of us tend to fit in learning something new around our existing schedules. This may mean for example, that you are trying to read this book and do the exercises while still working in C, Visual Basic, Ada etc. From personal experience, and from teaching others about Java, I can say that you will gain most by putting aside a significant amount of time and concentrating on the subject matter involved. This is not only because object orientation is so different, but also because you need to become familiar not only with the concepts but also with Java and its development environment.

So have a go, take a "leap of faith" and stick with it until the end. If, at the end, you still cannot see the point, then fair enough, but until then accept it.

2.5 Summary

In this chapter, we reviewed some of the terminology introduced in Chapter 1. We also considered the types of hierarchy which occur in object-oriented systems and which can at first be confusing. We then considered the pros and cons of object-oriented programming. You should now be ready to start to think in terms of objects. As has already been stated, this will at first seem a strange way to develop a software system, but in time it will become second nature. In the next chapter we examine how an object-oriented system might be developed and structured. This is done without reference to any source code, as the intention is to familiarize you with objects rather than with Java. It is all too easy to get through a book on Smalltalk, C++, Java etc. and understand the text but still have no idea how to start developing an object-oriented system.

2.6 Exercises

1. Research what other authors have said about single and multiple inheritance. Why do languages such as Smalltalk and Java not include multiple inheritance?
2. Look for terms such as class, method, member, member function, instance variable and constructor in the books listed in the further reading section. When you have found them, read their explanation of these terms and write down your understanding of their meaning.

2.7 Further Reading

Suggested further reading for this chapter includes Coad and Yourdon (1991), Winston and Narasimhan (1996) and Meyer (1988). In addition, all the books mentioned in Chapter 1 are still relevant.

Coad, P. and Yourdon, E. (1991). *Object-Oriented Analysis.* Yourdon Press, Englewood Cliffs, NJ.
Meyer, B. (1988). *Object-Oriented Software Construction.* Prentice Hall, Englewood Cliffs, NJ.
Winston, P. H. and Narasimhan, S. (1996). *On to JAVA.* Addison-Wesley, Reading, MA.

3 Why Object Orientation?

3.1 Introduction

The previous two chapters introduced the basic concepts behind object orientation and much of its terminology. It also explored some of the motivation which led to the object-oriented movement. This chapter looks at how object orientation addresses some of the issues which have been raised with procedural languages. To do this it looks at how a small extract of a program might be written in a language such as C, considers the problems faced by the C developer and then looks at how the same functionality might be achieved in an object-oriented language such as Java. Again, do not worry too much about the syntax you will be presented with – it will be Java, but it should not detract from the legibility of the examples.

3.2 The Procedural Approach

As has already been stated, object orientation provides four things:

1. Encapsulation
2. Abstraction
3. Inheritance
4. Polymorphism

It has been claimed that these four elements combine to provide a very powerful programming paradigm, but why? What is so good about object orientation?

3.2.1 A Naked Data Structure

Consider the following example of a "naked" data structure:

```
struct Date {
    int day;
    int month;
    int year;
}
```

This defines a data structure for recording dates. There are similar structures in many procedural languages, such as C, Pascal and Ada. It is naked because it has no defences against procedures accessing and modifying its contents.

So what is wrong with a structure such as this? Nothing, apart from the issue of visibility, that is, what can see this structure and what can update the contents of the structure. For example, code could set the day to −1, the month to 13 and the year to 9999. As far as the structure is concerned the information it holds is fine (that is day = −1, month = 13, year = 9999). This is because the structure only knows that it is supposed to hold integers; it knows nothing about dates *per se*. This is not surprising, it is only data.

3.2.2 Procedures for the Data Structure

This data is associated with procedures which perform operations on it. These operations might be to test whether the date represents a Saturday or a Sunday or part of the working week. It may be to change the date, in which case the procedure may also check to see that the date is a valid one.

For example:

- `isDayOfWeek(date);`
- `inMonth(date, 2);`
- `nextDay(date);`
- `setDay(date, 9, 23, 1946);`

How do we know that these procedures are related to the date structure we have just looked at? By the naming conventions of the procedures and by the fact that one of the parameters is a date (record).

The problem is that these procedures are not limited in what they can do to the data. For example the `setDay` procedure might have been implemented by a Briton who assumes that the date order is day, month and year. However, it may be used by an American who assumes that date order is month, day, year. Thus the meaning of `setDay(date, 9, 23, 1946)` will be interpreted very differently. The American views this as 23 September 1946, while the Briton views this as the 9th day of the 23rd month of 1946. In either case, there is nothing to stop the date record being updated with both versions. Obviously the `setDay()` procedure might check the new date to see whether it is legal, but then again it might not. The problem is that the data is naked and has no defence against what these procedures do to it. Indeed, it has no defence against what any of the procedures that can access it may do to it.

3.2.3 Packages

One possibility is of course to use a package construct. In languages such as Ada packages are commonplace and are used as a way of organizing code and restricting visibility. For example,

```
package Dates is
   type Date is...
   function isDayOfWeek(d: Date) return BOOLEAN;
```

```
function inMonth(d: Date, m: INTEGER) return
   BOOLEAN;
```
. . .

The package construct now provides some ring fencing of the data structure and a grouping of the data structure with the associated functions. In order to use this package a developer must import the package (for example using with and uses in Ada). They can then access the procedures and work with data of the specified type (in this case Date). There can even be data which is hidden from the package user within a *private part*. This therefore increases the ability to encapsulate the data (hide the data) from unwelcome attention.

3.3 Does Object Orientation Do Better?

This is an important question: "Does object orientation do any better" than the procedural approach described above? To answer this we will compare and contrast packages and classes before considering the role of inheritance.

3.3.1 Packages Versus Classes

It has been argued (to me at least) that a package is just like a class. It provides a template from which you can create executable code, it provides a wall around your data with well-defined gateways etc. However, there are a number of very significant differences between packages and classes.

Firstly, packages tend to be larger units (at least conceptually) than classes. For example, the TextIO package in Ada is essentially a library of textual IO facilities, rather than a single concept such as the class String in Java. Thus packages are not used to encapsulate a single small concept such as Date, but rather a whole set of related concepts (in the same ways as indeed they are used in Java itself). Thus a class is a finer level of granularity than a package even though it provides similar levels of encapsulation.

Secondly, packages still provide a relatively loose association between the data and the procedures. A package may actually deal with very many data structures with a wide range of procedures. The data and the procedures are related primarily via the related set of concepts represented by the package. In contrast a class tends to relate data and methods together very tightly in a single concept. Indeed, one of the guidelines presented later in this book relating to good class design is that, if a class represents more than one concept, split it into two classes.

Thus this close association between data and code means that the resulting concept is more than just a data structure (it is closer to a concrete realization of an abstract data type). For example:

```
class Date {
   private int day, month, year;
   public boolean isDayOfWeek() {..}
}
```

Anyone using an instance of Date now gets an object which can tell you whether it is a day of the week or not and can hold the appropriate data. Note that the isDayOfWeek() method takes no parameters – it doesn't need to, as it and the date are part of the same thing. This means that users of a Date object will never get their hands on the actual data fields which hold the date (i.e. the integers day, month and year). Instead, they are forced to go via the internal methods. This may only seem a small step, but it is a significant one: nothing outside the object may access the data within the object. In contrast, the data structure in the procedural version is not only held separately from the procedures, the values for day, month or year could be modified directly without the need to use the defined procedures.

For example, compare the differences between an ADA-esque excerpt from a program to manipulate dates:

```
d: Date;
d.day = 28;
setMonth(d, 2);
setYear(d, 1998);
isDayOfWeek(d);
inMonth(d, 2);
```

Note that it was necessary first to create the data and then to set the fields in the data structure. Here we have been good and have used the interface procedures to do this for month and year but not day. Once we had the data set up we could then call methods such as isDayOfWeek and inMonth on that data.

In contrast, the Java code uses a constructor to pass in the appropriate initialization information. How this is initialized internally is hidden from the user of the class Date. We then call methods such as isDayOfWeek() and isMonth(12) directly on the object date.

```
Date d = new Date(12, 2, 1998);
d.isDayOfWeek(); d.inMonth(12);
```

The thing to think about here is where would code be defined? Of course, at this stage you may well say that this is still only a form of encapsulation around the data. We will therefore look at inheritance next.

3.3.2 Inheritance

Inheritance is the key element which makes an object-oriented language more than an object-based language. An object-based language possesses the concept of objects, but not of inheritance. Indeed, inheritance is the thing which marks an object-oriented language as different from a procedural language. The key concept in inheritance is that one class can inherit data and methods from another, thus increasing the amount of code reuse occurring as well as simplifying the overall system. One of the most important features of inheritance (ironically) is that it allows the developer to get inside the encapsulation bubble in limited and controlled ways. This allows the subclass to take advantage of internal data structures and methods, without compromising the encapsulation afforded to objects. For example, let us define a subclass of the class Date (the keyword extends is used to indicate inheritance in Java):

```
class Birthday extends Date {
    private String name;
    private int age;
    public boolean isBirthday() {..}
}
```

The method isBirthday() could check to see if the current date matched the date represented by an instance of Birthday and return true if it does and false if it does not.

Note however, that the interesting thing here is that not only have I not had to define integers to represent the date, neither have I had to define methods to access such dates. These have both been inherited from the parent class Date.

In addition, I can now treat an instance of Birthday as either a Date or as a Birthday depending on what I want to do!

What would you do in languages such as C, Pascal or Ada83? One possibility is that you could define a new package Birthday, but that package would not extend Dates; it would have to import Dates, add interfaces to it etc. However, you certainly couldn't treat a Birthday package as a Dates package.

In a language such as Java, because of polymorphism, you can do exactly that. You can reuse existing code that only knew about Date, for example:

- public void test (Date d) {..}
- test(birthday);

This is because Birthday is indeed a type of Date as well as being a type of Birthday.

You can also use all of the features defined for Date on Birthdays:

- birthday.isDayOfWeek();

Indeed, you don't actually know where the method is defined. This method could be defined in the class Birthday (in which it would override that defined in the class Date). However, it could be defined in the class Date (if no such method is defined in Birthday). However, without looking at the source code there is no way of knowing!

Of course you can also use the new methods defined in the class Birthday on instances (objects) of this class. For example:

- birthday.isBirthday();

3.4 Summary

Classes in an object-oriented language provide a number of features that are not present in procedural languages. Hopefully, by the end of this book you will agree that they are useful additions to the developers toolbox. If not, give it time – one of the problems that we all face (myself included) is a reluctance to change. To summarize, the main points you should take from this chapter regarding object orientation are:

- Classes provide for inheritance.
- Inheritance provides for reuse.
- Inheritance provides for extension of data types.
- Inheritance allows for polymorphism.
- Inheritance is a unique feature of object orientation.
- Encapsulation is a good software engineering feature in object orientation.

4 Constructing an Object-Oriented System

4.1 Introduction

This chapter takes you through the design of a simple object-oriented system without considering implementation issues or the details of any particular language. Instead, this chapter illustrates how to use object orientation concepts to construct a software system. We first describe the application and then consider where to start looking for objects, what the objects should do and how they should do it. We conclude by discussing issues such as class inheritance, and answer questions such as "where is the structure of the program?".

4.2 The Application: Windscreen Wipe Simulation

This system aims to provide a diagnosis tutor for the equipment illustrated in Figure 4.1. Rather than use the wash–wipe system from a real car, students on a car mechanics diagnosis course use this software simulation. The software system mimics the actual system, so the behaviour of the pump depends on information provided by the relay and the water bottle.

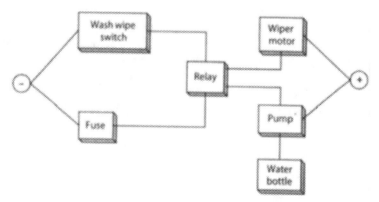

Figure 4.1 The windscreen wash–wipe system.

The operation of the wash–wipe system is controlled by a switch which can be in one of five positions: off, intermittent, slow, fast and wash. Each of these settings places the system into a different state:

Switch setting	System state
Off	The system is inactive.
Intermittent	The blades wipe the windscreen every few seconds.
Slow	The wiper blades wipe the windscreen continuously.
Fast	The wiper blades wipe the windscreen continuously and quickly.
Wash	The pump draws water from the water bottle and sprays it onto the windscreen.

For the pump and the wiper motor to work correctly, the relay must function correctly. The fuse must be intact for the pump or motor to operate.

4.3 Where Do We Start?

This is often a very difficult point for those new to object-oriented systems. That is, they have read the basics and understand simple diagrams, but do not know where to start. It is the old chestnut: "I understand the example but don't know how to apply the concepts myself". This is not unusual and, in the case of object orientation, is probably normal.

The answer to the question "Where do I start?" may at first seem somewhat obscure; you should start with the data. Remember that objects are things which exchange messages with each other. The things possess the data which is held by the system and the messages request actions that relate to the data. Thus, an object-oriented system is fundamentally concerned with data items.

Before we go on to consider the object-oriented view of the system, let us stop and think for a while. Ask yourself, "Where would I start if I was going to develop such a system in C or Pascal or even Ada?". In most cases, the answer is "with some form of functional decomposition". That is, you might think about the main functions of the system and break them down into subfunctions and so on. As a natural part of this exercise, you would identify the data required to support the desired functionality. Notice that the emphasis would be on the system's functionality.

Let us take this further and consider the functions we might identify for the example presented above:

Function	Description
Wash	Pump water from the water bottle to the windscreen.
Wipe	Move the windscreen wipers across the windscreen.

We would then identify important system variables and subfunctions to support the above functions.

Now let us go back to the object-oriented view of the world. In this view, we place a great deal more emphasis on the data items involved and consider the operations associated with them (effectively, the reverse of the functional decomposition view). This means that we start by attempting to identify the primary data items in the system; next, we look to see what operations are applied to, or performed on, the data items; finally, we group the data items and operations together to form objects. In identifying the operations, we may well have to consider additional data items, which may be separate objects or attributes of the current object. Identifying them is mostly a matter of skill and experience.

The object-oriented design approach considers the operations far less important than the data and their relationships. In the next section we examine the objects that might exist in our simulation system.

4.4 Identifying the Objects

We look at the system as a whole and ask what indicates the state of the system. We might say that the position of the switch or the status of the pump is significant. This results in the data items shown in Table 4.1.

The identification of the data items is considered in greater detail in Part 4. At this point, merely notice that we have not yet mentioned the functionality of the system or how it might fit together; we have only mentioned the significant items. As this is such a simple system, we can assume that each of these elements is an object and illustrate it in a simple object diagram (Figure 4.2).

Notice that I have named each object after the element associated with the data item (e.g. the element associated with the fuse condition is the fuse itself) and that the actual data item (e.g. the condition of the fuse) is an instance variable of the object. This is a very common way of naming objects and their instance variables. We now have the basic objects required for our application.

Table 4.1 Data items and their associated state information

Data item	States
switch setting	Is the switch set to off, intermittent, wipe, fast wipe or wash?
wiper motor	Is the motor working or not?
pump state	Is the pump working or not?
fuse condition	Has the fuse blown or not?
water bottle level	The current water level
relay status	Is current flowing or not?

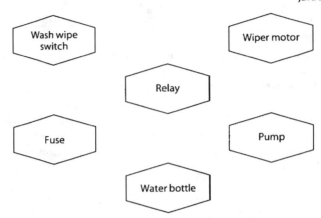

Figure 4.2 Objects in the simulation system[1].

4.5 Identifying the Services or Methods

At the moment, we have a set of objects, each of which can hold some data. For example, the water bottle can hold an integer indicating the current water level. Although object-oriented systems are structured around the data, we still need some procedural content to change the state of an object or to make the system achieve some goal. Therefore, we also need to consider the operations that a user of each object might require. Notice that the emphasis here is on the *user of the object* and what they *require of the object* rather than on what operations are performed on the data.

Let us start with the switch object. The switch state can take a number of values. As we do not want other objects to have direct access to this variable, we must identify the services which the switch should offer. As a user of a switch we want to be able to move it between its various settings. As these settings are essentially an enumerated type, we can have the concept of incrementing or decrementing the switch position. A switch must therefore provide a moveUp and a moveDown interface. Exactly how this is done depends on the programming language; for now, we concentrate on specifying the required facilities.

If we examine each object in our system and identify the required services, we may end up with Table 4.2.

We generated this table by examining each of the objects in isolation to identify the services which might reasonably be required. We may well identify further services when we attempt to put it all together.

Each of these services should relate to a method within the object. For example, the moveUp and moveDown services should relate to methods which change the state instance variable within the object. Using a generic pseudocode, the moveUp method, within the switch object, might contain the following code:

```
define method moveUp ()
   if state == "off" then
      state = "wash"
```

---

1   The hexagonal shape representing instances is based on the structured cloud used in Unified Modeling Language 0.8, described in Part 4 of this book.

Table 4.2 Object services

Object	Service	Description
switch	moveUp	Increment switch value
	moveDown	Decrement switch value
	state?	Return a value indicating the current switch state
fuse	working?	Indicate if the fuse has blown or not
wiper motor	working?	Indicate whether the wipers are working or not
relay	working?	Indicate whether the relay is active or not
pump	working?	Indicate whether the pump is active or not
water bottle	fill	Fill the water bottle with water
	extract	Remove some water from the water bottle
	empty	Empty the water bottle

```
elseif state == "wash" then
   state = "intermittent"
elseif state == "intermittent" then
   state = "slow"
elseif state == "slow" then
   state = "fast"
endif
end define method
```

This method changes the value of the `state` variable in `switch`. The new value of the instance variable depends on its previous value. You can define `moveDown` in a similar manner. Notice that the reference to the instance variable illustrates that it is global to the object. The `moveUp` method requires no parameters. In object-oriented systems, it is common for few parameters to be passed between methods (particularly of the same object), as it is the object which holds the data.

4.6 Refining the Objects

If we look back to Table 4.2, we can see that fuse, wiper motor, relay and pump all possess a service called `working?`. This is a hint that these objects may have something in common. Each of them presents the same interface to the outside world. If we then consider their attributes, they all possess a common instance variable. At this point, it is too early to say whether fuse, wiper motor, relay and pump are all instances of the same class of object (e.g. a `Component` class) or whether they are all instances of classes which inherit from some common superclass (see Figure 4.3). However, this is something we must bear in mind later.

4.7 Bringing It All Together

So far we have identified the primary objects in our system and the basic set of services they should present. These services were based solely on the data the objects

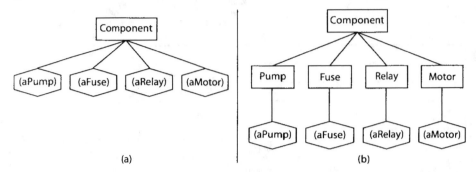

Figure 4.3 Possible classes for components in the simulation.

hold. We must now consider how to make our system function. To do this, we need to consider how it might be used. The system is part of a very simple diagnosis tutor; a student uses the system to learn about the effects of various faults on the operation of a real wiper system, without the need for expensive electronics. We therefore wish to allow a user of the system to carry out the following operations:

- change the state of a component device
- ask the motor what its new state is

The moveUp and moveDown operations on the switch change the switch's state. Similar operations can be provided for the fuse, the water bottle and the relay. For the fuse and the relay, we might provide a changeState interface using the following algorithm:

```
define method changeState()
   if state == "working" then
     state = "notWorking"
   else
     state = "working"
   endif
end define method
```

Discovering the state of the motor is more complicated. We have encountered a situation where one object's state (the value of its instance variable) is dependent on information provided by other objects. If we write down procedurally how the value of other objects affect the status of the pump, we might get the following pseudocode:

```
if fuse is working then
   if switch is not off then
     if relay is working then
       pump status = "working"
     endif
   endif
endif
```

This algorithm says that the pump status depends on the relay status, the switch setting and the fuse status. This is the sort of algorithm you might expect to find in a `main()` program. It links the subfunctions together and processes the data.

In an object-oriented language (such as Java), we do not have a main program in the same way that a C program has. Instead the `main()` method in Java is an initiating point for an object-oriented system. As it is associated with the class rather than an instance, it can trigger the creation of instances, but it is not itself part of those instances. This can be confusing at first; however, if you think of the `main()` method in Java as initiating a program that is outside the scope of the `main()` method, you are fairly close.

In an object-oriented system, well-mannered objects pass messages to one another. How then do we achieve the same effect as the above algorithm? The answer is that we must get the objects to pass messages requesting the appropriate information. One way to do that is to define a method in the pump object which gets the required information from the other objects and determines the motor's state. However, this requires the pump to have links to all the other objects so that it can send them messages. This is a little contrived and loses the structure of the underlying system. It also loses any modularity in the system. That is, if we want to add new components then we have to change the pump object, even if the new components only affect the switch. This approach also indicates that the developer is thinking too procedurally and not really in terms of objects.

In an object-oriented view of the system, the pump object only needs to know the state of the relay. It should therefore request this information from the relay. In turn, the relay must request information from the switches and the fuse.

Figure 4.4 illustrates the chain of messages initiated by the pump object:

1. pump sends a `working?` message to the relay
2. relay sends a `state?` message to the switch
   the switch replies to the relay
3. relay sends a second `working?` message to the fuse
   the fuse replies to the relay

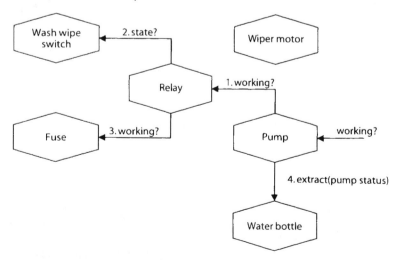

Figure 4.4 Collaborations between the objects for wash operation.

the relay replies to the pump
If the pump is working, then the pump object sends the final message to the water
bottle

4. pump sends a message `extract` to the water bottle

In step 4, a parameter is passed with the message because, unlike the previous
messages which merely requested state information, this message requests a change
in state. The parameter indicates the rate at which the pump draws water from the
water bottle.

The water bottle should not record the value of the pump's status as it does not
own this value. If it needs the motor's status in the future, it should request it from the
pump rather than using the (potentially obsolete) value passed to it previously.

In Figure 4.4, we assumed that the pump provided the service `working?`, which
allows the process to start. For completeness, the pseudocode of `working?` for the
pump object is:

```
define method working?()
  begin
    this.status = relay.working()
    if this.status == "working" then
      water_bottle.extract(this.status)
    endif
  end
end define method
```

This method is a lot simpler than the procedural program presented earlier. At no
point do we change the value of any variables which are not part of the pump,
although they may have been changed as a result of the messages being sent. Also, it
only shows us the part of the story that is directly relevant to the pump. This means
that it can be much more difficult to deduce the operation of an object-oriented
system merely by reading the source code. Some Java environments (such as
VisualCafé and Visual J++) alleviate this problem, to some extent, through the use of
sophisticated browsers.

4.8 Where Is the Structure?

People new to object orientation may be confused because they have lost one of the
key elements that they use to help them understand and structure a software system:
the main program body. This is because the objects and the interactions between
them are the cornerstone of the system. In many ways, Figure 4.4 shows the object-
oriented equivalent of a main program. This also highlights an important feature of
most object-oriented approaches: graphical illustrations. Many aspects of object
technology, for example object structure, class inheritance and message chains, are
most easily explained graphically.

Let us now consider the structure of our object-oriented system. It is dictated by
the messages which are sent between objects. That is, an object must possess a

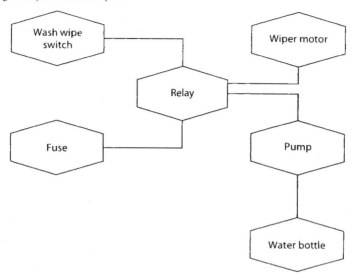

Figure 4.5 Wash–wipe system structure.

reference to another object in order to send it a message. The resulting system structure is illustrated in Figure 4.5.

In Java, this structure is achieved by making instance variables reference the appropriate objects. This is the structure which exists between the instances in the system and does not relate to the classes, which act as templates for the instances.

We now consider the classes that create the instances. We could assume that each object is an instance of an equivalent class (see Figure 4.6(a)). However, as has already been noted, some of the classes bear a very strong resemblance. In particular, the fuse, the relay, the motor and the pump share a number of common features. Table 4.3 compares the features (instance variables and services) of these objects.

Table 4.3 Comparison of components

	fuse	relay	motor	pump
instance variable	state	state	state	state
services	working?	working?	working?	working?

From this table, the objects differ only in name. This suggests that they are all instances of a common class such as Component (see Figure 4.6(b)). This class would possess an additional instance variable to simplify object identification.

If they are all instances of a common class, they must all behave in exactly the same way. However, we want the pump to start the analysis process when it receives the message working?, so it must possess a different definition of working? from fuse and relay. In other ways it is very similar to fuse and relay, so they can be instances of a class (say Component) and pump and motor can be instances of

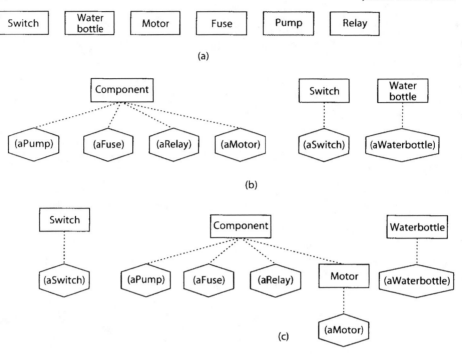

Figure 4.6 Possible class inheritance relationships.

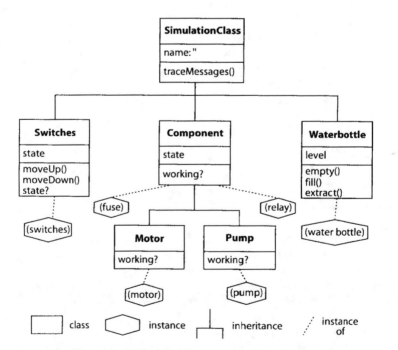

Figure 4.7 The final class hierarchy and instance diagram.

classes which inherit from Component (but redefine working?). This is illustrated in Figure 4.6(c). The full class diagram is presented in Figure 4.7.

4.9 Summary

In this chapter, you have seen how a very simple system can be broken down into objects. These objects combine to provide the overall functionality of the system. You have seen how the data to be represented determines the objects used and that the interactions between objects determine the structure of the system. You should also have noted that objects and their classes, methods and instance variables are identified by more of an evolutionary process than in languages that are not object-oriented.

4.10 Exercise

Take a system with which you are familiar and try to break it down into objects. Carry out a similar set of steps to those described above. Do not worry about how to implement the objects or the classes. Use whatever representation best fits your way of working to describe what the methods do (pseudocode or a programming language, such as C or Pascal, if you prefer). You can even use a flow chart if you are most comfortable with that. It is very important that you try to do this, as it is a useful exercise in learning to think in terms of objects.

4.11 Further Reading

A good place to start further reading on building object-oriented systems is with the first few chapters of Rumbaugh *et al.* (1991). In addition, Wirfs-Brock *et al.* (1990) is an excellent, non-language-specific introduction to structuring object-oriented systems. It uses a rather simplistic approach, which is ideal for learning about object-oriented system design but is not generally applicable. This is not a problem, as what you want to do at the moment is to get the background rather than specific techniques. Another good reference for further reading is Yourdon (1994).

Rumbaugh, J. *et al.* (1991). *Object-oriented modeling and design*. Prentice Hall, Englewood Cliffs, NJ.

Wirfs-Brock, R., Wilkerson, B. and Wiener, L. (1990). *Designing Object Oriented Software*. Prentice Hall, Englewood Cliffs, NJ.

Yourdon, E. (1994). *Object-Oriented Systems Design*. Prentice Hall, Englewood Cliffs, NJ.

5 A Brief History of Time, the Universe and Java

5.1 Introduction

I first encountered the Java language in April 1995. I was attending a conference in Amsterdam and, over breakfast with a number of American academics, was discussing suitable first programming languages. They mentioned a new language, called Java, that was quite similar to C++ but had many of the "dirty" parts of that language removed and some of the nice parts of languages such as Smalltalk added. I obtained and read the Java white paper. I thought that it looked like a nice language but that, like other object-oriented languages before it, it would not take off. After all, many people thought that Smalltalk was nicer than C++, but C++ still dominated, and languages such as Eiffel and Self were hardly being taken up at all. However, I had reckoned without the Internet and the World Wide Web. Since its launch in 1995, Java has become a force to be taken seriously.

In this chapter we encounter Java, the Sun Java Development Kit (JDK) and the Java environment. We also learn a little about the history of Java prior to the Java 2 Platform version of the JDK, which is discussed in detail in Chapter 6.

5.2 What Is Java?

Java can be viewed from a number of perspectives; in this it differs from many other programming languages, which can only be viewed as programming languages and nothing else. However, Java is more than just a programming language. Below we consider some of the ways to classify Java:

- *An object-oriented programming language* Java certainly provides the syntax and semantics of an object-oriented language. It is supported by a number of compilers which take programs written in Java and produce executable code. As you will see later, they tend to produce a byte code form which is then run on a virtual machine. As for the Java language itself, it is rather compact, unlike languages such as Ada, which are very large.

- *A programming environment* I refer here to the presence of the system-provided objects rather than any particular development environment. Unlike many languages (including C++), Java has associated with it a large (and fairly standard) set of classes. These classes make Java very powerful and promote a standard development style. You spend most of your time extending the "system" rather than programming from scratch. In a number of cases, these classes provide facilities which are considered part of the language in Ada, C and Pascal. The result is that Java is anything but a small programming system.

- *An operating environment* The operating environment is the Java Virtual Machine in which all Java programs execute. This is Java's own personal machine which has been ported to a variety of platforms and operating systems. Thus, Java can run (without recompilation) on a host of different systems.

- *The language of the Web* Java has received huge hype as the language which will bring the Web alive. However, in many ways Java is just an object-oriented language. There is no particular reason why Java should be any better as a Web language than Smalltalk or any other interpreted object-oriented language, such as Objective-C or Eiffel. However, Java got there first, and has the backing of both Netscape and Sun. It is therefore likely to remain the Web language.

Thus, it is quite possible to say that Java is a programming language, a set of extensible classes, an operating environment or even a Web development tool. It is, in fact, all of these.

5.3 Objects in Java

Almost everything in Java is an object; for example, strings, arrays, windows and even integers can be objects. Objects, in turn, are examples of classes of things; for example, the string "John Hunt" is an object of the class `String`. Thus, to program in Java, you define classes, create instances and apply operations to classes and objects.

However, unlike languages such as Smalltalk, which are considered pure object-oriented languages, Java also has standard types (such as integer) and procedural programming statements. This hybrid approach can make the transition to object orientation simpler. In some languages, such as C++, this can be a disadvantage, as the developer can avoid the object-oriented nature of the language. However, Java has no concept of a procedural program; instead, everything is held within an object (even the procedural elements).

5.4 History

Java's beginnings were not particularly auspicious. Like C before it, it rose phoenix-like from the ashes of a dropped project. The original project, code-named Green, was intended to develop "smart" consumer electronic devices (such as TV-top control boxes). It needed software to drive these small, potentially low-performance, but varied devices. The Green team did not want to use C or C++ due to technical difficulties with those languages (not least, problems associated with portability). They therefore decided to develop their own language and, by August 1991, a new object-oriented language was born. This language was called Oak. One rumour is that it was named after the tree outside the team leader's office; another is that Oak stands for "Object Application Kernel". However, at that time, it was just another programming language, which had some nice features and was good for client–server computing.

By 1993, the Green project had been renamed "First Person Inc.". It spent much of that year, and the start of the next, attempting to sell the hardware and software technology. However, the market was not there and Sun decided to drop the project and disband the team.

In mid-1993, the first Mosaic browser was released, and interest in the Internet (and in particular the World Wide Web) was growing. A number of the original project members felt that although the hardware element of the Green project might not be useful, the software language they had developed might well be perfect for the Web. They managed to convince Sun that it would be worth funding the software part of the project for a further year and Sun pumped $5 million into the software development during 1994.

In January 1995, Oak was renamed Java. This was, apparently, because Oak was already the name of a programming language; however, it may also be because Oak was not a particularly exciting name, whereas Java conjures up the right images.

In mid-1994, Java was used to build a new Web browser, called HotJava, which illustrated the potential of the Java language by allowing animated (rather than static) Web pages. This was the catalyst which really started things for the language. As Java was designed to be portable, secure and small, and to operate in real-time, it is ideally suited to the sort of environment that the Web imposes. However, it is worth noting that it is also an excellent object-oriented programming language in its own right and may well prove far more influential as a language for building standalone applications than as merely a language for animating the Web!

Since its launch in 1995, Java has caught the imagination of not only the computing community but also the populace in general. This is because of what it might do, rather than any marketing push provided by Sun: in his book *Just Java*, Peter van der Linden notes that, after Java's launch, Sun doubled the size of its Java marketing department from one person to two.

Sun released JDK 1.0 in 1996. This was the first release of the public domain developers' kit, which has become the benchmark specification for the Java platform. Since then there have been two further major releases of the JDK. The first is known as JDK 1.1 and was released early in 1997.

In December 1998 Sun released the Java 2 Platform (which had been known as JDK 1.2 during its beta testing phase). This version of Java represents the maturing of the Java platform, and we will look at this in more detail in the next chapter.

The wheel appears to have come full circle, as Sun is now talking of releasing small hand-held control devices for consumer products which contain a Java chip running Java programs. Thus Java will become a language for controlling consumer electronics (as it was originally intended to be).

5.5 Commercial Versions of Java

There are a number of commercial development environments for Java. These include IBM's VisualAge for Java, Microsoft's J++, Inprise's JBuilder, and Symantec's

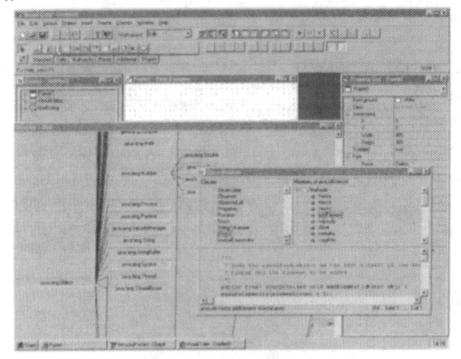

Figure 5.1 VisualCafé: an integrated development environment for Java.

VisualCafé, as well as Sun's own Java Workshop. These tools provide integrated development environments for Java (Figure 5.1). Compared with the very basic facilities of Sun's JDK, these tools are very sophisticated. Typically, they provide user interface-building tools, graphical class hierarchy browsers, dedicated class editors etc.

5.6 The Java Environment

Java is different from other development environments you may have used in that, when you write Java code, it does not execute on your host machine, even when it is compiled. Instead, it executes in a virtual machine, which in turn executes on your host computer[1]. In fact, this is part of the secret behind Java's portability – you can write code on one hardware platform and, without re-compilation, run it on another hardware platform with a completely different windowing system. In effect, your Java code always runs on the same machine: the Java Virtual Machine. There is, therefore, no concept of an "executable" in Java terms.

Instead of an executable file, you build up "class" files which hold the byte code form of the Java source. Figure 5.2 shows that a Java source file (with a .java

---

1   Java is compiled into a byte code format rather than a machine executable format. These byte codes are then executed by the virtual machine.

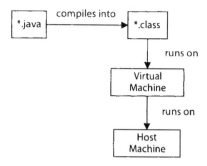

Figure 5.2 Java environment.

extension) is compiled into a byte encoded file (with a `.class` extension). The byte encoded form then runs on the virtual machine, which runs on the host machine.

5.6.1 The Java Developers' Kit

At present, Sun provides a public domain Java development environment which is known as the Java Developers' Kit (JDK)[2]. The first release of the JDK was version 1.0, in early 1996. Later in 1996, version 1.0.2 was made available and version 1.1 appeared in early 1997 (rapidly followed by the nearly identical versions 1.1.1–1.1.7).

Version 1.0.2 provided an improved set of graphic building classes, while version 1.1 implemented a new event-handling mechanism and revised the way in which native code is called from Java. The source code described in this book has been tested on versions 1.0, 1.0.2 and 1.1. The only source code which requires version 1.1 is the section dealing with graphical user interfaces (as it uses the new event-handling mechanism).

The JDK provides a number of tools, including a compiler, the virtual machine, a debugger and a documentation tool:

- **javac** is the Java language compiler. It is often read as "javack" rather than "java see", as the latter can cause confusion (i.e. it implies a Java to C converter!). It produces `.class` files containing the byte codes.

- **java** is the Java Virtual Machine, also known as the Java language run-time. It is a byte code interpreter which is implemented in two parts. The lower part is re-implemented for different platforms.

- **jdb** is the Java debugger. It is not as sophisticated as some debuggers, but can be very useful.

- **jar** is the Java archive tool. It can be used to combine (and compress) multiple files (in particular, class, image and sound files) into a single archive file. It enables you to deliver a Java application in a single file. This is particularly useful for

2 Sun has confused the issue by renaming JDK 1.2 the Java 2 Platform. In this book we take JDK 1.2 and Java 2 as the same thing, although technically there are a few differences – see the next chapter.

applets, which can be delivered by a single HTTP transaction rather than in a series of transactions.

- **javah** creates C header files and C stub files for a Java class. It allows code written in Java and C to work together. This book does not cover this issue.
- **javap** is the Java byte code disassembler.
- **javadoc** takes a Java source file and converts the class name, the methods and the variables into HTML documentation. It also searches for comments starting with /** and uses them to provide additional documentation.
- **appletviewer** allows applets to be run and viewed without the use of a browser. Applets are a special type of Java program which can be run from within a browser, such as Netscape Navigator (2.0 or higher) and Internet Explorer (3.0 or higher).

There is also a range of tools to support remote method invocation; they are not covered in this book. Note that different versions of the JDK provide slightly different versions of the tools.

The JDK is generally available and you can download it direct from Sun's Web site (http://java.sun.com/). Versions of the JDK can be downloaded for Solaris 2.x (both Sparc and x86), for Windows 95, 98 and NT, and for MacOS System 7 and above (although the Mac version tends to lag behind the versions for the other platforms). The source code in this book uses versions 1.1 and 1.2 (Java 2).

5.6.2 What Is JavaScript?

A rather confusing issue is that there is a "programming" language which can be used within HTML pages called JavaScript. This language is *not* Java and has no relationship with Java, other than a similarity with some of its syntax. However, you cannot define classes in JavaScript and thus you lose the potential power of object-oriented programming.

5.6.3 Applications and Applets

You can write two types of program in Java: applications and applets. The difference between them is essentially how they are run and what they can do:

- **applications** are standalone programs, which have the same access rights as any other standalone program.
- **applets** are special Java programs which can only execute within a Java-enabled browser or the appletviewer. They cannot access the local file store and must inherit from the applet class.

We will look at applets in more detail later in this book. However, we concentrate on the construction of applications, as I believe that this is where the biggest potential for Java lies. Applets tend to be used for animating a picture on a Web page. Of course, an applet may act as a client for a server, in which case it could be a substantial piece of code in its own right. The issues which are discussed for applications are true for such an applet).

5.6.4 Applications in Java

A number of large (and high-profile) applications have now been developed in Java. One of the very first, of course, was HotJava, the Web browser implemented by Sun to show Java's potential. Another is the Java Workshop, a visual development environment implemented in Java for Java. Sun have also produced a Web server implemented in Java, originally called Jeeves.

The World Wide Web consortium have produced a server in Java called Jigsaw. StarOffice for Java is a 100% pure Java application that provides the StarOffice Desktop on any Network Computer. StarOffice consists of the following components: word processing, spreadsheet, graphic and presentation programs; news and mail reader, event scheduler, an equation generator and an easy-to-use HTML editor. A similar suite of programs is Applix's Anyware Office. You can find out more about these applications at the Web sites mentioned in Table 5.1.

Table 5.1 Java application URLs

Application	URL
HotJava	http://www.javasoft.com/HotJava/
Java Workshop	http://www.sun.com/developer-products/java/
Jigsaw	http://www.w3.org/pub/Web/Jigsaw/
StarOffice	http://www.stardivision.com/
Anyware Office	http://www.applix.com/

5.7 Further Reading

There are a number of Java books produced by people from the Sun Java team, including Arnold and Gosling (1996), Gosling *et al.* (1996) and van der Linden (1996). Other authors include Flanagan (1996) and Cornell and Horstmann (1997).

Arnold, K. and Gosling, J. (1996). *The Java Programming Language*. Addison–Wesley, Reading, MA.
Cornell, G. and Horstmann, C. S. (1997). *Core JAVA*, 2nd edn. Prentice Hall, Englewood Cliffs, NJ.
Flanagan, D. (1996). *Java in a Nutshell*. O'Reilly and Associates.
Gosling, J., Joy, B. and Steele, G. (1996). *The Java Language Specification*. Addison–Wesley, Reading, MA.
van der Linden, P. (1996). *Just JAVA*. SunSoft Press/Prentice Hall, Englewood Cliffs, NJ.

6 Java 2 Platform: Java's Third Age?

6.1 The Three Ages of Java

Java has already undergone two ages in its evolution and now it is preparing for a third. The first two were its junior and adolescent phases and now Java 2 (JDK 1.2) aims to introduce its adult period. These periods represent the facilities provided by the language and thus its ability to construct robust real-world enterprise-oriented systems. So what have developers had up to now, and how does Java 2 improve on it?

6.1.1 Stage 1: Web Page Programming Language

This was the initial stage in Java's evolution (and covers version 1.0 of the Java Developers' Kit – JDK, released in the spring of 1996). It was quite a small language, containing only 200 or so classes. It provided basic graphical user interface facilities, rudimentary event handling, no database access but a compact safe language. Many of the classes either supported graphical components or provided basic data storage facilities. The language could be used to make Web pages come alive. It could also be used as a "personal programming" language. That is, it could be used to write small programs for an individual's personal use, but was not really suitable for large system development. This did not stop Java from being used in this way, and a number of successful systems were built. However, few intrinsic features directly supported such development. Sun saw the potential of this market and knew it could do better.

6.1.2 Stage 2: Application Development Language

In summer 1997 Sun released JDK 1.1. This was a major upgrade of the Java language. Not only did it include very many new classes (now well over 500) it also incorporated many language enhancements. For example:

- Reflection was added to the language. This allowed access to the internal definition of a class. This was particularly useful for tool developers.
- Delegation was used as the event model. This was a new, and far more powerful, event-handling model. It was used both in the GUI and in JavaBeans.
- JavaBeans were introduced. This is the Java software component model.
- Serialization of objects was made available. This was a facility embedded within the virtual machine which allowed objects (as opposed to ASCII text or numeric data) to be saved to a file. These objects could then be reloaded at a later date.

- The JDBC database interface was provided. This allowed access to very many database systems. This opened Java up as a client–server development environment.
- The Remote Method Interface was added. This allows objects executing in one virtual machine to directly call methods on an object in a different virtual machine.
- Signed applets. This allowed applets to move outside of the Java "sandbox" if the user trusted the supplier of the applet. This provided greater flexibility to the applet developer.

Other subtler, but equally significant changes, were made to many classes. In JDK 1.1, all classes[1] conformed to the JavaBeans naming conventions for accessing variables. For example, to set a value name a `set<Name>` method would be used, while to access a value a `get<Name>` method was used. This made the process of remembering the very many methods available easier.

At this stage, Java was well suited to the construction of real-world systems. It was a relatively simple matter to implement a Java program that accessed a database, retrieved some information and presented that information graphically or in table form to a user. It also allowed the straightforward construction of distributed applications using RMI. These programs could be run as standalone applications or as applets. However, the actual GUI interfaces were quite basic. For example, it was not possible to place a graphic on a button, or to provide tooltips over a button. In addition, there were no data-aware tables that could be used to directly display information obtained from a database. Third-party tools could be obtained to provide such facilities, but they were not part of Java. Again, Sun would rise to the challenge.

6.1.3 Stage 3: Enterprise Development Language

On 8 December 1998, Sun released JDK 1.2, which it rapidly renamed the Java 2 Platform[2]. This was yet another major upgrade to the language. It contains many features that have the potential to push Java from a simple application development language to an enterprise development language. That is, not only can relatively simple standalone systems be written, but also systems could now be implemented which integrate Java with business application middleware and back-end applications. As such, Java could be integrated with legacy systems (potentially written in non-object-oriented languages such as Cobol) via the Java IDL (an interface to CORBA-compliant Object Request Brokers (ORBs)).

In addition, the Java Foundation Classes (JFC) were included in Java 2. These are a major extension to the basic AWT as well as providing new facilities designed to simplify the construction of real-world applications. The JFC adapts the classic model–view–controller architecture for building user interfaces. It provides more

---

1   Actually, this should say almost all. For example, to obtain the size of a vector you do not use `getSize()`, you use `size()`!

2   Why change the name from JDK 1.2 to Java 2 Platform? This is really a marketing exercise as, during December 1998, if you tried to download Java 2, all the download pages talked about JDK 1.2. Indeed, the extra bits that Sun used to justify calling it the Java 2 Platform still required separate downloads as extensions to the JDK 1.2!

sophisticated graphical components (such as toolbars and buttons with graphics and tooltips) and support for data-aware components (such as tables). At the core of the JFC are the "Swing" components. These are the graphical elements of the JFC.

Many other classes were also improved. In some cases this represented improved performance, while in others it represented an extension of the facilities previously available. For example, the basic data structure classes had been extensively revised and extended. This made it much easier to enumerate over all the elements of a collection, as well as a new set of classes which provided for operations such as sorting and ordering.

The Java 2 Platform is thus Java at its best, as a mature development language. However, it does not stop there. Included in the Java 2 Platform is an extensions framework. This supports the dynamic downloading and installation of extensions to the Java platform. An extension is a group of Java packages that implement an API that extends the Java environment and is indicated by `javax.` in the package name. At present only two extensions are provided with the Java 2 Platform (these are the Java Servlet API and the Swing set). However, future extensions will be available from both Sun and third parties.

6.2 So What's in the Java 2 Platform?

If Java 2 is the embodiment of a third age for Java – what's in it? The core platform has been enhanced with the following features:

- *Security enhancements* Various security enhancements have been provided in Java 2. For example, a policy-based, easily configurable, fine-grained access control mechanism is provided. This introduces the concepts of "permissions" and "policy". When code is loaded, it is assigned "permissions" based on the security policy currently in effect. These control "read" and "write" access to files or directories, "connect" permissions to given hosts and ports etc. This approach improves upon the all or nothing approach of 1.0 and 1.1. It can also be extended to applications, beans, servlets etc.

- *Java IDL* The Java IDL compiler that maps IDL to Java. It also includes a Java ORB and IIOP support. This will allow Java to be easily and simply integrated with CORBA-compliant ORBs.

- *Swing* This is part of the JFC. Swing is a set of new GUI components which represent a significant improvement on the rather basic offering provided by the AWT. They are lightweight (that is implemented purely in Java) as opposed to many AWT components, which required peers implemented on the host machine. This improves the portability of the GUI. They also include the ability to use different "look and feels". These pluggable look and feels allow you to convert a display to any windowing environment (such as Windows, Macintosh or Motif) merely by selecting a different look and feel (see Figure 6.1). Note that the AWT package is still available and can be used instead of the newer Swing components if appropriate.

- *Java 2D* This is also part of the JFC. Note that although some people have been quoted as saying that Swing is pronounced Swing but spelt JFC, there are clear differences between Swing and the JFC. This is such an example: the Java 2D API is

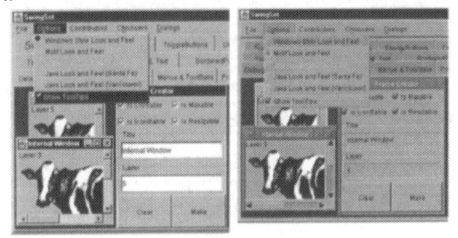

Figure 6.1 Using different "look and feels" (from the SwingSet demo).

not part of Swing, but is part of the JFC. The 2D API is a set of classes that provide extensive support for advanced 2D graphics and imaging. They go far beyond what was provided in the AWT (an example application implemented using the Java 2D API is illustrated in Figure 6.2. This is taken from J.E. Hunt and A. McManus, *Key Java: Advanced Tips and Techniques*, Springer-Verlag, 1998). For example, support is provided for line art, text and image compositing, as well as the provision of accurate colour space definitions and conversion. Note that this API is provided as a set of additions to the `java.awt` and `java.awt.image` packages (rather than as a separate package).

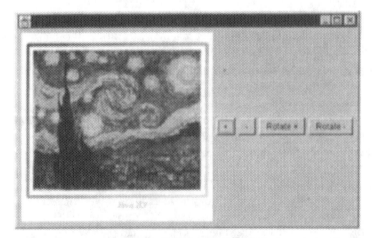

Figure 6.2 A simple 2D application.

- *Drag and Drop* Again, this is part of the JFC. This enables data transfer between a Java application and other applications (be they Java or native).

- *Accessibility* Another element of the JFC is the accessibility API. This provides access to all elements of the JFC and AWT allowing systems to interact directly with an application. For example, blind users may "speak" to the system, and the accessibility API would allow access to the same buttons and text fields as a visually able user might access. Thus the blind user could specify the selection box to access and the item in the selection box to select.

- *Application services* This contains a whole host of bits and bobs which have been added to the JFC. For example, keyboard navigation is included here and the undo mechanism for commands is available, as well as things such as custom cursors and a design tool to help in debugging graphic applications.

- *Collections* The collections API is a major enhancement of the data structure classes in Java. By data structure classes I am referring to classes such as `Vector` and `Hashtable` in the `java.util` package. The collection classes extend and refine the classes available. For example, there are classes such as `HashSet` (a general purpose `Set` implementation), `ArraySet` (a resizable array), `ArrayList` (an unsynchronized `Vector`), `LinkedList`, `HashMap` (an unsynchronized `Hashtable`) and `TreeMap` (a balanced binary tree), as well as `Vector` and `Hashtable`. It also includes a new iteration infrastructure which is more powerful and simpler to use, support for ordering (sorting) operations, and interfaces which support `Collection`, `Set`, `List` and `Map` functions.

- *Extensions Framework* This was mentioned earlier. All extensions are identified by the package name "javax".

- *Version identification* This addresses a long overdue weakness of the Java package framework; the inability to specify a particular package version.

- *Input method framework* This allows test editing components to receive Japanese, Chinese or Korean text.

- *Enhancements of existing APIs* These are enhancements to a number of APIs including the JavaBeans, RMI, Serialization, Audio JAR, Reflection, JDBC and JNI APIs. These enhancements are varied and include performance improvements, overcoming previous weaknesses and support for newly introduced features. Possibly the most significant are the performance enhancements which aim to improve memory allocation and garbage collection, compression for loaded classes and JIT compilers.

- *Others* There are a number of other introductions, such as Reference Objects that allow the programmer to maintain a reference to an object but which does not prevent the object from being reclaimed by the garbage collector. Another new feature is the Java Virtual Machine Debugger Interface which now provides low-level services for debugging.

From this you can see that Java 2 is more of a consolidation release than a whole new departure. This is probably no bad thing. The introduction of two completely different event-handling mechanisms in JDK 1.0 and JDK 1.1 led to incompatibilities, delays in the uptake of 1.1 and a great deal of reference material going out of date very quickly. It is also interesting to note that Sun has acknowledged the problems which faced early adopters of JDK 1.1 in terms of incompatible Web browsers. They have provided a browser plug-in which provides a Java Virtual Machine for Java 2.

Figure 6.3 Menus with icons (from SwingSet demo).

6.3 Analysis of the Java 2 Platform

The analysis is divided into two parts, covering the strengths and weaknesses of the Java 2 Platform.

6.3.1 Strengths

The Swing set provide a comprehensive set of components which at last make it possible to implement industry-standard GUIs in Java (for example including icons on menus; see Figure 6.3), while the collections API is beginning to move toward the level of support which Smalltalk programmers have enjoyed for years in constructing data structures. The security enhancements are both timely and sensible and open up much greater flexibility in controlling what a Java program can and cannot do. The introduction of Drag and Drop (finally) is a welcome addition, and important if Java applications are to be used on the desktop in a similar manner to many other applications. The performance enhancements introduced in JDK 1.2 are of course welcome, but the full potential will only be realized when the HotSpot run-time becomes available. The extensions framework provides a simple, standard and effective way of plugging third-party add-ons into the Java platform and could well be a key element of JDK 1.2. It is already being used extensively by Sun itself in providing a range of add-on facilities to Java (for example the Java Servlet API).

To return to Swing, many of its features are particularly significant. For example, the introduction of tooltips for buttons etc. is both effective and incredible simple to do (a tooltip for a button is illustrated in Figure 6.4). However, it makes the resulting application appear far more professional. Introducing dockable menu bars likewise improves the professional appearance of an application. The tree component and its associated classes are less easy to use, but result in great flexibility and adaptability (see Figure 6.5). These trees can grow, shrink or by modified on the fly. As they also adopt the pluggable look and feel approach, they can be made to mimic Windows

Figure 6.4 A button with a tooltip.

Figure 6.5 A simple table (from the SwingSet demo).

trees or Motif-style trees. The support for images allows the creation of much more powerful image-based applications.

6.3.2 Weaknesses

Although the performance of the early releases of JDK 1.2 was not particularly good (partly due to the inclusion of a great deal of debugging information), the performance of the final release is much better; however, as stated before, the HotSpot technology has yet to be included. Another problem with Java 2 is that versioning has only been applied to packages. It is not possible to specify different versions of classes. This is a pity, because that is exactly what is often required. Although there are workarounds for this, a package is often too large a grouping to work with.

A major bugbear of any of those who have been looking at early releases of Swing and the JDK 1.2 has been that of reliability. Basically, Swing has been full of "bugs". Indeed, seven different releases of the Swing set have appeared, two of these after Sun publicly stated it they would not be releasing any further version of the beta release of the Swing set as it was now stable. This does not bode well for the final release of the JDK 1.2. Indeed, if the JDK 1.1 is anything to go by, we could expect more than several "maintenance" releases of the JDK 1.2. If this happens, developers could well lose confidence in the JDK altogether. As Sun has already proved with the Swing set, this is not an easy thing to get right. Obviously, all these Swing releases have been either alpha or beta early releases, which should not expect to be 100% reliable, but let us hope that the final release is. It is notable that the final release of the 1.2 JDK was postponed by Sun in a bid to ensure that it was reliable, with four different candidate releases publically available for comment before the final version was released. During this period, Sun's Java Web site explained that a dedicated team of developers and tester were testing, retesting and regression testing every aspect of Java to ensure the quality of the product.

Finally, a weakness that is to some extent outside Sun's control is the time taken for tool vendors to provide support for the new release. It took many vendors at least 6 months to support JDK 1.1 and far longer for the browser vendors to move towards 1.1. If it takes as long for these vendors to move towards 1.2 this will have a negative effect on its viability (and that of Java). Although the Java 2 Browser plug-in may mitigate this effect to some extent.

6.4 Conclusions

In conclusion, the key elements of Java 2 for most developers are (not surprisingly) the Swing set and other JFC APIs, the performance enhancements and the collection classes. From personal experience, I did not really notice most of the other additions or enhancements. But perhaps that is the point: the other aspects of Java 2 should just fit in, and you gain the benefit without necessarily realizing why.

6.5 Online References

Java 1.2 (including Swing Set demo) is available through Sun's JavaSoft Web pages:

```
http://java.sun.com/
```

Also, check out the Swing home pages:

```
http://java.sun.com/products/jfc/swingdoc-current/
    index.html
```

JavaSoft article on Swing, parts 1 and 2:

```
http://developer.javasoft.com/developer/onlineTraining/
    swing/
http://developer.javasoft.com/developer/onlineTraining/
    swing2/
```

Also, check out the Java 2D home pages:

```
http://java.sun.com/products/java-media/2D/index.html
```

JavaSoft technical article on Java 2D:

```
http://developer.javasoft.com/developer/
    technicalArticles/monicap/2DGraphics/Intro/
    simple2D.html
```

7 Basic Java

7.1 Introduction

In the last two chapters, you learned a little about the history of Java and the Java development environment. In this chapter, you will encounter the Java language, the compiler, the debugger, the Java Virtual Machine and the `javadoc` utility.

Just to get you started, we will add two numbers together. First we do it in a procedural language, such as Pascal:

```
int a, b, c;
a := 1;
b := 2;
c := a + b;
```

This says something like, "create three variables to hold integer values (call them a, b and c). Store the value 1 into variable a and 2 into variable b. Add the two numbers together and save the result into the third variable, c". Now we look at how we could write the same thing in Java:[1]

```
Integer a b c;
a = new Integer(1);
b = new Integer(2);
c = new Integer(a + b);
```

As you can see, this looks basically the same (apart from the use of = rather than := and the need to state that we are going to use a new integer instance for each value). However, although the effect is the same, and the look similar, the meaning is dramatically different. In Java, the code says:

Define three temporary variables a, b and c. These variables will hold an object which is an instance of Integer or one of its subclasses. Create a new object of the class Integer and assign the value 1 to it. The object is then assigned to variable a. Create a new object of the class Integer and assign the value 2 to it. The object is then assigned to variable b. Take the value of the object in a, which is 1, and add that to the value of the object in b, which is 2. The result is then saved into a newly created instance of the class Integer. Then save this object into the variable c.

---

1 This is slightly contrived, as we could just as easily have used the built-in integer type. However, many situations require the Integer object, so it is a useful example.

The concepts of messages, classes, objects etc. are explained in more detail elsewhere. I hope that, by the end of this book, you can read the above definition and say "of course".

7.2 Setting Up the Development Environment

As was discussed in the last two chapters, the JDK comes with a number of tools, including a Java compiler (javac), a Java Virtual Machine (java), a tool for viewing applets (appletViewer), a rudimentary debugger (jdb) and a documentation tool (javadoc). You use these tools to create, debug, document and use Java programs. Depending on your environment and your platform, the actual details of how you install the JDK (or any set of Java tools) differ, and you should follow the guidelines provided.

Whatever your platform, you should be aware of the CLASSPATH environment variable. This variable tells Java where to look for class definitions, so it should at least point to the run-time library and the current directory. It may also point to other directories in which you have defined classes. In Windows 95 or 98, you may change CLASSPATH in the autoexec.bat file (Figure 7.1 shows my personal autoexec.bat) by adding the following declaration:

```
SET CLASSPATH=.;c:\java\lib\classes.zip
```

For Solaris 2.3, define CLASSPATH in your .cshrc file:

```
setenv CLASSPATH .:/usr/local/misc/Java/lib/
    classes.zip
```

Note that the default installations do not set up the classpath – they already know where to look for the classes. However, if you want to use packages at a later date you *will* need to set the classpath! You should also add the Java bin directory to your path. You should now be ready to use the Java tools.

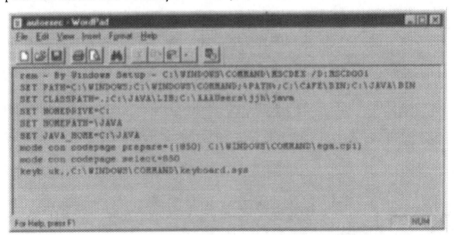

Figure 7.1 Setting up the autoexec.bat file for Java.

7.3 Compiling and Executing Java

```java
public class Hello {
  public static void main (String argv[]) {
    System.out.println("Hello World");
  }
}
```

Type in the program above very carefully to ensure that the syntax is correct. At this point, do not worry about what it means; we are only trying to get to grips with the tools provided by the JDK. Once you have typed in the text, save it to a file called:

```
Hello.java
```

Ensure that you use exactly the same capitalization as above. Next bring up a command line prompt. How you do this depends on the environment you are using. For example, in a UNIX box, it may involve opening an XTERM; on Windows 95/98, you may need to bring up the DOS prompt. You can then compile your Java program using the `javac` command:

```
> javac Hello.java
```

If it compiles successfully, it generates a `Hello.class` file which contains the byte codes. For example, on a Windows machine, the directory listing looks like this:

```
HELLO~1  JAV 344 22/01/97   14:20 Hello.java
HELLO~1  CLA 461 20/01/97   14:24 Hello.class
```

You can then run the generated byte codes on the Java Virtual Machine using the `java` program:

```
> java Hello
```

Notice that we do not provide an extension for the program, only the main part of the filename. You should then see the phrase "Hello World" appear in the window (see Figure 7.2).

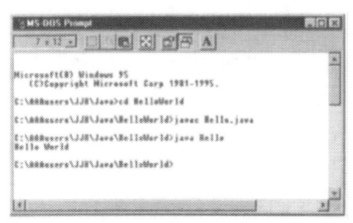

Figure 7.2 Compiling and running a Java program.

Congratulations! You have now written, compiled and run your first Java application.

7.4 Using the Java Debugger

Many books present you with source code to type in and execute, but give very little guidance on how to deal with errors. Therefore, in this section you get to type in some (intentionally) buggy Java code and compile it. This forces you to use tools such as the debugger to identify and correct the errors. After all, at this stage, you are more likely to write buggy Java than perfect Java.

Note that we are using the debugger supplied with JDK 1.1 for this example, as this is the commonest version of Java in current commercial use.

Type in the code below exactly as given:

```java
public class BuggyTest {

    public static void main (String args []) {
        BuggyTest anObject = new BuggyTest ();
        anObject.calculate (2, 0);
    }
    public void calculate (int a, int b) {
        int result = 0;
        result = a / b;
        System.out.println (result);
    }
}
```

Compile and run this program (see Figure 7.3). As you can see, a divide by zero exception was raised in the `calculate` method, which was called by the `main` method. In this case, it is simple to identify the problem. However, let us assume for a moment that the program is somewhat bigger and it is more difficult to identify the error.

One way of identifying the problem would be to place numerous print statements in the source code to determine variable values or execution paths. This is not the

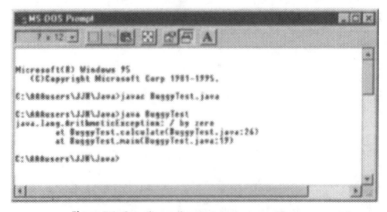

Figure 7.3 Compiling and running a program with errors.

best approach, as adding (or removing) these statements can introduce other errors. It is also time-consuming and cumbersome. The JDK provides a debugger, thus eliminating such concerns.

For anyone who has used tools such as VisualWorks, Visual C++ or Delphi, the debugger provided by the JDK is rudimentary at best (others are available, particularly with the commercial toolkits such as VisualCafé). However, the jdb is free and provides a minimum operating environment. To use the debugger, you must compile the Java program with the -g option:

```
> javac -g BuggyTest.java
```

Having done this, you can start the debugger:

```
> jdb BuggyTest
```

Notice that although we compile the file using the Java compiler, we do not use the Java Virtual Machine; instead, we run the byte code through the debugger (jdb). An annoying feature is that TCP/IP networking services must be running, even if you are not debugging a network application, in order for the jdb to operate.

Once you have started the debugger, you need to tell it what you want to do. For example, you can set a breakpoint, tell it to start running, display local variables etc. The main jdb control commands are presented in Table 7.1.

Table 7.1 Main control commands

run	executes loaded application
run class	starts specified class
load class	loads a class
gc	initiates garbage collection
exit (or quit)	exits jdb
!!	executes last command

Table 7.2 shows the basic jdb commands that provide information. You can see the wide range of jdb commands with the help command.

Table 7.2 Information access commands

dump	dumps an object's instance variables to the screen
help (or ?)	lists commands
list line	lists line of course code
locals	prints current local variables
memory	provides information on memory usage
methods	lists methods of a (named) class
print	prints details about an object or field
threads	lists the current threads
where	dumps stack of current thread

You can set a breakpoint in a method or relative to a line position in a .java file. Table 7.3 presents the breakpoint commands.

Table 7.3 Breakpoint commands

`stop in class.method`	sets a breakpoint in a specific method in the named class
`stop in class:line`	sets a breakpoint on a line in a .java file
`clear class.method`	clears a method breakpoint
`clear class:line`	clears a breakpoint
`step`	executes the current line
`cont`	continues execution from a breakpoint

The normal way of using the jdb is to set one or more breakpoints such that you can identify errors. You then run your program, which halts when it encounters a breakpoint. You can examine information about the local objects at that point. In some situations, you may decide to exit the debugger and change the class. In other situations, you may wish to move on to the next breakpoint.

Let us briefly consider the BuggyTest class example. The following is a typescript from running the jdb on a UNIX workstation:

```
1 bob.dcs.aber.ac.uk > javac -g BuggyTest.java
2 bob.dcs.aber.ac.uk > jdb BuggyTest
Initializing jdb...
0xee305738:class(BuggyTest)
```

At this point, we have started the jdb but have not actually done anything. The first thing we do is to set a breakpoint on the method calculate:

```
> stop in BuggyTest.calculate
Breakpoint set in BuggyTest.calculate
```

We now have a breakpoint and can run our application:

```
> run
run BuggyTest
Breakpoint hit: BuggyTest.calculate (BuggyTest:25)
main[1] running ...
```

The debugger halts when it encounters the breakpoint on the calculate method. We can now examine the state of the object and the values held by the method (using the locals keyword):

```
main[1] locals
Method arguments:
   this = BuggyTest@1dc60cb8
   a = 2
   b = 0
Local variables:
   result is not in scope.
```

We can see from this that the method halts just as it is called and before the first statement is evaluated (that is why `result` is not in the scope). We can continue until the anticipated exception is raised:

```
main[1] cont
main[1]
Uncaught exception:java.lang.ArithmeticException / by
    zero
  at BuggyTest.calculate(BuggyTest.java:26)
  at BuggyTest.main(BuggyTest.java:19)
  at sun.tools.debug.MainThread.run(Agent.java:55)
```

At this point, we can compare the message with the values held by the local variables and attempt to identify the problem:

```
main[1] locals
Method arguments:
  this = BuggyTest@1dc60cb8
  a = 2
  b = 0
Local variables:
  result = 0
```

If we examine the code, we see that a is divided by b, that is, 2 is divided by zero, giving rise to the exception. We can return to the class definition and change it.

```
main[1] quit
```

As you can see from this example, the jdb is not very sophisticated; however, it can be extremely useful in identifying bugs.

7.5 Using the Java Documentation Tool

Now that we have written our simple program, we wish to document it. This process can be simplified by using the javadoc utility, which processes our Java class to produce a set of Web pages which document its definition, interface and variables. You run the .java file through the javadoc program:

```
> javadoc BuggyTest.java
```

While it runs, you can see the following output:

```
C:\AAAusers\JJH\Java>javadoc BuggyTest
Loading source files for BuggyTest
Generating packages.html
Generating index
Generating tree

C:\AAAusers\JJH\Java>
```

This utility generates four .html files, which contain information about the packages available, the classes in the current package, an index of all variables and methods, and the class hierarchy involving the current class:

```
PACKAG~1    HTM 505 14/02/97 14:58 packages.html
PACKAG~2    HTM 341 14/02/97 14:58 Package-BuggyTest.html
ALLNAM~1    HTM 989 14/02/97 14:58 AllNames.html
TREE~1      HTM 378 14/02/97 14:58 tree.html
```

You can read these files using any Web browser. The BuggyTest class is very basic, and therefore these .html files are essentially empty.

7.6 Summary

You have now used a number of Java tools and written some Java code. You have also used some of the tools available to help you debug your code. You are now ready for the Java language itself!

7.7 Further Reading

If you are going to do any serious development in Java, then you should consider obtaining at least Volume 1 of Gosling and Yellin (1996), which concentrates on programming facilities. Volume 2 concentrates on the Abstract Window Toolkit graphical facilities.

Gosling, J. and Yellin, F. (1996). *The Java Application Programming Interface, Vol. 1: Core Packages*. Addison-Wesley, Reading, MA.

8 *Java Building Blocks*

8.1 Introduction

This chapter presents an introduction to the Java programming language. As such, it is not intended to be a comprehensive guide. It introduces the basic elements of the Java language, discusses the concept of classes and instances and how they are defined, presents methods and method definitions, and considers interface specifications.

8.2 The Basics of the Language

All Java programmers make extensive use of the existing classes, even when they write relatively trivial code. For example, the following version of the "Hello World" program reuses existing classes rather than just using the language (do not worry too much about the syntax of the definition or the parameters to the main method – we will return to them later):

```
public class HelloWorld {

  public static void main (String argv []) {

    String myName = "John Hunt";
    if (myName.endsWith("Hunt")) {
      System.out.println("Hello " + myName); }
    else {
      System.out.println("Hello World"); }
  }
}
```

In this example, I have reused the String class to represent the string "John Hunt" and to find a substring in it using the message endsWith(). Some of you may say that there is nothing unusual in this, and that many languages have string-handling extensions. However, in this case, it is the string contained within myName which decides how to handle the endsWith message and thus whether it contains the substring "Hunt". That is, the data itself handles the processing of the string! What is printed to standard output thus depends on which object receives the message. These features illustrate the extent to which existing classes are reused: you cannot help but reuse existing code in Java – you do so by the very act of programming.

As well as possessing objects and classes, Java also possesses an inheritance mechanism. This feature separates Java from object-based languages, such as Ada, which do not possess inheritance. For example, in the simple program above, I reuse the class `Object` (the root of all classes in Java) and the class `HelloWorld` automatically inherits all the features of `Object`.

Inheritance is very important in Java. It promotes the reuse of classes and enables the explicit representation of abstract concepts (such as the class `Dictionary`), which can then be turned into concrete concepts (such as the class `HashTable`). It is also one of the primary reasons why Java is so successful as a rapid application development tool – you inherit much of what you want and only define the ways in which your application differs from what is already available.

8.2.1 Some Terminology

We now recap some of the terminology introduced in Part 1 of this book, explaining it with reference to Java.

In Java programs, actions or operations are performed by passing *messages* to and from objects. An object (the *sender* of the message) uses a message to request that a procedure (referred to in Java as a *method*) be performed by another object (the *receiver* of the message). Just as procedure calls can contain parameters, so can messages.

Java is a typed language; however, the typing relates to the class of an object (or the interface that a class implements – we will return to this later) rather than its specific type. Thus, by saying that a method can take a parameter of a particular class, you actually mean that any instance of that class (or one of its subclasses) can be passed into that method.

8.2.2 The Message-Passing Mechanism

The Java message-passing mechanism is somewhat like a procedure call in a conventional language:

- The point of control moves to the receiver; the object sending a message is suspended until it receives a response.
- The receiver of a message is not determined when the code is created (at *compile time*); it is identified when the message is sent (at *run time*).

This *dynamic* (or *late*) binding mechanism is the feature which gives Java its polymorphic capabilities (see Chapter 1 for a discussion of polymorphism).

8.2.3 The Statement Terminator

In Java, the majority of statements terminate with a semi-colon (;):

```
System.out.println("Hello World");
```

8.3 Classes

A class is the basic building block in Java. Classes act as *templates* which are used to construct instances. Classes allow programmers to specify the *structure* of an object (i.e. its instance variables etc.) and the function of an object (i.e. its methods) separately from the object itself. This is important, as it would be extremely time-consuming (as well as inefficient) for programmers to define each object individually. Instead, they define classes and create *instances* of the classes.

8.3.1 Class Definitions

In Java, a class definition has the following format (note the keyword **static** before the class variable but not before the instance variable):

```
scopeOfClass class nameOfClass extends SuperClass {
    scope static type classVariable;
    scope type instanceVariable;
}
```

You need not remember this format precisely, as the meanings of the various parts of the class definition are explained later in the book. Indeed, the above is far from complete, but it illustrates the basic features. The following code is an example of a class definition:

```
public class Person extends Object {
    private int age = 0;
    public String name = "Bob";
}
```

This code defines a new class, Person, which is a subclass of the Object class (all classes extend Object by default; it is stated here only as an illustration). The new class possesses two *instance variables* called name and age. It has no class variables and no methods.

Notice that the age instance variable contains a value of type int (this is a basic data type), while the instance variable name possesses an object of the class String. Both variables are initialized: age to zero and name to the string "Bob".

Classes are not just used as templates. They have three further responsibilities: holding methods, providing facilities for inheritance and creating instances.

8.3.2 Classes and Messages

When a message is sent to an object, it is not the object which possesses the method but the class. This is for efficiency reasons: if each object possessed a copy of all the methods defined for the class then there would be a great deal of duplication. Instead, only the class possesses the method definitions. Thus, when an object receives a message, it searches its class for a method with the name in the message. If its own class does not possess a method with the appropriate name, it goes to the superclass and searches again. This search process continues up the class hierarchy until either an appropriate method is found or the class hierarchy terminates (with the class Object). If the hierarchy terminates, an error is raised.

If an appropriate method is found, then it executes *within the context of the object*, although the definition of the method resides in the class. Thus, different objects can execute the same method at the same time without conflict.

Do not confuse methods with instance variables. Each instance possesses its own copy of the instance variables (as each instance possesses its own state). Figure 8.1 illustrates this idea more clearly.

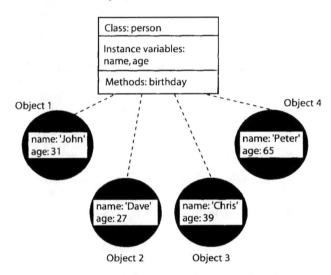

Figure 8.1 Multiple instance variables but a single method.

8.3.3 Instances and Instance Variables

In Java, an *object* is an *instance* of a *class*. All instances of a class share the same responses to messages (methods), but they contain different data (i.e. they possess a different "state"). For example, the instances of class Point all respond in the same way to messages inquiring about the value of the x-coordinate, but they may provide different values.

The class definition consists of variable declarations and method definitions. The state of each instance is maintained in one or more instance variables (also known as fields).

Figure 8.1 contains four instances of the class Person. Each instance contains copies of the instance variable definitions for name and age, thus enabling them to have their own values for these instance variables. In contrast, each instance references the single definition for the method birthday, which is held by the class.

8.3.4 Classes and Inheritance

It is through classes that an object inherits facilities from other types of object. That is, a subclass inherits properties from its superclass. For example, the Person definition above is a subclass of Object. Therefore, Person inherits all the methods and instance variables which were defined in Object (except those that were overwritten in Person).

Subclasses are used to refine the behaviour and data structures of a superclass. It should be noted that Java supports single inheritance, while some of the object-oriented languages (most notably C++) support multiple inheritance. Multiple inheritance is where a subclass can inherit from more than one superclass. However, difficulties can arise when attempting to determine where methods are executed. Java introduces the concept of *interfaces* to overcome one of the most significant problems with single inheritance. However, the discussion of Java interfaces comes later in the book.

An Example of Inheritance

To illustrate how single inheritance works, consider Figure 8.2. There are three classes: Class1 is a subclass of Object, Class2 is a subclass of Class1 and Class3 is a subclass of Class2.

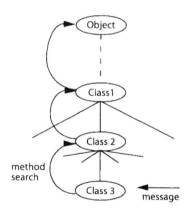

Figure 8.2 Class inheritance in Java.

When an instance of Class3 is created, it contains all the instance variables defined in classes 1 to 3 and class Object. If any instance variable has the same name as an instance variable in a higher class, then the Class3 instance uses the instance variable definition from the nearest class. That is, Class3 definitions take priority over Class2 and Class2 definitions take priority over Class1 etc.

We can send an instance of Class3 a message requesting that a particular method is executed. Remember that methods are held by classes and not by instances. This means that the system first finds the class of the instance (in this case Class3) and searches it for the required method. If the method is found, then the search stops and the method is executed. However, if the method is not found, then the system searches the superclass for Class3, in this case Class2. This process is repeated until the method is found. Eventually, the search through the superclasses may reach the class Object (which is the root class in the Java system). If the required method is not found here, then the search process terminates and the doesNotUnderstand: method in the class Object is executed instead. This method raises an exception stating that the message sent to the original instance is not understood.

This search process is repeated every time a message is sent to the instance of Class3. Thus, if the method which matches the original message sends a message to its own object (i.e. the instance of Class3), then the search for that method starts again in Class3 (even if it was found in Class1).

The Yo-Yo Problem

The process described above can pose a problem for a programmer trying to follow the execution of the system by tracing methods and method execution. This problem is known as the Yo-Yo problem (see Figure 8.3, which is based on the java.awt package) because, every time you encounter a message which is sent to "this" (the current object), you must start searching from your own class. This may result in jumping up and down the class hierarchy.

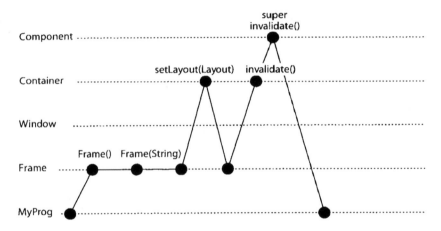

Figure 8.3 The yo-yo problem.

The problem occurs because you know that the execution search starts in the current instance's class, even if the method which sends the message is defined in a superclass of the current class. In Figure 8.3, the programmer starts the search in Class3, but finds the method definition in Class1; however this method sends a message to "this" which means that the programmer must restart the search in Class3. This time, the method definition is found in the class Object, and so on. Even with the browsing tools provided, this can still be a tedious and confusing process (particularly for those new to Java).

8.3.5 Instance Creation

A class creates an instance in response to a request, which is handled by a constructor. It may be confusing, but classes can possess class-specific methods and class instance variables. These are often referred to as class-side (or static) methods and variables and they can respond to a message as an instance would.

A programmer requests a new instance of a class using the following construct:

new ClassName();

Any parameters which need to be passed on to the class can be placed between the parentheses. They are then passed on to an appropriate constructor. Constructors are the most commonly defined class-side methods. They possess the same name as the class and are used to initialize a new instance of the class in an appropriate manner (you do not need to know the details of the process). The whole of this process is referred to as instantiation. An example of instantiating the class Person is presented below:

new Person("John Hunt", 33);

The class Person receives the message new, which causes the class method new to generate a new instance of the class, with its own copy of the instance variables age and name (see Figure 8.4). The name of the instance is "John Hunt" and the age is set to 33.

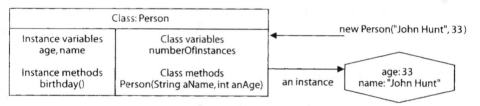

Figure 8.4 Instance creation.

The issue of classes having methods, some of which are intended for an instance of the class and some of which are intended for the class, is not as complicated as it may at first seem, not least because the language syntax used with Java tends to keep the two *sides* of classes pretty well distinct. To aid this, when developing most programmers define the class side before defining the instance side of the class. Some of the tools now available for Java also make this separation distinct and simplify the whole development process.

In an attempt to make it clearer, here are some definitions:

- *Instance variables* are defined in the class, but a copy is maintained in each instance, which has its own value.
- *Class (or static) variables* are defined in the class, with a single copy maintained in the class.
- *Instance methods* are defined in the class, with a single copy maintained in the class, but they are executed within the context of an object.
- *Class (or static) methods* are defined in the class, with a single copy maintained in the class, and executed within the context of the class.

The accessibility of these variables and methods depends on whether the programmer has made them public, private or protected. Some of these concepts are considered in greater detail later.

8.3.6 Constructors

A constructor is not a method but a special operator which is executed when a new instance of a class is created. Depending on the arguments passed to the class when the instance is generated, a different constructor can be called. For example, a class may need to have three fields initialized when it is instantiated. However, the programmer may allow the user of the class to provide one, two or three values. They can do this by defining constructors which take one, two or three parameters.

The syntax for a constructor is:

```
scopeofclass class classname {
    scopeofconstructor classname ( ... parameters ...) {
    ... statements ...
    }
}
```

By default, every class has a single constructor with no parameters. However, as soon as you define a constructor, the default constructor is no longer available. Notice that constructors, unlike methods, are not inherited.

8.3.7 Static Initialization Blocks

A class can also possess a static initialization block, which initializes the values to be held in class variables. This is useful if the initial values are not straightforward literals, but are related to some function (which may depend on other values held within the system).

```
class className {
    class variable definitions...
    static {
        ...initialization statements...
    }
}
```

Initialization blocks cannot call methods which may throw an exception back to the message sender (in this case, the initialization block) unless the initialization block explicitly handles the exception.

Static initialization blocks are only run when the class is loaded into the system. They are therefore only run once, and this is not under the control of the programmer.

The compiler cannot catch cycles between classes caused by static initialization blocks. Thus, the result can be unpredictable and depends on the point at which the cycle occurred and the class variables which were set. For example, assume that class A's initialization block calls a class method in class B. Class B is then loaded into the system; however, its initialization block calls a class method in class A. At this point, class A's initialization block has not completed and the correct functioning of its class methods may depend on class variables which have yet to be initialized.

8.3.8 Instance Initialization Blocks

Just as there are class initialization blocks, you can also define instance initialization blocks. These will be run just after the instance is created and just before the constructor is executed. If you have more than one constructor and want some initialization (which does not require parameterization) always to be executed, you could place this in an instance initialization block. Such a block is defined in a very similar manner to the static initialization block without the static keyword. For example:

```
class className {
    instance variable definitions...
    {
        ...instance initialization statements...
    }
}
```

8.3.9 Finalize Methods

In Java, memory is managed automatically for you by the Java Virtual Machine (JVM). You do not therefore have to destroy objects or reclaim the memory they use. However, there is a Java facility which allows you to execute a special method (referred to as a finalize method) when the JVM reclaims (or collects as garbage) an object. These methods are typically used for application-specific housekeeping and are not intended as destructor methods (which you may have seen in other languages).

You define a finalize method in the following way:

```
protected void finalize() throws Throwable {
    super.finalize();
    ...
}
```

Notice that the method is **protected**. This special modifier keyword limits the visibility of the method (we look at this further in Chapter 10). The **throws** Throwable element is an exception which may be raised by the finalize method defined in the superclass (again, we return to exceptions later in the book). Finally, the first statement in the method is a call to:

```
super.finalize();
```

This is a request to run the finalize method inherited by this class before running this version of the finalize method. This allows the finalize method to be extended rather than replaced.

8.3.10 Supplied Classes

There are very many classes in any Java system. For example, JDK 1.0 provided 139 and releases 1.0.2 and 1.1 both added classes, bringing the numbers up to 211 and 503 respectively. Java 2 added further classes, taking the count to over the 1000 mark. However, you only need to become familiar with a very few of them. The remaining classes provide facilities that you use without even realizing it.

8.4 Method Definitions

Methods provide a way of defining the behaviour of an object, i.e. what the object does. For example, a method may change the state of the object or it may retrieve some information. A method is the equivalent of a procedure in most other languages. A method can only be defined within the scope of an object. It has a specific structure:

```
access control modifier returnType methodName (args) {
    /* comments */
    local variable definitions
    statements
}
```

The *access control modifier* is one of the keywords which indicate the visibility of the method. The returnType is the type of the object returned, for example String or int. methodName represents the name of the method and args represents the types and names of the arguments. These arguments are accessible within the method.

8.4.1 The Comments Section

The /* comments */ section describes the operation performed by the method and any other useful information. Comments cannot be nested in Java, which can be awkward if you wish to comment out some code for later. For example, consider the following piece of Java:

```
/*
x = 12 * 4;
/* Now calculate y */
y = x * 23;
*/
```

The Java compiler reads this as a comment, followed by the code y = x * 23;, followed by the end of another comment. This causes an error. However, Java has two other types of comment. You can instruct the Java compiler to ignore everything until the end of the line, using the // indicator:

```
x = 12 * 4;
// Now calculate y
y = x * 23;
```

The final type of comment, the documentation comment, starts with /** and ends with */. Note the two asterisks at the beginning of this statement. They are

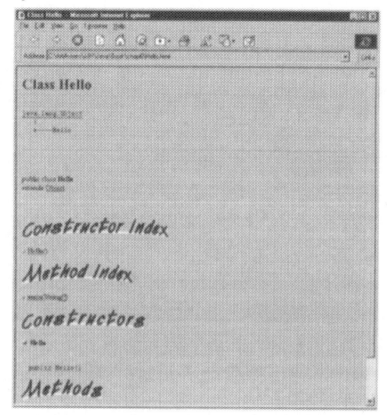

Figure 8.5 Viewing the javadoc-generated `Hello` class HTML page.

picked up and processed by the documentation utility (javadoc), which generates HTML pages that can be viewed in a Web browser (see Figure 8.5).

8.4.2 The Local Variables Section

In the local variable definition section, you define variables which are local to the method. These variables are typed and can appear anywhere in the method definition.

```
birthday()
   int newAge = 0;
   ...
```

8.4.3 The Statements Section

The statements section represents any legal set of Java statements that implement the behaviour of the method.

One of the uses of methods is to provide an interface between an object's internal data and the outside world. Such a method, often termed an accessor method, retrieves the value of an instance variable and makes it available to other objects. For example, the class Person has two instance variables age and name. The method getAge returns the age of an employee. Thus in response to the message getAge(), this method is executed and the value of the person's age is returned to the object sending the message.

In this situation the person's age is held explicitly. An equally valid internal representation for a Person would be to have an instance variable, dateOfBirth. The method getAge would need to calculate the age as the difference between the date of birth and the current date.

Notice that this would change the implementation of Person, but there would be no change as far as any other object in the system is concerned. This illustrates the encapsulation possible with Java (and other object-oriented programming languages).

8.4.4 The return Operator

Once a method has executed, an answer can be returned to the sender of the message. The value returned (whether an object, a basic type or an instance of a subclass) must match the return type specified in the method definition. The return expression in Java is the last expression executed in a method, although it need not be the last expression in the method.

The Java keyword to return a value is return (just as in C):

```
if (x == y)
   return x;
else
   return y;
```

In this case, the value of x or y is returned, depending upon whether x and y are equal or not.

8.4.5 An Example Method

Let us examine a simple method definition in Java. We wish to define a procedure to take in a number, add 10 to it and return the result.

```
public int addTen (int aNumber) {
   int result;
   result = aNumber + 10;
   return result;
}
```

Although the format may be slightly different from code that you have been used to, it is relatively straightforward. If you have C or C++ experience you might think that it is exactly the same as what you have seen before. Be careful with that idea – things are not always what they seem!

Let us look at some of the constituent parts of the method definition. The method name is addTen. Notice that every method name is followed by () whether it takes parameters or not. If it does, then the parameters are placed within the parentheses. In this case, the method has one parameter, called aNumber, of the basic type int. Just as in any other language, the parameter variable is limited to the scope of this method. The method also defines a temporary variable, result, also of the basic type int and limited to the scope of this method.

Variable names are identifiers that contain only letters and numbers and must start with a letter (the underscore, _, and the dollar sign, $, count as letters). Some examples are:

```
anObject  MyCar totalNumber $total
```

However, the Java convention is always to start a variable with a "normal" letter. Similarly the elements of a variable name are not separated by an underscore or a hyphen as in some language, rather by a capitalization convention. This is used consistently throughout Java, and most Java programmers adhere to this standard:

- *Private variables and methods* (i.e. instance or temporary variables and almost all methods) start with a lower-case letter.
- *Shared variables* (e.g. class-side variables) start with an upper-case letter.
- *Shared constants* are all in upper-case (e.g. TT_EOF).
- *Constructors and classes* always start with an upper-case letter.

Another convention is that if a variable or method name combines two or more words, then you should capitalize the first letter of each word, from the second word onwards, e.g. displayTotalPay, returnStudentName.

8.5 Interface Definitions

The Java *interface* construct is essentially a skeleton which specifies the protocol that a class must provide if it implements that interface. That is, it indicates the methods which must be available from any class which implements that interface. The interface itself does not define any functionality. The format for an interface is:

```
access-modifier interface interface-name {
   static variable definitions
   method headers...
}
```

The following interface specifies that any class implementing the OrganizerIO interface must provide add, get and remove methods. In addition, it specifies that the get method should return a string and that the remove method should return a boolean. The interface also specifies the parameters for the methods:

```
public interface OrganizerIO {
   public abstract void add(String string, Date date);
   public abstract String get(Date date);
   public abstract boolean remove(String string);
}
```

It is not necessary to define these methods as being abstract because they are abstract by default. Notice that you cannot define class-side (static) methods in an interface, as they cannot be abstract.

It may appear at this point that an interface is the same as an abstract class, however they differ in a number of ways:

- An interface cannot, by definition, provide any functionality. An abstract class can provide default functionality.
- Any class can implement one (or more) interfaces. A class can inherit from only one parent class.
- Interfaces are a compile-time feature; they influence the static analysis of the program being compiled. Abstract classes involve run-time issues associated with method selection, execution etc.
- An abstract class can inherit from an existing class. An interface abstracts a class from which it inherits.
- An interface can extend one or more interfaces by adding new protocols. A class cannot extend an interface (it can only implement it, or "fill it out").

In addition to acting as a contract with a class which specifies what that class (and its subclasses) must provide, an interface can also be used as a type specifier. This means that you can specify an interface and then use it to specify the type of object which a variable can hold. Thus, you can define an interface which is implemented by classes in completely different hierarchies. A method parameter, for example, can take instances of both those class hierarchies and only instances of those class hierarchies:

```
public class Bozo {
    . . .
    public void add (OrganizerIO temp) {
        . . .
    }
}
```

This means that the method add can take an instance of any class which implements the OrganizerIO interface.

Interfaces can also inherit from interfaces. Thus, for example, Records extends Workers, Employers and Clonable interfaces in the following example:

```
public interface Records extends Workers, Employers,
        Clonable {
    . . .
}
```

9 Java Constructs

9.1 Introduction

This chapter presents more of the Java language. It considers the representation and use of numbers, strings and characters. It also discusses assignments, literals and variables. Finally, it considers messages, message types and their precedence.

9.2 Numbers and Numeric Operators

9.2.1 Numeric Values

Numbers in Java can be examples of basic types, such as `int`, or objects in their own right (e.g. instances of the class `Integer`). This is because some data structure objects can only hold objects, so they can only hold a basic type (such as 3) when it is wrapped within an integer object:

```
Integer x = new Integer(3);
```

A number of classes provide for the types of numbers normally used, for example `Integer`, `Float`, `Double` and `Long`. These are all considered in greater detail later in the book. For the moment, we consider what numbers look like in Java.

Just as in most programming languages, a numeric value in Java is a series of numbers which may or may not have a preceding sign and may contain a decimal point:

```
25   -10   1996   12.45   0.13451345   -3.14
```

Unusually for a programming language, Java explicitly specifies the number of bytes which must be used for data types such as `short`, `int`, `long`, `float` and `double` (Table 9.1).

The Java language designers' purpose in specifying the number of bytes to use for each data type was to enhance the portability of Java implementations. In C, the number of bytes used for `int` and `long` is at the discretion of the compiler writers. The only constraint placed upon them is that `int` cannot be bigger than `long`. This means that a program that compiles successfully on one machine may prove unreliable and have errors when recompiled on another machine. This can make porting a program from one system to another extremely frustrating (ask anyone who has ever had to port a sizeable C system!).

Table 9.1 Standard numbers of bytes for numeric data types

Type	Bytes	Stores
byte	1	integers
short	2	integers
int	4	integers
long	8	integers
float	4	floating point numbers
double	8	floating point numbers

9.2.2 Arithmetic Operators

In general, the arithmetic operators available in Java are the same as in any other language. There are also comparison functions and truncation functions (see Table 9.2). Numbers can also be represented by objects which are instances of classes such as Integer and Float. These classes are all subclasses of the class Number and provide different facilities. However, some of the methods are fairly common (Table 9.3).

Table 9.2 Basic numeric operators

+	addition		==	equality
–	subtraction		<	less than
*	multiplication		>	greater than
/	division		!=	inequality
%	remainder		<=	less than or equal to
			>=	greater than or equal to

Table 9.3 Methods provided by numeric classes

equals()	equality
doubleValue()	conversion
toHexString()	conversion
valueOf(aString)	conversion (class-side)
toBinaryString()	conversion
toOctalString()	conversion

A number of the numeric classes also provide class variables, such as MAX_VALUE and MIN_VALUE (i.e. in Integer, Long, Double, Float etc.), and numbers such as NEGATIVE_INFINITY and POSITIVE_INFINITY (i.e. in Double and Float).

In addition, Java provides a class called Math. This class, which is a subclass of Object, provides the usual range of mathematical operations (see Table 9.4). All these methods are class (or static) methods available from the class Math. You do not have to create an instance of the class to use them.

Table 9.4 Mathematical functions provided by Math

max	maximum
ceil	round up
round	round to nearest
abs	absolute value
pow	raises one number to the power of the other

min	minimum
floor	round down
sqrt	square root
exp	exponential
random	random number generator

It is also interesting to notice that, to enhance the portability of Java, the language designers have stated that the definitions of many of the numeric methods must produce the same results as a set of published algorithms.

9.3 Characters and Strings

9.3.1 Characters

Just like numbers, characters in Java can be either basic types (such as char) or wrapped within the Character class:

```
Character aCharObject = new Character('J');
```

We consider this class and the operations it provides in greater detail later. For the moment, we consider what characters look like. In Java, a single character is defined by surrounding it with single quotes:

```
'J'    'a'    '@'    '1'    '$'
```

9.3.2 Strings

Strings in Java are direct subclasses of the Object class. As such, they are made up of individual elements, similar to strings in C. However, this is the only similarity between strings in C and Java. A Java string is not terminated by a null character and should not be treated as an array of characters. It should be treated as an object which responds to an appropriate range of messages (e.g. for manipulating or extracting substrings). The methods provided by the String class are listed in Table 9.5.

A string is defined by one or more characters placed between double quotes (rather than the single quotes used for characters):

```
"John Hunt"    "Tuesday"    "dog"
```

You cannot create a string by generating an array of characters. This can be the source of much confusion and frustration when an apparently correct piece of code does not work. A string containing a single character is not equivalent to that single character:

```
'a'  !=  "a"
```

Table 9.5 Methods provided by the class `String`

`charAt(int index)`	returns the character at position index
`compareTo(String aString)`	compares two strings lexicographically
`equals(String aString)`	compares two strings
`equalsIgnoreCase(String aString)`	compares two strings, ignoring the case of the characters
`indexOf(char aCharacter)`	returns the first index of the character in the receiving string
`substring(int start, int stop)`	creates substring from start to stop (in the receiving string)
`toLowerCase()`	returns the receiver in lower case letters
`toUpperCase()`	returns the receiver in upper case letters

The string "a" and the character 'a' are, at best, instances of different classes and, at worst, one may be an instance and one a basic type. The fact that the string contains only one character is just a coincidence.

To denote that a variable should take an instance of `String`, define it as being of type `String`:

```
String aVariable;
aVariable = "John";
```

9.4 Assignments

A variable name can refer to different objects at different times. You can make *assignments* to a variable name, using the = operator. It is often read as "becomes equal to" (even though it is not preceded by a colon, as in languages such as Ada).

Some examples of assignment statements follow:

```
currentEmployeeIndex = 1;
newIndex = oldIndex;
myName = "John Hunt";
```

Like all Java operators, the assignment operator returns a value. The result of an assignment is the value of that assignment (thus the value of the expression $x = 2 + 2$; is 4). This means that several assignments can be made in the same statement:

```
nextObject = newObject = oldObject;
```

The above example also illustrates a feature of Java style – variable names that indicate their contents. This technique is often used where a more meaningful name (such as `currentEmployeeIndex`) is not available (`temp` might be used in other languages).

Although variables in Java are strongly typed, this typing is perhaps not as strong as in languages such as Pascal and Ada. You can state that a variable is of type `Object`. As `Object` is a class, such a variable can possess instances of the class

Object or *one of its subclasses*! This means that a variable which holds a string may then be assigned a character or a vector (a type of data structure). This is quite legitimate:

```
Object temp;
temp = "John";
temp = new Character('a');
temp = new Vector();
```

An important point to note is that assignment is by reference when dealing with objects. This means that, in the following example, nextObject, newObject and oldObject all refer to the *same* object (as illustrated in Figure 9.1):

```
newObject = oldObject = new Vector();
nextObject = newObject;
```

As all three variables point to an instance of a container class (in this case Vector), if an update is made to the contents of any one of the variables, it is made for all three!

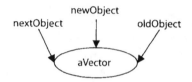

Figure 9.1 The result of a multiple assignment.

9.5 Variables

9.5.1 Temporary Variables

These variables exist only for the duration of some activity (e.g. the execution of a method). They can be defined anywhere within a method (as long as they are defined before they are used). The definition takes the form of the type (or class) of the variable and the variable name followed by any initialization required:

```
char aChar;
char anotherChar = 'a';
Object anObject;
String myName = "John Hunt";
```

The scope of a temporary variable depends on the context in which it is defined. For example, variables declared at the top level of a method are in scope from the point at which they are declared. However, block variables only have scope for the block within which they are defined (including nested blocks). Loop variables only have scope for the loop within which they are defined. Thus the scope of each of the following variables is different:

```
public int add (int a, int b) {
   int result = 0; r
   for (int i = 0; i < 5, i++) { ir
      if (a < i) {    ir
         int total = b;   tir
         total = total + c * i;   tir
      } ir
   } r
}
```

In the right-hand column, r indicates that result is in scope, i indicates the scope of the loop variable and t indicates the scope of the inner block variable, total.

9.5.2 Pseudo Variables

A pseudo variable is a special variable whose value is changed by the system, but which cannot be changed by the programmer. The value of a pseudo variable is determined by the current context and can be referenced within a method.

this is a pseudo variable which refers to the receiver of a message itself. The search for the corresponding method starts in the class of the receiver. To ensure that your source code does not become cluttered, Java assumes you mean this object if you just issue a reference to a method. The following statements have the same effect:

```
this.myName();
myName();
```

You can use this to pass a reference to the current object to another object:

```
otherObject.addLink(this);
```

super also refers to the message receiver, but the method search starts in the superclass of the receiver. It is often used if the functionality of a method is to be extended rather than overwritten:

```
public class StrangeExample {
   public void test() {
      System.out.println("In test");
   }
}


public class ExtendedStrangeExample extends
         StrangeExample {
   public static void main (String argv []) {
      ExtendedStrangeExample s;
      s = new ExtendedStrangeExample();
         s.test();
   }
```

```
    public void test() {
       System.out.println("Hi");
       super.test();
       System.out.println("John");
    }
}
```

The result of compiling and running these two classes is:

```
Hi
In test
John
```

Do not worry about the syntax or the meaning of the above example too much at the moment; just make sure you get the idea of things. If you decide to type in the above example, you must put each class in a separate file, as they are both public.

9.5.3 Variable Scope

Temporary variables are only available within the method in which they are defined. However, both class variables and instance variables are in scope (or are visible) at a number of levels. An instance variable can be defined to be visible (available) outside the class or the package, only within the package, within subclasses or only within the current class. The scope is specified by modifiers which precede the variable definition:

```
public String myName = "John Hunt";
```

9.5.4 Special Values – True, False and Null

The null value is an object that represents nothing or no object. It is not of any type nor it is an instance of any class (including Object). It should not be confused with the null pointer in languages such as C. It really does means *nothing* or *no value*.

The other two special values are boolean literals, representing truth and falsehood. You can wrap them in an instance of class Boolean, which provides a range of operations including the following methods:

- equals(Object object)
- booleanValue()
- toString

9.6 Messages and Message Selectors

9.6.1 Invoking Methods

Invoking a method is often referred to as *sending a message* to the object that owns the method. The expression which invokes a method is composed of a receiving

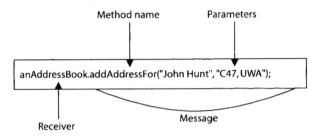

Figure 9.2 The components of a message expression.

object (the receiver), the method name and zero or more parameters. The combination of method name and parameters is often called the message, and it indicates, to the class of the receiving object, which method to execute. Figure 9.2 illustrates the main components of a message expression.

The value of an expression is determined by the definition of the method it invokes. Some methods are defined as returning no value (e.g. `void`), while others may return a basic type or object. In the following code, the result returned by the method `marries` is saved into the variable `newStatus`:

```
newStatus = thisPerson.marries(thatPerson);
```

9.6.2 Precedence

The rules governing precedence in Java are similar to those in other languages. Precedence refers to the order in which operators are evaluated in an expression. Many languages, such as C, explicitly specify the order of evaluation of expressions such as the following:

```
2 + 5 * 3 - 4 / 2;
```

Java is no exception. The rules regarding precedence are summarized in Table 9.6. The above expression would be evaluated as:

```
(2 + (5 * 3)) - (4 / 2);
```

Notice that if operators with the same precedence are encountered they are evaluated strictly from left to right.

9.7 Exercise: Hello World

9.7.1 Introduction

The aim of this practical exercise is to get you to write a very simple Java program and to use a number of the tools available in the Java Developers' Kit (or JDK).

Table 9.6 Operator precedence

Operation	Meaning	Precedence
++x --x	prefix increment/decrement	16
x++ x--	postfix increment/decrement	15
- ! ~	arithmetic negation/logical not/flip	14
(typename)	cast (type conversion)	13
* / %	multiplication/division/remainder	12
+ -	addition/subtraction	11
<< >> >>>	left and right bitwise operators	10
< > <= >=	relational operators	9
== !=	equality operators	8
&	bitwise and	7
^	bitwise exclusive or	6
|	bitwise or	5
&&	conditional and	4
||	conditional or	3
? :	conditional operators	2
=	assignment operator	1

9.7.2 What You Should Do

1. Get familiar with using an editor with Java. Ideally the editor used should be a Java-aware editor. One of the advantages of such an editor is that it highlights Java keywords, strings and comments etc.

   Two Java-aware editors which are available on the Web are:

   - KAWA – http://www.tek-tools.com/kawa/
   - UltraEdit – http://www.ultraedit.com/

   UltraEdit is also available from http://www.jttc.demon.co.uk/idm.htm

2. Write a simple hello world program.
3. Compile and run your program. Remember:

javac <filename>.java	compiles a Java program into byte codes.
java <filename>	is the virtual machine on which the byte codes execute.
java -cs<filename>	compiles (if necessary) and runs an application.

4. Use the jdb debugger if you have problems.

9.8 Summary

In this chapter and the previous, you have learnt about classes in Java, how they are defined, how instance variables are specified and how methods are constructed. You have also encountered many of the basic Java language structures.

10 *Control and Iteration*

10.1 Introduction

This chapter introduces control and iteration in Java. In Java, as in many other languages, the mainstay of the control and iteration processes are the if and switch statements and the for and while loops.

10.2 Control Structures

10.2.1 The if Statement

The basic format of an if statement in Java is the same as that in C. A test is performed and, depending on the result of the test, a statement is performed. A set of statements to be executed can be grouped together in curly brackets { }. For example:

```
if (a == 5)
   System.out.println("true")
else
   System.out.println("false");

if (a == 5) {
   System.out.print("a = 5");
   System.out.println("The answer is therefore true");
}
else {
   System.out.print("a != 5");
   System.out.println("The answer is therefore false");
}
```

Of course, the if statement need not include the optional else construct:

```
if (a == 5) {
   System.out.print("a = 5");
   System.out.println("The answer is therefore true");
}
```

You must have a boolean in a condition expression, so you cannot make the same equality mistake as in C. The following code always generates a compile-time error (as "=" indicates assignment):

```
if (a = 1) {
...
}
```

Unfortunately, assigning a boolean to a variable results in a boolean (all expressions return a result) and thus the following code is legal, but does not result in the intended behaviour (the string "Hello" is always printed on the console):

```
public class Test {
  public static void main (String args []) {
    boolean a = false;
    if (a = true)
      System.out.println("Hello");
  }
}
```

You can construct nested if statements, as in any other language:

```
if (count < 100)
  if (index < 10)
      {...}
  else
      {...}
else
  {...}
```

However, it is easy to get confused. Java does not provide an explicit if-then-elseif-else type of structure. In some languages, you can write:

```
if (n < 10)
  print ("less than 10");
else if (n < 100)
  print ("greater than 10 but less than 100");
else if (n < 1000)
  print ("greater than 100 but less then 1000");
else
  print ("greater than 1000");
```

This code is intended to be read as laid out above. However if we write it in Java, it should be laid out as below:

```
if (n < 10)
  print ("less than 10");
else if (n < 100)
    print ("greater than 10 but less than 100");
  else if (n < 1000)
      print ("> than 100 but < 1000");
```

```
else
   print ("> than 1000");
```

This code is comprised of three staements rather than one and has a very different meaning (although it may have the same effect). This can lead to the infamous "dangling else" problem. A much better solution is the switch statement.

10.2.2 The Conditional Operator

Java has inherited the conditional operator from C. This has both good and bad points. It is good because it is a very concise and efficient way of performing a test and carrying out one of two operations. It is bad because its terse nature is not clear to non-C programmers. However, it is a part of the language and all Java programmers must understand it.

The Java conditional operator has three operands which are separated by two symbols in the following format:

```
test expression ? true expression : false expression
```

The boolean expression determines whether the true or false expression is evaluated. For example, the following expression prints the maximum of two numbers:

```
m >= n ? System.out.println(m) : System.out.println(n);
```

The conditional operator, unlike an if statement, returns a value. It can therefore be used in an assignment statement. For example, we can assign the larger of two numbers to a third variable:

```
x = m >= n ? m : n;
```

Notice that this is becoming less readable (unless you are an experienced C programmer, in which case you would argue that it is obvious!).

10.2.3 The switch Statement

The conditional operator is not the only control statement that Java inherits from C; it also inherits the (flawed) C switch statement. This is a multi-way selection statement (similar to the case or select statements of some other programming languages). The structure of the switch statement is basically:

```
switch (expression) {
  case label1 :
    . . .
    break;
  case label2 :
    . . .
    break;
  . . .
  default: . . .
}
```

The expression returns an integer value and the case labels represent the possible values produced by the expression. Each case label is followed by one or more statements which are executed until a break (or return) statement is encountered. A switch statement may include a default statement which is executed if none of the case labels match the integer in the expression.

The switch statement has two major flaws. The first flaw is the need to "break" out of each case block. This is a major problem which has led to many software bugs. For example, in December 1989 the long-distance telephone service in the USA was disrupted by a software problem in the AT&T electronic switching systems. The problem was allegedly traced to the misuse of a break statement in a C program. The inclusion of such a feature has serious implications for the construction of high integrity software.

The second major flaw is the inability of the switch statement to deal with anything other than integer comparisons. There are many situations in which it would be far easier to write the following code:

```java
switch (student.getMark() ) {
case > 70 ...
...
}
```

Instead, you must convert the tested value into an integer and then test the integers explicitly:

```java
public class Grades {

  public static void main (String argv[]) {
    Grades g = new Grades();
    g.classify(60);
  }

  public void classify(int aNumber) {
    int temp = 0;
    System.out.println("The grade mark is " +
          aNumber);

    temp = aNumber / 10;

    switch (temp) {
      case 4 : System.out.println("Pass"); break;
      case 5 : System.out.println("2.2"); break;
      case 6 : System.out.println("2.1"); break;
      case 7 : case 8: case 9: case 10 :
        System.out.println("1st"); break;
      default : System.out.println("Fail");
    }
  }
}
```

The result of running this application is illustrated below:

```
C:>java Grades
The grade mark is 60
2.1
```

10.3 Iteration

Iteration in Java is accomplished using the for, while and do-while statements. Just like their counterparts in other languages, these statements repeat a sequence of instructions a given number of times.

10.3.1 for Loops

A for loop in Java is very similar to a for loop in C. It is used to step a variable through a series of values until a given test is false. Many languages have a very simple for loop, for example:

```
for i = 1 to 10 do
...
endfor;
```

In this construct, you do not need to specify the end condition, nor how the variable i is incremented; in Java, you must specify both:

```
for (initial-expression; test; increment-expression)
    statement
```

This has the disadvantage of making the for construct more complicated, but it does offer a great deal of control. One point to note with this for loop is that the boolean test expression indicates the condition that must hold while the loop is repeated. That is, it is a *while true* loop, rather than an *until true* loop. An example for loop is presented below:

```
for (n = 1; n <= 10; n = n + 1)
    System.out.println(n);
```

This loop assigns n the initial value 1. While n <= 10, it executes the println method and increments the value of n. We can repeat more than one statement if we enclose them in curly brackets { }.

As in C, you can use a comma-delimited list to initialize and increment (decrement) several variables in a for loop. The expressions separated by commas are evaluated from left to right:

```
for (i = 0, j = 10; i < 10; i++, j--)
    System.out.println (i + " : " + j);
```

10.3.2 while Loops

The while loop exists in almost all programming languages. In most cases, it has a basic form such as:

```
while (test expression)
    statement
```

This is also true for Java. The while expression controls the execution of one or more statements. If more than one statement is to be executed then the statements must be enclosed in curly brackets { }:

```
n = 1;
while (n <= 10) {
    System.out.println(n);
    n++;
}
```

The above loop tests to see whether the value of n is less than or equal to 10, and then prints the current value of n before incrementing it by one. This is repeated until the test expression returns false (i.e. n > 11).

You must assign n an initial value before the condition expression. If you do not provide an initial value for n, it defaults to null and the comparison with a numeric value raises an exception. It is interesting, and potentially useful, to note that "**while** (test) { }" is exactly equivalent to "**for** (; test ;) { }".

10.3.3 do Loops

In some cases, we want to execute the body of statements at least once; you can accomplish this with the do loop construct:

```
do
    statement
while (test expression);
```

This loop is guaranteed to execute at least once, as the test is only performed after the statement has been evaluated. As with the while loop, the do loop repeats until the condition is false. You can repeat more than one statement by bracketing a series of statements into a block using curly brackets { }:

```
n = 10;
do {
    System.out.println(n);
    n--;
} while (n > 0);
```

The above do loop prints the numbers from 10 down to 1 and terminates when n = 0.

10.3.4 An Example of Loops

As a concrete example of the `for` and `while` loops, consider the following class. It possesses a method which prints numbers from 0 to 1 less than the `MaxValue` class variable:

```java
public class Counter {
  // A class variable
  public static int MaxValue = 10;

  public static void main (String argv[]) {
    Counter c = new Counter();
    c.count();
  }

  public void count() {
    int i;
    System.out.println("----- For -------");
    for (i = 0; i < MaxValue; ++i) {
      System.out.print(" " + i);
    }
    System.out.println(" ");
    System.out.println("----- While -------");
    i = 0;
    while (i < MaxValue) {
      System.out.print(" " + i);
      ++i;
    }
    System.out.println(" ");
    System.out.println("--------------------");
  }
}
```

The result of running this application should be:

```
>java Counter
----- For -------
 0 1 2 3 4 5 6 7 8 9
----- While -------
 0 1 2 3 4 5 6 7 8 9
--------------------
```

10.4 Recursion

Recursion is a very powerful programming idiom found in many languages. Java is no exception. The following class illustrates how to use recursion to generate the factorial of a number. A factorial is a number calculated as a repeated series of multiplications. The factorial is the number (x) times itself for (x) iterations. A factorial number is written as the number of the factorial followed by an exclamation mark. For example, 4! is equal to 1×2×3×4 = 24.

```java
public class Factorial {

    public static void main (String argv[]) {
        Factorial f = new Factorial();
        System.out.println(f.factorial(5));
    }

    public int factorial (int aNumber) {
        System.out.println(aNumber);
        if (aNumber == 1) return 1;
        else return aNumber * factorial(--aNumber);
    }
}
```

The result of running this application is illustrated below:

```
C:>java Factorial
5
4
3
2
1
120
```

10.5 Exercise: Factorial

The aim of this exercise is to get you to use the loop facilities in Java. Above, an example of generating a factorial number using recursion is presented. This exercise requires that you implement a similar program, but using iteration loops rather than recursion.

10.5.1 What You Should Do

Create a Java application that will print the factorials of 2, 4, 6 and 10.

10.5.2 Notes

1. Remember `System.out.println()` takes a string as an argument and outputs that string to standard out followed by a new line.
2. Concatenating a string with anything produces a string which is the combination of the original string and the string representation of the object concatenated. For example, the following code results in the string "4":

```
"" + 4
```

10.6 Summary

You now know the basics of iteration and control in Java. You are now ready to consider a much larger application in Java.

This will involve you considering inheritance and reuse, encapsulation, data structures and the collection API in Java. These issues are covered in subsequent chapters.

11 The Person Class

11.1 Introduction

You should now be ready to write some Java code, so this chapter takes you through a worked example. It is a very simple example, in which you create a new class, define some instance variables and write a couple of methods.

11.2 Defining a Class

The Person class is to provide a very basic set of features. It must record a person's name and their age. It must also allow the person to have a birthday (and thus increment their age).

The first thing you need to do is define a Java class in a file with the same name as the class. Note that this is important: an error is generated if the class name and the file name are not the same. Java is case-sensitive (even if your host operating system is not), so person and Person are not the same.

11.2.1 Creating the Class

1. Create an empty file called Person.java using your favourite editor, such as KAWA or UltraEdit. If you have a tool such as Visual Café or JBuilder, you can use it instead (indeed, it will probably make your life much easier).
2. In the file, define a new class by typing in the following Java code:

```
public class Person {
   private int age = 0;
   private String name = "";
}
```

The above code defines the class Person (by default, it is a subclass of Object) and gives it two instance variables, name and age, which are only accessible from within the class. Note again that by default the java.lang package is imported. This contains the classes Object and String.

3. Compile the class by issuing the following command:

```
> javac Person.java
```

11.2.2 Defining a Class Comment

```
/**
 * Purpose: An example class to hold a person's name
 * and age.
 *
 * @author John Hunt
 * @version 07/02/97
 *
 */

public class Person {
  private int age = 0;
  private String name = "";
}
```

Normally I would also define a comment to go with this class to explain what it is intended to do. I would use the /** ... */ format of comment so that the javadoc utility can pick it up. The above listing illustrates the result of adding this comment using a Java-aware editor.

11.3 Defining a Method

We first define the main method. We then define a constructor which initializes the instance variables in the appropriate manner.

11.3.1 The main Method

Every Java application must have at least one main method where the execution begins. This method creates a new instance of the class and sends it the message birthday:

```
public static void main (String args []) {
  Person p = new Person();
  p.birthday();
}
```

This is essentially the same as that presented earlier in the book, so we do not re-analyze it.

11.3.2 The Constructor

As was explained in Chapter 8, a constructor allows parameters to be passed into a class when a new instance is created. However, we are keeping things simple here and relying on the simplest constructor (which is called with no parameters). The definition of this method is presented below (note that this means that the default automatic constructor is never generated for this class):

```
public Person () {
    System.out.println("In Person constructor");
    age = 33;
    name = "John Hunt";
}
```

This constructor prints out a message to the console and then initializes age (as the integer 33) and name (the string "John Hunt"). Once this method has executed, control returns to the point at which the instance was created (in our case, to the main method).

At this point your class definition should resemble that below. Notice that the instance variable definitions do not need to be at the start of the class:

```
/**
 * Purpose: An example class to hold a persons
 * name and age.
 *
 * @author John Hunt
 * @version 07/02/97
 *
 */

public class Person {
    private int age = 0;
    private String name = "";

    public static void main (String args []) {
        Person p = new Person();
        p.birthday();
    }

    public Person () {
        System.out.println("In Person constructor");
        age = 34;
        name = "John Hunt";
    }
}
```

11.3.3 The Accessor Methods

Now we can define some methods for accessing the instance variables. These are sometimes called *getter* methods. The two methods to be defined are getAge and getName.

The getAge method is defined as a public method (i.e. it is available outside the class) that returns the value of the instance variable age (which is specifically of type int):

```
public int getAge () {
    return age;
}
```

The getName method has exactly the same format, except that it returns an instance of String:

```
public String getName () {
   return name;
}
```

11.3.4 The Updater Method

We are now going to define a method which can update the value of the age instance variable. Such a method is known as an updater or *setter* method. This method is again public, but it does not return any value and is said to return void. It takes one parameter (of type int) called newAge. Note the way that the method names and the variable names start with a lower-case letter, but subsequent words start with a capital letter.

```
public void setAge (int newAge) {
   age = newAge;
}
```

11.3.5 The birthday Method

Having defined the methods that access the private instance variables (notice that nothing outside the class can modify these variables), we now define a method called birthday:

```
public void birthday () {
   int oldAge, newAge;
   oldAge = getAge();
   System.out.println("Happy birthday " + getName());
   System.out.print("You were " + oldAge);
   System.out.print(" but now you are ");
   newAge = oldAge + 1;
   setAge(newAge);
   System.out.println(age);
}
```

This last method prints out a birthday greeting and increments the person's age. It uses the other methods to change the current value of the instance variable age and to print a meaningful message to the user. This type of programming is known as variable-free programming, and is considered good style. Note that the call to print out information is System.out.println(). This indicates that the message println is sent to the contents of the variable out in the class system. In fact, this variable is bound to the standard output.

11.4 Creating an Instance

You should now execute the Java application you have created. You do this by running the byte code compiled from the file Person.java on the virtual machine. The result of compiling and running this application in Windows 95/98 is presented below:

```
C:>java Person
In Person constructor
Happy birthday John Hunt
You were 34 but now you are 35
```

Executing the byte code on the virtual machine causes an instance of Person to be created, the constructor to be called automatically and the message birthday to be sent to the new instance.

Once you have done this and are happy with what is happening, try to change the method definitions or add a new instance variable called address and define the appropriate methods for it. The complete Person class definition is presented below.

```java
public class Person {
  private int age = 0;
  private String name = "";
  public static void main (String args []) {
    Person p = new Person();
    p.birthday();
  }
  public Person () {
    System.out.println("In Person constructor");
    age = 33;
    name = "John Hunt";
  }
  public int getAge () {
    return age;
  }
  public void setAge (int newAge) {
    age = newAge;
  }
  public String getName () {
    return name;
  }
  public void birthday () {
    int oldAge, newAge;
    oldAge = getAge();
    System.out.println("Happy birthday " + getName());
    System.out.print("You were " + oldAge);
    System.out.print(" but now you are ");
    newAge = oldAge + 1;
    setAge(newAge);
    System.out.println(age);
  }
}
```

11.5 Exercise: Person

11.5.1 Introduction

The aim of this exercise is to get you to develop the Person class and manipulate instances of that class.

A Person has a name and age already. You should add an address instance variable and appropriate accessor and updater methods.

11.5.2 What You Should Do

1. Define the class Person so that it can represent a person's name and age. Note that the instance variables should be called name and age and should be made private, for example:

    ```
    private String name;
    ```

    Add a new instance variable to hold the address.

2. Write a main method in a separate class called Test. This class and its single method main should look like this:

    ```
    public class Test {
      public static void main (String args []) {
        Person p = new Person();
        p.setName ("John");
        p.setAge (34);
        p.setAddress ("94 High Street");
        System.out.println (p.getName () +
          " is " + p.getAge () +
          " lives at " +
            p.getAddress ());
      }
    }
    ```

3. Run and test this program.
4. Extend your main method in the class Test to use the birthday () message.
5. Extend the main method to create two instances of the Person class. Give one the name John and the other the name Paul. Increment the ages of each by different amounts.
6. Print out the values held in both objects.

11.5.3 Notes

1. Remember that System.out.println () takes a string as an argument and outputs that string to standard out followed by a new line.

2. Concatenating a string with anything produces a string which is the combination of the original string and the string representation of the object concatenated. For example, the following code results in the string "4":

```
"" + 4
```

3. `System.out.print()` does not start a new line; it merely prints the string passed to it.

4. If you use `System.out.print()` you should finish by using `System.out.println()` or `System.out.flush()` to ensure that the print buffer is flushed. If you do not do this then you might find that the last line of the output is not displayed.

12 *Classes, Inheritance and Abstraction*

12.1 Introduction

In this chapter, we consider some of the language features you saw in the last section of the book from an object-oriented point of view. This chapter discusses how you should use classes and what you should, and should not, use them for. It considers how you should use inheritance, abstraction and subclasses and highlights the use of constructors. It also tries to explain the use of (the oft misunderstood) main method.

12.2 Classes Revisited

The following is an incomplete example which illustrates many of the features found in class definitions. It is presented as a reminder without further explanation.

```
public class Person {
  // Define a class variable
  public static int numberCreated = 0;
  // Define an instance variable
  public String name = " ";

  // Define a class method
  public static void incrementNumberCreated() {
    numberCreated = numberCreated + 1;
  }

  // Define an instance method
  public void setName(String aName) {
    name = aName;
  }
  ...
}
```

Notice that the keyword static illustrates that the following element is on the class side (as opposed to the instance side).

12.2.1 What are Classes for?

In some object-oriented languages, classes are merely templates used to construct objects (or instances). In these languages, the class definition specifies the structure of the object and a separate mechanism is often used to create the object using this template.

In some other languages (for example Smalltalk-80), classes are objects in their own right; this means that they can not only create objects, they can also hold data, receive messages and execute methods just like any other object. Such object-oriented systems tend to have what is called a rich meta-model built upon the use of metaclasses. A metaclass is a special class whose sole instance is a class.

An object is an instance of something, so if a class is an object, it must be an instance of something. In the meta-model, a class is an instance of a metaclass. It should be noted that the metaclass concept is probably one of the most confusing parts of the whole of Smalltalk. This is partly due to the names used, but also because almost all of it is hidden from the developer. The developer is therefore only vaguely aware of it (if at all) during development.

Java adopts a position halfway between the two camps. That is, it has a weak meta-model in which classes can respond to messages and to requests for class variable values. However, Java does not provide the full power of the Smalltalk meta-model. This is because Smalltalk's meta-model is confusing and most developers never need to use it. Java's solution results in a simpler, cleaner and easier to understand model.

Thus, in Java, classes are not objects (in the true sense of the word), but are unique within a program and can:

- create instances
- be inherited by subclasses (and can inherit from existing classes)
- implement interfaces
- have class methods
- have class variables
- define instance methods
- define instance variables
- be sent messages

Objects (or instances), on the other hand, can:

- be created from a class
- have instance variables
- be sent messages
- execute instance methods
- have many copies in the system (all with their own data)

Thus a class is more than just a template for an object; it can also hold data and provide class specific behaviour. However, if you are confused by most of the above, remember: a class's two primary roles are to define instances and to allow inheritance.

12.2.2 Class-Side Methods

It may at first seem unclear what should normally go in an instance method as opposed to what should go in a class (or static) method when defining a new class. After all, they are both defined in the class. However, it is important to remember that one defines the behaviour of the instance and the other the behaviour of the class (it is a pity that these methods are designated by the keyword static as it is not obvious to the new programmer what static actually means). Class-side methods should only perform one of the following roles:

- *Instance creation* This role is very important as it is how you can use a class as the root of an application. It is common to see main methods which do nothing other than create a new instance of the class. For example:

```
public class Account {
   double balance = 0.0;

   public static void main (String args []) {
     Account account = new Account ();
   }

   ...remainder of class definition...
```

If you define such a method, but the class is not the root of the application, it is ignored. This makes it a very useful way of providing a test harness for a given class.

- *Answering inquiries about the class* This role can provide generally useful objects, frequently derived from class variables. For example, they may return the number of instances of this class that have been created.
- *Instance management* In this role, class-side methods control the number of instances created. For example, a class only allows a single instance to be created. Instance management methods may also be used to access an instance (e.g. randomly or in a given state).
- *Documentation* Methods for documentation can be very useful.
- *Examples* Occasionally, class methods are used to provide helpful examples which explain the operation of a class. This is good practice.
- *Testing* Class-side methods can be used to support the testing of an instance of a class. You can use them to create an instance, perform an operation and compare the result with a known value. If the values are different, the method can report an error. This is a very useful way of providing regression tests.
- *Support for one of the above roles*

Any other tasks should be performed by an instance method.

12.2.3 A Class or an Instance

In some situations, you may only need to create a single instance of a class and reference it wherever it is required. A continuing debate ponders whether it is worth creating such an instance or whether it is better to define the required behaviour in class methods and reference the class (which, after all, can be sent messages and have its class variables accessed). Invariably the answer to this is no, for the following reasons:

- Such an approach breaks the object-oriented model. Although this approach has been adopted by numerous Java authors (see Winston and Narasimhan (1996) for a particularly bad set of examples), it is not object-oriented and suggests that the programmer has not fully embraced the object-oriented model.
- The creation of an instance has a very low overhead. This is a key feature in Java and it has received extensive attention.
- You may require more than one instance sometime in the future. If you implement all the code on the class-side, you will have to move the methods to the instance side of the class.
- You may be tempted to treat the class as a global reference. This suggests that the implementation has been poorly thought out. It is unfortunate that a number of facilities provided by the Java system classes seem to support this use of a class as a global reference. For example, you can convert a numeric string into an integer using the `parseInt` class-side method of the class Integer:

```
Integer.parseInt("100");
```

This is essentially a way of making the `parseInt` method globally available. It is better to define the method on the class `String` and call it something like `toInteger`. If you do so, you can send any string a message requesting that it convert itself into an integer, rather than sending the `Integer` class such a request.

12.3 Inheritance in Classes

Inheritance is achieved in Java using the `extends` keyword (as was discussed in Chapter 8). Java is a single inheritance system, so a Java class can only inherit from a single class, which can, of course, implement zero or more interfaces. The following class definition builds on the class `Person` presented earlier:

```java
public class Student extends Person {
   private String subject = "Computer Science";
   public String getSubject() {
     return subject;
   }
}
```

This class extends the class `Person` by adding a new instance variable, `subject`, and a method to access it.

12.3.1 The Role of a Subclass

A subclass modifies the behaviour of its parent class. This modification should refine the class in one or more of these ways:

- Changes to the external protocol, the set of messages to which instances of the class respond.
- Changes in the implementation of the methods, the way in which the messages are handled.
- Additional behaviour which references inherited behaviour.

If a subclass does not provide one or more of the above, then it is incorrectly placed. For example, if a subclass implements a set of new methods, but does not refer to the instance variables or methods of the parent class, then the class is not really a subclass of the parent (it does not extend it).

For example, consider the class hierarchy illustrated in Figure 12.1. A generic (probably abstract) root class has been defined. This class defines a Conveyance which has doors, fuel (both with default values) and a method, startUp, that starts the engine of the conveyance. Three subclasses of Conveyance have also been defined: Dinghy, Car and Tank. Two of these subclasses are appropriate, but one should probably not inherit from Conveyance. We shall consider each in turn to determine their suitability.

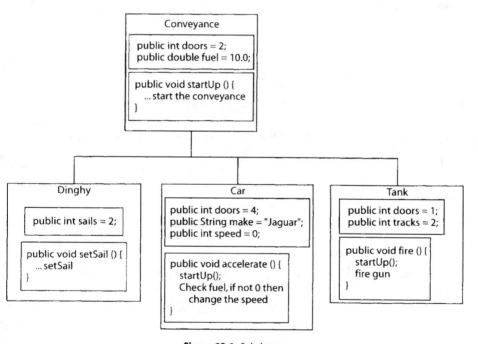

Figure 12.1 Subclasses.

The class Tank overrides the number of doors inherited, uses the startUp method within the method fire, and provides a new instance variable. It therefore matches all three of our criteria.

Similarly, the class Car overrides the number of doors and uses the method startUp. It also uses the instance variable fuel within a new method accelerate. It also, therefore, matches our criteria.

The class `Dinghy` defines a new instance variable `sails` and a new method `setSail`. As such, it does not use any of the features inherited from `Conveyance`. However, we might say that it has extended `Conveyance` by providing this instance variable and method. We must then consider the features provided by `Conveyance`. We can ask ourselves whether they make sense within the context of `Dinghy`. If we assume that a dinghy is a small sail-powered boat, with no cabin and no engine, then nothing inherited from `Conveyance` is useful. In this case, it is likely that `Conveyance` is misnamed, as it defines some sort of a motor vehicle, and the `Dinghy` class should not have extended it.

The exceptions to this rule are subclasses of `Object`. This is because `Object` is the root class of all classes in Java. As you must create a new class by subclassing it from an existing class, you can subclass from `Object` when there is no other appropriate class.

12.3.2 Capabilities of Classes

A subclass or class should accomplish one specific purpose; it should capture only one idea. If more than one idea is encapsulated in a class, you may reduce the chances for reuse, as well as contravene the laws of encapsulation in object-oriented systems. For example, you may have merged two concepts together so that one can directly access the data of another. This is rarely desirable.

Breaking a class down costs little but may produce major gains in reusability and flexibility. If you find that when you try to separate one class into two or more classes some of the code needs to be duplicated for each class, then the use of abstract classes can be very helpful. That is, you can place the common code into an abstract superclass to avoid unnecessary duplication.

The following guidelines may help you to decide whether to split the class with which you are working. Look at the comment describing the class (if there is no class comment, this is a bad sign in itself). Consider the following points:

- Is the comment short and clear. If not, is this a reflection on the class? Consider how the comment can be broken down into a series of short clear comments. Base the new classes around those comments.
- If the comment is short and clear, do the class and instance variables make sense within the context of the comment? If they do not, then the class needs to be re-evaluated. It may be that the comment is inappropriate, or the class and instance variables inappropriate.
- Look at the instance variable references (i.e. look at where the instance variable access methods are used). Is their use in line with the class comment? If not, then you should take appropriate action.

12.3.3 Restricting a Subclass

You can restrict the ability of a subclass to change what it inherits from its superclass. Indeed, you can also stop subclasses being created from a class. This is done using the keyword `final`. This keyword has different meanings depending on where it is used:

```
public final class LaserPrinter extends Printer {
```

No element of this class can be extended, so no subclass of `LaserPrinter` can be created.

```
public final int maximumMemory = 128;
```

The instance variable `maximumMemory` cannot have its value changed. It is a bit like specifying that a variable is a constant. You can also apply the keyword `final` to class variables.

```
public final void handshake() {
```

This states that this method cannot be overridden in a subclass. That is, a subclass cannot redefine `handshake()`; it must use the one that it inherits. You can also specify class methods as `final`.

Restricting the ability to overwrite part of, or all of, a class is a very useful feature. It is particularly important where the correct behaviour of the class and its subclasses relies on the correct functioning of particular methods, or the appropriate value of a variable etc. A class is normally only specified as `final` when it does not make sense to create a subclass of it. These situations need to be analyzed carefully to ensure that no unexpected scenarios are likely to occur.

12.4 Abstract Classes

An abstract class is a class from which you cannot create an object. It is missing one or more elements required to create a fully functioning instance. In contrast, a non-abstract (or concrete) class leaves nothing undefined and can be used to create a working instance. You may wonder what use an abstract class is. The answer is that you can group together elements which are to be shared among a number of classes without providing a complete implementation. In addition, you can force subclasses to provide specific methods, ensuring that implementers of a subclass at least supply appropriately named methods. You should therefore use abstract classes when:

- you wish to specify data or behaviour common to a set of classes, but insufficient for a single instance
- you wish to force subclasses to provide specific behaviour

In many cases, the two situations go together. Typically, the aspects of the class to be defined as abstract are specific to each class, while what has been implemented is common to all classes. For example, consider the following class (based loosely on the `Conveyance` class presented above):

```
public abstract class Conveyance {
    private int doors = 2;
    private double fuel = 5.0;
```

```
    private boolean running = false;
    public void startUp() {
      running = true;
      consumeFuel();
      while (fuel > 0) {
        consumeFuel();
      }
    }
    abstract void consumeFuel();
  }
```

This abstract class definition means that you cannot create an instance of Conveyance. Within the definition of Conveyance, we can see that the startUp method is defined, but the method consumeFuel is specified as abstract and no method body is provided. Any class which has one or more abstract methods is necessarily abstract (and must therefore have the keywords abstract class). However, a class can be abstract without specifying any abstract methods.

Any subclass of Conveyance must implement the consumeFuel method if instances are to be created from it. Each subclass can define how much fuel is consumed in a different manner. The following PetrolCar class provides a concrete class which builds on Conveyance:

```
  public class PetrolCar extends Conveyance {
    public static void main (String args []) {
      PetrolCar p = new PetrolCar();
      p.startUp();
    }
    public void consumeFuel () {
      fuel = fuel - 1.0;
      System.out.println(fuel);
    }
  }
```

The result of executing this class is illustrated below:

```
C:>java PetrolCar
4.0
3.0
2.0
1.0
0.0
```

We can also define a DieselCar class in which the fuel consumption rate is lower, for example:

```
  public class DieselCar extends Conveyance {
    public static void main (String args []) {
      DieselCar d = new DieselCar();
      d.startUp();
    }
```

```
public void consumeFuel () {
   fuel = fuel - 0.5;
   System.out.println(fuel);
 }
}
```

However, if all you wish to do is to specify that a set of methods should be defined by a subclass, then you may well be better off defining an interface. Interfaces never contain method bodies, nor do they declare instance variables, thus it is clearer that all you intend to do is to specify a particular protocol to be defined by those classes which implement the interface (see Chapter 6).

12.5 Constructors and Their Use

Constructors should only be used to initialize an instance of a class in an appropriate manner, and you should attempt to place all the initialization code in as few constructors as possible. For example, if there is only one initialization process but different numbers or combinations of parameters can be passed to the constructors, then you should define a single root constructor. The root constructor should represent the constructor with the most parameters. You should then define convenience constructors with fewer parameters. These constructors call the root constructor, using default values for the parameters which are not provided. Note the use of this followed by parameters. This is the way in which one constructor can directly call another constructor. For example:

```
public class Account {
   private double balance = 0.0;
   private String name = "";

   Account(double amount, String person) {
      balance = amount;
      name = person;
   }
   Account (String person) {
      this(0.0, person);
   }

   Account () {
      this(0.0, "man with no name");
   }
}
```

In this example, the three constructors each allow different amounts of information to be provided. However, the actual initialization only takes place within one method. Thus any changes to the way in which the initialization process is performed are localized to this one method.

An annoying feature of Java is that subclasses of Account do *not* inherit these constructors and must define their own.

12.6 The main Method

The main method should not be used to define the application program. This tends to happen when people move from C or C++ to Java, since in C the main function is exactly where the main functionality is placed. It is, therefore, unfortunate that the name main is used for this method. The main method should only ever do a very few things:

● Create an instance of the class within which it is defined. It should never create an instance of another class. If it does then you are not thinking in an object-oriented manner.

● Send the newly created instance a message so that it initializes itself.

● Send the newly created instance a message that triggers off the application's behaviour.

The PetrolCar and DieselCar classes are good examples of this. Both classes create a new instance (of the class) and send it the message startUp. Nothing else happens in the main method; all the work is done in the instance methods.

There is one situation in which you may break this rule. That is where the class you are defining is not intended to be the root class of the application. This class would not normally possess a main method and, if you define one, it is ignored when the class is used within a larger application (or applet). Therefore, you can use the main method to provide a test harness for the class. If you do not delete this main method, then it is available to those who modify or update the class at a later date. It can also act as a simple regression test.

13 Encapsulation and Polymorphism

13.1 Introduction

This chapter discusses the encapsulation and polymorphic features of Java. It illustrates how the encapsulation facilities can allow quite fine-grained control over the visibility of elements of your programs. The concept of packages is also discussed, along with some concrete examples. The polymorphic nature of Java concludes the chapter.

13.2 Encapsulation

In Java, you have a great deal of control over how much encapsulation is imposed on a class and an object. You achieve it by applying modifiers to classes, instance and class variables, and methods. Some of these modifiers refer to the concept of a package. For now, accept that a package is a group of associated classes.

13.2.1 Class Modifiers

You can change the visibility of a class by using a modifier keyword before the class keyword in the class definition, for example:

```
public class Person {...}
```

A public class is defined within its own file and is visible everywhere. A class that is local to a particular package has no modifier. It can be defined within a file containing other classes. At most, one of the classes in a file may be a public class.

13.2.2 Variable Modifiers

The amount of encapsulation imposed by a class is at the discretion of the programmer. You can allow complete access to everything within the class, or you can impose various levels of restrictions. In particular, you can control how much access another class has to the instance and class variables of a class. You do this by using a modifier keyword before the type of the variable, for example:

```
public static int MAX_VALUE = 100;
```

Table 13.1 The effect of a variable or method modifier

public	visible everywhere (the class must also be public)
no modifier	visible in current package
protected	visible in current package and in subclasses in other packages
private	visible only to current class

```
protected String name = "John Hunt";
private int count = 0;
```

Table 13.1 lists the modifiers and their meanings. Generally it is a good idea to impose as much encapsulation as possible. Thus everything should be hidden unless it has to be visible to other classes, in which case you should allow the minimum amount of visibility.

Notice that protected is weaker than using no modifier! You should use no modifier in preference to protected.

13.2.3 Method Modifiers

You can also limit the access of other classes to methods. You do this by using a modifier keyword before the return type of the method. The modifiers are the same as for variables:

```
public void setName(String name) {...}
private static int countInstances() {...}
protected final Object findKey() {...}
```

13.3 Packages

You can bring a set of related classes together in a single compilation unit by defining them all within one file. By default, this creates an implicit (unnamed) package; classes can access variables and methods which are only visible in the current package. However, only one of the classes can be publicly visible (the class with the same name as the file). A much better approach is to group the classes together into an explicit named package.

Packages are encapsulated units which can possess classes, interfaces and sub-packages. Packages are extremely useful:

● They allow you to associate related classes and interfaces.
● They resolve naming problems which would otherwise cause confusion.
● They allow some privacy for classes, methods and variables which should not be visible outside the package. You can provide a level of encapsulation such that only those elements which are intended to be public can be accessed from outside the package.

The JDK provides a number of packages, some of which are described briefly in the appendices. In general, you use these packages as the basis of your programs.

13.3.1 Declaring a Package

An explicit package is defined by the `package` keyword at the start of the file in which one or more classes (or interfaces) are defined:

```
package benchmarks;
```

Package names should be unique to ensure that there are no name conflicts. Java imposes a naming convention by which a package name is made up of a number of components separated by full stops (or periods). These components correspond to the location of the files. Thus if the files in a particular package are in a directory called `benchmarks` which is within a directory called `tests`, then the package name is given as:

```
package tests.benchmarks;
```

Notice that this assumes that all files associated with a single package are in the same directory. It also assumes that files in a separate package will be in a different directory. Any number of files can become part of a package; however, any one file can only specify a single package.

All components in the package name are relative to the contents of the `CLASSPATH` variable. This environment variable tells the java compiler where to start looking for class definitions. Thus, if the `CLASSPATH` variable is set to `C:\jjh\java`, then the following path is searched for the elements of the package:

```
c:\jjh\java\tests\benchmarks
```

All the files associated with the `tests.benchmarks` package should be in the `benchmarks` directory.

13.3.2 An Example Package

As an example, the files for the `book.chap13.lights` package are stored within a directory called `lights`, within a directory called `chap13`, within the `book` directory. The `lights` directory contains three classes which make up the contents of the lights package: `Light`, `WhiteLight` and `ColoredLight`. The header for the `Light.java` file contains the following code:

```
package book.chap13.lights;
import java.awt.*;
public abstract class Light extends Panel {...}
```

The `WhiteLight.java` and `ColoredLight.java` files are similar, for example:

```
package book.chap13.lights;
import java.awt.*;
public class ColoredLight extends WhiteLight {...}
```

The directory containing the `lights` package is listed below:

```
C:\AAAusers\JJH\Java\Book\chap13\lights>dir
```

```
COLORE~1 JAV        428 09/04/97 16:01 ColoredLight.java
LIGHT~1  CLA        695 09/04/97 15:55 Light.class
WHITEL~1 JAV        505 09/04/97 15:54 WhiteLight.java
LIGHT~1  JAV        634 09/04/97 15:54 Light.java
LIGHT               632 09/04/97 15:50 Light
WHITEL~1 CLA        631 09/04/97 15:55 WhiteLight.class
COLORE~1 CLA        655 09/04/97 16:01 ColoredLight.class
          7 file(s)  4,180 bytes
          2 dir(s) 89,227,264 bytes free
```

The CLASSPATH variable includes the path C:\AAAusers\JJH\Java, so the package specification, book.chap13.lights, completely specifies the files.

13.3.3 Accessing Package Elements

There are two ways to access an element of a package. One is to name the element in the package fully. For example, we can specify the Panel class by giving its full designation:

```
public abstract class Light extends java.awt.Panel
    {...}
```

This tells the Java compiler exactly where to look for the definition of the class Panel. However, this is laborious if we refer to the Panel class a number of times.

The alternative is to import the Panel class, which makes it available to the package within which we are currently working:

```
import java.awt.Panel;
public abstract class Light extends Panel {...}
```

However, in some situations, we wish to import a large number of elements from another package. Rather than generate a long list of import statements, we can import all the elements of a package at once using the * wildcard. For example:

```
import java.awt.*;
```

This imports all the elements of the java.awt package into the current package. Notice that this can slow down the compilation time considerably (although it has no effect on the run time performance).

13.3.4 An Example of Using a Package

The lights package described above has been used within a class outside the package. This class uses the ColoredLight class. It therefore imports it into the current package. For example:

```
import java.awt.Frame;
import java.awt.event.WindowListener;
```

```java
import book.chap13.lights.ColoredLight;

public class LightsGUI extends Frame implements
            WindowListener {
  public static void main (String args []) {
    Frame f = new LightsGUI();
  }

  public LightsGUI () {
    ...
    add("Center", new ColoredLight(true));
    ...
  }
  ...
}
```

Do not worry too much about what this class does (it draws a circle on a window), just notice that it has to import three classes from three separate packages in order to use Frame, WindowListener and ColoredLight.

13.4 Polymorphism

Polymorphism is the ability to send the same message to completely different objects, all of which respond to that message in their own way. Java's polymorphic abilities are derived from its use of dynamic (or late) binding. In addition, the same method name can be used with different parameters to allow apparently the same method to be declared a number of times within the same class.

13.4.1 Dynamic or Late Binding

Dynamic or late binding refers to the way in which Java decides which method should be run. Instead of determining the method at compile time (as a procedural language might), it determines it at run time. That is, it looks to see what class of object has received the message and then decides which method to run. As this decision is made at run time, there is some run-time overhead. However, there is also greater flexibility. For example, consider the following classes:

```java
public class Vehicle {

  public void drive() {
    System.out.println("Drive a vehicle");
  }
}

public class Car extends Vehicle {
```

```
public void drive() {
  System.out.println("Drive a car");
}
}
```

We can use these two classes within a test harness, as follows:

```
public class Example {

  public static void main(String args []) {

    Vehicle v = new Vehicle();
    Car c = new Car();
    v.drive();
    c.drive();
    v = c;
    v.drive();

  }
}
```

When this application is executed, the version of drive defined in the class Car is called twice, whereas the version in the superclass Vehicle is called only once:

```
C:\Book\chap13>java Example
Drive a vehicle
Drive a car
Drive a car

C:\Book\chap13>
```

The variable v was declared to be of type Vehicle. When it was assigned the instance of Car and it received the message drive, it responded with the Car version of drive, which was chosen at run time (based on the object held by v).

13.4.2 Method Selection

When the Java system selects a method in response to a message, it does so using three things:

- the class of the receiving object
- the name of the method
- the class (and order) of the parameters

The third element means that you can define two methods in the same class with the same name but with different parameters. The system works out which method you want to call at run time, by examining the parameters:

```
public class Lorry extends Vehicle {
```

```
   public void load (int i) {
      System.out.println("Loading integers " + i);
   }

   public void load (String s) {
      System.out.println("Loading strings " + s);
   }
}
```

This class, Lorry, has two methods called load, both of which take a single parameter. However, the parameters are of different types. This means that the Java system can distinguish between the two methods and thus no conflict arises. For example:

```
public class LorryExample {

   public static void main (String args []) {
      Lorry l = new Lorry();
      l.load(10);
      l.load("John");
   }
}
```

In this application, we use both versions of the load method, with the following result:

```
Loading integers 10
Loading strings John
```

You can also use this approach to provide class constructors.

13.5 Exercise: Managers and Employees

The aim of this exercise is that you should experiment with inheritance, polymorphism and method overriding.

13.5.1 What You Should Do

1. You should define at least three classes which should follow the structure illustrated below (you might like to make Employee a subclass of the Person class you implemented in an earlier chapter).

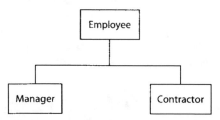

2. The employee class should define:
   - Instance variables
     - Name
     - Hours worked
   - Methods
     - Calculate pay (with an hourly rate of £5.00), which multiplies the hours worked by the hourly rate and returns the resulting value
3. The Manager class should:
   - Have a department instance variable
   - Override calculate pay and return a set salary of £400.00
   - Allow the department to be set to a given string
4. The Contractor class should:
   - Define a duration instance variable
   - Allow the duration of the contract to be defined
   - Use an hourly rate of £15.00

The following code should now be usable:

```java
public class Temp {

    public static void main (String [] args) {
        Employee e = new Manager("Bob", 23);
        System.out.println(e + e.calculatePay());
        e = new Contractor("Peter", 23);
        System.out.println(e + e.calculatePay());
    }
}
```

Try redefining the toString() method in Employee to print out the employee's name and the hours worked (what effect does it have?).

14 Data Structures

14.1 Introduction

Classes and objects merely package code and data together; you must still decide how to represent and maintain that data, for example in a list, as a tree, as part of a hash table or ordered in some manner. This chapter discusses how data structures are created and manipulated in Java. We consider a number of classes in the java.util package (see Appendix C), namely, Dictionary, Hashtable, Vector and Stack. We also consider how arrays are implemented in Java. The chapter concludes by considering automatic memory management. Note that an extended set of collections classes were added in Java 2 (JDK 1.2). These are discussed in some detail in Chapter 15.

14.2 Data Structure Classes

Figure 14.1 illustrates the relationships between the root class Object, the data structure classes and the Clonable and Serializable interfaces which they implement. The boxes indicate classes and the ovals indicate an interface.

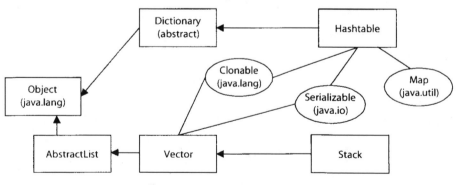

Figure 14.1 The data structure classes.

The root class, Object, is defined in the package java.lang. The other classes are all defined in the java.util package. Dictionary and AbstractList are abstract classes, which cannot be used to create instances. The other classes are all concrete classes, which can create instances.

14.3 The Abstract Class `Dictionary`

A `Dictionary` is a set of associations between a key and a value. It is an abstract subclass of `Object`. It is also the superclass of `Hashtable`. The elements in a `Dictionary` are unordered, but each has a definite name or *key*. Thus a `Dictionary` can be regarded as an unordered collection of object values with external keys (Table 14.1).

Table 14.1 The dictionary protocol

`get(Object aKey)`	returns the value associated with `aKey`.
`put(Object aKey,` `    object aValue)`	puts `aValue` into a dictionary with the external key `aKey`.
`keys()`	returns an enumeration of keys from the receiver.
`elements()`	returns an enumeration of the values in the receiver.
`remove(Object aKey)`	removes the key (and its corresponding value) from the dictionary.
`size()`	returns the number of keys in the receiver.

Notice that the key and the value must be objects (that is, you cannot use a primitive type, such as `int`, although you can use an integer object). Enumerations are explained in the next chapter.

14.4 The `Hashtable` Class

This is a concrete subclass of the abstract `Dictionary` class. It implements a simple hash table, such as that found in some other languages (e.g. Common LISP) or in libraries available for other languages (e.g. C). The great advantage of Java is that everyone has the same type of `Dictionary`. In Pascal or C, almost everyone has to invent their own or purchase a library to get the same functionality. This, of course, leads to problems of consistency between implementations.

You create an instance of a hash table using the `Hashtable` method with the parameters specified in Table 14.2.

The load factor is the point at which the hash table should grow and be rehashed. The load factor should be a real number between 0.0 and 1.0. When the number of entries is greater than the product of the load factor and the current capacity, the size of the hash table is increased and then it is rehashed. The new size of the hash table is twice the original size plus 1.

Table 14.2 The hash table constructor parameters

no parameters	creates a new empty hash table with a default initial capacity of 101
`int initialCapacity`	creates a new empty hash table of size `initialCapacity`. The load factor is 75 percent by default
`int initialCapacity` `float loadFactor`	creates a new hash table of size `initialCapacity` and the specified load factor

Here is a simple `Hashtable` example you might like to type in and try out. You must save it into a file called `Example.java`. You must also explicitly import the class `Hashtable`, as it is defined in a separate package called `java.util`.

```java
import java.util.Hashtable;

public class Example {
  public static void main (String args []) {
    Example e = new Example();
    e.example();
  }

  public void example () {
    Hashtable x = new Hashtable();
    x.put("jjh", "John");
    x.put("msw", "Myra");
    x.put("dec", "Denise");
    System.out.println(x.get("dec"));
    System.out.println(x.get("jjh"));
  }
}
```

In addition to the methods defined in `Dictionary`, `Hashtable` also provides the instance protocols shown in Table 14.3. The `Hashtable` class assumes that the key objects in the table implement the `hashCode` and the `equals` methods. In addition, for efficiency, the size of the hash table should be a prime number larger than the actual size required, and the key objects should never fill up more than 75 per cent of the space available in the hash table. For example, if the table is intended to hold 100 keys it should be created with a default size of 151.

Table 14.3 The hash table instance protocol

`clear()`	empties the hash table.
`clone()`	returns a "shallow" copy of the table (the table is duplicated, but the key and value references remain the same).
`contains(Object aValue)`	returns true if the table contains the value.
`containsKey(Object aKey)`	returns true if the table contains the key.
`rehash()`	rehashes the table into a larger table.
`toString()`	returns a string representation of the table.

A point to note is that, by default, all hash table methods return an object (i.e. an instance of type `Object`) even if the instance is really a subclass of `Object`. To access any variables or methods defined for the subclass it is necessary to cast the returned object into the correct class. For example, if the values in a hash table are strings then it is necessary to execute the following code:

```java
result = (String)aHashtable.get(aKey);
```

Note that it is not necessary for all the keys or elements in the hash table to be of the same class, as the only requirement is that they are instances of the class Object or one of its subclasses, which of course every class is.

14.5 The Vector Class

The Vector class is a concrete class which provides a similar facility to a linked list (or list structures in Lisp and Ordered Collections in Smalltalk) for objects. You can add elements to a vector, remove elements from it, check to see if an element is in it and process all the elements in it. In addition, the vector grows such that it possesses enough space to hold the elements within it. It is essentially an array of objects which can grow. You can access elements by their position in the vector. Notice that a vector of four elements is numbered 0 to 3. A vector cannot hold one of the primitive types such as int or boolean. Instead, they must be wrapped within a class such as Integer or Boolean. Tables 14.4 and 14.5 show the vector constructor parameters and the vector instance protocol, respectively.

Table 14.4 The vector constructor parameters

no parameters	creates an empty vector with a default size (10 in the JDK)
int initialCapacity	creates an empty vector of size initialCapacity
int initialCapacity int capacityIncrement	creates an empty vector of size initialCapacity and sets the growth increment to capacityIncrement

The methods which return the objects held within the vector always return objects of type Object (just as for hash tables). They must then be cast into the appropriate type. The following code presents a simple example of using a vector:

```java
import java.util.*;
public class VectorDemo {
  Vector names = new Vector(3, 2);

  public static void main (String argv []){
    VectorDemo v = new VectorDemo();
    v.example();
  }

  public void example () {
    names.addElement("John");
    names.addElement("Denise");
    names.addElement("Phoebe");
    System.out.println("The capacity is " +
            names.capacity());
    System.out.println("The size is " +
            names.size());
    names.insertElementAt("David", 2);
```

Table 14.5 The vector instance protocol

addElement(Object object)	adds the object to the end of the vector.
clone()	returns a duplicate of this vector. As the vector only holds references to the elements it holds, the elements themselves are not cloned
contains	returns true if the element is held in the vector
copyInto(Object anArray[])	copies the vector elements into the array. The array must be at least large enough to hold all the vector elements
elementAt(int index)	returns the element at the specified index
elements()	returns an enumeration of the elements in the vector
firstElement()	returns the first element in the vector without removing it from the vector
indexOf(Object Element)	returns the position of the first element matching the parameter within the vector
indexOf(Object Element, int index)	returns the position of the first element matching the parameter starting at the position specified by index
indexElementAt(Object object int index)	inserts the object at the position specified by index. If an object exists at that position, all objects with this and higher indexes are shifted up one position
isEmpty()	returns true if the vector holds no objects
lastElement()	returns the last element in the vector
lastIndexOf(Object element)	returns the position of the last occurrence of the element in the receiving vector
removeAllElements()	deletes all elements from the vector
removeElement(Object element)	deletes the specified element from the vector. Returns true if it is successful and false if the element was not a member of the receiving vector
removeElementAt(int index)	removes the element held at the position indicated by the index
setElementAt(Object object, int index)	replaces the element at the index with the new object

```
System.out.println("The capacity is now " +
        names.capacity());
System.out.println("The size is now " +
        names.size());
System.out.println("The last element is " +
        names.lastElement());
    }
}
```

The result of compiling and executing the VectorDemo is presented below:

```
C:>java VectorDemo
The capacity is 3
```

```
The size is 3
The capacity is now 5
The size is now 4
The last element is Phoebe
```

Vectors try to control the amount of storage they require by using the current capacity and two instance variables, capacityIncrement and elementCount. The capacity indicates the current maximum capacity of the vector, and the capacityIncrement determines the amount by which the vector grows in size once the current size (indicated by elementCount) exceeds the capacity.

To improve performance, the Vector class allows you to increase the size of the vector if you are about to add a large number of objects or to trim it down to size if the vector has grown larger than is currently needed. Notice the difference between ensureCapacity and setSize. This is summarized in Table 14.6.

Table 14.6 Vector management protocol

capacity()	returns the number of elements currently held in the vector
ensureCapacity(int minimumCapacity)	increases the amount of space available in the vector to that specified by the parameter minimumCapacity. If the capacity of the vector is greater than that specified no change is made
setSize(int newSize)	sets the number of elements that are currently held in the vector. If the new size is greater than the number of elements, then null values are added; if the number of elements exceeds the new size, those elements at positions newSize and greater are deleted
size()	returns the number of elements held by the receiving vector
trimToSize()	reduces the capacity of the vector to the current size. This frees up any unused storage space previously obtained by the vector

14.6 The Stack Class

The class Stack in JDK 1.1, a subclass of Vector, provides a basic stack object with the required last in, first out behaviour (see Table 14.7). It provides a single constructor, Stack, which creates a new empty stack.

Table 14.7 Stack instance protocol

empty()	returns true if the stack has no elements
peek()	returns the object at the top of the stack, without removing it from the stack
pop()	returns the object from the top of the stack and removes it from the stack
push(Object object)	places the object on the top of the stack
search(Object object)	returns the position of the object on the stack (or –1 if the object is not in the stack)

14.7 A Queue Class

You can easily define a Queue class in Java using the Vector class. Queues have a first in, first out behaviour, so you can use the addElement, firstElement and removeElement methods:

```java
import java.util.Vector;

public class Queue extends Vector {
  public final void add (Object object) {
    addElement(object);
  }
  public final Object peek () {
    return firstElement();
  }
  public final Object next () {
    Object result = firstElement();
    removeElement(result);
    return result;
  }
}
```

This class defines three new methods: add (Object object), peek and next. The add and peek methods are very straightforward, using the addElement and firstElement methods defined in Vector. The next method is not complex but has to use the firstElement method to obtain the object at the front of the queue so that it can remove this object and then return it.

14.8 Enumeration

Any object which is an instance of a class that implements the Enumeration interface produces a list of the elements it contains. You can access the list elements one at a time. The classes Hashtable and Vector (along with the collection classes above) implement the enumeration interface. You can access the elements contained in instances of these classes iteratively. This is an extremely useful feature, as any programmer who has used Lisp, Smalltalk or POP11 knows.

The elements method obtains an enumeration of an object's contents. The enumeration can then be accessed using the nextElement method, which returns successive elements from the list. The hasMoreElements method determines whether any further elements remain in the enumeration. This enumeration interface definition is presented below:

```java
public interface java.util.Enumeration {
  public abstract boolean hasMoreElements();
  public abstract Object nextElement();
}
```

You can use such an enumeration to apply the same message to all elements of a `Vector` (or collection). For example, to apply the `printself` message to all elements of a vector, we could write:

```
for (Enumeration e = aVector.elements() ;
  e.hasMoreElements() ; ) {
  temp = e.nextElement();
  temp.printself();
}
```

Enumeration has been superseded by iterators with Java 2; this is discussed in the next chapter.

14.9 Arrays

Arrays in Java are objects, like most other data types. Like arrays in any other language, they hold elements of data in an order specified by an index. They are zero-based arrays, as in C, which means that an array with 10 elements is indexed from 0 to 9.

To create a new array, you must specify the type of array object and the number of elements in the array. The number of elements is specified by an integer between square brackets. As an array is an instance, it is created in the usual way using the new operation:

```
new String[10];
```

This creates an array capable of holding 10 string objects. We can assign such an array instance to a variable by specifying that the variable holds an array. You do this by indicating the type of the array to be held by the variable along with the array indicator. Notice that we do not specify the number of array locations which are held by the array variable:

```
String names [];
String [] names;
```

Both of the above formats are legal; you should use the one with which you are more comfortable. Personally, I always use the former.

We now create an array and assign it to our variable:

```
String names [] = new String [4];
```

There is a short-cut way to create and initialize an array:

```
String names [] = {"John", "Denise", "Phoebe",
"James"};
```

This creates an array of four elements containing the strings "John", "Denise", "Phoebe" and "James". We can change any of these fields by specifying the appropriate index and replacing the existing value with a new string:

```
names [3] = "Isobel";
```

The above statement replaces the string "James" with the string "Isobel". Merely being able to put values into an array would be of little use; we can access the array locations in a similar manner:

```
System.out.println("The name in position 2 is " +
    names[1]);
```

The above statement results in the following string being printed:

```
The name in position 2 is Denise
```

As arrays are objects we can also obtain information from them. For example, to find out how many elements are in the array we can use the instance variable `length`:

```
names.length
```

Arrays are fixed in length when they are created, whereas vectors can change their length. To obtain the size of an array, you can access instance variable, `length`, but you must use a method, `size`, to determine the current size of a vector.

Arrays can be passed into and out of methods very simply by specifying the type of the array, the name of the variable to receive the array and the array indicator.

14.9.1 Arrays of Objects

The above examples have focused on arrays of `Strings`. You can also create arrays of any type of object (Figure 14.2), but this process is a little more complicated (it is actually the exactly the same for strings, but some of what is happening is hidden from you). For example, assuming we have a class `Person`, then we can create an array of `Persons`:

```
Person [] p = new Person[4];
```

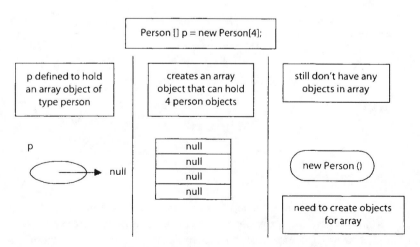

Figure 14.2 Creating an array of objects.

It is important to realize what this gives you. It provides a variable p which can hold a reference to an array object of Persons. At present this array is empty and *does not* hold references to any instances of Person. Note that this indicates that the array is actually an array of references to the instances "held" in the array as opposed to an array of those instances. This illustrated in Figure 14.3. To actually make it hold instances of Person we must add each person instance to the appropriate array location. For example:

```
p[0] = new Person();
p[1] = new Person();
p[2] = new Person();
p[3] = new Person();
```

This is illustrated in Figures 14.3 and 14.4. Thus the creation of an array of objects is a three-stage process:

1. Create a variable which can reference an array of the appropriate type of object.
2. Create the array object.
3. Fill the array object with instances of the appropriate type.

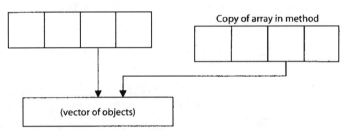

Figure 14.3 Passing an array into a method.

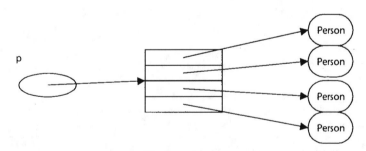

Figure 14.4 The complete array structure.

14.9.2 Basic Type Arrays

It should be noted that an array of basic types is exactly that. It is not an array of references to the basic types. Thus array of basic types is simpler and the generation of such an array produces an array containing the specified value or the default (zero) values, for example:

```
int totals [] = {0, 2, 5, 1, 7};
```

14.9.3 Multi-Dimensional Arrays

As in most high-level languages, multi-dimensional arrays can be defined in Java. This is done in the following manner:

```
String f [] [] = { {"John", "Denise", "Phoebe"},
                   {"Paul", "Fiona", "Andrew"}};
```

However, it is instructive to consider what this actually means. It states that a string array f can hold references to other string arrays which in turn can hold actual string objects. Thus to create these arrays and object for the Person class we would:

1. Define the variable P to hold a reference to an array of arrays

   ```
   Person p [][];
   ```

2. Create the multi-dimensional array

   ```
   p = new Person[2][];
   ```

   Note that we have to specify the first dimension, as it is necessary to allocate enough space for the required references. We do not have to specify the second dimension, as this can be specified in the subsequent array object creation messages.

3. Create the sub-arrays:

   ```
   p[0] = new Person[2];
   p[1] = new person[2];
   ```

4. Add instances to the two-dimensional array, for example:

   ```
   p[0][0] = new person("John");
   ```

As you can see from this last example, multi-dimensional arrays are accessed in exactly the same way as single-dimensional arrays with one index following another (note that each is within its own set of square brackets – [ ]).That is, you can access this two-dimensional array by specifying a particular position within the array using the same format:

```
System.out.println(matrix[2][2]);
```

It is also possible to have ragged arrays, as the second dimension is made up of separate array objects. For example, the following code defines a two-dimensional array in which the first row has four elements and the second has three.

```
String f [] [] = { {"John", "Denise",
                    "Phoebe", "Isobel"},
                   {"Paul", "Fiona", "Andrew"}};
```

Of course the way that multi-dimensional arrays are implemented in Java means that you can easily implement any number of dimensions required.

14.9.4 The Main Method

At this point you are ready to review the parameter passed into the main class method. As a reminder, it always has the following format:

```
public static void main (String args []) {
    ...
}
```

From this you can see that the parameter passed into the main method is an array of strings. This array holds any command line arguments passed into the program.

We now have enough information to write a simple program which parses the main method command line arguments:

```
public class ParseInput {
  public static void main (String args [] ) {
    if (args.length == 0) {
      System.out.println("No arguments");
    }
    else {
      for (i = 0; i < args.length; i++) {
        System.out.println("Argument number"
          + i + " is " + args[i]);
      }
    }
  }
}
```

This is a very simple program, but it provides the basics for a command line parser. Reread Sections 10.2 and 10.3 if you need to refresh your memory about how if statements and for loops work.

Arrays in Java are passed into methods by value (Figure 14.4). However, as they only hold a reference to the objects they contain, if those objects are modified internally the array outside the method is also modified. This can be the cause of extreme frustration when trying to debug programs. Arrays can also be returned from methods:

```
modifiers static-specifier type [] methodName (...)

public String [] returnNames () {
    ...
}
```

As an example of an array-based application, consider the following class ArrayDemo, which calculates the average of an array of numbers. This array is created in the main method and is passed into the processArray method as a parameter. Within this method, the values of the array are added together and the total is divided by the number of elements in the array (i.e. its length):

```
public class ArrayDemo {
  public static void main (String args []) {
```

```
    ArrayDemo d = new ArrayDemo();
    int anArray [] = {1, 4, 7, 9};
    d.processArray(anArray);
  }
  public void processArray (int myArray []) {
    int i, total = 0, average = 0;
    for (i = 0; i < (myArray.length); ++i){
      total = total + myArray[i];
    }
    average = total / myArray.length;
    System.out.println("The average was " + result);
  }
}
```

14.10 Memory Management

14.10.1 Why Have Automatic Memory Management?

Any discussion of data structures in Java needs to consider how Java handles memory. One of the many advantages of Java over languages such as C++ is that it automatically manages memory allocation and reuse. It is not uncommon to hear C++ programmers complaining about spending many hours attempting to track down a particularly awkward bug, only to find that it was a problem associated with memory allocation or pointer manipulation. Similarly, a regular problem for C++ developers is that of memory creep, which occurs when memory is allocated but is not freed up. The application either uses all available memory or runs out of space and produces a run-time error.

Most of the problems associated with memory allocation in languages such as C++ occur because programmers must not only concentrate on the (often complex) application logic but also on memory management. They must ensure that they allocate only the memory which is required and deallocate it when it is no longer required. This may sound simple, but it is no mean feat in a large complex application.

An interesting question to ask is "why do programmers have to manage memory allocation?". There are few programmers today who would expect to have to manage the registers being used by their programs, although 20 or 30 years ago the situation was very different. One answer to the memory management question, often cited by those who like to manage their own memory, is that "it is more efficient, you have more control, it is faster and leads to more compact code". Of course, if you wish to take these comments to their extreme, then we should all be programming in assembler. This would enable us all to produce faster, more efficient and more compact code than that produced by Pascal, C++ or Java.

The point about high-level languages, however, is that they are more productive, introduce fewer errors, are more expressive and are efficient enough (given modern computers and compiler technology). The memory management issue is somewhat similar. If the system automatically handles the allocation and deallocation of memory, then the programmer can concentrate on the application logic. This makes the programmer more productive, removes problems due to poor memory management and, when implemented efficiently, can still provide acceptable performance.

14.10.2　Memory Management in Java

Java provides automatic memory management. Essentially, it allocates a portion of memory as and when required. When memory is short, it looks for areas which are no longer referenced. These areas of memory are then freed up (deallocated) so that they can be reallocated. This process is often referred to as "garbage collection".

The Java Virtual Machine (JVM) uses an approach known as *mark and sweep* to identify objects which can be freed up. The garbage collection process searches from any root objects, i.e. objects from which the main method has been run, marking all the objects it finds. It then examines all the objects currently held in memory and deletes those objects which are not marked. It is at this point that an object's finalize method is executed.

A second process invoked with garbage collection is memory compaction. This involves moving all the allocated memory blocks together so that free memory is contiguous rather than fragmented.

14.10.3　When Is Garbage Collection Performed?

The garbage collection process runs in its own thread. That is, it runs at the same time as other processes within the JVM. It is initiated when the ratio of free memory versus total memory passes a certain point.

You can also explicitly indicate to the JVM that you wish the garbage collector to run. This can be useful if you are about to start a process which requires a large amount of memory and you think that there may be unneeded objects in the system. You can do this in one of two ways:

```
System.gc();
Runtime.getRuntime().gc();
```

However, calling System.gc is (allegedly) only an indication to the compiler that you would like garbage collection to happen. There is no guarantee that it will run. This is not made clear from the JDK documentation:

> Runs the garbage collector. Calling this method suggests that the Java Virtual Machine expend effort toward recycling unused objects in order to make the memory they currently occupy available for quick reuse. When control returns from the method call, the Java Virtual Machine has made its best effort to recycle all unused objects.

This explanation is misleading as it says that it "runs the garbage collector"!

14.10.4　Checking the Available Memory

You can find out the current state of your system (with regard to memory) using the Runtime environment object. This object allows you to obtain information about the current free memory, total memory etc.:

```java
public class MemoryStatus {

    public static void main (String args []) {
        MemoryStatus s = new MemoryStatus ();
        s.testMemory();
    }

    public void testMemory() {
        Runtime rt = Runtime.getRuntime ();
        long freeMemory = rt.freeMemory();
        long totalMemory = rt.totalMemory();

        System.out.println("Total memory is " +
            totalMemory + " and free memory is " +
                freeMemory);
        System.gc();
        freeMemory = rt.freeMemory();
        System.out.println("Total memory is " +
            totalMemory + " and free memory is now " +
                freeMemory);
    }
}
```

14.11 Exercise: Vectors

The aim of this exercise is to allow you a chance to use the very useful class Vector. This class is a growable array which can be used as a linked list structure or as an array.

14.11.1 What You Should Do

Your task is to implement a set data structure using an array.

A set is a data structure which will only hold a single instance of a particular type of object. That is, it will only hold a single instance of the string "john".

The class Set should define the following methods:

- add(Object) – Add an object to the set if it is not already present.
- remove(Object) – Remove an object from the set if it is already in the set.
- elements() – Return an enumeration of the elements in the Set (see the class Vector and the interface Enumeration).

14.11.2 Testing Your Set Class

You should test your newly defined class Set on the following application:

```java
public class Test {
  public static void main (String args []) {
    Set s = new Set();
    s.add("John");
    s.add("Paul");
    s.add("John");
    s.add(new Button("Exit"));
    s.add(new Button("Exit"));
    Enumeration e = s.elements();
    while (e.hasMoreElements()) {
      System.out.println(e.nextElement());
    }
  }
}
```

What is the result of running this program? Did it have any surprises for you?

14.11.3 Hints

1. You will need to import java.util.Vector into the file defining your class Set.
2. Define a class Set which contains a Vector (you can't subclass Vector!).
3. You should use the equals(Object) method to determine whether one object is the same as another.
4. Take advantage of the elements() method defined in Vector.

14.12 Summary

In this chapter you have encountered the various data structure classes which form the cornerstone of most implementations: Dictionary, Hashtable, Vector and Stack. If you come from a Lisp-style language, things like vectors should not have seemed too strange. However, if you come from languages such as C, Pascal or Ada, you may well have found the idea of a vector quite bizarre. Stick with it, try it out, implement some simple programs using it and you will soon find that it is easy to use and extremely useful. You will very quickly come to wonder why every language does not have the same facility!

14.13 Further Reading

Almost any good book on Java includes a detailed discussion of the classes used to construct data structures. However, particularly good references can be found in Cornell and Horstmann (1997).

Cornell, G. and Horstmann, C.S. (1997). *Core JAVA*, 2nd edn. Prentice Hall, Englewood Cliffs, NJ.

15 *The Collection API*

15.1 Introduction

Java 2 introduced a new set of collection classes. A collection, according to JavaSoft, is a single object representing a group of objects (such as Java's familiar `Vector` class). That is, they are a *collection* of other objects. Collections may also be referred to as containers (as they contain other objects). These collection classes are used as the basis for data structures.

The new collection classes extended the facilities provided by the utility classes `Vector` and `Hashtable`. These classes are called by names such as `HashSet`, `ArraySet`, `LinkedList` etc. Some of the collection classes (for example `ArrayList`) provide functionality similar to that of existing data structure classes, such as the `Vector` class, but have been optimized for performance. Like `Vector` and `Hashtable`, the collection classes can only hold objects; thus if you wish to hold the basic types within them, you need to wrap the basic type in the appropriate object wrapper. The Collections API is implemented as part of the `java.util` package.

15.2 What Is in the Collections API?

The collection classes and interfaces in Java 2 are collectively referred to as the Collections API. A *collection* is a group of objects (these objects are called the *elements* of the collection). Collections are the Java mechanism for building data structures of various sorts; it is therefore important to become familiar with the collection API and its functionality.

The interface `Collection` is the root of all collections in the API. Figure 15.1 summarizes the Collections API in Java 2. Some of the classes illustrated are abstract classes on which others built. In fact, the collection class hierarchy is a classic example of the use of interfaces and abstract classes and how they can be used to group together functionality as well as indicate what is expected of subclasses. Now might be a good time to stop and examine the collection API itself.

The Collections API can be divided up in the following manner:

- *Collection interfaces* There are four collection interfaces, which represent the core types of collections supported by the Collections API. These interfaces are `Collection`, `Set`, `List` and `Map`. We will look in more detail at these interfaces later.

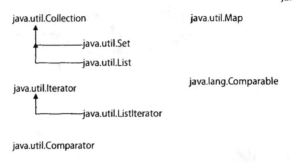

Figure 15.1 The interfaces defined in the Collections API.

- *Abstract implementations* These provide the abstract root classes for the collection hierarchy. They specify the behaviour which must be implemented by subclasses which provide the features of a Set, a List etc.
- *Concrete implementations* These are general purpose implementations of the core collection interfaces.
- *Anonymous implementations* These are classes which the developer does not instantiate, but which are returned by *static* factory methods in the classes Collections and Arrays. They are intended to enable pre-Collection API data structures to be converted into collections efficiently and effectively and to allow legacy APIs that return arrays to interoperate with new APIs that expect Collections.
- *Infrastructure* This grouping includes new interfaces for iteration and ordering as well as two new exceptions.
- *Array sorting and searching* As JavaSoft admit, the Arrays class static methods for sorting and searching arrays are not really part of the Collections API. However, they are being provided in Java 2 for the first time and they are useful in manipulating array-based data structures.

Figure 15.2 shows the Collections API class hierarchy.

Just as with the older utility data structure classes, the basic operations that are performed by the collection data structures include adding and removing elements, determining the size of the collection, querying the presence or absence of elements and iterating over the elements.

15.3 Collection Interfaces

The interfaces that comprise the collection hierarchy are designed to allow manipulation of collections in an implementation-independent fashion. This should allow for interoperability among unrelated APIs and applications that take collections as input or return them as output. This should reduce the effort required to design, implement, maintain and understand such APIs and applications. The Collections API should also help in the production of reusable software. The interfaces which form the basis of the Collections API are:

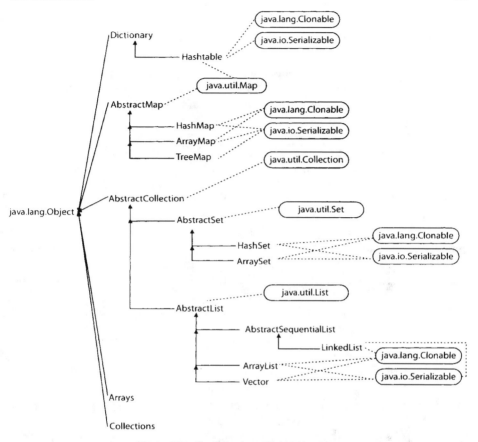

Figure 15.2 The Collections API class hierarchy.

- **Collection** This interface is the root of most of the Collections API. The only classes which do not implement this interface are the map-oriented classes (these are Hashtable, HashMap, ArrayMap and TreeMap).
- **Set** This interface represents the set data type. Sets contains all the elements put into them, in any order. Duplicates are not kept; adding equal objects many times results in only one such object in the set. This interface extends the Collection interface.
- **List** This interface defines an Ordered Collection data type (also known as a sequence). An ordered collection is a collection where the ordering is given by the order in which elements were added. This interface again extends the Collection interface.
- **Map** A map is an association between pairs of objects. One object often acts as the key to the other object (referred to as the value).

If you wish to define your own collection classes, then implementing one of these interfaces could be your starting point. The details of these interface are presented below.

15.3.1 Collection

The `Collection` interface is the interface which acts as the root of (almost) all collection classes. It defines the methods which all collections (except Map-type collections) must implement. Note that some of the implementing classes may decided that the implementation should throw an `Unsupported-OperationException` to indicate that they should not be used with this type of collection.

The interface defines methods for adding an element to a collection, accessing elements in a collection, removing an element from a collection and indicating the size of the collection. It also provides facilities which allow an iterator to be returned (these are similar to enumerations in JDK 1.1). The `toArray()` method also allows the collection to be converted into an array.

Any object can be stored into any collection (however, again implementations of a particular collection may limit the type of object they hold). This means that a collection can be a very flexible way of holding other objects. Typically, collections are used as data structures; however, they can also be used as temporary holding places for groups of calculations, results, classes etc.

The `Collection` interface defines the following (abstract) methods:

- `add(Object)` Ensures that this `Collection` contains the specified element (optional operation).
- `addAll(Collection)` Adds all of the elements in the specified `Collection` to this `Collection` (optional operation).
- `clear()` Removes all of the elements from this `Collection` (optional operation).
- `contains(Object)` Returns true if this `Collection` contains the specified element.
- `containsAll(Collection)` Returns true if this `Collection` contains all of the elements in the specified `Collection`.
- `equals(Object)` Compares the specified `Object` with this `Collection` for equality.
- `hashCode()` Returns the hash code value for this `Collection`.
- `isEmpty()` Returns true if this `Collection` contains no elements.
- `iterator()` Returns an `Iterator` over the elements in this `Collection`.
- `remove(Object)` Removes a single instance of the specified element from this `Collection`, if it is present (optional operation).
- `removeAll(Collection)` Removes from this `Collection` all of its elements that are contained in the specified `Collection` (optional operation).
- `retainAll(Collection)` Retains only the elements in this `Collection` that are contained in the specified `Collection` (optional operation).
- `size()` Returns the number of elements in this `Collection`.
- `toArray()` Returns an array containing all of the elements in this `Collection`.

You may note that some of the above methods are labelled "optional". This denotes that some implementations may not perform one or more of these operations. If they are called they should throw a run-time exception, the previously mentioned UnsupportedOperationException. This means that collection implementations must specify in their documentation which optional operations they support.

JavaSoft have introduced several terms to aid in this specification:

- Collections that do not support any modification operations (such as add, remove, clear) are referred to as unmodifiable. Collections that are not unmodifiable are referred to as modifiable.

- Collections that additionally guarantee that no change in the Collection will ever be observable via "query" operations (such as iterator, size, contains) are referred to as immutable. Collections that are not immutable are referred to as mutable.

- Lists that guarantee that their size will remain constant even though the elements may change are referred to as fixed-size. Lists that are not fixed-size are referred to as variable-size.

Some implementations may restrict what elements (or in the case of Maps, keys and values) may be stored. Possible restrictions include requiring elements to:

- be of a particular type
- be comparable to other elements in the collection
- be non-null
- obey some arbitrary predicate

If a programmer attempts to add an element that violates an implementation's restrictions, then that collection should generate a run-time exception. Under normal circumstances this should be one of:

- ClassCastException
- IllegalArgumentException
- NullPointerException

In addition, if a programmer tries to remove or test for such an element, then one of these exceptions may again be raised. However, this is not enforced and as such (depending on the implementation) no exception may be raised.

JavaSoft also state that all general purpose Collection implementation classes should provide two "standard" constructors: a void (no arguments) constructor, which creates an empty Collection, and a constructor with a single argument of type Collection, which creates a new Collection with the same elements as its argument. In effect, the latter constructor allows the user to copy any Collection, producing an equivalent Collection of the desired implementation type. Similarly, all general purpose Map implementations should provide a void (no arguments) constructor and a constructor that takes a single argument of type Map. There is no way to enforce these recommendations (as interfaces cannot contain constructors), but all of the general purpose Collection and Map implementations in Java 2 comply with this guideline.

15.3.2 Set

The interface Set is basically the same as the interface Collection, with the exception that it does not allow duplicates. That is, it is only possible to hold a single reference to an object in a set.

15.3.3 List

A list is an ordered collection of elements. That is, a list has a very specific sequence to the elements it contains. That order is determined by the order in which objects are added to the ordered collection/List instance. An implementation of the List interface can hold any type of object. Implementations of the List interface can be used in situations where the order in which the objects were added to the instance must be preserved. In general, List implementations will allow duplicate objects (although any particular implementation may reject duplicates and thus throw a run-time exception). They may allow null objects, although again any particular implementation may decide to reject null values.

There is a range of order-related messages which allow objects to be added and accessed with reference to the order in the List instance. For example, it is possible to access an object at a particular location, to find the positon of an object or the last position of an object using methods such as get(int), set(int Object), indexOf(Object), indexOf(Object, int) and lastIndexOf (Object). Note that, like arrays and Vectors, Lists are zero-based; thus the first location in a List is position zero. In addition, this interface inherits all the methods defined in the Collections interface.

To process Lists it would certainly be possible to iterate over the elements of the List using a standard for loop and the get(int) method. However, the time taken to access a particular object is linear with respect to its position in the list. It is therefore more efficient to use one of the Iterator access methods provided by a List. List provides a special Iterator, called a ListIterator, that allows element insertion and replacement and bidirectional access in addition to the normal Iterator operations. Two Iterator access methods are provided. One returns an iterator for the whole List, while the second returns an iterator that starts at a specified position in the List.

The methods defined in this interface (in addition to those inherited from Collection) are:

- addAll(int, Collection) Inserts all of the elements in the specified Collection into this List at the specified position (optional operation).
- get(int) Returns the element at the specified position in this List.
- indexOf(Object) Returns the index in this List of the first occurrence of the specified element, or –1 if the List does not contain this element.
- indexOf(Object, int) Returns the index in this List of the first occurrence of the specified element at or after the specified position, or –1 if the element is not found.

- lastIndexOf(Object) Returns the index in this List of the last occurrence of the specified element, or −1 if the List does not contain this element.
- lastIndexOf(Object, int) Returns the index in this List of the last occurrence of the specified element at or before the specified position, or −1 if the List does not contain this element.
- listIterator() Returns a ListIterator of the elements in this List (in proper sequence).
- listIterator(int) Returns a ListIterator of the elements in this List (in proper sequence), starting at the specified position in the List.
- remove(int) Removes the element at the specified position in this List (optional operation).
- removeRange(int, int) Removes from this List all of the elements whose index is between fromIndex, inclusive, and toIndex, exclusive (optional operation).
- set(int, Object) Replaces the element at the specified position in this List with the specified element (optional operation).

15.3.4 Map

A Map is a set of associations, each representing a key–value pair. The elements in a Map may be unordered, but each has a definite name or *key*. Although the values may be duplicated, keys cannot. In turn, a key can *map* to at most one value. Some Map implementations, like TreeMap and ArrayMap, make specific guarantees as to their order; others, like HashMap, do not.

The Map protocol allows either the keys to be viewed or the values to be viewed, or the keys to be used to access the values. JavaSoft have stated that all general purpose Map implementation classes should provide two "standard" constructors: a void (no arguments) constructor, which creates an empty Map, and a constructor with a single argument of type Map, which creates a new Map with the same key–value mappings as its argument. In effect, the latter constructor allows the user to copy any Map, producing an equivalent Map of the desired class.

- clear() Removes all mappings from this Map (optional operation).
- containsKey(Object) Returns true if this Map contains a mapping for the specified key.
- containsValue(Object) Returns true if this Map maps one or more keys to the specified value.
- entries() Returns a Collection view of the mappings contained in this Map.
- equals(Object) Compares the specified Object with this Map for equality.
- get(Object) Returns the value associated with aKey.
- hashCode() Returns the hash code value for this Map.
- isEmpty() Returns true if this Map contains no key–value mappings.
- keySet() Answers with a Set of keys from the receiver.

- `put(Object key, Object value)` Puts `value` into a dictionary with the external key `key`.
- `putAll(Map)` Copies all of the mappings from the specified `Map` to this `Map` (optional operation).
- `remove(Object)` Removes the mapping for this key from this `Map` if present (optional operation).
- `size()` Returns the number of key–value mappings in this `Map`.
- `values()` Answers with a `Collection` of the values in the receiver. Note that values are not necessarily unique (hence they are returned as a `Collection` rather than as a `Set`).

15.3.5 Comparisons

In order to sort a collection, the objects within the collection either need to be `Comparable` or they need to be able to be compared using a `Comparator`. `Comparable` and `Comparator` are two interfaces which can be implemented so that collections are classes can be sorted.

- `public interface Comparable` This interface defines the `compareTo (Object)`. This method should allow one object to be compared to another. The result of this comparison is referred to as the natural ordering of the objects. Arrays of `Objects` that implement this interface can be sorted automatically by `List.sort`. The interface assumes that concrete implementations of this interface will implement the `int compareTo(Object o)` method such that the method returns negative if the receiver is less than the object passed to the method, zero if they are equal and positive if the receiver is greater. Note many of the classes in the JDK now implement this interface.
- `public interface Comparator` This interface defines a comparison function which imposes a total ordering on some collection of `Objects`. Comparators can be passed to a sort method (such as `Arrays.sort`) to allow precise control over the sort order. The `Comparator` interface specifies one method: the `static int compare(Object, Object)` method. This method assumes that the result returned is negative if the first object is less than the second, zero if they are equal and a positive number if the first is greater than the second.

15.4 Abstract Implementations

A set of abstract classes are provided which implement the Collections API interfaces. These classes are `AbstractCollection`, `AbstractSet`, `AbstractList`, `AbstractSequentialList` and `AbstractMap`. They provide basic implementations for many of the methods specified in their associated interfaces (note the naming convention). The documentation provided with each class in the Java 2 release indicates which methods need to be implemented for a concrete class to be implemented. We shall consider each of these classes below.

15.4.1 `AbstractCollection`

The `AbstractCollection` class provides a skeleton implementation of a `Collection`. This implementation represents what is often referred to as a bag or multiset. Abstractly, a `Bag` can be considered to be any collection of objects, which can be of any class; these objects are the elements of the `Bag`. It is a general place-holder for collections of objects. There is no order assumed. It is the most general form of collection available in Java.

If you are confused by this description of a bag, think of it as a shopping bag. At a supermarket, you pick objects up from the shelves and place them in your shopping bag. For example, you pick up a pint of milk, a box of cornflakes, a packet of biscuits, three bags of potato crisps and a few bananas (see Figure 15.3).

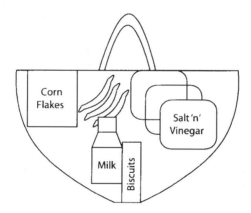

Figure 15.3 A shopping bag.

Each of the objects in the bag is a different type of thing, with different character-istics etc. There is no particular order to them – they will have moved about in the bag while you were shopping and while you brought them home. When you reach into the bag at home to remove the objects, the order in which they come out will not be predictable. If you think of a bag collection in these terms then you will not be far off the mark.

To create a concrete implementation of a `Bag` (or any other collection class) from the `AbstractCollection` class it is necessary to implement the following methods:

- `public Iterator iterator()` Returns an `Iterator` over the elements contained in this `Collection`. This object must implement the `hasNext` and `next` methods.

- `public int size()` Returns the number of elements in this `Collection`.

In addition, if the collection is to be modifiable, the subclass must implement the `add(Object)` method. This is because in the `AbstractCollection` class this method throws an `UnsupportedOperationException`. Note that the methods `equals(Object)` and `hashCode()` are inherited from `Object`.

15.4.2 `AbstractSet`

This abstract class is a direct subclass of `AbstractCollection`. It implements the `Set` interface. The only methods which are defined in this class are the methods `equals(Object)` and `hashCode()`. The `equals(Object)` method checks to see that the two objects are sets, that they have the same size and that all the objects in the set are equal. Note that it is assumed that the addition methods will conform to the `Set` constraint that duplicates are not allowed.

15.4.3 `AbstractList`

This abstract class provides a skeleton implementation of the `List` interface. Many methods are inherited from its direct superclass `AbstractCollection`. However, it defines methods such as `add(int, Object)`, `indexOf(Object)` and `indexOf(Object, int)` from the interface definition so that the basic structure of a `List` (`orderedCollection`) is provided. It uses an array to hold the data internally. The data structure used is optimized for random access. If sequential access is to be the most commonly used form of access, then the `AbstractSequentialList` class should be subclassed.

To create a concrete `List` collection class a subclass must implement the following methods:

- `get(int)` This returns the object held at the specified position.
- `size()` This returns the number of elements held in the collection.

In addition, if the `List` collection is modifiable the subclass must implement the `set(int, Object)` method. The default implementation will throw the `UnsupportedOperationException`. The assumption is also made that the `List` collection is of fixed size. This means that if the subclass is to be "growable" (that is can grow in size if necessary) then the subclass must also override the `add(int, Object)` and `remove(int)` methods. Note that it is not necessary to override the `add()` method. This is because the `add()` method actually calls the `add(int, Object)` method using the `size()` method to generate the position index.

15.4.4 `AbstractSequentialList`

This is essentially the same as the `AbstractList` class from which it inherits, except that the data structure and its access methods have been optimized for sequential access rather than random access. This means that it implements the "random access" methods (`get(int index)`, `set(int index, Object element)`, `set(int index, Object element)`, `add(int index, Object element)` and `remove(int index)`) on top of `List`'s `listIterator`, instead of the other way around.

To create a concrete subclass of this class, that subclass must implement:

- `public abstract ListIterator listIterator(int index)` Returns a `ListIterator` of the elements in this `List` (in proper sequence).

- `public abstract int size()` Returns the number of elements in this `List`.

In addition, for an unmodifiable `List`, the programmer should implement the `listIterator`'s hasNext, next, hasPrevious, previous and index methods. For a modifiable `List` the programmer should also implement the `listIterator`'s set method. For a variable-size list the programmer should additionally implement the `listIterator`'s remove and add methods. Remember that the get, set and remove methods all use the `List`'s `listInterator`.

15.4.5 **AbstractMap**

This abstract class provides a basic implementation for the `Map` interface. To create a concrete implementation of a map a subclass must implement:

- `public abstract Collection entries()` This method is expected to return a collection of all the key–value pairs in the map. It is expected to reflect the current state of the map, thus any changes made to the map should be reflected in the collection. Note that this collection is not expected to support the add or remove methods, and its `Iterator` should not support the remove method.

In addition, if a modifiable `Map` is to be defined, then the concrete subclass should override this class's put method (which otherwise throws an `UnsupportedOperationException`), and the `Iterator` returned by `entries().iterator()` must also implement its remove method.

15.5 Concrete Implementations

As stated earlier in this chapter, these classes are general purpose implementations of the core collection interfaces. They all inherit from appropriate abstract classes and thus provide good examples of how to create concrete versions of the various concepts such as lists and sets. The classes are summarized in Table 15.1. All the new classes (that is, those other than `Hashtable` and `Vector`) are unsynchronized, as this greatly improves their performance. They can be synchronized by using a synchronizing wrapper, which can be obtained using the appropriate `Collection` class's static method. For example, to generate a synchronized version of a collection class you can use the static method `Collection.synchronized Collection(Collection c)`.

As the concrete collection classes implement the appropriate associated interfaces, we will not list the complete set of methods for each class. Instead, we will only look at the new classes and consider the inheritance relationships between the classes and what constructors they provide. In some cases an example of using that class is also provided.

Table 15.1 Concrete collection classes

HashSet	Implements a Set
ArraySet	Intended for small sets (faster creation and iteration than HashSet)
ArrayList	An unsynchronized Vector
LinkedList	A doubly-linked List, which may provide better performance if insertion and deletion occur frequently
Vector	As in JDK 1.1. Included for legacy applications
HashMap	An unsynchronized Hashtable
ArrayMap	Intended for small hash tables (faster creation and iteration than HashMap).
TreeMap	A balanced binary tree implementation of the Map interface. Unlike Hashtable, imposes an ordering on its elements
Hashtable	As in JDK 1.1. Included for legacy applications

15.5.1 **HashSet**

This class is a direct subclass of the AbstractSet class. It implements the Set interface as well as the java.lang.Clonable and java.io.Serializable interfaces.

The HashSet class provides the following constructors:

- HashSet() Constructs a new, empty HashSet; the backing HashMap has default capacity and load factor. The default capacity and load factor for a HashMap are 101 and 75%.
- HashSet(Collection) Constructs a new HashSet containing the elements in the specified Collection.
- HashSet(int) Constructs a new, empty HashSet; the backing HashMap has the specified initial capacity and default load factor (75%).
- HashSet(int, float) Constructs a new, empty HashSet; the backing HashMap has the specified initial capacity and the specified load factor.

For example, consider the following simple Test class. This class creates a simple set and adds four strings to it (one of which is a duplicate):

```java
import java.util.*;

public class Test {
  public static void main(String args []) {
    HashSet set = new HashSet(10);
    set.add("John");
    set.add("Denise");
    set.add("Phoebe");
    set.add("John");
    Iterator it = set.iterator();
    while (it.hasNext()) {
      System.out.println(it.next());
    }
```

```
    }
  }
```

Note that an iterator is used to process all the elements in the set. Iteration over collections are described in more detail later in this chapter. The result of executing this class is:

```
C:>java Test
John
Phoebe
Denise
```

15.5.2 ArraySet

This class is a direct subclass of the AbstractSet class. It implements the Set interface as well as the java.lang.Clonable and java.io.Serializable interfaces. It is intended for use with small sets which are likely to be frequently modified. It will give *extremely* poor performance for large sets.

The ArraySet class provides the following constructors:

- ArraySet() Constructs a new, empty ArraySet; the backing ArrayList has default initial capacity (10) and capacity increment (0). If the increment is zero then the size of the ArrayList is doubled each time the current capacity is exceeded.
- ArraySet(Collection) Constructs a new ArraySet containing the elements in the specified Collection.
- ArraySet(int) Constructs a new, empty ArraySet; the backing ArrayList has the specified initial capacity and default capacity increment.

15.5.3 ArrayList

This is a concrete subclass of the AbstractList class. It is a resizable list collection. Essentially this is an unsynchronized Vector. Like a Vector, it has an initial capacity and an increment. Again like Vector, its default capacity is 10 and its default increment is zero. If the increment is zero then the size of the ArrayList doubles each time the capacity is exceeded. Also like Vector, it possesses methods to manipulate its size, such as ensureCapacity(int), trimToSize() and size().

The ArrayList class provides the following constructors:

- ArrayList() Constructs an array list with a capacity of 10 and an increment of 0.
- ArrayList(Collection) Constructs an ArrayList containing the elements of the specified Collection, in the order they are returned by the Collection's iterator. The increment is defaulted to zero.
- ArrayList(int) Constructs an empty ArrayList with the specified initial capacity and the default increment.
- ArrayList(int, int) Constructs an empty ArrayList with the specified initial capacity and capacity increment.

As an example, consider the following Test class modified to use an ArrayList. This class creates a simple set and adds four strings to it (one of which is a duplicate):

```java
import java.util.*;

public class Test {
  public static void main(String args []) {
    ArrayList list = new ArrayList(10);
    list.add("John");
    list.add("Denise");
    list.add("Phoebe");
    list.add("John");
    Iterator it = list.iterator();
    while (it.hasNext()) {
      System.out.println(it.next());
    }
  }
}
```

The results obtained from running this example are illustrated below:

```
C:>java Test
John
Phoebe
Denise
John
```

Note that ArrayList allows duplicates.

15.5.4 LinkedList

The LinkedList class is a concrete subclass of the AbstractSequential-List class. It provides a doubly linked list implementation of the List interface. This class is particularly good for sequential access-oriented operations and for insertions and deletions. It provides the following constructors:

- LinkedList() Constructs an empty LinkedList.
- LinkedList(Collection) Constructs a LinkedList containing the elements of the specified Collection, in the order they are returned by the Collection's iterator.

The LinkedList class also provides the following additional methods for adding objects to the front and back of a list:

- addFirst(Object) Inserts the given element at the beginning of this List.
- addLast(Object) Appends the given element to the end of this List.

In turn it also provides the following additional access methods:

- getFirst() Returns the first element in this List.

- getLast() Returns the last element in this List.

The following deletion methods are also defined:

- removeFirst() Removes and returns the first element from this List.
- removeLast() Removes and returns the last element from this List.

15.5.5 **HashMap**

This class is a concrete subclass of the AbstractMap class. It is essentially an unsynchronized Hashtable. As with the Hashtable class it possesses a default capacity and loading factor. In HashMap these are 101 and 75% respectively. The constructors provided by HashMap are:

- HashMap() Constructs a new, empty HashMap with a default capacity of 101 and load factor of 75%.
- HashMap(int) Constructs a new, empty HashMap with the specified initial capacity and default load factor.
- HashMap(int, float) Constructs a new, empty HashMap with the specified initial capacity and the specified load factor.
- HashMap(Map) Constructs a new HashMap with the same mappings as the given Map.

An example of using a HashMap is provided below:

```
import java.util.*;

public class MapTest {
  public static void main(String args []) {
    HashMap table = new HashMap(10);
    table.put("John", "C47");
    table.put("Denise", "D57");
    table.put("Phoebe", "A12");
    table.put("Isobel", "E56");
    System.out.println("Johns office is " +
      table.get("John"));
  }
}
```

The result of executing this class is:

```
c:> java MapTest
Johns office is C47
```

15.5.6 **ArrayMap**

This is a concrete subclass of AbstractMap. It is intended for small, but fast, hash tables. It is implemented on top of an ArrayList and overrides the entries(), clone() and put(key, value) methods. In an ArrayMap the key–value pairs are guaranteed to be in the order in which they were inserted. If a key–value pair is removed and a mapping for the same key is inserted at a later time, the mapping goes to the end of the map.

`ArrayMap` provides the following constructors:

- `ArrayMap()` Constructs a new, empty `ArrayMap`; the backing `ArrayList` has default initial capacity and capacity increment.
- `ArrayMap(int)` Constructs a new, empty `ArrayMap`; the backing `ArrayList` has the specified initial capacity and default capacity increment.
- `ArrayMap(Map)` Constructs a new `ArrayMap` containing the mappings in the specified `Map`.

15.5.7 `TreeMap`

This class is a concrete subclass of the `AbstractMap` class and implements a binary tree as the data structure for holding the mappings from keys to values. the binary tree is ordered on the keys and thus guarantees that the key–value pairs are in key order. This class thus provides guaranteed $\log(n)$ time cost for the `containsKey`, `get`, `put` and `remove` operations.

It provides the following constructors:

- `TreeMap()` Constructs a new, empty `TreeMap`, sorted according to the keys' natural sort method.
- `TreeMap(Comparator)` Constructs a new, empty `TreeMap`, sorted according to the given comparator.
- `TreeMap(Map)` Constructs a new `TreeMap` containing the same mappings as the given `Map`, sorted according to the keys' natural sort method.

15.6 The `Collections` class

The `Collections` class is a general utility class of the Collections API. It provides many very useful (static) methods which can be used to wrap collections in a synchronized wrapping, to search and sort collections, to find the minimum or maximum value in a collection and create unmodifiable versions of modifiable collections. Note that this class provides no instance-side methods – all the methods are static.

The following list summarises the set of methods available:

- `binarySearch(List, Object)` performs a binary search on the list for the specified object.
- `binarySearch(List, Object, Comparator)` performs a binary search on the list for the specified object using the specified comparator.
- `enumeration(Collection)` returns an enumeration object for the specified collection.

- `max(Collection)` Returns the object which is the maximum value for the normal comparison methods for its elements.

- `max(Collection, Comparator)` Returns the maximum element of the given `Collection`, according to the order induced by the specified `Comparator`.

- `min(Collection)` Returns the object which is the minimum value for the normal comparison methods for its elements.

- `min(Collection, Comparator)` Returns the minimum element of the given `Collection`, according to the order induced by the specified `Comparator`.

- `nCopies(int, Object)` Generates a list containing the specified number of copies of the object. This list is immutable.

- `sort(List)` Sorts the specified `List` into ascending order, according to the natural comparison method of its elements.

- `sort(List, Comparator)` Sorts the specified `List` according to the order induced by the specified `Comparator`.

- `subList(List, int, int)` Generates a sublist consisting of the elements of the specified list between the first and second indexes. The first index is inclusive; the second index is exclusive.

- `synchronizedCollection(Collection)` Returns the `Collection` wrapped in a synchronization wrapper.

- `synchronizedList(List)` Returns the `List` wrapped in a synchronization wrapper.

- `synchronizedMap(Map)` Returns the `Map` wrapped in a synchronization wrapper.

- `synchronizedSet(Set)` Returns the `Set` wrapped in a synchronization wrapper.

- `unmodifiableCollection(Collection)` Returns a version of the `Collection` which is unmodifiable.

- `unmodifiableList(List)` Returns a version of the `List` which is unmodifiable.

- `unmodifiableMap(Map)` Returns a version of the `Map` which is unmodifiable.

- `unmodifiableSet(Set)` Returns a version of the `Set` which is unmodifiable.

15.7 Iteration Over Collections

Just as with the classes `Vector` and `Hashtable`, it is possible to iterate over the contents of any of the collection classes. In JDK 1.1 implementations of the `Enumeration` interface were used to perform this iteration. In Java 2 iterators are used. The change in name is intended to indicate that iterators are more powerful and are meaningful (in that a number of the methods have changed their name to be more obvious). For example, the hasMoreElements() method of Enumeration is replaced by hasNext(), as the method next() is used to access the next element in the iteration. It is also possible to modify the collection underlying the iteration while the iteration is in progress. In time it is expected that the Iterator will replace the Enumeration.

The Iterator interface is one of two interfaces (the ListIterator is the other) which provide for iteration. This interface defines the following (abstract) methods which are implemented by any concrete iterator:

- hasNext() This returns true if there is at least one more element to process.
- next() Returns the next element in the collection to process. Note that to access the first element in the iteration the method next() must first be called.
- remove() This method deletes the last element returned by the method next() from the underlying collection.

The Iterator interface has a direct subinterface, the ListIterator interface. This interface extends the concept of iterators to allow much greater manipulation of the underlying collection as well as the ability to process elements of the iteration in either direction (i.e. backwards as well as forwards).

The ListIterator interface defines the following (abstract) methods which are implemented by any concrete ListIterator:

- add(Object) Adds the Object to the underlying list. The object is added at the current point in the iteration. Thus a subsequent call to next() would return this object.
- hasNext() Returns true if there is at least one more element to return using the next() method.
- hasPrevious() Returns true if there is at least one more element to return using the previous() method.
- next() Returns the next element in the collection to process. Note that to access the first element in the iteration, the method next() must first be called.
- nextIndex() Returns the index of the element that would be returned by a subsequent call to next.
- previous() Returns the element before the current element in the iteration.
- previousIndex() Returns the index of the element that would be returned by a subsequent call to previous().
- remove() Removes from the List the last element that was returned by next() or previous().
- set(Object) Replaces the last element returned by next or previous with the specified element.

15.8 Array Sorting and Searching

The Arrays class provides a set of utility methods for sorting and searching arrays as well as for converting arrays to lists. There are a wide range of sorting and searching methods for different basic data types (such as `byte`, `short` and `long`) as well as for objects (reference types). The search methods are all of the format `binarySearch(<array of type>, <data of type>)`; for example `binarySearch(byte[], byte)`. In turn, the sorting methods are all of the format `sort(<array of type>)`; for example `sort(short[])`. For arrays of type `Object`, an additional sorting method is provided in which the type of comparator to be used can be specified (`sort(Object [], comparator)`). The `toList` method takes an array of type `Object` and returns a list.

15.9 Choosing a Collection Class

It can sometimes be confusing for those new to the Collections API to decide which collection class to use. Some make the mistake of always using an array (because it is similar to the constructs that they are used to). However, this is failing to understand the way one should work with collections (data structures) in Java. To this end the decision tree in Figure 15.4 may be of use.

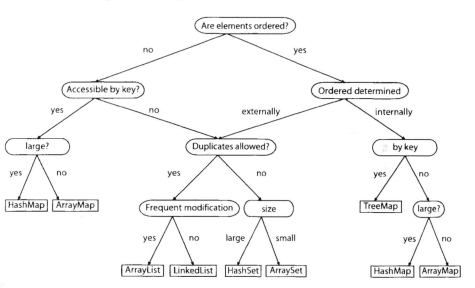

Figure 15.4 Selecting which collection class to use.

The most commonly used collection classes are `HashSet`, `ArrayList`, `HashMap` and `LinkedList`.

15.10 Summary

It is likely that, just as in Smalltalk, these classes will become the most used classes in Java. The various collection API interfaces and classes will form the basis of the data structures you build and will be the cornerstone of most of your implementations. For those of you coming from a Lisp-style language these concepts won't have seemed too strange. However, for those of you coming from languages such as C, Pascal or Ada you may well have found the ideas of a bag and a set quite bizarre. Stick with them, try them out, implement some simple programs using them and you will soon find that they are easy to use and extremely useful. You will very quickly come to wonder why every language doesn't have the same facilities!

16 *An Object-Oriented Organizer*

16.1 Introduction

This chapter presents a detailed example application constructed using the data structure classes. The application is intended as an electronic Personal Organizer. It contains an address book, a diary (or appointments section) and a section for notes. The remainder of this chapter describes one way of implementing such an Organizer. At the end of the chapter, there is a programming exercise.

16.2 The `Organizer` Class

This application involves more than one class and has a more complex architecture than anything you have seen so far (see Figure 16.1). It also illustrates another important concept in object orientation, that of an object within an object. These are often referred to as *part-of* hierarchies, i.e. one object is *part-of* another. This should not be confused with the class hierarchy, which is a *kind-of* hierarchy.

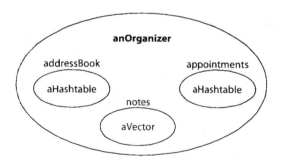

Figure 16.1 The structure of an `anOrganizer` object.

An instance of the `Organizer` class contains three other objects. These objects are held in the instance variables `addressBook`, `appointments` and `notes`. The instances within `addressBook` and appointments are `Hashtable` objects, while the notes instance variable holds a `Vector` object.

16.3 The Class Definition

The purpose of the Organizer class is to provides some of the facilities of a Personal Organizer. The class definition is illustrated below. We shall build this definition up throughout the chapter:

```java
import java.util.*;

public class Organizer {

    // Instance variable definitions
    private Hashtable addressBook = new Hashtable();
    private Hashtable appointments = new Hashtable();
    private Vector notes = new Vector();
    ...
    // all methods go here
    ...
}
```

We have defined the class and its instance variables. Notice that we have made the instance variables private. This ensures that objects outside the Organizer class cannot access the variables directly; they must access the information via specified interfaces. Also notice that we have imported the java.util package, as we are using both the Hashtable and Vector classes. In addition, we have initialized the instance variables so that they hold the appropriate objects.

16.4 The Updating Protocol

Now we define the methods for the *updating* protocol. That is, we define all the methods associated with adding new information to the Organizer.

The addNote method adds a new note to the notes instance variable. It is an extremely simple method that requires no additional explanation:

```java
public void addNote(String aNote) {
    notes.addElement(aNote);
}
```

The addAddress method adds a new address to the addressBook. It first checks to see if the name provided is already in the address book. If it is, an error message is generated; otherwise the name and address are added to the book. Notice that we use another instance method addressFor (part of the accessing protocol) to determine whether the addressee is already present; if not, it returns the result null (you can use the null value instead of any object, in this case, a string). The addAddress method is illustrated below:

```java
public void addAddress(String name, String location) {
    String alreadyThere;
```

```
    alreadyThere = addressFor(name);
    if (alreadyThere == null) {
      addressBook.put(name, location);
      System.out.println("Added " + name +
            " to the address book");
    }
    else
      System.out.println("An entry for " + name +
            " is already present");
  }
```

The method for adding a new appointment is essentially the same as the addAddress method:

```
public void newAppointment(String anAppointment,
            String aDate) {
    String alreadyThere;
    alreadyThere = appointmentFor(aDate);
    if (alreadyThere == null) {
      appointments.put(aDate, anAppointment);
      System.out.println("Added " + anAppointment +
            " for " + aDate);
    }
    else
      System.out.println("An entry for " + aDate +
            " is already present");
  }
```

16.5 The Accessing Protocol

Next, we define the methods associated with obtaining information from the Organizer. That is, we define all the methods used to access information within the instance variables.

The addressFor method retrieves an address from the address book. Although the return type of the method is String, it can also return a null value. Also, notice that we must cast the result obtained from the hash table addressBook to a String:

```
public String addressFor(String name) {
    String address;
    address = (String) addressBook.get(name);
    if (address == null)
      System.out.println("No address for " + name);
    return address;
  }
```

The appointmentFor method retrieves an appointment from the appointments instance variable. It is essentially the same as the addressFor method:

```
public String appointmentFor(String aDate) {
  String appointment;
  appointment = (String) appointments.get(aDate);
  if (appointment == null)
    System.out.println("No appointment for " + aDate);
  return appointment;
}
```

Finally, the printNotes method displays all the notes which have been made in the Organizer:

```
public void printNotes() {
  String item;
  System.out.println("\n\t Notes");
  System.out.println("\t-------\n");
  for (Enumeration enum = notes.elements();
        enum.hasMoreElements(); ) {
    item = (String) enum.nextElement();
    System.out.println(item);
  }
}
```

The above method uses special characters, known as escape characters, which help to control the printed text. The characters \t and \n indicate a tab and a line feed, respectively.

16.6 The Main Method

Once you have defined all the methods, you are ready to use your Organizer. The Organizer class is not intended as an application in its own right. Instead, it is intended to be used with other classes as part of a larger application. However, it is good Java style to provide a main method. In a class which is not expected to be the top-level class in an application, this method can provide a test harness which illustrates the typical use of the class. When the class is used as part of a larger application the main method is ignored. The main method in the Organizer class has been used in just such a way:

```
public static void main (String args [] ) {
  Organizer organizer = new Organizer();
  System.out.println("Adding test information\n");
  organizer.addAddress("John", "Room 47");
  organizer.addAddress("Myra", "Room 42");
  organizer.newAppointment("Meeting with MEng",
        "10/10/97");
  organizer.addNote("I must do all my work");
  System.out.println("\nNow performing tests\n");
  System.out.println("Johns address is " +
```

```
        organizer.addressFor("John"));
  System.out.println("Appointments for 10/10/97 are "
        + organizer.appointmentFor("10/10/97"));
  organizer.printNotes();
}
```

This method shows how the Organizer can be used. It creates a new Organizer and adds some entries to it (see Figure 16.2).

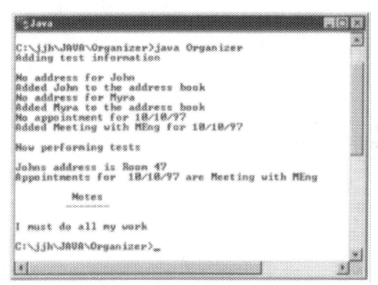

Figure 16.2 Running the Organizer as an application.

Try your Organizer out in a similar way. Extend its functionality. For example, provide a way of deleting an address or replacing it with a new one.

16.7 Exercise: the Financial Manager Project

In the remainder of this book, you develop a small project which provides the basic functionality of a Financial Manager application:

1. Add a deposit to a current account for a specified amount.
2. Make a payment (withdrawal) from a current account for a specified amount.
3. Get the current balance of a current account.
4. Print a statement of all payments and deposits made, in the order in which they happened, to the Transcript.

Create a subclass of Object (for example, FinancialManager) to hold the current balance and handle deposits and withdrawals. You should be able to specify the user's name and initial balance to the constructor. Use a Vector class to hold the statement. Create a test class with a main method that resembles the following code:

```
public class Test {
  public static void main (String args []) {
    FinancialManager fm =
          new FinancialManager("John", 0.0);
    fm.deposit(25.00);
    fm.withdraw(12.00);
    fm.deposit(10.00);
    fm.deposit(5.00);
    fm.withdraw(8.00);
    System.out.println("The current balance is " +
          fm.balance());
    fm.statement();
  }
}
```

The output from this Test class is:

```
The current balance is 20.0
Statement:
Deposit   0.0
Deposit   25.0
Withdraw 12.0
Deposit   10.0
Deposit   5.0
Withdraw 8.0
```

Part 2

Java Developers' Handbook

17 *Graphic Programming Using the Abstract Window Toolkit*

17.1 Introduction

This chapter describes how to create graphical displays using the standard JDK windowing and graphical classes. It does not cover the construction of graphical user interfaces, which are discussed in the next chapter.

In this chapter we consider windows in Java, how you create them and how you can draw and write in them. Such windows can be used to display graphs, images, text, lines and shapes (such as boxes and circles).

17.2 Windows as Objects

In Java, almost everything is an object; it is said to be a pure object-oriented language. This issue was considered earlier, but some of the implications may well have passed you by. Windows and their contents are also objects; when you create a window, you create an object which knows how to display itself on the computer screen. You must tell it what to display, although the framework within which the associated method (paint) is called is hidden from you. You should bear the following points in mind during your reading of this chapter and the next; they will help you understand what you are required to do:

- You create a window by instantiating an object.
- You define what the window displays by creating subclasses of system provided classes (such as Panel).
- You can send messages to the window to change its state, perform an operation and display a graphic object.
- The window object can send messages to other objects in response to user (or program) actions.
- Everything displayed by a window is an object and is potentially subject to all of the above.

This approach may very well contrast with your previous experience. In many other windowing systems, you must call the appropriate functions in order to obtain a window, providing default behaviour either by pointers to functions or by associating some event with a particular function. You also determine what is displayed in the window by calling various functions on the window.

In the object-oriented world, you define how a subclass of the windowing classes responds to events, for example what it does in response to a request to paint itself. All the windowing functionality and window display code is encapsulated within the window itself.

17.3 Windows in Java

Of course, the above description is a little simplistic. It ignores the issues of how a window is created, initialized and displayed, and how its contents are generated. In pre-Java 2, these are handled by the classes Frame, Component and Container (or their subclasses)[1].

- *Frames* provide the basic structure for a window: borders, a label and some basic functionality (e.g. resizing).
- *Components* are graphical objects displayed in a frame. Some other languages refer to them as widgets. Examples of components are lines, circles, boxes and text.
- *Containers* are special types of component which are made up of one or more components (or containers). All the components within a container (such as a panel) can be treated as a single entity.

Windows have a component hierarchy which is used (among other things) to determine how and when elements of the window are drawn. The component hierarchy is rooted with the frame, within which components and containers can be added. Figure 17.1 illustrates a component hierarchy for a window with a frame, two containers (subclasses of Panel, which is itself a direct subclass of Container) and a few basic components. Note that this figure illustrates a part-of relationship and not inheritance.

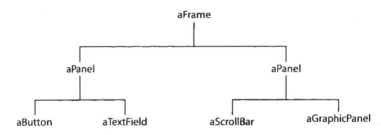

Figure 17.1 The component hierarchy for a sample window.

When the Java Virtual Machine (JVM) needs to redraw the window displayed by the above hierarchy, it starts with the highest component (the frame) and asks it to redraw itself. It then works down the hierarchy to the bottom components, asking each to redraw itself. In this way each component draws itself before any components

---

1   Java 2 also contains these classes and their Swing equivalents; see Chapter 20.

that it contains. This process is handled by the windowing framework. The user generally only has to redefine the paint method to change the way in which a component is drawn.

17.4 The Abstract Window Toolkit

The Abstract Window Toolkit (AWT) is a generic platform-independent windowing system. It allows you to write graphical Java programs which have (almost) the same look and feel, whatever the host platform. For example, the graphical applications presented within this section of the book were written on a Windows 95 PC and a Solaris 2.5 Sun. This is because these are the machines available to me and, depending on the time of day, I may be working on one or the other. I do not need to worry about the host environment, only about the AWT.

This is, of course, not a new idea. The VisualWorks development environment for Smalltalk, from ParcPlace-Digitalk, has had such a system since the early 1990s. However, that does not reduce its usefulness. Such toolkits greatly reduce the problems which software vendors often face when attempting to deliver their systems on different platforms. Indeed, a small software house with which I am involved is moving to Java primarily because of the benefits that the AWT offers.

The AWT is made up of a number of associated packages that provide the Java side of the windowing environment. At some point, these facilities must be converted into calls to the host windowing system; however, such operations are extremely well hidden from the Java programmer, who does not need to know anything about them. The following packages comprise the AWT:

- `java.awt` is the main AWT package, which provides the primary classes with which most Java programmers become familiar: `Frame`, `Component`, `Container`, `Button`, `Menu`, `Label` and many more.
- `java.awt.image` provides classes which allow graphic images (such as those in GIF or JPEG formats) to be manipulated and displayed.
- `java.awt.peer` defines a set of interfaces which are used when creating peer objects. Peers are objects which allow the functionality of an interface to remain the same, even though the way in which the interface is displayed changes.
- `java.awt.event` is the AWT event model, introduced in JDK 1.1, and is catered for by classes defined within this package. This is another package with which all Java programmers who use graphics are likely to become familiar.
- `java.awt.datatransfer` provides three classes and a number of interfaces which support mechanisms to transfer data using cut, copy and paste style operations and clipboards. In JDK 1.1, however, this package only provides a Clipboard API; the Drag and Drop API associated with this package is in the following releases JDK 1.2/Java 2.

The package with which we are concerned in this chapter is the `java.awt` package (see Appendix E). Figure 17.2 presents the primary classes used in graphics programming and their relationships. In the figure, ovals indicate interface definitions and rectangles represent classes. For further information on the primary classes you should consult the online documentation provided with your toolkit.

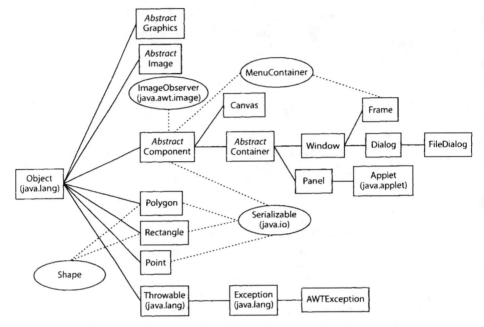

Figure 17.2 Part of the `java.awt` package.

17.5 The `Component` Class

The `Component` class, an abstract subclass of `Object`, defines the basic functionality for all graphic components in the AWT. As all graphic elements are objects, it is their responsibility to determine what their visual effect should be. It is also their responsibility to draw (and redraw) themselves and to respond to actions. For example, although a button may be told that it should be disabled, it is the button's responsibility to decide how to illustrate this to the user (perhaps "greyed-out", or not displayed at all). The point is that the button component decides this. The `Component` class defines many methods, some of which are listed below:

- `paint(Graphics)` paints the component.
- `repaint()` repaints the component.
- `setVisible(boolean)` shows the component if the flag is true or hides it if the flag is false.
- `isVisible()` checks if the component is visible.

The following methods are associated with the component size, shape and location on the display:

- `setBounds(int, int, int, int)` reshapes the component to the specified bounding box.
- `setBounds(Rectangle)` reshapes the component to the specified bounding box.

- getBounds () returns the current bounds.
- getMaximumSize () returns the maximum size.
- getMinimumSize () returns the minimum size.
- getPreferredSize () returns the preferred size.
- getSize () returns the current size.
- setSize (Dimension) resizes the component to the specified dimension.
- setSize (int, int) resizes the component to the specified width and height.
- getLocation () returns the current location of this component.
- getLocationOnScreen () returns the current location of this component in the screen's coordinate space.
- contains (int, int) checks whether this component contains the specified (x, y) location, relative to the coordinate system.
- contains (Point) checks whether this component contains the specified point, relative to the coordinate system of this component.

In many situations, you want to be able to modify the background and foreground colours associated with a component. You can use the following methods :

- getBackground ()
- setBackground (Color)
- setForeground (Color)
- getForeground ()

The class also defines methods associated with the cursor and font being used:

- getCursor () gets the cursor set on this component.
- setCursor (Cursor) sets the cursor image to a predefined cursor.
- getFont () gets the font of the component.
- setFont (Font) sets the font of the component.

Finally, there are a number of component-related methods:

- getName () gets the name of the component.
- getParent () gets the parent of the component.
- isShowing () checks if this component is showing on screen.
- isValid () checks if this component is valid.
- setName (String) sets the name of the component to the specified string.

17.5.1 Painting Graphical Displays

You may have noted above that there are two methods paint () and repaint (). These were described as:

- paint (Graphics) paints the component.
- repaint () repaints the component.

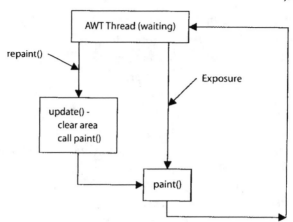

Figure 17.3 How a graphics context is repainted.

In fact, there is a third method which is also used with the repainting process. This is the `update(Graphics)` method, which we will come back to. This simple separation hides a very important feature of the basic graphics facilities in Java – the painting of graphic contexts is handled by a separate "intelligent" thread (which we will refer to as the AWT thread). The way in which this thread works is illustrated in Figure 17.3. If for any reason the graphics display needs to be repainted (for example due to part of the display being uncovered) then the AWT thread will directly run the `paint()` method. However, it will only run the `paint()` method on the part of the display which needs to be repainted. This means that if the `paint()` method performs some operation that changes its display each time it is executed, then only part of the display will be updated. For example, consider the following classes:

```java
import java.awt.*;

public class Test extends Frame {
  public Test() {
    add("Center", new TestCanvas());
    setSize(100, 100);
    setVisible(true);
  }
  public static void main (String args []) {
    new Test();
  }
}


class TestCanvas extends Canvas {
  String [] names = {"John", "Denise", "Phoebe",
    "Isobel"};
  int pointer = 0;

  public void paint (Graphics g) {
```

```
      g.drawString(names[pointer], 50, 50);
      pointer++;
      if (pointer == names.length)
        pointer = 0;
  }
}
```

The Test class merely adds the TestCanvas to its centre (we will look at this again later). The TestCanvas class, however, cycles through the four strings in the string array names whenever the paint method is called. That is, the class implements the paint() method such that each time the method is called a different string is displayed. However, if only part of the current window is obscured and then uncovered, the display presented in Figure 17.4 could result (this is actually a mixture of the top half of the string Denise and the bottom half of the string Phoebe). This illustrates that the paint() method should merely draw the current information not change it.

Figure 17.4 A corrupted display.

If your program requires some changes to be made then those should be performed outside of the paint() method and then repaint() should be called. repaint() in turn calls the update(Graphics) method, which ensures that the whole of the display will be painted (rather than just part of it). This is illustrated in Figure 17.3. Herein lies the confusion: you implement one method but call a different method (that is, you implement paint(Graphics) but call repaint()). Note that for efficiency you may also wish to redefine the update(Graphics) method.

17.6 The Container Class

The Container class is a direct subclass of Component. It allows one or more components (or containers) to be handled as a unit. Conceptually, it means that a group of component objects can be treated as a single (composite) object for certain operations. It possesses a single constructor, Container(), which creates a new instance of a container.

The protocol for the Container class contains a large number of methods for adding and removing components, for redrawing the display and for handling events. This last issue is not covered in this chapter.

- add(Component) adds the specified component to the container.
- getComponentAt(int, int) locates the component that contains the x, y position in the receiver.

- `getComponentAt(Point)` locates the component that contains the specified point.
- `getComponentCount()` returns the number of components in this panel.
- `getComponents()` gets all the components in this container.
- `remove(Component)` removes the specified component from this container.
- `removeAll()` removes all the components from this container.

This class also includes methods for dealing with the maximum, minimum and preferred sizes of the component. These are important when resizing the window and for enabling the layout manager to generate (reasonably) good displays on different platforms:

- `getMaximumSize()` returns the maximum container size.
- `getMinimumSize()` returns the minimum container size.
- `getPreferredSize()` returns the preferred container size.

Finally, the `Container` class also allows you to specify a layout manager. A layout manager handles how components should be laid out in a window. For example, they may be laid out according to a grid, or they may just fill the space available as effectively as possible. Layout managers are discussed in detail in the next chapter.

- `setLayout(LayoutManager)` sets the layout manager.
- `getLayout()` gets the layout manager.

17.7 The `Panel` Class

The `Panel` class (a direct subclass of `Container`) defines a generic container which uses a layout manager to determine where to place components. The `Panel` class provides the following constructors:

- `Panel()` creates a new panel. The default layout for all panels is `FlowLayout`. This is the simplest way of laying out components.
- `Panel(LayoutManager layout)` creates a new panel with the specified layout manager.

This class is used extensively to create containers for components.

17.8 The `Frame` Class

The `Frame` class defines an object which provides the outer rectangular box of a window. It is a direct subclass of the `Window` class, which defines windows which have no borders or menus. The `Frame` class includes the window borders, the title and associated buttons (such as the minimize, maximize and close buttons). Within this outer frame the rest of the window can be drawn.

An example of using the Frame class to create a very simple window object is presented below. It inherits from the Frame class, which provides all the basic facilities it requires, and from the Component class which sets the size of the window (setSize(200, 100)) and its visibility (setVisible(true)):

```java
import java.awt.*;

public class SimpleExample extends Frame {
  public SimpleExample (String name) {
    super("Hello : " + name);
    setSize(200, 100);
    setVisible(true);
  }

  public static void main (String argv []) {
    SimpleExample win = new SimpleExample(argv [0]);
  }
}
```

Note that we could have used pack() instead of setSize() if the ExampleCanvas had specified what size it wished to be.

You can execute this code to produce the window displayed in Figure 17.5. by providing a parameter which forms part of the window label:

```
c:>java SimpleExample John
```

Figure 17.5 A basic frame window.

You must close the window by killing the Java process because we have not defined what happens when the Exit button is pressed.

The Frame class provides two constructors:

- Frame() constructs a new unlabelled window that is initially invisible.
- Frame(String title) constructs a new, initially invisible, window with the specified title as its label.

The Frame class defines an extensive set of class-side variables which indicate different types of cursor, including CROSSHAIR_CURSOR, DEFAULT_CURSOR, HAND_CURSOR, MOVE_CURSOR, TEXT_CURSOR and WAIT_CURSOR. The Frame protocol provides the following methods:

- getTitle() returns the receiving window object's current label.
- isResizable() returns true if the user can resize the receiving window object.

- `setIconImage(Image)` sets the image to display when the receiving window is iconized.
- `setResizable(boolean)` allows the programmer to indicate whether the receiving window should be resizable or not.
- `setTitle(String)` sets the title for the receiving window to the specified title.

17.9 The `Graphics` Class

The abstract `Graphics` class, a direct subclass of `Object` for all graphics contexts, allows an application to draw components on various devices or onto off-screen images.

A graphics context is an object which works with windows to display graphical objects (determining how the graphic object should be rendered). You should never need to create a graphics context as this part of the AWT framework is hidden from most programmers. However, you need to know how to use a graphics context.

In the `paint(Graphics)` method, you normally send messages to the specified graphics context to tell it what to display (e.g. a string, an image, a line or a rectangle). The context can translate what is being displayed, clip an area or perform logical operations (Table 17.1).

Table 17.1 The `Graphics` protocol – drawing methods

`clearRect(int x, int y, int width, int height)`	Fills the specified rectangle with the current background colour
`copyArea(int x, int y, int width, int height, int deltax, int deltay)`	Copies an area of the component
`draw3DRect(int x, int y, int width, int height, boolean raised)`	Draws a 3-D highlighted outline of the specified rectangle
`drawArc(int x, int y, int width, int height, int startAngle, int arcAngle)`	Draws the outline of an arc covering the specified rectangle
`drawLine(int x1, int y1, int x2, int y2)`	Draws a line between the specified points
`drawOval(int x, int y, int width, int height)`	Draws the outline of an oval covering the specified rectangle
`drawPolygon(int[] xPoints, int[] yPoints, int nPoints)`	Draws the outline of a polygon, defined by arrays of coordinates
`drawPolygon(Polygon polygon)`	Draws the outline of a polygon, defined by the specified object
`drawRect(int x, int y, int width, int height)`	Draws the outline of the specified rectangle
`drawRoundRect(int x, int y, int width, int height, int arcWidth, int arcHeight)`	Draws the outline of the specified rounded corner rectangle

Filled versions of many of these are also available, for example:

- `fill3DRect(int x, int y, int width, int height, boolean raised)`
- `fillArc(int x, int y, int width, int height, int startAngle, int arcAngle)`
- `fillLine(int x1, int y1, int x2, int y2)`
- `fillOval(int x, int y, int width, int height)`
- `fillPolygon(int[] xPoints, int[] yPoints, int nPoints)`
- `fillPolygon(Polygon polygon)`
- `fillRect(int x, int y, int width, int height)`
- `fillRoundRect(int x, int y, int width, int height, int arcWidth, int arcHeight)`

You can also draw characters and strings, and display images on a drawing context (Table 17.2).

Table 17.2 The `Graphics` protocol – characters, strings and images

`drawChars(char[] buf, int offset, int count, int x, int y)`	Draws the specified characters using the current font and colour
`drawString(String string, int x, int y)`	Draws the specified `String` using the current font and colour
`DrawImage(Image image, int x, int y, Color bgcolor, ImageObserver observer)`	Draws as much of the specified image as is currently available at the specified coordinate (x, y) with the given solid background colour
`drawImage(Image image, int x, int y, ImageObserver observer)`	Draws as much of the specified image as is currently available at the specified coordinate (x, y)
`drawImage(Image image, int x, int y, int width, int height, Color bgcolor, ImageObserver observer)`	Draws as much of the specified image as has already been scaled to fit inside the specified rectangle with the given solid background colour
`drawImage(Image image, int x, int y, int width, int height, ImageObserver observer)`	Draws as much of the specified image as has already been scaled to fit inside the specified rectangle

Translation and clipping operations are also supported:

- `translate(int x, int y)` translates the origin of the graphics context to the point (x, y) in the current coordinate system.
- `clipRect(int x1, int y1, int x2, int y2)` intersects the current clip with the specified rectangle.
- `setClip(int x1, int y1, int x2, int y2)` sets the current clip to the rectangle specified by the given coordinates.
- `getClip()` returns a `Shape` object representing the current clipping area.

- setClip(Shape shape) sets the current clipping area to an arbitrary clip shape. Takes as a parameter any object whose class implements the Shape interface.

- getClipBounds() returns the bounding rectangle of the current clipping area.

You can also obtain and change the current drawing colour and font.

- getColor() gets the current colour.
- getFont() gets the current font.
- setColor(Color color) sets the current colour as specified.
- setFont(Font font) sets the font for all subsequent text rendering operations.

Finally, logical graphical operations are also supported:

- setPaintMode() sets the logical pixel operation function to the Paint, or overwrite, mode.

- setXORMode(Color color) sets the logical pixel operation function to the XOR mode, which alternates pixels between the current colour and the specified XOR alternation colour.

17.10 A Worked Graphical Application

We will work through a very simple application which uses a Frame and a Panel to illustrate the ideas presented in this chapter. The aim of the application is to create a graphical window which displays a string, draws a rectangle around that string and draws some coloured lines (see Figure 17.6).

Figure 17.6 A simple graphic application.

This graphic application is constructed from two classes: ExampleFrame and ExamplePanel. In order to emphasize that they are two completely separate classes, whose instances work together to generate the above window, I have defined them both as public classes (and they must therefore be defined in separate .java files).

17.10.1 The ExampleFrame Class

The ExampleFrame class is a concrete class which directly inherits from the Frame class. This class does four main things:

- Creates a bordered window by calling the super constructor (super (label)).
- Places a canvas on the window using the add () method.
- Sets the size of the window and displays the window using the setSize () and setVisible(true) methods.
- Registers itself as the object which should handle any window events which occur. This allows us to provide a way of terminating the window once it is created (see the next chapter for further detail).

The construction of the frame is quite straightforward. Of course, if we add more panels to the window, then it could get substantially more complex. The source code for the ExampleFrame class is defined in the file ExampleFrame.java:

```java
import java.awt.*;
import java.awt.event.*;
public class ExampleFrame extends Frame
            implements WindowListener {
  public static void main (String args []) {
    ExampleFrame exampleFrame =
        new ExampleFrame("Graphics Example");
  }

  public ExampleFrame (String label) {
    // Call the super constructor to add the label
    super(label);
    // Create and add the canvas to the frame
    add(new ExamplePanel());
    // Set the window size to that required
    setSize(150, 100);
    // Display the window
    setVisible(true);
    // Set up a listener for the window
    addWindowListener(this);
  }

  public void windowClosed(WindowEvent event) {}
  public void windowOpened(WindowEvent event) {}
  public void windowDeiconified(WindowEvent event) {}
  public void windowIconified(WindowEvent event) {}
  public void windowActivated(WindowEvent event) {}
  public void windowDeactivated(WindowEvent event) {}
  public void windowClosing(WindowEvent event) {
    System.exit(0);
  }
}
```

The ExampleFrame class also implements an interface called WindowListener. This interface specifies a set of methods (which must, of course, be defined by the implementing class) which specify how to handle various events which occur in the window. The only method of interest is the windowClosing method, which executes whenever the window's Close button is activated. We can use this to provide a more controlled way of closing a window than that used in the earlier frame example. We send the exit message, with the parameter 0, to the System object to terminate the application.

17.10.2 The ExamplePanel Class

The ExamplePanel class, a subclass of Panel, defines what should be displayed by the application. It is, if you like, the drawing surface displayed within the window frame. This class defines a single method, paint (Graphics g), which defines the operations that display the contents of the window. In this case, it draws a string, places a rectangle around the string and then displays a set of red and blue lines. To ensure that any methods using paint do not have problems with colours, it resets the original colour before terminating. The methods used to change the colour and draw the string, the rectangle and the lines are all defined by the Graphics class. The source code for this class is defined in the file ExampleCanvas.java:

```java
import java.awt.*;

public class ExampleCanvas extends Canvas {
  String string = "Hello John";

  // This method is automatically executed whenever
  // Java requires the window to be displayed.
  public void paint (Graphics g) {
    int i;

    // Get original colour
    Colour originalColour = g.getColour();

    // Write some text into the window
    g.drawString(string, 40, 20);
    g.drawRect(35, 8, (string.length() * 7), 14);

    // Now draw some lines
    for (i = 20 ; i < 50; i = i + 3) {

      // Set the colour of the line and draw it
      if ((i % 2) == 0)
        {g.setColour(Colour.blue);}
      else
        {g.setColour(Colour.red);};
      g.drawLine(25, (70 - i), 100, (5 + i));
    }
```

```
        // Restore original colour
        g.setColour(originalColour);
    }
}
```

17.11 Exercise: Graphical Hello World

This exercise aims to get you to write a simple graphical application using some of the features you have seen during the lecture sessions.

17.11.1 What You Should Do

Your task is to write a graphic application that will display a message in a window. This message should be whatever has been passed to the application as a command line argument (or "hello world" if no input is provided).

Thus your program should be started in the following manner (assuming your root class is called Hello):

```
> java Hello "Hello John"
```

17.11.2 Hints

1. Create a subclass of Frame to act as the root window of your application.
2. Give your window a title.
3. Define a Canvas with a paint method.
4. Get the paint method to print the message passed into the application.
5. Add the canvas to the frame.

17.11.2 Note

You will need to make the message, passed into the application as a parameter, available to the canvas.

17.12 Advanced Exercise: Graphing

This advanced exercise aims to give you more experience with the graphical side of Java.

In this exercise you should read a series of integer values from the command line and display them as a line graph within a Java application.

17.12.1 What You Should Do

Your task is to write a graphic application that will display in a window the graph defined by a series of integer values.

The *y* values should be 0 to 100 and the *x* values should be 0 to 10.

Thus your program should be started in the following manner (assuming your root class is called Grapher):

```
> java Grapher 10 50 70 35 24 7 15 8
```

Note that you do not have to supply all 10 values and that you may wish to decide on your *x* and *y* scales once you have read all the numbers input.

17.12.2 Hints

1. Follow a similar approach to that used in the last exercise. That is, create a subclass of Frame to act as the root window of your application.
2. Give your window a title.
3. Define a Canvas with a paint method.
4. Your paint method should now draw a series of lines as defined by the input points.
5. Be careful about where the origin of your window is relative to your graph.
6. Add the canvas to the frame.

17.12.3 Note

You will need to make the data, passed into the application as a parameter, available to the canvas.

17.13 Further Reading

The current AWT documentation provided by the JDK tells you much about the methods provided by a particular class, but little about how to use them. However, there are very many books available which describe the Java AWT.

Cornell and Horstmann (1997) has two very good chapters on the AWT, covering most aspects of interest to the casual developer. An excellent book dedicated to the AWT is Geary and McClellan (1997). This book provides detailed coverage of the AWT and 30 additional components which build on the AWT components. These additional components are referred to as the Graphic Java Toolkit (GJT).

In addition, you should make extensive use of the online documentation provided by your system. A number of the toolkit vendors, such as Symantec and Microsoft, provide additional graphic classes which can be extremely useful (although they may tie your future development to these toolkits).

Cornell, G. and Horstmann, C.S. (1997). *Core JAVA,* 2nd edn. Prentice Hall, Englewood Cliffs, NJ.

Geary, D.M. and McClellan, A.L. (1997). *Graphic Java.* SunSoft Press.

18 *User Interface Programming*

18.1 Introduction

In the last chapter you saw how to create a window and place a panel on it that allows you to draw graphic objects (lines, rectangles, etc.). However, today's graphical user interfaces (GUIs) go far beyond this, allowing buttons, input and output fields, selection lists, menus etc. The Abstract Window Toolkit (AWT) provides many classes which directly support these types of facility. As Java is a pure object-oriented language, a button is an object, a menu is an object, a text field is an object and so is a selection list. Thus to create a GUI in Java, you create the window and instances of the facilities you require; then you add these instances to the window instance. You use the Frame and Panel classes, just as you did in the previous chapter, to display such GUI component objects. Of course life is not quite as simple as this; you need to take into account how the various components in the window should be laid out, what the window should do in response to an event (such as a user clicking a button) and how to terminate the window cleanly. In the last chapter, you briefly saw part of this when the WindowListener interface was used to catch the windowClosing event.

In this chapter, we consider how events can be caught and handled and the range of GUI facilities provided by the AWT. In the next chapter we look at how to lay out components in a window.

18.2 The Event Delegation Model

Version 1.1 of JDK introduced a new event model into Java. This event model is much cleaner than the previous approach and should result in simpler, clear and more maintainable code. However, partly due to the introduction of new terminology, many find the new model confusing. This is typically because they have already become familiar with the previous approach or they are familiar with how language X did it.

18.2.1 The Philosophy Behind the Event Model

When trying to understand the event model in Java there are a few things you should remember. You must not forget that you are generating objects (including windows, components in windows and events), which themselves generate other objects or send messages. You must, therefore, construct objects which work within this framework.

The way in which Java handles input to a user interface is part of a concept which was called the Model–View–Controller (MVC) architecture in Smalltalk. This concept states that it is a good idea to separate the application program (the model) from the user display (the view) and from the object which controls what happens on the display (the controller) (see Hunt (1997)).

This means that different interfaces can be used with the same application, without the application knowing about it (see Figure 18.1). The intention is that any part of the system can be changed without affecting the operation of the other parts. For example, the way that the graphical interface displays the information can be changed without modifying the actual application or the textual interface. Indeed, the application need not know what type of interface is connected to it.

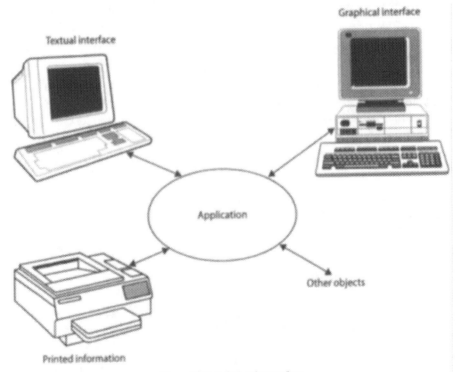

Figure 18.1 Splitting the interface.

The MVC architecture aims to separate the user interface from the underlying information model to enable:

- Reusability of application and user interface components.
- Separate development of the application and user interface.
- Inheritance from different parts of the class hierarchy.
- Control-style classes which provide common features separately from how those features are displayed.

To achieve the MVC architecture, Java provides two facilities:

- The observer/observable model which allows application programs and user interfaces to be loosely coupled.
- Listeners which act as controllers handling various events.

Listeners are objects which "listen" for a particular event and then react to it. For example, when a button is clicked by the user, the listener is notified and decides what action to take. This approach is known, in Java, as an *Event Delegation Model* because the responsibility for handling an event, which occurs in one object, is held by another object.

18.2.2 A Partial Example

A user constructs a GUI application by defining the graphic objects to be displayed, adding them to the display and associating them with a listener object. The listener object then handles the events which are generated for that object. This requires the user interface class (typically a subclass of Frame) to implement one or more interfaces which ensure that the window responds to the correct events from the JVM infrastructure. For example, if we want a window to respond to an action on a frame button, such as the Close button, then the window must implement the WindowListener interface:

```
public class simpleGUI extends Frame
            implements WindowListener{
   protected Button exitbutton;

   ...display construction code...

   public void windowClosed(WindowEvent event)
   public void windowOpened(WindowEvent event)
   public void windowDeiconified(WindowEvent event)
   public void windowIconified(WindowEvent event)
   public void windowActivated(WindoWEvent event)
   public void windowDeactivated(WindowEvent event)

   public void windowClosing(WindowEvent event)
      System.exit(0);
   }
}
```

The WindowListener interface defines the set of window methods listed above. When an event occurs, the appropriate message is sent to the object along with the initiating event, which can then be handled in the appropriate manner. In this case, we have only defined the windowClosing method using the exit(int) method defined on the system object.

In the above example, we also wish to create a button which is displayed on the interface and which allows the user to exit without using the border frame buttons (some window managers on UNIX do not provide a Close Window frame button). To do this, we create a button and a listener for the action on the button:

```
exitButtonController = new ExitButtonController(this);
exitbutton = new Button(" Exit ");
exitButton.addActionListener(exitButtonController);
```

This code creates a listener object, `ExitButtonController`, and a labelled button. It then adds the `exitButtonController` as the listener for the button. The `ExitButtonController` class provides a single instance method `actionPerformed` which initiates the `System.exit(0)` method.

The resulting class and instance structures are illustrated in Figure 18.2. As you can see from this diagram, the separation of interface and control is conceptually very clean.

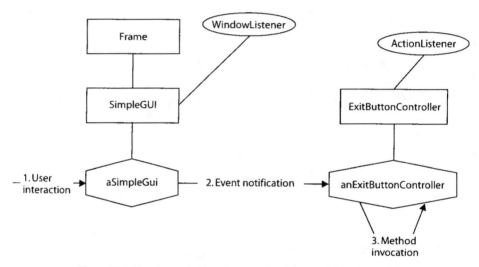

Figure 18.2 The class and object diagram using the event delegation model.

The `ExitButtonController` class definition is presented below. You do not have to call such a class a "controller"; you can equally call it an `ExitButtonEventListener`. However, the listeners are the interface definitions. By choosing a different name, we make it clear that we are talking about the classes which provide the execution control.

```
class ExitButtonController implements ActionListener {
  protected Frame view;
  public ExitButtonController(Frame win) {
    view = win;
  }
  public void actionPerformed(ActionEvent event) {
    System.exit(0);
  }
}
```

Notice that the `ExitButtonController` class does not inherit from any particular class (other than `Object`). It implements the `ActionListener` interface. Listeners are defined as classes which implement various interfaces. This should not be a surprise, as the listener objects must decide what to do with particular events on an application-specific basis: there is little the system-provided class could do. Instead, the interfaces ensure that the implementing classes provide the protocol required by the Java event delegation model.

18.2.3 The Listener Interfaces

There are a number of interfaces associated with the event delegation model defined in the package `java.awt.event`. Table 18.1 presents the listener interfaces, the methods which are triggered in response to events and the objects which originate the events. Using this table, you can see that if you wish to handle an action on a button, list or text field you must define an object which implements the `ActionListener`. This interface defines a single method, `action-performed()`. Your listener class must therefore define this method.

18.3 GUI Component Classes

The components defined by the AWT which support the range of facilities commonly found on a GUI are relatively limited. Anyone who has used tools such as Delphi, Visual C++ or VisualWorks will probably be disappointed. This situation will change over time, however the facilities provided by release 1.1 of the JDK are those indicated in Figure 18.3 (see Appendix E for the complete hierarchy). The only elements not illustrated in this diagram are the `Dialog` and `FileDialog` classes. The most commonly used of these classes are discussed briefly below. The remaining classes are summarized at the end of this section.

18.3.1 The `Button` Class

The `Button` class defines a labelled button component. Such buttons, typically, are rectangular in shape, have a textual label and cause a method to execute when the user selects the button. The `Button` class defines two constructors and two listener methods:

- `Button()` constructs a button with no label.
- `Button(String)` constructs a button with the specified label.
- `addActionListener(ActionListener)` adds the specified listener to receive action events from this button.
- removeActionListener(ActionListener) removes the specified listener so that it no longer receives events from this button.

The method protocol includes:

- `setlabel(String)`, which sets the button label.
- `getlabel()`, which returns the current button label.

Table 18.1 The listeners used with the event delegation model

Interface	Triggered methods	Originating object
ActionListener	actionPerformed (ActionEvent)	Button, List, MenuItem, TextField
Itemlistener	itemStateChanged (itemEvent)	Checkbox, CheckboxMenuItem, Choice
WindowListener The argument to these methods is WindowEvent	windowClosing windowOpened windowIconified windowDeiconified windowClosed windowActivated windowDeactivated	Dialog, Frame
ComponentListener The argument to these methods is ComponentEvent	componentMoved componentHidden componentResized componentShown	Dialog, Frame
AdjustmentListener	adjustmentValueChanged (AdjustmentEvent)	Scrollbar
Itemlistener	itemStateChanged (itemevent)	Checkbox, CheckboxMenuItem, Choice, List
MouseMotionListener	mouseDragged (MouseEvent) mouseMoved (MouseEvent)	Canvas, Dialog, Frame, Panel, Window
MouseListener	mousePressed (MouseEvent) mouseReleased (MouseEvent) mouseEntered (MouseEvent) mouseExited (MouseEvent) mouseClicked (MouseEvent)	Canvas, Dialog, Frame, Panel, Window
KeyListener	keyPressed (KeyEvent) keyReleased (KeyEvent) keyTyped (KeyEvent)	Component
TextListener	textValueChanged (TextEvent)	TextComponent

18.3.2 The Checkbox Class

A checkbox object is a graphical component which comprises a label, a toggle and a state. The state can be either true or false, which is represented graphically by a selected or unselected checkbox (see Figure 18.4). This application is defined in a class RadioTest, which is based on the SimpleGUI class presented in this chapter. A checkbox can be part of a group within which only one checkbox can be selected. Such groups are often known as radio buttons.

Figure 18.3 The AWT user interface components.

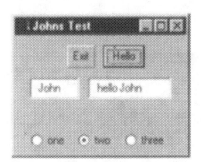

Figure 18.4 Using checkboxes.

The Checkbox class defines a number of constructors:

- checkbox() constructs a checkbox with an empty label.
- Checkbox(String) constructs a checkbox with the specified label.
- Checkbox(String, boolean) constructs a checkbox, with the specified label, set to a specified state.

- `Checkbox(String, boolean, CheckboxGroup)` constructs a checkbox with the specified label, set to the specified state, and in the specified checkbox group. There is also a version of this constructor which swaps the order of the state and group.

The method protocol for the `Checkbox` class includes methods to access the label associated with the checkbox item:

- `getlabel()` returns the label of the checkbox.
- `setlabel(String)` sets this label of the checkbox.

The `Checkbox` class possesses methods to obtain and set the state of the checkbox item:

- `getstate()` returns the boolean state of the checkbox.
- `setstate(boolean)` sets the checkbox to the specified boolean state.

Two methods enable you to set the checkbox group:

- `getCheckboxGroup()` returns the checkbox group containing the receiver.
- `setCheckboxGroup(CheckboxGroup)` sets the checkbox group of the receiver.

There are also two methods to set and delete a listener object:

- `addItemListener(ItemListener)` adds the specified item listener to receive item events from this checkbox.
- `removeItemListener(ItemListener)` removes the specified item listener so that it no longer receives item events from this checkbox.

18.3.3 The `CheckboxGroup` Class

The `CheckboxGroup` class creates an object which associates a set of checkboxes in a radio button relationship. Only one checkbox within a group may be set to true at any one time.

The `CheckboxGroup` class has a single constructor which creates a new instance. The method protocol for this class includes:

- `getSelectedCheckbox()` which returns the currently selected checkbox.
- `setSelectedCheckbox(Checkbox)` sets the current choice to the specified checkbox.

An example of constructing a set of checkboxes and a checkbox group is presented below:

```
CheckboxGroup g = new CheckboxGroupo;
add(one = new Checkbox("one", g, false));
add(two = new Checkbox("two", g, true));
add(three = new Checkbox("three", g, false));
```

This is, essentially, the source code used to generate the checkbox group displayed in Figure 18.4.

18.3.4 The Label Class

The Label class is used to construct a textual label for display within a window. It is an output-only field which can be modified dynamically. It possesses three class variables which specify the alignment of the text within the label:

- CENTER
- LEFT
- RIGHT

The Label class defines three constructor methods:

- Label() constructs an empty label.
- Label(String) constructs a new label with the specified string.
- Label(String, int) constructs a new label with the specified string of text and alignment.

The Label class provides methods for getting and setting the label and its alignment:

- gettext() gets the text of this label.
- setText(String) sets the text for this label to the specified text.
- getalignment() gets the current alignment of this label.
- setalignment(int) sets the alignment for the receiving label.

18.3.5 The TextComponent Class

TextComponent is a generic class which provides a component which allows you to edit text. It is of primary importance because it is the direct superclass of TextField and TextArea. These classes inherit some of the features of a TextComponent. In particular, it defines the listener methods:

- addTextListener(TextListener) adds the specified text event listener to handle events generated by the receiver.
- removeTextListener(TextListener) removes the specified text event listener so that it no longer handles events from the receiver.

This class also defines methods which allow you to specify whether the text can be edited, what the text is and which part of the text is selected:

- seteditable(boolean) sets the specified boolean to indicate whether or not the receiver can be edited by the user. If it is false, the TextComponent is read-only.
- setText(String) sets the text displayed by the receiver.
- getSelectedText() returns the selected text contained in the receiver.

18.3.6 The TextField Class

This class manages the display (and editing) of a single line of text. It is a direct subclass of TextComponent and adds the following constructors:

- `TextField()` constructs a new empty `TextField`.
- `TextField(int)` constructs an empty `TextField` with the specified number of columns.
- `TextField(String)` constructs a new `TextField` initialized with the specified text.
- `TextField(String, int)` constructs a new `TextField` initialized with the specified text and columns.

`TextField` also defines some additional method protocol:

- `addActionListener(ActionListener)` links the receiving object to an action listener.
- `setcolumns(int)` sets the number of columns in the receiver.

18.3.7 The `TextArea` Class

This class, also a direct subclass of `TextComponent`, provides a graphical component for displaying and editing multiple lines of text.

It defines a number of class variables which indicate the number of scrollbars required:

- `SCROLLBARS_BOTH`
- `SCROLLBARS_HORIZONTAL_ONLY`
- `SCROLLBARS_NONE`
- `SCROLLBARS_VERTICAL_ONLY`

The `TextArea` class provides five constructors:

- `TextArea()` constructs a new `TextArea`.
- `TextArea(int, int)` constructs an empty `TextArea` with the specified number of rows and columns.
- `TextArea(String)` constructs a `TextArea` which displays the specified text.
- `TextArea(String, int, int)` constructs a `TextArea` with the specified text and number of rows and columns.
- `TextArea(String, int, int, int)` constructs a `TextArea` with the specified text, number of rows and columns, and scrollbar visibility.

The `TextArea` class provides a large number of methods, including:

- `append(String)` which appends the given text to the end
- `insert(String, int)`, which inserts the string into the receiver at the specified point.
- `setcolumns(int)`, which sets the number of columns for the receiver
- `setrows(int)`, which sets the number of rows for the receiver.

18.4 Additional AWT Classes

There are a number of other classes with which you should become familiar (Table 18.2; see Appendix E).

Table 18.2 Other AWT classes

Class	Description
Choice	Provides a choice button which presents a number of selections. The label shows the current choice.
List	Provides single (and multiple) selection lists.
Scrollbar	Allows a variable's value to be modified within a range. They can be used with a canvas to provide a scrollable region (you may also use a ScrollPane, new in JDK 1.1).
MenuBar	Provides an object which generates a platform-dependent representation of a window's menu bar.
MenuItem	Generates an option on a menu.
Menu	Defines a menu on a menu bar.
PopupMenu	Defines a dynamically generated and displayed menu which can pop up at a specific point within a window. (This class was new in JDK 1.l.)
Dialog	Generates a simple window which receives data from a user. It can be modal or non-modal.
FileDialog	Defines a file selection dialog appropriate to the current platform, thus removing the need for the user to write different dialogs for each platform. It is a modal dialog.

Additional documentation for all these classes is available online within the java.awt package documentation (see also Appendix E).

18.5 Exercise: Text Editor

Figure 18.5 shows the window generated by a simple java application called Edit. The aim of this exercise is for you to implement a simple editor (without attempting to provide any file-saving or loading facilities).

18.5.1 What You Should Do

You should implement the above application using the following classes:

- Button
- Panel
- Frame
- TextArea

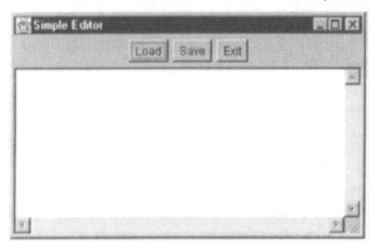

Figure 18.5 The simple text editor.

The buttons Load and Save should print a warning message in the standard out stating that they have not been implemented yet. The exit button should function correctly.

You might like to add a button "New" which will clear the text currently displayed in the TextArea.

18.5.2 Hints

1. The class Edit should be a subclass of Frame and should implement the ActionListener and WindowListener interfaces.
2. When instantiated, the class Edit should create a button panel (which displays three buttons labelled Exit, Load and Save) and a TextArea and display them within a window. Note: to add the button panel, add it to the north of the window (e.g. add(buttonpanel, "North")); add the text area to the centre (e.g. add(textArea, "Center")).

19 *Managing Component Layout*

19.1 Introduction

A layout manager is an object which works with a graphical application, and the host platform, to determine the best way to display the objects in the window. The programmer does not need to worry about what happens if a user resizes a window, works on a different platform or (if you are developing applets) uses a Web browser.

Layout managers help to produce portable, presentable user interfaces. In the JDK there are a number of different layout managers which use different philosophies to handle the way in which they lay out components: FlowLayout, BorderLayout, Grid-Layout, GridBagLayout and CardLayout (for notebook-style interfaces). Note that if you are using a Java IDE such as Visual Café or VisualAge for Java you will find that additional layout managers are provided. Indeed, if you wish you can define your own layout managers by subclassing the appropriate class or implementing the appropriate interface.

19.2 The FlowLayout Manager

This is the simplest layout manager. It lays the components out in a row across a window. When there is no more space left, it starts on the next row, and so on until no more space is left. The display in Figure 19.1 could be generated using a FlowLayout object.

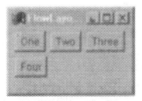

Figure 19.1 Using a flow layout manager.

The class which generated this application is presented below (the buttons do not actually do anything):

```
import java.awt.*;

public class FlowLayoutExample extends Frame {

    public static void main (String argv []) {
```

```
        FlowLayoutExample f = new FlowLayoutExample();
    }

    public FlowLayoutExample () {
      setTitle("FlowLayout Example");

      setLayout(new FlowLayout(FlowLayout.LEFT));

      add(new Button("One"));
      add(new Button("Two"));
      add(new Button("Three"));
      add(new Button("Four"));

      setSize(150, 100);
      setVisible(true);
    }
}
```

Most of what this Frame subclass does should be familiar to you by now. It sets the label for the frame, creates some buttons and adds them to the window, and sets the frame size and whether it should be visible or not. However, it also creates a FlowLayout manager which is initialized using left alignment (the default alignment is "center"). The layout manager object determines where within the window frame the components are placed.

The FlowLayout class defines three class variables which indicate the type of alignment required:

● CENTER
● LEFT
● RIGHT

The FlowLayout class defines three constructors:

● FlowLayout() constructs a flow layout with a centred alignment and default 5 unit horizontal and vertical gaps.
● FlowLayout(int) constructs a flow layout with the specified alignment and a default 5 unit horizontal and vertical gap.
● FlowLayout(int, int, int) constructs a new flow layout with the specified alignment and horizontal and vertical gaps.

Although the FlowLayout class does define instance methods, they are not normally used by the user. Note that this is the default layout for a panel.

19.3 The BorderLayout Manager

The BorderLayout class defines a layout manager which has a concept of four outer points and a central point (labelled North, East, South, West and Center). This

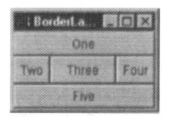

Figure 19.2 Using a border layout manager.

window·is divided up as illustrated in Figure 19.2. Of course, you do not have to place components at all available locations. If you omit one (or more) locations, the others stretch to fill up the space. The border layout is the default layout for frames and panels.

To add components to a window which has a border layout manager, you use a version of the add method which takes a position indicator (such as "South") as well as the component to add. For example, we can change the FlowLayout example to work with borders and produce the display in Figure 19.2.

```java
public class BorderLayoutExample extends Frame {
   ... as before

   public BorderLayoutExample () {
     setTitle("BorderLayout Example");
     setLayout(new BorderLayout());
     add("North", new Button("One"));
     add("West", new Button("Two"));
     add("Center", new Button("Three"));
     add("East", new Button("Four"));
     add("South", new Button("Five"));
     ... as before
   }
}
```

The BorderLayout class defines five class variables:

- CENTER
- EAST
- NORTH
- SOUTH
- WEST

It also defines two constructors:

- BorderLayout() constructs a border layout with no gaps between the components.
- BorderLayout(int, int) constructs a border layout with the specified gaps.

19.4 The GridLayout Manager

The GridLayout manager defines a two-dimensional grid onto which components are added. The default order of addition is from left to right and top to bottom. Figure 19.3 shows an example of using a two-by-two grid. It was created by defining a grid layout manager and then adding the four buttons:

```
public class GridLayoutExample extends Frame {
  ... as before
  public GridLayoutExample () {
    setTitle("GridLayout Example");
    setLayout(new GridLayout(2, 2));
    add(new Button("One"));
    add(new Button("Two"));
    add(new Button("Three"));
    add(new Button("Four"));
    ... as before
  }
}
```

Figure 19.3 Using a grid layout manager.

The GridLayout class defines the following constructors:

- GridLayout() creates a grid layout with one column per component, in a single row.
- GridLayout(int, int) creates a grid layout with the specified rows and columns.
- GridLayout(int, int, int, int) creates a grid layout with the specified rows, columns, and horizontal and vertical gaps.

19.5 The GridBagLayout Manager

The GridBagLayout manager is a powerful and flexible layout manager which is more complex to use than the other layout managers. This layout manager uses a dynamically created grid to lay components out. However, a component can stretch across more then one column and row, the columns and rows may not be of equal size, and they do not need to be filled in order.

The GridBagLayout class provides a single constructor GridBagLayout () and a number of instance methods which help control the way in which components are laid out.

To position a component object, a GridBagLayout object uses a GridBag-Constraints object, which specifies constraints on how to position a component (for example, its initial *x* and *y* location, width and height), how to distribute the component objects, and how to resize and align them.

The display in Figure 19.4 was constructed using a GridBagLayout object and a GridBagConstraint object.

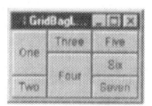

Figure 19.4 Using a grid bag layout manager.

The class definition that uses this layout manager is a little more complex than that for the previous layout managers:

```
import java.awt.*;

public class GridBagLayoutExample extends Frame {

    private GridBagLayout layout;
    private GridBagConstraints constraints;

    public static void main (String argv []) {
      GridBagLayoutExample f = new
        GridBagLayoutExample();
    }

    public GridBagLayoutExample () {
      // Create the layout manager and
      //the constraint object
      layout = new GridBagLayout();
      constraints = new GridBagConstraints();

      // Set layout characteristics
      constraints.weightx = 1.0;
      constraints.weighty = 1.0;
      constraints.fill = GridBagConstraints.BOTH;

      setTitle("GridBagLayout Example");
      setLayout(layout);

      // Add the buttons
```

```
    addButton(0,  0,  1,  2,  "One");
    addButton(0,  2,  1,  4,  "Two");
    addButton(1,  0,  1,  1,  "Three");
    addButton(1,  1,  1,  4,  "Four");
    addButton(2,  0,  1,  1,  "Five");
    addButton(2,  1,  1,  1,  "Six");
    addButton(2,  2,  1,  1,  "Seven");

    setSize(150, 100);
    setVisible(true);
  }

private void addButton(int x,  int y,  int w,  int h,
         String s) {
    Button button = new Button(s);
    constraints.gridx = x;
    constraints.gridy = y;
    constraints.gridwidth = w;
    constraints.gridheight = h;
    layout.setConstraints(button, constraints);
    add(button);
  }
}
```

There are two parts to the layout features used in this class: the layout constraints and the positioning of the components. The general layout principles are controlled by a GridBagConstraint object. You must set the instance variables as shown in Table 19.1.

The grid coordinates of a component are determined by instance variables on the constraints object:

- gridx, gridy together specify the top left of the component's display area. The top-left cell has address (gridx=0, gridy=0).
- gridwidth, gridheight together specify the number of cells in a row and column in the component's display area. The default value is 1.

Once these constraints have been set, you must associate them with a particular component (or container). In the above class, each button is associated with a set of constraints for the layout manager using the setConstraints() method.

Finally, the component is added to the layout manager using the add(component) method. We did not have to create a new GridBagConstraint object for each button; instead, we reset the positioning instance variables of a single constraint object.

19.6 The CardLayout Manager

This is a layout manager for a container that contains several "cards". Only one card is visible at a time and the user can flip through the cards. It possesses two constructors:

Table 19.1 The instance variables of a `GridBagConstraint` object

fill	Determines how to resize a component that is smaller than the display area:	
	NONE	do not resize (the default)
	HORIZONTAL	fill the display area horizontally, but do not change the height
	VERTICAL	fill the display area vertically, but do not change the width
	BOTH	fill the display area entirely
ipadx ipady	Specify how much to pad out the component (beyond its minimum size).	
insets	Specifies the space between the component and the edges of its display area.	
anchor	Determines where to place a component that is smaller than the display area:	
	CENTER (the default)	
	NORTH	SOUTH
	NORTHEAST	SOUTHEAST
	NORTHWEST	SOUTHWEST
	EAST	WEST
weightx weighty	Determine how to distribute space; this is important for specifying resizing behaviour. Unless you specify a weight for at least one component in a row (weightx) and column (weighty), all the components clump together in the centre of their container. When the weight is zero (the default), any extra space is put between the grid of cells and the edges of the container.	

- `CardLayout ()` creates a card layout with gaps of size zero.
- `CardLayout (int, int)` creates a card layout with the specified gaps.

The primary methods in this class are:

- `first (Container)` which flips to the first card.
- `last (Container)` which flips to the last card.
- `next (Container)` which flips to the next card.

19.7 A Simple GUI Example

In this section we present a very simple GUI class. An instance of this class generated the window displayed in Figure 19.5. This application performs the following functions:

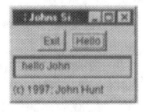

Figure 19.5 A simple graphical application.

- Displays the string "hello John" in a text box in response to the user clicking on the Hello button.
- Exits the application in response to the user clicking on the Exit button.

It combines the layout managers presented in this chapter with the components introduced in the previous one. It also makes use of the event delegation model introduced in the last chapter.

The structure of this interface is essentially the same as that presented in Figure 19.2. The main difference is that the controller class is called SimpleController and it handles two button events: the Exit button and the Hello button.

The class SimpleGUI should not contain any surprises for you. It creates a new panel on which it adds two buttons. These buttons use a listener object to handle the events generated. The window itself acts as a window listener enabling it to handle operations such as closing the window. In addition, it uses a border layout to position buttons on the panel, as well as the panel, text field and label on the frame.

```java
import java.awt.*;
import java.awt.event.*;

public class SimpleGUI extends Frame
            implements WindowListener{
  protected Button exitButton, helloButton;
  protected TextField field1;
  private SimpleController controller;
  public static void main (String args []) {
    Frame f = new SimpleGUI();
  }

  public SimpleGUI () {
    setTitle("Johns Simple GUI");
    controller = new SimpleController(this);

    // Set up panel for buttons (using a flow layout)
    Panel b = new Panel();
    b.setLayout(new FlowLayout(FlowLayout.CENTER));

    exitButton = new Button("Exit");
    exitButton.addActionListener(controller);
    b.add(exitButton);

    helloButton = new Button("Hello");
    helloButton.addActionListener(controller);
    b.add(helloButton);

    // Add the button panel to the frame
    add("North", b);
```

```
    // Create a non-editable text field and add that
    field1 = new TextField(10);
    field1.setEditable(false);
    add("Center", field1);

    // Put a label in the frame
    Label label = new Label("(c) 1997: John Hunt");
    add("South", label);

    // Make the frame handle window events
    addWindowListener(this);

    // Resize and show the window
    setSize(160, 110);
    setVisible(true);;
  }

  public void windowClosed(WindowEvent event) {}
  public void windowOpened(WindowEvent event) {}
  public void windowDeiconified(WindowEvent event) {}
  public void windowIconified(WindowEvent event) {}
  public void windowActivated(WindowEvent event) {}
  public void windowDeactivated(WindowEvent event) {}
  public void windowClosing(WindowEvent event) {
    System.exit(0);
  }
}

class SimpleController implements ActionListener {
  SimpleGUI view;

  public SimpleController (SimpleGUI win) {
    view = win;
  }

  public void actionPerformed(ActionEvent event) {
    // You can get the source object of an event
    Object source = event.getSource();

    // You can then compare the event source with
    // actual objects.
    if (source == view.exitButton)
      System.exit(0);
    else if (source == view.helloButton)
      view.field1.setText("hello John");
  }
}
```

You could have a different controller for each button. In such a situation, you do not need to test to see which button generated an event (thus eliminating the if statement that selects the action). This is a more object-oriented approach and it is used in the next chapter.

19.8 Exercise: GUIs in Java

In this exercise you will get to construct a graphical user interface using the Button class, the Panel and Frame classes and some layout managers.

19.8.1 What You Should Do

You should implement an interface which resembles that in Figure 19.6. To do this you will need to use different containers (Panels) with different layout managers, all embedded within the top-level frame.

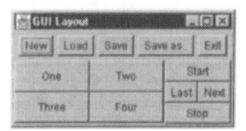

Figure 19.6 The GUI to be created in the exercise.

19.8.2 Hints

1. Create a subclass of Frame to act as the root window of your application.
2. Use the default border layout of the Frame class to organize the top-level containers.
3. Use at least three panels.
4. Use a FlowLayout for the top panel, a GridLayout for the bottom left panel and a BorderLayout for the bottom right panel.
5. Remember that the buttons don't do anything yet.

20 *Putting the Swing into Java*

20.1 Introduction

We have already mentioned the Java Foundation Classes (JFC), Swing and the Java 2 release of the Java Developers' Kit (JDK 1.2) in this book. However, many of you won't be sure of the relationships between AWT, Swing, JFC and the JDK, nor indeed what Swing actually provides. This chapter cuts through the hype and shows you what Swing will mean for you.

20.2 Swing, the JFC and the JDK

Lets start by talking about Swing. What is it? It has been stated that the overall goal of the Swing project was "to build a set of extensible GUI components to enable developers to more rapidly develop powerful Java front ends for commercial applications" (see http://java.sub.com/products/jfc/swingdoc-static/ swing_arch.html). That's all well and good, but what does it mean to you and me? In real terms, it means that Swing provides a set of graphical components which allow user interfaces to be constructed which provide commercial quality (and functionality) with the minimum of effort. For example, many users are now familiar with the idea of brief reminders being displayed when they leave their cursor over a button for a short period. In Swing, these are referred to as tooltips and are simple and straightforward to implement. Prior to Swing, however, the equivalent functionality would have to have been provided by developers themselves catching mouse events, waiting a period of time and then popping up a small window with the tooltip displayed inside it. None of this would have been trivial.

What else does Swing provide? Firstly, all components in Swing are 100% pure Java (referred to as lightweight). This means that the windows should look the same whatever platform they are on and should be easier to maintain (for Sun). As all graphical components are "lightweight", their appearance is controlled purely by the Java code (without the need for platform-dependent peers – as in JDK 1.0 and 1.1). In Swing, a separate user interface "view" component performs the actual rendering of the component on the screen. This allows different views to be plugged in. This in turn allows the idea of different "look and feels". This means that it should be possible for a UNIX developer to select the Win95/98/NT look and feel to see what the interface would look like on that platform. It also means that it is easier to deploy the same software on different platforms, but with interfaces that match the interface manager on that particular platform. This separation of view from the actual component is based on a modified version of the Model–View–Controller architecture (described later).

Swing also provides a greatly increased set of facilities for graphical user interfaces, including trees, icons on buttons, dockable menu bars, menus with icons, borders, additional layout managers and improved support for fonts and colours.

So does this mean that the AWT (the Abstract Window Kit) of versions 1.0 and 1.1 of Java is being thrown out of the window? Not exactly – the AWT will still be available and systems can be constructed using both the AWT and Swing (although there are some limitations). However, as the AWT knows nothing about different "look and feels" and mixes both lightweight (pure Java) and heavyweight (native) components, any AWT windows may not be consistent with the Swing windows. From the point of view of the developer, it makes little sense to continue to use the AWT when all of the AWT's facilities (and more) are replicated in Swing. So why is the AWT still part of Java? Well, in fact much of Swing is implemented on the foundations provided by the AWT. Indeed, much of what an AWT developer already knows will go a long way to helping with getting started with Swing, as will be shown by this chapter. Indeed, all the layout managers will still be used.

So that's Swing, but what is its relationship to the JFC and the JDK? Essentially, Swing is a core component of the JFC, along with Java2D, Accessibility and Drag and Drop. It is the largest element of the JFC (as it stands now) and will therefore be taken by many to equate to the JFC. Indeed, one insider has said that it is "spelt JFC but pronounced Swing". However, as can be seem from the above list, this is not the case. As this chapter is about Swing we will not digress into Java2D, the Accessibility API or Drag and Drop, except to say that each is a significant development, with Java2D being a major improvement over the basic facilities in previous versions of the JDK.

So where does that leave Java 2? In many ways, Java 2 is the JFC plus various enhancements which consolidate JDK 1.1. For example, Java 2 includes numerous collection classes for data structures that greatly improve on the basic set of facilities provided with JDK 1.0 and 1.1. Equally, the performance enhancements provided will be welcome; however, it is the Swing set of components that will grab the attention.

20.3 What is the MVC?

We have already said that Swing is based on a modified version of the Model–View–Controller (MVC) architecture. So what is the MVC? The MVC is not a new idea (it originated in Smalltalk), but the concept has been used in many places. The intention of the MVC architecture is the separation of the user display from the control of user input and from the underlying information model, as illustrated in Figure 20.1 (Krasner and Pope, 1988). This is often referred to as model-driven programming (i.e. the separation of GUIs from the data that they present). There are a number of reasons why this is useful:

- Reusability of application and/or user interface components
- The ability to develop the application and user interface separately
- The ability to inherit from different parts of the class hierarchy
- The ability to define control style classes which provide common features separately from how these features may be displayed

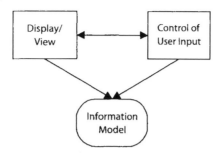

Figure 20.1 The Model–View–Controller architecture.

This means that different interfaces can be used with the same application, without the application knowing about it. It also means that any part of the system can be changed without affecting the operation of the other. For example, the way that the graphical interface (the look) displays the information could be changed without modifying the actual application or how input is handled (the feel). Indeed, the application need not know what type of interface is currently connected to it at all. Prior to Swing it was certainly possible to build GUIs based on the MVC in Java (Hunt, 1997). However, Swing makes the concept of separating the data from the display and control fundamental to its operation.

20.4 Swinging the MVC into Action

Swing uses a modified version of the traditional Model–View–Controller architecture. This is because in practice the view and the controller need to be tightly bound. Indeed, in Smalltalk it was common to find that many classes in the view hierarchy had associated classes in the controller hierarchy, and that if you used one particular view then you had to use the associated controller. For myself, I have found over the last year or so that I have moved to defining my controllers as inner classes to my views, so that while I am separating them logically, they are directly tied together. This is essentially the conclusion which the Swing development team came to. Thus in Swing there is a model object (for holding the data) and a UI object for managing the view and the control. For example, even a button has a separate model: in the case of the class javax.swing.JButton, any model used must implement the javax.swing.ButtonModel interface.

However, even this description fails to capture a subtlety introduced by Swing – "UI delegates". In order to allow different look and feels to be plugged in, each view controller combination actually has a "UI delegate" associated with it. It is the UI delegate which actually draws the component, although it is the component itself which is responsible for handling the display and user input (see Figure 20.2).

In Figure 21.2, the data-specific Model is separated from the JComponent (the root of many of Swing's GUI components) which possesses both the view and the controller. In turn, the controller uses a separate UI delegate to actually draw the component in a window. Thus Swing both provides leverage for model-driven programming and for pluggable look and feels.

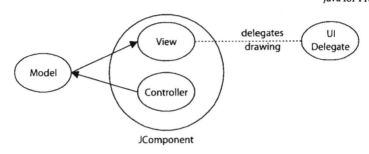

Figure 20.2 The modified MVC in Swing.

So what does this mean for the developer? Does it mean that to use a button you must first create a model of the data displayed by a button? No: in the case of simple components such as buttons and labels, when you construct the GUI component an appropriate model is created automatically. However, for more complex GUI components, such as trees, you first need to create the model (in terms of DefaultMutableTreeNodes) and then instantiate the JTree GUI component on top of it. The JTree GUI component then displays the information held in the model.

20.5 Transitioning to Swing

In the remainder of this chapter we will look at how to convert a relatively simple AWT-based application to a Swing-based one. We will adopt this strategy, as many readers will have experience of the AWT, either due to earlier chapters in this book or previous experience with Java. It also highlights the similarities and differences between Swing and the AWT. The application we shall use provides a very simplistic picture tool. However, it possesses many of the features which will be of interest to Java developers. We shall first look at how this application is implemented in the AWT and then at what changes we need to make to move it over to Swing. (Note that depending on whether you are using the Swing release with JDK 1.1 or the Java2/JDK 1.2 release, you will need to sue different import statements. The Swing release requires an import statement of the form import com.sun.java.swing.* compared with a JDK 1.2 Beta import statement import java.awt.swing.*. The final release of the JDK 1.2, known as Java 2, has the Swing set in javax.swing.*. Thus Swing has become part of the Standard Java Extensions (as indicated by the use of javax). Throughout this chapter we will assume that Java2/JDK 1.2 is being used.)

20.5.1 The Simple Gallery Application

The Gallery application allows a user to display GIF or JPEG images. It is intended as a simple personal image viewer. It does not include any zoom facility, nor does it allow for editing of the images. The simple AWT-based gallery application is illustrated in Figure 20.3. This figure shows a GIF image (my daughter at four months old!). Users can load images, resize the window and exit the application. The program is implemented by two classes, SimpleGallery and PicturePanel within the gallery package. Listing 20.1 presents the SimpleGallery class.

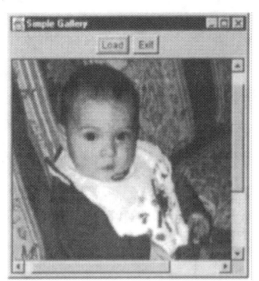

Figure 20.3 The SimpleGallery application.

Listing 20.1 *SimpleGallery*

```java
package gallery;

import java.awt.*;
import java.awt.event.*;

public class SimpleGallery extends Frame {
  PicturePanel picturePanel;
  public static void main(String args []) {
    new SimpleGallery("Simple Gallery");
  }

  public SimpleGallery(String label) {
    super(label);
    // registers window handler
    addWindowListener(new WindowHandler());
    // creates and adds button panel
    Panel panel = new Panel();
    ButtonPanelController bpc = new
      ButtonPanelController();
    Button b = new Button("Load");
    b.addActionListener(bpc);
    panel.add(b);
    b = new Button("Exit");
    b.addActionListener(bpc);
    panel.add(b);
    add("North", panel);
```

```
    // Creates and adds picture panel to main frame
    picturePanel = new PicturePanel();
    ScrollPane pane = new
      ScrollPane(ScrollPane.SCROLLBARS_ALWAYS);
    pane.add(picturePanel);
    add("Center", pane);

    pack();
    setVisible(true);
  }

  // Inner class to handle window events
  class WindowHandler extends WindowAdapter {
    public void windowClosing(WindowEvent event) {
      System.exit(0);
    }
  }

  // Inner class to handle button events
  class ButtonPanelController implements
      ActionListener {
    public void actionPerformed(ActionEvent event) {
      String cmd = event.getActionCommand();
      if (cmd.equals("Load")) {
        FileDialog fd = new
          FileDialog(SimpleGallery.this, "Select
          Image", FileDialog.LOAD);
        fd.setVisible(true);
        picturePanel.setImageFilename(fd.getFile());
      } else {
        System.exit(0);
      }
    }
  }
}
```

This class is not particularly complex, nor indeed does it make use of many AWT facilities. As such, it is representative of a wide spectrum of interfaces. It possesses a main frame, to which are added two subpanels, one containing two buttons and one containing an instance of a drawing panel. It also possesses two inner classes which handle the events generated when users click on the buttons or the window frame's buttons. These are presented as inner classes as they provide access to the encompassing object (e.g. SimpleGallery.this refers to the object containing the ButtonPanelController). In particular, the ButtonPanelController class uses the FileDialog class to present the user with a selection box from which to select the appropriate GIF or JPEG file.

The PicturePanel class is a little more complex. This class must load a GIF or JPEG image from a file displayed within the drawing area of the panel. This class is listed in Listing 20.2.

Listing 20.2 *The* PicturePanel *class*

```java
package gallery;

import java.awt.*;
import java.awt.image.*;

public class PicturePanel extends Panel implements
    ImageObserver {
  private String imageFilename;
  private Image image;

  // Repaint the panels display whenever the graphics
  // have been corrupted or a new image is to be
  // displayed
  public void paint(Graphics gc) {
  // Note drawImage returns immediately.
  // An image observer is required to determine
  // when the image has been fully loaded (see
  // imageUpdate().
  if (image != null)
    gc.drawImage(image, 1, 1, this);
  }

  // Specifies the image to load and then triggers the
  // loading of the image
  public void setImageFilename(String filename) {
    imageFilename = filename;
    loadImage();
  }

  // Load the image using the appropriate toolkit for
  // the current platform
  private void loadImage() {
    try {
      Toolkit toolkit = Toolkit.getDefaultToolkit();
      image = toolkit.getImage(imageFilename);
    } catch(Exception e) {System.out.println("Problem
      loading image");}
  }

/**
    * This method is used to determine whether the
```

```
 * image being displayed has been fully loaded or
 * not. If it returns true then the image still
 * requires more information. If it returns false
 * then the image has been successfully loaded
 * or an error has occurred.
 */
public boolean imageUpdate(Image img,
        int infoflags,
        int x,
        int y,
        int width,
        int height) {
    if (ImageObserver.PROPERTIES == infoflags) return
        true;
    else if (ImageObserver.ERROR == infoflags) {
        System.out.println("Error in image - image
          display aborted");
        return false;
    } else return true;
}

// Need to specify the size of the panel
public Dimension getPreferredSize() {return new
    Dimension(400, 400); }
}
```

The PicturePanel class is made more complex due to the way in which it must load the image from a file. As Java was originally intended for use with the Internet, it allows an image to be loaded in parts. Thus any object which tries to load an image must monitor the loading process to determine when it has finished. This is done by implementing the ImageObserver interface and thus the imageUpdate method. This is further complicated by the need to use a platform-specific toolkit to actually load the image in the first place. Once the image is loaded it is quite simple to actually draw it in the panel by redefining the paint(Graphics) method to execute the drawImage() method on the graphics context passed to it. The paint(Graphics) method is executed whenever part (or all) of the display is corrupted, or whenever the repaint() method is called.

20.6 A Swinging Gallery

We are now ready to port this application to Swing. So where do we start? The first thing is to convert classes such as Frame, Button and Panel to their Swing equivalents. In general, the graphical components in Swing are prefixed by a J; thus the Swing version of Button is JButton etc. Table 20.1 presents some comparisons.

Table 20.1 Mapping AWT to Swing components

AWT name	Swing name	AWT name	Swing name
Button	JButton	CheckBox	JCheckBox
Frame	JFrame	ScrollBar	JScrollBar
Panel	JPanel	Label	JLabel
Menu	JMenu	List	JList
TextField	JTextField	TextArea	JTextArea

You should be careful of merely assuming that the Swing versions of components will be exactly the same as the AWT versions. In general they provide more functionality. In some cases they have changed their names because their functionality has changed so much (for example, FileDialog is now JFileChooser). In other cases new classes have been introduced to provide a better way of implementing features. For example, to generate a radio button in the AWT a developer used a CheckBox object within a checkbox group; in Swing we now have the JRadioButton class.

So far, so good – we have now changed all the Buttons, Panels and Frames to become JButton, JPanel and JFrame. Next we need to obtain the top level JFrame's content pane. For example, this is done in Listing 20.3 in the following manner: Container pane = getContentPane(). This is new – you never had to get hold of a frame's content pane in the AWT. Indeed, did a frame have a content pane in the AWT? So what is this content pane? In Swing, JFrame, JDialog and JApplet are top-level containers. These top-level containers provide the framework within which other (lightweight) components can draw themselves. This framework is implemented by the content pane. Without a content pane lightweight components such as JButton, JLabel etc. could not be drawn. Thus lightweight components must be drawn within some form of top-level container (or within a component which is eventually drawn within a top-level container). Effectively, the content pane is the link to the host platform: it is a heavyweight AWT component (in fact an instance of Container) which can render itself on the host platform's windowing system.

Once you have got hold of the JFrame's content pane, you must then make sure that all the components displayed within the window are added to the content pane and not the JFrame. For the gallery application (now named SwingGallery) the structure of the application is therefore that illustrated in Figure 20.4.

For the main SwingGallery class, we can now start to think about taking advantage of some of the new features of Swing to improve the look and feel of our application. For example, we can add icons to our buttons. This is very easy to do: the ImageIcon class can be used to create an image which can be used as an icon for a button. One of the constructors for this class takes a string specifying the location of the image to use (for example, ImageIcon buttonIcon = new ImageIcon("load.gif");). Now we need to modify the constructor used to create the actual button so that the newly created icon is passed to it as one of its parameters (such as JButton b = new JButton("Load", buttonIcon);), and that is all there is too it. We can also add keyboard short-cuts

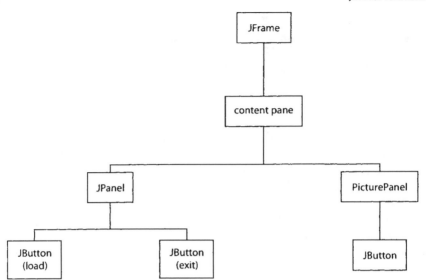

Figure 20.4 The structure of the `SwingGallery` GUI.

using the `setAcceleratorKey(char)` (or `setMnemonic(char)` if you are using the Swing release rather than the JDK 1.2 beta release – `setMnemonic` was omitted from that release by accident!). Finally, we can also add tooltips to buttons using the `setToolTip(String)` method (for example `b.setToolTipText("Loads a picture");`).

For the `SwingGallery` we have now completed the porting process. However, we can have some fun by adding the option to use different look and feels. This can be done by defining two radio buttons which will select either the basic look and feel or a Motif-style look and feel and adding them to a button group. The associated `RadioButtonHandler` then loads into `UIManager` whichever look and feel has been selected (for example, `UIManager.setLookAndFeel("javax.swing.motif.MotifLookAndFeel");`). Essentially, this will cause the Swing components to change their UI delegates to ones which draw, in this case, Motif-style components. To ensure that all components update their display, one of the Swing utility facilities is used (for example `SwingUtilities.updateComponentTreeUI();`). Thus to change the whole display's look and feel we only need to write a few lines of Java. Note that this process may throw an exception if an unavailable look and feel has been specified. The specification of the `SwingGallery` class is presented in Listing 20.3.

Listing 20.3 The `SwingGallery` class

```
package swing.gallery;

import java.awt.Container;
import java.awt.event.*;
import javax.swing.*;
import javax.swing.border.*;
```

```java
// Now need to make class a subclass of JFrame
public class SwingGallery extends JFrame {
  PicturePanel picturePanel;
  public static void main(String args []) {
    new SwingGallery("Swing Gallery");
  }

  public SwingGallery(String label) {
    super(label);

    // Need to get the JFrames content pane
    Container pane = getContentPane();
    // To stop autoclose of window
    set DefaultCloseOperation
      (WindowConstants.DO_NOTHING_ON_CLOSE);

    addWindowListener(new WindowHandler());

    // Now use a JPanel instead of Panel (can set a
    // border)
    JPanel p = new JPanel();
    p.setBorder(BorderFactory.createEtchedBorder());

    ButtonPanelController bpc = new
      ButtonPanelController();
    // Now use JButtons instead of Button which can
    // take an icon
    ImageIcon buttonIcon = new ImageIcon("load.gif");
    JButton b = new JButton("Load", buttonIcon);
    // Can now set a key board short cut and tooltips
    b.setKeyAccelerator('l');
    b.setToolTipText("Loads a picture");
    b.addActionListener(bpc);
    p.add(b);

    b = new JButton("Exit");
    b.setKeyAccelerator('x');
    b.setToolTipText("Exits from application");
    b.addActionListener(bpc);
    p.add(b);

    // VERY IMPORTANT: Now add the panel to the
    // content pane
    pane.add("North", p);

    picturePanel = new PicturePanel();
```

```java
      // Now use a JScrollPane
      JScrollPane scrollPane = new
        JScrollPane(picturePanel,
        ScrollPaneConstants.VERTICAL_SCROLLBAR_ALWAYS,
        ScrollPaneConstants.HORIZONTAL_SCROLLBAR_ALWAYS
      );

      pane.add("Center", scrollPane);

      // Some extra bits to show some of Swings look and
      // feel
      // Illustrate use of different look and feel using
      // radio buttons
      JCheckBox motifButton = new JCheckBox("Motif");
      motifButton.setActionCommand("motif");
      motifButton.setToolTipText("Selects the Motif look
        and feel");
      JCheckBox basicButton = new JCheckBox("Basic",
        true);
      basicButton.setActionCommand("basic");
      basicButton.setToolTipText("Selects the Basic look
        and feel");
      RadioButtonHandler rbh = new
                  RadioButtonHandler(this);
      motifButton.addItemListener(rbh);
      basicButton.addItemListener(rbh);

      ButtonGroup buttonGroup = new ButtonGroup();
      buttonGroup.add(motifButton);
      buttonGroup.add(basicButton);

      p = new JPanel();
      p.setAlignmentX(LEFT_ALIGNMENT);
      p.setBorder(new BevelBorder(BevelBorder.RAISED));

      p.add(motifButton);
      p.add(basicButton);

      pane.add("South", p);

      pack();
      setVisible(true);
    }

    // Inner class to handle window events
  class WindowHandler extends WindowAdapter {
    public void windowClosing(WindowEvent event) {
```

```
        System.exit(0);
    }
}


// Inner class to handle button events
class ButtonPanelController implements
    ActionListener {
  public void actionPerformed(ActionEvent event) {
    String cmd = event.getActionCommand();
    if (cmd.equals("Load")) {
      // Now need to use Swing file dialog
      JFileChooser fd = new JFileChooser(".");
      fd.setPrompt("Select Image");
      fd.showDialog(SwingGallery.this);
      String filename =
        (fd.getSelectedFile()).getName();
      picturePanel.setImageFilename(filename);
    } else {
      System.exit(0);
    }
  }
}


// New inner class to handle radio button look and
// feel options
class RadioButtonHandler implements ItemListener {
  private JFrame frame;
  public RadioButtonHandler (JFrame frame)
    {this.frame = frame;}
  public void itemStateChanged(ItemEvent event) {
    String lookAndFeel;
    String option =
      ((JCheckBox)event.getItem()).getActionCommand();
    if (option.equals("motif")) {lookAndFeel =
      "java.awt.swing.motif.MotifLookAndFeel";
    } else {lookAndFeel =
        "javax.swing.basic.BasicLookAndFeel";}
    // This is where the look and feel gets set
    try {
      UIManager.setLookAndFeel(lookAndFeel);
      SwingUtilities.updateComponentTreeUI(frame);
      frame.pack();
    } catch (Exception exc) {
      System.err.println("could not load
        LookAndFeel: " + lookAndFeel);
    }
  }
```

```
      }
   }
```

We now need to look at the `PicturePanel` class. In Swing we can make this class much simpler. Of course we need to change references from `Panel` to `JPanel`; however, we can now use the `JButton` class to display the image and the `ImageIcon` class to load it. Thus our `JPanel` merely creates a `JButton` object using only an `Image` (i.e. no string label) and adds it to itself. When a new image is to be displayed a new `JButton` object is created with the new image. The Swing version of the `PicturePanel` class is presented in Listing 20.5.

Listing 20.5 *The Swing version of* `PicturePanel`

```java
package swing.gallery;

import javax.swing.*;

// Now make this a subclass of JPanel
public class PicturePanel extends JPanel {
   private String imageFilename;
   private JButton image;
   public void setImageFilename(String filename) {
      imageFilename = filename;
      loadImage();
   }
   // Use a button with the image as an icon - a lot
   // easier
   private void loadImage() {
      if (image != null) remove(image);
      ImageIcon picture = new ImageIcon(imageFilename);
      image = new JButton(picture);
      add(image);
   }
}
```

The result of running our new Swing-based application is presented in Figure 20.5 using both the basic and the Motif look and feels.

20.7 Things to Remember

This section briefly summarizes some of the things you need to remember when you are porting an AWT interface to Swing (or writing a Swing interface from scratch):

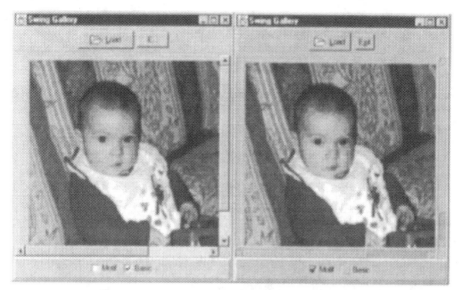

Figure 20.5 The SwingGallery application (in basic and Motif).

1. You need to get hold of the top-level components content pane before you can add anything to it. You can do this using the getContentPane() method.
2. All Swing components have an associated model. For buttons and labels etc. this model is created for you; for more complex components you need to create it before creating the GUI component (on it).
3. You need to be careful about mixing lightweight Swing components with heavyweight AWT components. This can cause problems with the use of different look and feels as well as refreshing displays.
4. We have ignored whole areas of Swing in this article. For example, the buttons in the SwingGallery application might well have been better implemented as a dockable menu bar (see java.awt.swing.JToolBar).
5. At present you will need to import Swing from different places depending on whether you are using Swing with JDK 1.1 or Java 2/JDK 1.2.
6. Swing has not been fully released yet and as such is subject to change and possesses a number of undesirable "features".

20.8 References

Krasner, G.E. and Pope, S.T. (1988). A cookbook for using the Model–View–Controller user interface paradigm in Smalltalk-80. *JOOP* 1(3), 26–49.
Hunt, J.E. (1997). Constructing modular user interfaces in Java. *Java Report* 2(8), 25–32.

20.9 Online References

The Swing home pages:

```
http://java.sun.com/products/jfc/swingdoc-current/
    index.html
```

Java 2/JDK 1.2:

```
http://java.sun.com/
```

The Swing Connection:

```
http://java.sun.com/products/jfc/swingdoc-current/doc/
    index.html
```

The JFC Home Page:

```
http://java.sun.com/products/jfc/index.html
```

The Java Tutorial: Using the JFC "Swing" Release:

```
http://java.sun.com/docs/books/tutorial/post1.0/ui/
    swing.html
```

21 *Swing Data Model Case Study*

21.1 Introduction

This chapter presents an example of a Swing component which uses a complex data model. In this case we will examine the JTree swing component, which requires a data model which represents the tree being displayed. The JTree component renders the tree data model; thus if the data model changes, the tree rendered by JTree also changes. To illustrate these ideas we will construct a simple application which displays all the classes inherited by a specified class. Note that a second Swing package will be used: javax.swing.table.*.

21.2 The JTree Swing Component

A JTree is a Swing component that can be used to display hierarchical data (in a similar manner to the way in which the Windows Explorer tool displays information about the directories and files on a PC). An example of the JTree displaying such data, taken from the SwingSet demonstration provided with Swing, is illustrated in Figure 21.1. Within a tree each row contains exactly one item of data, and every tree has a root (in this case labelled Music) from which other nodes *descend*. Nodes at the end of the tree which cannot possess children are called leaf nodes. Non-leaf nodes (which are also non-root nodes) can have any number of children (including zero). A node is made into a leaf node by calling setAllowsChildren(false) on the node.

Figure 21.1 A JTree component displaying hierarchical data.

Note that the JTree component does not contain the data being displayed; rather, it renders or displays a view onto that data (this is illustrated in Figure 21.2). This is due to the Model–View–Controller architecture underlying Swing components (as discussed in the last chapter). Essentially, the JTree component is the View and Controller, while the data defining the hierarchical tree structure is the model.

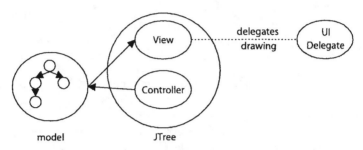

Figure 21.2 The JTree architecture.

A node in the tree data model can either be visible (that is, currently displayed in the JTree component) or hidden (for example, there may be more nodes under Jazz in Figure 21.1; however, at present they are hidden). A node may also be expanded, such as the node labelled "Help" in the figure or collapsed, such as the node labelled "A Hard Day's Night". Note that in Figure 21.1 expanded nodes are denoted by a box containing a minus sign and collapsed nodes are denoted by a box containing a plus sign. This is dependent upon the look and feel currently being used and is different in both the Metal and Motif look and feels.

You can programmatically add nodes to the tree, expand or collapse whole paths, or highlight individual nodes or whole paths. You can pick up whether a node has been clicked once or twice and you can catch events which cause the tree to expand or collapse, as well as interrogate the JTree component to find out what it is currently displaying. All in all, the JTree component is a very powerful and flexible GUI component.

You can also identify which node is selected and when this selection changes (using the TreeSelectionListener interface).

21.2.1 The JTree Constructors

The JTree swing component defines the following JTree constructors:

- JTree() Returns a JTree with a sample model. Useful for testing (for example to ensure that your TreeSelectionListener class is operating correctly).
- JTree(Hashtable) Constructs a JTree with each element of the Hashtable as the child of a root node.
- JTree(Object[]) Constructs a JTree with each element of the object array as the child of a root node.
- JTree(TreeModel) Constructs an instance of JTree using the JTreeModel as the data model to be displayed.

- JTree(TreeNode) Returns a JTree with an instance of JTreeModel as its data model, rooted at the TreeNode passed to the constructor which is defined as a leaf node (i.e. it does not allow child nodes).

- JTree(TreeNode, boolean) Constructs a JTree with an instance of JTreeModel as its data model. The boolean parameter is passed into the constructor of JTreeModel, which will determine how JTreeModel tests for leafness. If the flag passed in is true, leafness is determined by messaging getAllowsChildren; otherwise isLeaf is messaged.

- JTree(Vector) Constructs a JTree with each element of the vector as the child of a root node.

The set of constructors described above allows a JTree component to be constructed from an existing data structure (e.g. a Vector, Array or Hashtable) to be building directly from a TreeModel and rooted on a single tree node.

21.2.2 The JTree API

The JTree swing component has an extensive API which would run to too many pages to list here. Instead, the key methods of the JTree component are highlighted and the reader is pointed to the JDK documentation for more information.

Tree Expansion and Contraction

Setting the TreeExpansionListener

- public void addTreeExpansionListener(TreeExpansionListener tel) Adds tel as interested in receiving TreeExpansion events.

- public void removeTreeExpansionListener(TreeExpansionListener tel) Removes tel as being interested in receiving TreeExpansion events.

Expanding and Collapsing Trees

- expandPath(TreePath path) Ensures that the last item identified in path is expanded and visible.

- public void expandRow(int row) Ensures that the item identified by row is expanded.

- public void collapsePath(TreePath path) Ensures that the last item identified in path is collapsed and visible.

- public void collapseRow(int row) Ensures that the item identified by row is collapsed.

Testing for Expansion

- public boolean isExpanded(TreePath path) Returns true if the value identified by path is currently expanded; returns false if any of the values in path are currently not being displayed.

- `public boolean isExpanded(int row)` Returns true if the value identified by `row` is currently expanded.
- `public boolean isCollapsed(TreePath path)` Returns true if the value identified by `path` is currently collapsed; returns false if any of the values in `path` are currently not being displayed.
- `public boolean isCollapsed(int row)` Returns true if the value identified by `row` is currently collapsed.

Tree Selection

Setting the `TreeSelectionListener`

- `public void addTreeSelectionListener(TreeSelectionListener tsl)` Adds `tsl` as interested in receiving `TreeSelection` events.
- `removeTreeSelectionListener public void removeTreeSelectionListener(TreeSelectionListener tsl)` Removes `tsl` as being interested in receiving `TreeSelection` events.

Obtaining the Selection Path

- `public TreePath getSelectionPath()` Returns the path to the first selected value, or null if nothing is currently selected.
- `public TreePath[] getSelectionPaths()` Returns the path of the selected values, or null if nothing is current selected.
- `public int[] getSelectionRows()` Returns all of the currently selected rows.
- `public int getSelectionCount()` Returns the number of nodes selected.

Manipulating Tree Selection

- `public void clearSelection()` Clears the selection.
- `public void addSelectionPath(TreePath path)` Adds the path identified by `path` to the current selection. If any component of `path` is not visible it will be made visible.
- `public void addSelectionPaths(TreePath[] paths)` Adds each path in `paths` to the current selection. If any component of any of the paths is not visible it will be made visible.
- `public void addSelectionRow(int rows)` Adds the paths at each of the rows in `rows` to the current selection.
- `public void addSelectionRows(int[] rows)` Adds the paths at each of the rows in `rows` to the current selection.
- `public void removeSelectionPath(TreePath path)` Removes the path identified by `path` from the current selection.
- `public void removeSelectionPaths(TreePath[] paths)` Removes the paths identified by `paths` from the current selection.

- `public void removeSelectionRow(int row)` Removes the path at the index `row` from the current selection.
- `public void removeSelectionRows(int[] rows)` Removes the paths that are selected at each of the indices in `rows`.
- `public void setSelectionPath(TreePath path)` Sets the selection to the value identified by `path`. If any component of `path` is not currently visible it will be made visible.
- `public void setSelectionPaths(TreePath[] paths)` Sets the selection to `paths`. If any component in any of the paths is not currently visible it will be made visible.
- `public void setSelectionRow(int row)` Sets the selection to the path at index `row`.
- `public void setSelectionRows(int[] rows)` The selection is set to the paths for the items at each of the rows in `rows`.

Testing

- `public boolean isPathSelected(TreePath path)` Returns true if the item identified by `path` is currently selected.
- `public boolean isSelectionEmpty()` Returns true if the selection is currently empty.
- `public boolean isRowSelected(int row)` Returns true if the row identified by `row` is selected.

21.2.3 Changing the Model

These methods are used to changing the model currently being displayed by the `JTree` component:

- `public TreeModel getModel()` Returns the `TreeModel` that is providing the data.
- `public void setModel(TreeModel newModel)` Sets the `TreeModel` that will provide the data.

Note that in the Swing release 1.0.2 the `setModel(TreeModel)` method is missing, and this is why the example presented later in this chapter does not use it. Instead it has to embark on a rather convoluted way of modifying the display.

21.3 The JTree Package

In addition to the `Jtree` class there is also a `tree` package. This package is under Swing in a package called `tree` (thus it is `javax.swing.tree` or `com.sun.java.swing.tree.*` depending on your version of Swing). However, the `tree` package provides a very useful set of interfaces and classes for building tree data structures (which also happen to work with the `JTree` Swing component). This is probably the best way to think about this package. The `tree` package defines seven interfaces and four classes, which are described below.

21.3.1 Interfaces

These interfaces are used to specify the facilities required by nodes in a tree, by cell editors and renderers etc. Details of the interfaces are left as a reference to the `swing.tree` package API.

- `MutableTreeNode`
- `RowMapper`
- `TreeCellEditor` Adds to `CellEditor` the extensions necessary to configure an editor in a tree.
- `TreeCellRenderer`
- `TreeModel` The interface that defines a suitable data model for a `JTree`.
- `TreeNode`
- `TreeSelectionModel` This interface represents the current state of the selection for the tree component.

21.3.2 Classes

The classes in the `swing.tree` package provide the basics for tree creation and selection. In particular, the `DefaultMutableTreeNode` and `DefaultTreeModel` implement the basic facilities of a `MutableTreeNode` and a `TreeModel`.

- `DefaultMutableTreeNode` This is a general purpose node in a tree data structure. It can be used to construct the tree data model used with the `JTree` Swing component. However, it can also be used to construct tree data structures in general.
- `DefaultTreeModel` A simple tree data model that uses `TreeNodes`. This class can also be used to construct the tree data model used with the `JTree` Swing component.
- `DefaultTreeSelectionModel` Implementation of `TreeSelectionModel`.
- `TreePathRepresents` A path to a node.

21.3.3 The `DefaultMutableTreeNode` Class

This class implements the `MutableTreeNode` interface to provide a basic implementation of a tree node for use in building a tree data model for the `JTree` Swing component. A tree node may have at most one parent and zero or more children. `DefaultMutableTreeNode` provides operations for examining and modifying a node's parent and children and also operations for examining the tree that the node is a part of.

A node's tree is the set of all nodes that can be reached by starting at the node and following all the possible links to parents and children. A node with no parent is the root of its tree; a node with no children is a leaf. A tree may consist of many subtrees, each node acting as the root for its own subtree. `DefaultMutableTreeNode` also provides enumerations for efficiently traversing a tree or subtree in various orders or for following the path between two nodes.

This class provides the following constructors:

- `DefaultMutableTreeNode()` Creates a tree node that has no parent and no children, but which allows children.

- `DefaultMutableTreeNode(java.lang.Object userObject)` Creates a tree node with no parent and no children, but which allows children, and initializes it with the specified user object.

- `DefaultMutableTreeNode(java.lang.Object userObject, boolean allowsChildren)` Creates a tree node with no parent and no children, initialized with the specified user object, and which allows children only if specified.

While the full set of methods defined for this class are not provided below, the key methods are listed (for further methods the reader is directed to the JDK API documentation).

Modifying the Tree

These methods are used to modify the contents of the tree associated with a given tree node.

- `void add(MutableTreeNode newChild)` Adds the `MutableTreeNode` as a child of the receiving node.

- `void insert(MutableTreeNode newChild, int childIndex)` Removes `newChild` from its present parent (if it has a parent), sets the child's parent to this node, and then adds the child to this node's child array at index `childIndex`.

- `void remove(int childIndex)` Removes the child at the specified index from this node's children and sets that node's parent to null.

- `void remove(MutableTreeNode aChild)` Removes `aChild` from this node's child array, giving it a null parent.

- `void removeAllChildren()` Removes all of this node's children, setting their parents to null.

- `void removeFromParent()` Removes the subtree rooted at this node from the tree, giving this node a null parent.

Enumerating Over the Tree

These methods allow the elements in a tree to be iterated over. Note that the enumeration interface is used rather than the newer `Iterator` interface defined in the JFC `Collection` classes:

- `java.util.Enumeration    breadthFirstEnumeration()` Creates and returns an enumeration that traverses the subtree rooted at this node in breadth-first order.
- `java.util.Enumeration depthFirstEnumeration()` Creates and returns an enumeration that traverses the subtree rooted at this node in depth-first order.
- `java.util.Enumeration children()` Creates and returns a forward-order enumeration of this node's children.

Obtaining the Path

These methods allow the developer to obtain information about the path containing the current node.

- `TreeNode getParent()` Returns this node's parent or null if this node has no parent.
- `TreeNode[] getPath()` Returns the path from the root to get to this node.
- `TreeNode getRoot()` Returns the root of the tree that contains this node.

Testing the Tree

These methods allow the tree (or subtree) containing the current node to be tested:

- `boolean isLeaf()` Returns true if this node has no children.
- `boolean isNodeAncestor(TreeNode anotherNode)` Returns true if anotherNode is an ancestor of this node – if it is this node, this node's parent or an ancestor of this node's parent.
- `boolean isNodeChild(TreeNode aNode)` Returns true if aNode is a child of this node.
- `boolean isRoot()` Returns true if this node is the root of the tree.

21.4 Building the Data Model

This section discusses the process by which the data model for the `JTree` component, used in the simple class hierarchy browser tool (described in detail later in the chapter), is constructed. In this example a class called `TreeGenerator` possesses a single static (class-side) method called `createDataModel`. This method is used to build a tree of `DefaultMutableTreeNodes`, the root of which is returned. This is then used elsewhere in an application by a `JTree` Swing component or by anything else which requires a tree data structure. Branches in the tree are indicated by a vector inside the current level vector and nodes are indicated by strings.

```
package browser;

// As we are working with trees need to import
```

```
// the tree package. Note JTree is in the swing
// package.
import javax.swing.tree.*;
import java.util.*;

public class TreeGenerator {

    /**
     * This method converts a vector into a tree data
     * model.
     * @param vector of contents of tree
     * @returns DefaultmutableTreeNode
     */
    public static DefaultMutableTreeNode
        createDataModel(Vector tree) {
      DefaultMutableTreeNode top, last, current =
        null; // Root of tree

      // Get the node at the top of the tree
        top = new DefaultMutableTreeNode
          ((String)tree.lastElement());
        tree.removeElement(tree.lastElement());
        last = top;

      // Process vector of strings in reverse order
      // adding each node to the tree
        for (int i = tree.size(); i > 0; i--) {
          Object element = tree.elementAt(i - 1);
          if (element instanceof String) {
            current = new
              DefaultMutableTreeNode(element);
          } else {
            current =
              createDataModel((Vector)element);
          }
          last.add(current);
          last = current;
        }
        return top;
    }
}
```

This method makes clear that a tree data model can be constructed without reference to the Swing component JTree. It also illustrates that the tree data model could now be used for any one of a number of purposes, as we have created a generic tree data structure which can be processed just like any other data structure. As we now have a tree data model we are ready to build an application around this class.

21.5 Building the GUI Application

The application we are going to consider is illustrated in Figure 21.3. It takes the fully qualified name of a class (which includes its package specification) and constructs a tree of the classes it inherits from (using the reflection API described later in this book). A new class inheritance hierarchy can be displayed at any time by clicking on the open button (indicated by the open file button icon). The second icon indicates the "exit" button.

Figure 21.3 The browser application displaying JTree's hierarchy.

The buttons across the top of the browser application are actually held in a toolbar and are thus dockable. The first button indicates that a new tree is to be opened for a new class, while the second button is used to exit the application.

As can be seen from the figure this browser is displaying the Windows look and feel. Figure 21.4 illustrates the same application run with the Motif look and feel. As you can see, the data is exactly the same; the only difference is that the way in which the tree is drawn is different.

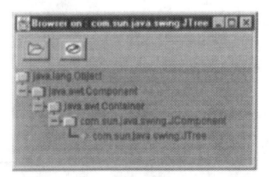

Figure 21.4 The browser using the Motif look and feel.

To create this application, all that is required is that the DefaultMutable-TreeNode, returned by the static method of the TreeGenerator class, is passed to a suitable JTree constructor. To provide a scrollable view on the tree, so that scrollbars allow parts of the tree that are hidden to be viewed, the JTree component is placed inside a JScrollPane. This is then added to the JFrame's content pane. The JScrollPane is held in an instance variable treeView. This is all handled by the setClass(String) method. This means that for a different class to be displayed the setClass method can remove the current treeView and build a new data structure, JTree component and JScrollPane. This is only necessary because of the setModel() omission in Swing 1.0.2. If this had not been omitted, all that would have been required would be to set a new model for an existing JTree component.

The remainder of this application handles changing the tree being displayed, changing the look and feel, adding the toolbar and handling button events etc.

The browser application code is presented below. As you have seen most of the features before we will not examine this class in detail.

```
package browser;

/*
 * Import both the AWT package and the swing package
 */
import java.awt.*;
import java.awt.event.*;
import javax.swing.*;
// As we are working with trees also need to import
// the tree package. Note JTree is in the swing
// package.
import javax.swing.tree.*;
import java.util.*;
/**
 * This class provides a simple graphical browser for
 * viewing class inheritance hierarchies.
 * @author John Hunt
 * @version 1.0
 */
public class Browser extends JFrame {
    private DefaultMutableTreeNode root;
    private String classname;
    private Class classObject;
    private JTree tree;
    private JScrollPane treeView;

    /**
     * Used to initiate the execution of the application
     */
    public static void main (String args []) {
        if (args.length == 0)
            System.out.println("Usage: java Browser <fully
                qualified class name>");
```

```
    else
      new Browser(args[0]);
}

/**
 * Constructor used to create an instance of a
 * Browser on a particular class. For example:
 * <p>
 * new Browser("java.awt.Frame");
 * <p>
 * @param classname The class for which the
 * inheritance hierarchy is to be displayed.
 */
public Browser(String classname) {
  super("Browser on : " + classname);

  // Create the class hierachy for classname
  setClass(classname);

  // Get the content pane
  Container pane = getContentPane();

  // Handle window events
  addWindowListener(new WindowHandler());

  //-------------------
  // Create a tool bar
  //-------------------
  JToolBar toolBar = new JToolBar();

  // Instantiate the handler for the toolbar buttons
  ActionHandler handler = new ActionHandler(this);

  // Define the new class button
  ImageIcon buttonIcon = new ImageIcon("load.gif");
  JButton button = new JButton(buttonIcon);
  button.setToolTipText("New class hierarchy");
  button.addActionListener(handler);
  toolBar.add(button);

  // Now create the exit button
  buttonIcon = new ImageIcon("exit.gif");
  button =new JButton(buttonIcon);
  button.setToolTipText("Exit browser");
  button.setActionCommand("Exit");
  button.addActionListener(handler);
  toolBar.add(button);
```

```
    // Add the toolbar to the window
    // using the content pane.
    pane.add(toolBar, BorderLayout.NORTH);

    // Set the look and feel to the Windows look and
    // feel
    if (!UIManager.getLookAndFeel().getName().equals
        ("Windows")) {
      try {
        UIManager.setLookAndFeel("javax.swing.
          plaf.windows.WindowsLookAndFeel");
        SwingUtilities.updateComponentTreeUI(this);
      } catch (Exception exc) {
        System.err.println("could not load Windows
          LookAndFeel");
      }
    }

    // Set the size of the window and make it visible
    pack();
    setVisible(true);
  }

  /**
   * Used to create the tree to be displayed by the
   * JTree GUI component.
   *
   * @return DefaultMutableNode root of tree
   */
  private DefaultMutableTreeNode createTreeNodes() {
    Vector names = new Vector(10,10); // Holds list of
      // classes in reverse order
    DefaultMutableTreeNode root = null; // Root of
                                        // tree

    // Use reflection to obtain the class object for
    // the specified classname. Using this object
    // obtain the superclass. Repeat this process
    // until the class Object has been found - all
    // classes inherit from Object in Java.
    try {
      classObject = Class.forName(classname);
      Class superClass = classObject.getSuperclass();
      String superclassname = superClass.getName();
      names.addElement(superclassname);
```

```java
  while (!superclassname.equals
      ("java.lang.Object")) {
    superClass = superClass.getSuperclass();
    superclassname = superClass.getName();
    names.addElement(superclassname);
  }

  names.insertElementAt(classname, 0);
  names.trimToSize();

  // the vector of class names will be converted
  // into a tree data structure - note single
  // inheritance means a single branched tree.
  root = TreeGenerator.createDataModel(names);
} catch (ClassNotFoundException e)
    {System.out.println("Error: Class not
    found");}
  return root;
}

/**
 * Takes a string representing the class to generate
 * the hierarchy for and constructs a tree model
 * which is placed in a JTree GUI component which
 * is added to the windows content pane.
 *
 * @param classname Name of class to display
 */
protected void setClass(String classname) {
  this.classname = classname;

  // Get the windows content frame
  Container container = getContentPane();

  // If a tree is currently being displayed, remove
  // it from the window
  if (treeView != null)
    container.remove(treeView);
  // Create the nodes.
  root = createTreeNodes();
  tree = new JTree(root);
  tree.getSelectionModel().setSelectionMode
    (TreeSelectionModel.SINGLE_TREE_SELECTION);

  // Create the scroll pane and add the tree to it.
  treeView = new JScrollPane(tree);
```

```
      // Add tree view to the content pane
      container.add(treeView);

      // Change title at top of window
      setTitle("Browser on : " + classname);
   }
}

/**
 * Helper class used to handle window events
 */
class WindowHandler extends WindowAdapter {
  public void windowClosing(WindowEvent e)
    {System.exit(0);}
}

/**
 * Provides the listener for the tool bar in the
 * Browser class
 */
class ActionHandler implements ActionListener {
  Browser frame;
  /**
   * Constructor takes a reference to the Browser
   * object so that it can reference this object when
   * a new class is to be displayed
   */
  public ActionHandler(Browser f) {
    frame = f;
  }
  public void actionPerformed(ActionEvent event) {
    String cmd = event.getActionCommand();
    // Select the action to perform depending on the
    // button pressed
    if (cmd.equals("Exit")) {
      System.exit(0);
    } else {
      // Use a CLassRequestDialog to obtain the name
      // of the new class to display. Use the setClass
      // method of Browser to change the class being
      // displayed and repack the window.
      ClassRequestDialog crd = new
        ClassRequestDialog(frame);
      crd.setVisible(true);
      String newclass = crd.getText();
```

```
  // Check to see if the cancel button was selected
  // (returns null)
    if (!newclass.equals("")) {
      frame.setClass(newclass);
      frame.pack();
    }
  }
}
}
```

To execute this application type java browser.Browser <fully qualified class name>. For example:

```
java browser.Browser javax.swing.Jtree
```

Note the use of the package browser in running the application.

21.6 Online Resources

The Swing Connection:

```
http://java.sun.com/products/jfc/swingdoc-current/doc/
   index.html
```

The Java Tutorial: Using the JFC "Swing" Release:

```
http://java.sun.com/docs/books/tutorial/post1.0/ui/
   swing.html
```

(see section entitled "How to Use Trees").
The JFC Home Page:

```
http://java.sun.com/products/jfc/index.html
```

22 *Observers and Observables*

22.1 Introduction

This chapter introduces the dependency mechanism. This is a mechanism, provided by the Java language, which allows a change in one object to result in a method in another object running. This is a very powerful mechanism, which can be particularly useful in creating GUI applications.

22.2 The Dependency Mechanism

There are a number of different relationships between objects in an object-oriented system. We have already considered several of these earlier in this book:

- Inheritance (class to class relationships)
- Instantiation (class to instance relationships)
- *Part-of* or contains (instance to instance relationships)

However, there is another important relationship supported by many object-oriented languages, such as Smalltalk and Java. This is the dependency relationship, where the state or behaviour of one object is dependent on the state of another object. Figure 22.1 indicates that there is a set of dependency relationships between the objects A to F. Object A is dependent on some aspect of objects B and D. In turn object B is dependent on some aspect of object C and so on.

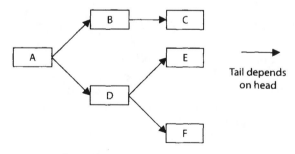

Figure 22.1 Dependency between objects.

22.2.1 Why Do We Want Dependency?

The reasons for dependency are all down to *change*. We wish to communicate the fact that an object has changed its value to another object, which may be interested in either the fact of the change or the new value effected by the change. The dependency mechanism provides a way of communicating such events in a generic, implementation-independent, manner.

An obvious question is "why not just get the object to send messages to those interested in it?". The answer is that if you know the objects that are interested, then you can send messages to them. However, if all you know is that at some time, at a later date, some object may need to know something about the state of an object (but you do not know what that other object might be) then you cannot arrange to send messages to it.

The dependency mechanism allows any object whose class is a subclass of Observable to act as the source of a dependency. Any object that implements the Observer interface can act as the dependent object.

We do not need to know what might be interested in the object. We merely need to know that it might be involved in a dependency relationship. The (hidden) dependency mechanism takes care of informing the unknown objects about the updates.

22.2.2 How Does Dependency Work?

The dependency mechanism is implemented in the class Observable within the java.util package. This class is a direct subclass of Object, so any class can inherit from Observable and thus take part in a dependency relationship.

In Java terminology, the head of the dependent relationship (i.e. the object on which other objects depend) is referred to as the observable object, while the dependent object is referred to as the observer object. The observable object allows other objects to observe its current state. An observable object can have zero or more observers, which are notified of changes to the object's state by the notify-Observers method.

You can browse the Observable class to explore the dependency mechanism. The basic implementation, inherited from Observable, associates a vector of other objects with the observable object. This vector holds the objects which are dependent on the object (collectively, these objects are known as the object's observers). For example, in Figure 22.2, the object ObjectA has two observers, ObjectB and ObjectC. The links to the dependent objects are held by ObjectA in a list of observers called obs. ObjectA cannot access this vector as it is private to the Observable class. However, it can obtain the number of observers using the countObservers method.

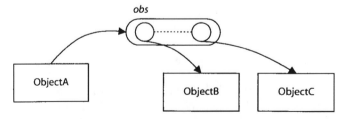

Figure 22.2 An object and its observers.

22.2.3 Constructing Dependencies

The `addObserver` message adds an object to a dependency list. For example, we can construct the above dependencies:

```
ObjectA.addObserver(ObjectB);
ObjectA.addObserver(ObjectC);
```

Duplicates cannot be held in the list of observers. If you attempt to add an object to the list of observers more than once, it is only recorded once (and thus is only told of changes once).

An observable object holds a vector of objects which depend on it, but an object cannot access information about the objects on which it depends. For example, there are no references from `ObjectB` or `ObjectC` back to `ObjectA` in Figure 22.2. This may seem a bit strange at first; however, once you understand how the dependency mechanism works, as realized by the `Observable` class and the `Observer` interface, you will see why things are this way round.

You can remove dependencies once they have been created. The following code removes `ObjectB` from the observer list of `ObjectA`:

```
ObjectA.deleteObserver(ObjectB);
```

22.2.4 A Simple Dependency Example

We develop further the following very simple dependency example during the chapter. It creates two objects and a dependency between them. The objects are instances of the classes `DataObject` and `ObserverObject`, which are direct subclasses of `Observable` and `Object`, respectively. Place the classes in appropriate `.java` files (i.e. `DataObject.java` and `ObserverObject.java`).

```java
import java.util.Observable;
public class DataObject extends Observable {
}
```

The `update` method is explained below; it is used here merely to allow the `ObserverObject` to implement the `Observer` interface:

```java
import java.util.Observer;
import java.util.Observable;

public class ObserverObject implements Observer {
    public void update(Observable o, Object arg){
        System.out.println("Object " + o + " has
            changed");
    }
}
```

We now have two classes which can take part in a dependency relationship. To illustrate how objects of these classes can be related, define the following class in a file called `TestHarness.java`. Although, in general, I do not condone using separate objects to illustrate how other objects work, in this case it ensures that you understand that the dependency relationships are handled automatically via the inherited facilities.

```java
public class TestHarness {
  public static void main(String args []) {
    TestHarness t = new TestHarness();
    t.test();
  }
  public void test () {
    DataObject temp1 = new DataObject();
    ObserverObject temp2 = new ObserverObject();
    temp1.addObserver(temp2);
    System.out.println(temp1.countObservers());
  }
}
```

The result of println is the value 1, although our DataObject class is empty! From the point of view of the DataObject class, dependency is an invisible mechanism which works behind the scenes. Of course, this is not really the case. The dependency mechanism has been inherited from Observable and is implemented via message sends and method executions just like any behaviour provided by an object.

22.2.5 Making Dependency Work for You

We have now considered how to construct a dependency relationship. We want this relationship to inform the dependent objects that a change has occurred in the object on which they depend.

To do this we use two sets of methods. One set, the "changed" methods, states that something has changed. The other set, the "update" methods, is used to state what type of update is required.

Figure 22.3 illustrates the sequence of messages which are sent in response when an object changes. That is, when ObjectA is sent the setChanged and notifyObservers messages (usually by itself), all its observers are sent an update message. From the point of view of ObjectA, much of this behaviour is hidden; in fact, so much so that a point of confusion relates to the sending of one

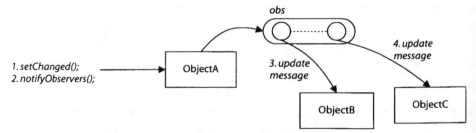

Figure 22.3 The dependency mechanism in action.

message (the `notifyObservers` message) and the execution of another method (the `update` method). A programmer defining Objects A, B and C:

- sends one (or more) `setChanged` messages to `ObjectA`
- sends a `notifyObservers` message to `ObjectA`
- defines an update method in `ObjectB` and `ObjectC`

The confusion stems from the need to send one message but define another. However, if you think about how you are linking into the existing dependency framework, it can make more sense. The change message is a message to the dependency mechanism asking it to notify the object's dependants about a change. The dependency mechanism is inherited and is generic across applications, but system developers cannot know when the change message should be sent – that is application-specific. It is, therefore, the application developer's responsibility to send the change messages. For example, you may only want dependants to be told of certain changes, such as updates to one field on an input screen, etc.

Similarly, there is no way that the system developers can know how the dependants should update themselves. The update message could display the new value produced by the originating object, perform some calculation, or access a database. As the update methods are defined in an interface, they do nothing; they are abstract methods. Nothing is said anywhere in the system about what an observer should do when the object changes.

In the simple example above, we need to specify what `ObjectB` and `ObjectC` should do when `ObjectA` changes. This requires defining update methods (as we did very briefly in the `ObserverObject` example presented earlier).

22.2.6 The "Changed" Methods

There are three messages which inform an object that it has changed and should notify its observers:

- `setChanged()` indicates to the observable object that something has happened which should be passed on to any observers next time they are notified of a change. It is very useful to separate out specifying that something has changed from the actual notification action. You can determine that observers must be notified at one point in an object's execution (when data is entered), but trigger the notification at another point (at the end of some execution cycle). Interestingly, the Smalltalk dependency mechanism does not provide this flexibility.

- `notifyObservers()` informs the observers that something has changed (but not what the change was). It calls the `notifyObservers(Object object)` method with a null parameter.

- `notifyObservers(Object object)` notifies the observers that something has changed and what the change was. This is done by sending the update message to the objects in the `obs` vector. The update method takes two parameters: the current object and the object passed into the `notifyObservers` method. It assumes that the change can be represented as an object, so if the change results in the number 24, it must be wrapped in an `Integer` object.

The first point to note about the changed messages is that they are sent to the object which has changed in some way. They inform the object that it has changed and that this change should be passed on to any observers. The changed messages do not effect the change or notify the observers.

The notifyObservers messages trigger off the update part of the dependency mechanism. The only difference between the messages relates to the amount of information provided. The simplest notification message (and the one with the least information) is the notifyObservers() message. This can be useful when you want to make sure that the dependants assume nothing about the object to which the change is happening.

The way these messages are implemented is that the setChanged method sets a boolean flag, changed, to true. This flag is examined by the notify-Observers(Object) method; if the flag is set to true, it notifies the objects in the obs vector that they need to update themselves and resets the changed flag to false. If the changed flag is already false, it does nothing.

22.3 The Observer Interface

The Observer interface defines the abstract update method which must be implemented by objects which wish to take part in a dependency:

```
public interface Observer {
    void update(Observable observable, Object arg);
}
```

As with all interfaces, any concrete class that implements this interface must provide the body of the update method. Any class implementing this interface can be guaranteed to work with the notification methods used in an observer object.

The first parameter passed to this method is the observable object. If ObjectA is sent a setChanged message followed by a notifyObservers message, then ObjectB and ObjectC are sent the update message with the first parameter set to ObjectA.

The value of the arg parameter depends on the version of notifyObservers which was sent to ObjectA. If no parameters were sent, then the value of arg is null. If one parameter was sent, arg holds the parameter. This means that the developer can decide how much information the observer object can work with.

22.4 Extending the Dependency Example

This section provides an example of how the dependency mechanism works. We use the DataObject and ObserverObject classes defined in Section 22.2.4.

The first thing we do is to define some instance variables (age, name and address), a constructor and an updater, age, in DataObject:

```java
import java.util.Observable;

public class DataObject extends Observable {
    String name = "";
    int age = 0;
    String address = "";

    public DataObject (String aName,
        int years, String anAddress) {
        name = aName;
        age = years;
        address = anAddress;
    }

    public void age (int years) {
        age = years;
        setChanged();
        notifyObservers("age");
    }

    public String toString() {
        return "(DataObject: " + name + " of " + address
                + " who is " + age + ")";
    }

}
```

The updater method, `age`, which sets the `age` instance variable, also informs itself that it has changed (using `setChanged`) and that this fact should be passed on to its dependants (using `notifyObservers ("age")`). This is a typical usage of the `notifyObservers` message. That is, it informs the notification mechanism about the type of change which has taken place. It also illustrates good style: it informs this object about the change which has taken place. It is very poor style to have an object send an instance of `DataObject` the message `age`, followed by the changed messages. It implies that something outside the `DataObject` decides when to inform its observers.

Next we define how an instance of `ObserverObject` responds to the change in a `DataObject`; we define an update method:

```java
import java.util.Observer;
import java.util.Observable;

public class ObserverObject implements Observer {

    public void update(Observable o, Object arg){
        if (arg == "age")
            System.out.println("Object " + o +
                    " has changed its " + arg);
        else
```

```
        System.out.println("Don't know how to handle
            changes to " + arg);
    }
}
```

As this is just a simple example, all it does is print a string on the console that reports the change. We use the `TestHarness` class we defined earlier to try out this simple example. We use the new `DataObject` constructor to create the observable object and the `age` updater to change the observable object's age:

```
public class TestHarness {

    public static void main(String args []) {
        TestHarness t = new TestHarness();
        t.test();
    }

    public void test () {
        DataObject temp1 =
            new DataObject("John", 33, "C47");
        ObserverObject temp2 = new ObserverObject();
        temp1.addObserver(temp2);
        System.out.println(temp1.countObservers());
        temp1.age(34);
    }
}
```

The result of executing this class is illustrated below:

```
C:\AAAusers\JJH\Java\Book\chap22>java TestHarness

1
Object (DataObject: John of C47 who is 34) has changed
its age

C:\AAAusers\JJH\Java\Book\chap22>
```

The `ObserverObject` has been informed of the change of `age`, although we did not define a method to do this directly.

In the simple example presented above, you should note (and understand) the following points:

- `DataObject` does not have a reference to, nor does it know anything about, an `ObserverObject`.
- The `ObserverObject` does not reference a `DataObject` internally.
- The link between `temp1` and `temp2` is external to both objects.

It can be difficult to debug and maintain relationships which have been implemented using the dependency mechanism (as the message chain is partly hidden). Therefore, you should exercise care in its use.

22.5 Exercise: Dependency and the Financial Manager

Try to modify the `FinancialManager` example by adding a `monitor` class to send the user a message if the bank balance dips below a certain threshold.

22.6 Summary

This chapter has introduced the dependency mechanism in Java as implemented by the `Observable` class and `Observer` interface. This relationship is quite complex, but the user interface classes make extensive use of it and you should gain some experience with it.

23 *A GUI Case Study*

23.1 Introduction

In this chapter, we consider how to construct an object-oriented graphical application. Many people use languages such as C++ to develop the graphical user interface (GUI) of their system, but then resort to C for the remainder of the system. However, in many cases these people do not construct the GUI in an object-oriented manner. They use the facilities available, but tend to pack everything together. In this chapter, we attempt to consider how a GUI can be constructed using a tried and tested object-oriented approach.

We shall construct the Account application shown in Figure 23.1. This application allows a user to keep track of a current account balance using two buttons which indicate whether the amount input should be treated as a deposit or a withdrawal. The amount is entered by the user into the first text field and the current balance is displayed in the second text field. The user can exit from the application in a controlled manner using the Exit button.

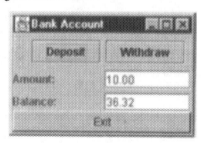

Figure 23.1 The GUI for the Account application using Swing components.

To construct this application, we use a number of concepts which have been introduced over the last few chapters:

- The Model–View–Controller architecture (which is also known as the Model–View–Handler architecture
- Event listeners (via the Java event delegation model)
- Dependency via observers and observables
- Frames, panels and layout managers
- The Swing set of GUI components

If you have read the last few chapters, none of the above should be a surprise to you. However, you may not be clear on how they may be used within a "real" application.

23.1.1 The Model–View–Handler Architecture

The Model–View–Handler (MVC)[1] architecture separates the interface objects (the views) from the objects which handle user input (the Handlers) from the application (the model). It has already been described in Chapter 20. However, it is an architecture which you can usefully employ when constructing your own graphical applications.

Figure 23.2 illustrates the overall structure of the Account application. Notice that there are direct links between the interface (or view) object and the Handler objects. However, although the interface and the Handler objects have links to the application (anAccount), the application knows nothing about the interface or the Handlers. This means that it is independent of the interface, and its Handlers and can be associated with various different interfaces. Any of the elements can be modified without the need to change the others.

Figure 23.3 illustrates the system interaction. It shows the various messages sent when a user clicks on the deposit button. You should notice the following points:

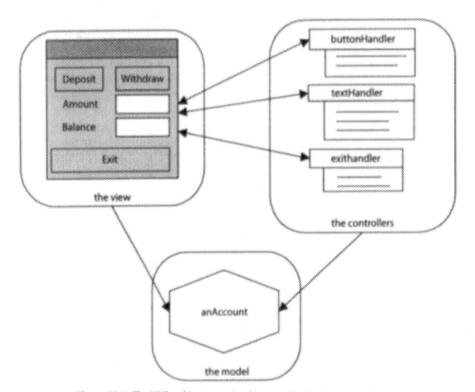

Figure 23.2 The MVC architecture as implemented by the Account application.

---

1   Note that the abbreviation MVC is used here, but in this case we are calling the controllers Handlers as they handle events – MVC was developed before Java so some of the terminology differs.

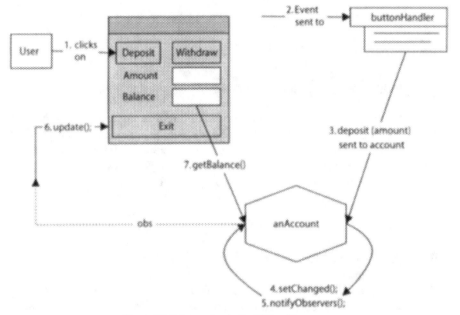

Figure 23.3 Interaction in the MVC architecture.

- Neither the display nor the Handler holds the balance. It is obtained from the account whenever it is needed.
- The Handler relies on the event delegation model to determine that it should do something.
- When the Handler asks the model to change it does not tell the display. The display finds out about the change through the dependency mechanism.
- The account is unaware that the message deposit(amount) comes from the Handler. Any object can send a deposit message and the account still informs its dependants about the change.

23.1.2 Event Listeners

In this system, the Handlers are registered as event listeners for the input elements on the interface. The buttonHandler deals with inputs associated with the Deposit and Withdraw buttons. The fieldHandler deals with inputs to the amount field (when the user presses the Return key). Finally, the exitHandler deals with inputs associated with the Exit button.

23.1.3 Observers and Observables

Although Figure 23.2 illustrates that there is no direct link from the account object to the interface, the dependency mechanism can inform any object interested in the state of the account object that a change has occurred. Thus, the interface object can register itself as an observer of the account object. When a deposit or withdrawal is made, the account object informs its observers (including the interface object) that its balance has changed and they should update themselves. The account object does not have to know about the interface object.

23.1.4 Frames, Panels and Layout Managers

The interface object is made up of a number of objects such as a frame, a number of panels and graphic components (buttons and text fields). Layout managers control the way in which these objects are arranged within the window frame. The exit button Handler can be used without any modification from previous examples. The abstract `buttonHandler` class is a reusable class for any object acting as a Handler within an MVC architecture; it is the superclass of the `buttonPanelHandler` class.

23.2 The Class Structure

In this section, we consider each of the classes defined as part of the Account application. The instance structure is considered in the next section. The classes are:

- `AccountInterface`
- `WindowHandler`
- `ButtonHandler`
- `TextHandler`
- `ExitButtonHandler`
- `ButtonPanelHandler`
- `ButtonPanel`
- `TextPanel`
- `Account`

The `Account` class and the `AccountInterface` class are the only public classes. All the other GUI classes are defined within the same file as the `AccountInterface` class.

23.2.1 The `AccountInterface` Class

This is the root class of the whole application. It is the only class with a main method and thus represents the entry point for the application. The `AccountInterface` class is a direct subclass of `Frame` and it implements the `WindowListener` and `Observer` interfaces (see Figure 23.4). It defines a constructor which builds up the window to be displayed to the user by instantiating the `buttonPanel`, the `TextPanel` and a button component. It also registers as an observer of the account object, sets the size of the window and makes itself visible.

Instances of this class only hold references to the text fields (which need to be accessed and updated), the exit button and its Handler, and the account object. The other objects are expected to maintain references to the `accountInterface` object so that they can obtain information from it. You do not need to provide an explicit link from the

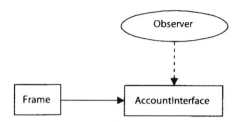

Figure 23.4 The AccountInterface class.

accountInterface to these objects as they receive information via the event delegation mechanism (i.e. they are event listeners associated with the window). This buffers the accountInterface from changes in the other objects.

The accountInterface class also defines an instance method, update, which defines how instances of this class should respond when the account object reports a change. In this case, the response is that the current balance, held by the account object, is displayed in the second balance text field.

```
import java.utils;
import javax.swing.*;
import java.awt.*;
public class AccountInterface extends JFrame
implements Observer {
  protected TextPanel textPanel;
  protected Account account = new Account(0.0);

  public static void main (String args []) {
    Frame f = new AccountInterface();
  }

  public AccountInterface () {
    super("Bank Account");

    /* Get the JFrames content pane */
    Container pane = getContentPane();

    /* Add the interface as an observer of the account */
    account.addObserver(this);

    /* Create the Toolbar object and its Handler */
    JToolBar toolbar = new JToolBar();
    toolbar.add(new ButtonPanel(this));
    pane.add("North", toolbar);

    /* Next set up the text panel */
    textPanel = new TextPanel();
    pane.add("Center", textPanel);
```

```
/* Now add the exit button and its handler */
Button exitButton = new Button(" Exit ");
exitButton.addActionListener(new
   ExitButtonHandler(this));
pane.add("South", exitButton);

/* Finally add the listener for the whole window */
addWindowListener(new WindowHandler());

/* Now set the size of the window and make it
   visible */
pack();
setVisible(true);
}

/* The update method is called whenever an observed
   object (in this case the account, wishes to
   notify an observer that a change had occurred */
public void update (Observable o, Object arg) {
  textPanel.balanceField.setText
    (account.stringBalance());
  }
}
```

23.2.2 The WindowHandler Class

This class handles window events. It is a direct subclass of the WindowAdapter, which is a convenience call which provides null implementations of all the methods specified in the WindowListener interface. This means that it is only necessary to implement the windowClosing() method, as the remaining methods are provided as null body implementation in the superclass.

```
class WindowHandler extends WindowAdapter {
  public void windowClosing(WindowEvent event) {
    System.exit(0);
  }
}
```

23.2.3 The JPanel Classes

There are two JPanel classes used in this application (see Figure 23.5). They inherit from the JPanel class and define what should be displayed on an area of the window. The ButtonPanel class defines two button components. The TextPanel class defines two labels and two text fields.

Both classes create instances of Handler classes which define what should happen when a user provides some input (either via the mouse or as text). The Handler

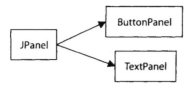

Figure 23.5 The JPanel classes.

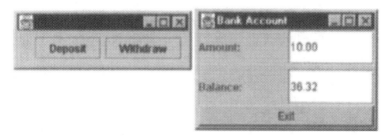

Figure 23.6 The dockable toolbar used with the application.

classes are described in the next subsection. Note that the ButtonPanel is displayed within a JToolBar which provides a dockable toolbar for the application (see for example Figure 23.6).

The ButtonPanel Class

The ButtonPanel class definition uses elements from the Swing package and java.awt and java.awt.event packages (as do most of the remaining classes):

```
class ButtonPanel extends JPanel {
  public ButtonPanel (AccountInterface win) {
    ButtonPanelHandler panelHandler =
            new ButtonPanelHandler(win);
    JButton button = new JButton("Deposit");
    button.addActionListener(panelHandler);
    add("East", button);

    button = new JButton("Withdraw");
    button.addActionListener(panelHandler);
    add("West", button);
  }
}
```

When this class is instantiated, it first creates a listener for the two buttons, ButtonPanelHandler. It then creates the buttons and places them within the panel (the flow layout manager is the default for panels). This class assumes nothing about the container within which it is used. Thus it can be used in many different situations, with different containers and different applications. This illustrates one of the advantages of making part of the display an object.

The `TextPanel` Class

The TextPanel class provides a similar facility for textual elements of the display. It defines four graphic components which are displayed in a two-by-two grid. The text fields handle the amount (inputField) and the current balance (balanceField). Note that it creates a separate Handler (TextHandler) to handle events and makes this Handler the listener for the inputField:

```java
class TextPanel extends JPanel {
  protected JTextField inputField, balanceField;

  public TextPanel () {
    TextHandler panelHandler = new TextHandler(this);

    setLayout(new GridLayout(2, 2, 5, 5));

    add(new JLabel("Amount: "));
    inputField = new JTextField(8);
    inputField.addActionListener(panelHandler);
    add(inputField);

    add(new JLabel("Balance: "));

    balanceField = new JTextField(8);
    add(balanceField);
  }
}
```

23.2.4 The Handler Classes

The Handler classes provide the actions to be performed when specified events occur. They do this by implementing the ActionListener interface (see Figure 23.7).

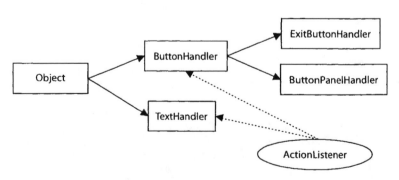

Figure 23.7 The Handler classes.

There is one abstract superclass, ButtonHandler. The concrete Exit-ButtonHandler, ButtonPanelHandler and TextHandler classes are used in conjunction with the panel objects (or the exit button component).

The ButtonHandler Class

This is an abstract superclass for all classes which handle events generated by buttons (or containers which possess buttons). It is abstract because it does not attempt to define the actionPerformed method specified by the Action-Listener interface. It defines one instance variable, view, and one constructor which initializes the instance variable. The instance variable provides a link between a view and the event handler (this is why Swing modifies the MVC so that the view and controller are part of the Swing component).

```java
abstract class ButtonHandler implements ActionListener
{
   protected AccountInterface view;
   public ButtonHandler (AccountInterface win) {
      view = win;
   }
}
```

The ExitButtonHandler Class

This class is a concrete subclass of ButtonHandler. It specifies the action to be performed when the user presses the Exit button. In this case, the message exit is sent to the system object and the application terminates.

```java
class ExitButtonHandler extends ButtonHandler {

   public ExitButtonHandler (AccountInterface win) {
      super (win);
   }

   public void actionPerformed (ActionEvent event) {
      System.exit(0);
   }
}
```

Note that the actionPerformed method does not perform any checks on the event or determine the button pressed. This is because it is only ever called when the button pressed event is triggered. This is a very clean and simple way of specifying what should happen when a button is pressed. We can create a unique Handler class for each button. The disadvantage of this approach is the proliferation of classes (and .class) files that it produces. An alternative approach is presented by the ButtonPanelHandler class. The approach that you take depends on personal preference and the nature of the application.

The *ButtonPanelHandler* Class

This class deals with events on both the Deposit and Withdraw buttons. This means that it must determine which button was pressed. It does this by sending the getActionCommand message to the event object. This method returns the action command associated with the button pressed. By default the action command is the label of the button. The method can then compare action command string with the string "Withdraw" to determine which action to actually perform.

Text fields always return a string. You must convert the string into a numeric form (in this case, a double) to use it with the deposit and withdraw methods. The class method valueOf (defined on class Double) is used to create an instance of Double. The actual value is then obtained by sending this object the doubleValue message.

Once the input amount has been obtained, an if statement sends either the withdraw or the deposit message to the account held by the top level view (hence the need to provide a link to the AccountInterface object).

```java
class ButtonPanelHandler extends ButtonHandler {
  public ButtonPanelHandler(AccountInterface win) {
    super(win);
  }
  public void actionPerformed(ActionEvent event) {
    String cmd = event.getActionCommand();
    double amount;
    // Converts the numerical strings in the text
    // input field to a double
    amount = (Double.valueOf
      (view.textPanel.inputField.getText()))
      .doubleValue();
    // Depending on which button is pressed, the
    // amount is either deposited or withdrawn
    if (cmd.equals("Withdraw"))
      view.account.withdraw(amount);
    else
      view.account.deposit(amount);
  }
}
```

The *TextHandler* Class

This class handles the events generated for the inputField. An event is generated when the user presses Return while the cursor is within the text field. When this happens a message is printed on the console. It is an extremely simple event listener, but it illustrates that event listeners need not be complex.

```java
class TextHandler implements ActionListener {
  protected TextPanel panel;
  public TextHandler (TextPanel aPanel) {
```

```
    panel = aPanel;
  }
  public void actionPerformed(ActionEvent event) {
    System.out.println("Input is " +
        (panel.inputField.getText()));
  }
}
```

23.2.5 The Account Class

The Account class defines the application used with the GUI. It is a very simple application which maintains a numeric value of type double (the current account balance). It uses two methods to add or subtract amounts from this balance (deposit and withdraw, respectively). The dependency mechanism is used to inform objects observing account instances that a change has taken place.

```
import java.util.Observable;

public class Account extends Observable {
  private double balance = 0.0;

  public Account (double initialBalance) {
    setBalance(initialBalance);
  }

  private void setBalance (double anAmount) {
    balance = 0.0;
    deposit(anAmount);
  }

  public void deposit (double anAmount) {
    balance += anAmount;
    setChanged();
    notifyObservers();
  }

  public void withdraw (double anAmount) {
    balance -= anAmount;
    setChanged();
    notifyObservers();
  }

  public String stringBalance () {
    return String.valueOf(balance);
  }
}
```

Note that the `setBalance(double)` method ensures that, when the balance is set, the same notification takes place as when an amount is deposited. Also note that the current balance is returned as a string. This is a convenience method for objects working with the `account` object.

23.3 The Instance Structure

Figure 23.8 presents the instance structure of the GUI. As you can see from this diagram, this application's user interface is extremely object-oriented. Not only are the graphical components objects (buttons, labels and text fields), the elements which handle events on the objects are also objects.

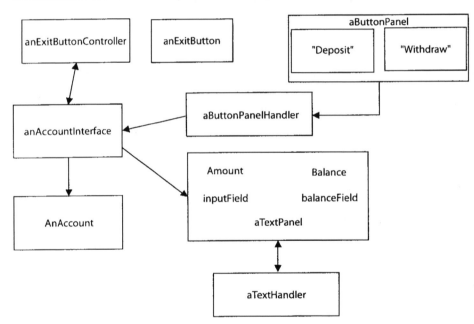

Figure 23.8 The instance structure of the application.

The Exit button Handler has been reused from the examples presented in the previous two chapters. This illustrates one of the benefits of this approach, the reusability of interface components. In addition, the application code (represented by the account object) is independent of the interface and its event handlers (Handlers). If this was a real application, we might well have very many classes representing the application rather than just the single class presented above.

23.4 Exercise: a GUI for the Financial Manager

As an exercise you should try to construct a GUI for the financial manager application. You can either start from scratch or build on the simple application presented above.

23.5 Summary

You should not have found anything surprising in this chapter, as we have covered all of the aspects before. However, you may not have visualized them working together in the way presented here. Remember that the aim of this chapter has been to apply object-oriented techniques to the construction of the GUI, in the same way that we apply them to the construction of the application.

You can write a Java program which is not object-oriented. The same is true of the user interface aspects of Java. In the case of the example, you could place all of the application within a single `AccountInterface` class, which would hold the application code, the window definition and the event-handling code.

However, the less object-oriented you make the interface part of your application, the less reusable, the less robust to change and the less effective it becomes. You lose the following advantages:

- reusability of parts of the system
- the ability to inherit from different parts of the class hierarchy
- modularity of system code
- resilience to change
- encapsulation of the application

Although these issues might not be a problem for an application as simple as that presented here, for real-world systems they are certainly significant. I hope that you are now aware of the benefits of adopting the MVC architecture and will try to adopt this approach in your own systems. Of course, you may find that the resulting system appears overly complex at first. However, if you persevere with it, the approach will become second nature.

23.6 Further Reading

One place to read about the concepts behind the MVC architecture is within the Smalltalk community. Smalltalk explicitly uses the MVC architecture to promote object-oriented reusable interfaces. A good place to start is with Hunt (1997), which considers how the MVC architecture can be implemented within Java. Another article in the *Java Report* (Sevareid, 1997) also provides an excellent introduction to the event delegation model.

Hunt, J. E. (1997). Constructing Modular User Interfaces in Java, *Java Report*.
Sevareid, J. (1997). The JDK 1.1's New Delegation Event Model, *Java Report*, pp. 59–79.

24 Combining Graphics and GUI Components

24.1 Introduction

This chapter aims to bring together the graphic elements described earlier in the book with the user interface components (such as buttons and layout managers) from the last few chapters. It presents a case study of a drawing tool akin to tools such as Visio, xfig or MacDraw.

24.2 The SwingDraw Application

The SwingDraw application allows a user to draw diagrams using squares, circles, lines and text. The user can also select, resize and reposition any of these graphic objects. At present, no delete option is provided (although this would be a simple addition). SwingDraw is implemented using the Swing set of components as defined in the 1.0.2 release of Swing. This means that buttons with icons, menus with icons, dockable menu bars and different look and feels can be used. This application was implemented using this release of Swing and release 1.1.6 of the JDK. This configuration was selected as many developers will be forced to use the 1.1.* version of JDK for some time to come. These developers are not precluded from using the Swing set, and this chapter illustrates how straightforward it is.

When users start the SwingDraw application, they see the interface shown in Figure 24.1. It has a menu bar across the top, a dockable toolbar below the menu bar and a scrollable drawing area below. The first button clears the drawing area. The second and third buttons are not implemented but are intended to allow a user to load and save drawings. The next four buttons set the drawing mode which determines whether a line, a square, a circle or text is added when the mouse is clicked in the drawing area. The final button allows the user to exit the application. These buttons are duplicated on the applications menus (as illustrated in Figure 24.2).

Once a graphic component has been added to the drawing, the user can select it by clicking over the component with the mouse. The selected component is redrawn in red and is surrounded by four small boxes. The user can then move it around (no resize function is provided).

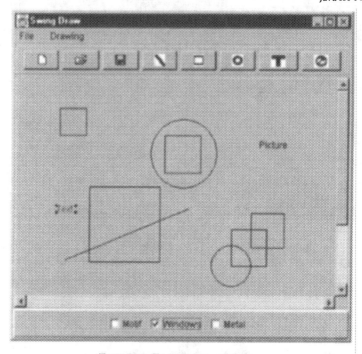

Figure 24.1 The SwingDraw application.

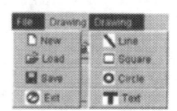

Figure 24.2 The File and Drawing menus.

24.3 The Structure of the Application

The interface is made up of a number of elements (see Figure 24.3): the menu bar, the panel of buttons across the top of the window, a scroll pane containing the drawing panel, and the window frame (implemented by the SwingDraw class).

Figure 24.4 shows the same information as Figure 24.3, but as a containment hierarchy, which means that one object is contained within another. In Figure 24.4, the lower level objects are contained in the higher level objects. It is important to visualize this as the majority of Java interfaces are built up in this way, using layout managers. Note that the DrawToolBar object actually contains another object called ButtonPanel. It is the ButtonPanel that holds the various buttons.

Figure 24.5 illustrates the inheritance structure between the classes used in the SwingDraw application. This class hierarchy is typical of an application which incorporates user interface features with graphical elements. For example, there is a subclass of Frame with the main Draw application class. The Model–View–

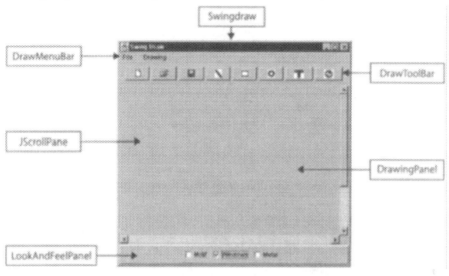

Figure 24.3 The objects in the SwingDraw interface.

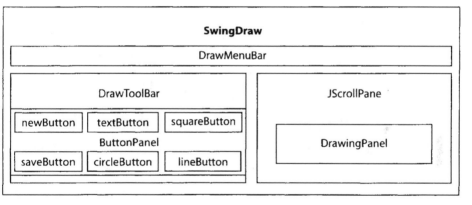

Figure 24.4 The containment hierarchy of the SwingDraw interface.

Controller structure has a controller class (DrawingController), a model subclass (Drawing) and a view class (DrawingPanel).

There are four types of drawing object: Circle, Line, Square and TextFigure. The only difference between these classes is what is drawn on the graphics context representing the view. The Figure class, from which they all inherit, defines the common attributes used by all objects within a Drawing (e.g. *x* and *y* location and size).

The ButtonPanel and ButtonPanelController classes display the buttons and deal with user interactions.

Although exceptions are not introduced until Chapter 27, the Drawing class uses an exception whenever the user adds a component which it does not know about. Exceptions are well suited for such a scenario and it is a good example of how they should be used.

The final class in the SwingDraw application is the TextDialog class. Dialogs are model windows which the user must handle before continuing. This is, therefore, a good way of obtaining the text to be displayed.

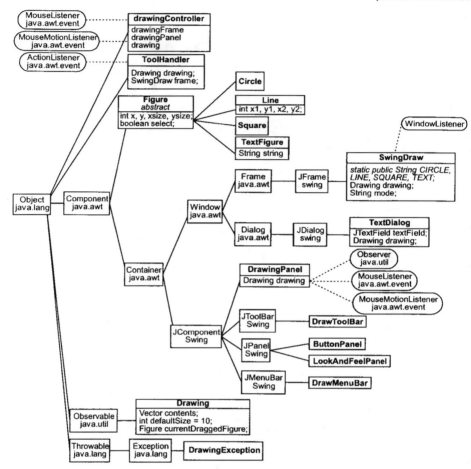

Figure 24.5 Inheritance in SwingDraw.

In Figure 24.4, the classes in bold are part of the `draw` package which defines the SwingDraw application. The other classes are extended by the SwingDraw classes. Solid lines indicate the extension of a parent class (shown to the left of the subclass). Additional classes are used with the application but are not presented in this figure (for example, `Vector` and `Button`). Also note that interfaces are presented in oval boxes and dashed lines indicate the implementation of an interface.

However, the inheritance hierarchy is only part of the story for any object-oriented application. Figure 24.6 shows how the objects relate to one another within a working application. The `SwingDraw` application object does not possess any links to the objects displayed within it. This is because the user interacts with the application via the event delegation model; individual controllers handle user interaction and the observer–observable mechanism refreshes the drawing display. This separates the interface from the drawing elements and the button action elements of the application.

The `JScrollPane` is an AWT class which handles scrolling panels. As SwingDraw does not manipulate the scrolling panel from within the application, it does not need to maintain a reference to this object.

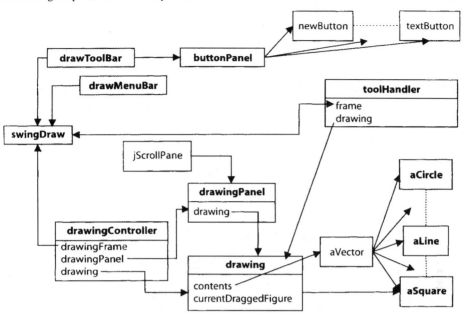

Figure 24.6 The object relationships.

The Drawing, DrawingPanel and DrawingController classes exhibit the classic MVC structure. The view and the controller classes (DrawingPanel and DrawingController) know about each other and the drawing, whereas the drawing knows nothing about the view or the controller. The view is notified of changes in the drawing through the dependency mechanism implemented through the observer–observable class and interface.

Drawing is a relatively simple model which merely records a set of graphical objects in a Vector. These can be any type of object and can be displayed in any way. It is the objects themselves which determine what they look like when drawn.

24.4 The Interactions Between Objects

We have now examined the physical structure of the application, but not how the objects within that application interact. In many situations this can be extracted from the source code of the application (with varying degrees of difficulty). However, in the case of an application such as SwingDraw, which is made up of a number of different interacting components, it is useful to describe the system interactions explicitly.

The diagrams illustrating the interactions between the objects use the following conventions:

- a solid arrow indicates a message send
- a dashed arrow indicates an instance creation
- a square box indicates a class

- a round box indicates an instance
- a name in brackets indicates the type of instance
- numbers indicate the sequence of message sends

These diagrams are based on the mechanism diagrams described by Rumbaugh *et al.* (1991) and discussed in more detail in Part 4.

24.4.1 The Draw Constructor

When the SwingDraw application is initiated, the main method in the SwingDraw class is executed. This method creates an instance of the class SwingDraw, executing the SwingDraw constructor. The operations performed by the constructor are summarized in Figure 24.7.

The constructor sets up the environment for the application. It creates the drawing object, its panel (and as part of this operation its controller), and the toolbar and its menu bar, as well as the drawing itself. It also makes itself the listener for window events and sets the default drawing mode to "circle". It also sets its size (using pack()) and then makes itself visible.

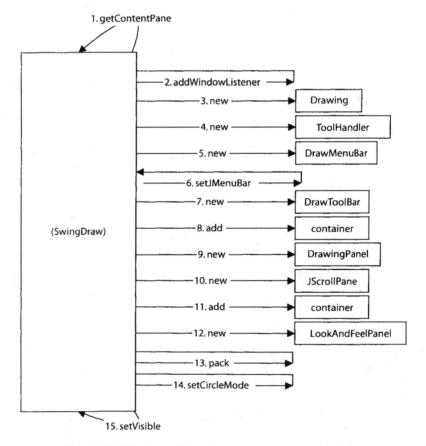

Figure 24.7 The actions performed by the SwingDraw constructor.

24.4.2 Changing the Type of Graphic Object

One interesting thing to look at is what happens when the user selects one of the buttons in the button panel held in the toolbar panel.

The button panel is an object into which each of the buttons has been placed (user interfaces in Java tend to be built up from components and types of container in a hierarchical manner; see Figure 24.3). The toolController handles the events generated (as part of the event delegation model which we saw earlier in the book). When an event is generated the actionPerformed method of the tool-Controller sends the drawing object the appropriate set*Mode method.

Figure 24.8 shows what happens when the user clicks on the Square button. The setSquareMode method sets the mode variable of the drawing object to the string "Square". The mode values are defined as class variables: "Line", "Circle", "Square" and "Text". The same effect would result if the user selected one of the Drawing menu options (i.e. the actionPerformed(ActionEvent) method of the toolHandler would be executed).

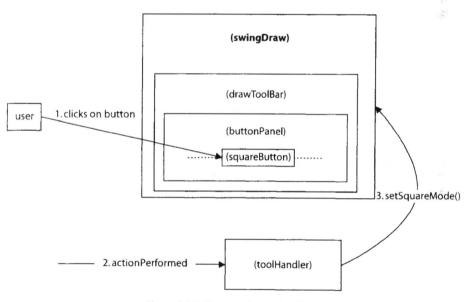

Figure 24.8 Changing the graphic object.

24.4.3 Adding a Graphic Object

A user adds a graphic object to the drawing displayed by the drawingPanel by pressing the mouse button. We do not distinguish between the mouse buttons, although it can be done quite simply by using the getModifiers method and comparing the result with the class variables button1_Mask, button2_Mask and button3_Mask.

Figure 24.9 illustrates what happens when the user presses and releases a mouse button over a blank part of the drawing area to create a new component.

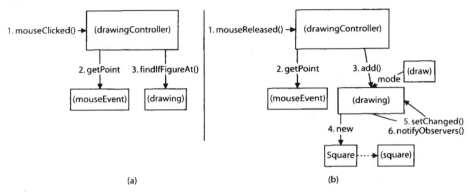

Figure 24.9 Adding a graphic component.

When the user presses the mouse button, a mouseClicked message is sent to the drawingController, which decides what action to perform in response (see Figure 24.9(a)). In SwingDraw, it obtains the cursor point at which the event was generated by sending a getPoint message to the mouseEvent. If a graphic object is already at this location, it is highlighted. In this case, we assume that there is no graphic object at the current cursor location and it becomes the start point of a new object.

When the user releases the mouse button, the mouseReleased message is sent to the drawingController (see Figure 24.9(b)). The drawing controller finds the new cursor location (the end point of the object to be added) by sending the getPoint message to the mouseEvent object. It then sends an add message to the drawing object, specifying the type of object (determined by the mode instance variables). The drawing object creates a new instance of the appropriate class and adds it to the vector held in its contents field. Then the drawing object sends itself the setChanged and notifyObservers messages so that its dependants can be informed of the change. The dependency mechanism sends the update message to the drawingPanel, which sends itself a repaint message. The paint method then asks each of the graphic objects to draw itself on the graphics context (i.e. the screen).

This section has outlined the most difficult part of constructing a graphical view – working out what is sent where, by what and when. The thing to remember is that you are slotting your application-specific code into a number of generic frameworks, in particular, the observer–observable dependency mechanism, the event delegation model and the hierarchical construction of interfaces. At this stage it is often much easier to look at what someone else has done and use it as the basis of what you require, although it is still important to become familiar with these frameworks and their use.

24.4.4 Moving a Graphic Object

A user moves a graphic object by clicking the mouse button, dragging the mouse and releasing the button (see Figure 24.10). This application must handle the button pressed, mouse dragged and button released events.

Figure 24.10(a) illustrates the interactions which occur when the mouse is clicked over a graphic object. Essentially, it is the same as in Figure 24.9, except that the object is sent the message select. This changes the state of the graphic object,

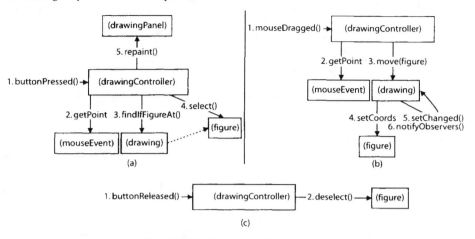

Figure 24.10 Moving a graphic component.

which alters its display. By default, an object displays with a solid black line. When it is selected, it displays with a red line and a small red box at each corner.

Figure 24.10(b) illustrates what happens as the mouse is dragged. A move message (with the figure as parameter) is sent to the drawing object, which uses the setCoords method to change the figure's position. The setChanged and notifyObservers messages are then used to inform observers of the drawing that something has changed. The update method of the drawingPanel executes and the window is repainted.

When the mouse button is released (Figure 24.10(c)), the currently selected figure is deselected.

24.5 The Classes

This section presents the classes in the SwingDraw application. As these classes build on concepts already presented in the last few chapters, they will be presented in their entirety with annotations highlighting specific points of their implementations. If you find any aspect of a class confusing, please refer to the chapter discussing the related issue.

24.5.1 The SwingDraw Class

The SwingDraw class provides the main window for the application:

```
package swingdrawing;

import java.awt.*;
import java.awt.event.*;
```

```java
import javax.swing.*;

public class SwingDraw extends JFrame {
  protected static String CIRCLE = "Circle",
    SQUARE = "Square",
       LINE = "Line", TEXT = "Text";

  private Drawing drawing;
  protected String mode;

  public static void main(String args []) {
    new SwingDraw("Swing Draw");
  }

  public SwingDraw(String label) {
    super(label);

    // Need to get the JFrames content pane
    Container pane = getContentPane();

    // Set the window handler so that the window can
    // be closed
    addWindowListener(new WindowHandler());

    // Create the drawing data model
    drawing = new Drawing();
    // Create the handler to be used by the toolbar
    // and the menubar
    ToolHandler toolHandler = new ToolHandler(this,
       drawing);

    // Build up the menu structure. Note the method
    // used to set the menu for the frame is
    // setJMenuBar and not setMenuBar (which
    // is inherited from Frame).
    setJMenuBar(new DrawMenuBar(toolHandler));

    // Now build the toolbar across the top of the
    // window
    pane.add("North", new DrawToolBar(toolHandler));

    // Now build the drawing area which forms the
    // majority of the interface. Note that the view
    // (the drawingPanel) is itself displayed within a
    // JScrollPane so that a scrollable drawing area
    // is provided.
```

```
    JScrollPane scrollPane = new JScrollPane(new
      DrawingPanel(this, drawing),
      ScrollPaneConstants.VERTICAL_SCROLLBAR_ALWAYS,
      ScrollPaneConstants.HORIZONTAL_SCROLLBAR_ALWAYS
    );

    pane.add("Center", scrollPane);

    // Illustrate use of different look and feel using
    // radio buttons
    pane.add("South", new LookAndFeelPanel(this));
    // Initialize the size of the window, set the
    // current mode and make the window visible.
    pack();
    setCircleMode();
    setVisible(true);
  }

  public void setSquareMode () {
    mode = SwingDraw.SQUARE;
  }

  public void setCircleMode () {
    mode = SwingDraw.CIRCLE;
  }

  public void setLineMode () {
    mode = SwingDraw.LINE;
  }

  public void setTextMode() {
    mode = SwingDraw.TEXT;
  }

  // Inner class to handle window events
  class WindowHandler extends WindowAdapter {
    public void windowClosing(WindowEvent event) {
      System.exit(0);
    }
  }
}
```

24.5.2 The DrawMenuBar class

The draw menu class is a subclass of the JmenuBar class which defines the contents of the menu bar for the SwingDraw application. It does this by creating two JMenu objects and adding them to the menu bar. Each JMenu implements a drop-down menu from the menu bar. The createMenuItem() method is used to create the individual menu items to be displayed on each menu. This method takes a string and a ActionListener and create a menu item with an icon based on the string (which is also used as the menu label).

```java
package swingdrawing;

import java.awt.event.*;
import javax.swing.*;

public class DrawMenuBar extends JMenuBar {
    public DrawMenuBar (ActionListener handler) {

        // Now create the File menu
        JMenu menu = new JMenu("File");
        menu.add(createMenuItem("New", handler));
        menu.add(createMenuItem("Load", handler));
        menu.addSeparator();
        menu.add(createMenuItem("Save", handler));
        menu.addSeparator();
        menu.add(createMenuItem("Exit", handler));
        // Add this menu to the menu bar itself
        add(menu);

        // Now create the drawing style menu
        menu = new JMenu("Drawing");
        menu.add(createMenuItem("Line", handler));
        menu.add(createMenuItem("Square", handler));
        menu.addSeparator();
        menu.add(createMenuItem("Circle", handler));
        menu.addSeparator();
        menu.add(createMenuItem("Text", handler));
        // Add menu to menu bar itself
        add(menu);
    }

    private JMenuItem createMenuItem(String label,
ActionListener handler) {
        JMenuItem mi = new JMenuItem(label);
        mi.setHorizontalTextPosition(JButton.RIGHT);
        mi.setIcon(new ImageIcon(label + ".gif"));
        mi.addActionListener(handler);
        return mi;
    }
}
```

24.5.3 The `DrawToolBar` and `ButtonPanel` Classes

The `DrawToolBar` class is a subclass of `JToolBar`. This allows the `DrawToolBar` to act like a dockable tool bar. It contains a single object, which is the `ButtonPanel`. The `ButtonPanel` class, a subclass of `JPanel`, handles the display of the buttons. It simplifies the construction of the user interface. A simple flow manager places the buttons on the panel and the whole panel is added to the draw application window using a border manager. Note that the method `createButton` takes an `ActionListener` and two strings. It then creates a `JButton` which displays an icon whose file is based on the label passed to it and which includes tooltips. Note that this means that it would be relatively straightforward to internationalize the creation of the buttons.

```java
package swingdrawing;

import javax.swing.*;
import java.awt.event.ActionListener;

/**
 * Provides a tool bar using a ButtonPanel class
 */
public class DrawToolBar extends JToolBar {
  public DrawToolBar(ActionListener handler) {
    add(new ButtonPanel(handler));
  }
}

/**
 * Defines a set of buttons with icons in a panel.
 * At present the buttons are hard coded, but could be
 * loaded from a preferences file.
 */
class ButtonPanel extends JPanel {
  ButtonPanel (ActionListener handler) {
    add(createButton(handler, "New",
      "Creates new drawing"));
    add(createButton(handler, "Load",
      "Loads a drawing"));
    add(createButton(handler, "Save",
      "Saves a drawing"));
    add(createButton(handler, "Line",
      "Sets line mode"));
    add(createButton(handler, "Square",
      "Sets square mode"));
    add(createButton(handler, "Circle",
      "Sets circle mode"));
```

```
      add(createButton(handler, "Text",
        "Sets text mode"));
      add(createButton(handler, "Exit",
        "Exits from application"));
  }

  private JButton createButton(ActionListener handler,
        String cmd, = String tips) {
    ImageIcon icon = new ImageIcon(cmd + ".gif");
    JButton button = new JButton(icon);
    // Need to set the action command for this button
    // as no text label has been provided.
    button.setActionCommand(cmd);
    button.setToolTipText(tips);
    button.addActionListener(handler);
    return button;
  }
}
```

24.5.4 The ToolHandler Class

The ToolHandler class defines, in the actionPerformed method, what happens when each of the buttons in the ButtonPanel is pressed or the menu options in the DrawMenuBar selected. The response of most buttons is to call a method on another object (primarily to set the drawing object mode).

```
package swingdrawing;

import java.awt.event.ActionListener;
import java.awt.event.ActionEvent;

class ToolHandler implements ActionListener {
  SwingDraw drawFrame;
  Drawing drawing;
  ToolHandler (SwingDraw draw, Drawing d) {
    drawFrame = draw;
    drawing = d;
  }
  public void actionPerformed(ActionEvent event) {
    String cmd = event.getActionCommand();
    if (cmd.equals("New")) {
      drawing.newDrawing();
    } else if (cmd.equals("Save")) {
      System.out.println("Save: Not implemented");
    } else if (cmd.equals("Load")) {
      System.out.println("Load: Not implemented");
```

```
      } else if (cmd.equals("Line"))
        drawFrame.setLineMode();
      else if (cmd.equals("Square"))
        drawFrame.setSquareMode();
      else if (cmd.equals("Circle"))
        drawFrame.setCircleMode();
      else if (cmd.equals("Text"))
        drawFrame.setTextMode();
      else {
        System.exit(0);
      }
    }
  }
}
```

24.5.5 The Drawing Class

The Drawing class is a subclass of Observable (so that it can act as the source of a dependency relationship). The instance variable, currentDraggedFigure, indicates a figure whose size is determined by the user dragging the cursor. It is not a particularly good way to implement this function, but it does keep things simple.

```
package swingdraw;

import java.util.*;
import java.awt.*;

public class Drawing extends Observable {
  private Vector contents = new Vector();
  private int defaultSize = 10;
  private Figure currentDraggedFigure = null;

  public void add (String comp, Point point1,
         Point point2, int size, String string)
         {Figure fig;
    if (currentDraggedFigure != null){
      contents.removeElement(currentDraggedFigure);
      currentDraggedFigure = null;
    }
    try {
      if (comp == Draw.SQUARE)
        fig = new Square(point2, size);
      else if (comp == Draw.CIRCLE)
        fig = new Circle(point2, size);
      else if (comp == Draw.LINE)
        fig = new Line(point1, point2);
      else if (comp == Draw.TEXT)
```

```
        fig = new TextFigure(point2, string);
      else
        throw new DrawingException("Unknown figure:
          " + comp);
      contents.addElement(fig);
    setChanged();
    notifyObservers();
  }
  catch (DrawingException e) {
    System.out.println("Unknown figure");
  }
}

public void move(Figure fig, Point point) {
  fig.setCoords(point.x, point.y);
  setChanged();
  notifyObservers();
}

public void addDraggedFigure (String comp,
      Point point, Point endPoint, int size) {
  if (currentDraggedFigure != null)
    contents.removeElement(currentDraggedFigure);
  currentDraggedFigure = null;
  add(comp, point, endPoint, size, null);
  currentDraggedFigure =
      (Figure) contents.lastElement();
}

public void remove (Object object) {
  contents.removeElement(object);
  setChanged();
  notifyObservers();
}

public Enumeration elements () {
  return contents.elements();
  }

public Figure findIfFigureAt(Point point) {
    Enumeration e = contents.elements();
  Figure fig;
  while (e.hasMoreElements()) {
    fig = (Figure)e.nextElement();
  if (fig.contains(point))
    return fig;
  }
```

```
    return null;
  }

  public void newDrawing () {
    contents = new Vector();
    setChanged();
    notifyObservers();
  }
}
```

24.5.6 The DrawingPanel Class

The DrawingPanel class is a subclass of the Panel class. It provides the view for the drawing data model. This uses the classical MVC architecture and has a drawing (data model), a drawingPanel (the view) and a drawing-Controller (the controller).

Note that it is a subclass of JComponent. This is because JPanel produced undesired behaviour in the 1.0.2 release of Swing in this application.

The DrawingPanel instantiates its own DrawingController to handle mouse events. This class could really be an inner class of the DrawingPanel; however, for clarity in this example it is left as a top-level class.

```
package swingdraw;

import java.awt.*;
import java.util.*;
import javax.swing.*;

public class DrawingPanel extends JComponent
  implements Observer {

  private Drawing drawing;

  DrawingPanel (JFrame frame, Drawing d) {
    drawing = d;
    drawing.addObserver(this);

    // Create the controller associated with this
    // DrawingPanel
    DrawingController controller = new
      DrawingController(frame, this, drawing);
    addMouseListener(controller);
    addMouseMotionListener(controller);
  }

  // Changes name from paint to paintComponent
```

```java
public void paintComponent(Graphics g) {
  Figure afig;
  Enumeration e = drawing.elements();
  while (e.hasMoreElements()) {
    afig = (Figure)e.nextElement();
    afig.paint(g);
  }
}

/**
 * Defines the dimensions of the drawing panel
 */
public Dimension getPreferredSize() {
  return new Dimension(400, 400);
}

/* Observer methods */

public void update(Observable object, Object arg) {
  repaint();
}
}
```

The getPreferredSize method returns a dimension which indicates the size that we would like the panel to be. This method is required so that the layout managers can determine the optimum layout for the interface.

24.5.7 The DrawingController Class

The DrawingController class provides the control class for the MVC architecture used with the drawing (model) and DrawingPanel (view) classes. In particular, it handles the mouse events in the DrawingPanel.

It implements the MouseListener and MouseMotion-Listener interfaces, which catch the mouse events. We also define a number of other mouse event methods (such as mouseEntered and mouseExited).

```java
package swingdrawing;

import java.awt.*;
import java.awt.event.*;
import javax.swing.JFrame;

public class DrawingController
    implements MouseListener, MouseMotionListener {
  Figure fig;
  Draw drawingFrame;
```

```
DrawingPanel drawingPanel;
Drawing drawing;
Point startPoint;
int xDiff = 0, yDiff = 0;
Cursor oldCursor;
DrawingController (Draw draw, DrawingPanel
  drawPanel,
        Drawing drawModel) {
  drawingFrame = draw;
  drawingPanel = drawPanel;
  drawing = drawModel;
}


/* Mouse listener methods */
public void mouseClicked(MouseEvent e) {}
public void mousePressed(MouseEvent e) {
  Figure figUnderCursor =
        drawing.findIfFigureAt(e.getPoint());
  if (figUnderCursor != null){
    fig = figUnderCursor;
    fig.select();
    startPoint = null;
    drawingPanel.repaint();
  }
  else
    startPoint = e.getPoint();
}


public void mouseReleased(MouseEvent e) {
  String s = "";
  if (startPoint != null) {
    if (drawingFrame.mode == Draw.TEXT) {
      TextDialog d =
        new TextDialog(drawingFrame, drawing);
      d.setVisible(true);
      s = d.getString();
    }
    Point currentPoint = e.getPoint();
    Point endPoint = getPoint(currentPoint);
    drawing.add(drawingFrame.mode,
      startPoint,
      endPoint,
      Math.max(xDiff, yDiff),
      s);
  }
  else {
    fig.deselect();
```

```java
      fig = null;
      drawingPanel.repaint();
  }
}

public void mouseEntered(MouseEvent e) {
  oldCursor = drawingPanel.getCursor();
  drawingPanel.setCursor(new
      Cursor(Cursor.CROSSHAIR_CURSOR));
}

public void mouseExited (MouseEvent e) {
  drawingPanel.setCursor(oldCursor);
}

/* Mouse Motion Listener methods */
public void mouseDragged(MouseEvent e) {
  if ((startPoint != null) &&
      (drawingFrame.mode != Draw.TEXT))
    drawing.addDraggedFigure(drawingFrame.mode,
      startPoint,
      getPoint(e.getPoint()),
      Math.max(xDiff, yDiff));
  else if (fig != null)
    drawing.move(fig, e.getPoint());
}

public void mouseMoved(MouseEvent e) {}
private Point getPoint (Point currentPoint) {
  if (drawingFrame.mode == Draw.LINE)
    return currentPoint;
  else if (startPoint.equals(currentPoint))
    return currentPoint;
  else {
    xDiff = Math.abs(startPoint.x - currentPoint.x);
    yDiff = Math.abs(startPoint.y - currentPoint.y);

    if ((xDiff < 10) && (yDiff < 10))
      return currentPoint;
    else {
      Point newPoint =
        new Point(Math.min(startPoint.x,
          currentPoint.x),
          Math.min(startPoint.y,
            currentPoint.y));
      return newPoint;
    }
```

```
      }
    }
  }
```

24.5.8 The LookAndFeelPanel Class

The LookAndFeelPanel class creates a panel which contains checkboxes to indicate the type of look and feel to be used by the SwingDraw application. At present, three look and feels are supported: "Motif", "Windows" and "Metal". The class creates the appropriate JCheckBox to be used to select different look and feels and places them within ButtonGroup. It then adds them to itself so that when it is displayed the buttons will appear. The createJCheckBox method is used to create each checkbox object. Note that the metal look is the default selection. The RadioButtonHandler class is used to respond to the itemStateChanged method, which is called when a different checkbox is selected.

```java
package swingdrawing;

import java.awt.*;
import java.awt.event.*;
import javax.swing.*;
import javax.swing.border.*;

public class LookAndFeelPanel extends JPanel {
  private static String Motif = "Motif";
  private static String Windows = "Windows";
  private static String Metal = "Metal";

  public LookAndFeelPanel(JFrame frame) {
    RadioButtonHandler rbh = new
RadioButtonHandler(frame);
    ButtonGroup buttonGroup = new ButtonGroup();
    JCheckBox motifButton = createRadioButton(rbh,
    Motif, "Selects the Motif look and feel",
    buttonGroup);
    JCheckBox windowsButton = createRadioButton(rbh,
    Windows, "Selects the Windows look and feel",
    buttonGroup);
    JCheckBox metalButton = createRadioButton(rbh,
    Metal, "Selects the Metal look and feel",
    buttonGroup);
    metalButton.setSelected(true);

    // Now configure the look of this panel and add
    // the buttons
    setAlignmentX(LEFT_ALIGNMENT);
```

```java
    setBorder(new BevelBorder(BevelBorder.RAISED));

    add(motifButton);
    add(windowsButton);
    add(metalButton);
  }
  private JCheckBox createRadioButton(ItemListener
      handler,
      String label,
      String tips,
      ButtonGroup group) {
    JCheckBox button = new JCheckBox(label);
    button.setActionCommand(label);
    button.setToolTipText(tips);
    button.addItemListener(handler);
    group.add(button);
    return button;
  }

  // Inner class to handler itemlistener events
  class RadioButtonHandler implements ItemListener {
    private String motif = "javax.swing.
      plaf.motif.MotifLookAndFeel";
    private String windows = "javax.swing.
      plaf.windows.WindowsLookAndFeel" ;
    private String metal = "javax.swing.plaf.
      metal.MetalLookAndFeel";
    private JFrame frame;
    public RadioButtonHandler (JFrame frame) {
      this.frame = frame;
    }
    public void itemStateChanged(ItemEvent event) {
      String lookAndFeel;
      String option = ((JCheckBox)event.getItem())
        .getActionCommand();
      if (option.equals(Motif)) {
        lookAndFeel = motif;
      } else if (option.equals(Windows)) {
        lookAndFeel = windows;
      } else {
        lookAndFeel = metal;
      }

      try {
        UIManager.setLookAndFeel(lookAndFeel);
        SwingUtilities.updateComponentTreeUI(frame);
        frame.pack();
```

```
      } catch (Exception exp) {
        System.err.println("Could not load
          LookAndFeel: " + lookAndFeel);
      }
    }
  }
}
```

24.5.9 The DrawingException Class

This is a very simple class which is a minimal extension of the Exception class. It explicitly catches the DrawingException if it is raised in the Drawing class.

```
package swingdraw;
public class DrawingException extends Exception {
  DrawingException (String message) {
    super(message);
  }
}
```

24.5.10 The Figure Class

The Figure class (an abstract superclass and a subclass of Component) captures all the elements which are common to graphic objects which are displayed within a drawing. The x and y instance variables define the cursor position when the mouse is clicked; the xsize and ysize instance variables define the size of the object.

```
package swingdraw;

import java.awt.*;

public abstract class Figure extends Component {
  int x, y, xsize, ysize;
  boolean selected = false;

  Figure () {
    this(1, 1);
  }

  Figure (Point point, int size) {
    this(point.x, point.y, size);
  }

  Figure (Point point, int aSize, int bSize) {
    this(point.x, point.y, aSize, bSize);
```

```
  }

  Figure (int a, int b) {
    this(a, b, 10);
  }

  Figure (int a, int b, int c) {
    x = a;
    y = b;
    xsize = c;
    ysize = c;
  }

  Figure (int a, int b, int c, int d) {
    x = a;
    y = b;
    xsize = c;
    ysize = d;
  }

  public void setCoords (int a, int b) {
    x = a;
    y = b;
  }

  public void setFigureSize(int x) {
    xsize = x;
    ysize = x;
  }

  public Point getStartPoint() {
    return new Point(x, y);
  }

  public boolean contains (int a, int b) {
    boolean result = false;
    if ((a >= x) && (a <= (x + xsize)))
      if ((b >= y) && (b <= (y + ysize)))
        result = true;
    return result;
  }

  public boolean contains (Point point) {
    return contains(point.x, point.y);
  }

  /** The subclasses of this class are expected to
```

```
    extend the method paint */
  public void paint(Graphics g) {
    displayFigure(g);
  }

  public void drawselectededBoxes (Graphics g) {
    g.fillRect(x - 2, y - 2, 4, 4);
    g.fillRect(x - 2, (y + ysize), 4, 4);
    g.fillRect((x + xsize), y - 2, 4, 4);
    g.fillRect((x + xsize), (y + ysize), 4, 4);
  }

  public void displayFigure (Graphics g) {
    if (selected){
      g.setColor(Color.red);
      drawselectededBoxes(g);
    }
    else
      g.setColor(Color.black);
  }

  public void selected () {
    selected = true;
  }

  public void deselected () {
    selected = false;
  }
}
```

The constructors provided by this class allow an instance of Figure to be generated in a number of different ways. The constructors which take fewer parameters are convenience constructors for those taking larger numbers of parameters. This focuses the functionality into one or two places.

24.5.11 The Square Class

This is a subclass of Figure that specifies how to draw a rectangle in a drawing. It extends the paint method inherited from Figure.

```
package swingdraw;

import java.awt.*;

class Square extends Figure {
  Square(Point p, int s) {
```

```java
    super(p, s);
  }
  public void paint (Graphics g) {
    super.paint(g);
    g.drawRect(x, y, xsize, ysize);
  }
}
```

24.5.12 The Circle Class

This is another subclass of Figure. It extends the paint method by drawing a circle:

```java
package swingdraw;

import java.awt.*;

class Circle extends Figure {
  Circle (Point p, int aSize) {
    super(p, aSize);
  }
  public void paint (Graphics g) {
    super.paint(g);
    g.drawOval(x, y, xsize, ysize);
  }
}
```

24.5.13 The Line Class

This is another subclass of Figure. It is more complex, as the way in which a line is selected and moved differs from that inherited from Figure.

```java
package swingdraw;

import java.awt.*;

class Line extends Figure {
  int x1, y1, x2, y2;
  Line(Point p1, Point p2) {
    x1 = p1.x;
    y1 = p1.y;
    x2 = p2.x;
    y2 = p2.y;
  }
```

```java
public void paint (Graphics g) {
  super.paint(g);
  g.drawLine(x1, y1, x2, y2);
}

public void drawSelectedBoxes(Graphics g) {
  g.fillRect(x1 - 2, y1 - 2, 4, 4);
  g.fillRect(x2 - 2, y2 - 2, 4, 4);
}

public void setEndPoint(int a, int b) {
  x2 = a;
  y2 = b;
}

public void setEndPoint(Point point) {
  setEndPoint(point.x, point.y);
}

public void setStartPoint(int a, int b) {
  x1 = a;
  y1 = b;
}

public void setStartPoint(Point point) {
  setStartPoint(point.x, point.y);
}

public void setCoords(int a, int b) {
  if ((a > (x1 - 10)) && (a < (x1 + 10)))
    if ((b > (y1 - 10)) && (b < (y1 + 10)))
      setStartPoint(a, b);
  if ((a > (x2 - 10)) && (a < (x2 + 10)))
    if ((b > (y2 - 10)) && (b < (y2 + 10)))
      setEndPoint (a, b);
}

public Point getStartPoint() {
  return new Point(x1, y1);
}

public Point getEndPoint() {
  return new Point(x2, y2);
}

public boolean contains (int a, int b) {
  if ((a > (x1 - 10)) && (a < (x1 + 10)))
```

```
      if ((b > (y1 - 10)) && (b < (y1 + 10)))
         return true;
    if ((a > (x2 - 10)) && (a < (x2 + 10)))
      if ((b > (y2 - 10)) && (b < (y2 + 10)))
         return true;
    return false;
  }
}
```

24.5.14 The TextFigure Class

This is also a subclass of Figure. It redefines some of the inherited behaviour. In particular, it redefines the contains method and the drawSelectedBoxes method:

```
package swingdraw;

import java.awt.*;

class TextFigure extends Figure {
  private String string = "";

  TextFigure(Point p, String s) {
    super(p, (s.length() * 6), 10);
    string = s;
  }

  public void paint (Graphics g) {
    super.paint(g);
    g.drawString(string, x, y);
  }

  public boolean contains (int a, int b) {
    boolean result = false;
    if ((a >= x) && (a <= (x + xsize)))
      if ((b >= (y - ysize)) && (b <= y))
        result = true;
    return result;
  }

  public void drawSelectedBoxes (Graphics g) {
    g.fillRect(x - 2, y - 2, 4, 4);
    g.fillRect(x - 2, (y - ysize), 4, 4);
    g.fillRect((x + xsize), y - 2, 4, 4);
    g.fillRect((x + xsize), (y - ysize), 4, 4);
  }
}
```

24.5.15 The `TextDialog` Class

When users wish to add a new TextFigure to the drawing, they are prompted for the text by a dialog box. This dialog box is implemented by the TextDialog class (a direct subclass of JDialog). It is a simple window which uses only a label and a text field. Notice how it passes information back to the application using the getString() method.

```java
package swingdraw;

import java.awt.*;
import javax.swing.*;

class TextDialog extends JDialog implements
ActionListener {

  JTextField textField;
  Drawing drawing;
  TextDialog (JFrame parent, Drawing d,
    String label) {
      super(parent, "Text Dialog", true);
      drawing = d;

      Container pane = getContentPane();

      pane.add("North", new JLabel(label));

      textField = new JTextField(12);
      pane.add("Center", textField);
      textField.addActionListener(this);

    pack();
  }

  public void actionPerformed (ActionEvent e) {
    dispose();
  }

  public String getString () {
    return textField.getText();
  }
}
```

The getString method obtains the string from the dialog using the getText method of the textField.

24.6 Exercises

You could develop the SwingDraw application further by adding the following features:

- *A delete option* You can add a button labelled Delete to the window. It should set the mode to "delete". The drawingPanel must be altered so that the mouseReleased method sends a delete message to the drawing. The drawing must find and remove the appropriate graphic object and send the changed message to itself.

- *Save and load options* This involves saving the elements in the contents field of the drawing object in such a way that they can be restored at a later date. You can use serialization (see Chapter 29).

- *A resize option* This involves identifying which of the boxes surrounding the selected object is being dragged and altering the sizes appropriately.

24.7 Summary

This chapter introduced a larger application which includes mouse events and scrollable panes, as well as mixing Java's graphics facilities with its user interface facilities and Swing. Remember that you can download the source code for this application from the Springer Web site (see p. xxv).

24.8 Reference

Rumbaugh, J. *et al.* (1991). *Object-oriented modeling and design.* Prentice Hall, Englewood Cliffs, NJ.

25 *Applets and the Internet*

25.1 Introduction

Java burst onto the computer scene back in 1995. At that time, it looked unlikely that any new programming language could become as influential as Java has within just a few years. However, Java had an ace up its sleeve. This ace was not that it was a pure object-oriented language, nor that it compiled to an intermediate form which could run, without recompilation, on different platforms. Rather, it was that it could be used with the rapidly growing Internet to produce programs which could run within a Web browser (such as Netscape Navigator or Internet Explorer). The first Web browser to show this was HotJava, which was also written in Java. The fact that it could run programs within Web pages caught people's imagination, and the rest, as they say, is history.

A Java applet is a program which can run within a Web browser (or the JDK appletviewer) as illustrated in Figure 25.1. That is all that it is. That "all" hides a lot, as

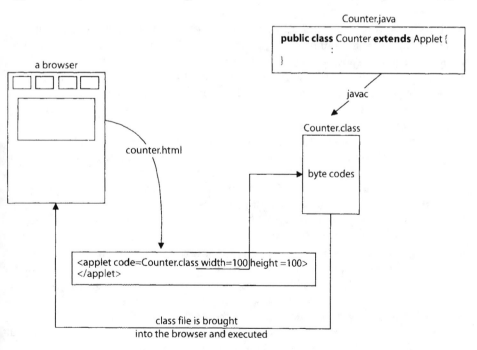

Figure 25.1 Loading an applet into a browser.

299

anyone who has attempted to build Web systems in C, CGI scripts, TCP/IP etc. can tell you. From the point of view of constructing applications, Java applets hide issues such as communications protocols and hardware platforms from you. You are concerned only with constructing useful, reliable, maintainable applications (which just happen to run within a Web browser).

The name "applet" originally signified a small program which should be run within a larger program (such as a Web browser), much in the way that a piglet indicates a small pig. However, there is no reason why an applet should be particularly small, just as there is no reason why an application should be particularly large. Indeed, numerous applets are now being implemented which are large applications in their own right. They are merely applets because their users access them via a Web browser (either locally or remotely).

The primary class which makes applets possible is the `Applet` class, defined in `java.Applet`, which is a subclass of `Panel`. This in itself tells you something about the way in which an applet operates (but we shall come back to that later).

The `Applet` class must be the superclass of any class which acts as the root for an application which is to be accessed by a Web browser or the JDK appletviewer. This is because it provides a standard interface between the application and its operating environment which allows the parent application to provide information to, and obtain information from, the applet (and vice versa).

25.2 Applet Security

Applets differ from applications in another important respect. Applets have far less access to the host environment than applications. This is to provide some degree of protection against rogue applets (you may be welcoming programs written by someone else onto your machine – you don't want them tampering with your environment).

There were a number of security scares over applets and Web browsers during 1996–1998; however these tended to be due to limitations in the Web browsers' implementations of the Java security model. The security model is quite straight-forward: *by default, applets are not allowed to do anything which may harm your host environment*. This means that applets cannot access your local file store, run local programs, access information about the host machine or communicate with other machines (other than the server from which they were downloaded). Note that in Java 2 the security model has undergone major enhancements.

In some cases, applets have slightly more access. If an applet is loaded into a browser using the load local file option, rather than over the Internet, it can connect to other hosts, load Java libraries and find out information about the user.

The JDK appletviewer can also execute applets. The appletviewer mimics the behaviour of a Web browser when running an applet. However, it allows significantly greater permission to the applets. In fact, the only difference between an application and an applet running in the appletviewer is that the applet cannot delete a file (see Table 25.1).

Applets may be signed, which means that the supplier of the applet is registered along with the applet. If you trust the supplier, you can give the applet greater freedom. Signed applets were introduced in JDK 1.1, but they will prove invaluable to organizations wishing to make use of Java for distributed solutions to applications as diverse as

Table 25.1 Applet and application permissions for JDK 1.1

Operation	Remote	Local	Appletviewer	Application
Read local file	No	No	Yes	Yes
Write local file	No	No	Yes	Yes
Obtain file information	No	No	Yes	Yes
Delete file	No	No	No	Yes
Run local executable	No	No	Yes	Yes
Load Java library	No	Yes	Yes	Yes
Call exit	No	No	Yes	Yes
Connect to other host	No	Yes	Yes	Yes

MIS and Computer-Aided Engineering (within an organizational intranet). Java 2 has further enhanced the applet security mechanism with security policies that can be applied to classes, packages or whole systems (applets and applications).

25.3 The `Applet` Class

Figure 25.2 illustrates the inheritance hierarchy from `Object`. Applets can contain graphic components and containers, redraw themselves, and operate inside a containing object.

Figure 25.2 The `Applet` inheritance hierarchy.

The fact that applets are a subclass of `Panel` provides the key to the way in which they are used[1]. In essence, the encapsulating application (e.g. Netscape) acts as the frame within which the applet displays. If you think of the Web browser as providing the subclass of `Frame` within which your applet displays, you begin to understand how they operate. A consequence of this is that applets do not need to define a `main` method (indeed if they do it is ignored when running under a Web browser). Instead, a series of messages are sent by the encapsulating application to the applet (the browser–applet protocol illustrated in Figure 25.3). These messages trigger various methods, the most important of which is the `init` method. Others include the `start`, `stop` and `destroy` methods (the sequence of messages between the browser and the applet is illustrated in Figure 25.3).

- `void init()`
  The browser sends the `init` message to the applet once it has constructed the applet and completed the background work. The `init` method should carry out

---

1 Java 2 has introduced a new Swing-compatible applet called `JApplet`. Like a `JFrame`, it has a content pane to which you should add components; otherwise it is just like an applet.

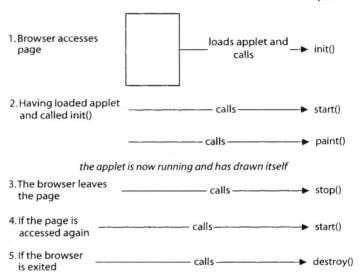

Figure 25.3 The browser–applet protocol.

all initialization because an applet cannot link to other objects or generate graphic displays until it has been created, for security reasons (and thus does not possess a constructor).

● void start()
After sending the init message to the applet, the browser then sends it the start message. The start message is sent every time the user returns to the Web page containing the applet. Thus the start method may execute more than once. You should, therefore, place code which should only be run once in the init method, and code which should be run every time the applet is started in the start method.

● void stop()
The stop message is automatically sent to the applet whenever the user leaves the Web page containing the applet. Leaving a Web page does not terminate the applet; it merely suspends it. Anything which must be tidied up before the applet is suspended should be placed in the stop method.

● void destroy()
The destroy message is sent to an applet when the browser terminates normally. You do not need to close the window (panel) in which the applet is running as the browser does that. However, you can use the destroy method to tidy up any system resources your applet uses. If the applet is running when the user quits the browser, the stop method executes before the destroy method.

25.4 Working with Applets

The actual process of constructing a system to be run as an applet is not complex. I use the term "program" to refer to the Java code in order to avoid confusion between applets and applications.

1. The root class of the program must inherit from the Applet class.

2. It must then define the init method, which should define all elements of the program which need to be initialized once. This is the code which would have been placed in a constructor within a normal application.

3. You may need to select a layout manager. As Applet is a subclass of Panel, it uses the flow layout manager. If you wish to use a different layout (such as BorderLayout), you must set it. You can do this in the init method.

4. You may define the start, stop and destroy methods.

5. You must define a Web page to hold the applet using HTML (see Figure 25.1).

Once you have done these things you have done enough to run the applet. Of course, you still need to define what the applet does, but those definitions are the same as for any Java program. As Applet is a subclass of Panel, all the graphic and GUI classes and methods which you can use with a Panel are also available within an Applet.

25.5 The Account Applet

You can develop an applet as an application first and then port it to an applet later. This can make the debugging and testing of the applet easier. It is certainly a useful way to illustrate the differences between a standalone application and an applet. Therefore we amend the Account application presented in earlier in this book to make it an applet, following these steps:

1. Make the root class inherit from Applet rather than Frame.

2. Remove the WindowListener interface and method definitions (applets cannot close themselves, so there is no reason to handle window-closing events).

3. Delete the main method.

4. Define an init method and move the contents of the constructor into it.

5. Set the layout manager to the border layout manager.

6. Delete the constructor.

7. Remove window resizing, visibility and title methods. An applet does not define its window title or its size. These operations are performed by the Web browser using parameters passed to it by the HTML on the initiating Web page.

8. Define an HTML file for the applet.

25.5.1 Change the Root Class Definition

We must change the parent class and remove the WindowListener.

```
import java.applet.*;
import java.awt.*;
import java.util.Observable;
import java.util.Observer;
public class AccountApplet extends Applet
            implements Observer {
```

```
    protected TextPanel textPanel;
    protected Account account = new Account(0.0);
    ...remainder of class definition...
}
```

Compare this class definition with that presented in Chapter 23, and notice that we have also deleted the links to the Exit button and the Exit button controller. They have no meaning for the applet. We have also changed the name of the root class from AccountInterface to AccountApplet, just to avoid confusion. Finally, in order to inherit from the Applet class, we have imported the java.applet package.

25.5.2 Define the init Method

We must move the contents of the constructor into this method. We have removed the references to the Exit button and its controller. We have also removed the setTitle, addWindowListener(this), setSize(180, 140) and setVisible(true) calls. Thus the init method is quite a bit smaller than the original constructor:

```
public void init () {

    /* Add the interface as an observer of the account */
    account.addObserver(this);

    /* Specify layout manager as flow is the default */
    setLayout( new BorderLayout());

    /* Create the Button panel object and
       its controller */
    ButtonPanel buttonPanel = new ButtonPanel(this);
    add("North", buttonPanel);

    /* Next set up the text panel */
    textPanel = new TextPanel();
    add("Center", textPanel);
}
```

In the above method, we have set the layout manager as suggested earlier. We can delete the empty constructor and the methods implementing the Window-Listener interface (such as WindowClosed and windowClosing). We have now done enough to run this program as an applet. You must execute the appletviewer on the HTML file:

```
C: >appletviewer account.HTML
```

Figure 25.4 shows the result in the JDK appletviewer.

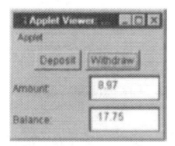

Figure 25.4 Running the Account applet.

25.6 A Brief Introduction to HTML

One area which was ignored above is the definition of a Web page within which to run the applet. You do this using the Hypertext Markup Language (HTML) which tells a Web browser how to lay out a Web page. The basics of the language are quite straightforward, although the language as a whole is quite large. Essentially, an HTML page is made up of the following parts:

● A title, indicated by `<title>` some text `</title>`.
● A body, indicated by `<body>` some text `</body>`.

Notice that the keywords used in HTML have a starting element and an ending element. Thus whatever is being laid out is surrounded by two keywords (or tags). Some tags merely indicate a particular feature, for example:

● `<p>` tells the browser to start a new paragraph.
● `<hr>` tells the browser to insert a horizontal line.

A complete description of HTML is beyond the scope of this book. However, there are many books on HTML available and you should read one of them for further information.

25.7 The `<APPLET>` HTML Tag

The `<APPLET>` tag is an extension to the original HTML. However, almost all browsers available today support it. Browsers created before the advent of Java are programmed to ignore tags they do not understand.

The `<APPLET>` tag allows you to specify which class to run, the size and position of the applet, the data to pass into the applet, and some text to display if the browser does not understand the tag. The `<APPLET>` tag has the following basic format:

```
<APPLET CODE=classfile WIDTH=pixels HEIGHT=pixels
   ...optional applet information>
</APPLET>
```

Table 25.2 Mandatory applet tag fields

Field	Description
code	Specifies the name of the file containing the root applet class, which should be in the same directory as the HTML file. As an alternative, you can specify an object field.
object	Specifies the name of the file that contains a serialized representation of an applet. The applet is deserialized. The init method is not invoked, but the start method is. This is because before the applet could be serialized it must have been initialized, started and then stopped. As an alternative, you can specify a code field.
width	Specifies the width, in pixels, of the applet.

Certain fields must appear within the <APPLET> tag Table 25.2). The field names can be in upper or lower case; thus WIDTH is equivalent to width.

We now know enough to look at the HTML file that defines the Web page containing the account applet (in a file called Account.HTML):

```
<HTML>
<TITLE>Account Applet</TITLE>
<BODY>
<APPLET CODE="AccountApplet.class"
    WIDTH=180 HEIGHT=100>
</APPLET>
</BODY>
</HTML>
```

This specifies that the Web browser (or appletviewer) should run the applet defined in the AccountApplet.class file. Notice that we specify the byte-encoded compiled version, rather than the .java file. This means that any language which can be compiled into Java byte codes can be accessed in this way. The applet is displayed in a window 180 pixels wide by 100 pixels high.

The HTML <applet> tag provides a range of optional fields, which provide additional information for the applet or the Web browser. In the following full syntax description, required elements are in bold, optional elements are in regular typeface, and elements you specify are in italic:

```
<APPLET
    CODEBASE = codebaseURL
    ARCHIVE = archiveList
    CODE = appletFile    or OBJECT = serializedApplet
    ALT = alternateText
    NAME = appletInstanceName
    WIDTH = pixels HEIGHT = pixels
    ALIGN = alignment
    VSPACE = pixels HSPACE = pixels
>
<PARAM NAME = appletAttribute1 VALUE = value>
<PARAM NAME = appletAttribute2 VALUE = value>
```

Table 25.3 Optional applet tag fields

Field	Description
CODEBASE	Specifies the base URL, i.e. the directory that contains the applet's code. If it is not specified, then the document's URL is used.
ARCHIVE	Describes one or more archives, containing classes and other resources, that are "preloaded".
ALT	Specifies any text that should be displayed if the browser understands the applet tag but cannot run Java applets.
NAME	Specifies a name for the applet instance, which makes it possible for applets on the same page to find (and communicate with) each other.
ALIGN	Specifies the alignment of the applet (left, right, top, middle, baseline and bottom).
VSPACE	Specifies the number of pixels above and below the applet.
HSPACE	Specifies the number of pixels on each side of the applet.
<PARAM NAME ...>	Specifies an applet-specific attribute.
alternateHTML	Specifies text which is used instead of the applet, if the Web browser does not understand the applet tag. This text can use other HTML tags.

```
   . . .
   alternateHTML
   </APPLET>
```

These fields are described in Table 25.3.

Applets access their attributes with the getParameter method. Parameters always return their values as strings. For example, if the HTML file includes the following tag:

```
<PARAM NAME=pictureSize VALUE="100">
```

The applet can access this information in the following manner:

```
int size =
Integer.parseInt(getParameter("pictureSize"));
```

We have to use the class-side parseInt method to convert the string "100" to the integer 100. If the parameter name, pictureSize, had been omitted, the value null would have been returned. Also note that parameter names are case-sensitive; you must use exactly the same case to get the value.

25.8 Accessing HTML Files

Although it is outside the scope of this book, and many of you are already familiar with Web browsers, this section introduces the concept of a Uniform Resource Locator (URL). A URL consists of the address of a file on the Internet and a scheme for interpreting that file. The particular scheme of interest for HTML files is the Hypertext Transfer Protocol (HTTP). For example, to access the HTML file described above, you provide the following URL as the address:

Table 25.4 The structure of a URL

Section	Example
Scheme	`http:`
Separator	`//`
Computer name	`www`
Domain name	`aber.ac.uk`
Path to the file	`~jjh/JavaBook/chap23/Account.HTML`

`http://www.aber.ac.uk/~jjh/JavaBook/chap25/Account.HTML`

Table 25.4 shows how a URL is constructed.

You can access HTML files locally, by replacing the `http:` scheme with the `file:` scheme and omitting the Internet address. For example, if the file is on the C drive of your PC you may access it by specifying the following URL:

`file:///c:/users/jjh/JavaBook/chap25/Account.HTML`

25.9 Network Programming

The `java.net` package provides a number of classes which can be used for network programming (Table 25.5).

Table 25.5 Network programming classes

Class	Description
`DatagramPacket`	Implements a connectionless packet delivery service. Each message is routed from one machine to another based solely on information contained within that packet. Multiple packets sent from one machine to another may be routed differently, and may arrive in any order.
`DatagramSocket`	Represents a socket for sending and receiving datagram packets.
`HttpURLConnection`	Supports HTTP-specific features.
`InetAddress`	Represents an Internet Protocol (IP) address.
`MulticastSocket`	Represents a (UDP) `DatagramSocket`, with additional capabilities for joining "groups" of other multicast hosts on the Internet.
`ServerSocket`	Waits for a request to come in over the network, performs some operation based on it, and then possibly returns a result to the requester.
`Socket`	Represents an end point for communication between two machines.

We focus on the URL class to illustrate how one of the networking classes can be used (see Chapter 30 of this book, about sockets, for more information). The URL class allows a URL instance to act as a reference for a resource available either locally or via the Web. You create the instance using one of the URL class constructors:

- URL(String) creates a URL object from the String representation.
- URL(String protocol, String host, int port, String file) creates a URL object from the specified protocol, host, port number and file.
- URL(String protocol, String host, String file) creates an absolute URL from the specified protocol name, host name and file name.
- URL(URL context, String spec) creates a URL by parsing the specification within the context.

If an error occurs when constructing the URL object, the constructors throw the MalformedURLException. You must, therefore, catch this exception when working with the URL class.

```
import java.net.*;

...class definition

public void example () {
   try {
     URL url = new URL("http://www.aber.ac.uk/~jjh/
       Acc");
     ...further Java
   }
   catch (MalformedURLException e) {
     System.out.println("Ooops");
   }
...remainder of method and class
```

Once you have obtained a URL, there are a number of methods available for accessing the information (Table 25.6).

Table 25.6 URL methods

Method	Description
equals(Object)	Compares two URLs.
getContent()	Returns an object possessing the contents of the receiver URL.
getFile()	Returns the string file name of the receiver URL.
getHost()	Returns the string host name of the receiver URL, if applicable.
getPort()	Returns the integer port number of the receiver URL.
getProtocol()	Returns the string protocol name of the receiver URL.
openStream()	Opens a stream connection to the receiver URL and returns an InputStream for reading from that connection.
sameFile(URL)	Compares two URLs and returns true if they match.

25.10 Summary

This chapter has illustrated how applets can be defined within Java. It has also shown how they can be accessed via a Web browser or the appletviewer. It also considered how Java applets can access resources on the Internet via URLs.

Applets open up a huge potential for applications which would have been too difficult to contemplate only a short time ago (except by the dedicated and knowledgeable few).

25.11 Further Reading

You may wish to delve further into HTML and TCP/IP as well as Java applets. There are many books on HTML available, including Scharf (1995).

TCP/IP stands for Transmission Control Protocol/Internet Protocol. TCP uses IP as its underlying protocol for routing and delivering information to the correct address. TCP takes care of creating, managing and closing the end-to-end connection which exists during the transfer of information. FTP (File Transfer Protocol) uses TCP, which in turn supports HTTP. A good book to start with on TCP/IP is Parker (1994).

There is a wide range of books which consider applets in great detail. Indeed, the majority of books on Java concentrate on applets. However, Cornell and Horstmann (1997) provide some excellent examples without becoming applet-obsessed.

Cornell, G. and Horstmann, C.S. (1997). *Core JAVA*, 2nd edn. Prentice Hall, Englewood Cliffs, NJ.
Parker, T. (1994). *Teach yourself TCP/IP in 14 Days*. Sams Publishing, Indianapolis.
Scharf, D. (1995). *HTML Visual Quick Reference*. Que Corporation.

25.12 Exercise: Tic-Tac-Toe Applet

The aim of this exercise is to write a very simple Tic-Tac-Toe (or Noughts and Crosses) applet.

25.12.1 What You Should Do

The applet should place a X or a O in a square depending on which turn should be made. To keep things simple it is assumed that this is a two-player game in which the applet merely displays the result of each move. It is up to the players to identify a win situation. (Note that if you use the JButton class from the Swing components you could use icons for the Xs and Os, but you need to use the JApplet class and its content pane). An example of what the display should look like is presented in Figure 25.5.

The HTML used to run the applet is:

```
<applet code=TicTacToe.class width=160 height=120>
</applet>
```

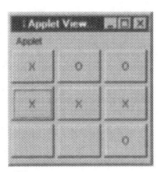

Figure 25.5 The Tic-Tac-Toe applet.

You should not try to do anything complicated.

You need to respond to a mouse click and then to place a X or O in the appropriate location. You could so this using a MouseListener and the paint() method. However, the above example actually makes use of the Button class and the GridLayout manager to do the work.

25.12.2 Notes

If you use the approach I used then the following may be useful for you to know:

1. Use an ActionListener.
2. You can change the label on a button using the setLabel(<string>) method.
3. The GridLayout manager has a constructor which takes four arguments: the first two are the size of the grid and the second two are the horizontal and vertical gaps.

26 *Concurrency*

26.1 Introduction

This chapter presents, and explains a short example, of how concurrency can be accomplished within Java.

26.2 Concurrent Processes

The concepts behind object-oriented programming lend themselves particularly well to the concepts associated with concurrency. For example, a system can be described as a set of discrete objects communicating with one another when necessary. In most Java implementations, only one object may execute at any one moment. However, conceptually at least, there is no reason why this restriction should be enforced. The basic concepts behind object orientation still hold, even if each object executes within a separate independent process.

Traditionally, a message send is treated like a procedural call, in which the calling object's execution is blocked until a response is returned. However, we can extend this model quite simply to view each object as a concurrently executable program module, with activity starting when the object is created and continuing even when a message is sent to another object (unless the response is required for further processing). In this model, there may be very many (concurrent) objects executing at the same time. Of course, this introduces issues associated with resource allocation etc., but no more so than in any concurrent system.

One implication of the concurrent object model is that objects are larger than in the traditional single execution thread approach, because of the overhead of having each object as a process. A process scheduler for handling these processes and resource allocation mechanisms mean that it is not feasible to have integers, characters etc. as separate processes.

Java has limited built-in support for concurrency. It does support processes and synchronization of methods; however, the processor scheduler (part of the Java Virtual Machine (JVM)) implements a naïve non-preemptive scheduling policy, with limited support for rescheduling within a particular priority level. Further, once a high-priority process is running, no lower priority process runs until the high-priority process suspends or terminates. For these reasons, the basic Java system contains only a few processes, and typical applications using concurrency do not create more than a few tens of processes.

26.3 Threads

A Java process is a preemptive lightweight process termed a *thread*. Every thread (process) has an associated priority, and a Java thread runs to completion unless a higher priority process attempts to gain control. Java does not share the processor time among processes of the same priority. Threads with a higher priority are executed before threads with a lower priority. A thread with a higher priority may interrupt a thread with a lower priority. By default, a process inherits the same priority as the process which spawned it. You can change the priority of a process by using the setPriority message.

A thread is a "lightweight" process because it does not possess its own address space and it is not treated as a separate entity by the host operating system. Instead, it exists within a single machine process using the same address space.

It is useful to get a clear idea of the difference between a thread (running within a single machine process) and a multi-process system.

26.3.1 Thread States

The thread which is currently executing is termed the active thread. A thread can also be suspended (i.e. waiting to use the processor) or stopped (waiting for some resource). Figure 26.1 illustrates the thread states and the messages which cause the state to change.

Notice that a thread is considered to be alive unless it has been stopped (when it can be considered dead). A live thread can be running, suspended, sleeping, interrupted, waiting etc. The runnable state indicates that the thread can be executed by the processor, but it is not currently executing. This is because an equal or higher priority process is already executing and the thread must wait until the processor becomes free. Note that suspend and resume are deprecated in Java 2.

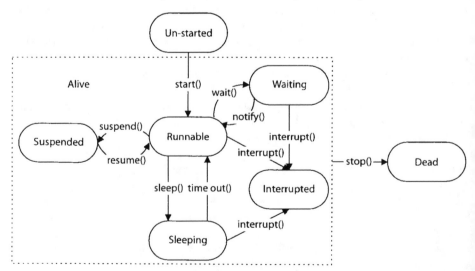

Figure 26.1 Thread states.

26.3.2 Creating a Thread

There are two ways in which to initiate a new thread of execution (this chapter considers only the first way):

- Create a subclass of the Thread class and redefine the run method to perform the set of actions that the thread is intended to do. For example:

```
public class Scroller extends Thread {
  public void run () {
    while (true) {
      ...scroll a message...
    }
  }
}
...
Thread t = new Scroller();
```

- Define a new class that implements the Runnable interface. It must define the run method and can be started by passing an instance of the class to a new Thread instance. For example:

```
public class Scroller implements Runnable {
  public void run () {
    while (true) {
      ...scroll a message...
    }
  }
}
...
Thread t = new Thread(new Scroller());
```

In both cases, we define a class which specifies the operations or actions that the new thread (of execution) performs. Thus, a thread is an independent object running on the processor (in this case, the JVM). As a thread is an object, it can be treated just like any other object: it can be sent messages, it can have instance variables and it can provide methods. Thus, the multi-threaded aspects of Java all conform to the object-oriented model. This greatly simplifies the creation of multi-threaded systems as well as the maintainability and clarity of the resulting software.

Once a new instance of a thread is created, it must be started. Before it is started, it cannot run, although it exists (see Figure 26.1).

26.3.3 Thread Groups

You can group threads into a ThreadGroup. Indeed, by default, every thread is part of the group of the thread which created it. The thread group defines a set of threads which can be treated as a whole. For example, they can all be suspended, resumed or stopped. A thread group can be made up of other thread groups (referred to as sub-thread groups) as well as individual threads. The primary use of thread groups is as a way to enforce security policies by dynamically restricting thread operation access to members of the same group.

26.4 The Thread Class

The Thread class defines all the facilities required to create a class which can execute within its own lightweight process (within the JVM) (Tables 26.1 and 26.2).

Table 26.1 Thread class variables

MIN_PRIORITY	An integer which defines the minimum priority of a thread.
NORM_PRIORITY	An integer which defines the default priority of a thread (5 in JDK 1.1 and below).
MAX_PRIORITY	An integer which defines the maximum priority of a thread (10 in JDK 1.1 and below).

Table 26.2 Methods that change the state of a thread (see Figure 26.1)

start()	Schedules the thread (makes it runnable).
resume()	Reschedules a thread which has been suspended.
suspend()	Unschedules the thread temporarily. It must wait until it receives a resume(0) message before it can claim the processor.
stop()	Unschedules the thread permanently. That is, it changes the process state to "dead".
sleep(long milliseconds)	Suspends the thread for the specified number of milliseconds.
yield()	Forces the thread to relinquish the processor momentarily, thus allowing other threads to execute.

There are a number of methods that obtain information about the status of the process:

● isAlive() tests to see whether the thread has started execution and has not yet terminated.

● isInterrupted() tests to see whether the thread has been interrupted.

The run method specifies what the thread does. This method must be overwritten in any subclasses of Thread (the method defined in Thread does nothing unless it has a class implementing the Runnable interface available to it). The specification of the run method is:

```
public void run() {...}
```

There are messages associated with a thread's priority, including:

● setPriority(int priority), which sets the priority of the thread.

- getPriority(), which returns the priority of the thread.

Every thread has a unique name. If you do not provide one, then a name is automatically generated by the system. There are two methods that access and set a thread's name:

- getName() obtains the name of the thread.
- setName(String string) sets the name of the thread to the string parameter.

26.4.1 Implementing a Thread

To create a class which can be executed as a separate thread, you must define either a new subclass of Thread or a class which implements the Runnable interface.

To create a subclass of Thread, you must follow these steps:

1. Define a new subclass of Thread.
2. Define the run method.

```
class SampleThread extends Thread {
  String string;
  public SampleThread (String aString) {
    string = aString;
  }
  public void run () {
    while (isAlive()) {
      System.out.print(string);
    }
  }
}
```

3. Create an instance of the class.
4. Send the start message to the thread instance. This schedules the new thread and causes the run method to execute.

```
SampleThread thread = new
SampleThread ("SampleThread");
thread.start();
```

To implement the Runnable interface, you must follow these steps:

1. Define a class which implements the Runnable interface.
2. Define the run method in this class.
3. Create an instance of this class.
4. Create an instance of the Thread class using the Thread(Runnable target) constructor.
5. Send the message start to the thread instance (not the instance which implements the Runnable interface). This schedules the new thread, which in turn initiates the run method on the Runnable object.

26.4.2 Synchronization

Semaphores provide a simple means of synchronization between multiple threads. If two processes are executing and one must not pass a certain point until the other has completed some operation, then a semaphore between the two threads can indicate to the first process that the operation has been completed.

The `Thread` class provides facilities for simple synchronization on methods within the same class. The `synchronized` keyword specifies that the associated methods cannot run at the same time as other synchronized methods defined by the class. Each instance has a single semaphore. If one method is executing, others must wait for it to finish.

You can use the `synchronized` keyword in two ways. The first version allows control over exactly which parts of a method are protected by the synchronized keyword:

```
public void nextSlice() {
  synchronized (this) {
    . . .
  }
}
```

The second approach is simpler (but it synchronizes the whole method). If the whole method is synchronized, the javadoc tool includes this fact in the resultant documentation files.

```
public synchronized void nextSlice() {
  . . .
}
```

The advantage of the synchronized flag approach is simplicity and efficiency. The disadvantage is that it does not directly support more complex synchronization.

In some situations, you want one thread to wait for another thread to complete before it continues past a certain point. You can specify this using the join method. This method waits for the receiving thread to die before allowing the sending thread to continue:

```
. . .
anotherThread.join();
...code executes after another thread terminates
```

Other versions of `join` specify a certain amount of time to wait before continuing, for example `join(long milliseconds)`. If the receiving thread has not terminated after the time specified in milliseconds, the sending thread resumes.

26.5 A Time-Slicing Example

This example shows how to achieve time slicing using Java. The basic idea behind the effective control of multiple processes within Java is the introduction of a high-priority process. This process wakes up every few milliseconds and regroups the processes in a waiting queue of lower processes. It then goes back to "sleep". It thus slices time between the various processes at the lower priority.

26.5.1 Using Schedulers

If it is necessary to develop a preemptive scheduler (that is, one that shares processor time between a given number of processes), then you can do it by using the facilities provided by the standard scheduler. This results in two schedulers: the system scheduler and a user-defined scheduler.

The system scheduler still enables a process to execute. For example, it is still this scheduler which suspends or interrupts a process. The user-defined scheduler manages the queue of user processes waiting to be handed to the system scheduler whenever it "wakes up". Of course, in order to gain control of the processor, the user-defined scheduler must have a higher priority than all other user processes. It can then interrupt the user processes and select which process to initiate.

The key to the user-defined scheduler is that it "wakes up" every few milliseconds. You can use the `sleep(milliseconds)` message to suspend the scheduler process until the associated timer sends the process a resume message. The resume message causes it to take control of the processor again.

When the process is awake, it can determine which of the processes currently waiting to use the processor to resume. One way to do this is with an index indicating the currently executing process. This index can be incremented to indicate the next process to resume; this ensures that a different process is resumed every time the scheduler process "goes back to sleep".

26.5.2 The Time-Slicing Source Code

This example is based on a new subclass of `Thread` called `TimeSlice`. It is a high-priority thread which cycles between a sleep state and a running state. When it runs, it selects a new process for execution using the `nextSlice` method. You can achieve this sleeping and slicing cycle by spawning a new process (with the highest allowable priority).

The `TimeSlice` class sets up the processes to be sliced in `initialize-TimeSlicing()` and initiates the time-slicing operation within the `run` method. The sleep message can throw an instance of the `InterruptedException` class. You must therefore handle this exception (for example, within a `try-catch` block, as discussed in the previous chapter).

The `initializeTimeSlicing` method sets the priority of the `TimeSlice` thread to the highest priority available. It creates three new processes, and gives each of them the normal priority. It then starts and suspends each of these processes. Notice that the instances are held in an instance variable, `threads`. Having set up the threads, the `start` message is sent to the object, which schedules the `TimeSlice` thread object and sends it the message `run`.

```
import java.util.*;

public class TimeSlice extends Thread {
```

```java
  private Vector threads = new Vector(3);
  private SampleThread currentThread;
  private int index = 0;

  public static void main (String args []) {
    TimeSlice timeSlicer = new TimeSlice();
    timeSlicer.initializeTimeSlicing();
  }

  public void initializeTimeSlicing() {
    int i;
    SampleThread aThread;
    System.out.println("Initializing Time Slicing");
    setPriority(Thread.MAX_PRIORITY);
    threads.addElement(new SampleThread("a"));
    threads.addElement(new SampleThread("b"));
    threads.addElement(new SampleThread("c"));
    for (i = 0; i < threads.size(); i++) {
      aThread = (SampleThread)threads.elementAt(i);
      aThread.setPriority(Thread.NORM_PRIORITY);
      aThread.start();
      aThread.suspend();
    }
    start();
  }

  public void run () {
    System.out.println("Starting time slicing");
    while (isAlive()) {
      nextSlice();
      try {
        sleep(100);
        System.out.println("\n-----");
      }
      catch (InterruptedException e) {
        System.out.println("Interrupted stopping..");
        stop();
      }
    }
  }

  public void nextSlice () {
    if (currentThread != null) {
      currentThread.suspend();
    }
    index++;
    if (index == threads.size()) {
```

```
      index = 0;
    }
    currentThread =
      (SampleThread) threads.elementAt (index) ;
    currentThread. resume () ;
  }
}
```

The run method defined for TimeSlice continuously loops while the thread is active. This is common behaviour for a run method and is better style than looping while true (for threads). The run method first calls the nextSlice method, which selects the next thread to execute and then sends itself to sleep for 100 milliseconds. The selected thread can then execute until the 100 milliseconds are up. Then the lower priority process suspends and the TimeSlice thread resumes. The call to sleep is wrapped in a try-catch block so that if an InterruptedException is raised, it is handled locally.

The nextSlice method first suspends the current (lower priority) thread and then selects the next thread to execute. This is where the real business of the time-slicing operation occurs. The algorithm describing this method's operation is:

1. Find the current executing lower priority thread.
2. Suspend it.
3. Select a new thread to resume.
4. Send the selected thread the resume message.

This is a very simple algorithm, but it works! The implementation uses an index to record the position of the current thread within the vector of threads. This index is incremented each time nextSlice is called. When the index is greater than the number of threads, it is reset to zero (vectors are indexed from zero). The current thread object is held in the currentThread instance variable.

To test out the effects of this approach to time-slicing, the main method creates a new TimeSlice instance and sends it the initializeTimeSlicing message.

The SampleThread class is a very simple process which extends Thread. It merely prints a string, passed to it by its constructor, onto the console while it is active:

```
class SampleThread extends Thread {
  String string;
  public SampleThread (String aString) {
    string = aString;
  }
  public void run () {
    while (isAlive()) {
      System.out.print(string);
    }
  }
}
```

Figure 26.2 Running the TimeSlice application.

Figure 26.2 shows the result of running the TimeSlice application.

26.6 Thread Interaction

In Java threads can interact in a manner controlled by wait and notify flags. These flags are used to allow one thread to indicate to other threads that they are waiting or that they can continue. The wait and notify mechanism is based around a common object which acts as the communications mechanism for the semaphores. If one thread reaches a point where it must wait on another object until it is allowed to continue (because the thread is in a consumer–producer relationship with another thread) then that thread is guaranteed to be blocked until it receives a notify message. This is illustrated in Figure 26.3, where thread 1 is suspended once it issues the wait message to the common object. It is only resumed once thread 2 sends the notify message to the common object.

There are in fact three methods provided for the synchronization of threads:

- wait() This message causes the send to be suspended/blocked until a notify or notifyAll message is sent to the common object.

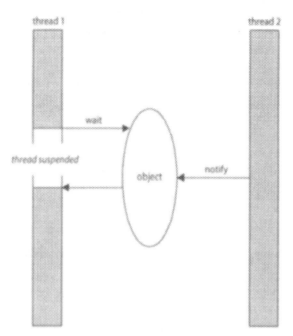

Figure 26.3 Thred interactions.

- notify() This message allows the next thread in the common objects thread to queue to resume processing. If there are two or more threads waiting on this object, only the first is unblocked. If there are no threads waiting on the receiver object then the notify message has no effect (that is, the notify is not recorded for future waits()).

- notifyAll() This message unblocks all threads currently waiting on the receiving object.

These methods are all defined in Object, thus allowing any object to be used as the common object between two or more threads.

These methods must be executed within a synchronized block which is synchronized on the common object.

For example, let us assume that we have a queue object in which one thread adds information to a queue and another thread removes it. In the thread that consumes (removes) data from the queue we might have the following:

```
synchronized (queue) {
   queue.wait();
   newData = queue.next();
}
```

while in the producer thread we might have the following:

```
synchronized (queue) {
   queue.add(object);
   queue.notify();
}
```

Note that the operations to add and remove information to and from the queue are also placed in the synchronized block so that they are not interrupted by the processor (thus avoiding potential inconsistencies).

One final aspect to this process is that the wait() method may throw the InterruptedException if another thread has interrupted this thread. You must therefore wrap the call to wait within a try-catch block.

27 *Exception Handling*

27.1 Introduction

This chapter considers exception handling and how it is implemented in Java. You are introduced to the object model of exception handling, to the throwing and catching of exceptions, and to the defining of new exceptions and exception-specific constructs.

27.2 What Is an Exception?

In Java, almost everything is an object, including exceptions. All exceptions must extend the class `Throwable` or one of its subclasses, which allows an exception to be thrown or raised. Figure 27.1 presents the `Exception` class hierarchy.

The `Throwable` class has two subclasses: `Error` and `Exception`. Errors are unchecked exceptions generated at run time. These are errors from which it is

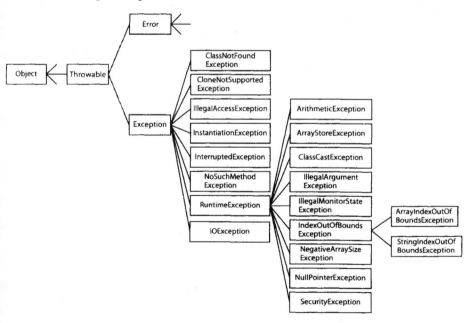

Figure 27.1 Part of the `Exception` class hierarchy.

unlikely that a program can recover (such as out of memory errors). Your methods are not expected to deal with them and the compiler does not check that the methods deal with them.

There are two types of Exception subclass. One set, the checked exceptions, ensures that problems, such as a file not being available, are explicitly dealt with. The other set, unchecked exceptions, deals with problems which may occur at run time but which are not due to the environment.

Your methods must deal with checked exceptions. The compiler checks to see that methods only throw exceptions which they can deal with (or which are passed up to other methods to handle).

An exception can be thrown explicitly by your code or implicitly by the operations you perform. In either case, an exception is an object, and you must instantiate it before you do anything with it. You do this by sending the throw message to an instance of the appropriate exception. For example, to raise an Arithmetic-Exception for a divide by zero error, we write:

throw new ArithmeticException("Division By Zero");

The exception is caught by the first handler (try block) which is defined on the ArithmeticException (or one of its parent signals).

27.3 What Is Exception Handling?

An exception moves the flow of control from one place to another. In most situations, this is because a problem occurs which cannot be handled locally, but can be handled in another part of the system. The problem is usually some sort of error (such as dividing by zero), although it can be any problem (for example, identifying that the postcode specified with an address does not match). The purpose of an exception, therefore, is to handle an error condition when it happens at run time.

The terminology used in exception handling is listed in Table 27.1.

Table 27.1 Terms used in exception handling

Exception	An error which is generated at run time
Raising an exception	Generating a new exception
Throwing an exception	Triggering a generated exception
Handling an exception	Processing code that deals with the error
Handler	The code that deals with the error (referred to as the catch block)
Signal	A particular type of exception (such as *out of bounds* or *divide by zero*)

It is worth considering why you should wish to handle an exception; after all, the system does not allow an error to go unnoticed. For example, if we try to divide by zero, then the system generates an error. This may mean that the user has entered an incorrect value, and we do not want users to be presented with a dialog suggesting that they enter the system debugger. We can use exceptions to force the user to correct the mistake and rerun the calculation.

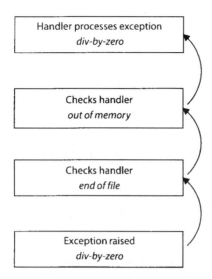

Figure 27.2 Searching through the execution stack.

Different types of error produce different types of exception. For example, if the error is caused by dividing an integer by zero, then the exception is a *divide by zero* exception. The type of exception is identified by objects called signals which possess exception handlers. Each handler can deal with exceptions associated with its class of signal (and its subclasses).

An exception is initiated when it is thrown. The system searches back up the execution stack until it finds a handler which can deal with the exception (i.e. it searches for a `try` block of the appropriate type). The associated handler then processes the exception. This may involve performing some remedial action or terminating the current execution in a controlled manner. In some cases, it may be possible to restart executing the code.

As a handler can only deal with an exception of a specified class (or subclass), an exception may pass through a number of other blocks before it finds one that can process it.

Figure 27.2 illustrates a situation in which a *divide by zero* exception is raised. This exception is passed up the execution stack, where it encounters an exception handler defined for an *End of File* exception. This handler cannot handle the *divide by zero* exception, so it is passed further up the execution stack. It then encounters a handler for an *out of memory* exception. Again, it cannot deal with a *divide by zero* exception and the exception is passed further up the execution stack until it finds a handler defined for the *divide by zero* exception. This handler then processes the exception.

In Java, exceptions are objects and you create and throw an exception by sending messages.

27.4 Throwing an Exception

It is necessary to handle the `IOException` when performing IO using files. This can be done by delegating responsibility for the exception back up the execution chain. You do this using the `throws` clause after the method name declaration (but before the method body):

```
public void handleInput () throws IOException {
    ...
}
```

However, this approach is too simplistic and relies on someone else doing something sensible with the `IOException`. There are three choices with exceptions:

- Declare the exception in the `throws` clause and let the exception pass back up the call stack.
- Catch the exception and handle it within the method.
- Catch the exception and map it to your own exceptions by throwing a new exception.

Passing the exception back up the execution stack is acceptable as long as you know that it is dealt with sensibly. Java forces you either to handle the exception locally or to pass it back up the execution stack explicitly in order to ensure that you think about what should happen if the exception occurs. You must consider carefully whether to throw or handle the exception.

The general syntax for passing the exception out of a method is:

```
access-modifier return-type method-name(parameters)
        throws exception-class {
    ...method body...
}
```

where `exception-class` indicates the class of exception handled. Subclasses of the named exception class are also handled in this way.

27.5 Catching an Exception

You can catch an exception by implementing the `try-catch-finally` construct. This construct is broken into three parts:

- *try block*
  The `try` block indicates the code which is to be monitored for the exceptions listed in the `catch` expressions.
- *catch expressions*
  You can use an optional `catch` expression to indicate what to do when certain classes of exception occur (e.g. resolve the problem or generate a warning message). If no `catch` expression is included, the defining methods must use the `throws` clause.
- *finally block*
  The optional `finally` block runs after the `try` block exits (whether or not this is due to an exception being raised). You can use it to clean up any resources, close files etc.

This construct may at first seem confusing. However, once you have worked with it for a while you will find it less daunting. Typically, you use the same incantation of the construct; concentrate on the details of the code within the try block and do not worry about the exception handling mechanism.

The following example uses the construct to read data from a file and process it. The try block incorporates the file access code, and the code in the catch block states what should happen if an IOException is raised. In this case, it prints a message. The message in the finally block is always printed. It brings together many of the aspects of the Java language. It includes a vector, a switch statement, and while and for loops.

```java
import java.io.*;
import java.util.*;

public class Grades {

  public static void main (String argv []){
    Grades grades = new Grades();
    grades.calculateGrades();
  }

  // Instance variables
  Vector names = new Vector();
  Vector marks = new Vector();

  public void calculateGrades () {
    int i;

    loadData("input.data");

    for (i = 0; i < names.size(); i++) {
      System.out.print(names.elementAt(i));
      System.out.println("\t " + marks.elementAt(i));
    }
  }

  public void loadData (String filename) {
    // Define local variables
    FileInputStream inputFile;
    Reader reader;
    StreamTokenizer st;
    String aString;
    int aNumber, next;

    try {
      // Set up link to file and token reader
```

```
         inputFile = new FileReader("input.data");
         reader = new BufferedReader(inputFile);
         st = new StreamTokenizer(reader);
         System.out.println("----------------------------");

         // Read contents of file
         while ((next = st.nextToken()) != st.TT_EOF) {
            switch (next) {
             case st.TT_NUMBER: {
               aNumber = (int) st.nval;
               System.out.println("--------------------");
               marks.addElement(new Integer(aNumber));
               break;
             }
             default : {
               aString = st.sval;
               System.out.println(aString);
               names.addElement(aString);
             }
            }
         } // End of while
         // Now close the file
         inputFile.close();
      }
      catch (IOException e) {
        System.out.println("Whoops, we have a problem");
      }
      finally {
        System.out.println("All's well that ends
          well!");
      }
   }
}
```

The Grades application reads data from a file called input.data which has the following format:

```
"Bob" 45 "Paul" 32 "Peter" 76 "Mike" 29 "John" 56
```

The loadData method uses the FileInputStream, BufferedReader and StreamTokenizer classes to read the file. The data is placed in one of two vectors depending on the type of data (either string or integer). This code is wrapped up in a try block. If this code raises an IOException, the message "Whoops, we have a problem" is printed. Once the try block is processed, the finally block prints out "All's well ends well!". The calculateGrades method loads in the data file and prints out the data in the two vectors as a table. Figure 27.3 shows the result of executing the Grades application.

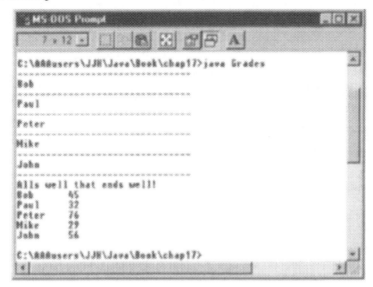

Figure 27.3 Running the Grades application.

27.6 Defining an Exception

You can define your own exceptions, which can give you more control over what happens in particular circumstances. To define an exception, you create a subclass of the Exception class or one of its subclasses. For example, to define a DivideByZeroException, we can extend the Exception class and generate an appropriate message:

```
public class DivideByZeroException extends Exception {
  public Object offender;

  public DivideByZeroException (Object anObject) {
    super("Divide by zero in " + anObject);
    offender = anObject;
  }
}
```

This class explicitly handles divide by zero exceptions. We could have made it a subclass of ArithmeticException; however, it is an unchecked exception and we wish to force the programmer to handle this exception if it is raised. The following code is an example of how we might use DivideByZeroException:

```
public class Example {
  int x, y;

  public static void main (String args []) {
    Example temp = new Example(5, 0);
```

```
    try {
      temp.test();
    }
    catch (DivideByZeroException exception) {
      System.out.println("Oops");
    }
  }

  public Example(int a, int b) {
    x = a;
    y = b;
  }

  public void test() throws DivideByZeroException {
    if (y == 0)
      throw new DivideByZeroException(this);
    else
      System.out.println(x / y);
  }
}
```

In this example, we check to see if the divisor is zero. If it is, we create a new instance of the DivideByZeroException class and throw it. The test method delegates responsibility for this exception to the calling method (in this case, the main method). The main method catches the exception and prints a message.

27.7 Exercise: Custom Exceptions

The aim of this exercise is to define and use your own exception. The exception should be used to handle situations where the first parameter to a method is larger than the second. Your exception class should indicate this to the developer.

27.7.1 What You Should Do

1. You should first define your own exception class. Call this class MyException.
2. You should then write a method (in another class) which uses the method presented below.
3. Your method should catch and handle any MyExceptions which are raised.
4. Try out your code using a range of values.

Your code should use this method:

```
  public void test(int a, int b) throws MyException {
    if (a > b)
```

```
      throw new MyException();
   else
      System.out.println("The numbers are " + a +
         " and " + b);
}
```

28 *Streams and Files*

28.1 Introduction

This chapter discusses the second most used class hierarchy in Java: the Stream classes. The Stream classes are used (among other things) for accessing files.

Notice that the Stream classes and hierarchies are quite large and complex. You should therefore not worry if you are unable to grasp the facilities provided by all the classes (or indeed how they relate to each other). This chapter does not attempt to provide a complete description of the classes; rather, it tries to offer a taste of what streams can do and why they are provided. You should refer to the Java online reference material for further details.

28.2 Streams

28.2.1 What Is a Stream?

Streams are objects which serve as sources or sinks of data. At first this concept can seem a bit strange. The easiest way to think of a stream is as a conduit of data flowing from or into a pool.

There are a number of types of stream in the Java system, and each has a wide range of uses. Figure 28.1 illustrates part of the structure of the Stream class hierarchy (see Appendix D for the complete structure of the java.io package, of which the Stream classes form part). The abstract InputStream and OutputStream classes are the root classes of the stream hierarchies. Below them are stream classes for reading, writing, accessing external files etc.

A stream may be input only (InputStream) or output only (OutputStream); it may be specialized for handling files (FileInputStream); and it may be an internal stream (which acts as a source or sink for data internal to the system) or an external stream (which is the source or sink for data external to the system). A string is a typical example of an internal source or sink; a file is a typical example of an external source or sink.

Typically, a stream is connected to an external device or a collection of data. If a stream is connected to an external device (for example, a file), then it acts as an interface to that device. It allows messages to be sent to and received from the external device object, enabling it to accomplish various activities, including input

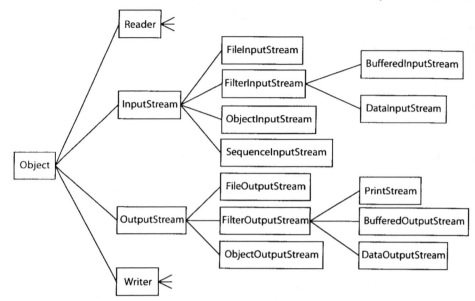

Figure 28.1 The structure of part of the Stream class hierarchies.

and output. If a stream is connected to a collection (such as a string) it acts as a way to process the contents of the collection. In both cases, the stream views the source (or sink) of the data as being able to provide (or receive) a data item on request.

Tables 28.1–28.4 list the methods and classes used by input and output streams.

Table 28.1 InputStream class methods

close()	Closes the receiving input stream and releases resources
read()	Answers the next byte of data in the receiver stream
read(byte b [])	Reads bytes of data into the array from the receiver
read(byte b [], int offSet, int length)	Reads bytes of data into the array, starting at offSet and finishing at offSet plus length

Table 28.2 OutputStream class methods

close()	Closes the receiving output stream and releases resources
flush()	Flushes the output stream such that any buffered output is written
write (int b)	Writes a byte, b, to the receiving stream
write (byte b [])	Writes the contents of the array, b, to the receiving stream.
write(byte b [], int offSet, int length)	Writes all data elements of the array, b, to the receiver stream starting at offSet and finishing at offSet plus length.

Table 28.3 The input stream classes

`FileInputStream`	Reads data from a file
`FilterInputStream`	Superclass of all classes that filter input streams
`ObjectInputStream`	Reads data and objects from a file (used with a `FileInputStream`)
`SequenceInputStream`	Enables several input streams to be linked serially
`BufferedInputStream`	Buffers input to reduce number of reads
`DataInputStream`	Reads primitive Java data types from an underlying input stream

Table 28.4 The output stream classes

`FileOutputStream`	Writes data to a file
`FilterOutputStream`	Superclass of all classes that filter output streams
`ObjectOutputStream`	Saves data and objects to a file (used with a `fileOutputStream`)
`BufferedOutputStream`	Buffers writing to an underlying stream for efficiency
`PrintWriter`	Handles output of non-byte data
`DataOutputStream`	Writes primitive data types to an output stream

28.2.2 Readers and Writers: Character Streams

Specialist class hierarchies (Figure 28.2) intended for reading and writing character streams form part of the `java.io` package (see Appendix D) and return characters (rather than bytes).

Versions 1.0 and 1.0.2 did not contain such classes. They have been introduced because they simplify the task of writing programs that are not dependent on a specific character encoding. They make it easier to write a program that works with ASCII, Unicode etc., which is important if you are developing systems which might be used in different parts of the world, using different encodings to represent features of different languages. By default, Java uses Unicode, an international standard character encoding.

The `Reader` classes convert bytes from a byte input stream into characters in Java's Unicode representation. In turn, the `Writer` classes convert characters into bytes and then write those bytes to a byte output stream. Typically, you do not use these classes directly. You instantiate them and use them in conjunction with an object, such as a stream tokenizer.

The `Reader` class (Table 28.5) is the abstract root class for all streams that read characters. Its subclasses must override the `read(char[], int, int)` and `close` methods, at least. However, most subclasses override other methods and provide functionality.

The `Writer` class (Table 28.6) is the abstract root class for all streams that write characters. Subclasses of this class must override the `write(char[], int, int)`, `flush` and `close` methods, at least. They may also override other methods and provide additional methods.

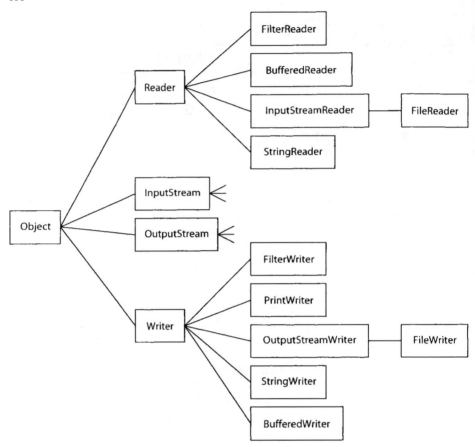

Figure 28.2 The Reader and Writer hierarchies

Table 28.5 The Reader class protocol

close()	Closes a stream
read()	Reads a single character
read(char charBuffer [])	Reads characters into an array
read(char charBuffer [], int offSet, int length)	Reads characters into a portion of an array, starting at offSet and up to offSet plus length
ready()	Indicates whether the stream is ready to be read from

The constructors of the FileReader class (Table 28.7) assume that the default character encoding and the default byte-buffer size are appropriate. You can specify these values yourself, by constructing an InputStreamReader on a File-InputStream.

The constructors of the FileWriter class (Table 28.8) assume that the default character encoding and the default byte-buffer size are acceptable. To specify these values yourself, construct an OutputStreamWriter on a FileOutput-Stream.

Table 28.6 The Writer class protocol

close()	Closes the stream, flushing it first
flush()	Flushes the stream by writing buffered characters to the byte stream, which is also flushed
write(int character)	Writes a single character
write(char charBuffer [])	Writes out an array of characters
write(char charBuffer [], int offSet, int length)	Writes a portion of an array of characters, starting at offSet and finishing at offSet plus length
write(String string)	Writes a string to a stream
write(String string, int offSet, int length)	Writes a portion of a string starting at offSet and finishing at offSet plus length

Table 28.7 The Reader classes

BufferedReader	A stream that provides for the efficient buffering of characters being read
FilterReader	Abstract class for reading filtered character streams
StringReader	A character stream whose source is a string
InputStreamReader	A stream that translates bytes into characters according to a specified character encoding
FileReader	Convenience class for reading character files

Table 28.8 The Writer classes

BufferedWriter	A class that provides for the efficient buffering of characters being written
FilterWriter	Abstract class for writing filtered character streams
StringWriter	A character stream whose sink is a string
OutputStreamReader	A class that translates characters into bytes according to a specified character encoding
FileWriter	Convenience class for writing character files
PrintWriter	A class that prints formatted representations of objects to a text output stream

28.2.3 Stream Tokenizers

The StreamTokenizer class takes an input stream and parses it into "tokens" that are read one at a time. You can control the parsing process, enabling identifiers, numbers, quoted strings, and various comment styles (including C and C++ style comments) to be parsed. You can also tell a stream tokenizer to ignore line terminators or to return identifiers in lower case.

A stream tokenizer provides the next available token in response to the nextToken message. The result may be a string or a number from the underlying streams. This process can be repeated until the nextToken message returns the value TT_EOF, indicating that the end of the file has been reached. The stream tokenizer allows a much higher level of response from the system than is possible using the byte or character input streams. This saves you a lot of work (although it may at first seem very confusing).

28.2.4 Using the IO Classes

Streams are often combined to provide the required functionality. Figure 28.3 illustrates one way of reading characters (as opposed to bytes) from a file. It uses a character stream in combination with other objects to obtain the data in the file. We shall endeavour to consider each of the objects involved separately and to explain what they do and why the objects all work together.

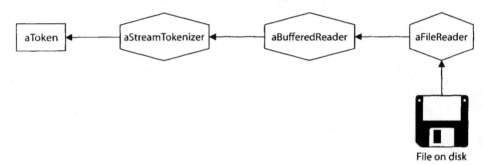

File on disk

Figure 28.3 Reading strings and numbers from a file.

The FileReader class (a subclass of InputStreamReader) defines an object that translates the bytes from a file into a character stream. This is advisable, as character streams are potentially more efficient than byte streams (partly due to the way in which the byte-oriented streams were originally implemented in Java).

Character streams are often used in collaboration with an instance of BufferedReader. This class processes text from a character input stream (such as FileReader), buffering characters to provide for the efficient reading of characters, strings and lines. You can override the default buffer size. Notice that each request to the buffered reader causes a corresponding request to be made to the underlying character reader. In object-oriented terms, the character reader object is responsible for reading individual characters on request. The buffered reader object is responsible for buffering such requests for efficiency.

Next, a stream tokenizer reads individual tokens. The result may be a string or a number from the underlying streams.

The following source code illustrates how to use these classes:

```
inputFile = new FileReader("input.data");
reader = new BufferedReader(inputFile);
tokens = new StreamTokenizer(reader);

while ((next = tokens.nextToken()) != tokens.TT_EOF) {
    switch (next) {
```

```
    case tokens.TT_NUMBER: {
      aNumber = (int) tokens.nval;
      ...
    }
    default : {
      aString = tokens.sval;
      ...
    }
  }
}
inputFile.close();
```

28.3 Files

28.3.1 Accessing File Information

To access a file, you must first have a filename to work with. A filename is created by one of the constructors of the `File` class (Table 28.9).

Table 28.9 `File` class constructors

`File (String path)`	Creates an instance that represents the file with the given path
`File (String path, String name)`	Creates an instance that represents the file with the given path and name
`File (File dir, String name)`	Creates an instance that represents the file in the given directory and with the given name

The `File` class also defines a number of class variables which provide information on the platform's directory separator characters:

```
File.separator
```

You may wish to check to see whether a file exists before attempting to access it (to be sure there is something to read from or to make sure you do not overwrite an existing file; see Table 28.10). You do this with the `exists` message, which returns true if the file is present and false if it is not.

A `File` object can be used with a `FileReader` or `FileWriter` constructor to build a stream between a file and an application.

28.3.2 The `FileReader` Class Constructors

- `FileReader(String fileName)` takes a string which defines the file.
- `FileReader(File file)` takes an instance of a file.

These constructors both throw `FileNotFoundException`.

Table 28.10 `File` messages

`canRead()`	Tests whether the specified file can be read
`canWrite()`	Tests whether the specified file can be written
`delete()`	Deletes the specified file
`getParent()`	Returns the parent directory of the file
`getPath()`	Returns the pathname of the file
`isDirectory()`	Tests whether the file is a directory
`isFile()`	Tests whether the file is a "normal" file
`lastModified()`	Returns the time that the file was last modified
`list()`	Returns a list of the files in the directory specified by this `File` object
`list (FileFilter filter)`	Returns a list of the files in the directory that satisfy the specified filter
`mkdir()`	Creates a directory whose pathname is specified by the receiver
`mkdirs()`	Creates a directory and any necessary parent directories
`renameTo(File)`	Renames the file to have the pathname given by the `File` argument
`toString()`	Returns a string representation of the object

28.8.3 The `FileWriter` Class Constructors

● `FileWriter(String fileName)` creates a stream to the specified file.
● `FileWriter(String fileName, boolean append)` creates a stream to the specified file.
● `FileWriter(File file)` creates a stream to the file specified by the instance of the class `File`.

These constructors throw `IOException`.

28.3.4 The `BufferedReader` Class Constructors

● `BufferedReader(Reader reader)` creates a buffering character input stream that uses a default size of input buffer.
● `BufferedReader(Reader reader, int size)` creates a buffering character input stream that uses an input buffer of the specified size.

28.3.5 The `BufferedWriter` Class Constructors

● `BufferedWriter(Writer writer)` creates a buffered character output stream that uses a default size of output buffer.
● `BufferedWriter(Writer writer, int size)` creates a buffered character output stream that uses an output buffer of the specified size.

28.3.6 The `StreamTokenizer` Class

The constructors available for `StreamTokenizer` include:

- `StreamTokenizer(Reader reader)` creates a tokenizer that parses the given character stream.
- `StreamTokenizer(InputStream inputStream)` creates a tokenizer that parses the specified input stream.

The `StreamTokenizer` protocol includes:

- `nextToken` obtains the next token in the input stream.
- `ttype` indicates the type of the token just parsed. This can be a string (`TT_WORD`), a number (`TT_NUMBER`), the end of the line (`TT_EOL`) or the end of the file (`TT_EOF`).
- `sval` holds the current string (if `ttype` indicates a string).
- `nval` holds the current number (if `ttype` indicates a number).

28.3.7 The `PrintWriter` Class Constructors

The constructors available for the `PrintWriter` class include:

- `PrintWriter(OutputStream outputStream)` creates a new Print-Writer from an existing `OutputStream`.
- `PrintWriter(OutputStream outputStream, boolean autoflush)` creates a new `PrintWriter`, with or without automatic line flushing, from an existing `OutputStream`.
- `PrintWriter(Writer writer)` creates a new `PrintWriter` on a `writer` object.
- `PrintWriter(Writer writer, boolean autoflush)` creates a new `PrintWriter`, with or without automatic line flushing, on a `writer` object.

A `PrintWriter` object responds to a variety of printing messages including all the `print` and `println` methods used with the `System.out` stream.

28.3.8 Handling File IO Errors

Java knows that IO operations (such as accessing a file) can lead to exceptions being raised. For example, if you read from a file which does not exist, then an exception is raised and your system is left in an unstable state with streams open.

Java does not allow you to do nothing with an exception. You must either handle the exception or delegate responsibility for handling it. The next chapter considers how you can handle, generate and define exceptions. In this chapter, we merely consider how to delegate responsibility for the exception.

You delegate responsibility for an exception by specifying in a method header that the method should throw an exception of a particular class (or subclass) back up the execution stack:

```
public void example () throws IOException {
   . . .
}
```

The IOException is the root of all exceptions raised during IO operations. In this case, every IOException, and all subclasses of IOException, are passed out of the method example.

28.4 Accessing a File

This section presents a simple application, FileDemo, which illustrates how the contents of a file can be accessed. The application uses the classes described earlier in this chapter, including FileReader, BufferedReader and Stream-Tokenizer.

Notice that it uses a separate Grades class to determine the grade that should be allocated for a given mark. It is common object-oriented style to place a large chunk of functionality into a class in its own right. This may at first seem very procedural; however, Grades provides a particular type of operation which may be used in different situations in different classes, and it makes most sense to provide it as a reusable component.

```
import java.io.*;
import java.util.*;

public class FileDemo {
   Vector records = new Vector();

   public static void main (String argv[])
            throws IOException {
      FileDemo d = new FileDemo();
      d.loadData("input.data");
   }

   public void loadData (String filename)
            throws IOException {
      // Define local variables
      FileReader inputFile;
      Reader reader;
      StreamTokenizer tokens;
      Grades g = new Grades();
      String aString;
      int aNumber, next;

      // Set up link to file and token reader.

      inputFile = new FileReader(filename);
```

```
        reader = new BufferedReader(inputFile);
        tokens = new StreamTokenizer(reader);

        System.out.println("-----------------------");

        // Read contents of file using nextToken.
        while ((next = tokens.nextToken()) !=
            tokens.TT_EOF) {
          switch (next) {
            // Check to see the type of token returned
            // TT_WORD indicates a string
            case tokens.TT_NUMBER: {
              aNumber = (int) tokens.nval;
              g.classify(aNumber);
              records.addElement(new Integer(aNumber));
              System.out.println("--------------------");
              break;
            }
            default : {
              aString = tokens.sval;
              System.out.println(aString);
            }
          }
        }
        // Now close the file
        inputFile.close();
    }
}
```

The sample data file `input.data` contains:

   `"Bob" 45 "Paul" 32 "Peter" 76 "Mike" 29 "John" 56`

The result of executing this application is illustrated in Figure 28.4.

28.5 Creating a File

As a contrast, the `FileOutDemo` application illustrates how output can be written to a file. Notice that connecting to a file for output is essentially the same as connecting to a file for input. The primary difference is that instead of using a `StreamTokenizer`, we use a `PrintWriter`. This class is really the same class as `FileDemo`, with two new methods: `printGrades` and `writeData`. The following code presents only the new or changed parts of the class definition:

```
public class FileOutDemo {
  public static void main (String argv [])
```

Figure 28.4 Running FileDemo.

```
        throws IOException {
  FileOutDemo f = new FileOutDemo();
  f.printGrades();
}

public void printGrades () throws IOException {
  loadData("input.data");
  writeData("output.data");
}

public void loadData (String filename)
        throws IOException {
  ... as for FileDemo ...
}

public void writeData(String filename)
        throws IOException {
  Enumeration item;
  Integer aMark;
  FileWriter outputFile;
  BufferedWriter writer;
  PrintWriter output;

  // Link a stream to the file
  outputFile = new FileWriter(filename);
  writer = new BufferedWriter(outputFile);
```

```
    output = new PrintWriter(writer);

    // Write data to the file
    output.println("The file contains " +
        records.size() + " records");
    for (item = records.elements();
          item.hasMoreElements();) {
      aMark = (Integer) item.nextElement();
      output.println(aMark);
    }

    // Lastly don't forget to close the file
    output.close();
  }
}
```

The result of executing this application is presented in Figure 28.5.

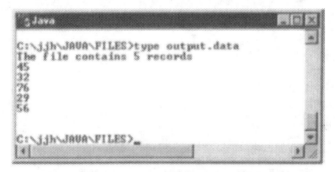

Figure 28.5 Running the FileOutDemo application.

28.6 Input from the Console

You can obtain input from the user via the console using an InputStream. This is similar to generating output to the console. The global object System possesses both output and input streams. The output stream has been used extensively in the examples throughout this book. The input stream can be used to obtain information from the user. This is illustrated in the following, very simple, example application:

```
import java.io.*;
public class TestReader {
  public static void main (String args [])
              throws IOException {
    TestReader t = new TestReader();
    t.printMenu();
  }
```

```
public void printMenu() throws IOException {
  char ch;
  System.out.println("The options available are:");
  System.out.println(" 1. File");
  System.out.println(" 2. Exit");
  System.out.print("Please make a selection: ");

  ch = (char)System.in.read();

  System.out.println("\n The input was " + ch);
  }
}
```

The result of executing the above application is illustrated in Figure 28.6.

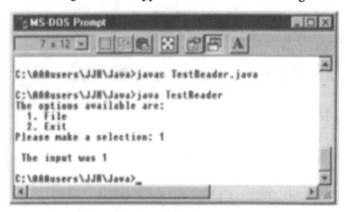

Figure 28.6 Running the `TestReader` application

28.7 Exercise: IO for the Text Editor

In Figure 28.6 the window generated by a simple java application called Edit (this was implemented as an earlier practical). You will use this class in this practical. The aim of the practical is for you to write the methods which this application will use to save and retrieve text from a file.

The class `Edit` is a subclass of `Frame` and implements the `ActionListener` interface. Thus an instance of `Edit` can create a window and can handle `ActionEvents`.

When instantiated, the class `Edit` creates a button panel (which displays three buttons labelled exit, load and save) and a `TextArea` and displays them within a window (Figure 28.7). The event-handling code has already been implemented for the buttons. When the Exit button is pressed, the system terminates, when the Load button is pressed a method called `loadText()` is called, while when the Save button is pressed a method `saveText()` is executed.

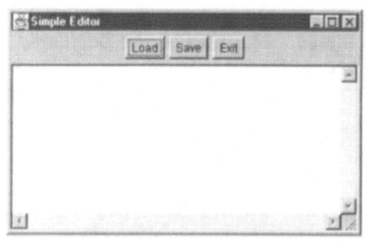

Figure 28.7 Running the Simple Editor application.

28.7.1 What You Should Do

Your task is to implement the saveText() and loadText() methods. At present both methods are missing most of their functionality. Only the ability to read or write to, or from, the text area was provided when you created this application earlier in the book. You must use the facilities in the java.io package to read and write the text obtained. You could also use the FileDialog class (from the java.awt package) to allow the user to select file names.

The classes which are likely to be of use to you are:

- java.awt
  - FileDialog
  - Dialog
- java.io
  - FileReader
  - BufferedReader
  - FileWriter
  - BufferedWriter
  - PrintWriter

28.8 Summary

In this chapter, you have encountered streams and their use in file input and output. Many simple Java applications and applets do not access files. However, if you need to store information or share it between applications, then you need to interact with the host file system. You have now seen the basic facilities available, and should spend some time exploring the stream and file facilities available in Java.

29 *Serialization*

29.1 Introduction

If you save object information without serialization, then you can only save the ASCII version of the data held by the object. You need to reconstruct the data into objects when you read the text file, which means that you have to indicate that certain data is associated with certain objects and that certain objects are related. This is very time-consuming and error-prone. It is also very unlikely that the ASCII data written out by someone else is in the right format for your system.

This was the only way of creating persistent data in the JDK versions 1.0 and 1.0.2. However, in JDK version 1.1 serialization was introduced to simplify this operation.

Serialization allows you to store objects directly to a file in a compact and encoded form. You do not need to convert the objects or reconstruct them when you load them back in. In addition, everyone else who uses serialization can read and write your files. This is useful not only for portability but also for sharing objects.

The name, serialization, comes from situations which can arise when saving more than one related object to a file. For example, in Figure 29.1 four objects are related by references and are held by another object Family (within a vector).

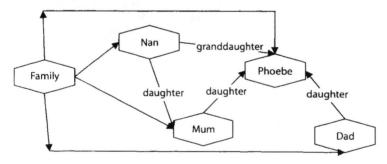

Figure 29.1 Related objects.

If, when we want to save the whole family to file, we merely save each object independently, we also have to save copies of the objects that they reference. In the above example, we would end up with multiple copies of Phoebe. If we can determine whether an object has already been saved to disk, then we can record a reference to the previously saved object, so that the original structure can be restored at a later date. This reference is referred to as a serial number (hence the name serialization).

Each object is stored to disk with its own serial number. If an object has been stored, then a reference to its serial number is included with any object which references it. For example, if Phoebe has serial number 1 then, when Mum, Dad or Nan are saved, they merely record that they reference the object with serial number 1.

29.1.1 Saving Objects

To save an object to a file, you use the ObjectOutputStream class. However, an ObjectOutputStream must use a stream, such as FileOutputStream, to write data into a file:

```
FileOutputStream file = new FileOutputStream("data");
ObjectOutputStream output = new
ObjectOutputStream(file);
output.writeObject(family);
file.close();
```

The above code results in all the objects held by family being saved to the file data using serialization. This illustrates that, although you may find the concepts confusing, serialization is easy to work with.

29.1.2 Reading Objects

To read objects which have been saved to file back into an application, you need to use the ObjectInputStream class. You must also use an input stream, such as FileInputStream, to read the (byte) data from the file:

```
FileInputStream file = new FileInputStream("data");
ObjectInputStream input = new ObjectInputStream(file);
Family family = (Family) input.readObject();
file.close();
```

Notice that you must cast the object retrieved by the readObject method into the appropriate class (just as with vectors and hash tables).

29.2 The ObjectOutputStream Class

The ObjectOutputStream class defines a single constructor which creates an ObjectOutputStream that writes to the specified OutputStream:

```
ObjectOutputStream(OutputStream output)
        throws IOException
```

The ObjectOutputStream class provides the protocol shown in Table 29.1.

Table 29.1 The protocol for the `ObjectOutputStream` class

`close()`	Closes the stream
`flush()`	Flushes the stream
`write(byte b[])`	Writes an array of bytes
`write(byte b[], int offSet, int length)`	Writes a sub array of bytes
`write(int anInt)`	Writes a byte
`writeBoolean(boolean bool)`	Writes a boolean
`writeByte(int anInt)`	Writes an 8 bit byte
`writeBytes(String string)`	Writes a string as a sequence of bytes
`writeChar(int character)`	Writes a 16 bit character
`writeChars(String string)`	Writes a string as a sequence of characters
`writeDouble(double aDouble)`	Writes a 64 bit `double`
`writeFloat(float aFloat)`	Writes a 32 bit `float`
`writeInt(int anInt)`	Writes a 32 bit `int`
`writeLong(long aLong)`	Writes a 64 bit `long`
`writeObject(Object object)`	Writes the specified object
`writeShort(int aShort)`	Writes a 16 bit `short`

29.3 The `ObjectInputStream` class

The `ObjectInputStream` class defines a single constructor which creates an `ObjectInputStream` that reads from the specified `InputStream`:

```
ObjectInputStream(InputStream input)
        throws IOException, StreamCorruptedException
```

The `ObjectInputStream` class defines the protocol shown in Table 29.2.

29.4 The `Serializable` Interface

Any class whose objects are to be used as part of a serializable application must implement the `Serializable` interface (if you examine the diagrams in the appendices, you can see that many classes, such as `Vector`, implement the `Serializable` interface). The serialization interface is a flag indicating that a class can be serialized. It means that user-defined classes can also be serialized without the need to define any new methods. All the instance variables of an object are written onto the output stream automatically. When the object is restored the instance variable information is automatically restored.

In some situations, you may need to implement the methods specified by the `Serializable` interface. For example, you may not need to save the information held in all the instance variables, but only those which cannot be regenerated, thus

Table 29.2 The protocol for the `ObjectInputStream` class

`close()`	Closes the input stream
`read()`	Reads a byte of data
`read(byte charBuffer[], int offSet, int length)`	Reads into an array of bytes
`readBoolean()`	Reads in a boolean
`readByte()`	Reads an 8 bit byte
`readChar()`	Reads a 16 bit `char`
`readDouble()`	Reads a 64 bit `double`
`readFloat()`	Reads a 32 bit `float`
`readInt()`	Reads a 32 bit `int`
`readLine()`	Reads a line that has been terminated by a \n, \r, \ r\n or EOF
`readLong()`	Reads a 64 bit `long`
`readObject()`	Read an object from the receiver
`readShort()`	Reads a 16 bit `short`
`readUnsignedByte()`	Reads an unsigned 8 bit byte
`readUnsignedShort()`	Reads an unsigned 16 bit `short`

minimizing the size of the serialized objects on disk. A user-defined class can define the `readObject` and `writeObject` methods. The `Serializable` interface definition for these two methods is:

```
private void writeObject
    (java.io.ObjectOutputStream out)
  throws IOException
private void readObject(java.io.ObjectInputStream in)
  throws IOException, ClassNotFoundException;
```

The `writeObject` method must write onto the output stream, `out`, the information required to restore the object. In turn, the `readObject` method is expected to read that information back into an object, setting instance variables as appropriate from the `in` stream. In either case, you should use the write or read methods defined on the appropriate streams to handle the instance variable data.

If you are confused by what these methods do, then think of it this way: "these methods define what information is saved to the file or restored from the file, for a particular class of object".

If you try to save an object which is not serializable, then the `NotSerializableException` is thrown. This exception identifies the class of the non-serializable object.

Notice that the way in which you define how an object can be saved to a file or restored from a file is classic object orientation. That is, the object itself defines how it should be saved to a file. The parameter to `writeObject` is the stream which is linked to the file, but the stream does not decide what is written.

29.5 A Simple Serialization Application

This section describes a very simple application which creates a set of person objects and a family object, and implements relationships as illustrated in Figure 29.1. The Family class defines how members are added to the family and how the writeObject and readObject methods are implemented (notice that we did not need to define these, as the objects could have been serialized automatically). Finally, the Person class defines the functionality of person objects (such as how to add daughters and granddaughters) and how to implement readObject and writeObject.

29.5.1 The Person Class

The Person class implements the Serializable interface by defining the methods writeObject and readObject.

The writeObject method writes out the contents of each of the instance variables in turn. Of course, an instance variable might well reference another person object and serialization comes into play.

The readObject method reads each of the objects from the input stream in the same order as they were written out. We could have provided additional strings to identify the instance variables being saved or loaded.

An additional method, toString, is used by the output stream to print a textual representation of the object.

```
import java.io.*;
public class Person implements Serializable {
   private String title;
   private Person daughter;
   private Person granddaughter;
   public Person(String string) {title = string;}
   public String name () {return title;}

   public void addDaughter(Person person) {
      daughter = person;
   }

   public void addGrandDaughter(Person person) {
      granddaughter = person;
   }

   public String toString() {
      String result;
      result = "Person: " + title;
      if (daughter != null)
         result = result + " : daughter " +
               daughter.name();
      if (granddaughter != null)
```

```
        result = result + " granddaughter " +
            granddaughter.name();
    return result;
}

private void writeObject(ObjectOutputStream out)
            throws IOException {
    out.writeObject(title);
    out.writeObject(daughter);
    out.writeObject(granddaughter);
}

private void readObject(ObjectInputStream in)
        throws IOException, ClassNotFoundException {
    title = (String)in.readObject();
    daughter = (Person)in.readObject();
    granddaughter = (Person)in.readObject();
}
}
```

29.5.2 The Family Class

The definition of the Family class is considerably simpler than the Person class, as all it does is act as an interface to a vector. As vectors already know how to save their contents to a file, we merely need to write the whole vector to the output stream. When we come to read the objects back in from a file we can read the whole vector in one go (remembering to cast the result returned by readObject to Vector).

```
import java.util.Vector;
import java.util.Enumeration;
import java.io.*;
public class Family implements Serializable {

    private Vector members = new Vector();

    public void addFamilyMember(Person person) {
        members.addElement(person);
    }

    public void printFamily() {
        Person member;
        for (Enumeration e = members.elements();
                e.hasMoreElements() ; ) {
            member = (Person)e.nextElement();
            System.out.println(member);
        }
```

```
    }

    private void writeObject(ObjectOutputStream out)
            throws IOException {
      out.writeObject(members);
    }

    private void readObject(ObjectInputStream in)
        throws IOException, ClassNotFoundException {
      members = (Vector)in.readObject();
    }
}
```

29.5.3 The Test Class

The Test class provides a test harness for the serializable classes. The setUpAndSave method instantiates a family object and constructs a set of person objects as illustrated in Figure 29.1. It then saves this structure to a file called family.data. The data is not saved into any instance variables and is not passed between this method and the load method. The load method loads objects in from the family.data file.

```
  import java.io.*;

  public class Test {

    public static void main (String args [])
        throws IOException, ClassNotFoundException {
      Test t = new Test();
      t.setUpAndSave();
      t.load();
    }

    public void setUpAndSave() throws IOException {
      Family family = new Family();
      Person nan = new Person("Nan");
      Person dad = new Person("Dad");
      Person mum = new Person("Mum");
      Person phoebe = new Person("Phoebe");
      dad.addDaughter(phoebe);
      mum.addDaughter(phoebe);
      nan.addGrandDaughter(phoebe);
      nan.addDaughter(mum);
      family.addFamilyMember(dad);
      family.addFamilyMember(mum);
      family.addFamilyMember(nan);
      family.addFamilyMember(phoebe);
```

```
    family.printFamily();
    System.out.println("\nSaving family to object
            file");
    FileOutputStream file =
            new FileOutputStream("family.data");
    ObjectOutputStream output =
            new ObjectOutputStream(file);
    output.writeObject(family);
    file.close();

    System.out.println("Family saved");
  }

  public void load() throws IOException,
          ClassNotFoundException {
    System.out.println("\nLoading new family from
            file");
    FileInputStream file =
            new FileInputStream("family.data");
    ObjectInputStream input =
            new ObjectInputStream(file);
    Family family = (Family) input.readObject();
    file.close();
    System.out.println("New family loaded\n");
    family.printFamily();
  }
}
```

Figure 29.2 shows that the same information is printed in both methods. The serialization process was a success! One copy of each object is stored to the file, and

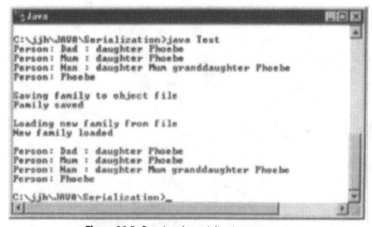

Figure 29.2 Running the serialization example.

each subsequent reference to that object is replaced with a serial number (see Figure 29.3).

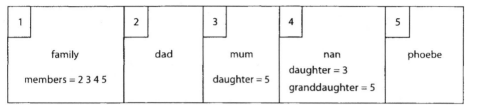

Figure 29.3 The file structure for the Family application.

29.6 Exercise: Using Files with the Financial Manager

This application builds on the one started in Chapter 16. The Financial Manager application keeps a record of deposits and withdrawals from a current account. It also keeps an up-to-date balance and allows statements to be printed.

A problem with the version in Chapter 16 is that there is no way of permanently storing the account information. As soon as the FinancialManager object is destroyed (or the reference to it is lost), then all the information associated with it is also lost. This exercise extends the existing application so that it can:

- save the current statement to a file
- load an existing statement from a file

You must provide two new interfaces, one to load a file and one to save a file. These files contain a formatted version of the information held in the statement. If you were to use a text file then the format might be:

```
<type of action> <amount> newline
```

For example:

```
deposit 24.00
withdraw 13.00
```

It is significantly easier to use serialization, as it makes accessing the contents of the file much easier. You must check to see that the file exists before loading it.

If you are successful, then the following main method should give the same result from both FinancialManager objects.

```
public class Test {

    public static void main (String args []) {
        FinancialManager fm = new FinancialManager();
        fm.deposit(25.00);
        fm.withdraw(12.00);
        fm.deposit(10.00);
        fm.deposit(5.00);
```

```
    fm.withdraw(8.00);

    System.out.println("The current balance is " +
            fm.balance();
    fm.statement();
    fm.save("account1");

    FinancialManager anotherFM = new
            FinancialManager();
    anotherFM.load("account1");

    System.out.println("\n");
    anotherFM.statement();
    System.out.println("The loaded balance is " +
            anotherFM.balance());
    }
}
```

The result of running this Test class is shown below:

```
C:Book\chap29\finance>java Test
The current balance is 20.0
Statement:
Deposit 0.0
Deposit 25.0
Withdraw  12.0
Deposit 10.0
Deposit 5.0
Withdraw  8.0

Statement:
Deposit 0.0
Deposit 25.0
Withdraw  12.0
Deposit 10.0
Deposit 5.0
Withdraw  8.0
The loaded balance is 20.0
```

29.7 Summary

In this chapter you have encountered object input and output streams and their use in storing and retrieving objects from file. This is another way of sharing information (in this case objects) between applications. It also provides a way of providing object persistence. You should now spend some time exploring the object input and output stream facilities available in your Java system.

30 Sockets in Java

30.1 Introduction

A "socket" is an end point in a communication link between separate processes. In Java, sockets are objects which provide a way of exchanging information between two processes in a straightforward and platform-independent manner (see the classes in the java.net package). In fact, sockets in Java are very straightforward, as you will see in this chapter.

30.2 Socket to Socket Communication

When two processes wish to communicate they can do so via sockets. Each process has a socket which is connected to the other's socket. One process can then write information out to the socket, while the second process can read information back in from its socket. To achieve this, the streams model, already used for file access, is exploited. Associated with each socket are two streams, one for input and one for output. Thus to pass information from one process to another you write that information out to the output stream of one socket and read it from the input stream of another socket (assuming the two sockets are connected). This is illustrated in Figure 30.1. This has the great advantage that, once the network connection has been made, passing information between processes is not significantly different from reading and writing information with any other stream.

30.3 Setting up a Connection

To set up the connection, one process must be running a program that is waiting for a connection, while the other must try to reach the first. The first is referred to as a server socket while the second is referred to just as a socket.

For the second process to connect to the first (the server socket) it must know what machine the first is running on and which port it is connected to. A port number is a logical point of communication on a computer. Port numbers in the TCP/IP system are 16 bit numbers in the range 0–65536 (a description of TCP/IP is beyond the scope of this book; see Parker (1994) for further information). Generally, port numbers below 1024 are reserved for pre-defined services (which means that you should avoid

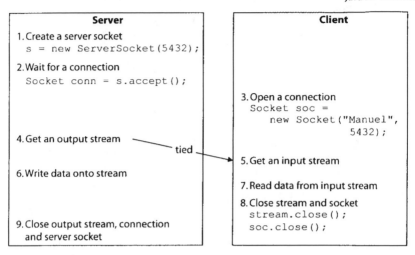

Figure 30.1 Socket to socket communication.

using them unless you wish to communicate with one of those services, such as telnet, SMTP mail or ftp).

For example, in Figure 30.1 the server socket connects to port 5432. In turn, the client socket connects to the machine on which the server is executing and then to port number 5432 on that machine. Nothing happens until the server socket accepts the connection. At that point the sockets are connected and the socket streams are bound to each other.

30.4 An Example Client–Server Application

30.4.1 The System Structure

Figure 30.2 illustrates the basic structure of the system we are trying to build. There will be a server object running on one machine and a client object running on another. The client will connect up to the server using sockets in order to obtain information.

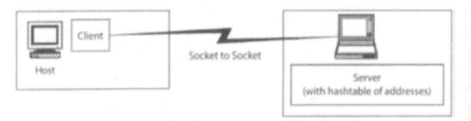

Figure 30.2 The simple client–server application.

The actual application being implemented is an address book. The addresses of employees of a company are held in a hash table. This hash table is set up in the `Servers` constructor, but could equally be held in a database etc.

30.4.2 Implementing the Server Application

We shall describe the server application first. This is the Java application program that will service requests from client applets for information. To do this it must provide a server socket for clients to connect to. Listing 30.1 presents the annotated source code for the `Server` class.

Listing 30.1 The Server application

```java
import java.net.*;
import java.io.*;
import java.util.*;

public class Server {
  // Instance variable to hold names and addresses
  private Hashtable addressTable;

  // Main method to start the erver application
  public static void main (String args []) {
    Server s = new Server();
    s.start();
  }

  public Server() {
    // Set up names and addresses
    addressTable = new Hashtable(10);
    addressTable.put("John",   "C45");
    addressTable.put("Denise", "C44");
    addressTable.put("Phoebe", "B52");
    addressTable.put("Isobel", "E23");
  }

  public void start() {
    // Set up the server socket
    ServerSocket serverSocket = null;
    Socket socket;
    InputStream socketIn;
    OutputStream socketOut;
    DataInputStream dataInputStream;
    DataOutputStream dataOutputStream;
    ObjectInputStream objectInputStream;
    ObjectOutputStream objectOutputStream;
```

```java
// Register service on port 1234
try {
  serverSocket = new ServerSocket(1234);
} catch (IOException e) {System.out.println
      ("Server socket registration failed");}

// Wait for a connection from a client
while (true) {
  try {
    // Wait here and listen for a connection
    socket = serverSocket.accept();
    socketIn = socket.getInputStream();
    dataInputStream = new
      DataInputStream(socketIn);
    objectInputStream = new
      ObjectInputStream(dataInputStream);
    String queryString =
      (String)objectInputStream.readObject();

    // Now obtain information from addressTable
    // need to cast the result of a string as
    // Object is returned by default.
    String result =
      (String)addressTable.get(queryString);

    // Return information to client
    // Get a communications stream from the socket
    socketOut = socket.getOutputStream();
    dataOutputStream = new
      DataOutputStream(socketOut);
    objectOutputStream = new
      ObjectOutputStream(dataOutputStream);
    objectOutputStream.writeObject(result);

    // Now close the connections, but not the
    // server socket
    dataInputStream.close();
    dataOutputStream.close();
    socketIn.close();
    socketOut.close();
    socket.close();
  } catch (IOException e) {
    System.out.println("Error during socket
      communications: " + e.getMessage());
    e.printStackTrace();
  } catch (ClassNotFoundException e) {
```

```
        System.out.println("Error reading object in
          from socket: " + e.getMessage());
        e.printStackTrace();
      }
    }
  }
}
```

Essentially the Server in Listing 30.1 sets up the addressTable to contain a hash table of the names and addresses available. It then waits for a client to connect to it. This is done by creating a serverSocket (in this case on port 1234). It then enters a loop where it continually waits for connections, processes requests and waits for the next connection. When the connection is made, it uses the input stream of its socket to obtain the information provided by the client. Note that although this is a socket to socket communication, as streams are used, the way to pass an object is exactly the same as writing that object out to a file. Thus serialization is used to pass the string between the two processes (remember a Java string is an object). It then queries the addressTable and returns the result (again using serialization to write the string to the output stream). Having done all this it closes its connection to the socket. It is now ready for the next query. As you can see from this, the program is actually very straightforward. This is thanks primarily to the Java ServerSocket and Stream classes that hide a great deal of the implementation details often associated with socket communications.

30.4.3 Implementing the Client application

The client application is essentially a very simple program that creates a link to the server application. To do this it creates a socket that connects to the server's host machine, and in our case this socket is connected to port 1234. It then uses an object output stream to pass a string to the server. Having done that, it waits for the server to provide a response. The response is the result of querying the database for the address associated with the supplied name. This is then printed out with an appropriate message.

The annotated source code for the Client applet is presented in Listing 30.2.

Listing 30.2 The Client applet

```
import java.net.*;
import java.io.*;
public class Client {

  public static void main (String args []) {
    String query = null;
    if (args.length == 0) {
      System.out.println("Usage: java Client <name>");
    } else {
```

```java
    query = args[0];
}

try {
  // First get a socket connection to the Server
  // object
  Socket socket = new Socket("jhunthome", 1234);
  OutputStream outputStream =
    socket.getOutputStream();
  DataOutputStream dataOutputStream = new
    DataOutputStream(outputStream);
  ObjectOutputStream objectOutputStream = new
    ObjectOutputStream(dataOutputStream);
  // Now send a query requesting the required
  // information
  objectOutputStream.writeObject(query);

  // Now get the response
  InputStream inputStream =
    socket.getInputStream();
  DataInputStream dataInputStream = new
    DataInputStream(inputStream);
  ObjectInputStream objectInputStream = new
    ObjectInputStream(dataInputStream);

  String results =
    (String)objectInputStream.readObject();

  // Once we get the result - print it out
  if (results == null) {
    System.out.println("No address is held for " +
      query);
  } else {
    System.out.println("Address for " + query + "
      is : ");
    System.out.println(results);
  }

  dataOutputStream.close();
  dataInputStream.close();
  outputStream.close();
  inputStream.close();
  socket.close();

} catch (IOException e) {
  System.out.println("Error during socket
    communications: " + e.getMessage());
```

```
      e.printStackTrace();
    } catch (ClassNotFoundException e) {
      System.out.println("Error reading object in from
        socket: " + e.getMessage());
      e.printStackTrace();
    }
  }
}
```

An example of using the client to query the server is presented below:

```
C:\jjh\JAVA\chap30>java chap30.Client James
No address is held for James

C:\jjh\JAVA\chap30>java chap30.Client Phoebe
Address for Phoebe is :
B52
```

30.5 Further Reading

Parker, T. (1994) *Teach Yourself TCP/IP in 14 Days*. Sams Publishing, Indianapolis.

31 Java and Remote Method Invocation

31.1 Introduction

In the last chapter we looked at how an applet could communicate with a server application using sockets. This approach is relatively straightforward to use and exploits the widely adopted Sockets communication model. However, Java offers another way of enabling Java programs (both applets and applications) to communicate – Remote Method Invocation (or RMI). Indeed, RMI is surprisingly simple to use and may well be preferable to sockets for Java-to-Java communication. This is because the resulting software is simpler and easier to maintain than using sockets. For example, a distributed software system resembles a software system executing within a single virtual machine except for the addition of one line to a client and two lines to a server! Note that all RMI classes are in the `java.rmi` package or one of its subpackages, such as `server`.

31.2 Remote Method Invocation

Remote Method Invocation is one of the facilities provided in Java for implementing distributed systems (others include Sockets and interfaces to CORBA-compliant ORBs). RMI is similar in concept to Remote Procedure Calls (RPC) for procedural languages. Essentially, an object can invoke a method on another object in a separate process (potentially on a different machine).

RMI is surprisingly straightforward, merely requiring the developer to:

- define a remote interface (which specifies what methods are available remotely)
- subclass an appropriate RMI server class
- run the `rmic` compiler on the server class to generate the stub and skeleton files used with RMI
- register the remote object with the RMI registry

The remote object is then available for use. In turn, the client need only obtain a reference to the remote object (via the registry) to be able to invoke remote methods on it. We will look at each of these steps in a little more detail.

Note that the registry is a central resource that records the names of remote objects and references to them. Using the registry, clients can obtain a reference that allows them to communicate with the remote server.

31.2.1 The Remote Interface

A remote interface specifies the methods that will be available remotely from an RMI server object. All objects which are going to make themselves available remotely must implement a remote interface. To define a remote interface you must follow a number of steps:

- Define a new interface.
- Make this interface extend the interface java.rmi.Remote.
- Define any methods which are going to be available remotely (these methods must be public).
- Each method must declare that it throws the java.rmi.RemoteException.

As an example, consider the remote interface definition in Listing 31.1. This listing shows the RMIInterface interface to be used by the RMIServer.

Listing 31.1 *The RMIInterface remote interface*

```
package myrmi;

/**
 * The remote interface used to indicate which
 * methods are remotely available.
 */
public interface RMIInterface extends
    java.rmi.Remote {
  public String query(String request)
         throws java.rmi.RemoteException;
}
```

31.2.2 Subclassing a Server Class

Once you have defined a remote interface, you can start to define the server class that implements this interface. To do this you need to:

- Specify the remote interface(s) being implemented by the server.
- Optionally subclass a remote server (e.g. java.rmi.server.Unicast-RemoteObject).
- Provide implementations for the methods specified in the remote interface.
- Define a constructor for the server. This constructor must throw the java.rmi.RemoteException.
- Create and install the java.rmi.RMISecurityManager.

These steps sound complex, but are in reality straightforward. For example, Listing 31.2 illustrates the source code for the RMIServer remote object class. As you can see, it implements the RMIInterface interface and thus the query(String) method. It defines a null parameter constructor that throws the

RemoteException exception (as indicated above). Within this constructor, it first calls super(). This invokes the null argument constructor[1] of the java.rmi.server.UnicastRemoteObject. By doing this, the remote object is "exported" so that it can handle calls to the remote object on an anonymous port (actually 1099). Next, the constructor calls the initialize() method. This method merely sets up a vector of vectors containing the test data. For a real system, this data might be extracted from other systems or a database. Once inside a try block, the constructor then uses the setSecurityManager() method of the System class to install a newly created instance of the RMISecurityManagar. Note that we do not need to know much about this security manager to be able to use it.

Listing 31.2 The RMIServer class

```java
package myrmi;

import java.rmi.*;
import java.rmi.server.UnicastRemoteObject;
import java.util.Vector;

/**
 * An RMI server. This server records the partners of
 * various people. It will then return the name of a
 * person's partner or the string "Unknown".
 */
public class RMIServer extends UnicastRemoteObject
implements RMIInterface {
  private Vector data = new Vector();

/**
 * This constructor initialises the simple data
 * structure holding the information and registers
 * this object with the rmiregistry.
 * @throws RemoteException
 */
public RMIServer() throws RemoteException {
  super();
  initialize();
  try {
    System.setSecurityManager(new
      RMISecurityManager());
    System.out.println("Set security manager");
    Naming.rebind("//hal.dcs.aber.ac.uk/RMIServer",
      this);
```

---

1 This would actually happen by default, but it is included here to indicate the operations occurring.

```
      System.out.println("RMIServer bound in registry");
    } catch (Exception e) {
      System.out.println("RMIServer error " +
        e.getMessage());
      e.printStackTrace();
    }
}

/**
  * Initialises the internal data structure with sample
  * data. A better solution would be to hold this
  * information in a database, but for simplicity it is
  * held internally.
  */
public void initialize() {
  addRecord("John", "Denise");
  addRecord("Paul", "Fiona");
  addRecord("Peter", "Maureen");
  addRecord("Bernard", "Liz");
}

// Adds the information to the data structure. Note
// the data is added twice so that if a name is found
// the following name is always the persons partner
// (or null)
private void addRecord(String s1, String s2) {
  Vector details = new Vector();
  details.addElement(s1); details.addElement(s2);
  data.addElement(details);
  details = new Vector();
  details.addElement(s2); details.addElement(s1);
  data.addElement(details);
}

/**
  * This method is the externally published method that
  * may be called by any remote object which has
  * obtained a reference for the remote object
  * @returns String
  * @throws java.rmi.RemoteException
  */
public String query(String request) throws
java.rmi.RemoteException {
  String result = "Unknown";
  for (int i=0; i < data.size(); i++) {
    Vector record = (Vector)data.elementAt(i);
    String person = (String)record.elementAt(0);
```

```
        if (person.equals(request))
            result = (String)record.elementAt(1);
    }
    return result;
}

/**
 * Test harness for RMIServer
 */
public static void main(String args []) {
    try {
        new RMIServer();
    } catch (RemoteException e) {
        System.out.println("RMIServer error " +
            e.getMessage());
        e.printStackTrace();
    }
}
}
```

The other thing to note is the call to `rebind()` sent to the class `Naming`. This is actually the process used to register this object with the RMI registry. This allows another object in a different process to obtain a reference to this object. Essentially, the registry maintains a table of remote objects and how to reference them (i.e. the machine and port they are connected to). This process is illustrated in Figure 31.1.

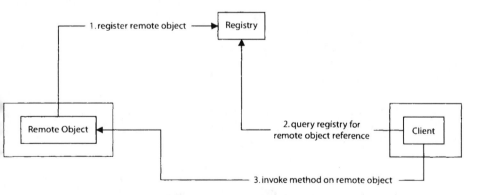

Figure 31.1 How the registry manages RMI references.

If you do not want to use the default port, a different port can be specified when the object is registered with the registry. For example, `//hal.dcs.aber.ac.uk:1234/RMIServer` would connect the `RMIServer` to port `1234`.

31.2.3 Running the rmic Compiler

Once you have defined the server class and successfully compiled it, you can then run the rmic compiler. This compiler is applied to the .class file rather than the .java file. For example, to execute the rmic compiler on the RMIServer class just created we would issue the following command at the command line:

```
rmic myrmi.RMIServer
```

Note that I have specified the package within which the RMIServer is implemented. This produces two additional .class files:

- RMIServer_Skel.class
- RMIServer_Stub.class

These files define the skeleton and stub files used to interface between the server and any clients. Essentially, the skeleton connects the server to the RMI framework, while the stub acts as a proxy server in the client's environment. This is illustrated in Figure 31.2.

Figure 31.2 Using the skeleton and stub classes.

31.2.4 Starting the Registry

We are now nearly ready to deploy our RMI server object. However, we must first start the RMI registry so that it can record the location and name of the server object. This is done by executing the rmiregistry command. This command produces no output and is typically run in the background. For example, on Windows 95/98/NT you can issue the following command from the command line:

```
start rmiregistry
```

If start is not available, you can use javaw. In fact, on a Windows machine you can merely execute rmiregistry within a DOS window and it will start to execute. However, if you terminate the window you will terminate the rmiregistry process (hence the use of start or javaw).

The registry runs on port 1099 by default. If you want to start the registry on a different port, specify the port number in the command. For example, to run the registry on port 1234 use:

```
start rmiregistry 1234
```

You can now start the server object. As the RMIServer class implements the main method, this remote object can be initiated in the normal manner:

```
java myrmi.RMIServer
```

31.3 The RMIClient

As we now have a server object that is running and has registered itself with the RMI registry, we can now create a client object. In our case we want to create a class which will obtain a string from the command line and print out the result returned from the RMIServer object. Listing 31.3 presents the RMIClient class definition.

Listing 31.3 The RMIClient class

```java
package myrmi;

import java.rmi.*;

/**
 * A simple client class used to conneсct to the
 * RMIServer remote object and query it for the
 * partner of the specified person.
 */
public class RMIClient {
  private String question;
  public RMIClient(String string) {
    question = string;
    try {
      System.out.println("Attempting to gain reference
        to the remote object");
      RMIInterface remoteObject =
          (RMIInterface)Naming.lookup
            ("//hal.dcs.aber.ac.uk/RMIServer");
      System.out.println("Reference to remote object
          obtained");
      // Get string from remote object
      System.out.println("Issuing query to remote
          object");
      String reply = remoteObject.query(question);
      System.out.println(" \n" + question + "s partner
          is " + reply);
    } catch (Exception e) {
      System.out.println("RMIClient error " +
          e.getMessage());
      e.printStackTrace();
    }
  }

  /**
   * Test harness for RMIClientBean
   */
```

```
public static void main(String args []) {
  if (args.length == 1)
    new RMIClient(args[0]);
  else
    System.out.println("Usage: java RMIClient
        <name>");
}
}
```

The RMIClient is an extremely simple class. It obtains the first command line parameter and uses that as the query to pass to the RMIServer. It obtains a reference to the RMIServer from the rmiregistry (the confusingly named class Naming). For example:

```
(RMIInterface)Naming.lookup("//hal.dcs.aber.ac.uk/
    RMIServer");
```

Note that it has to specify the machine on which the server is running as well as the name given to the server. Also, note that the object returned by the lookup method must be cast to the remote interface type (in this case RMIInterface). The resulting object can now be used in just the same way as a local object. In fact, it is a local object (the stub object). The calls are then passed on to the actual server object via the RMI framework.

The result of executing the rmiregistry, the RMIServer and the RMIClient are illustrated in Figure 31.3.

31.4 Converting to an Applet

If we wish to convert the RMIClient into an applet, then there are three things we need to do:

1. Provide a graphical interface to be displayed within the Web browser or appletviewer.
2. Implement an init() method to set up this GUI.
3. Implement an actionPerformed(ActionEvent) method to obtain the result of querying the RMIServer.

The resulting applet is presented in Listing 31.4 (the RMIApplet class). This applet is presented in Figure 31.4, where it is running inside the appletviewer. As can be seen from this example, although the code used to access the RMIServer has been moved from the constructor of the RMIClient into the action-Performed(ActionEvent) method of the RMIApplet, the code is actually the same. Thus using the RMI within an applet is as straightforward as using it within an application.

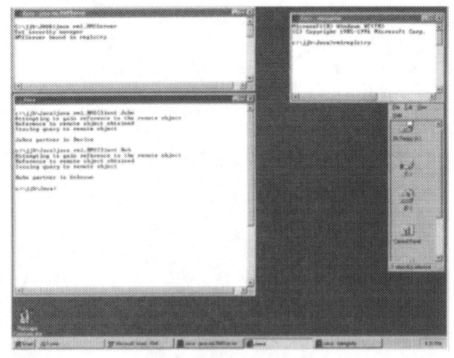

Figure 31.3 Running the RMI example.

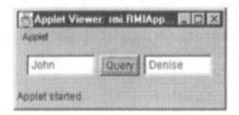

Figure 31.4 Running the RMIApplet in the appletviewer.

Listing 31.4 *The* RMIApplet *class*

```
package myrmi;

import java.rmi.*;
import java.awt.*;
import java.awt.event.*;

/**
 * A simple client applet to illustrate how RMI can be
 * used in applets.
 */
```

```java
public class RMIApplet extends java.applet.Applet
implements ActionListener {
  private TextField input, output;
  public void init() {
    // Build up the display
    Panel p = new Panel();
    input = new TextField(8);
    p.add(input);
    Button b = new Button("Query");
    b.addActionListener(this);
    p.add(b);
    output = new TextField(8);
    p.add(output);
    add(p);
  }
  /**
   * Method stipulated by the ActionListener interface
   */
  public void actionPerformed(ActionEvent event) {
    String query = input.getText();
    try {
      RMIInterface remoteObject =
        (RMIInterface)Naming.lookup
          ("//hal.dcs.aber.ac.uk/RMIServer");
      // Get string from remote object
      String reply = remoteObject.query(query);
      output.setText(reply);
    } catch (Exception e) {
      System.out.println("RMIApplet error " +
        e.getMessage());
      e.printStackTrace();
    }
  }
}
```

31.5 Performance

A concern, which is often expressed with reference to RMI in Java, is that there must be a performance penalty (compared with using plain sockets). As RMI is built on top of sockets, but provides additional support via the RMI registry for locating objects and providing skeletons and stubs as required, there must of course be some performance penalty. However, depending on how you use sockets in Java, the relative performance of RMI may be a surprise.

To illustrate this, Table 31.1 presents the performance of RMI versus two different implementations that make use of sockets. To keep the performance trials similar, all

Table 31.1 Comparative performance of RMI and sockets

Test application	Average of 100 exchanges
RMI	39 ms
Serialization and sockets	17 ms
UTF conversion and sockets	4002 ms

three applications passed one string from the client to the server and returned another string 100 times. Averages were calculated for the two-step send and retrieve process. One of the socket implementations uses the UTF read and write string methods. The other socket implementation uses serialization. In serialization, the object to be sent via the socket is "serialized" into a form that can be restored at the other end. At present, this approach can only work between Java programs (just as RMI can only be used to connect different Java programs). In contrast, the UTF approach writes strings in a platform-independent manner that could be used between Java and any programming language.

All tests were carried out on a 133 MHz Pentium PC with 32 MByte of memory, using the standard JDK 1.1.5 virtual machine, without optimization turned on (in the javac compiler).

As can be seen from Table 31.1, RMI is twice as slow as serialization and sockets; however, the conversion to UTF format strings is significantly slower (100 times slower!). This appears to be due to the writeUTF() and readUTF() methods. These methods are written in Java (as opposed to being part of the JVM as is the case with serialization – which is also used by RMI) or implemented in native code. In addition, this Java does not look particularly optimal.

Thus the use of sockets in the blind belief that they will always be faster than RMI is not true. The performance penalty which is incurred by RMI (relative to serialization and sockets) does need to be considered; however, the resulting programs are far, far simpler. For comparison, the serialization test programs are presented in Listing 31.5. If you compare these with the RMI class presented earlier (upon which the test applications were based), you can see that it is quite a bit more complicated.

Listing 31.5 *Serialization and sockets server and client code*

```java
import java.net.*;
import java.io.*;

/**
 * Simple server class which provides address for
 * named people using a simple protocol (e.g. name =
 * 'John'). The socket to socket communication
 * facilities of Java are used to connect a client to
 * this server.
 */
public class SerializationServer {

    // Starts the server application
```

```java
public static void main (String args []) {
  SerializationServer s = new SerializationServer();
  s.start();
}

/**
 * Provides the main server loop:
 * 1. Wait for a connection
 * 2. Obtain a reuqest for an address
 * 3. Query the database
 * 4. Respond with a null string or the address
 */
public void start() {
  // Set up the server socket
  ServerSocket serverSocket = null;
  Socket socket;
  InputStream socketIn;
  OutputStream socketOut;
  ObjectInputStream objectInputStream;
  ObjectOutputStream objectOutputStream;
  String queryString;

  // Register service on port 1234
  try {
    serverSocket = new ServerSocket(1234);
  } catch (IOException e)
    {System.out.println("Server socket registration
    failed");}

  try {
    // Wait here and listen for a connection
    socket = serverSocket.accept();
    socketIn = socket.getInputStream();
    objectInputStream = new
      ObjectInputStream(socketIn);
    // Get a communications stream from the socket
    socketOut = socket.getOutputStream();
    objectOutputStream = new
      ObjectOutputStream(socketOut);

    queryString =
      (String)objectInputStream.readObject();
    // Wait for data from a client
    while (!queryString.equals("end")) {
      // Return information to client
      objectOutputStream.writeObject("John");
```

```
        queryString =
          (String)objectInputStream.readObject();
      }

      // Now close the connections, but not the server
      // socket
      objectInputStream.close();
      objectOutputStream.close();
      socketIn.close();
      socketOut.close();
      socket.close();
    } catch (Exception e) {
      System.out.println("Error during socket
        communications" + e.getMessage());
      e.printStackTrace();
    }
  }
}

import java.net.*;
import java.io.*;

/**
 * A simple client to test client / server via sockets
 */
public class SerializationClient {
  private String query = "name";
  private Socket socket;
  private OutputStream outputStream;
  private ObjectOutputStream objectOutputStream;
  private InputStream inputStream;
  private ObjectInputStream objectInputStream;

  public static void main(String args []) {
    SerializationClient c;
    if (args.length == 0) {
      c = new SerializationClient();
    } else {
      c = new SerializationClient(args[0]);
    }
    c.test();
  }

  // Method used to initialize an applet.
  // Sets up the applet panel.
  public SerializationClient () {
    this("manuel.dcs.aber.ac.uk");
```

```java
    }

    public SerializationClient(String s) {
      try {
        // First get a socket connection to the Server
        // object
        socket = new Socket(s, 1234);
        outputStream = socket.getOutputStream();
        objectOutputStream = new
          ObjectOutputStream(outputStream);

        // New get the input streams
        inputStream = socket.getInputStream();
        objectInputStream = new
          ObjectInputStream(inputStream);
      } catch (Exception e) {
        System.out.println("Error during socket
          communications");
        System.out.println(e.getMessage());
      }
    }

    public void test() {
      String result;

      long first = 0, second = 0, total = 0;

      try {
        for (int j = 0; j < 10; j++) {
          System.out.println("Round: " + j);
          first = System.currentTimeMillis();
          for (int i = 0; i < 10; i++) {
            // Now send a query to the server specifying
            // the name to search for
            objectOutputStream.writeObject("name");
            result =
              (String)objectInputStream.readObject();
          }
          second = System.currentTimeMillis();
          total = total + (second - first);
        }

        objectOutputStream.writeObject("end");

        System.out.println("total : " + total + "
          Average: " + (total / 10));
```

```
        // Close streams and socket
        objectOutputStream.close();
        objectInputStream.close();
        outputStream.close();
        inputStream.close();
        socket.close();
    } catch (Exception e) {
        System.out.println("Error during test method");
        System.out.println(e.getMessage());
    }
  }
}
```

31.6 Exercise: RMI Hello World

The aim of this exercise is to define a simple distributed program using Remote Method Invocation (RMI). This will be a distributed version of the "Hello World" program.

31.6.1 What You Should Do

First define the interface and classes required:

1. You should define an interface which extends the `java.rmi.Remote` interface and specifies a public method `printHelloWorld()` which throws the `java.rmi.RemoteException`.
2. You should define a class which will print hello world in response to a request to execute a `printHelloWorld()` request.
3. This class needs to use `Naming.rebind(server, this)` to make itself available for remote access.
4. You should then define a separate class which obtains a reference to the remote class using `Naming.lookup(Server)`.
5. Using this reference call `printHelloWorld()` remotely.
6. Next use the `rmic` compiler to create the stubs and skeletons required.
7. Now start the RMI registry using:

   ```
   start rmiregistry      (Win95/98/NT)
   rmiregistry &          (UNIX)
   ```

   Remember to start the remote objects program first.
8. Now run the calling objects program.

32 *Servlets: Serving Java up on the Web*

32.1 Introduction

Java has primarily been a language used to implement browser-side programs, also known as applets, when it comes to the Web. However, with the Java servlet API, the power of Java can be applied to server-side software as well as client, browser-side, software. This chapter tells you how servlets are written, what they are used for and how they interact with browser requests.

Just as applets are (at least conceptually) small applications, in the same way as a piglet is a little pig, servlets are programs that run on the Web server. Of course, just as with applets, the size of a servlet is not restricted and it may be anything from a few lines of code to many thousands (or more) lines of code.

The key is that a servlet runs on the server and will respond to requests from a client, either from HTML pages or indeed applets. Thus a servlet is used in situations where CGI (Common Gateway Interface) scripts might be used. These scripts are more often than not implemented in Perl (a scripting language) and sometimes in C. So why should you write a servlet in Java rather than write a Perl script? The primary reasons are that:

- Java is a high-level language with very many good software engineering features. In contrast, Perl is a difficult language to write, can be hard to comprehend and certainly difficult to maintain. Ask anyone who has written a particularly difficult bit of Perl to detail what that code does just a few days later. Many will find it hard to give you a detailed answer.

- Java code is platform-independent. Thus a servlet is platform-independent. In contrast, a Perl script (or indeed a C program) may well be platform-dependent.

Table 32.1 summarizes the contrast between Servlets and CGI scripts. Essentially, Servlets offer a great deal to the developer over Perl CGI scripts. For example, the Web server loads servlets only once. They can therefore maintain state and resources between multiple information requests. In contrast, CGI scripts are run each time they are called. They are thus transient and cannot hold the system state.

32.2 How Servlets Work

Just as applets have a browser–applet protocol, servlets have a server–servlet protocol. Servlets work in the manner illustrated in Figure 32.1.

Table 32.1 CGI–servlet comparison

	CGI scripts	**Servlets**
Persistence	No	Yes
Speed	Lower	Higher
Platform	Specific	Independent
Extensible	Hard	Hey! It's just Java
Invocation	Possible	Only through server
Maintainability	Poor	Good
Comprehensibility	Poor	Good
Accessibility	Limited	Good

Figure 32.1 Browser–server–servlet interaction.

- *Step 1*: A user using a Web browser requests some information from the Web server via an http request.
- *Step 2*: The Web server receives the request. If the request is for a straightforward HTML page then the appropriate HTML file will be loaded. If the request is to a servlet, then the servlet invoker will load and initiate the servlet (unless it was already running). This is done by running the servlet on a Java virtual machine (JVM).
- *Step 3*: The servlet's init() method is then executed. This method is the equivalent of the init() method defined for applets. That is, it is executed only once, when the servlet is first created. It should be used in the same way as the init() method for applets, that is, as the servlet's initialization method (rather than defining a constructor). The init() method must complete before any requests are handled.
- *Step 4*: The servlet will receive the HTTP request and perform some type of process. Each request is handled by its own thread (lightweight Java process). Depending upon the request, one of the following methods will be called to handle the request:
  - doGet – handles GET, conditional GET and HEAD requests
  - doPost – handles POST requests
  - doPut – handles PUT requests
  - doDelete – handles DELETE requests.
- *Step 5*: The servlet will return a response back to the Web server from one of the above methods.

- *Step 6*: The Web server will forward the response to the client.
- *Step 7*: When requested, the Web server will terminate the servlet. This may be done by the Web server administrator. At this time the destroy() method is called. This method runs only once and is used to "tidy" up any system resources used by the servlet etc. For the servlet to be run again, it must be reloaded by the Web server.

There are some things to note about servlets as opposed to applets.

Firstly, the servlet and its environment is completely under the control of those deploying it. That is, you have control of which JVM is used, and you are independent of the user's browser. This is important, as it removes concerns associated with the so-called "browser wars".

Secondly, a servlet is not constrained by the applet sandbox. This means that a servlet can reside behind a firewall and can communicate with any and all systems that it needs to. For example, JavaIDL can be used to connected to a CORBA-compliant Object Request Broker (ORB) or sockets can be used to connect to legacy systems (for example implemented in C).

Thirdly, the client Web browser does not communicate directly with the servlet. Rather, the browser communicates with the Web server, which in turn communicates with the servlet. Thus if the Web server is secure behind a firewall, then the servlet is also secure.

32.3 The Structure of the Servlet API

The Servlet API is made up of a number of packages, including the javax. servlet and javax.servlet.http packages. Note that these package names do not start with java but with javax. This indicates that they are a Java standard extension to the basic Java platform (a standard introduced with JDK 1.2/Java 2). This means that a Java vendor does not have to support this API (although many vendors are already supporting it). You can obtain the Java Servlet Development Kit 2.0 (the JSDK 2.0) from Sun's Java Web site (see http://java.sun.com, products/). This development kit can be used to develop and test server extensions based on the servlet API. Included in the development kit is the servlet source code, reference documentation and tutorial as well as a standalone server (called servlet-runner) that can be used to test servlets before running them on a servlet-enabled Web server.

The JSDK 2.0 serves as the reference implementation for the Java Servlet API and can be used with JDK 1.1.*. If you are interested in developing servlets with JDK 1.2/Java 2, there is no need to use this JSDK, as the servlet API is bundled with JDK1.2/Java 2.

The key classes and interfaces in the Servlet API are presented below and are illustrated in Figure 32.2.

- Servlet This interface defines all the methods that a servlet must respond to (including init() and destroy()). Classes that implement this interface can be used as servlets.

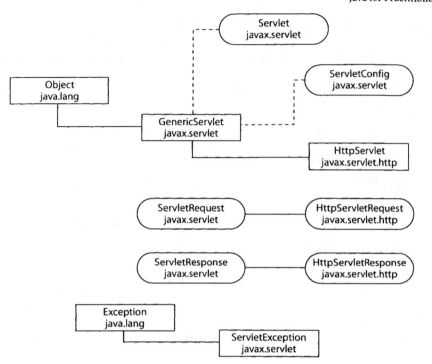

Figure 32.2 Java servlet classes and their inheritance relationships.

- HttpServlet This is an abstract class that is intended to simplify writing HTTP servlets. It extends the GenericServlet base class and provides a framework for handling the HTTP protocol. The methods that are overridden by subclasses are doGet, doPost, doPut, doDelete and getServletInfo. The four do* methods have already been mentioned. The getServletInfo method provides information through a service's administrative interfaces. Note that a developer need only override one of these methods and not all of them.

- HttpServletRequest This is an interface specification which extends the ServletRequest interface. It provides a definition for an object which provides data from the client to the servlet for use in the HttpServlets' methods.

- HttpServletResponse This is an interface specification which extends the ServletResponse interface. It defines the protocol for an object that manipulate HTTP protocol-specified header information and return data to its client.

These are the main interfaces and class used by a servlet. Of course, these are not the only classes and interfaces available; however, they are the key ones.

32.4 An Example Servlet

As we have now considered how servlets work as well as what the structure of a servlet is, we will look at a simple implementation. Listing 32.1 presents the

SampleServer class. This is a fully functional (if somewhat limited) servlet. It responds to POST requests for information. Essentially, a user inputs a name on a Web page and "submits" the information on that page to the Web server. The Web server in turn loads and runs this servlet. The servlet responds by generate an HTML page which includes the name of the wife of the specified man.

Note that the init() method, although it is used to set up the hashtable of names, first classes the super.init() method. This illustrates how the init() method should be overridden. That is, the super version of the method should be called first (super causes the method search to start in the parent class rather than the current class).

The doPost() method responds to requests generated by a Web client via the post option on the method parameter of the form tag (see later). There are actually two ways in which a Web client can send information to a server: POST and GET. We will only look at the approach used with posted information.

This method is overridden in a subclass of the GenericServlet class (or as in this case one of its subclasses). It takes two parameters, one a request object and one a response object. The request object is used to access the information provided when the client "posted" the request. In this case it will be used to access the name text field on an HTML page. In turn, the response object is used to return the result (which is probably going to be in the form of HTML). To use the response object the developer of the servlet must set entity headers in the response, access the output stream of the response and use this output stream to write any response data. The headers that are set should include content type and encoding. If a writer is to be used to write response data, the content type must be set before the writer is accessed. In general, the servlet implementer must write the headers before the response data because the headers can be flushed at any time after the data starts to be written.

To set the content type of the response, the setContentType() method is used. This method may only be invoked once for each execution of the doPost() method.

Notice that the doPost() method throws two types of exception: the IOException and the ServletException. The IOException may be thrown during the process of reading from the request object or writing to the response object. In turn, the ServletException may be thrown if the request could not be handled.

Listing 32.1 The SamplerServer.java file

```
import java.util.*;
import javax.servlet.*; import javax.servlet.http.*;

public class SampleServer extends HttpServlet {
   Hashtable table = new Hashtable();
   public void init(ServletConfig sc)
      throws ServletException {
    super.init(sc);

    // Set up info for servlet example
```

```
      table.put("John",  "Denise");
      table.put("Paul",  "Fiona");
      table.put("Peter", "Karen");
   }

   public void doPost(HttpServletRequest req,
         HttpServletResponse res)
         throws ServletException,
            IOException {
      // Set the content type header of the response
      res.setContentType("text/html");

      // Get the output stream to write the html out to
      PrintWriter output. res.getWriter();

      // Get value passed to servlet from the html page
      String name = req.getParameter("Name");
      // Generate response in HTML
      String result = table.get(name);
      output.println("<html>\n<head><body>");
      output.println("<title>Example</title></head>");
      output.println("<p>");
      output.println("The wife of " + name +
         " is " + result);
      output.println("</p></body></html>");
      output.flush();
   }

   public void destroy() {
      super.destroy();
      // Anything specific to this application
   }
}
```

Note that to generate the HTML which is output back to the Web server and subsequently to the Web browser we actually use a PrintWriter and the println method. This is exactly the same as if we were writing to a stream for any other purpose (such as writing to a file or a socket).

Also note that in this case, although the init() method is actually used to set up the hashtable to be used by the doPost() method, the destroy() method does not need to be included. It is presented here to illustrate how it should be overridden. That is, the super version of the method should be called first.

Having defined the servlet, we now need to define an HTML page which will request services on that servlet. Listing 32.2 provides just such an HTML page (which appears in a browser as shown in Figure 32.3). This HTML page is very simple. It uses a form to allow a user to enter a name. This name is passed to the servlet when the

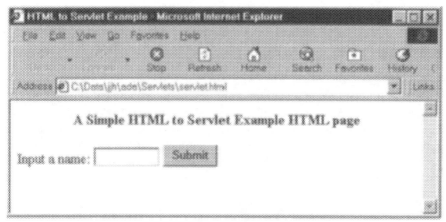

Figure 32.3 The HTML page used to access the servlet.

submit button is pressed. Notice that the form header tag specifies the action to perform when the Submit button is pressed. Thus in this case it specifies the SimpleServer servlet. It does this by specifying the Web server from which the servlet should be downloaded and then the directory on that server containing the servlet (plus the name of the servlet). Note that in this case the method associated with the action is POST – thus the doPost() method will be called on the servlet.

Listing 32.2 The HTML page

```
<HTML>
<HEAD>
<TITLE> HTML to Servlet Example</title>
</HEAD>
<BODY>
<FORM action="http://www.ttc.demon.co.uk/servlet/
SimpleServer" method = "POST">
Input a name:
<INPUT type=text name=name size=10>
<INPUT type=submit value="Submit">
</FORM>
</BODY>
</HTML>
```

A form rather than an applet was used in this example, as the client is significantly simpler, particularly for this very simple system. However, it is important to realize that rather than a form, the request could have come from an applet.

HTML forms provide a way of interacting with a Web page that requires no scripting or applet writing. In addition, almost every type of browser, from whichever vendor, supports HTML forms. This makes the form a very sensible choice for Web developers. As forms are just HTML, they follow the familiar tag structure seen with other HTML constructs. They possess a start tag and an end tag.

Between these tags you can use standard HTML to lay out your form, as well as special forms tags to provide for interactivity. These forms tags include buttons, text fields and text areas, selection boxes etc.

One button used with a form is of particular interest: the Submit button. This button (illustrated in Listing 32.2 and Figure 32.3) invokes a Web server-side action by requesting some service. This service could be provided by a CGI script, or, as in this case, by a servlet. The effect of the user selecting the Submit button is that all the input information (in Listing 32.2 the information entered into the text field) is collected together and sent to the to the server along with the service requested. In our case this results in the server loading and initializing the servlet and then invoking the doPost() method. The information collected from the form is provided to the servlet via the HttpServletRequest object.

Once the SampleServer processes the request it returns a response in terms of HTML as described earlier. The resulting Web page is illustrated in Figure 32.4.

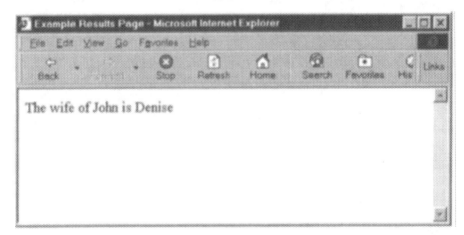

Figure 32.4 The result of querying the servlet.

32.5 Why Use Servlets?

There are a wide range of situations in which you might wish to use servlets. The example given here is for processing data POSTed over HTTPS using an HTML form. This example could be extended further and could be used as the basis of an e-commerce system. For example, an order-entry and processing system could be implemented in this way. The servlet could receive and process the information provided. It could then generate a transaction which could be passed to the enterprise's main sales system and on to the deployment and payment systems (remember that a servlet is not restricted in what it can connect to in the way that an applet would be).

Another situation in which you might want to use a servlet might be the provision of real-time updates to a Web page. Rather than gaining a static Web page generated, say, the night before, the Web page viewed by the user could present the latest data. This could be used to view the current state of stocks and shares etc.

A servlet can also be used to help balance the load on a server. If a server receives a request for a service, but decides that the current server is too heavily loaded, it could forward that request to other servers and servlets, thus allowing a single logical service to be presented to the user which actually exploits multiple servers.

32.6 Summary

Java servlets are an enormously useful extension to the standard Java platform. They can be used instead of CGI scripts and offer greater portability, maintainability and reliability than such scripts. In addition they are not constrained by the "sandbox" in the way that Java applets are constrained. It is likely that they will be used in many client–server Web-based applications using XML and HTML rather than applets.

32.7 Further Reading

Moss, K. (1998). *Java Servlets.* McGraw-Hill, New York.

Servlet download:

```
http://java.sun.com/products/
```

33 *Java Database Connectivity*

33.1 Introduction

Officially JDBC is not an acronym; however, to all intents and purposes it stands for Java DataBase Connectivity. This is the mechanism by which relational databases are access in Java. Java is an (almost) pure object-oriented language; however, although there are some object-oriented databases available, many database systems presently in commercial use are relational. It is therefore necessary for any object-oriented language which is to be used for commercial development to provide an interface to such databases. Unfortunately, each database vendor provides its own proprietary (and different) API. In many cases these are little more than variations on a theme, but they tend to be incompatible. This means that if you were to write a program that was designed to interface with one database system, it is unlikely that it would automatically work with another.

Of course, one of the philosophies of Java is *"write once, run anywhere"*. This means that we do not want to have to rewrite our Java code just because it is using a different database on a different platform (or even the same platform). JDBC is Sun's attempt to provide a vendor-independent interface to any relational database system. This is possible, as most vendors implement most (if not all) of the standard SQL, thus allowing a common denominator. SQL stands for Structured Query Language and is used to obtain information from relational databases. SQL is a large topic in its own right and is beyond the scope of this chapter. Reference is therefore made to appropriate books at the end of the chapter.

One potential problem with such an approach is that although the developers' interface is the same, different implementations of an application would be needed to link to different databases. In the JDBC this is overcome by providing different back-end drivers. Developers are now insulated from the details of the various relational database systems that they may be using and have a greater chance of producing portable code.

In the remainder of this chapter we consider JDBC and these database drivers in more detail. We then look at some examples of typical database operations and consider the implications for applets.

33.2 What Is JDBC?

The JDBC allows a Java developer to connect to a database, to interact with that database via SQL, and of course to use those results within a Java application or applet. The combination of Java and JDBC allows information held in databases to be easily and quickly published on the Web (via an applet). It also provides a bridge that supports the Open Database Connectivity (ODBC) standard. The first version of the JDBC was released in the summer of 1996. It is an important addition to Java's armoury, as the JDBC provides programmers with a language and environment that is platform- and database vendor-independent. This is (almost) unique. Most developers who use the ODBC C API are database vendor-independent, but find it nontrivial to port their C applications to different platforms due to windowing differences, hardware-dependent language features etc.

ODBC is a database access standard developed by Microsoft. This standard has been widely adopted, not only by the vendors of Windows-based databases but by others as well. For example, a number of databases more normally associated with UNIX-based systems or IBM mainframes now offer an ODBC interface. Essentially, ODBC is a basic SQL interface to a database system that assumes only "standard" SQL features. Thus specialist facilities provided by different database vendors cannot be accessed. In many ways, JDBC has similar aims to ODBC. However, one major different is that JDBC allows different database drivers (interfaces) to be used, one of which is the ODBC driver.

At present, the JDBC only allows connection to, and interaction with, a database via SQL. Features such as those found in tools like Delphi and Visual Basic are not available. For example, there are no database controls, form designers or query builders. Of course, it is likely that such tools will become available either from Sun or from third-party vendors. This situation will change in the future, as many JFC components (or Java Foundation Classes) are data-aware. The JFC provides an enhanced set of tools including GUI components and is due to appear in release 1.2 of Sun's JDK.

The JDBC is able to connect to any database by using different (back-end) drivers. These act as the interfaces between the JDBC and databases such as Oracle, Sybase, Microsoft Access and shareware systems such as MiniSQL. The idea is that the front end presented to the developer is the same whatever the database system, while the appropriate back-end is loaded as required. The JDBC then passes the programmer's SQL to the database via the back-end. Java is not the first system to adopt this approach; however, a novel feature of the JDBC is that more than one driver can be loaded at a time. The system will then try each driver until one is found that is compatible with the database system being used. Thus multiple drivers can be provided, and at run time the appropriate one is identified and used. This is illustrated in Figure 33.1.

Figure 33.1 illustrates some of the most commonly used methods provided by the JDBC along with two database drivers (namely the MiniSQL driver and the ODBC driver; note that any number could have been provided). Such a setup would allow a Java program to connect to an mSQL database via the mSQL driver and to any database that supports the ODBC standard through the ODBC driver. The getConnection(), executeQuery() and executeUpdate() methods will be looked at in more detail later in this chapter.

There are an increasing number of database drivers becoming available for JDBC. At present, databases such as Oracle, Sybase and Ingres all have their own drivers. This allows features of those databases to be exploited. However, even databases that

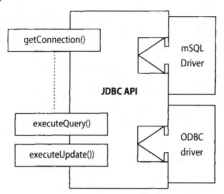

Figure 33.1 The structure of the JDBC.

are not directly supported can be accessed via the ODBC driver, thus making a huge range of databases available to the Java developer.

There is a very definite series of steps that must be performed by any JDBC program. These involve loading an appropriate driver, connecting to a database, executing SQL statements and closing the connection made. These are discussed in more detail later in this article.

33.3 What the Driver Provides

What actually is a driver? In practice, it provides the concrete implementation for a number of interfaces defined in the `java.sql` package. In particular, it defines implementations for the interfaces and classes (such as `Driver`, `Connection`, `Statement` and `ResultSet`) which form a major part of the SQL API. Each of these will be considered in more detail later. However, essentially they comprise the way to connect to a database, to pass SQL statements to be executed to that database and to examine the results returned. Note that, unlike some object-to-relational database interfaces, JDBC does not try to objectify the results of querying a relational database. Instead, the results are returned in a table-like format within a results set. It is then up to the developer to decide how to handle the information retrieved.

33.4 Registering Drivers

As part of the JDBC API a JDBC driver manager is provided. This is the part of the JDBC that handles the drivers currently available to a JDBC application. It is therefore necessary to "register" a driver with the driver manager. There are three ways of doing this:

1. Passing a command line option to a Java application using the `-Dproperty =value parameter`. For example:

```
java ●-Djdbc.drivers=jdbc.odbc.JdbcOdbcDriver queryDB
```

2. For applets it is possible to set the jdbc.drivers system property. In HotJava this can be done in the properties file of the .hotjava directory. For example:

```
jdbc.drivers=jdbc.odbc.JdbcOdbcDriver:
    imaginary.sql.iMsqlDriver
```

3. Programmatically by requesting the class of the driver to be loaded using the static method forName() in the class Class. For example:

```
Class.forName("sun.jdbc.odbc.JdbcOdbcDriver");
Class.forName("COM.imaginary.sql.msql.MsqlDriver");
```

This will cause the associated class (in this case the driver) to be loaded into the running application.

As was mentioned earlier, you can install more than one driver in your JDBC program. When a request is made to make a connection to a database each one will be tried in turn until one accepts that request. However, using more than one driver will slow down both system start-up (as each must be loaded) as well as your run-time program (as each may need to be tried in turn). For this reason, it may be best to select the most appropriate driver and stick with that one.

The JDBC ODBC driver is provided as part of Sun's JDK 1.1. However, other drivers can be obtained and used with the JDBC. For example, the mSQL driver mentioned above was downloaded from the Web and installed in an appropriate directory. In this way, database vendors can supply their own proprietary database drivers which developers can then utilize in their own applications.

33.5 Opening a Connection

Listing 33.1 presents a simple class that uses the ODBC driver to connect to a Microsoft Access database. We must first make the JDBC API available, which is done by importing the SQL package. Next the application loads the JDBC ODBC driver and then requests that the DriverManager makes a connection with the database testDB. Note that to make this connection a string (called url) is passed to the driver manager along with the user id and the password.

Listing 33.1 TestConnect.java

```
import java.sql.*;
public class TestConnect {

  public static void main (String args []) {
    String url = "jdbc:odbc:testDB";

    if (args.length < 2) {
      System.out.println("Usage: java TestConnect
        userid password");
      System.exit(1);
```

```
    }

    String userid = args[0];
    String password = args[1];

    try {
      Class.forName("sun.jdbc.odbc.JdbcOdbcDriver");
      Connection con =DriverManager.getConnection(url,
        userid, password);
      con.close();
      System.out.println("All okay");
    } catch (Exception e) {
      System.out.println(e.getMessage());
      e.printStackTrace();
    }
  }
}
```

The string specifying the database to connect to is formed from a JDBC URL. This is a URL that is comprised of three parts:

1. The JDBC protocol indicator (jdbc:)
2. The appropriate sub-protocol such as odbc:
3. The driver-specific components (in this case JdbcOdbcDriver)

URLs are used as the Java program accessing the database may be running as a standalone application or may be an applet needing to connect to the database via the Web. Note that different database drivers will require different driver-specific components. In particular, the mSQL driver requires a URL of the following format:

```
jdbc:msql://hal.aber.ac.uk:1112/testDB
```

In this case it is necessary to provide the host name, the port on that host to connect to and the database to be used.

Once a connection has successfully been made to the database, the program then does nothing other than to close that connection. This is important, as some database drivers require the program to close the connection while others leave it as optional. If you are using multiple drivers it is best to close the connection.

Note that the attempt to load the driver and make the connection we placed within a try-catch block. This is because both operations can raise exceptions and these must be caught and handled (as they are not run-time exceptions). The forName() method raises the ClassNotFoundException if it cannot find the class which represents the specified driver. In turn, the getConnection() static method raises the SQLException if the specified database cannot be found.

The try-catch block works by trapping any exceptions raised in the try part within the catch part (assuming the exception raised is an instance of the specified class of exception or one of its subclasses).

An example of using this application is presented below:

```
java TestConnect jeh popeye
```

Here I am passing in the user id jeh and the password popeye.

33.6 Obtaining Data from a Database

Having made a connection with a database we are now in a position to obtain information from it. Listing 33.2 builds on the application in Listing 33.1 by querying the
database for some information. This is done by obtaining a Statement object from
the Connection object. SQL statements without parameters are normally
executed using Statement objects. However, if the same SQL statement is executed
many times, it is more efficient to use a PreparedStatement. In this example we
will stick with the Statement object.

Listing 33.2 TestQuery.java

```
import java.sql.*;
public class TestQuery {

  public static void main (String args []) {
    String url = "jdbc:odbc:testdb";

    if (args.length < 2) {
      System.out.println("Usage: java TestQuery userid
        password");
      System.exit(1);
    }

    String userid = args[0];
    String password = args[1];

    try {
      Class.forName("sun.jdbc.odbc.JdbcOdbcDriver");
      Connection con =DriverManager.getConnection(url,
        userid, password);

      Statement statement = con.createStatement();
      ResultSet results =
        statement.executeQuery("SELECT address FROM
            addresses
          WHERE name = 'John' ");
      System.out.println("Addresses for John:");
      while (results.next()) {
```

```
        System.out.println(results.getString
          ("address"));
      }
      statement.close();

      con.close();
    } catch (Exception e) {
      System.out.println(e.getMessage());
      e.printStackTrace();
    }
  }
}
```

Having obtained the statement object we are now ready to pass it some SQL. This is done as a string within which the actual SQL statements are specified. In this case the SQL statement is:

```
SELECT address
   FROM addresses
   WHERE name = 'John'
```

This is pure SQL. The SELECT statement allows data to be obtained from the tables in the database. In this case the SQL states that the address field (column) of the table addresses should be retrieved where the name field of that row equals 'John'.

This string is passed to the statement object via the executeQuery() method. This method also generates an SQLException if a problem occurs. The method passes the SQL to the driver previously selected by the driver manager. The driver in turn passes the SQL on to the database system. The result is then returned to the driver which in turn returns it to the user's program as an instance of ResultsSet. A results set is a table of data within which each row contains the data which matched the SQL statement. Within the row, the columns contain the fields specified by the SQL. A ResultSet maintains a cursor pointing to its current row of data. Initially the cursor is positioned before the first row. The next() method moves the cursor to the next row.

The ResultsSet class defines a variety of get methods for obtain information out of the ResultsSet table, for example getBoolean(), getByte(), getString() and getDate(). These methods are provided by the JDBC driver and attempt to convert the underlying data to the specified Java type and return a suitable Java value. In Listing 33.2 we merely print out each address in turn using next() method to move the table cursor on.

Finally, the statement and the connection are closed. In many cases it is desirable to immediately release a statement's database and JDBC resources instead of waiting for this to happen when it is automatically closed; the close method provides this immediate release.

33.7 Creating a Table

So far we have examined how to connect to a database and how to query that database for information. However, we have not considered how that database is created. Obviously the database may not be created by a Java application – for example, it could be generated by a legacy system. However, in many situations it is necessary for the tables in the database to be updated (if not created) by a JDBC program. Listing 33.3 presents a modified version of Listing 33.2. This listing shows how a statement object can be used to create a table and how information can be inserted into that table. Again the strings passed to the statement are pure SQL; however, this time we have used the executeUpdate() method of the Statement class.

Listing 33.3 `TestCreate.java`

```java
import java.sql.*;
public class TestCreate {

  public static void main (String args []) {
    String url = "jdbc:odbc:testdb";
    if (args.length < 2) {
      System.out.println("Usage java TestCreate userid
        password");
      System.exit(1);
    }
    String userid = args[0];
    String password = args[1];

    try {
      Class.forName("sun.jdbc.odbc.JdbcOdbcDriver");
      Connection con =DriverManager.getConnection(url,
        userid, password);
      Statement statement = con.createStatement();

      statement.executeUpdate(
        "CREATE TABLE addresses (name char(15),
          address char(3))");
      statement.executeUpdate(
        "INSERT INTO addresses (name, address)
          VALUES('John', 'C46')");
      statement.executeUpdate(
        "INSERT INTO addresses (name, address)
          VALUES('Myra', 'C40')");

      statement.close();
      con.close();
```

```
    } catch (Exception e) {
      System.out.println(e.getMessage());
      e.printStackTrace();
    }
  }
}
```

The executeUpdate() is intended for SQL statements which will change the state of the database, such as INSERT, DELETE and CREATE. It does not return a result set; rather it returns an integer indicating the row count of the executed SQL. You can either use this value or ignore it (as in Listing 33.3).

33.8 Applets and Databases

By default, applets are not allowed to load libraries or read and write files. In addition, applets are not allowed to open sockets to machines other than those they originated from. These restrictions cause a number of problems for those wishing to develop applets that work with databases. For example, many drivers rely on the ability to load native code libraries that actually generate the connection to the specified database. One way around these restrictions is to turn them off in the browser being used. This is acceptable for an intranet being used within a single organization; however, it is not acceptable as a general solution.

Another possibility is to use drivers that are 100% pure Java, such as the mSQl driver. However, even using an mSQL driver, the applet is still restricted to connecting to a database on the originating host. Thus the developers must ensure that the Web server that serves the applets is running on the same host as the mSQL daemon. This may or may not be a problem.

Another option is to use a separate database server application (note "appli cation" and not "applet") which runs on the same host as the Web server. Applets can then connect to the database server application requesting that it connect to databases, execute updates, perform queries etc. The database server application is then the program that connects to and interacts with the database. In such a setup the applet does not directly communicate with the database system and is thus not hindered by the restrictions imposed on applets. This is illustrated in Figure 33.2. In this figure a user's browser has connected to the Web server and downloaded the applet. The applet then connects to the database server application. The server application then connects to the database management system on another host.

With the advent of signed applets some of the above problems go away, however signed applets are far from universal. In addition many organizations are using browsers which do not support them yet.

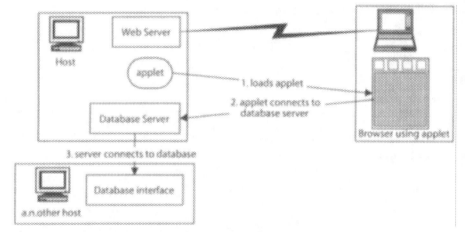

Figure 33.2 Using JDBC within an applet.

33.9 Online References

Sun's JDBC home page can be found at

`http://java.sun.com/products/jdbc`

Information on available JDBC drivers can be obtained from

`http://java.sun.com/products/jdbc/jdbc.drivers.html`

mSQL is available for anonymous ftp from

`ftp://bond.edu.au/pub/Minerva/msql`

The mSQL JDBC driver is available from

`http://www.imaginary.com/~borg/Java/java.html`

33.10 References

Hamilton, G., Cattell, R. and Fisher, M. (1997). *JDBC Database Access With Java: A Tutorial and Annotated Reference.* Addison-Wesley, Reading, MA.
Jepson, B. (1997). *Java Database Programming.* John Wiley and Sons, New York.
Microsoft (1997). *Microsoft ODBC 3.0 Software Development Kit and Programmer's Reference.* Microsoft Press, Redmond, WA.
Reese, G. (1997). *Database Programming with JDBC and Java.* O'Reilly.
Stephens, R.K. (1997). *Teach yourself SQL in 21 days,* 2nd edn. Sams.

33.11 Mini SQL

Mini SQL or mSQL is a lightweight database server originally developed as part of the Minerva Network Management Environment. Its creator, David Hughes, has continued its development and makes mSQL available as a shareware product for a very small fee. MSQL provides fast access to stored data with low memory requirements through a subset of ANSI SQL (i.e. it does not support views or subqueries etc.). It is available for UNIX-compatible operating systems as well as for Windows95/98/NT and OS/2. However, it is worth noting that the UNIX version tends to be ahead of the PC-oriented versions. The mSQL package includes the database engine, a terminal "monitor" program, a database administration program, a schema viewer and C and Java language APIs. A Java JDBC driver for mSQL is also available.

mSQL is a very popular choice among Java developers because it is available on a wide variety of platforms, the mSQL driver is 100% Pure Java (and thus there is no problem about loading a native library when writing applets) and of course it is shareware. The downside is that the performance of mSQL is not as good as that of commercial database systems. With regard to applets it is worth noting that an applet (by default) is not allowed to make a network connection to any other computer other than the machine from which it was loaded. Thus the Web server and the mSQL demon must be running on the same machine.

For more information on mSQL see:

Jepson, B. (1998) *Official Guide to Mini SQL 2.0.* John Wiley, New York.

34 *JavaBeans Software Components*

34.1 Introduction

Many developers have now heard of JavaBeans, but may be unsure of what they are or how to write a JavaBean (often referred to just as a Bean). JavaBeans are a relatively new addition to Java, having been added to the JDK 1.1 release with additional facilities being available in the Beans Development Kit (BDK), the most recent release of which was made available in early 1998. The goal of JavaBeans is to define a *software component model* for Java (see the JavaBeans documentation at `http://splash.javasoft.com/beans/`). Examples of Beans might be spreadsheets, database interfaces, word processors, graphic components such as buttons or business graphs.

One of the most confusing elements in JavaBeans is the use of the `java.beans` package and the BDK. The java.beans package provides classes and interfaces which are primarily useful to programmers who are developing tools to support and manipulate Beans. The BDK provides additional support for the JavaBeans API, a test Bean development tool (the "BeanBox"), sample Beans and documentation. In the example presented here, you will notice that no classes or interfaces provided by either are used. The only element used is the BeanBox tool. This is because any class can be treated as a Bean as long as certain naming conventions are followed.

The Beans component model is intended to be similar in concept to Visual Basic's VBX and OCX component architecture and to Delphi's VCL, but without the need to follow a rigid programming model. This makes the generation of Beans simpler, but at times requires the developer to define numerous methods for accessing Bean properties. For further information on JavaBeans see Englander (1997), Hunt (1997) and Flanagan (1997).

In the remainder of this chapter we shall review the concept of JavaBeans and then consider how a JavaBean is defined. We shall also examine one particular example of how a simple Java class can be converted into a Bean and used within the BeanBox developer tool.

34.2 JavaBeans

A JavaBean is an ordinary Java class which must describe itself following a specified naming convention or by using a `BeanInfo` object. This approach is in contrast with some other component models (notably Delphi's VCL) in which components must inherit from a particular ancestor class. This can be a point of confusion for JavaBean developers, who might well attempt to find the `Bean` class within which to wrap their code. Instead, any class in Java can be converted into a Bean as long as it follows the Bean's naming conventions or defines a `BeanInfo` object (the only caveat being that if a Bean has a visual appearance which can be used within a tool builder then the Bean must inherit from the AWT class `Component` or one of its subclasses). The great advantage of this approach is its simplicity; the disadvantage is that, at first sight, it appears that there is nothing concrete that defines a Bean.

34.2.1 Properties, Events and Methods

A JavaBean is defined (at least to the user of the Bean) by three things. These are

- *Properties* These are the attributes of the Bean which can be modified by anything outside of the Bean. They are often referred to as being "published" or "exposed" by the Bean. In effect, a property is an instance variable on the class defining the Bean which is accessed via specific `get` and `set` methods. For example, if we have a property `max`, then we would have:
  - a private instance variable `max`
  - `setMax()` and `getMax()` methods,

  Note that the methods which are used to set and get the value of the property max have the format `set<property name>` and `get<property name>`. This will be discussed again in more detail later.
- *Events* These are used to allow one component to communicate with another component. The event model used is the Delegation Event Model introduced to the AWT (Abstract Window Toolkit) in JDK 1.1 (see Hunt (1997) and Flanagan (1997)).
- *Methods* These are public methods (which do not match the naming conventions used in Beans) that can be used to directly request some service of a Bean.

34.2.2 The Beans Conventions

There are a number of conventions associated with JavaBeans. The first of these was mentioned in Section 34.2.1, and relates to properties; others relate to method, events, the `BeanInfo` object and the visual representation of Beans.

Properties

To make a private instance variable into a published property, "getter" and "setter" methods should be provided which match the following format:

```
public <property type> get<Property Name> ( )
public void set<Property Name> (<property type>
    parameter)
```

In addition, if the property is a boolean property then by convention this is indicated by

```
public boolean is<property name>
```

For example, isRollOver() properties can be read, read/write or write-only and can be simple, indexed, bound or constrained. The simplest of these, "simple", will be used in this chapter. This indicates a property containing a single value.

Events

Event handling in JavaBeans is exactly the same as event handling in JDK 1.1 of the AWT. This means that there are sources of events (in this case Beans), event objects and receivers of events (or listeners). However, JavaBeans imposes some restrictions on the naming of the methods associated with events in order that it can determine the events fixed by a Bean automatically. This means that the methods used to register event listeners must match the following conventions:

```
public void add<listener type> (<listener type>
     listener)
public void remove<listener type> (<listener type>
     listener)
```

Note that this assumes that an appropriate listener interface has been defined.

Methods

Any method which is public, but does not match the above conventions, is assumed to be one which is published by the Bean. Such methods may be called by other Beans directly or any Java code. Note that a limitation in the BeanBox used in the example presented below is that it can only deal with public methods which return no value and take no parameters.

Graphic Beans

Any Bean which has a visual representation which can be used within a Bean development tool such as the BeanBox must subclass the component class or one of its subclasses. This will allow it to use the standard AWT facilities to draw itself in the development tool.

BeanInfo Object Naming

The BeanInfo object, if present, is expected to have a name which matches the following convention:

```
<BeanName>BeanInfo
```

34.2.3 The BeanInfo Object

A BeanInfo object is an object which provides information on a Bean's properties and methods. This can be used if the developers of a Bean have not followed the Bean naming conventions or if they wish to provide additional information etc. BeanInfo is actually an interface which must be implemented by any class providing Bean information. A convenience class, SimpleBeanInfo, defined in the JavaBeans API, provides default implementations for the methods specified in the `BeanInfo` interface.

34.3 Defining JavaBeans

Listings 34.1 and 34.2 define two simple JavaBeans which are intended to work together.

The Counter Bean

The first Bean, the Counter Bean, counts up to a maximum value and then either resets its counter or notifies an Alarm Bean (via an event), depending on the state of the property `rollOver`, that it has reached its maximum value.

The initial value and the maximum values for the counter are also properties. Notice that the naming conventions imposed by JavaBeans have been followed and thus no `BeanInfo` object is required. We therefore know that the private instance variables `count`, `listeners` and `label` are not properties, as they do not have the necessary `get` or `set` methods.

The `increment()` method in the Counter Bean is used to increment the value of the `count` instance variable. If this reaches the `maxValue`, the counter is either reset or the `MaxValueEvent` is generated. This is then sent to any objects which have registered themselves as listeners of this event with the `Counter`.

The class `Counter` actually extends the class `Panel` in order that the Bean can have a visual representation in a "BeanBox"-style tool. `Panel` has been used so that not only can we set the background and foreground colours (features inherited from `Component` via `Panel`), we can also add other components to the display (in this case a simple text label object). This text label will be used to display the current value of the `count` variable (via the `setText()` method). We have also defined a `getMinimumSize()` method which will be used by a development tool to determine the minimum size to allocate to the visual representation of the Bean. The Counter Bean is illustrated in Figure 34.1.

Listing 34.1 The `Counter.java` file

```java
package sunw.demo.counter;

import java.awt.*;
import java.util.*;

public class Counter extends java.awt.Panel {

    private long count;

    private Vector listeners = new Vector();
    private Label label;
    private long initialValue, maxValue;
```

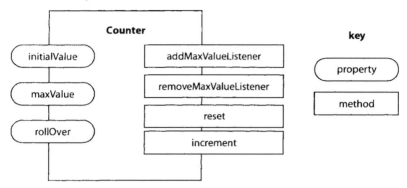

Figure 34.1 The Counter Bean.

```java
private boolean rollOver = true;

public Counter() {
  setBackground(Color.blue);
  setForeground(Color.white);
  label = new Label(" ");
  add(label);
}
public Dimension getMinimumSize() {return new
  Dimension(30, 30);}
public void setInitialValue(long init) {initialValue
  = init;}
public long getInitialValue () {return
  initialValue;}
public void setMaxValue(long max) {maxValue = max;}
public long getMaxValue () {return maxValue;}
public void setRollOver(boolean state) {rollOver =
  state;}
public boolean getRollOver () {return rollOver;}
public boolean isRollOver (){return rollOver;}
public synchronized void addMaxValueListener
    (MaxValueListener l){
  listeners.addElement(l);
}

public synchronized void removeMaxValueListener
    (MaxValueListener l) {
  listeners.removeElement(l);
}

public void reset() {count = initialValue;}
public void increment() {
  if (count != maxValue) {
```

```
        count++;
        label.setText(count + "");
      }
    else {
      if (isRollOver())
        reset();
      else {
        MaxValueEvent mve = new MaxValueEvent(this);
        synchronized (this) {
          MaxValueListener ml;
          Enumeration e = listeners.elements();
          while (e.hasMoreElements()) {
            ml = (MaxValueListener)e.nextElement();
            ml.maxValueReached(mve);
          }
        }
      }
    }
  }
}
```

The Alarm Bean

For the Alarm Bean we have subclassed Canvas, as we only need to display a coloured square in one of two colours, depending on whether it has been triggered or not. Triggered is a property which can either be set via the property tool editor or when the maxValueReached() method is executed. The result is that the box displayed by the Alarm Bean is white when not triggered and red when triggered.

Listing 34.2 The Alarm.java file

```
package sunw.demo.counter;

import java.awt.*;

public class Alarm extends Canvas implements
    MaxValueListener {
  private boolean triggered = false;
  public Alarm () {
    setBackground(Color.white);
  }
  public boolean isTriggered() {return triggered;}
  public void setTriggered(boolean state) {triggered =
    state;}
  public boolean getTriggered() {return triggered;}
  public Dimension getMinimumSize() {return new
    Dimension(30, 30);}
```

```
   public void maxValueReached(MaxValueEvent e) {
      setTriggered(true);
      setBackground(Color.red);
   }
}
```

The MaxValueEvent and MaxValueListener classes

Two additional classes are defined in Listings 34.3 and 34.4. These classes are not Beans but are auxiliary classes used by the previous two Beans. They define a simple event and an event listener interface. The event class, MaxValueEvent, defines the event which will be generated by the Counter Bean but caught by the Alarm Bean. It extends the java.util.EventObject class which is the root class of all event classes.

In turn, the MaxValueListener defines an interface which specifies that any object registering itself as a MaxValueListener (a receiver of an event) must define the maxValueReached() method. For example, the Alarm Bean will act as just such a listener for the Counter Bean, and therefore it implements the maxValueReached() method (see Listing 34.4).

Finally, in order for the Alarm Bean to register as a listener with the Counter Bean, the Counter Bean must define the appropriate addMaxValueListener() and removeMaxValueListener() methods. These methods add or remove listeners from a vector (held in the instance variable listeners). As we want to ensure that no one tries to update the list of listeners while we are informing them of the occurrence of MaxValueEvent, these methods must be synchronized, as must the part of the increment() method which calls the maxValueReached() method on each of the listeners.

Listing 34.3 The MaxValueEvent.java file

```
package sunw.demo.counter;

public class MaxValueEvent extends
    java.util.EventObject {
  public MaxValueEvent(Object object) {
    super(object);
  }
}
```

Listing 34.4 The MaxValueListener.java file

```
package sunw.demo.counter;

public interface MaxValueListener extends
    java.util.EventListener {
  void maxValueReached(MaxValueEvent m);
}
```

Packaging the Beans

We are now in a position to package our two Beans (and auxiliary classes) so that they can be used by the BeanBox tool. The BeanBox tool expects Beans to be placed in a JAR file within a directory called jars (Beans can be loaded from other directories using the load jar option from the BeanBox file menu). A JAR file is a ZIP format archive file with an optional manifest file (JAR stands for Java Archive file). For tools such as the BeanBox, the manifest file is required as it provides the BeanBox with information on which files are Beans (see Listing 34.5). The statement Java-Bean: <boolean> is used to indicate whether the preceding class is a Bean or not.

Listing 34.5 The manifest.tmp file

```
Name:  counter/MaxValueListener.class
Java-Bean:  False

Name:  counter/MaxValueEvent.class
Java-Bean:  False

Name:  counter/Counter.class
Java-Bean:  True

Name:  counter/Alarm.class
Java-Bean:  True
```

Constructing the JAR file and placing the JAR file in an appropriate directory, can be done manually or by using a make file. The actual JAR tool can be used to construct a JAR file for the example classes described above using (note that this assumes that the *.class files are held in a subdirectory called counter):

```
jar cvfm c:\bdk\jars\counter.jar manifest.tmp
    counter\*.class
```

The options specify that a new JAR file should be created and the *.class files added to it. The first parameter specifies where the JAR file should be placed, the second parameter specifies the name of the manifest file and the third parameter specifies where to look for the files to archive.

Using the Beans

The result of running the BeanBox tool, having created the JAR file, is illustrated in Figure 34.2. As you can see, the two Beans have been added to the ToolBox menu. The BeanBox window itself illustrates the effect of using the two Beans. Each Bean has been added to the window and the properties of the Counter Bean have been set in the Property editor (e.g. the maxValue is 4 and the rollOver property is false). Note that the property editor is generated automatically by the BeanBox with the appropriate properties displayed with the appropriate types. A third Bean, a button Bean, has been added and used to call the increment() method on the Counter Bean. In turn, the Counter Bean has been connected to the Alarm Bean via the event

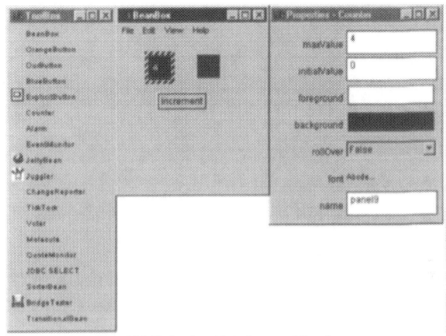

Figure 34.2 The BeanBox with the Counter and Alarm Beans.

MaxValueEvent. In the figure, the Counter has reached its maximum value and the event has been sent to the Alarm Bean, which has changed its colour to red (from its default white).

34.4 Summary

As you can see from this chapter, and the simple example presented, it is very easy to define a JavaBean. The model used is very simple; communication is via methods or event delegation, and standard Java resources such as JAR and interfaces make it work. As more and more tools are appearing for Beans the influence and effect of Beans will undoubtedly grow. Such tools will also simplify the task of defining a Bean, minimizing the need for manually defining set and get methods.

34.5 References

Englander, R. (1997). *Developing JavaBeans*. O'Reilly.
Flanagan, D. (1997). *Java in a Nutshell*. O'Reilly.
Hunt, J. (1997). *Java and Object Orientation: An Introduction*. Springer-Verlag, London.

35 *Java Native Interface*

35.1 Introduction

There are some situations in which it is necessary or desirable to use a language other than Java. For example, you may need to integrate a Java application with an existing (legacy) system or use specific facilities provided by a particular language (such as numerical packages in FORTRAN). Part of the overall system may be time-critical or require low-level access to hardware (in which case you may use C).

In any of these situations, linking Java to the associated system is referred to as linking it to native code. This can be done either from Java to the relevant language or vice versa.

35.2 Properties of the Java Native Interface

The are a number of properties of the Java Native Interface (more normally referred to as the JNI). These are summarized below:

- *Greater potential performance* If there is a particular part of a system which is processor-intensive, but which is not providing the required performance, then reimplementing such functionality in C may provide the answer. If such functionality is implemented in C, then optimizing C compilers can be used to obtain the best possible performance. Note that the optimizations performed by the JDK compiler are minimal and certainly not a patch on what a true optimizing C compiler can achieve. However, it is also worth noting that in using C you will not only tie your application to a particular platform, there will also be some overhead involved in loading the C library!

- *Ability to load libraries* The JNI allows Java applications to take advantage of the very many legacy C libraries available. This can be useful not only for linking in legacy code but also for taking advantage of task- or domain-specific software (such as scientific or mathematical libraries).

- *Some initial overheads* There are of course some overheads associated with loading the C library and care needs to be taken that this does not outweigh any performance improvement obtained through using C. Of course, if a legacy system is being integrated with Java then this is not necessarily an issue.

- *Reduced portability* As part of your application is now written in a language (such as C) which is compiled into a platform-specific executable, you will either need to provide multiple libraries for different platforms (and maintain those different versions) or you will be tied to a single platform. This destroys the "write once, run anywhere" philosophy of Java.

- *Parameter passing – overly complicated* As you will see later, parameter passing in the JNI is not necessarily as straightforward as it could be. This is due to the fact that Java and languages such as C use fundamentally different ways of representing data (such as strings).

- *Really aimed at C* You may have noticed that in the preceding discussion I have continually referred to C as the implementation language being used. This is because the JNI is aimed primarily at C. Thus although it is called the "Java Native Interface" it would probably be better named the "Java C Interface".

- *Third-party tools support C++ (Twin Peaks)* If you wish to interface Java to C++ then you must either do it via a C layer or use third-party products such as Twin Peaks.

35.3 The Basics of the JNI

The are five steps to the integration of Java and C. These are the steps you must follow to implement a native method. They are:

- Define a class with native methods
- Create C header file
- Create C stub file
- Write the C program/functions
- Combine C code, header files and stub file into a dynamic loadable library

We shall consider each step in more detail below.

35.3.1 Define a Class with Native Methods

The JNI provides a number of facilities which allow C functions to be integrated into a Java application. In particular, it uses the keyword `native`. This keyword indicates that a particular method is implemented using native code (e.g. another language):

```
public class HelloWorld {
    public native void hello();
}
```

This example declares that the method `hello()` is provided by a separate implementation. Notice that it is an abstract method as it does not possess a method body. This will be provided by the C implementation. To actually access the C implementation of the native method `hello()`, the class must (statically) load the appropriate C library. For example:

```
public class HelloWorld {
    public native void hello();
    static { System.loadLibrary("nativeHello"); }
}
```

Note that instances of this class can be used in exactly the same was as instances of any other class. The C implementation of the method `hello()` is encapsulated within the instance of `HelloWorld`. For example:

```
public class Test {
  public static void main (String args []) {
    HelloWorld h = new HelloWorld();
    h.hello();
  }
}
```

35.3.2 Create the C Header and Stub Files

These files are created automatically using the `javah` tool provided with the JDK. To do this you apply the `javah` tool twice: first to create the header file and then to create the stub file.

- Use `javah` to create the C header file, for example:

  ```
  javah HelloWorld
  ```

  This produces the `HelloWorld.h` file.
- Use `javah -stubs` to create the stub, for example:

  ```
  javah -stubs HelloWorld
  ```

  This produces the `HelloWorld.c` file

Note that you should not manually edit these files as they are auto-generated and any regeneration of these files will overwrite the existing files. Also notice that `javah` uses the `.class` file, not the `.java` file. Thus you must have compiled the `.java` file before you use the `javah` tool.

35.3.3 Write the C Program/Function

We are now ready to write the corresponding C function. The function must be named following rules laid down by the JNI:

- The C function name must be the concatenation of the class and the method.
- If the class is defined within a given package, then the name should be prefixed by the package name.
- Use an underscore to separate the various parts of the name.

By these rules, the above example expects a C function called `HelloWorld_hello`:

```
#include <stdio.h>
#include "HelloWorld.h2"
#include <StubPreamble.h>

void HelloWorld_hello(struct HHelloWorld *) {
```

```
    printf("Hello Native World!\n");
}
```

For the moment, do not worry about the struct being passed into the method; what this is will become clear later. For now just treat it as the appropriate way to define this method.

At the head of this file, we have included the header file generated by the javah tool. We have also included the StubPreamble.h file (which in this case is assumed to be in an include path). This file defines the structures used by the JNI as well as various utility macros for converting between Java and C data types. This file can be found in the JDK /include directory.

When you save your C program to a file do not call it classname.c, as the javah tool automatically uses that name for the stub file. Instead, call it something like classname_prg.c. In the above example, we could save it to HelloWorld_prg.c. We are now ready to compile the two C files and link them. That is, you should compile the stub file and the file containing your C program. Every compiler will do this in its own way, but as an example the following illustrates a generic compilation command:

```
cc HelloWorld.c NativeHello.c -o nativeHello.so
```

35.3.4 Load Library

You are now ready to load the C library into the Java environment using the loadLibrary() method available from the System object. For example:

```
System.loadLibrary("nativeHello");
```

35.4 Parameter Passing

Parameter passing between Java and C is not trivial. This is because, firstly, different C compilers will specify different sizes for different data types, whereas Java is standardized, and secondly because Java objects do not map directly onto anything in C. In this section we will consider how data can be transferred between C and Java in the JNI.

35.4.1 Basic Data Types

The basic types in Java are of fixed size. That is, their size is part of the language specification. In contrast, this is left up to the compiler vendor to decide in C. Thus a mapping for these data types from Java to C which is guaranteed to work is required. Table 35.1 illustrates this mapping. You will note that this mapping is quite conservative and uses long for everything except the Java data type Long. This data type is mapped to the int64_t standard.

Table 35.1 Relationships between Java and C data types

Java	C
boolean	long
byte	long
char	long (the Unicode value)
short	long
int	long
long	int64_t

For example, let us assume that we wish to implement a version of the `hello` method which took an integer that indicated the number of times to print out the "hello" message. In the Java class we might write:

```
public class HelloWorld {
  public native void hello(int loop);
    static { System.loadLibrary("nativeHello"); }
}
```

In the C program we would now need to receive the integer and loop the appropriate number of times. As the loop is of type `int`, we need to receive it as a C `long`. For example:

```
#include <stdio.h>
#include "HelloWorld.h"
#include <StubPreamble.h>

void HelloWorld_hello(struct HHelloWorld *, long loop) {
  for (int i=0; i < loop; i++)
    printf("Hello Native World!\n");
}
```

We can now call this method in exactly the same way as we would call any other Java method which takes an integer:

```
public class Test {
  public static void main (String args []) {
    HelloWorld h = new HelloWorld();
    h.hello(5);
  }
}
```

In this case we would print out the message "Hello Native World" five times.

35.4.2 Java Strings

We will now consider passing strings between Java and C. Remember that Java Strings are objects, and as such are quite different from C strings (which are essentially an array of characters terminated by the appropriate control character). Indeed, Java strings are passed to C programs as being of type `Hjava_lang_String *`. This now means that in order to access a Java string in a C program we need to convert it to a C string. There are a number of utility functions provided which help the programmer to do this (these functions can be found in `javaString.h` in the JDK `include` directory). These include:

- `void javaStringPrint(Hjava_lang_String *)` This function prints a Java string.
- `int javaStringLength(Hjava_lang_String *)` This function returns the length of the Java string. This can be useful, as the length of the string is used with other helper functions.
- `char *makeCString(Hjava_lang_String *s)` This function converts a Java String to a C string for short-term use. This is because the memory used for the string is allocated from the heap rather from longer term memory. This method will free the used memory as soon as the all references to it go out of scope.
- `char *allocCString(Hjava_lang_string *s)` This function uses `malloc()` to create a `char` array for longer term use of a string. Note that you must free memory allocated for this string once you have finished with it.
- `char *javaString2CString(Hjava_lang_String *, char *, int)` This function copies the characters of the `String` object into a C string buffer. The C string's address is returned.
- `Hjava_lang_String *makeJavaString(char *, int)` This function converts a C string back into a Java string so that information can be passed back to Java.

As an example of string passing in the JNI we will extend our native `hello` method to take a Java string to be used in the call to `printf` rather than the literal string "Hello Native World". In the Java class we might write:

```
public class HelloWorld {
    public native void hello(String text, int loop);
    static { System.loadLibrary("nativeHello"); }
}
```

In the C program we would now need to receive the string and convert it into something we can actually work with. Remember that Java strings are of type `Hjava_lang_String *` in C; thus the string parameter is of this type. We then use the `makeCString()` utility function to convert the string to a C string.

```
#include <stdio.h>
#include "HelloWorld.h"
#include <StubPreamble.h>
#include <javaString.h>

void HelloWorld_hello(struct HHelloWorld *,
        struct Hjava_lang_String *s,
```

```
            long loop) {
    char *text = char makeCString(s);
    for (int i=0; i < loop; i++)
        printf("%s\n", text);
}
```

Again the hello Java method is called in just the same way as any other Java method which takes a string. For example:

```
public class Test {
    public static void main (String args []) {
        HelloWorld h = new HelloWorld();
        h.hello("Hi John", 5);
    }
}
```

In this case we would print out the message "Hi John" five times.

35.4.3 References to Other Objects

We have now looked at passing basic data types and strings to C. However, there are many situations when what is really required is the ability to pass an object to C and then interrogate it in the C program. This is certainly possible, and this section looks at how objects are passed to, and accessed in, C programs. In fact, any Java object can be passed to C, which makes the link between Java and C very flexible. As with strings, there are a set of structures as well as utility macros and functions to help with the interface between the Java object world and the C world (for more information look at the files included in the StubPreamble.h file in the include directory of the JDK). In particular it provides the unhand macro, which de-handles the Java object. This allows the Java object to be referenced in the same way as C structure containing a pointer to other data items.

We can now return the first parameter passed to the C function. This has apparently appeared by magic, as it was never specified in any of the Java methods we have looked at. In fact, this is a reference to the object to which the call to run the native method was sent. That is, it is the this pseudo-variable which is automatically passed to the C function. This allows the C function to access the instance variables and methods of the (conceptually) encompassing object.

To illustrate these ideas we will define a class Person which holds a string in an instance variable name and possesses a native method hello. For example:

```
public class Person {
    public String name = "John";
    public native void hello();
}
```

As before, we need to compile this class and then generate the header and stub files using the javah tool. Having done this we can now write the C function. This time it will be called Person_hello(...), as the class is now called Person. As the first parameter passed to the C function is actually the reference to the object within which the `hello` method is "executing", we can now use this as the way to access the instance variable `name`. To do this we use the `unhand()` function to access the object and reference the name variable (as though it was a pointer). This returns a reference to the Java string which is passed to the `makeCString()` function which converts it to a C string. We are then able to print the message "Hello John":

```c
#include <stdio.h>
#include <StubPreamble.h>
#include <javaString.h>
#include "Person.h"

void Person_hello(struct HPerson *this) {

  char *name;
  name = makeCString(unhand(this)->name);
  printf("\n Hello %s \n", name);
}
```

Calling methods on an object is very similar.

35.5 Exercise: Native Hello World

The aim of this exercise is integrate a DLL implemented in C into your Java code.

35.5.1 What You Should Do

The file `Hello.c` has the following C function defined:

```c
/*
 * Native version of the hello world program
 */
#include <stdio.h>
#include "HelloWorld.h"
#include <StubPreamble.h>

void HelloWorld_hello(struct HHelloWorld *h,
    long count) {
  for (; count > 0; count-) {
    printf("Hello Native World! \n");
  }
}
```

You should write a class which contains a native method which relies on the above function for its implementation.

35.5.2 Notes

1. You should load the DLL library in the class which possesses the native method.
2. Remember: the name of the C function is formed from the name of the class and the name of the method.
3. Write some code which calls the native method (and see what happens).

36 *Byte Code Protection*

36.1 Introduction

An issue for anyone involved in deploying Java applications is how to protect your Java. This is an issue because the Java byte codes which are produced by the `javac` compiler can be de-compiled by the `javap` tool (provided as part of the JDK). This means that unscrupulous end users can de-compile your byte codes and do whatever they wish with the source code. For example, consider the very simple code presented below:

```
public class Example {
  private static String name = "John";
  public static void main (String args []) {
    System.out.println("Hello " + name);
  }
}
```

This was then compiled and de-compiled. The end result is:

```
Compiled from Example.java
public synchronized class Example extends
    java.lang.Object
  /* ACC_SUPER bit set */
{
  private static java.lang.String name;
  public static void main(java.lang.String[]);
  public Example();
  static static {};
}

Method void main(java.lang.String[])
    0 getstatic #12 <Field java.io.PrintStream out>
    3 new #6 <Class java.lang.StringBuffer>
    6 dup
    7 ldc #1 <String "Hello ">
    9 invokespecial #9 <Method
      java.lang.StringBuffer(java.lang.String)>
   12 getstatic #11 <Field java.lang.String name>
   15 invokevirtual #10 <Method java.lang.StringBuffer
      append(java.lang.String)>
```

```
18 invokevirtual  #14 <Method java.lang.String
   toString()>
21 invokevirtual  #13 <Method void
   println(java.lang.String)>
24 return
```

Obviously this would take a little work to reorganize the code. However, it is not secure and a determined enough person(s) could spend the necessary time to obtain detailed descriptions of your system. Third parties are also supplying "better" de-compilers (for example, see Mocha `http://www.geocities.com/Colosseum/Arena/9636/mocha-b1.zip` and OEW for Java `http://www.isg.de/OEW/Java/demo.html`).

One way to deal with this is to use a native code compiler. However, as has already been said, this reduces the portability of your system and may require a separate compiled version for each platform (which does away with one of the big advantages of Java).

Another way to protect your code from access by an unscrupulous user is to use an obfuscator (encryptor). The primary purpose of an obfuscator is to rename identifiers to make it difficult for other people to decode your classes. The identifiers are renamed to be short and cryptic, which also reduces the size of the class files. Jzipper is both an obfuscator and a GUI-based zip tool (see `http://www.oriondevel.com/JZipper/`). It is a 100% pure Java application that allows you to package up your code into a zip file and obfuscate it. Others include Hashjava (`http://www.sbktech.org/hashjava/form.html`) and Jshrink (`http://www.e-t.com/jshrink.html`). For example, after using Jshrink on Example we get:

```java
import java.io.PrintStream;
public synchronized class Example {
  private static String 0;
  public static void main(String astring[])
  { System.out.println(new StringBuffer(
     "Hello ").append(0).toString());
  }
  static
  {
    0 = "John";
  }
}
```

Note that Jshrink is careful not to change the external interface of the class; however, many obfuscators do make such a change.

Of course, there are some caveats. Firstly, you must obfuscate every class that is used in an applet – otherwise, the Java Virtual Machine (JVM) won't be able to match class and method identifiers. This means that you cannot obfuscate classes that you want to provide external access to (e.g. as part of a library).

In addition, any code that references an identifier by a string will fail (as the identifier has been renamed but the string has not been). An example of problem code would be `getClass().getMethod("toString", null)`. However, this type of code is not found in many applications. Most obfuscators work around these problems, but they do limit the obfuscators' effectiveness.

However, the use of an obfuscator can have a number of detrimental impacts on:

- *Maintenance* – you will need to remember to obfuscate each version or release of your system in its entirety for the obfuscator to work. This may lead to a large configuration problem.
- *Deployment* – you will now need to redeploy the whole of an application/applet if you change, extend or otherwise modify your original source code. You cannot just deploy the modified classes, as the obfuscation process may well have generated different identifiers for classes, methods or variables.
- *Warnings* – when the system crashes at run time a stack trace is printed out to help developers identify what went wrong. With obfuscated code this is made much more difficult. The stack trace lists the shortened, obfuscated, names of methods and classes! This can make debugging and error tracing harder.
- *Reflection* – as has already been hinted at, the obfuscator cannot deal with "strings" used to represent classes etc. For example, `Class.forName ("java.awt.Frame")`, would not be obfuscated. This is not a problem in many applications, but for those using JDBC, reflection etc. this can mean that obfuscation is not an option. Many tools may well use reflection and thus this can be a real issue.

37 Java, IDL and Object Request Brokers

37.1 Introduction

This chapter considers the new Java IDL facilities provided as part of JDK 1.2/Java 2. To do this it is divided into two parts. The first part describes the CORBA standard for Object Request Brokers (ORBs). The second part then describes Java IDL and its interface to a CORBA-compliant ORB as well as the ORB provided as part of Java IDL.

37.2 CORBA

The Common Object Request Broker Architecture (CORBA) is a standard produced by the Object Management Group (OMG) in collaboration with many organizations (which are members of the OMG). The OMG adopts and publishes interfaces; it publishes "standards", but never gets involved in the creation, selling or re-selling of software. This is accomplished via a competitive selection process based on proposals generated outside the OMG. Interface documents published by the OMG give the standard interface; implementations of those specifications are available from other companies, such as Hewlett-Packard and Sun, which develop software systems that they can then sell as matching one of these specifications.

CORBA specifies the architecture of CORBA-compliant Object Request Brokers (ORBs). An ORB is a mechanism that allows objects to communicate between processes, processors, hardware, operating systems etc. Calls in an ORB are treated as client–server calls. That is, the calling object is halted until a reply is received. The structure of a request from one object on one machine to another object on another machine is illustrated in Figure 37.1.

However, although the process is as illustrated in Figure 37.1, to the programmer the call appears as illustrated in Figure 37.2. That is, it appears to the programmer that the server object is held locally and that the message is sent from the client to a local object. This greatly simplifies the programming task.

The way in which this process works is that, when a client requests information from, or a service provided by, a remote object, the client stub and the ORB cooperate to pass the request on to the implementation skeleton. The skeleton then passes the request on to the actual object. Once the object has processed the request (returning the required data etc.), the skeleton takes any results produced and uses the ORB to

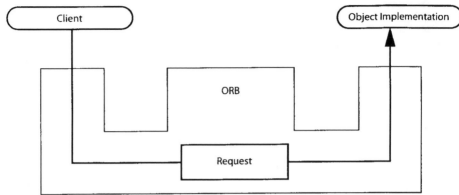

Figure 37.1 What actually happens.

Figure 37.2 How the system appears to the programmer.

pass those results back to the client stub. The stub then passes the results to the client object.

In order to facilitate this process, the ORB needs to do a number of things. In particular, it needs to keep track of where the objects are and handle any conversions or translations required when crossing platform boundaries (both machine and operating system boundaries). It may also need to handle the creation and deletion of objects as well as activating objects before passing requests to them. In particular, it must handle object references persistently.

To facilitate the integration of different languages into the ORB framework, Interface Definition Languages (IDLs) are provided. A number of IDLs have now been provided for Java (for example, ORBIX provides a CORBA-compliant ORB and a Java IDL). An IDL defines the interfaces provided by an object. This information is used to produce client stubs and implementation skeletons. The components of CORBA are shown in Figure 37.3.

37.3 Java IDL

In JDK 1.2/Java 2 a new feature has been added called Java IDL. This allows IDL speci-fications to be compiled into Java interfaces so that Java programs can work with a CORBA-compliant ORB. This means that both Java applications and Java applets can now work seamlessly with any ORB and thus with any systems connected to that ORB (or via IIOP – Internet Inter-ORB Protocol – with other ORBs). Thus an applet can communicate with a legacy system via an ORB in a clean, implementation-independent manner.

To implement a distributed application which uses the Java IDL ORB you should use the following steps:

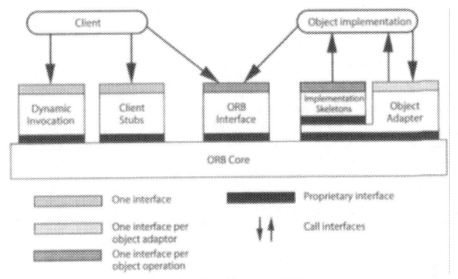

Figure 37.3 The components of CORBA.

- Define an IDL interface.
- Use the idltojava compiler on the IDL specification to generate the appropriate Java interface and stub and skeleton files.
- Implement a Server class as a concrete implement of the appropriate Java interface.
- Implement a Client class as a concrete implementation of the appropriate interface.
- Compile all the Java code.
- Initiate the name server
- Run the server and the client

This section looks in more detail at Java IDL and works through a simple example client server application.

37.3.1 Java ORB

Included in the Java IDL are a fully compliant Java ORB for distributed computing using IIOP communication and stub and server classes for linking Java objects to an ORB. The Java ORB is compliant with the CORBA/IIOP 2.0 Specification. The Java IDL ORB supports only transient CORBA objects. These are objects whose lifetimes are limited by their server process's lifetime. Once the process is terminated the objects maintained by those processes are also terminated.

37.3.2 Java Name Server

Java IDL also provides a transient name server to organize objects into a tree directory structure. The name server is initiated by executing tnameserv at the command line, for example:

```
tnameserv -ORBInitialPort 1234
```

The number following the -ORBInitialPort option indicates the port number to connect the name server to. In this case we have connected it to port number 1234. As described in Chapter 31, port numbers below 1024 are usually restricted for system services, and so should not be used for the name server. The name server can be stopped by terminating the process running the name server.

The name server stores object references by name in a tree structure similar to a file directory. A client may look up or resolve object references by name. Because the name server is an ordinary Java IDL transient server, the entire directory structure of names is lost each time tnameserv stops running.

The name server is transient because when it is terminated all the references it maintains are lost. Thus they are not persistent between sessions of the name server. The name server is compliant with the Naming Service Specification described in CORBAservices: Common Object Services Specification.

37.3.3 Converting IDL to Java

To implement an object which will work with an ORB, it is necessary to map an IDL specification (the CORBA side of an object's interface) to the required implementation language – in this case Java. Note that in order to convert IDL specifications to Java specifications it is necessary to use the idltojava compiler. This tool must be downloaded separately from the JDK release (quite why this is is unclear to me). The idltojava compiler can be downloaded from the following URL (note that this URL takes you to the Java Developers' Connection pages. To access these pages you must be a member of the JDC. Membership costs nothing and can be done at any time):

```
http://developer.java.sun.com/developer/earlyAccess/
    jdk12/idltojava.html
```

The result of downloading the idltojava compiler is a .exe file (if you are on a Windows machine). This file will unbundle the idltojava compiler once run. You will then be ready to use the idltojava tool.

Using the idltojava compiler you can now compile an IDL interface into a Java interface and the other .java files needed, including a client stub and a server skeleton.

For example, consider the following IDL specification for an interface called OrbHello, which contains a single operation helloWorld

```
module Hello {
    interface OrbHello {
        string helloWorld();
    };
};
```

Assuming that this IDL is defined in a file called OrbHello.idl, then using the idltojava compiler we would call the idltojava tool thus:

```
idltojava OrbHello.idl
```

Note that `idltojava` is currently hard-coded to use the C++ preprocessor supplied with Microsoft Visual C++. To switch off the pre-processor use `-fo-cpp` as an option to the `idltojava` command, for example:

```
idltojava -fno-cpp OrbHello.idl
```

To change the preprocessor used, set the two environment variables CPP and CPARGS. The CPP variable should be set to the full pathname of the preprocessor to be used and set CPARGS to the complete list of arguments to be passed to the preprocessor.

The result of running the `idltojava` tool on the `OrbHello.idl` file is that five files are created in a subdirectory called `Hello`. These five file are:

- `_OrbHelloImplBase.java` This is an abstract class which will be used as the superclass of the server object once it is implemented. It provides the basic CORBA functionality for the server. It implements the `OrbHello.java` interface.

- `_OrbHelloStub.java` This is an abstract class which will be used as the superclass of any clients that wish to reference a server object. It provides the basic CORBA functionality for the client. It implements the `OrbHello.java` interface.

- `OrbHello.java` This is the Java interface version of the IDL interface presented above. It is presented below:

```
package Hello;
public interface OrbHello extends
    org.omg.CORBA.Object {
  String helloWorld();
}
```

As you can see from this, this is a normal Java interface version of the IDL interface. Note that it extends the `org.omg.CORBA.Object`, specifying standard CORBA object functionality, as well as specifying a single method `helloWorld()`.

- `OrbHelloHelper.java` This is a final class that provides helper functions (including the `narrow()` method) required to cast CORBA object references to their Java types.

- `OrbHelloHolder.java` This is a final class that holds a public instance member of type `OrbHello`. It provides operations for out and inout arguments, which CORBA has but which do not map easily to Java's semantics.

You are now ready to implement the server and client classes. To do this you must provide concrete implementations for the `_OrbHelloImplBase` class and `_OrbHelloStub` interface.

37.3.4 Implementing the Server

The Server is comprised of two classes: the `Servant` class and the `OrbServer` class. The `Servant` class is a concrete subclass of the `_OrbHelloImplBase` abstract class. The Servant class implements the behaviour of all the operations and attributes of the interface it supports. In this case it only needs to implement the helloWorld() method. The OrbServer class initiates the application Servant. To do this it must first provide a reference to an ORB instance so that it can make the Servant object available (register it with the ORB). To register the Servant object, the OrbServer application must inform the name server of the Servant object and what it should be called by within the ORB.

Why is it necessary to have both Servant and Server classes? It is necessary because only servers can create new objects which can be registered with the ORB. Thus the OrbServer class is essentially a factory object which creates a new Servant object which is registered with the ORB.

The _OrbhelloImplBase class, which must be subclassed by Servant, is presented below:

```java
package Hello;
public abstract class _OrbHelloImplBase extends
  org.omg.CORBA.DynamicImplementation implements
  Hello.OrbHello {
  // Constructor
  public _OrbHelloImplBase() {
    super();
  }
  // Type strings for this class and its superclases
  private static final String _type_ids[] = {
    "IDL:Hello/OrbHello:1.0"
  };

  public String[] _ids() { return (String[])
    _type_ids.clone(); }

  private static java.util.Dictionary _methods = new
    java.util.Hashtable();
  static {
    _methods.put("helloWorld", new
      java.lang.Integer(0));
  }
  // DSI Dispatch call
  public void invoke(org.omg.CORBA.ServerRequest r) {
    switch (((java.lang.Integer)
        _methods.get(r.op_name())).intValue()) {
      case 0: // Hello.OrbHello.helloWorld
        {
        org.omg.CORBA.NVList _list =
          _orb().create_list(0);
        r.params(_list);
        String ___result;
```

```
            ___result = this.helloWorld();
        org.omg.CORBA.Any __result =
          _orb().create_any();
        __result.insert_string(___result);
        r.result(__result);
        }
        break;
        default:
          throw new org.omg.CORBA.BAD_OPERATION(0,
            org.omg.CORBA.CompletionStatus.
            COMPLETED_MAYBE);
    }
  }
}
```

The `Servant` class is relatively straightforward. It merely implements the `_OrbHelloImplBase` abstract class, which in this case means that it implements a single method with the signature `public String sayHello()` (as specified by the `OrbHello` interface. This method returns the string "Hello ORB of communications". Note that there are specific packages which need to be imported in order to implement the server above and beyond the packages which are required for the actual Java application.

```
import Hello.*; // The directory containing the stub
                //files
import org.omg.CosNaming.*;
// Imports the naming service package
import org.omg.CosNaming.NamingContextPackage.*;
        // Specifies exceptions thrown by
        // the name service
import org.omg.CORBA.*;    // The main CORBA package

class Servant extends _OrbHelloImplBase {
  public String sayHello() {
    return "Hello ORB of communications.";
  }
}
```

The `OrbServer` class defines the `public static void main` method used to initiate the application. It performs the following steps:

- Obtains a reference to the ORB.
- Instantiates the `Servant` class and registers it with the ORB.
- Obtains a reference to the name server, which is initially returned as a CORBA object and must be converted to the appropriate type.
- Binds the name to be used to identify the object within the ORB name server.
- Waits for a client to request a method on this object via the ORB.

The source code for the OrbServer class is presented below. It performs the above steps. Each step is commented in detail and thus the source will be used as the main point of documentation. Note that a number of the ORB-related methods throw exceptions and thus the whole method will be wrapped in a try-catch block.

```java
public class OrbServer {

  public static void main(String args[]) {
    try {
      // Obtain a reference to the orb
      ORB orb = ORB.init(args, null);

      // Instantiate Servant and register it with orb
      Servant servant = new Servant();
      orb.connect(servant);

      // Next obtain a reference to the name server.
      org.omg.CORBA.Object nameServerObject =
        orb.resolve_initial_references("NameService");
      // Now need to perform the equivalent of casting
      // it to a name server as it is currently an
      // CORBA object this is done using the narrow
      // utility method.
      NamingContext nameServer =
          NamingContextHelper.narrow(nameServerObject);
      // Next bind the name to be used to identify the
      // object within the orb name server
      NameComponent name =
          new NameComponent("OrbHelloWorld", "");
      NameComponent path[] = {name};

      // Register the servant object with the given
      // name in the name server.
      // This means that a client can gain a reference
      // to servant by requesting "OrbHelloWorld"
      nameServer.rebind(path, servant);

      // Now wait for a client to request a method on
      // this object via the orb. Note we need to
      // specify which Object class we are referring
      // to as there is also a class called Object in
      // the CORBA package.
      java.lang.Object obj = new java.lang.Object();
      synchronized (obj) {
        sync.wait();
      }
```

```
    } catch (Exception e) {
      e.printStackTrace(System.out); }
  }
}
```

You are now ready to implement the client.

37.3.5 Implementing the Client

The Client class is a separate object which will communicate with the server via the ORB (in much the same way as the client example in Chapter 31). To do this the client must:

- Obtain a reference to the ORB.
- Using the orb object, obtain a reference to the name server (once again converting it to the appropriate type).
- Next, obtain a reference to the remote object. This is done by requesting that the name server "resolve" the reference for the remote object named "OrbHelloWorld".
- Now call the appropriate method on the remote object.

The source code for the OrbClient class is presented below. Again note that the appropriate packages must be imported.

```
import Hello.*;
import org.omg.CosNaming.*;
import org.omg.CORBA.*;

public class OrbClient {
  public static void main(String args[]) {
    try {
      // create and initialize the ORB
      ORB orb = ORB.init(args, null);

      // Next obtain a reference to the name server.
      org.omg.CORBA.Object nameServerObject =
        orb.resolve_initial_references("NameService");
      // Now "cast" it to the name server class
      NamingContext nameServer =
        NamingContextHelper.narrow(nameServerObject);

      // Now obtain a reference to the remote object.
      NameComponent name =
        new NameComponent("OrbHelloWorld", "");
      NameComponent path[] = {name};
      Hello servant =
        HelloHelper.narrow(nameServer.resolve(path));
```

```
        // We can now call the remote method on the
        // remote object. Communication between this
        // object and the remote object are handled by
        // the ORB.
        String hello = servant.sayHello();
        System.out.println(hello);
    } catch (Exception e) {
        e.printStackTrace(System.out);  }
    }
}
```

37.3.6 Compiling the Server and Client

You are now ready to compile your distributed application. This means that you must compile all the `.java` files that have been created by you and which have been generated automatically by the `idltojava` compiler. This should happen automatically when you run the `javac` compiler on the client and server classes.

37.3.7 Running the Application

You are now in a position to run your distributed application. To do this you should have already started the name server (we will assume it is running on port 1234). You can now initiate the OrbServer server application. This is done in the following manner:

```
java OrbServer -ORBInitialPort 1234
```

Note that a `-ORBInitialPort` command line option has been passed to the OrbServer application with the port number being used by the name server. This information is used by helper classes to connect to the name server.

The final part of this application is to run the client application. Once again you need to specify the port on which the name server is running. Thus the client is initiated in the following manner:

```
java OrbClient -ORBInitialPort 1234
```

37.3.8 Java IDL and RMI

As you can see from the description in this chapter, IDL and RMI are very similar in structure and concept. It is primarily the syntax used to initiate the operations and register the objects which differs, so why should you use one versus the other? Essentially it comes down to interoperability. RMI is a Java-to-Java mechanism, while Java IDL is a Java-to-ORB communications mechanism which allows it to communicate with a very wide range of languages (including C, C++, Cobol and Smalltalk). From a purely performance aspect, if you are performing Java-to-Java communications RMI is a lot faster than using an ORB (as it has less to do), whereas using Java IDL is more flexible. One interesting development is that work is currently being undertaken on an RMI to IDL interface which will allow MRI to communicate with ORBs as well as other Java applications – this will be extremely interesting!

37.4 Online References

`idltojava` tool:

```
http://developer.java.sun.com/developer/earlyAccess/
    jdk12/idltojava.html
```

Object Management Group:

```
http://www.omg.org/
```

OMG technical library:

```
http://www.omg.org/cgi-bin/doclist.pl
```

CORBAservices: Common Object Services Specification:

```
http://www.omg.org/corba/csindx.htm
```

38 *Inner Classes and Reflection*

38.1 Introduction

One of the new features of JDK 1.1 was the addition of inner classes. These are classes defined with the scope of an outer (or top-level) class. These inner classes can be defined within the main body of a class, within a block of statements or (anonymously) within an expression. This chapter introduces inner classes and considers where and when they should be used. It also briefly introduces the reflection API before providing an example of using an inner class to provide a way of generalizing reusable software.

38.2 What Are Inner Classes?

Inner classes are classes which exist inside other, top-level, classes. They possess very specific properties, which include being:

- defined within the scope of an existing class or a method inside an existing class
- able to access the outer class's instance and class variables (except nested classes which are explained later in this chapter)
- able to access the outer class's `this` variable (by prefixing it with the name of the outer classes). This does not apply to nested classes
- able to be an interface specification
- able to have default, private, protected or public visibility
- able to be anonymous (that is not be explicitly named)
- abstract

There are also a number of limitations on non-nested inner classes compared with their outer (top-level) class relatives. They cannot:

- declare static methods or variables
- have constructors

For example, in the following class `Employee`, two inner classes are defined that are used to represent an address and a wage. Thus the structure of the class is as illustrated in Figure 38.1.

The source code for the class and its two inner classes, is presented below:

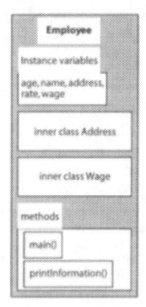

Figure 38.1 The structure of the Employee class.

```java
public class Employee {
    int age = 0;
    public String name = "Bob";
    double rate = 12.45;
    Address address;
    Wage wage;
    public Employee (String aName, int number,
        String aStreet, String aCity,
        double ratePerHour, int hours) {
      name = aName;
      rate = ratePerHour;
      address = new Address(number, aStreet, aCity);
      wage = new Wage(hours);
    }

    // Inner class -------------------------------------
    class Address {
      int number = 0;
      String street = "";
      String city = "";
      Address (int num, String aStreet, String aCity) {
        number = num;
        street = aStreet;
        city = aCity;
      }
      void printDetails() {
```

```
      System.out.println(number + " " + street +
        " , " + city);
    }
  }

  // Inner class ------------------------------------
  class Wage {
    int hoursWorked = 0;

    Wage (int hours) {
      hoursWorked = hours;
    }
    void printDetails() {
      System.out.println("Pay packet = " +
        hoursWorked * rate);
    }
  }

  public static void main (String args []) {
    Employee e = new Employee("John", 33,
        "High Street", "Bath", 2.45, 36);
    e.printInformation();
  }
  public void printInformation() {
    System.out.println("\nFor Employee: " + name);
    address.printDetails();
    wage.printDetails();
  }
}
```

The result of executing this application is:

```
C:>java Employee

For Employee: John
33 High Street , Bath
Pay packet = 88.2
```

The rate variable referenced by the printDetails method of the Wage class refers to an instance variable in the encapsulating class Employee. Thus inner classes can access variables and methods from the enclosing class.

In many ways, the top-level class can act as an object package containing zero or more inner classes. This is particularly useful for component-oriented development. In addition, the ability to define a particular piece of code which can be created and passed to where it is needed is very important. For example, C provides function pointers while Smalltalk uses block objects (objects that represent code). Java provides the inner class and anonymous inner classes in particular.

38.3 Types of Inner Class

38.3.1 Nested Top-Level Classes

A nested top-level class or interface is exactly like a normal outer class except that it has been placed within an existing class. Such classes are declared static and must be declared within an existing outer class (although they can be nested up to any depth). Such classes are grouped together within an outer class for convenience and may be treated like any normal class (although they must be referenced either via their outer class or imported directly using the import statement – import outerClassName.innerClassName;). That is, these classes may be referenceable by objects outside the top-level class (depending upon their visibility). Instances can be created from them (assuming they are not interfaces or abstract classes), and they can inherit from any appropriate class (but not from their own outer class).

38.3.2 Member Inner Classes

These are the sort of classes illustrated in the Employee example above. They are classes which are defined within the scope of an existing class but outside of any method.

38.3.3 Method-Level/Local Inner Classes

These are classes which are defined within a method. They have the scope of the enclosing block and thus they may only be visible for part of a method's execution. They can access the enclosing class(es) and any local final variables and parameters. An example of a method-level class is illustrated below:

```
public class Test extends Frame {

  public Test() {
    setUpWindowHandler();
    ...
  }

  public void setUpWindowHandler() {

    // --- method level / local inner class
    class Handler extends WindowAdapter {
      public void windowClosing(WindowEvent e) {
        System.exit(0);}
      }
    }

    Handler h = new Handler();
```

```
        addWindowListener(h);
    }
}
```

In this example, the method setUpWindowHandler first declares a local class Handler which implements a single method windowCLosing(Window-Event). Once it has done this it declares a variable h to hold a new instance of the handler class. It then passes this as a parameter to the method addWindowListener. The class Handler cannot be instantiated outside the scope of this method (although an instance of handler can be used outside the method, as this example shows).

38.3.4 Anonymous Inner Classes

Anonymous inner classes are classes which are generated and instantiated on the fly. An interface or existing class (which may be abstract) is used as the template of the new anonymous class. The anonymous class then defines a new behaviour required and is immediately instantiated. No programmatic reference to the anonymous class is maintained for the programmer and no further instances of the class can be created (except via methods such as clone()). For example:

```
ActionListener handler =
        new ActionListener {
    public void actionPerformed(ActionEvent event) {
        System.out.println("An event occurred");}};
```

This example creates a class based on the ActionListener interface which requires that the actionPerformed(ActionEvent) method is implemented. This anonymous class implements that method within the outer curly brackets. It is therefore a concrete implementation of a ActionListener and can be used anywhere that the ActionListener interface is specified.

As you can see from this example, anonymous classes can produce very compact code. However, it can become obscure to read and so care needs to be taken with its use.

38.4 How and When Should I Use Inner Classes?

38.4.1 As Helper Classes

Inner classes are often used as helper classes to perform some specific function (such as implementing a particular action), to implement some generic features (such as an interface to be used thoughout the outer class but nowhere else) or to provide a particular view on to some data (by providing an iterator or enumerator etc.). In general, they are not used as a "cheap" way of packing a whole set of classes together and so that they only need to reference the top-level class. However, it is worth noting that this is a programming idiom which could be used.

38.4.2 As Event Handlers

A very common use of an inner class is with the AWT. An inner class can be used to implement a particular listener or to subclass a particular adapter. This has the benefit of separating out the control aspect of the interface from the display elements. It also means that the event handler inner class can inherit from a different class to the encompassing class. For example, in the following code the outer class inherits from the class Frame, but the inner class inherits from the class WindowAdapter (thus we do not have to provide null implementation methods for the event handlers we do not wish to use in the WindowListener interface:

```
import java.awt.*; import java.awt.event.*;
public class Hello extends Frame {
  public static void main (String args []) {new
    Hello(args[0]);}
  public Hello (String label) {
    add(new Label(label));
    addWindowListener(new WindowHandler());
    pack();
    setVisible(true);
  }
  // ---- inner class event handler
  private class WindowHandler extends WindowAdapter {
    public void windowClosing(WindowEvent e)
      {System.exit(0);}
  }
}
```

38.4.3 An Anonymous Event Handlers

Anonymous inner classes can also be used to provide a similar facility to the above. However, the resulting code is far less readable (and for large anonymous classes can be very difficult to follow). However, for classes that are only ever going to be used once, they may have a role to play. For example, if we convert the above into an anonymous class then the resulting source code might look like:

```
import java.awt.*; import java.awt.event.*;

public class Hello extends Frame {
  public static void main (String args []) { new
    Hello(args[0]);}
  public Hello (String label) {
    add(new Label(label));
    addWindowListener(new WindowAdapter () {
      public void windowClosing(WindowEvent e) {
        System.exit(0);
      }});
```

```
    pack();
    setVisible(true);
}}
```

As you can see from this, the anonymous class has been embedded into the call to addWindowListener(). This is a common style that you will find used in many situations. However, it renders the code far from clear – unless you are expecting an inner class at this point. Indeed, I have come across inner classes which span pages like this – which makes it very difficult to fathom what is going on!

You should therefore be careful of liberally sprinkling your code with inner classes (particularly anonymous inner classes), as if they are not properly documented the source code can become hard to follow. Note that as of JDK 1.1.* the javadoc facility does not pick up inner classes and cannot therefore provide a way of documenting them!

38.4.4 Laying out a Java Class with Inner Classes

You should try to follow these guidelines when laying out a Java class which contains named inner classes:

- Try to avoid mixing variables, methods and inner classes when laying out the class – this will only lead to confusion. Instead, group variable declarations together, methods together and inner classes together. You don't need to worry about which comes first as the Java compiler is a multiple pass compiler which will sort out forward references.
- Remember that the built-in make facility may miss inner classes referenced in other classes. You may therefore find that when you recompile you do not get the expected behaviour.
- Don't use an outer class as a cheap global "database". One temptation is to treat the outer class as a global blackboard onto which you can write global data (this providing a limited scope global database). This is not a good programming style and may jeopardize future development.

38.4.5 Inner Class Guidelines

This section provides some guidelines on the definition and implementation of inner classes:

- Make an inner class private by default. That way you will stop the outer class merely being a "cheap" package. If you have to make the inner classes non-private then at least you must make this decision explicitly.
- Use nested level inner classes for separate but related objects.
- Use member inner classes as helper classes which support a particular functionality or abstraction.
- Use method-based inner classes for local shared functionality
- Use method-based inner classes carefully.

- Avoiding using lots of anonymous classes – they are confusing and difficult to maintain
- Be careful how you document inner classes.

38.5 The Reflection API

The Java Reflection API (implemented by the `java.lang.reflect` package) allows access to information about Java classes and objects. It greatly simplifies the task of building tools such as inspectors, debuggers, component builders and test support tools because it gives the tools access to information about the methods and their visibility, the class and instance variables, the constructors etc.

If your security policy allows it, then the Reflection API (also sometimes referred to as introspection) can be used to:

- obtain class or instance information
- construct new class instances and new arrays
- access and modify class and instance variables
- invoke methods on classes and instances

The Reflection API provides new classes based on the class `Class`:

- `Field` represents a field in a class or instance. It allows you to obtain information about the field and to access or modify the data held by the field.
- `Method` represents a method in a class or instance. It allows you to obtain information about the method's parameters, return type and checked exceptions. It also provides an `invoke` method which is used to execute the actual method in a class or on an object.
- `Constructor` represents a class constructor. You can use it to obtain information about a constructor's parameter. It can also create a new instance of the associated class using the represented constructor.

The Reflection API also extends the class `Class`. The new methods give information about a class or instance and return a field, method or constructor instance, for example `getField`, `getMethod`, `getConstructor`, `getFields`, `getMethods` and `getConstructors`. The following code implements a class called `Inspector`, which uses the class `Class` to obtain various items of information about a given class. For each class it obtains information about the constructors, interfaces, methods and variables that the class defines. It also finds out which class it inherits from.

```
import java.lang.reflect.*;
import java.util.*;

public class Inspector {

    private Vector constructors = new Vector();
    private Vector classMethods = new Vector();
```

```java
private Vector classVariables = new Vector();
private Vector instanceMethods = new Vector();
private Vector instanceVariables = new Vector();
private String name = "";
private Class superClass;
private Class cls;
private Vector interfaces = new Vector();

public Inspector(String classname) {
  int mod;
  name = classname;
  try {
    System.out.println("Loading class : " +
      classname);
    cls = Class.forName(classname); // Loads the
                                    // class object
    System.out.println("Class load successful");

    // Find the superclass
    setSuperClass(cls.getSuperclass());
    // Find the constructors
    Constructor cons[] =
      cls.getDeclaredConstructors();
    if (cons != null) {
      for (int i = 0; i < cons.length; i++) {
        addConstructor(cons[i]);
      }
    }
    // Find the interfaces
    Class ints[] = cls.getInterfaces();
    if (ints != null) {
      for (int i = 0; i < ints.length; i++) {
        addInterface(ints[i]);
      }
    }
    // Find the methods declared in this class
    // and distinguish between the instance and
    // class methods.
    Method methods[] = cls.getDeclaredMethods();
    if (methods != null) {
      Method m;
      for (int i = 0; i < methods.length; i++) {
        m = methods[i];
        mod = m.getModifiers();
        if (Modifier.isStatic(mod)) {
          addClassMethod(m);
        } else {
```

```
              addInstanceMethod(methods[i]);
          }
       }
     }
     // Find the variables of the class and
     // distinguish between instance and class
     Field fields[] = cls.getDeclaredFields();
     if (fields != null) {
       Field f;
       for (int i = 0; i < fields.length; i++) {
         f = fields[i];
         mod = f.getModifiers();
         if (Modifier.isStatic(mod)) {
           addClassVariable(f);
         } else {
           addInstanceVariable(fields[i]);
         }
       }
     }
   } catch (java.lang.ClassNotFoundException e) {
     System.out.println("Error loading " + cls);
   }
}

public void addClassMethod(Method meth) {
  classMethods.addElement(meth);
}

public void addClassVariable (Field field ) {
  classVariables.addElement(field);
}

public void addConstructor(Constructor cons) {
  constructors.addElement(cons);
}

public void addInstanceMethod(Method meth) {
  instanceMethods.addElement(meth);
}

public void addInstanceVariable (Field field ) {
  instanceVariables.addElement(field);
}

public void addInterface(Class anInterface) {
  interfaces.addElement(anInterface);
}
```

```java
public String getName ( ) {
  return name;
}

public Class getSuperClass() {
  return superClass;
}

public void setSuperClass(Class superClass) {
  this.superClass = superClass;
}

/**
 * Returns a String that represents the value of
 * this object.
 */
public String toString() {
  StringBuffer result = new StringBuffer("Class
    details for " + name + "\n");
  if (superClass != null) {
    result.append("\tSuperclass: " + getSuperClass()
      + "\n");
  }
  if (!constructors.isEmpty()) {
    result.append("Constructors: \n");
    Enumeration e = constructors.elements();
    while (e.hasMoreElements()) {
      result.append("\t" + e.nextElement() + "\n");
    }
  }

  if (!interfaces.isEmpty()) {
    result.append("Interfaces: \n");
    Enumeration e = interfaces.elements();
    while (e.hasMoreElements()) {
      result.append("\t" + e.nextElement() + "\n");
    }
  }

  if (!classVariables.isEmpty()) {
    result.append("Class Variables \n");
    Enumeration e = classVariables.elements();
    while (e.hasMoreElements()) {
      result.append("\t" + e.nextElement() + "\n");
    }
  }
```

```java
    if (!classMethods.isEmpty()) {
      result.append("Class Methods \n");
      Enumeration e = classMethods.elements();
      while (e.hasMoreElements()) {
        result.append("\t" + e.nextElement() + "\n");
      }
    }

    if (!instanceVariables.isEmpty()) {
      result.append("Instance Variables \n");
      Enumeration e = instanceVariables.elements();
      while (e.hasMoreElements()) {
        result.append("\t" + e.nextElement() + "\n");
      }
    }

    if (!instanceMethods.isEmpty()) {
      result.append("Instance Methods \n");
      Enumeration e = instanceMethods.elements();
      while (e.hasMoreElements()) {
        result.append("\t" + e.nextElement() + "\n");
      }
    }

    return result.toString();
  }
  // Main method for Inspector application
  public static void main(java.lang.String[] args) {
    if (args.length < 1) {
      System.out.println("Usage java Inspector <fully
        qualified class name>");
      System.exit(1);
    }
    Inspector insp = new Inspector(args[0]);
    System.out.println(insp);
  }
}
```

Note that we had to wrap much of the code directly involved with reflection in a try-catch block. This is because a number of the reflection methods throw the ClassNotFoundException if the specified class cannot be loaded. The results of running the Inspector on itself are presented below:

```
C:\jjh\JAVA\practioners\chap38>java Inspector
Inspector
Loading class : Inspector
```

```
Class load successful
Class details for Inspector
      Superclass: class java.lang.Object
Constructors:
      public Inspector(java.lang.String)
Class Methods
      public static void
        Inspector.main(java.lang.String[])
Instance Variables
      private java.util.Vector Inspector.constructors
      private java.util.Vector Inspector.classMethods
      private java.util.Vector
        Inspector.classVariables
      private java.util.Vector
        Inspector.instanceMethods
      private java.util.Vector
        Inspector.instanceVariables
      private java.lang.String Inspector.name
      private java.lang.Class Inspector.superClass
      private java.lang.Class Inspector.cls
      private java.util.Vector Inspector.interfaces
Instance Methods
      public void
        Inspector.addClassMethod(java.lang.reflect.
        Method)
      public void
        Inspector.addClassVariable(java.lang.reflect.
        Field)
      public void
        Inspector.addConstructor(java.lang.reflect.
        Constructor)
      public void
        Inspector.addInstanceMethod(java.lang.reflect.
        Method)
      public void
        Inspector.addInstanceVariable(java.lang.
        reflect.Field)
      public void
        Inspector.addInterface(java.lang.Class)
      public java.lang.String Inspector.getName()
      public java.lang.Class Inspector.getSuperClass()
      public void
        Inspector.setSuperClass(java.lang.Class)
      public java.lang.String Inspector.toString()
```

Part 3

Java Art and Style

39 *Java Style Guidelines*

39.1 Introduction

Good programming style in any language helps promote the readability, clarity and comprehensibility of your code. In many languages, there are established standards to which many people adhere (sometimes without realizing it). For example, the way in which a C or Pascal program is indented is a standard. However, style guidelines which have evolved for these procedural languages do not cover many of the issues which are important in Java. As languages that are not object-oriented do not have concepts of classes, instances and methods, they do not have standards for dealing with them.

Of course, you should not forget all the pearls of wisdom and programming practices that you have learnt using other languages. There are a number of acknowledged bad practices which are not specific to Java (for example, the use of `goto`-style constructs). In this chapter, we assume that you do not need an explanation of the basic concepts; instead, we try to concentrate on style issues specific to Java.

39.2 Code Layout

Java has inherited much of its language style from C, and many programmers have adopted a C style for program layout. Indeed, if you examine the system-provided classes (the source code of which is available within the JDK; for example, on a PC, look in the directories within `JDK1.1\src\java\`), this style has been used throughout. Thus an `if-then` statement is laid out in the same way as in a C program:

```
if (size == 20) {
   total = total * size;
}
```

For more information on the style of C programming see Kernighan and Ritchie (1988).

39.3 Variables

39.3.1 Naming Variables

In Java, variable names such as `t1`, `i`, `j` or `temp` should rarely be used. Variable names should be descriptive (semantic variables) or should indicate the type of object which the variable holds (typed variables). The approach that you choose depends on personal style and the situation in which the variables are used.

Semantic Variable Names

Instance and class variables tend to have semantic names. The semantic approach has the advantage that you need to assume less about what the variable is used for. Since subclasses can inherit instance and class variables, the point at which they are defined and the point at which they are used may be very distant. Thus any contextual meaning and commentary provided with their definition is lost. Examples of semantic variable names include:

```
score
currentWorkingMemory
TotalPopulationSize
```

Typed Variable Names

The typed approach is often adopted for parameter names to indicate the class of object that is required by the method. For example:

```
add(Object anObject)
push(Object object)
```

Some methods use both the semantic and typed approaches:

```
put(Object key, Object object)
```

Temporary Variables

Temporary variables, which are local to a method, often have a mixture of semantic and typed names. They may also have temp or tmp as part of their name to indicate their temporary nature. Larger methods often have semantic local variable names due to the additional complexity of such methods.

If you must use very short variable names (which are acceptable, for example, as counters in loops), stick to the traditional names. For example, using variables such as i, j, k for counters is a shorthand (inherited from FORTRAN) with which most people are familiar. Similarly, a temporary generic exception is often named e in Java; you can adopt the same convention.

Multiple Part Variable Names

If the variable name is made up of more than one word, the words should not be separated by - or _, but by giving the first letter of all but the first word an initial capital:

```
theDateToday   employeeRecord   objectInList
```

This approach is often referred to as title case (or modified title case for names starting with a lower-case letter). Whether the first word in the variable is capitalized or not depends on the type of variable. Table 39.1 summarizes the conventions.

Table 39.1 Variable naming conventions

Variable type	Convention
Class variable	Upper-case
Class names	Initial capital
Temporary variables	Lower-case
Instance variables	Lower-case
Method parameters	Lower-case

In the system-provided classes, the parts of a class variable name are separated by underscores:

```
Double.MAX_VALUE
StreamTokenizer.TT_EOF
```

You should follow this convention, but the Java system classes do not adhere rigidly to it. Some classes, such as File, use a title case approach and others, such as Color, ignore the convention completely:

```
File.pathSeparator
Color.red
```

39.3.2 Using Variables

- *Instance variables* should be used to hold local data or references to other objects. The other objects should be involved in some form of collaboration with the object (otherwise it does not need a reference to them).
- *Class variables* should be used as "constant" values which are referenced by all instances of a class. They should never be used as a form of global variable (such a use is frequently an indication that a solution has not been designed with the proper amount of care and attention). Occasionally, a class may use its class variables to hold information about the instances, such as the number of instances created. However, this information should be private to the class.

Defining and Initializing Instance and Class Variables

You can declare class and instance variables anywhere within the body of a class. However, it is good style to declare them at the beginning. It is easier to follow the class structure if all the class variables (statically defined variables) are declared first, followed by the instance variables. If another programmer can find all such declarations in the same place, the code is easier to understand and maintain.

You should initialize variables when you declare them. If you cannot initialize them with the actual value to be used, then you should use a default value and set the actual value as soon as possible. For class variables you may do this within a static initialization block; for instance variables, you may do it within a constructor or an init method (depending on whether it is a standalone application or an applet).

One reason that you should initialize a variable is that it provides an indication to others of the information to be held by the variable. For example, stating that a variable can hold a string does not say very much. However, if you initialize the variable with the string "Mr Joe Bloggs" it says much more. The other reason that you should initialize a variable is that the Java compiler does not warn you about uninitialized class and instance variables (they are set to null). Your code may attempt to use a variable which has not been initialized, thus raising an exception.

Defining Temporary Variables

Temporary variables can be defined anywhere within a method body. However, it is good style to declare them at the start of the method as, once again, this is easier to read. It also implies that the programmer has given some thought to the variables that are required.

As a variable can be declared where and when it is used, it is common to find a variable declared within a loop. This means that it is declared every time the loop is executed:

```
for (i = 0; i < 10; ++i) {
   Integer count = new Integer(i);
}
```

This is very bad style, but is an easy mistake to fall into if variables are declared anywhere.

Accessing Instance and Class Variables

In general it is always better to access instance and class variables via intermediate methods, referred to as *accessor* (or *getter* and *setter*) methods, rather than accessing or setting them directly. This is called variable-free programming and it promotes the modularity of your methods. It insulates the methods against changes in the way the object (or class) holds instance (or class) information. This is a very important concept, as direct access to instance variables can limit the power of subclassing.

You can also protect variables from undesired changes. For example, you can put preconditions on an access method, or return a copy of the contents of the variable so that it cannot be directly affected. To implement this, you should make judicious use of the Java visibility modifiers described earlier in the book.

39.4 Classes

39.4.1 Naming Classes

The naming of a class is extremely important. The class is the core element in any object-oriented program and its name has huge semantic meaning which can greatly affect the clarity of the program. Examples of Java system classes include:

```
HashTable
FileInputStream
SecurityManager
```

The above names are good examples of how a name can describe a class. The name of a class is used by most developers to indicate its purpose or intent. This is partly due to the fact that it is the class name which is used when searching for appropriate classes (for example, by using the documentation generated by `javadoc`).

You should therefore use descriptive class names; classes with names such as `MyClass` or `ProjectClass1` are of little use. However, class names should not be so specific that they make it appear that the class is unlikely to be of use except in one specific situation (unless, of course. this is the case). For example, in an application that records details about university lecturers, a class with a name such as `ComputerScienceDepartmentLecturer` is probably not appropriate, unless it really does relate only to lecturers in the Computer Science department. If this is the case, you need to ask yourself in what way computer science lecturers are different from other lecturers.

39.4.2 The Role of a Class

A subclass or class should accomplish one specific purpose; that is, it should capture only one idea. If more than one idea is encapsulated in a class, you should break the class down into its constituent parts. This guideline leads to small classes (in terms of methods, instance variables and code). Breaking a class down costs little but may produce major gains in reusability and flexibility.

A subclass should only be used to modify the behaviour of its parent class. This modification should be a refinement of the class and should therefore extend the behaviour of the class in some way. For example, a subclass may redefine one or more of the methods, add methods which use the inherited behaviour, or add class or instance variables. A subclass which does not do at least one of these is inappropriate.

39.4.3 Creating New Data Structure Classes

When working with data structures, there is always the question of whether to create a new data structure class to hold your data or whether to define a class which holds the data within one of its instance variables and then provide methods which access that variable.

For example, let us assume that we wish to define a new class, called `Account`, which holds information on deposits and withdrawals. We believe that we should use a hash table to hold the actual data, but should `Account` be a subclass of `HashTable` or of something else (for example, `Object`, with an instance variable holding an instance of `HashTable`)? Of course, it depends on what you are going to do with the `Account` class. If it provides a new data structure class (in some way), even if it is only for your application, then you should consider making it a subclass of `HashTable`. However, if you need to provide a functionally complex class which just happens to contain a hash table, then it is almost certainly better to make it a subclass of `Object`.

There is another point to consider: if `Account` is a subclass of `HashTable`, then any instance of `Account` responds to the whole of the `HashTable` protocol. You should ask yourself whether this is what you want, or whether a more limited protocol (one appropriate to an account object) is more suitable.

39.4.4 Class Comments

Every class, whether abstract or concrete, should have a class comment. This comment is the basic documentation for the class. It should, therefore, tell a developer creating a subclass from the class, or a user of the class, what they need to know. The comment may also contain:

- information about the author
- a history of modifications to the class
- the purpose, type and status of the class
- information about instance and class variables (including the class of object they hold and their use)
- information about collaborations between this class and others
- example usage
- copyright information
- class-specific information, such as the things that a subclass of an abstract class is expected to redefine

You should place the class comment just before the class, using the /** */ form of syntax which allows javadoc to pick up the comment and generate HTML documentation. A common trick is to use /** followed by **/:

```
/**
   This is a javadoc comment
**/
```

This makes it easy to find the start and end of javadoc comments by searching for the two asterisks. You can use tags such as @author, @see and @version to ensure that these items are highlighted. For methods, you can use @return, @param and @exception to document the return value, any parameter values and any exceptions raised.

Finally, to help with the layout of the comment once it is converted into HTML, you can embed HTML tags within the comment. For example, <p> forces a new paragraph.

39.4.5 Using a Class or an Instance

In situations where only a single instance of a class is required, it is better style to define a class which is instantiated once than to provide the required behaviour in class-side methods.

Using a class instead of an instance is very poor style, breaks the rules of object orientation and may have implications for the future maintenance of the system.

39.5 Interfaces

An interface is a way of specifying the protocol which should be implemented by a set of objects which are members of different class hierarchies. You should use an interface in the following situations:

- as a specification mechanism, where one or more classes are intended to provide the same functionality
- where one or more (as yet undefined) user classes are anticipated and you must ensure that they provide the correct protocol
- where you must specify the type of a variable for a set of (as yet undefined) user classes

The above points assume that the classes come from different parts of the class hierarchy. If all classes have the same superclass, then you can use an abstract super-class instead of an interface.

39.6 Enumerated Types

Java does not provide explicitly for enumerated types. However, an interface can mimic part of the functionality of an enumerated type. In such an interface, only public static variables are defined. These variables are assigned numeric values which can indicate their ordering. For example, the following interface defines the equivalent of a Week enumerated type:

```java
public interface Week {
    public static final Monday = 1;
    public static final Tuesday = 2;
    public static final Wednesday = 3;
    public static final Thursday = 4;
    public static final Friday = 5;
}
```

Any class which implements this interface can then reference the variables Monday, Tuesday etc. directly and can compare them:

```java
If (Monday < Tuesday) ...
```

Of course, a class does not need to implement this interface; it could reference Monday via the interface:

```java
Week.Monday
```

39.7 Methods

39.7.1 Naming Methods

A method name should always start with a lower-case letter. If the method name is made up of more than one element then each element after the first should start with a capital letter (modified title case):

```java
account deposit(100);
account printStatement();
```

The naming of methods is as important as the naming of classes. An appropriate method name not only makes the code easier to read, it also aids in reuse. You should select a method's name to illustrate the method's purpose. In addition, many programmers try to select a name which makes it possible to read an expression containing the method in a similar manner to reading a sentence.

In many situations, you define multiple methods with the same name but different parameters. This is possible because Java identifies a method by both its name and its parameter classes. Thus, different methods can be supplied to deal with different situations, resulting in less complex code and more flexibility. For example:

```
statement deposit(100);
statement deposit(date, 100);
statement deposit(100, date);
```

Methods which return true and false as the result of a test follow a common naming format throughout the Java system. These methods use a verb such as `is` or `equals` concatenated with whatever is being tested. In some cases, the method name expresses the test itself:

```
equals(Object)
startsWith(String)
isAlive()
isInterrupted()
```

In the first case, the method tests to see whether the receiver is the same as the parameter. This method name is used in many different classes (for example, `Integer` and `String`).

In the second example, the method only tests part of the receiver, and its name reflects that. In the next two cases, some aspect of the receiver is tested. The third method tests whether a process is active, and the value being tested for is used as part of the method name.

39.7.2 Using Methods

In general, you should put a method as high up in the inheritance hierarchy as possible (as long as it makes sense to do so). The higher the method, the more visible it is to classes in other branches of the hierarchy, and the more method-level reuse you can achieve.

Think carefully about the purpose and placement of methods within a class. Just as a class should have a specific purpose, a method should also have a single purpose. If a method performs more than one function, then you should divide it into separate methods. In general terms, a method should be no longer than one A4 page.

Deciding how to break up the desired functionality into elements can be difficult in a procedural programming language. In Java, it is made more difficult by considerations of object encapsulation and reuse. However, you can bear the following questions in mind when determining whether your code is correctly placed within the methods:

- If the method does not refer to any aspect of the object (i.e. it does not use `super`, `this`, instance variables etc.), what does it do? Should it be there?

- How many objects does the method reference? A method should only send messages to a limited set of objects. This promotes maintainability, comprehensibility and modularity.
- Have you used accessor methods to access instance variables? Variable-free programming can greatly insulate the method from changes within the object.
- Is the behaviour encapsulated by the method intended for public or private (to the object) use? If it is a mixture of the two, then the method should be decomposed into two or more methods. The private code should be placed in a method which is defined to be private. This indicates to a developer (and enforces) that the method is not intended for external use.
- Does the method rely more on the behaviour of other objects than on its own object (that is, a series of messages is being sent to some object other than `this`)? If so, the method may be better placed in another object (or objects).

This last point is worth considering in slightly more detail. The series of messages in such a method may be better placed in a method in the class of the receiver object. This is because it really describes behaviour associated with that object. By placing it with the receiver object's class, all modifications to the behaviour of the receiver are encapsulated in that object. In addition, this behaviour may be useful to other objects; if you encode it within the receiver's class, other objects can gain access to that behaviour (rather than duplicating it in a number of places).

It is not easy to achieve good reuse of method-level code when code is poorly placed. Most messages should be sent to this. Structuring the code appropriately is probably one of the hardest things to do well in object-oriented programming; however, if you do it correctly, it can pay very high dividends.

39.7.3 Class Methods and Instance Methods

The distinction between class and instance methods was discussed in more detail in Chapter 12. The main points are presented here as they are relevant to considerations of style in Java.

You should use the main method to create instances and invoke the initial behaviour. You should use other class methods for the following purposes only:

- Information about the class
- Instance management and information
- Documentation and examples
- Testing facilities (regression-style)
- Support for one of the above

Any other purposes should be performed by an instance method.

39.7.4 Static Initialization Blocks

You should only use a static initialization block to initialize class variables which cannot be initialized by a simple initialization clause. It is easy to produce cyclic static initialization blocks and the result of such initialization is likely to be incorrect.

A static initialization block should immediately follow the class variable declarations and precede any method definitions (e.g. the main method).

39.7.5 Constructors

You should only use a constructor to initialize an instance of a class in an appropriate manner. Do not place instance-style functionality within the constructor. Instead, provide a separate method and call it from the constructor so that you can reinitialize the object later if necessary.

39.7.6 The `finalize` Method

This method is executed when the garbage collector picks up an object. You should only use it to perform housekeeping operations which can be left until the object is destroyed. Do not place operations which should be performed as soon as all references to the object are removed (for example, closing a file) in the `finalize` method because you cannot guarantee exactly when the garbage collector will deal with the object.

39.7.7 Programming in Terms of Objects

It is all too easy, when you first start with Java, to write procedure-oriented code within methods. Indeed, many publicly available Java classes contain code which has clearly been written by a C or C++ programmer rather than by someone writing in an object-oriented manner. In Java, you should try to think in terms of objects.

39.7.8 Positioning of Methods

Just as with variables, you should present class methods first followed by instance methods. How you arrange the class methods is a matter of personal style – there is no real standard (as yet). However, you should at least follow these guidelines:

- Place the static initialization block immediately after the variable declarations.
- Group all constructors together.
- Place the main method before general-purpose class methods.
- Group related class methods together.

Figure 39.1 shows a recommended order of methods.

39.8 Scoping

Scope modifiers can be applied to classes, class and instance variables, and methods. In general, you should attempt to hide as much as possible from other objects; you should only make public items that must be public.

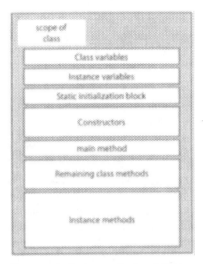

Figure 39.1 The layout of a class definition.

- When you decide that you must make a class public, limit access to it as much as possible.
- If a class or instance variable cannot be private, limit access to it. That is, use the default modifier in preference to protected (by default, the variable is only visible in the current package; protected means that it is visible in the package and in subclasses in other packages).
- If you do not want to allow something to be changed, make it final. You can make classes, instance or class variables, and methods final.
- Make a method private unless it is needed outside the class. If it is needed, limit access to it as much as possible.

If you are unclear about the modifiers and their meaning, refer to back to their definitions.

39.9 Statement Labels

One part of the Java language which has not been discussed in this book is the use of statement labels. You can use labels in conjunction with the break and continue statements.

You label a statement by preceding it with a word followed by a colon:

```
label: statement
```

Although we have only considered the break statement within the context of a switch statement, you can use a break statement to terminate any loop or block of code (for loops, if statements etc.). If the break statement is unlabelled then it terminates the innermost loop or block. However, if you label a statement, you can break out to the level of the label through any number of loops or blocks:

```
if (x == 3)
   outer: for (i = 0; i < 10; ++i) {
      for (j = 0; j < 10; ++j) {
         if ((i + j) == 19)
            break outer;
      }
   }
```

You can also use the continue statement within a loop. It jumps to the end of the loop and causes the condition to be evaluated. If the condition allows the loop to continue, then the next iteration of the loop is executed. You can use a label with the continue statement to jump to an outer loop rather than just an inner loop.

It can be argued that the use of a labelled break or continue is not a form of goto, as they are more controlled. That is, they can only be used to jump from one part of the code to another within a loop (or a block). However, it is as easy to produce obfuscating code with break, continue and label as it is with goto. Good programming style should remove the need to use these parts of the Java language. If you find you need to use them, then you are probably producing a poorly thought-out implementation.

39.10 Reference

Kernighan, B.W. and Ritchie, D.M. (1988). *The C Programming Language*, 2nd edn. Prentice Hall, Englewood Cliffs, NJ.

40 Common Java Bugs and Programmer Errors

40.1 Introduction

As with any language there are common errors (or bugs) which programmers make. In some cases these are picked up by the compiler, but there are still many which slip through the net. It is always useful for someone learning Java (or indeed for those who have more experience but wish to check their own programming style) to become familiar with the types of mistake that can be made. It is also useful to know what problems exist in the language itself. This chapter deals with these issues.

40.2 Programmer errors

40.2.1 Single Character Errors

Although Java has tried to ensure that single character errors are at least unlikely, it still retains their potential. For example, although Java has attempted to ensure that the old C classic bug relating to the use of the single equals (=) assignment character instead of the double equals (==) equality test within a conditional statement has been eradicated via its use of the `boolean` type, it has failed to remove it altogether. For example, the following is legal Java:

```java
boolean flag;
if (flag = true) {...}
```

The problem is that Java has defined such conditional statements to expect a boolean value and that the assignment statement is an expression which returns the value assigned (in this case a `boolean`). This is a double-edged sword, as it is possible to write `a = b = c = 0;`. Of course, the downside is that the result of assigning true to the variable `flag` is the value true. Thus the conditional code fragment above is accepted by the compiler. Java programmers might well argue that the above is poor style and that any Java programmers worth their salt would have used the following:

```java
if (flag) {...}
```

However the potential for this type of error still remains (although diminished when compared with C).

An interestingly different single character error relates to comments. In some languages (most notably Ada) the only type of comment allowed is a single-line comment which is terminated by the end of line. However, in Java (and many other languages) multi-line comments are allowed, with the comment started and terminated by specific combinations of letters (in the case of Java by / * and * / or / * * and * /). However, Java allows one comment to start within another; that is, it does not recognize the / * as being special. Thus it is quite possible to write the following code:

```
/* This is the start of a comment /
if (true) {
  Test5 = new test5();
  System.out.println("Done the test");
}
/* This is another comment */
System.out.println ("The end");
```

The result is that the if statement is taken to be part of the comment, as a single * was missed from the first comment.

40.2.2 Inappropriate Use of ==

There are many situations where in another programming language you might use = or == to indicate equality, whereas in Java you must use an appropriate method. This is because == in Java represents equality of objects (when used with reference types, e.g. objects; that is, do two reference type variables hold the same value?). As reference type variables all hold the address of the object they refer too, this is an address-oriented comparison. Thus in the following example, the address of the string referenced by the variable name is compared with the address of the literal string object. As these are not the same object, they will have different addresses. This means that the result of executing this code will be that the string "Go away" will be printed to standard out.

```
String name = "John";
if (name == "John") {
  System.out.println("Hello John");
} else {
  System.out.println("Go away");
}
```

In Java it is often necessary to use a method to determine the equality of two reference types. For example, the String class defines a number of methods which can be used to compare two strings: equals(String), equalsIgnoreCase (String), compareTo(String), regionMatches(int, String, int, int). Thus we could rewrite the above example as:

```
String name = "John";
if (name.equals("John")) {
  System.out.println("Hello John");
} else {
```

```
      System.out.println ("Go away");
}
```

This code now functions in the intended manner. That is, the string "Hello John" is printed to the standard out.

Note that this situation does not arise for basic or fundamental types such as int, float, double, boolean and char, as they are not referenced by an address. Thus 3 == 3 really does compare the value 3 with the value 3.

40.2.3 Adding a Return Type to a Constructor

A very common error which is not picked up immediately by the compiler is to attempt to write a construct but to give it a return type (such as void). For example:

```
public class Test extends Frame {
  public void Test (String title) {
     setTitle (title);
        pack ();
        setVisible (true);
  }
}
```

This will compile without any error message. However, if we subsequently try to create an instance of this class using the Test (String) constructor the compiler will complain, stating that there is no such constructor. The problem is that the compiler sees public void Test (String title) {...} as a normal method which just happens to have the same name as the class. Thus we have defined a method Test (String) in the class Test rather than a constructor. What we should have written was:

```
public class Test extends Frame {
  public Test (String title) {
     setTitle (title);
        pack ();
        setVisible (true);
  }
}
```

This can be a particularly annoying mistake which can take a great deal of time to identify the first time it is encountered.

40.2.4 Constructor Inheritance (Not)

Another mistake which many new developers to Java make is assuming that constructors are inherited in the same way as methods are inherited. However, in Java constructors are not inherited. Thus if you define a single-parameter constructor in class A, and wish to use the same constructor in its subclass B, you will need to define a second constructor in class B which merely calls the parent's constructor. This can result in excessive constructor definitions. For example:

```
public class Parent {
  String name;
  public Parent(String string) {
    name = string;
  }
}

public class Child extends Parent {
  public Child(String string) {
    super(string); // calls constructor in parent
                   // class
  }
}
```

40.2.5 Zero Parameter Constructor

When a class is defined, it will always have at least one constructor. If the developer does not define any constructors, then a default zero parameter constructor is automatically constructed. However, as soon as any constructors are explicitly defined this default constructor is removed. This is not normally a problem. However, what is not so clear is that a subclass will always call the parent class's zero parameter constructor if no other constructor has been explicitly called (using the super (...) call). Thus if a parent class does not have a zero parameter constructor a compile-time exception will be generated. For example:

```
Child.java:12: No constructor matching Parent() found
  in class Parent.

  public Child() {
       ^

1 error
```

40.2.6 Floating-Point Problems

An interesting effect of the IEEE 754 floating-point specification used in Java is that if you multiply some numbers together you may end up with an unexpected result. For example, the result of multiplying 3 * 1.1 is actually 3.3000000000000003, not 3.3. This is because 1.1 cannot be represented exactly in floating-point form. This of course means that some rounding error should be expected. This often surprises new Java programmers. Also, Java does not raise an exception when an arithmetic operation results in a non-numeric result because the IEEE 754 specification includes the values positive infinity, negative infinity, negative zero and not-a-number. This means that even if the result of some operation is infinity or not a number Java can return an appropriate value.

40.2.7 Overflow

This focuses on mistakes made by developers when they do not realize what will happen to a numerical value if overflow occurs. The problem with overflow is that when a numerical value (for example, an integer) reaches its maximum positive value, if 1 is added to this the value turns negative. For example, given the following Java code:

```
int i = Integer.MAX_VALUE;
System.out.println(i);
i++;
System.out.println(i);
```

the results obtained when running this code are:

```
2147483647
-2147483648
```

No warning is given for this and any program experiencing this will continue to function (probably incorrectly). However, in languages such as Ada there are two types of integer value, one which behaves in the same manner to Java numerics (including the wrapper classes), called *modular*, and one which will generate an exception in overflow situations. In Ada 95 the integer type is defined as:

> An integer_type_definition defines an integer type; it defines either a signed integer type, or a modular integer type. The base range of a signed integer type includes at least the values of the specified range. A modular type is an integer type with all arithmetic modulo a specified positive modulus; such a type corresponds to an unsigned type with wrap-around semantics.

Programmers can then decide which version they wish to use (this is somewhat akin to having two types of exception class, Exceptions and RuntimeExceptions, which may or may not be caught!).

40.2.8 Random Number Generator

Another issue is the use of the random number generator class (Random) which only operates appropriately if the numbers generated are from consecutive sequences. However, if the programmer uses various different "next" methods (e.g. nextInt() or nextDouble()) this results in non-adjacent numbers being generated which will not in general yield a well-designed "random" sequence.

40.2.9 Initialization of Objects

This category really relates to poor style or undesired behaviour, in that it can adversely affect a program's performance. For example, the class Vector can be constructed with a variety of different values as parameters to its constructors. Some of these values will generate a run-time error and some will result in undocumented behaviour. This is undesirable (although probably not critical). Examples of these are presented in Table 40.1 for the class Vector.

Table 40.1 Initializing `Vectors`

Constructor parameters	Result
`new Vector(-1)`	Run-time exception raised
`new Vector(-1, 2)`	Run-time exception raised
`new Vector(-1, 0)`	Run-time exception raised
`new Vector(-1, -1)`	Run-time exception raised
`new Vector(0)`	Runs but doubles in capacity each time capacity is reached (e.g. capacity is 0, 1, 2, 4, 8 etc.)
`new Vector(1, 0)`	Runs but doubles in capacity each time capacity is reached
`new Vector(1, -1)`	If increment is negative, results in doubling of capacity each time capacity is reached
`new Vector(0, -1)`	As above

40.3 Language Weaknesses

We have identified 12 different categories under which Java related defects can be classified. These 12 categories were developed from an analysis of published defects from a variety of sources and experimental findings. The process which was used to generate the initial set (of unclassified defects) involved the following steps:

1. Identify a set of defects from experimental findings.
2. Expand that set from analysis of the Java Language Specification.
3. Search the Web for on-line sources of defects (such as those provided by Sun and links from the Gamelan site, as well as laboratories carrying out analysis of the Java environment, such as the University of Washington).
4. Search through the comp.lang.java.* newsgroups, examining defects reported.
5. Analyze reports on the Java type system (such as those produced by the University of Cambridge).
6. Analyze published research, such as the "Java Security" book (McGraw and Felten, 1997).

Some of the defects found were duplicates and some were issues associated with ambiguities in language specifications. This generated a set of 127 different defects. Of these 127, there were 9 which could be attributed to flaws in the language (for example allowing a boolean to be assigned within a conditional part of an `if` statement), 69 were actual bugs in either the javac compiler or run-time (for JDK 1.1.*), 3 could be attributed to programmer errors and 7 were programmer style errors (such as failing to use the `switch` statement correctly). This is summarised in Table 40.2.

We analysed the 127 defects in detail to generate the 12 different categories. The generation of the categories used the following protocol:

1. Define an initial set of categories (what were they).
2. Select a defect and allocate it to an existing category.

Table 40.2 Analyzed defects

Type reported	Number	Explanation
Language omissions	40	Omissions from the Java language specification or the inner class specification
Language flaws	9	Errors in the language specification (relative to perceived use)
Bugs	59	Errors in the runtime or compiler (relative to the language specifications)
Programmer errors	3	Errors which can be introduced by a programmer due to the language specifications
Stylistic weaknesses	15	Specified Java features which are likely to cause problems

3. If no appropriate category exists, define a new category.
4. If defects remain to be analysed, return to step 2.

The result is the final set of 12 categories presented in Table 40.3.

Table 40.3 The 12 Java-related defect categories

Category	No.	Category	No.
Type safety	1+	Compile-time errors (for the javac compiler)	42
Numeric operations	7	Inheritance	9
Unspecified behaviour	44	Reflection	7
Use of final/implementation of final	3	Initialization of objects	7
Visibility	3	Single character errors	2
Security	5	Run-time	2

40.3.1 Type Safety

A language is type safe if the evaluation of any expression will produce a value of a type compatible with the type assigned to the value by the type system (unless an exception is raised). Showing that a language is type safe is a first step towards ensuring that applications written in that language will not compromise the security of the system on which they run. Indeed, some of the breaches in Java security that have been reported in the literature have exploited bugs in Java implementations to break the type system (see Section 40.3.9).

Since testing alone can never show that there are no bugs in a system, type safety has to be mathematically proved. A formal semantics for the type model of the language in question must be developed and then used to prove that program execution preserves types.

Various people have been working on the type safety of Java. Sophia Drossopoulou and Susan Eisenbach at the Imperial College of Science, Technology and Medicine, University of London, have analyzed a subset of the Java language and shown it to be type safe. This is being carried out within the SLURP group (Sound Languages Underpin Reliable Programming). They are continuing their work by enlarging the subset of Java which is analysed (Drossopoulou and Eisenbach, 1997; Drossopoulou et al. 1997; Drossopoulou and Eisenbach, 1998).

This work is complemented by that of Don Syme at the University of Cambridge, UK, who has developed a tool for proof checking by machine and applied it to the subset of Java originally analysed by Drossopoulou and Eisenbach (Syme, 1997). By automating the proof checking Don Syme was able to clarify significant details in the earlier work and detect errors and omissions. He was also able to independently rediscover a significant flaw in the Java language specification that had been found by developers of a Java implementation (Perera and Bertelsen, 1997).

The results described above have generally supported the safety of Java. However, Vijay Saraswat, at AT&T Research, Florham Park, NJ, has reported a flaw in Java's type system. He claims that, because of the way the Java type space is organized at run time, the Java Virtual Machine can be tricked into accepting one class as if it were a different class (Saraswat, 1997). It could be argued that this is an implementation issue and that the Java *language* could still be type safe. Indeed, Vijay Saraswat goes on to show in his paper how the JVM design can be fixed to overcome the problem.

Clearly, more work is needed before we can be sure that the Java language is type safe. This work is in progress. Ensuring the reliability of implementations is another matter and would require a completely formal development. Some work along these lines is under way. Richard Cohen, at Computational Logic Inc., Austin, TX, has formally developed a subset of the JVM, called the Defensive Java Virtual Machine (dJVM) (Cohen, 1997) and Zhenyu Qian, at the University of Bremen, has formally defined a large subset of the JVM instructions (Qian, 1997). A rigorous formal development of a complete Java implementation is still some way off. However, Java should be small enough, and formal methods sufficiently well advanced now, that such a development may well be feasible.

40.3.2 Compile-Time Errors (for the `javac` Compiler)

Compile-time errors are errors in the `javac` 1.1.* compilers (and, of course in JDK 1.2, but we are not concerned with those here as JDK 1.2 is still in beta at the time of writing). Of the 127 defects we studied in detail, 42 of them were compile-time errors. These of course may be fixed in subsequent releases, but are present in versions of the compiler in current use. In general they are errors in the compiler (i.e. bugs) rather than elements which are in conflict with the Java language specification. For example, the following code will cause the `javac` compiler to hang:

```
class A { class B { class C extends B {} } }
```

This appears to be a problem relating to cyclic references within inner classes. It is interesting to note how many of the 127 defects are actually related to the inner class specification. In fact, 36 defects can directly be attributed to the addition of inner classes. Of these, 26 are compiler bugs and 10 are in the "unspecified behaviour" category. Table 40.4 summarizes the effects of the introduction of the inner class specification (and associated syntax changes) on the 12 categories.

Table 40.4 The effect of the introduction of inner classes

Category	No.	Category	No.
Unspecified behaviour	10	Compile-time errors	21
Final keyword	3	Visibility	1
Inheritance	1		

40.3.3 Divide by Zero

This category relates to a reported compile-time omission. In some versions of the javac compiler, no compile-time warning is given when the compiler encounters a compile-time constant that would result in the raising of an Arithmetic-Exception. For example,

```
int i = 1 / 0;
```

compiles but would generate a run-time error in versions of javac prior to 1.1.3.

40.3.4 Inheritance

This category relates to defects associated with inheritance between classes, between interfaces and classes, and between different interfaces. In general, the defects within this category can be broken down into two different sub-categories: *accessibility* and *allowable inherited features/members*.

Accessibility relates to the accessibility of methods or variables (whether static or non-static). For example, the default access allows a class to extend an abstract class in another package which it cannot subsequently implement, for example:

```
package a;
public abstract class First { abstract void test(); }

package b;
public class Second extends First {void test () { ... }}
```

The problem with this is that the method test in the first class is not visible in the second package and this test() cannot implement it. Other similar defects include transformations of this which should have the same result as super but which can render a visible member inaccessible. Note that at present it is possible to specify that an abstract method is private (thus stopping any subclass from overwriting that method).

Allowable inherited features/members relates to issues associated with inheritance which compromise specifications. For example, an inner method is not allowed to have any static members; however, an inner member can inherit from a class that possesses static members (this is allowed by javac in JDK 1.1). The result is a malformed inner class.

40.3.5 Unspecified Behaviour

Perhaps surprisingly, given Java's original aims, this is the largest category within the 12 we have identified, with 44 different situations in which Java's behaviour is undefined (although it may not be the most significant category from the point of view of the developer). However, even here it is possible to identify two subcategories of defects. One relates to undocumented features and the other to undefined behaviour.

The former is probably less important than the latter. For example, in the former subcategory we have the fact that all interfaces inherit from the class `Object` (and thus implicitly contain abstract methods for all the methods defined within the class `Object`). This means that it is possible to invoke all `Object` operations on an instance given a reference to an interface type.

The latter subcategory, undefined behaviour, is more serious as it includes situations which have been left unspecified within the language or the behaviour of the compiler. These are not features which can be exploited if you know about them; rather, they are features which each compiler writer will have to work out for themselves. For example, it is not specified what the requirements on the method `test()` are for the `throws` clause in the following example. This is because it is not specified whether it should throw X, Y or both:

```
interface A {void print() throws X;}
interface B {void print() throws Y;}
interface C extends A, B {}
class D {
void test(C c) throws ??? /* what */ {c.print();}
}
```

The presence of unspecified behaviour is particularly concerning, as different compiler writers may make different decisions about how to resolve the undefined behaviour! This compromises the "write once, run anyway" aim of Java.

One point to note is that many of the defects in this category relate to inner classes. It appears that this is where the largest number of "gaps" exist in the Java language specifications. For example, the inner class specification explicitly allows a class to extend a top-level inner class. However, the result is that it allows the following cyclic reference:

```
class X extends Y.Z {...}
class Y extends X.Z {...}
```

It therefore appears that within the area of inner classes developers may find that the code they have written works on one platform with one compiler but not on another platform or another compiler. Java 2 eliminates many of these problems.

It is also interesting to note that the task scheduler within the JDK operates in different ways depending on whether you are using the UNIX or Win32 versions. The Win32 version is pre-emptive, whereas the UNIX version is not. Thus programs may exhibit different behaviour depending upon which machine they are running on!

40.3.6 Reflection

This category relates to defects in the core reflection API. This could be viewed as just an example of defects within the class library; however, as the reflection API will be

essentially to all tool builders and is the foundation upon which the JavaBeans introspection facilities are built it is particularly significant. The defects in this category
include omissions in the behaviour of classes and methods within the reflection API
such as the behaviour of the getFields() method. This method claims to return
all publicly accessible members; however, it actually returns all public members
(whether they are accessible or not). In addition, it also includes situations where the
result of using the reflection API to access a data item is different from accessing it
directly. For example, below the instance variable i is accessible in the class C;
however, the reflection API uses the accessibility of the class defining this variable to
determine whether it is accessible or not (in this case it therefore determines that it is
not):

```
package a;
class A { public Integer i; }
public class B extends A { }

package b;
public class C extends a.B {
  void test() throws Exception {
    i = new Integer(5); //okay
    java.lang.reflect.Field f =
      this.getClass().getField("i");
    f.set(this, new Integer(6)); // generates a
                                 // runtime error
}}
```

40.3.7 Use of Keyword `final`/Implementation of `final`

There are two subcategories within this category. These subcategories relate to the
use of the final modifier with methods and classes while the second relates to the
initialization of blank final fields.

final Modifier for Methods

It is possible to declare that a method is both abstract and final. For example:

```
public abstract class Test2 { abstract final void
  test(); }
```

In such situations it is therefore impossible to implement the abstract method.
The result is that no instances of the offending class (or its subclasses) can ever be
created.

Initialization of Blank final Fields

In Java 1.1 the use of the keyword final has been extended. These extensions
include the introduction of a blank final field. This is a field which is specified as
final but which is not set until a later date (after which time it cannot be changed).
However, related defects arise from this definition. The first is that the inner class

specification requires blank `final` variables to be initialized in every constructor (presumably to ensure that they are initialized). This allows a blank `final` field to be assigned more than once (within separate constructors). For example, it allows the following:

```
class Test {
   final int i;
   Test (int n) { i = 0; }
   Test () {
     this(5);
     i = 5;
   }
}
```

This Java code allows the final non-static integer variable "i" to be set twice when the class `test` is instantiated using the `Test()` constructor. This should cause at least a run-time exception. Again, Java 2 fixes this.

40.3.8 Visibility

This category describes defects relating to the visibility rules in Java. These are typically bugs in the way in which `javac` has been implemented. They can at times compromise the security of classes. For example, a protected static variable should not be visible in a different package. However, if a class in a different package extends the static variable's class, then the static variable becomes visible:

```
package p1;
public class A { protected static int x; }

package p2;
class B extends p1.B {
   void test() {
     B.x = 5;
     new B().x = 5;
}}
```

Interestingly, a number of the visibility bugs are associated with inner classes (again). For example, `javac` allows an inner class to have the same name as a lexically enclosing class (which the inner class specification explicitly prohibits), for example:

```
class A { void test() { class A {} } }
```

Other similar bugs relate to problems referencing inherited (and protected) inner classes as well as cyclic references to inner interfaces.

40.3.9 Security

Any high-integrity system must be secure. There are two aspects to this. First, the system must protect the data it is processing from casual observers. Second, it must not allow itself to be corrupted, either accidentally or maliciously. Clearly, the degree of security will depend on the application. A system that is processing HIV test records must maintain the confidentiality of the people being tested, whereas a system processing weather data for a Space Shuttle launch, although safety critical, need not be confidential. On the other hand, every high-integrity system must protect itself from corruption. If the system is corrupted then its integrity can no longer be guaranteed.

Object-oriented development presents a number of challenges for security. Can we be sure that *all* the classes higher up the class hierarchy upon which we depend are themselves secure? Is it possible for someone to replace one of these classes with a class that could compromise the security of our system, either by leaking data or by providing a trapdoor through which a Trojan horse may be introduced?

Applets are of particular concern from the security point of view. They are embedded in Web pages and may be activated without the user being aware of their existence. Although considerable effort has gone into making the applet mechanism secure, implementation bugs can, and have, introduced loopholes that enable this security to be broken. Systems that use applets require careful analysis of security issues and of the environments within which the systems will execute. An understanding of the holes in Java's "sandbox" and other security mechanisms is also necessary.

40.3.10 Run time

The run-time environment executes the byte codes compiled by the `javac` (or similar) compiler. In general the run-time environment does not appear to present many problems. However, there have been a couple of run-time defects reported. One indicated that the run-time environment and the compiler used different scoping tests, such that the compiler accepted the code but the run-time did not. For example, `javac` allows a static method to implement a non-static abstract method. However, at run time, an `IllegalAccessError: Unimplemented interface method` error is raised. For example;

```
class X { public static void test() {} }
interface Y { void test(); }
class Z extends X implements Y {}
class A {
  public static void main (String args []) {
    Y y = new Z();
    y.test(); // runtime error
  }
}
```

40.4 References

Cohen, R.M. (1997). *The Defensive Java Virtual Machine Specification (Version 0.5)*. Computational Logic, Inc, Austin TX.

Drossopoulou, S. and Eisenbach, S. (1997). Java is type safe – probably. 11th European Conference on Object Oriented Programming, June 1997. `http://src.doc.ic.ac.uk/public/ic.doc/ALA/papers/S.Drossopoulou/JavaSoundEcoop.ps`

Drossopoulou, S. and Eisenbach, S. (1998). Towards an Operations Semantics and Proof of Type Soundness for Java. `http://www-dse.doc.ic.ac.uk/~dpw/papers/towards.ps`.

Drossopoulou, S., Eisenbach, S. and Khurshid, S. (1997). *Is the Java Type System Sound?* `http://www-ala.doc.ic.ac.uk/papers/S.Drossopoulou/JavaSoundJour.ps`.

Perera, R. and Bertelsen, P. (1997). *The Unofficial Java Bug Report,* June. `http://www2.vo.lu/homepage/gmid/java.htm`

Qian, Z. (1997). *A Formal Specification of Java Virtual Machine Instructions.* `http://informatik.uni-bremen.de/~qian/abs-fsjvm.html#end`

Saraswat, V. (1997). *Java is not Type-Safe.* `http://www.research.att.com/~vj/bug.html`.

SLURP Group: `http://outoften.doc.ic.ac.uk/projects/slurp/`.

Syme, D. (1997). *Proving Java Type Soundness.* `http://www.cl.cam.ac.uk/users/drs1004/reports/java.ps`.

41 *Reliable Java Systems*

41.1 Introduction

The construction of high-integrity or high-reliability systems in an object-oriented language, and in Java in particular, introduces some very specific issues. These issues include security, the ambiguities in the language and common programmer bugs. These are considered further in the remainder of this chapter.

"High integrity" is a rather ill-defined term. Here we are applying it to any system that, because of its nature or application, must provide the utmost reliability and confidence. Such a system must be unlikely to fail but, if it does fail, it should do so in a non-catastrophic manner, i.e. it must give the wider application a chance to detect and recover from the failure. A high-integrity application may be one that is safety-critical in that its failure might endanger life, limb or property. Alternatively, it may be one on which people depend for their livelihood or one on which a significant enterprise depends for its success. Note that, in the modern world where computers and the Internet are ubiquitous, a system which was never designed with integrity in mind nor intended for use in critical applications may well find itself being so used. A software component may be downloaded from the Internet and incorporated into a larger system. In time, its existence becomes hidden and the larger system may be used in a critical application without proper consideration being given to the integrity of its components.

41.1.1 Security

Any high-integrity system must be secure. Security is discussed in Section 40.3.9, so we shall not elaborate further here.

41.1.2 Language features

Issues associated with type safety, language ambiguities and common programmer bugs need to be considered. A language is type safe if the evaluation of any expression will produce a value of a type compatible with the type assigned to the value by the type system (unless an exception is raised). Showing that a language is type safe is a first step towards ensuring that applications written in that language will not compromise the security of the system on which they run. Indeed, some of the breaches in Java security that have been reported in the literature have exploited bugs in Java implementations to break the type system.

From the point of view of language flaws, the Java development team missed a prime opportunity to rid the programming world of one of the worst language constructs of all time: the C-style switch statement. There are two major flaws with the Java switch statement. The first is the need to "break" out of each case block. This is a major problem that has led to many software bugs. For example, in December 1989 the long-distance telephone service in the USA was disrupted by a software problem in the AT&T electronic switching systems. The problem was allegedly traced to a misuse of a break statement in a switch statement in a C program (Neumann, 1995). As can be seen from this, the inclusion of such a feature has serious implications for the construction of high-integrity software.

The second major flaw is the inability of the switch statement to deal with anything other than integer comparisons. There are many situations in which it would be far easier to say something like:

```
switch (student.getMark() ) {
  case > 70 ...
  ...
}
```

Instead it is necessary to convert the value to be tested into an integer and then test the expected integer results explicitly. This obviously introduces additional complexity and promotes the introduction of errors.

Since Java was defined with safety considerations in mind, possibly most surprising of all is the presence of unspecified behaviour in the Java language. Section 40.3.5 presents an example of this. The presence of unspecified behaviour is particularly concerning, as different compiler writers may make different decisions about how to resolve the undefined behaviour! Thus a developer may produce different source code, depending upon the compiler used. This then raises the question of what happens when the resulting byte codes are executed in different (or the same) virtual machine.

Finally, Java includes a number of features that actively promote programmer errors. For example, consider the following Java code, which contains a common programmer error (note that this code compiles successfully):

```
import java.awt.*;
public class Foo extends Frame {
  public void Foo() {
    Button b = new Button("Test");
    add("Center", b);
    pack();
    setVisible(true);
  }
  public static void main(String args []) {
    new Foo();
  }
}
```

The intention of this code is that when the user compiles and run this class, a window containing a single button labelled "Test" will be displayed. However, the programmer did not define a constructor (a special method with the same name as the class but no return type). Instead a normal method was defined with the same name as the class which returned void. The null parameter constructor was automatically created for them and it is this that was run. Of course, this auto-created constructor did not create a button and open the window! The problems here are that Java first automatically created a constructor and then allowed a method to have exactly the same name as the class (with the same capitalization). If either of these things were disallowed, then the compiler could have picked up on this and warned the programmer.

41.1.3 The Environment

Java is intended to be "write once, run anywhere". However, at present it is closer to "write once, test everywhere". This is due to differences in virtual machine implementations, internal details relating to how system-provided classes are implemented and platform dependencies. Thus if a developer's software works correctly on one platform with one virtual machine, although it may not need to be recompiled for other platforms, it is still necessary to test it on all platforms.

41.1.4 The javac Compiler

The javac compiler provided as part of the JDK 1.1 is not bug-free. It contains a number of bugs that are primarily related to the newest addition to Java – inner classes. There are a few points that should be noted about inner classes. Firstly, they can access variables and methods from the enclosing class. Secondly, inner classes are not usable outside the scope of the outer class. Thirdly, when an instance of the outer class is created its inner class is also instantiated. Fourthly, local inner classes can be defined within the scope of a method and are only accessible within that method's scope. No additional syntax has been provided to define an inner class, although there have been a number of associated syntax additions, such as the ability to qualify a new statement.

As inner classes are a new addition to Java, developers may well make mistakes with their use. However, there appears to be a problem relating to cyclic references within inner classes in at least one of the 1.1.* releases of Java. If a developer's code relies on the presence of an error in the way inner classes are handled by the javac compiler, then this could compromise the integrity of the software itself, and cause major problems as new releases of the compiler are made available (which may plug the hole).

Another example of a compiler bug is that in some versions no compile-time warning is given when the compiler encounters a compile-time constant that would result in the raising of an ArithmeticException.

41.1.5 Language Maturity

Since its release Java has been subject to extensive change. Not only have there been three major releases since 1995, but there have been many beta releases available for public review. Obviously a beta release cannot be expected to be of the same standard as the final release, so it is not surprising that these versions have contained bugs. However, the Java 1.1 final release ended up having seven subsequent releases to fix bugs present in the compiler or virtual machine plus two additional releases (1.1.7A and 1.1.7B). This is not acceptable in a language intended for use in mission-critical applications!

It is likely that the language will stabilize in the very near future, even given the above discussion. Indeed, work is already under way to produce an ISO standard for Java. In March, 1997, Sun submitted an application to ISO/IEC JTC 1 to become a Recognized Publically Available Specification (PAS) submitter for Java. The ISO/IEC JTC 1 is the International Organization for Standardization/International Electro-technical Commission Joint Technical Committee 1. In 1995, the JTC 1 launched a program whereby an organization could act as submitters of PAS to enable the rapid approval of international standards. This enables organizations to evaluate, define and submit specifications to JTC 1 to facilitate development of industry standards. Although Sun had to resubmit its submission, it was successful and has been accepted as a PAS submitter. Sun is now in the process of preparing to submit Java (and the APIs which are currently stable) as the initial Java standard. Such a standard could be in place within seven months of submission[1].

41.2 Impact

All of the points raised above have an impact on the way in which reliable object-oriented Java programs should be developed and deployed. In particular, they affect issues such as the reusability of code and the amount and nature of testing required.

41.2.1 The Reusability of Code

One problem that may be encountered due to the issues discussed above is that code that worked acceptably in one release of Java may not work in another (even between "bug-fix" releases). This may be because a "feature" of that version of the compiler or run-time environment was being exploited. As a newer version of the compiler becomes available that feature may be eliminated. This can typically happen during a major upgrade of a language or a compiler. However, as there are many new features in recent releases of Java (1.1. and 1.2) and defects in the compiler and run-time, it may be difficult for developers to be sure that they are not exploiting some "illegal" loophole.

In addition, Java developers typically consider that their code really is "write once, run anywhere". However, experience has shown this not to be the case. However, if Java classes are made publicly available it is unlikely that developers will have tested their classes on all possible platforms. Thus developers' confidence in Java's ability to "run anywhere" may be undermined. If not, the opposite position of "blind trust" could be catastrophic.

---

1   Information on the JTC 1 can be found on the Web via ANSI (which administers the JTC 1) at http://www.ansi.org/.

41.2.2 Testing

The testing of code in a subclass, as well as that inherited from existing classes, is an important issue. Just because code inherited from a parent class works in that class does not mean that it works in the subclass. As Java itself possesses no assertion-checking mechanisms, it is not possible for one piece of code to check the actions of another. For example, if a parent method calls a method in a subclass, it cannot check the result using any built-in mechanisms. Of course, assertion mechanisms can be added to Java (Hunt and Long, 1998).

In addition, developers must remember to test their software on each platform that it will be deployed on. This means that they should consider test plans that include method, class, integration and system testing on all deployment platforms.

As the language is changing so rapidly, and new versions of the JDK are being made available at regular intervals, developers need to be even more careful about fixing on a particular version for the duration of a project. The problem that this raises with Java is that even selecting a major release of the JDK (such as 1.1) may not be sufficient. For example, between JDK 1.1.2 and JDK 1.1.3 a number of bugs were fixed which were re-introduced in JDK 1.1.4. Thus even upgrading within a set of "bug-fix" releases may not necessarily be the best thing! Certainly if a development team does upgrade the compiler and virtual machine it needs to repeat all the tests which have already been performed to ensure that the software is not adversely affected by the new release. The situation becomes even worse when Java Development Environments (JDEs) are taken into account. Many of these possess behaviour that does not match that of the JDK. This means that if a development team uses such a JDE it is liable to produce code that does not operate acceptably on other platforms.

41.2.3 Dynamic Loading of Classes

One of the features of Java is its ability to dynamically load classes in the virtual machine at run time. It does this by searching the current directory and the CLASSPATH for the named class. However, this means that one version of a class in one environment is not necessarily the same as a class with the same name in another environment. Thus although an application works fine with one version of class X, when deployed it may pick up another class called X and fail. Other than manually ensuring that the correct version of the class X is being used, there is no way of overcoming this problem. Note that the serial version ID can be used to ensure that a specific version of a class is being used. However, it can be tedious to do this for every single class that is being used.

The 1.2 release of the JDK (Java 2) does introduce package versioning. Versioning allows package-level version control, where applications and applets can identify, at run time, the version of a specific Java Runtime Environment, VM, or class package. Thus if developers specify a particular version of a package, they can be sure that they will get the class associated with that version. This obviously assumes that the developers are using packages (which they should be) and that one version of a package will only ever possess one version of a class (no matter where that package is located).

41.2.4 Class Authentication Signatures

In order to ensure that classes are not corrupted, they can be signed with a non-forgeable signature that can be checked when the class is loaded. This mechanism provides confidence that the class that is actually loaded is the one intended and that it has not been replaced by another, either accidentally or deliberately.

41.2.5 Quality Control Procedures

The application of drastic quality control measures is necessary if an application is truly mission-critical or requires very high levels of reliability. For example, one may specify that certain language features (such as inner classes or anonymous classes) or specific classes will not be used within the application.

41.2.6 The Use of Code Quality Analysis Software

Code quality is best assured by the use of quality analysis and metrics gathering software. This software (such as "lint" or QAC (Programming Research Ltd, 1996) for the C language) can be used to generate various reports and statistics about the software which, in turn, can be used in the quality control process. For example, one may stipulate that no method should be longer than so many lines of code, or have greater than some specified complexity. These tools can also identify common problems, such as unreachable code, which may indicate a programming error undetectable by the compiler. The more sophisticated tools are capable of carrying out a complete flow analysis of a piece of code, thereby highlighting problems such as uninitialized variables or variables set but not used.

It is interesting to note that it has been suggested that one of the motivations behind Java was to eliminate the need for tools such as QAC.

41.2.7 Rapid Application Development Tools

Rapid application development tools (RAD tools) can help a development team to explore the capabilities of Java. In particular, they are a useful source of experience for new additions to the language, such as inner classes. Unfortunately, they tend to lag behind the latest release of the JDK. This means that it can take six months or more for such tools to be fully compliant with the latest version of the Java language. This can minimize their usefulness.

41.3 Minimization Strategies

The strategies proposed in this section are divided into two. The first set are intended to deal with issues associated with specific categories presented above. The second set are intended as general guidelines which cut across all categories.

41.3.1 Specific Strategies

1. Care needs to be taken when using packages and either private or default visibility members.
2. Care should also be taken with the use of the `final` modifier on both methods and fields. Where it is used, developers should ensure that its use will not compromise their systems (in particular care should be exercised with blank final fields).
3. Don't rely on the compiler being able to correctly identify undesirable behaviour such as unassigned values, division by a zero constant or unreachable code. (Note that `javac` usually identifies each of these, but there are certain circumstances in which it either fails to diagnose them or diagnoses them incorrectly).
4. Don't rely on reflection to act in exactly the same way as the run-time virtual machine when it comes to visibility.
5. Developers should become familiar with the classes in the Java API. In particular, this may mean studying the source code for frequently used classes to ensure they understand the effects of their actions in extreme cases (for example, the `Vector` class).
6. Care should be taken when developing classes that will be used by third parties to ensure that the classes' visibility will not be compromised.
7. Avoid new features until they have been fully tested by the user community. In particular, avoid using inner classes until the current defects have been resolved.
8. Ensure that any house styles used minimize the chance of single-character errors (for example boolean tests should be used without performing an equality test e.g. `if (!flag)` or `while (flag)`).
9. Only use up-to-date browsers with the latest security updates (see McGraw and Felten (1997) for more on this).

41.3.2 General Strategies

1. Be wary of using third-party software which is only made available in `.class` format. You need to be able to check its source to ensure that it will not compromise the integrity of your own code.
2. Avoid using areas of Java where behaviour is undefined (this implies that the developer knows what is not defined!). If you must use them, then stick to one environment on one machine (as the undefined behaviour may be implemented differently in other environments).
3. Stick with a known working version of the JDK until a new version has been explored by the user community. Don't jump to a new version just because it has been released.
4. Stay in touch with on-line resources such as `comp.lang.java.*`, The Unofficial Java Bug Report (`http://www2.vo.lu/homepages/gmid/`) and the Sun Microsystems Bugs Report (`http://www.javasoft.com/products/jdk/1.1/knownbugs/`) to ensure that you learn about significant bugs as soon as they are found.

5. Note that many of the above strategies rely on the developer being familiar with the types of defects currently reported and their implications. It is therefore important for those developing high-integrity systems in Java to maintain a watchful eye on all appropriate sources of information. This is probably the most important single strategy that can be recommended.

41.4 Consequences for Java Software Development

Given the strategies presented in the last subsection, there are some consequences for both the type of system that can be built with Java and how those systems are built. In particular:

- If you wish to ensure that your program and its data are safe then do not construct applets; build applications only. That is, do not rely on browsers and the Internet unless you have to. If you require a system that has a distributed element, why not rely on a central database (via JDBC), RMI or a CORBA-compliant ORB? This may seem to be at odds with the philosophy of Java, but Java security and browser security are still relatively new and are evolving all the time.

- When developing Java code, attempt to use quality assurance tools (such as QAC for C [QAC]) when and where available. Just because Java tries to be safer does not mean that it actually is safer.

- Just because a class has successfully compiled using the `javac` compiler does not indicate that it is safe to use. This means that merely compiling a class is no guarantee that when it is deployed (made available for use by others) it will be either useful or reliable (obviously one would encourage testing of such classes before making them available for use by others, but that is a separate issue).

- Don't trust the compiler to identify misbehaviour accurately. In many situations `javac` is capable of warning developers that some code is either uninitialized, unreachable or undesirable (e.g. will generate a run-time error). However, developers cannot guarantee that it will do so in all such situations. They should therefore not rely on the compiler to provide such warnings.

- Apply drastic measures if your application is truly mission critical or requires very high levels of reliability. For example, specify that certain language features or classes will not be used within your applications.

- Assess how significant reliability is and decide at that point whether Java will allow you to achieve your aim.

- Develop to a particular version of Java and stick with that version. This is good practice in most situations, as it is rarely a good idea to change version during project development. In the case of Java 1.1 many developers were forced to stick with Java 1.0 (or at least the 1.0 features of 1.1) because the browser they were using did not support 1.1. An additional consideration may be that by the time the next major release of Java arrives, all (or at least most of the serious) bugs will have been eradicated from the previous version of Java. Any that do remain may be well documented by that stage.

- If your development needs to make use of the latest version of Java or the latest additions to the language (such as inner classes), attempt to minimize the risks incurred by keeping up to date with the latest bug reports.

- Do not pick up and use PD class libraries for Java from the Internet without first analyzing them to determine whether their behaviour is acceptable. This may appear to go against the open nature of Java; however, part of this is the provision of source code (as well as .class files) and thus is really an acknowledgement of the fragility of some areas of Java.

- An additional set of tests (to those normally defined) should be used to explicitly identify whether known defects are affecting a development. For example, if inner classes are being used in the development of a package to be distributed to users, define tests that will attempt to exploit known inner class defects.

It should be noted that these strategies and their effects do not relate to specific defects. This is because, as new features are introduced, new versions of tools are released and more experience is gained, the specific set of defects will alter. Therefore these strategies do not (and cannot) deal with specific defects and should not be taken as any form of immunity from any set of defects. Rather, they should be taken as a description of current best practice.

41.5 Further Reading and References

Further details on testing and the use of assertions to perform run-time tests can be found in Hunt, J. and McManus, A. (1998). *Key Java: Advanced Tips and Techniques*. Springer-Verlag, London.

Hunt, J. and Long, F. (1998). Implementing assertions in Java. *Java Developers Journal*, 3(1).

McGraw, G. and Felten, E.W. (1997). *Java Security: Hostile Applets, Holes and Antidotes*. John Wiley, New York.

Neumann, P.G. (1995). *Computer Related Risks*, Addison-Wesley, Reading, MA, pp. 14–15.

Programming Research Ltd (1996) *QAC: Deep Flow static analyser: Users Guide*, Programming Research Ltd., http://www.prqa.co.uk/.

Sun Microsystems Bugs Reports. http://www.javasoft.com/products/jdk/1.1/knownbugs/.

The Unofficial Java Bug Report. http://www2.vo.lu/homepages/gmid/.

42 *Performance Optimization*

42.1 Introduction

This chapter addresses the question "How can I optimize performance in my Java system?". A number of different techniques are considered, including optimization using the tools provided with Sun's Java Developers' Kit (JDK), the use of Just-In-Time (JIT) compilers, native code compilation, the Java profiler and the appropriate use of Java programming language constructs and classes. A useful source of information on Java optimization can be found at http://www.cs.cmu.edu/~jch/java/.

42.1.1 Sun's JDK

Because it is free, the standard javac compiler and JVM (or the cut-down Java Runtime Environment, JRE) are the one most widely used environment for distribution. We shall therefore consider what optimizations are possible using this environment. Note that we are primarily concerned with the JDK 1.1.*, as this is the environment that most developers will currently (and for the foreseeable future) be using.

In Sun's JDK, you may have noticed the "optimize" flag -O available on the javac. What optimizing does it actually do? The answer, in fact, is very little. It strips out all debugging information, which can make the class size smaller, it removes some (but not all) redundant code, and it attempts to make some method calls in-line. But that is it (at present). For those of you who are familiar with optimization in languages such as C this will seem very little. However, in time it is likely that this will improve.

Of course, unlike languages such as C, compilation is not the end of the story. The resulting byte codes are then "executed" by a virtual machine. The standard Java Virtual Machine works within strict memory constraints. When it starts, it takes 1 Mbyte of memory from the underlying OS. During the life of the program, it can request up to a maximum of 16 Mbyte (versions of Java before 1.1 used values much less than this). The startup and maximum heap sizes can be configured using the -ms and -mx flags (the heap is the block of memory that your Java program can use for new object instances). For example, the following command starts the virtual machine with 4 Mbyte out of a maximum of 24 Mbyte:

```
java -ms4m -mx24m MyClass
```

If you find that you are getting out-of-memory errors, or that the application as a whole slows down when large amounts of data are in memory (causing the GC to be called more often), try increasing the maximum size of the heap. Note that once the virtual machine has requested memory from the operating system, it will not return it (even when it doesn't need that much memory any more).

Another impact on the performance of a system is the garbage collector. The garbage collector is a process that hunts around in memory looking for objects which are no longer being used and from which memory can be reclaimed. This simplifies the programmer's task and reduces the chances of memory leaks etc. The standard JVM runs the garbage collector (GC) asynchronously. This means that the GC will be called when explicitly requested by the application; when memory is very low; and every now-and-then in a background thread. However, this may mean that the garbage collector is called when you least want it to execute (for example at a particular performance-critical moment). Luckily, the virtual machine provides a number of flags to help control the garbage collector.

The JVM can be instructed to stop running garbage collection asynchronously with the -noasyncgc flag. In this case, garbage collections will only be run when the JVM runs out of memory or when explicitly called. This means that you can call the GC during some idle operation (such as during user input). The GC will actually only execute if it needs to. Thus even if you call the GC, it will not necessarily execute. You do not therefore need to worry about calling the GC unnecessarily. For example, the following code allows you to find out the amount of free memory before and after calling the garbage collector (System.gc()).

```
System.out.println(runtime.totalMemory( ) -
    runtime.freeMemory( ));
System.gc( ); // calls garbage collector
System.out.println(runtime.totalMemory( ) -
    runtime.freeMemory( ));
```

42.1.2 Just-In-Time Compilers

Just-In-Time (JIT) compilers are now widely available, and make a very significant improvement to the speed of Java code. Most browsers use a JIT to speed up Java applets. Note that JITs are part of the virtual machine, and are not to be confused with the Java source code compilers, such as javac.

When a method is called for the first time, the Java byte code is compiled (just in time for its first use), and executed as native code. The compiled code is stored for any subsequent calls to the method. The compilation phase is very fast and does not introduce a noticeable delay. The improvement is execution speed can be dramatic, particularly with processor-intensive code.

JavaSoft has now made available Symantec's JIT virtual machine as part of its Performance Pack for Windows. This is freely available for download at the JavaSoft Web site. It integrates transparently with the Java Development Kit (JDK) or the Java Runtime Environment (JRE).

The new version of the JDK 1.2/Java 2 will include a JIT compiler as standard. This JIT compiler is likely to provide a major boost to the performance of Java systems.

42.1.3 Native Code

The previous discussion has focused on the use of the `javac` compiler and the Java Virtual Machine. However, if you are intending to deploy an application on a specific platform, then you can choose to compile it into a native executable. Bear in mind, though, that the speed of the executable is only as good as the compiler and its run-time library – in some situations you may find that there is little improvement in performance over a good JIT.

For example, IBM's High Performance Compiler for Java (for AIX, OS/2, Windows 95/98, Windows NT) compiles Java byte code into optimized platform-specific native (object) code. The resulting code is (generally) significantly faster than the byte code executed in Sun's Java Virtual Machine or a JIT compiler. The degree of performance improvement, however, does depend upon the application. At present this native code compiler is in beta release and supports most of the JDK 1.1.* API (see `http://www.alphaWorks.ibm.com/Home/`). SuperCede 2.0 also provides a facility to create a `.exe` version of your Java system (see `http://www.supercede.com/`).

However, you should be aware that some tools for turning Java code into a native executable simply package the classes into a file and call on the original virtual machine.

42.1.4 Profiling

The standard Java virtual machine can help you to identify the speed-critical areas in your code. If you run your application with the `-prof:MyClass.prof` flag, it will write profiling information to the file `MyClass.prof`. The format of this (large) file is, as yet, undocumented. However, the most useful information is at the beginning, where it lists all of the methods that were called during the life of the application, the calling method, the number of times the method was called, and the time spent in the method. The list is ordered by the number of times a method is called. This option has been changed in Java 2.

The volume of profile information can be a little daunting, but there are a number of tools available that help you interpret the information. HyperProf is a good example of this, written entirely in Java. It also includes a smart graphical display of the profile results, which, while not being terribly useful, is definitely worth a look!

42.1.5 Coding Styles

As well as a having good understanding of the tools available to you, knowing how the language itself works can lead to some simple improvements in performance. As a simple example, consider the following code, which returns a string representation of the contents of a (non-empty) `Vector`.

```
String result = "[" + elementAt(0);
for (int i = 1; i < size(); i++)
  result += ", " + elementAt(i);
return result + "]";
```

String concatenation in Java is performed by converting the string into a `StringBuffer` and using the `append()` method. Each time the `for` loop executes, Java converts `result` into a `StringBuffer`, appends the string literal and the element string, converts the whole lot back into a string and assigns it to `result`. If you use a `StringBuffer` explicitly, as in the next code example, there is only one conversion between the `StringBuffer` and the `String`, resulting in a *threefold* increase in speed:

```
StringBuffer result = new StringBuffer("[");
result.append(elementAt(0));
for (int i = 1; i < size(); i++) {
  result.append(", ");
  result.append(elementAt(i).toString());
}
result.append("]");
return result.toString();
```

You should become familiar with the very many techniques/appropriate programming constructs which can achieve similar results (for further details see Hunt and McManus (1998)).

42.2 Further Reading

Further details on this topic can be found in:

Hunt, J. and McManus, J. (1998). *Key Java: Advanced Tips and Techniques.* Springer-Verlag, London.

43 *Java Self-Test Examination*

43.1 Introduction

At this point you have covered all the areas of Java that you need to be a proficient and effective Java practitioner. After this chapter we will be concentrating on designing object-oriented systems rather than Java-specific features. This chapter therefore provides a point at which you can test your own knowledge of Java before continuing with the book. For those of you intending to take Sun's Certified Java Programmer 1.1[1] examination it also allows you to practise the style of questions used in the examination. It should not be used as a way of learning Java; nor should it be treated as a form of revision. However, testing one's knowledge as a way of identifying gaps is always useful.

Some care has been taken to ensure that the style of questions is the same as that of the actual certification exam, but that no questions from the examination are actually included. The style is based on one person's experience of taking the Java Certification examination, and it should therefore not be assumed that this mock exam is an exact reflection of the actual exam.

This mock examination consists of 65 questions (the actual exam consists of 60 questions). Just as in the actual examination a mixture of styles of question are included. These range between questions that require a single answer and those that require one or more answers. The former are indicated by:

● Select the most appropriate answer.

The latter are indicated by:

● Select all correct answers.

Note that a question that has the above request may require only one correct option; it is for you to decide. However, if you do not identify all the correct options for that question you will score zero for that question. One free-format question is included as an example of that style of questioning.

As in the actual exam you should not attempt to identify any trends relating to As, Bs or Cs. That is, do not assume that because the answer A has not appeared for a while there is a good chance that it will soon.

For the actual examination the pass mark is 70%. You should therefore aim to achieve at least 46 correct answers in this mock examination. The correct answers are give at the end of the examination.

---

1 **Disclaimer:** This mock examination is in no way sanctioned by Sun Microsystems and no guarantees are provided about the similarity of these questions to those in the actual exam.

43.2 Java Multiple Choice Exam

Q. 1
Which colour is used to indicate instance methods in the standard "javadoc" format documentation?

    A. blue
    B. red
    C. purple
    D. orange

Select the most appropriate answer.

Q. 2
What is the correct ordering for the `import`, `class` and `package` declarations when found in a single file?

    A. `package, import, class`
    B. `class, import, package`
    C. `import, package, class`
    D. `package, class, import`

Select the most appropriate answer.

Q. 3
Which methods can be legally applied to a string object?

    A. `equals(String)`
    B. `equals(Object)`
    C. `trim()`
    D. `round()`
    E. `toString()`

Select all correct answers.

Q. 4
What is the parameter specification for the `public static void main` method?

    A. `String args []`
    B. `String [] args`
    C. `Strings args []`
    D. `String args`

Select all correct answers.

Q. 5

What does the zeroth element of the string array passed to the `public static void main` method contain?

 A. The name of the program
 B. The number of arguments
 C. The first argument if one is present

Select the most appropriate answer.

Q. 6

Which of the following are Java keywords?

 A. `goto`
 B. `malloc`
 C. `extends`
 D. `FALSE`

Select all correct answers

Q. 7

What will be the result of compiling the following code?

```
public class Test {
  public static void main (String args []) {
    int age;
    age = age + 1;
    System.out.println("The age is " + age);
  }
}
```

 A. Compiles and runs with no output
 B. Compiles and runs, printing out *The age is 1*
 C. Compiles but generates a run-time error
 D. Does not compile
 E. Compiles but generates a compile-time error

Select the most appropriate answer.

Q. 8

Which of these is the correct format to use to create the literal char value a?

 A. `'a'`
 B. `"a"`
 C. `new Character(a)`
 D. `\000a`

Select the most appropriate answer.

Q.9
What is the legal range of a byte integral type?

  A. 0–65, 535
  B. (–128)–127
  C. (–32,768)–32,767
  D. (–256)–255

Select the most appropriate answer.

Q.10
Which of the following is illegal?

  A. **int** i = 32;
  B. **float** f = 45.0;
  C. **double** d = 45.0;

Select the most appropriate answer.

Q.11
What will be the result of compiling the following code?

```
public class Test {
   static int age;
   public static void main (String args []) {
      age = age + 1;
      System.out.println ("The age is " + age);
   }
}
```

  A. Compiles and runs with no output
  B. Compiles and runs, printing out *The age is 1*
  C. Compiles but generates a run-time error
  D. Does not compile
  E. Compiles but generates a compile-time error

Select the most appropriate answer.

Q.12
Which of the following are correct?

  A. 128 >> 1 gives 64
  B. 128 >>> 1 gives 64
  C. 128 >> 1 gives –64
  D. 128 >>> 1 gives –64

Select all correct answers

Q. 13

Which of the following return true?

```
A. "john" == "john"
B. "john".equals("john")
C. "john" = "john"
D. "john".equals(new Button("john"))
```

Select all correct answers.

Q. 14

Which of the following do not lead to a run-time error?

```
A. "john" + " was " + " here"
B. "john" + 3
C. 3 + 5
D. 5 + 5.5
```

Select all correct answers.

Q. 15

Which of the following are so called "short circuit" logical operators?

```
A. &
B. | |
C. & &
D. |
```

Select all correct answers.

Q. 16

Which of the following are acceptable?

```
A. Object o = new Button("A");
B. Boolean flag = true;
C. Panel p = new Frame();
D. Frame f = new Panel();
E. Panel p = new Applet();
```

Select all correct answers.

Q. 17

What is the result of compiling and running the following code?

```
public class Test {
  static int total = 10;
  public static void main (String args []) {
    new Test();
  }
  public Test () {
    System.out.println("In test");
```

```
System.out.println(this);
int temp = this.total;
if (temp > 5) {
  System.out.println(temp);
}
}
}
```

A. The class will not compile
B. The compiler reports an error at line 2
C. The compiler reports an error at line 9
D. The value 10 is one of the elements printed to the standard output
E. The class compiles but generates a run-time error

Select all correct answers.

Q. 18
Which of the following is correct?

```
A. String temp [] = new String {"j" "a" "z"};
B. String temp [] = { "j " " b" "c"};
C. String temp = {"a", "b", "c"};
D. String temp [] = {"a", "b", "c"};
```

Select the most appropriate answer.

Q. 19
What is the correct declaration of an abstract method that is intended to be public?

```
A. public abstract void add();
B. public abstract void add() {}
C. public abstract add();
D. public virtual add();
```

Select the most appropriate answer.

Q. 20
Under what situations do you obtain a default constructor?

A. When you define any class
B. When the class has no other constructors
C. When you define at least one constructor

Select the most appropriate answer.

Q. 21
Given the following code:

```
public class Test {
  . . .
}
```

Which of the following can be used to define a constructor for this class?

```
A. public void Test() {...}
B. public Test() {...}
C. public static Test() {...}
D. public static void Test() {...}
```

Select the most appropriate answer.

Q.22

Which of the following are acceptable to the Java compiler?

```
A. if (2 == 3) System.out.println("Hi");
B. if (2 = 3) System.out.println("Hi");
C. if (true) System.out.println("Hi");
D. if (2 != 3) System.out.println("Hi");
E. if (aString.equals("hello"))
               System.out.println("Hi");
```

Select all correct answers.

Q.23

Assuming that a method contains code which may raise an Exception (but not a RuntimeException), what is the correct way for a method to indicate that it expects the caller to handle that exception?

A. **throw** Exception
B. **throws** Exception
C. **new** Exception
D. Don't need to specify anything

Select the most appropriate answer.

Q.24

What is the result of executing the following code using the parameters 4 and 0?

```
public void divide(int a, int b) {
   try {
      int c = a / b;
   } catch (Exception e) {
      System.out.print("Exception ");
   } finally {
      System.out.println("Finally");
   }
}
```

A. Prints out: Exception Finally
B. Prints out: Finally
C. Prints out: Exception
D. No output

Select the most appropriate answer.

Q.25

Which of the following is a legal return type of a method overloading the following method?

```
public void add(int a) {...}
```

A. **void**
B. **int**
C. Can be anything

Select the most appropriate answer.

Q.26

Which of the following statements is correct for a method which is overriding the following method?

```
public void add(int a) {...}
```

A. The overriding method must return `void`
B. The overriding method must return `int`
C. The overriding method can return whatever it likes

Select the most appropriate answer.

Q.27

Given the following classes defined in separate files:

```
class Vehicle {
  public void drive() {
    System.out.println("Vehicle: drive");
  }
}

class Car extends Vehicle {
  public void drive() {
    System.out.println("Car: drive");
  }
}

public class Test {
  public static void main (String args []) {
    Vehicle v;
    Car c;
    v = new Vehicle();
    c = new Car();
    v.drive();
    c.drive();
    v = c;
    v.drive();
  }
}
```

What will be the effect of compiling and running this class `Test`?

A. Generates a compiler error on the statement v= c;
B. Generates a run-time error on the statement v= c;
C. Prints out:
```
Vehicle: drive
Car: drive
Car: drive
```
D. Prints out:
```
Vehicle: drive
Car: drive
Vehicle: drive
```

Select the most appropriate answer.

Q. 28

Where in a constructor, can you place a call to a constructor defined in the super class?

A. Anywhere
B. The first statement in the constructor
C. The last statement in the constructor
D. You can't call super in a constructor

Select the most appropriate answer.

Q. 29

Which variables can an inner class access from the class which encapsulates it?

A. All static variables
B. All final variables
C. All instance variables
D. Only final instance variables
E. Only final static variables

Select all correct answers.

Q. 30

What class must an inner class extend?

A. The top-level class
B. The Object class
C. Any class or interface
D. It must extend an interface

Select the most appropriate answer.

Q. 31

In the following code, which is the earliest statement where the object originally held in e may be garbage collected?

```
 1. public class Test {
  2. public static void main (String args []) {
    3. Employee e = new Employee ("Bob", 48);
    4. e.calculatePay();
    5. System.out.println(e.printDetails());
    6. e = null;
    7. e = new Employee ("Denise", 36);
    8. e.calculatePay();
    9. System.out.println(e.printDetails());
   10. }
 11. }
```

A. Line 10
B. Line 11
C. Line 7
D. Line 8
E. Never

Select the most appropriate answer.

Q. 32

What is the name of the interface that can be used to define a class that can execute within its own thread?

A. Runnable
B. Run
C. Threadable
D. Thread
E. Executable

Select the most appropriate answer.

Q. 33

What is the name of the method used to schedule a thread for execution?

A. `init();`
B. `start();`
C. `run();`
D. `resume();`
E. `sleep();`

Select the most appropriate answer.

Q. 34
Which methods may cause a thread to stop executing?

```
A. sleep();
B. stop();
C. yield();
D. wait();
E. notify();
F. notifyAll()
G. synchronized()
```

Select all correct answers.

Q. 35
Write code to create a text field able to display 10 characters (assuming a fixed size font) displaying the initial string "hello".

Q. 36
Which of the following methods are defined on the Graphics class?

```
A. drawLine(int, int, int, int)
B. drawImage(Image, int, int, ImageObserver)
C. drawString(String, int, int)
D. add(Component);
E. setVisible(boolean);
F. setLayout(Object);
```

Select all correct answers.

Q. 37
Which of the following layout managers honours the preferred size of a component?

```
A. CardLayout
B. FlowLayout
C. BorderLayout
D. GridLayout
```

Select all correct answers.

Q. 38
Given the following code what is the effect of a being 5?

```
public class Test {
  public void add(int a) {
    loop: for (int i = 1; i < 3; i++){
      for (int j = 1; j < 3; j++) {
        if (a == 5) {
          break loop;
        }
        System.out.println(i * j);
```

```
        }
      }
    }
  }
```

A. Generate a run-time error
B. Throw an `ArrayIndexOutOfBoundsException`
C. Print the values: 1, 2, 2, 4
D. Produces no output

Select the most appropriate answer.

Q. 39

What is the effect of issuing a `wait()` method on an object?

A. If a `notify()` method has already been sent to that object then it has no effect
B. The object issuing the call to `wait()` will halt until another object sends a `notify()` or `notifyAll()` method
C. An exception will be raised
D. The object issuing the call to wait() will be automatically synchronized with any other objects using the receiving object

Select the most appropriate answer.

Q. 40

The layout of a container can be altered using which of the following methods?

A. `setLayout(aLayoutManager);`
B. `addLayout(aLayoutManager);`
C. `layout(aLayoutManager);`
D. `setLayoutManager(aLayoutManager);`

Select all correct answers.

Q. 41

Using a `FlowLayout` manager, which is the correct way to add elements to a container?

A. `add(component);`
B. `add("Center", component);`
C. `add(x, y, component);`
D. `set(component);`

Select the most appropriate answer.

Q. 42

Given that a Button can generate an ActionEvent which listener would you expect to have to implement, in a class which would handle this event?

- A. FocusListener
- B. ComponentListener
- C. WindowListener
- D. ActionListener
- E. ItemListener

Select the most appropriate answer.

Q. 43

Which of the following are valid return types for listener methods?

- A. boolean
- B. the type of event handled
- C. void
- D. Component

Select the most appropriate answer.

Q. 44

Assuming we have a class which implements the ActionListener interface, which method should be used to register this with a Button?

- A. addListener(*);
- B. addActionListener(*);
- C. addButtonListener(*);
- D. setListener(*);

Select the most appropriate answer.

Q. 45

In order to cause the paint (Graphics) method to execute, which of the following is the most appropriate method to call?

- A. paint()
- B. repaint()
- C. paint(Graphics)
- D. update(Graphics)
- E. None – you should never cause paint(Graphics) to execute

Select the most appropriate answer.

Q. 46

Which of the following illustrates the correct way to pass a parameter into an applet?

A. `<applet code=Test.class age=33 width=100 height=100>`
B. `<param name=age value=33>`
C. `<applet code=Test.class name=age value=33 width=100 height=100>`
D. `<applet Test 33>`

Select the most appropriate answer.

Q. 47

Which of the following correctly illustrate how an `InputStreamReader` can be created?

A. **new** `InputStreamReader(new FileInputStream("data"));`
B. **new** `InputStreamReader(new FileReader("data"));`
C. **new** `InputStreamReader(new BufferedReader("data"));`
D. **new** `InputStreamReader("data");`
E. **new** `InputStreamReader(System.in);`

Select all correct answers.

Q. 48

What is the permanent effect on the file system of writing data to a new `FileWriter("report")`, given that the file `report` already exists?

A. The data is appended to the file
B. The file is replaced with a new file
C. An exception is raised as the file already exists
D. The data is written to random locations within the file

Select the most appropriate answer.

Q. 49

What is the effect of adding the sixth element to a vector created in the following manner?

new `Vector(5, 10);`

A. An `IndexOutOfBounds` exception is raised.
B. The vector grows in size to a capacity of 10 elements
C. The vector grows in size to a capacity of 15 elements
D. Nothing, the vector will have grown when the fifth element was added

Select the most appropriate answer.

Q.50

What is the result of executing the following code when the value of x is 2?

```
switch (x) {
  case 1:
    System.out.println(1);
  case 2:
  case 3:
    System.out.println(3);
  case 4:
    System.out.println(4);
}
```

A. Nothing is printed out
B. The value 3 is printed out
C. The values 3 and 4 are printed out
D. The values 1, 3 and 4 are printed out

Select the most appropriate answer.

Q.51

Consider the following example:

```
class First {
  public First (String s) {
    System.out.println(s);
  }
}
public class Second extends First {
  public static void main(String args []) {
    new Second();
  }
}
```

What is the result of compiling and running the Second class?

A. Nothing happens
B. A string is printed to the standard out
C. An instance of the class First is generated
D. An instance of the class Second is created
E. An exception is raised at run time stating that there is no null parameter constructor in class First.
F. The class Second will not compile as there is no null parameter constructor in the class First

Select the most appropriate answer.

Q. 52

What is the result of executing the following fragment of code?

```java
boolean flag = false;
if (flag = true) {
    System.out.println("true");
} else {
    System.out.println("false");
}
```

A. `true` is printed to standard out
B. `false` is printed to standard out
C. An exception is raised
D. Nothing happens

Select the most appropriate answer.

Q. 53

Consider the following classes:

```java
public class Test {
    public static void test() {
        this.print();
    }
    public static void print() {
        System.out.println("Test");
    }
    public static void main(String args []) {
        test();
    }
}
```

What is the result of compiling and running this class?

A. The string `Test` is printed to the standard out
B. A run-time exception is raised stating that an object has not been created
C. Nothing is printed to the standard output
D. An exception is raised stating that the method `test` cannot be found
E. An exception is raised stating that the variable `this` can only be used within an instance
F. The class fails to compile, stating that the variable `this` is undefined

Select all correct answers.

Q. 54

Examine the following class definition:

```java
public class Test {
  public static void test() {
    print();
  }
  public static void print() {
    System.out.println("Test");
  }
  public void print() {
    System.out.println("Another Test");
  }
}
```

What is the result of compiling this class?

A. A successful compilation

B. A warning stating that the class has no main method

C. An error stating that there is a duplicated method

D. An error stating that the method test () will call one or other of the print () methods

Select the most appropriate answer.

Q. 55

What is the result of compiling and executing the following Java class?

```java
public class ThreadTest extends Thread {
  public void run() {
    System.out.println("In run");
    suspend();
    resume();
    System.out.println("Leaving run");
  }

  public static void main(String args []) {
    (new ThreadTest()).start();
  }
}
```

A. Compilation will fail in the method main

B. Compilation will fail in the method run

C. A warning will be generated for method run

D. The string "In run" will be printed to standard out

E. Both strings will be printed to standard out

F. Nothing will happen.

Select the most appropriate answer.

Q. 56

Given the following sequence of Java statements

```
1.  StringBuffer sb = new StringBuffer("abc");
2.  String s = new String("abc");
3.  sb.append("def");
4.  s.append("def");
5.  sb.insert(1, "zzz");
6.  s.concat(sb);
7.  s.trim();
```

which of the following statements are true?

A. The compiler would generate an error for line 1
B. The compiler would generate an error for line 2
C. The compiler would generate an error for line 3
D. The compiler would generate an error for line 4
E. The compiler would generate an error for line 5
F. The compiler would generate an error for line 6
G. The compiler would generate an error for line 7

Select all correct answers.

Q. 57

What is the result of executing the following Java class?

```
import java.awt.*;

public class FrameTest extends Frame {
  public FrameTest() {
      add (new Button("First"));
      add (new Button("Second"));
      add (new Button("Third"));
      pack();
      setVisible(true);
  }
  public static void main(String args []) {
    new FrameTest();
  }
}
```

Select from the following options:

A. Nothing happens
B. Three buttons are displayed across a window
C. A run-time exception is generated (no layout manager specified)
D. Only the "First" button is displayed
E. Only the "Second" button is displayed
F. Only the "Third" button is displayed

Select the most appropriate answer.

Q. 58
Consider the following tags and attributes of tags:

1. CODEBASE
2. ALT
3. NAME
4. CLASS
5. JAVAC
6. HORIZONTALSPACE
7. VERTICALSPACE
8. WIDTH
9. PARAM
10. JAR

Which of the above can be used within the <APPLET> and </APPLET> tags?

A. lines 1, 2, 3
B. lines 2, 5, 6, 7
C. lines 3, 4, 5
D. lines 8, 9, 10
E. lines 8, 9

Select all correct answers.

Q. 59
Which of the following is a legal way to construct a RandomAccessFile?

A. RandomAccessFile("data", "r");
B. RandomAccessFile("r", "data");
C. RandomAccessFile("data", "read");
D. RandomAccessFile("read", "data");

Select the most appropriate answer.

Q. 60
Carefully examine the following code:

```java
public class StaticTest {
  static {
    System.out.println("Hi there");
  }
  public void print() {
    System.out.println("Hello");
  }
  public static void main(String args []) {
    StaticTest st1 = new StaticTest();
    st1.print();
    StaticTest st2 = new StaticTest();
    st2.print();
  }
}
```

When will the string "Hi there" be printed?

A. Never
B. Each time a new instance is created
C. Once when the class is first loaded into the Java Virtual Machine
D. Only when the static method is called explicitly

Select the most appropriate answer.

Q.61

Consider the following program:

```
public class Test {
  public static void main (String args []) {
    boolean a = false;
    if (a = true)
      System.out.println ("Hello");
    else
      System.out.println ("Goodbye");
  }
}
```

What is the result?

A. Program produces no output but terminates correctly
B. Program does not terminate.
C. Prints out "Hello"
D. Prints out "Goodbye"

Select the most appropriate answer.

Q.62

Examine the following code, which includes an inner class:

```
public final class Test4 implements A {
  class Inner {
    void test () {
      if (Test4.this.flag); {
        sample ();
      }
    }
  }
  private boolean flag = false;
  public void sample () {
    System.out.println ("Sample");
  }
  public Test4 () {
    (new Inner ()).test ();
  }
  public static void main(String args []) {
```

```
      new Test4();
   }
}
```

What is the result?

A. Prints out "Sample"
B. Program produces no output but terminates correctly
C. Program does not terminate
D. The program will not compile

Select the most appropriate answer.

Q. 63

Carefully examine the following class:

```
public class Test5 {
  public static void main (String args []) {
    /* This is the start of a comment
    if (true) {
      Test5 = new test5();
      System.out.println("Done the test");
    }
    /* This is another comment */
    System.out.println ("The end");
  }
}
```

What is the result?

A. Prints out "Done the test" and nothing else
B. Program produces no output but terminates correctly
C. Program does not terminate
D. The program will not compile
E. The program generates a run-time exception
F. The program prints out "The end" and nothing else
G. The program prints out "Done the test" and "The end"

Select the most appropriate answer.

Q. 64

The following code defines a simple applet:

```
import java.applet.Applet;
import java.awt.*;

public class Sample extends Applet {
  private String text = "Hello World";
  public void init() {
    add(new Label(text));
  }
}
```

```
   public Sample (String string) {
      text = string;
   }
}
```

It is accessed from the following HTML page:

```
<HTML>
<TITLE>Sample Applet</TITLE>
<BODY>
<APPLET code="Sample.class" width=200 height=200></
APPLET>
</BODY>
</HTML>
```

What is the result of compiling and running this applet?

A. Prints "Hello World"
B. Generates a run-time error
C. Does nothing
D. Generates a compile time error

Select the most appropriate answer.

Q.65
Examine the following code:

```
public class Calc {
   public static void main (String args []) {
      int total = 0;
      for (int i = 0, j = 10; total > 30; ++i, --j) {
         System.out.println(" i = " + i + " : j = " + j);
         total += (i + j);
      }
      System.out.println("Total " + total);
   }
}
```

Does this code:

A. Produce a run-time error?
B. Produce a compile-time error?
C. Print out "Total 0"?
D. Generate the following as output?
```
   i = 0 : j = 10
   i = 1 : j = 9
   i = 2 : j = 8
   Total 30
```

Please select the most appropriate answer.

43.3 Answers to Java Certification Mock Exam

1. B	2. A	3. A, B, C, E	4. A, B	5. C
6. A, C	7. D	8. A	9. B	10. B
11. B	12. A,B	13. A, B	14. A, B, C, D	15.B, C
16. A, E	17. D	18. D	19. A	20. B
21. B	22. A, C, D, E	23. B	24. A	25. C
26. A	27. C	28. B	29. A, B, C	30. C
31. C	32. A	33. B	34. A, B, C, D	35. **new** TextField ("hello", 10)
36. A, B, C	37. B	38. D	39. B	40. A
41. A	42. D	43. C	44. B	45. B
46. B	47. A, E	48. B	49. C	50. C
51. F	52. A	53. F	54. C	55. D
56. D, F	57. F	58. A, E	59. A	60. C
61. C	62. A	63. F	64. B	65. C

43.4 Further Reading

Some useful references for the Java certification exam provided by Sun Microsystems are listed below.

The Sun Educational Services Web pages:

    http:/www.sun.com/service/suned/cert/

For some on-line sample questions see:

    http:/www.sun.com/service/suned/cert/scjp11_quest.html

In addition, there are two books available which are aimed specifically at helping you to pass the Certification exam. These are:

Boone, B. (1997). *Java Certification for Programmers and Developers.* McGraw-Hill, New York. On-line information can be found at http://mcgraw-hill.inforonics.com/cgi/getarec?mgh31641

Roberts, S. and Heller, P. (1997). *Java 1.1 Certification Study Guide.* Sybex. On-line information can be found at http://www.sybex.com/cgi-bin/bookpg.pl?2069back.html.

Part 4

Object-Oriented Design

44 *Object-Oriented Analysis and Design*

44.1 Introduction

This chapter surveys the most significant object-oriented design and analysis methods to emerge since the late 1980s. It concentrates primarily on OOA (Coad and Yourdon, 1991), Booch (Booch, 1991, 1994), Object Modeling Technique (Rumbaugh *et al.*, 1991), Objectory (Jacobson *et al.*, 1992) and Fusion (Coleman *et al.*, 1994). It also introduces the Unified Modeling Language (Booch *et al*, 1996; Booch and Rumbaugh, 1995).

This chapter does not aim to deal comprehensively with either the range of methods available or the fine details of each approach. Rather, it provides an overview of the design process and the strengths and weaknesses of some important and reasonably representative methods.

44.2 Object-Oriented Design Methods

The object-oriented design methods we will consider are all architecture-driven, incremental and iterative. They do not adopt the more traditional waterfall software development model; instead they adopt an approach which is more akin to the spiral model of Boehm (1988). This reflects developers' experiences when creating object-oriented systems – the object-oriented development process is more incremental than that for procedural systems, with less distinct barriers between analysis, design and implementation. Some organizations take this process to the extreme and adopt an evolutionary development approach. This approach delivers system functions to users in very small steps and revises project plans in the light of experience and user feedback. This philosophy has proved very successful for organizations that have fully embraced it and has led to earlier business benefits and successful end-products from large development projects. However, as with all things, care needs to be taken with this approach.

44.3 Object-Oriented Analysis

We first consider the Object-Oriented Analysis approach (OOA) of Coad and Yourdon (1991). The identification of objects and classes is a crucial task in object-oriented analysis and design, but many techniques ignore this issue. For example, both the Booch method and OMT do not deal with it at all. They indicate that it is a highly creative process that can be based on the identification of nouns and verbs in an informal verbal description of the problem domain. A different approach is to use a method such as OOA as the first part of the design process and then to use another object-oriented design method for the later parts of the process.

OOA helps designers identify the detailed requirements of their software, rather than how the software should be structured or implemented. It aims to describe the existing system and how it operates, and how the software system should interact with it. One of the claims of OOA is that it helps the designer to package the requirements of the system in an appropriate manner (for object-oriented systems?) and to reduce the risk of the software failing to meet the customer's requirements. In effect, OOA helps to build the Object Model that we look at in more detail when we look at OMT.

There are five activities within OOA which direct the analyst during the analysis process:

● Finding classes and objects in the domain.
● Identifying structures (among those classes and objects). Structures are relationships such as *is-a* and *part-of.*
● Identifying subjects (related objects).
● Defining attributes (the data elements of the objects).
● Defining services (the active parts of objects that indicate what the object does).

These are not sequential steps: as information becomes available, the analyst performs the appropriate activity. The intention is that the analyst can work in whatever way the domain expert finds it easiest to express the knowledge. Thus, the analyst may go deeper into one activity than the others as the domain expert provides greater information in that area. Equally, the analyst may jump around between activities, identifying classes one minute and services the next.

44.4 The Booch Method

The Booch method (also known as Booch, Object-Oriented Development or OOD) is one of the earliest recognizable object-oriented design methods. It was first described in a paper published in 1986 and has become widely adopted since the publication of a book describing the method (Booch, 1991, 1994).

The Booch method provides a step-by-step guide to the design of an object-oriented system. Although Booch's books discuss the analysis phase, they do so in too little detail compared with the design phase.

44.4.1 The Steps in the Booch Method

● *Identification of classes and objects* involves analyzing the problem domain and the system requirements to identify the set of classes required. This is not trivial and relies on a suitable requirements analysis.

- *Identification of the semantics of classes and objects* involves identifying the services offered and required by an object. A service is a function performed by an object and, during this step, the overall system functionality is devolved among the objects. This is another non-trivial step and it may result in modifications to the classes and objects identified in the last step.
- *Identification of the relationships between classes and objects* involves identifying links between objects as well as inheritance between classes. This step may identify new services required of objects.
- *Implementation of classes and objects* attempts to consider how to implement the classes and objects, how to define the attributes and provide services. This involves considering algorithms. This process may lead to modifications in the deliverables of all of the above steps and may force the designer to return to some or all of the above steps.

During these steps, the designer produces

- Class diagrams, which illustrate the classes in the system and their relationships.
- Object diagrams, which illustrate the actual objects in the system and their relationships.
- Module diagrams, which package the classes and objects into modules. These modules illustrate the influence Ada had on the development of the Booch method (Booch, 1987).
- Process diagrams, which package processes and processors.
- State transition diagrams and timing diagrams, which describe the dynamic behaviour of the system (the other diagrams describe the static structure of the system).

Booch recommends an incremental and iterative development of a system through the refinement of different yet consistent logical and physical views of that system.

44.4.2 Strengths and Weaknesses

The biggest problem for a designer approaching the Booch method for the first time is that the plethora of different notations is supported by a poorly defined and loose process (although the revision to the method described in Booch (1994) addresses this to some extent). It does not give step-by-step guidance and possesses very few mechanisms for determining the system's requirements. Its main strengths are its (mainly graphical) notations, which cover most aspects of the design of an object-oriented system, and its greatest weakness is the lack of sufficient guidance in the generation of these diagrams.

44.5 The Object Modeling Technique

The Object Modeling Technique (OMT) is an object-oriented design method which aims to construct a series of models which refine the system design until the final model is suitable for implementation. The design process is divided into three phases:

- The Analysis Phase attempts to model the problem domain.
- The Design Phase structures the results of the analysis phase in an appropriate manner.
- The Implementation Phase takes into account target language constructs.

44.5.1 The Analysis Phase

Three types of model are produced by the analysis phase:

- *The object model* represents the static structure of the domain. It describes the objects, their classes and the relationships between the objects. For example, the object model might represent the fact that a department object possesses a single manager (object) but many employees (objects). The notation is based on an extension of the basic entity–relationship notation.
- *The dynamic model* represents the behaviour of the system. It expresses what happens in the domain, when it occurs and what effect it has. It does not represent how the behaviour is achieved. The formalism used to express the dynamic model is based on a variation of finite state machines called statecharts. These were developed by Harel and others (1987, 1988) to represent dynamic behaviour in real-time avionic control systems. Statecharts indicate the states of the system, the transitions between states, their sequence and the events which cause the state change.
- *The functional model* describes how system functions are performed. It uses data flow diagrams which illustrate the sources and sinks of data as well as the data being exchanged. They contain no sequencing information or control structures.

The relationship between these three models is important, as each model adds to the designer's understanding of the domain:

- The object model defines the objects which hold the state variables referenced in the dynamic model and are the sources and sinks referenced in the functional model.
- The dynamic model indicates when the behaviour in the functional model occurs and what triggers it.
- The functional model explains why an event transition leads from one state to another in the dynamic model.

You do not build these models sequentially; changes to any one of the models may have a knock-on effect in the other models. Typically the designer starts with the object model, then considers the dynamic model and finally the functional model, but the process is iterative.

The analysis process is described in considerable detail and provides by step-by-step guidance. This ensures that the developer knows what to do at any time to advance the three models.

44.5.2 The Design Phase

The design phase of OMT builds upon the models produced during the analysis phase:

- *The system design step* breaks the system down into subsystems and determines the overall architecture to be used.
- *The object design step* decides on the algorithms to be used for the methods. The methods are identified by examining the three analysis models for each class etc.

Each of the steps gives some guidelines for their respective tasks; however, far less support is provided for the designer than in the analysis phase. For example, there is no systematic guidance for the identification of subsystems, although the issues involved are discussed (resource management, batch versus interactive modes etc.). This means that it can be difficult to identify where to start, how to proceed and what to do next.

44.5.3 The Implementation Phase

The implementation phase codifies the system and object designs into the target language. This phase provides some very useful information on how to implement features used in the model-based design process used, but it lacks the step-by-step guidance which would be useful for those new to object orientation.

44.5.4 Strengths and Weaknesses

OMT's greatest strength is the level of step-by-step support which it provides during the analysis phase. However, it is much weaker in its guidance during the design and implementation phases, where it provides general guidelines (and some heuristics).

44.6 The Objectory Method

The driving force behind the Objectory method (Jacobson, 1991) is the concept of a *use case*. A use case is a particular interaction between the system and a user of that system (an actor) for a particular purpose (or function). The users of the system may be human or machine. A complete set of use cases therefore describes a system's functionality based around what actors should be able to do with the system. The Objectory method has three phases which produce a set of models.

44.6.1 The Requirements Phase

The requirements phase uses a natural language description of what the system should do to build three models.

- *The use case model* describes the interactions between actors and the system. Each use case specifies the actions which are performed and their sequence. Any alternatives are also documented. This can be done in natural language or using state transition diagrams.
- *The domain model* describes the objects, classes and associations between objects in the domain. It uses a modified entity–relationship model.
- *The user interface descriptions* contain mock-ups of the various interfaces between actors and the system. User interfaces are represented as pictures of windows while other interfaces are described by protocols.

44.6.2 The Analysis Phase

The analysis phase produces the analysis model and a set of subsystem descriptions. The analysis model is a refinement of the domain object model produced in the requirements phase. It contains behavioural information as well as control objects which are linked to use cases. The analysis model also possesses entity objects (which exist beyond a single use case) and interface objects (which handle system–actor interaction). The subsystem descriptions partition the system around objects which are involved in similar activities and which are closely coupled. This organization structures the rest of the design process.

44.6.3 The Construction Phase

The construction phase refines the models produced in the analysis phase. For example, inter-object communication is refined and facilities provided by the target language are considered. This phase produces three models:

- Block models represent the functional modules of the system.
- Block interfaces specify the public operations performed by blocks.
- Block specifications are optional descriptions of block behaviour in the form of finite state machines.

The final stage is to implement the blocks in the target language.

44.6.4 Strengths and Weaknesses

The most significant aspect of Objectory is its use of use cases, which join the building blocks of the method. Objectory is unique among the methods considered here, as it provides a unifying framework for the design process. However, it still lacks the step-by-step support which would simplify the whole design process.

44.7 The Fusion Method

The majority of object-oriented design methods currently available, including those described in this chapter, take a systematic approach to the design process. However, in almost all cases this process is rather weak, providing insufficient direction or support to the developer. In addition, methods such as OMT rely on a "bottom up" approach. This means that the developer must focus on the identification of appropriate classes and their interfaces without necessarily having the information to enable them to do this in an appropriate manner for the overall system. Little reference is made to the system's overall functionality when determining class functionality etc. Indeed, some methods provide little more than some vague guidelines and anecdotal heuristics.

In contrast, Fusion explicitly attempts to provide a systematic approach to object-oriented software development. In many ways, the Fusion method is a mixture of a range of other approaches (indeed, the authors of the method acknowledge that there is little new in the approach, other than that they have put it all together in a single method; see Figure 44.1).

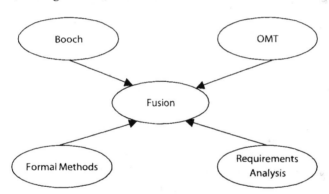

Figure 44.1 Some of the influences on Fusion.

As with other object-oriented design methods, Fusion is based around the construction of appropriate models that capture different elements of the system and different knowledge. These models are built up during three distinct phases:

- *The analysis phase* produces models that describe the high-level constraints from which the design models are developed.
- *The design phase* produces a set of models that describe how the system behaves in terms of a collection of interacting objects.
- *The implementation phase* describes how to map the design models onto implementation language constructs.

Within each phase a set of detailed steps attempts to guide the developer through the Fusion process. These steps include checks to ensure the consistency and completeness of the emerging design. In addition, the output of one step acts as the input for the next.

Fusion's greatest weakness is its complexity – it really requires a sophisticated CASE tool. Without such a tool, it is almost impossible to produce a consistent and complete design.

44.8 The Unified Modeling Language

The Unified Modeling Language (UML) is an attempt by Grady Booch, Ivar Jacobson and James Rumbaugh to build on the experiences of the Booch, Object Modeling Technique (OMT) and Objectory methods. Their aim is to produce a single common and widely useable modelling language for these methods and, working with other methodologists, for other methods. This means that UML focuses on a standard language and not a standard process, which reflects what happens in reality: a particular notation is adopted as the means of communication on a specific project and between projects. However, between projects (and, sometimes, within projects), different design methods are adopted as appropriate. For example, a design method intended for the domain of real-time avionics systems may not be suitable for designing a small payroll system. The UML is an attempt to develop a common meta-model which unifies semantics and from which a common notation can be built.

44.9 Summary

In this chapter, we have reviewed a number of object-oriented analysis and design methods and the Unified Modeling Language. We have briefly considered the features, strengths and weaknesses of each method.

In all these systems, during the design process it is often difficult to identify commonalities between classes at the implementation level. This means that, during the implementation phase, experienced object-oriented technicians should look for situations in which they can move implementation-level components up the class hierarchy. This can greatly increase the amount of reuse within a software system and may lead to the introduction of abstract classes that contain the common code.

The problem with this is that the implemented class hierarchy no longer reflects the design class hierarchy. It is therefore necessary to have a free flow of information between the implementation and design phases in an object-oriented project.

44.10 References

Boehm, B.W. (1988). A spiral model of software development and enhancement. *IEEE Computer*, May, pp. 61–72.

Booch, G. (1987). *Software Components with Ada*. Benjamin Cummings, Menlo Park, CA.

Booch, G. (1991). *Object-Oriented Design with Applications*. Benjamin Cummings, Redwood City, CA.

Booch, G. (1994). *Object-Oriented Analysis and Design with Applications*, 2nd edn. Benjamin Cummings, Redwood City, CA.

Booch, G. and Rumbaugh, J. (1995). *The Unified Method Documentation Set*, Version 0.8. Rational Software Corporation (available at http://www.rational.com/ot/uml.html/).

Booch, G., Jacobson, I. and Rumbaugh, J. (1996). *The Unified Modeling Language for Object Oriented Development, Documentation Set*, Version 0.91 Addendum, UML Update. Rational Software Corporation (available at http://www.rational.com/ot/uml.html/).

Coad, P. and Yourdon, E. (1991). *Object-Oriented Analysis*. Yourdon Press, Englewood Cliffs, NJ.

Coleman, D., Arnold, P., Bodoff, S., Dollin, C., Gilchrist, H., Hayes, F. and Jeremes, P. (1994). *Object Oriented Development: The Fusion Method*. Prentice Hall, Englewood Cliffs, NJ.

Harel, D. (1988). On visual formalisms. *Communications of the ACM*, **31**(5), 514–30.

Harel, D. *et al.* (1987). On the formal semantics of Statecharts. *Proceedings of the 2nd IEEE Symposium on Logic in Computer Science*, pp. 54–64.

Jacobson, I. *et al.* (1992). Object-Oriented Software Engineering: A Use Case Driven Approach. Addison-Wesley, Reading, MA.

Rumbaugh, J. *et al.* (1991). *Object-Oriented Modeling and Design*. Prentice Hall, Englewood Cliffs, NJ.

45 *OMT and UML*

45.1 Introduction

This is a very brief chapter outlining the design method to be used for the remainder of this part of the book. As you will see it is an amalgam of the use case analysis phase of Objectory, the methodology of OMT and the UML notation. This is because such a combination represents current best practice in the software industry. It also indicates the way in which the unified design method is itself developing.

45.2 Objectory: Use Case Analysis

Ivar Jacobson and his colleagues developed use case analysis as part of the Objectory design method. With the advent of the unified method initiative, use case analysis has been introduced into the UML. It is widely accepted as being an extremely useful first step in the analysis and design of an object-oriented system.

A use case analysis provides insights into the identification of how a system will be used and what (at the top level) the system is required to do. In an non-object-oriented approach this phase might be considered to represent a requirements analysis. However, a detailed study of the system's requirements may already have been performed (for example using OOA). The use case analysis therefore puts the requirements into the context of the system being defined.

The intention of the use case analysis is to identify how the system is to be used and what it is expected to do in response to this use. This involves identifying the external users of the system (human or machine) and the required system functionality. The users of the system and the roles they play are referred to as *actors*, while the functions requested and their sequence are called *use cases*. The combination of the actors and the use cases are referred to as the *use case model*.

45.3 The OMT Methodology

The OMT methodology is a prescriptive method for the construction of object-oriented design. That is, it provides extensive guidance (at least during the analysis phase) for the construction of object-oriented designs. It consists of phases that progress a design from (relatively) early requirements analysis through detailed design to the implementation.

The *analysis phase* is concerned with understanding and modelling the application and the domain within which it operates. OMT suggests that the initial input to the analysis phase is a problem statement that describes the problem to be solved and provides a conceptual overview of the proposed system. This problem statement may be a textual description (as suggested by the authors) or a more formal description, as provided by a technique such as Object-Oriented Analysis (OOA) or one of the software engineering structured analysis methods.

The *design phase* is made up of two sub-phases. The system design phase is concerned with the overall architecture of the system. The object design phase attempts to produce a practical design; this involves moving the focus away from conceptual objects and towards computer implementation objects.

The *implementation phase* considers how the design should be implemented. It considers, among other issues, mapping a design onto an object-oriented language, a database system or a language that is not object-oriented.

45.4 The UML Notation

The Unified Modeling Language (UML) is part of a development to merge (unify) the concepts in the Booch, Objectory and OMT methods (Booch and Rumbaugh, 1995; Booch *et al.*, 1996). The method is still under development (and has taken a low profile recently); however, the notation underlying this method is complete. This notation is now the focus of a great deal of interest. For example, Microsoft Corporation, Hewlett-Packard, Oracle and Texas Instruments have all endorsed the UML.

The UML is a third-generation object-oriented modelling language (Rational, 1996) that adapts and extends the published notations used in the works of Booch, Rumbaugh and Jacobson (Booch, 1994; Rumbaugh *et al.*, 1991; Jacobson *et al.*, 1992). Many others, such as Fusion (Coleman *et al.*, 1994), Harel's statecharts (Harel *et al.*, 1987; Harel, 1988) and CORBA (Ben-Natan, 1995), as illustrated in Figure 45.1, also influence it.

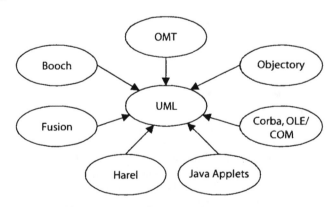

Figure 45.1 The influences on the UML notation.

The UML is intended to form a single common widely useable modelling language for a range of object-oriented design methods (including Booch, Objectory and OMT). It is also intended that it should be applicable in a wide range of applications and domains. For example, it should be equally applicable to client–server applications and real-time control applications.

The justification for UML is that different organizations, applications and domains require (and use) different design methods. An organization may develop its own methods or modify other methods through experience. Different parts of the same organization may use different methods. The notation that they use acts as a language to communicate the ideas represented in part (or all) of the design.

For example, the production of shrink-wrapped off-the-shelf software is different from the creation of one-off bespoke software; however, both activities may be carried out by a software company. Such an organization may well wish to exchange ideas, designs or parts of a design among its departments or operational units. This kind of exchange relies on the availability of a common language; UML provides such a language.

At present, version 1.2 of the UML has been released. It has been accepted by the Object Management Group (OMG) as a standard (this is an ongoing process and is part of the OMG's call for information on object-oriented methods). For the latest information on the UML (and other developments on the unification front) see the Rational Software Corporation's Web site (http://www.rational.com/).

For further information, see version 1.0 of the UML documentation set. There is also a series of books on the UML, including a Reference Manual and a User Guide (Booch *et al.*, 1997). Other books are becoming available, for example a Process Book (which, at the time of writing, is still in the pipeline) and Fowler and Scott (1997).

45.4.1 The Meta-Model

The UML is built upon a common meta-model that defines the semantics of the language. On top of this, there is a common notation that interprets these semantics in an easily (human) comprehensible manner.

A meta-model describes the constituents of a model and its relationships. It is a model that documents how another model can be defined. Such models are important because they provide a single common and unambiguous statement of the syntax and semantics of a model. A meta-model allows CASE tool builders to do more than provide diagramming tools. The meta-model serves several purposes:

- Defining the syntax and describing the semantics of the UML's concepts.
- Providing a (reasonably) formal basis for the UML.
- Providing a description of the elements of the UML.
- Providing the basis for the interchange of models between vendors' tools.

In the normal course of events, a user of the UML (or indeed of a tool that supports the UML) need not know about the meta-model. However, for the developers of the UML and for tool vendors in general the meta-model is a valuable, indeed essential, feature.

At present, the UML meta-model is defined in terms of the UML and textual annotations (although this may appear to be infinitely recursive, it is possible). Work on the meta-model is still progressing; the authors of the UML are attempting to make it more formal and simpler.

45.4.2 The Models

The UML defines a number of models and their notations:

- *Use case diagrams* organize the use cases that encompass a system's behaviour (they are based on the use case diagrams of Objectory).
- *Class diagrams* express the static structure of the system (they derive from the Booch and OMT methods), for example the *part-of* and *is-a* relationships between classes and objects. The class diagrams also encompass the object diagrams. Therefore in this book we refer to them as the Object Model (as in OMT).
- *Sequence diagrams* deal with the time-ordered sequence of transactions between objects.
- *Collaboration diagrams* indicate the order of messages between specified objects. They complement sequence diagrams as they illustrate essentially the same information. However, sequence diagrams highlight the actual sequence, while collaboration diagrams highlight the structure required to support the message sequence.
- *State machine diagrams* are based on statecharts, like those in OMT. They capture the dynamic behaviour of the system.
- *Component diagrams* represent the development view of the system, that is, how the system should be developed into software modules. You can also use them to represent concepts such as dynamic libraries.
- *Deployment diagrams* attempt to capture the topology of the system once it is deployed. They reflect the physical topology upon which the software system is to execute.

45.5 Combining the Three Approaches

The three approaches are combined here such that the use case acts as the initiating point for many of the OMT's (prescriptive) phases. That is, the use case model dictates the formation of the models in OMT's analysis phase, as indicated in Figure 45.2:

- The use case model helps identify the primary objects in the object model.
- It helps specify the top-level behaviour of the system in the dynamic model.
- It helps determine the inputs and outputs provided by, and expected by, the actors for the functional model.

In addition, use cases may also influence how the system is organized into subsystems as they indicate associated behaviours. In the implementation phase, the

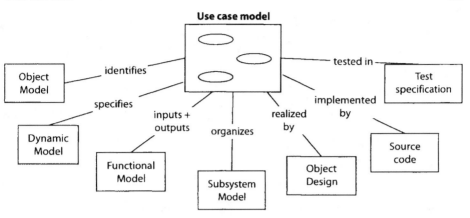

Figure 45.2 Using the use case model in OMT.

use cases may identify suitable scenarios and expected results for integration or system testing.

In turn, the UML is used to document the results of the OMT analysis (as opposed to OMT's own notation). This is because the OMT notation is weaker than the UML and is incapable of representing information that is essential for the construction of robust designs.

46 *Use Case Analysis*

46.1 Introduction

This chapter provides an introduction to an object-oriented design method based on the Object Modeling Technique (OMT) and use case analysis from the Objectory design method (Jacobson *et al.*, 1993). Subsequent chapters discuss the whole of the analysis and design process based on OMT, while this chapter presents the use case analysis taken from Objectory. This chapter (and subsequent chapters) should not be treated as a definitive or complete description of the method (see Rumbaugh *et al.* (1990) and Derr (1995)); rather, the intention is to present the flavour of these approaches allowing you, the reader, to explore them further elsewhere.

The remainder of this chapter introduces the use case analysis process, the notation used to represent use cases and the steps performed to generate a use case. A worked example is presented at the end of the chapter.

46.2 Use Case Diagrams

Use case diagrams explain how a system (or subsystem) is used. The elements that interact with the system can be humans, other computers or dumb devices that process or produce data. The diagrams thus present a collection of use cases which illustrate what the system is expected to do in terms of its external services or interfaces. Such diagrams are very important for illustrating the overall system functionality (to both technical and non-technical personnel). They can act as the context within which the rest of the system is defined.

The large rectangle in Figure 46.1 indicates the boundaries of the system (a telephone help desk adviser). The rectangles on either side of the system indicate external actors (in this case a Service Engineer and a Telephonist) which interact with the system. An actor represents a specific role played by a user. The ovals inside the system box indicate the actual use cases. For example, both the actors need to be able to "load a casebase".

The notation for actors is based on "stereotypes" (which are discussed in more detail later). An actor is a class with a stereotype: <<actor>> indicates the actor stereotype and the stick figure is the actor stereotype icon. Although we have used the class icon (a box) as well as the stereotype icon (the stick man), we could have used only one of them if we had so wished.

Each individual use case can have a name, a description explaining what it does, and a list of its responsibilities, attributes and operations. It may also describe its

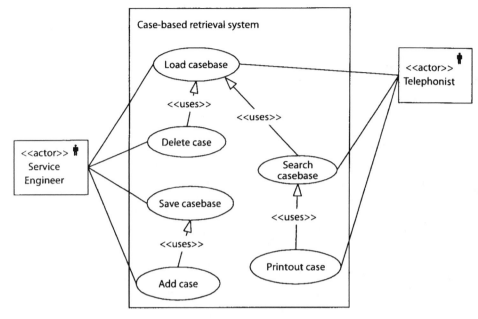

Figure 46.1 Use case diagram.

behaviour in the form of a statechart. The most appropriate form of description for a use case differs from one domain to another and thus the format should be chosen as appropriate. This illustrates the flexibility of the UML; it does not prescribe the actual format of a use case.

You can use sequence diagrams and collaboration diagrams with use case diagrams to illustrate the sequence of interactions between the system and the actors (see Chapter 48). You should also annotate use cases with a statement of purpose, to place the use case in context.

Finally, the relationship between use case diagrams and class diagrams is that use cases are peers of classes. Depending on the size of the system, they can be grouped with the object model in a package or remain totally independent.

46.3 Actors

An actor can be anything that interacts with the system: a human user, another computer system, a dumb terminal, a sensor, a device to be controlled etc. However, an actor not only represents the user, but also the role that the user plays at that point in time. For example, in a small company the accountant might act as the data entry clerk at one time, the internal auditor at another and as the payroll administrator at yet another time. A different actor could represent each of the roles, although the same person might perform them all. To stress the difference between actors and users, Jacobson *et al.* (1992) says that they think of an actor as "a class, that is, a description of a behaviour", while a user is described as playing "several roles" which are "many actors".

Identification of the actors in the system is not trivial and, as Jacobson *et al.* (1992) point out, "all actors are seldom found at once". Jacobson goes on to state that a "good starting point is often to check why the system is to be designed?". Having done this it should be possible to identify the main users of the system and what they need to do with it. From these users and their needs you can identify actors. Identification of human actors is usually relatively straightforward, but it is often much more difficult to identify non-human actors. In general, as the rest of the use case model develops, these actors "come out in the wash". For a simple online ATM system the actors may be the *customer*, the *bank clerk* and the *bank manager*.

The notation used in this book for an actor is based on that presented by the UML.

46.4 Use Cases

When an actor interacts with a system it is for a specified purpose. The achievement of this purpose involves following one or more steps. If there are multiple steps, they may be in a specific sequence to achieve the desired purpose. For example, to obtain money from a cash dispenser (ATM), you must insert your card, type in your PIN, select the type of transaction you require, specify the amount of money required, take the card and then take the money. If you attempt to change this sequence (e.g. you type in your PIN before inserting your card), you cannot obtain your money. The combination of the purpose and the specified sequence of steps forms a use case.

An individual use case can be represented in a number of ways: the two most common are as natural language descriptions and as state transition diagrams. Whichever approach is adopted, the same information should be captured. The most appropriate form may depend on the availability of support tools for the state machine notation.

The collection of all use cases for a system defines the functionality of that system. The identification of use cases is based on the identification of actors. Each actor does one or more things to the system, each of which is a use case. Each actor must have at least one use case (and may be involved in many use cases). Whether each use case is unique (or merely a duplication of another use case) may only be determined once all the use cases are identified and defined. To help in identifying the use cases, you can ask the following questions (Jacobson *et al.*, 1992):

- What are the main tasks of each actor?
- Will the actor have to read/write/change any of the system information?
- Will the actor have to inform the system about outside changes?
- Does the actor wish to be informed about unexpected changes?

Early in the analysis process it is often enough just to identify the possible use cases and not worry about their details. Once a reasonable set of uses is identified, you may be able to analyze the systems requirements in greater detail in order to flesh out the use cases. Use case identification tends to be iterative and should not be treated as a single-step process for all but the simplest of systems.

Having identified the use cases, we can identify the steps performed within each use case. In many cases this can help to identify omissions and over-generalizations in the problem statement or domain understanding. For the simple online ATM system mentioned above, a typical use case might be:

A Customer who wants to find out what their current balance initiates the Check account use case. This is accomplished by:

1. Typing in the account number

2. Typing the PIN

3. Requesting the current balance of the account (this may be on screen or a printout)

4. Receiving the balance

Notice that the first element of the use case is a statement of its purpose. This is then followed by the sequence of steps performed by the use case. The steps described above are referred to as the *basic course* of the use case, that is, the normal way in which the use case executes. In general, use cases only possess a single basic course, but they may possess one or more *alternative courses*. These alternatives deal with exceptional situations or errors. For example, what if the customer does not have a current account? What happens if they do not log off the system?

46.5 Use Case Models

The identification of the actors and the use cases helps to specify the limits of the system. That is, anything that is an actor is outside the system, whereas anything that is a use case is within the system boundaries. This means that you can draw a line around the use cases to indicate the boundary of the system in terms which both a developer and a user can understand. This can help to clarify misunderstandings between users and developers over what is the system's responsibility and what is not. A partial use case model for the simple account system is presented below.

46.6 Interface Descriptions

Having defined the actors in the system and the uses they make of the system, the next step is often to specify the interfaces between the actors and the system. For human users of the system, these interfaces may well be graphical user interfaces (GUIs). You can draw them with a drawing tool or develop a mock-up using some form of interface simulation software. These interfaces can be very useful in confirming the users' needs and their anticipated use, as well as helping to keep them involved in the development.

As the use cases specify the sequences of operations to be performed, the GUIs can mimic the desired system behaviour. This is a good way of confirming that the use case is correct. For non-human interfaces, any proposed communications protocols can be defined and checked (for example, that the interacting system is capable of sending and receiving the appropriate information).

46.7 Online ATM Use Case Analysis

The system to be analyzed is a (very) simple online ATM system (Figure 46.2). Such a system maintains information on customers, their current accounts, and the deposits and withdrawals they make, as well as any direct debits they have set up (a direct debit is a regular direct payment from one bank account to another). There are two types of user of the systems: bank clerks and bank managers. Each has access to different parts of the online ATM system. Note that this does not mean that a bank manager cannot act as a bank clerk – remember that actors represent roles played by potential (in this case human) users.

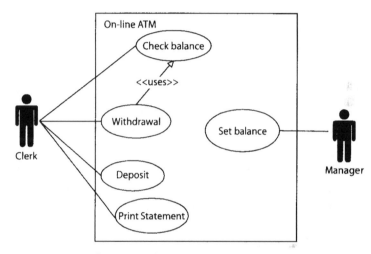

Figure 46.2 The online ATM use case diagram.

Having identified the actors in the system we are now in a position to identify what they do and hence the use cases. As noted earlier, we can consider a number of questions that will help in identifying the use cases. We shall do this for the clerk actor as an example of how the process works. Each of the questions is considered below:

- *What are the main tasks of the clerk actor?* A bank clerk will wish to find out the amount of money in a bank account. They will also want to be able to deposit and withdraw money for customers. In the case of withdrawing money they should be able to do so if there are sufficient funds in the customer's account. This indicates that there are at least three use cases for *balance checking, deposits* and *withdrawals*.

- *Will the clerk have to read/write/change any of the system information?* As this is a banking system we do not want the clerks to be able to directly change customer account details (only a manager is allowed to do that). However, we do want them to be able to deposit and withdraw funds that will indirectly change a customer's data. We do not want clerks to be able to change a customer's balance, but we do want them to be able to access it. All of this supports the three use cases identified by the previous question. In addition, we want a clerk to be able to print a customer's bank statement. We therefore need a fourth use case for the clerk: "print statement".

- *Will the clerk have to inform the system about outside changes?* In this particular system the answer is no. However, in a real banking system we might identify information such as changes of address, employer, martial status etc. that we would like the clerk to be able to alter on the customer's behalf.

- *Does the clerk wish to be informed about unexpected changes?* Again, due to the simplicity of this application the answer is no; however, in the real system the answer might not be so clear-cut.

This leaves us with four use cases for the clerk that must be analyzed in further detail. The basic course for the *check balance* use case was presented earlier in this chapter. We shall therefore present the basic course for the remaining use cases.

46.7.1 *Deposit* Use Case

The *deposit* use case is started by a clerk in response to a customer who wishes to place additional funds into his or her current account. This is accomplished by:

1. Typing in the account number
2. Typing in the PIN
3. Placing funds in an appropriate receptacle
4. Receiving acknowledgement of the deposit

46.7.2 *Withdrawal* Use Case

A customer who wishes to obtain funds from a current account causes the clerk to initiate the *withdrawal* use case. This is accomplished by:

1. Typing in the account number
2. Typing in the PIN
3. Requesting a specified amount from their account
4. The online ATM system confirming availability of funds
5. Receiving the specified amount of money

For the *withdrawal* use case we shall also consider an *alternative course* of steps. This course will present the series of steps that should be performed when the customer does not have sufficient funds in the current account to meet the withdrawal requested:

1. Typing in the account number
2. Typing in the PIN
3. Requesting a specified amount from their account
4. The online ATM system rejects the request due to lack of funds
5. Receiving the notification of failure

The identification of the remaining use cases and their basic courses (as well as any additional alternative courses) is left as an exercise for the reader due to space constraints.

46.7.3 Interface Descriptions

The interface for this system is quite straightforward. The user is presented with the *logon screen*, which allows the selection of one of the four uses cases (presented as options). This is illustrated in Figure 46.3. Note that the bottom options have their associated buttons greyed out, as no user has yet logged on. Depending upon the option selected by the user, the logon, deposit and withdrawal, check balance or set balance screen is presented.

Figure 46.3 Main logon screen.

The logon screen is illustrated in Figure 46.4. The result of an authorized user of the system logging on is that the "check balance", "withdraw and deposit" and "set balance" options are enabled. The check balance screen is illustrated in Figure 46.5. This interface requires information such as the account number and PIN to allow access to a customer account.

The deposit and withdraw (transaction) screen is presented in Figure 46.6. Note again that an account number is required. The amount specified can then be withdrawn or deposited depending upon the option selected.

The set balance screen is presented in Figure 46.7. Note that a security code is required as well as the account number and new balance. The security code is checked against the current user. If the current user is not a manager or if the security code is not correct an error message is displayed. If the security code is correct, the account specified by the account number has its balance reset to that specified in the new balance field.

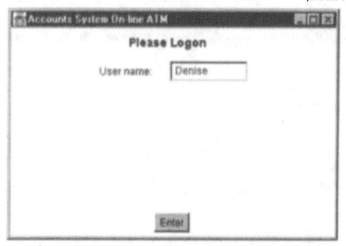

Figure 46.4 The logon screen.

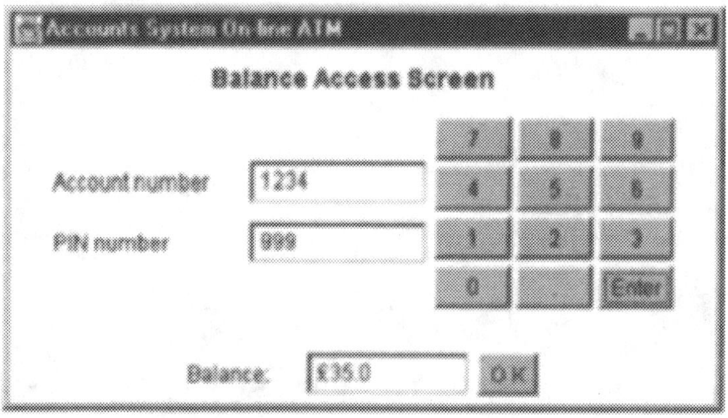

Figure 46.5 The check balance screen.

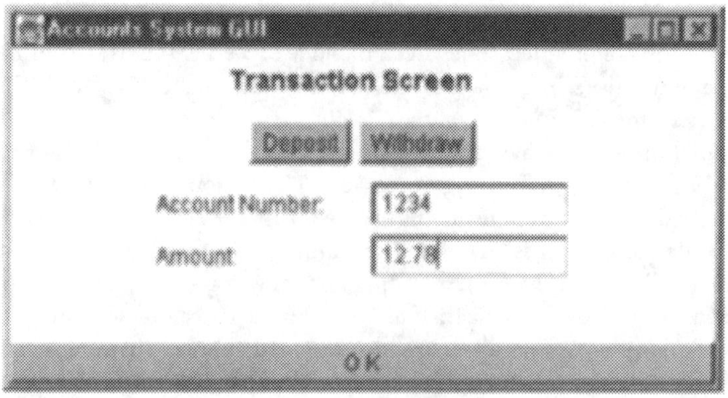

Figure 46.6 The transaction screen.

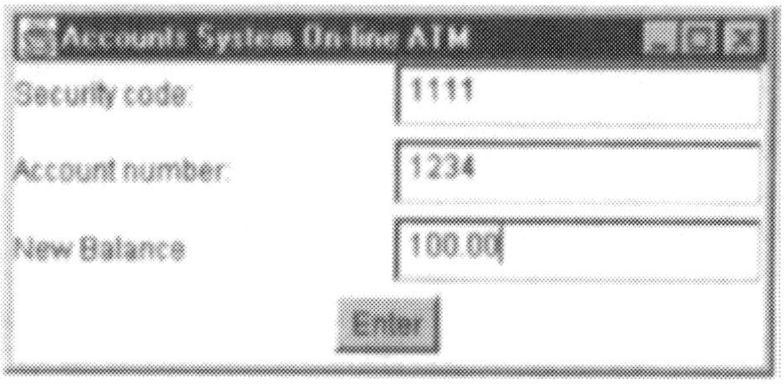

Figure 46.7 The set balance screen.

Finally, the print statement screen is illustrated in Figure 46.8. This screen accepts the customer's account number and then prints the associated statement into the scrollable text area below.

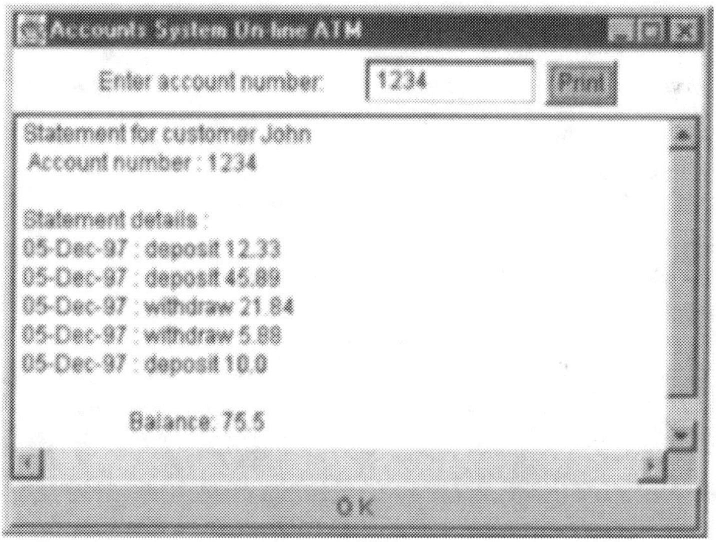

Figure 46.8 The print statement screen.

47 *The Analysis Phase: Object Modelling*

47.1 Introduction

The OMT analysis phase is concerned with producing a precise, concise, under-standable and correct representation of the real world. This representation is presented as a series of models. In particular, OMT defines an *object model*, a *dynamic model* and a *functional model*. In this chapter we consider the generation and definition of the object model.

47.2 The Object Model

The object model is the key element of the OMT and the UML. It is the first step in the OMT and the unifying element of a UML model. The object model is essentially comprised of the class and object diagrams. These diagrams illustrate the static structure of a system via the important classes and objects in the system and how they relate to each other. The UML documentation currently talks about class diagrams (and within this about object diagrams) stating that "class diagrams show generic descriptions of possible systems and object diagrams show particular instantiations of systems and their behaviour". It goes on to state that class diagrams contain classes while object diagrams contain objects, but that it is possible to mix the two. However, it discusses both under the title *class diagrams*. To avoid confusion, we adopt the term Object Model to cover both sets of diagrams (following the approach adopted in both the Booch and OMT methods).

The information for the object model comes from:

- the problem statement (written in natural language, according to OMT)
- a requirements analysis process such as OOA or an exploratory technique such as Class, Responsibility, Collboration (CRC)
- the domain experts
- general knowledge of the real world
- the use case model (if you have constructed one)

OMT claims that object models promote communication between computer professionals and application-domain experts (what do *you* think?). OMT suggests the following steps as an appropriate way in which to construct an object model:

- Identify objects and classes.
- Prepare a data dictionary.
- Identify associations (including aggregations) between objects.
- Identify attributes of objects and links.
- Organize and simplify object classes using inheritance.
- Verify that access paths exist for likely queries.
- Iterate and refine the model.
- Group classes into modules.

You should not take the sequence of these steps too strictly; object-oriented analysis and design is rarely completed in a truly linear manner. You are likely to perform some steps to a greater depth as the process goes on. In addition, some steps may lead to revisions in other steps and, once an initial design is produced, it will doubtless require revisions. You should consider these steps as a set of processes, the order of which may be influenced by the domain, the expertise available, the application etc. However, you should probably always start with the process of identifying objects and classes.

In the remainder of this chapter we shall consider each of these steps in turn.

47.3 Identifying Classes

This section considers how classes are represented as well as how they are identified.

47.3.1 Representing Classes

A class is drawn as a solid-outline rectangle with three components. The class name (in bold type) is in the top part, a list of attributes is in the middle part and a list of operations is in the bottom part (Figure 47.1).

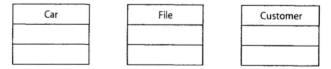

Figure 47.1 Example classes.

A class *stereotype* tells the reader what "kind" of class it is (for example, exceptions, controllers, interfaces, etc.). You show the stereotype as a normal font text string between << >> centred above the class name (see Figure 47.16).

However, UML makes no assumptions about the range of stereotypes that exist, and designers are free to develop their own. Other (language-specific) class properties can also be indicated in the class name compartment. For example, in Figure 47.16 the Window class is an abstract class.

47.3.2 Representing Objects

An object in the UML is drawn as a rectangle divided into two sections. The upper section contains the *objectName : className* underlined.[1] The object name is optional, but the class name is compulsory. In Figure 47.2, the object is repMobile1 and the class is Car.

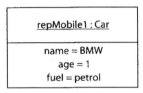

Figure 47.2 An object.

You can also indicate how many objects of a particular class are anticipated by entering the maximum value, range etc. in the top compartment. The lack of any number indicates that a single object is intended. The lower compartment contains a list of attributes and their values in the format *name type = value* (although the type is usually omitted). You can suppress the bottom compartment for clarity.

47.3.3 Generating Objects and Classes

The first step in constructing the object model is to identify the objects in the domain and their classes. Such objects may include:

- physical entities such as petrol pumps, engines and locks
- logical entities such as employee records, purchases and speed
- soft entities such as tokens, expressions or data streams,
- conceptual entities such as needs, requirements or constraints

As long as an item makes sense for the application and the domain, then it is a candidate object or class. The only things you should avoid are objects that relate to the proposed computer implementation.

OMT suggests that you identify these candidate objects by looking in the textual problem description. It indicates that classes are often found by identifying nouns in the description. However, if you have a more formal problem specification it may be easier to identify a set of potential classes. If you have used the use case analysis method you may also be able to identify the topmost objects directly from the use

---

1   Prior to the 0.91 version of the UML objects were drawn as a hexagon with straight sides and a slight peak at the top and bottom. If you are familiar with Booch clouds, you can think of it as a structured cloud. This was a major notational change which the UML authors made so that they did not have to invent a different symbol every time they had a type–instance relationship. However, it means that the distinction between objects and classes in diagrams is minimal and can easily lead to confusion. If you wish to make the distinction clearer you are free to continue to use the structured cloud symbol. Most people would understand what was meant.

case diagrams. Techniques such as CRC are also used as exploratory stages to help identify initial classes.

Do not worry about getting it right at this point or about identifying classes which should not be there. Inappropriate classes are filtered out later on; for the moment, attempt to find anything that could be a class. Once you have a comprehensive list of candidate classes, you can discard any unnecessary or incorrect ones by using the following criteria:

- *Are any of the classes redundant?* If two or more classes express the same information then one is redundant. For example, customer and user may be different names for the same thing.

- *Are any of the classes irrelevant?* A class may be outside the scope of the system to be built even if it is part of the domain. For example, although porters work in a hospital, they are probably not relevant to a hospital bed allocation system.

- *Are any of the classes vague?* Some classes may represent ill-defined concepts. For example, *history provision* is vague – of what is it a history?

- *Are any of the classes really attributes of other classes?* For example, name, address, salary and job title tend to be attributes of an employee object rather than objects in their own right. This can be tricky, as it is often possible to represent something as both a class and an attribute. You can leave the decision until later. If a class possesses only one type of information and has no operations, then it should probably be an attribute.

- *Are any of the classes really operations?* If a class appears to describe an operation that is applied to objects and not manipulated in its own right then it is not a class. For example, a telephone call is a sequence of actions performed by a caller. In the implementation, you may wish to make this an object; however, at this point in the design we are trying to produce a model of the application domain (i.e. not an implementation model).

- *Does the name of the class represent its intrinsic nature and not its role in the application?* For example, the class `Person` might represent an object in a restaurant booking system, but the class `Customer` is a better representation of its role in the system.

- *Is a class really an implementation construct?* Processes, algorithms, interrupts and exceptions are implementation concepts and tend not to be related to the application domain.

47.3.4 Identifying Classes for the Online ATM System

The first step is to identify all candidate classes (even if later they may be identified as superfluous). In addition, a customer can only have one account, and we will assume that an account is associated with just one customer. For example, in our online ATM system (this may be done directly from the use case analysis) we might identify customer, clerk, manager etc. directly. We may go on to question what classes are required to support the use cases. For example, we might identify Account, Balance, Transfer, Deposit, Withdrawal and Direct Payment. This would result in the initial set of classes illustrated in Figure 47.3.

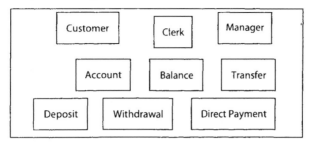

Figure 47.3 Initial set of classes.

Other classes may then be identified, such as Account History, Statement, Trans-action, Amount, Account Number and PIN. This would result in the extended set of classes illustrated in Figure 47.4. Note that we have not attempted to rationalize these classes, merely to identify potential classes.

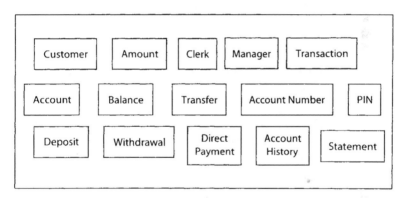

Figure 47.4 Additional classes.

47.3.5 Rationalizing Classes

We shall consider each of the questions presented earlier for removing unnecessary or incorrect classes.

- *Are any of the classes redundant?* If we examine Figure 47.4 it would appear that the Account History class and the Statement class are representing essentially the same information – historical data relating to the bank account. We can therefore remove the more generic and potentially less semantically meaningful Account History. There may also be duplication between Account and Balance, but this is not yet clear.

- *Are any of the classes irrelevant?* None of the classes identified so far appears to be outside the scope of this system.

- *Are any of the classes vague?* It is not clear what the Amount class represents. However, we will leave the renaming of this class until we have completed the rationalization of the classes, as the role may then become clearer.

- *Are any of the classes really attributes of other classes?* This is a tricky question, as it may be unclear whether a particular class will possess more than one item of information in the final design. However, in our system it is possible to identify some classes as being attributes of another class. For example, the Balance is probably just a numeric value and should be an attribute of the Account class. In turn, the Account Number and PIN are merely sequences of digits and should be attributes of the Customer class.

At this point it is unclear whether the Amount should be a class or an attribute of the Deposit or Withdrawal classes. We will therefore leave the Amount class for now.

● *Are any of the classes really operations?* If we consider the classes in Figure 47.4, there are a number of classes that appear to be operations; for example, Deposit, Withdrawal and Transfer. These might well evolve into classes for the implementation; however, here we are trying to represent the application domain. They are therefore inappropriate and need to be removed.

● *Does the name of the class represent its intrinsic nature and not its role in the application?* If we consider the classes in Figure 47.4, all the classes appear to fit the application. However, if we consider the role of the clerk and the manager it may be argued that the manager is actually a privileged user (as a manager does not actually manage the application). However, to allow the semantics of the system to remain clear we will leave the manager class alone for now.

● *Is a class really an implementation construct?* None of the classes in our system appears to fall into this category.

This leaves us with the classes presented in Figure 47.5. Of course, you might well have produced a completely different set of classes. Remember that the design process, such as that being described here, is still more of an art than a science, and rarely is there a single correct answer.

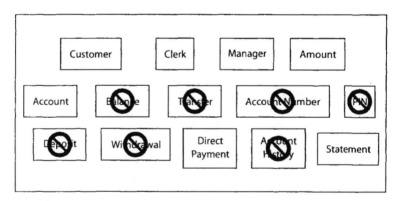

Figure 47.5 The refined set of classes.

47.4 Preparing a Data Dictionary

A data dictionary provides a definition for each of the terms or words used in the evolving analysis models. Each entry precisely describes each object class, its scope, any assumptions or restrictions on its use, and its attributes and operations (once they are known).

47.4.1 The Online ATM Data Dictionary

We are now in a position to start to define our data dictionary for our simple online ATM application. Given the remaining classes presented in Figure 47.5, our data dictionary will resemble that presented in Table 47.1.

Table 47.1 The data dictionary.

Name	Description	Assumptions	Attributes
Customer	Client of Bank with a Current Account		Account Number PIN
Clerk	User of system		
Manager	Privileged user of system	Can change balance directly	
Account	Holds information on a Customer's account		Balance
Statement	Historical record of deposits, Withdrawals and direct debits to and from the account	Is an ordered record	
Transaction	This represents the amount deposited, withdrawn or debited. It therefore represents a transaction	Can represent type of transaction	Amount
Direct Debit	Records the details of the Direct Debit payment	Works with a transaction	

As a result of producing the data dictionary we have removed the Amount class and added it as an attribute of the Transaction class. The data dictionary should be updated as and when attributes, operations and new classes are identified.

47.5 Identifying Associations

47.5.1 Representing Associations

An association, drawn as a solid line (see Figure 47.6), represents a relationship between classes or objects. An association between classes may have a name and an optional direction arrowhead that shows which way it is to be read. For example, in Figure 47.6 the relationship called hasEngine is read from the Car class to the Engine class. In addition, each end of an association is a *role*. A role may have a name that illustrates how its class is viewed by the other class. In Figure 47.6, the engine sees the car as a name and the car sees the engine as a specified type (e.g. Petrol, Diesel or Electric).

Figure 47.6 Association between classes and links between objects.

Each role (i.e. each end of the association) indicates the multiplicity of its class, which is how many instances of the class can be associated with one instance of the other class. This is indicated by a text expression on the role:* (indicating zero or more), a number or a range (e.g. 0..3). If there is no expression, there is exactly one association (see Figure 47.7). You can specify that the multiple objects should be ordered using the text {Ordered}. You can also annotate the association with additional text (such as {Sorted}) but this is primarily for the reader's benefit and has no meaning in UML.

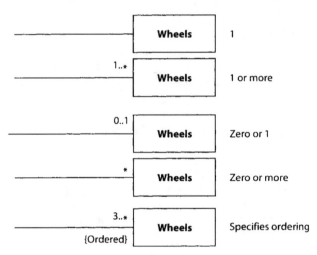

Figure 47.7 Annotated associations.

In some situations an association needs attributes. This means that you need to treat the association as a class (see Figure 47.8) These associations have a dashed line from the association line to the association class. This class is just like any other class

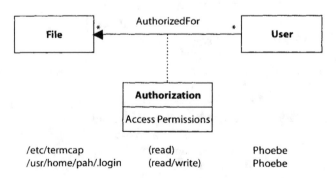

Figure 47.8 Associations with attributes.

and can have a name, attributes and operations. In Figure 47.8, the associations show an access permissions attribute which indicates the type of access allowed for each user for each file.

Aggregation indicates that one or more objects are dependent on another object for their existence (*part-whole* relationships). For example, in Figure 47.9, the Micro-Computer is formed from the Monitor, the System box, the Mouse and the Keyboard. They are all needed for the fully functioning MicroComputer. An empty diamond shows aggregation on the role attached to the whole object.

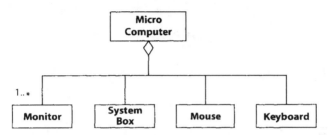

Figure 47.9 Aggregation tree notation.

It is sometimes useful to differentiate between by-value and by-reference references (see Figure 47.10). If the aggregation symbol is not filled, it indicates a by-reference implementation (i.e. a pointer or other reference); if the aggregation symbol is filled, it indicates a by-value implementation (i.e. a class that is embedded within another class).

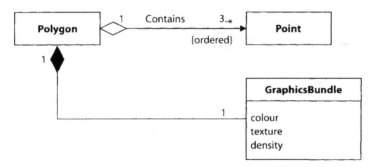

Figure 47.10 Reference implementation.

A qualified association is an association that requires both the object and the qualifier to identify uniquely the other object involved in the association. It is shown as a box between the association and the class. For example, in Figure 47.11 you need the catalogue and the part number to identify a unique part. Notice that the qualifier is part of the association, not the class.

A ternary (or higher order) association is drawn as a diamond with one line path to each of the participating classes (see Figure 47.12). This is the traditional entity–relationship model symbol for an association (the diamond is omitted from the binary association to save space). Ternary associations are very rare and higher

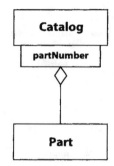

Figure 47.11 Qualified associations.

order associations are almost non-existent. However, you can model them if necessary.

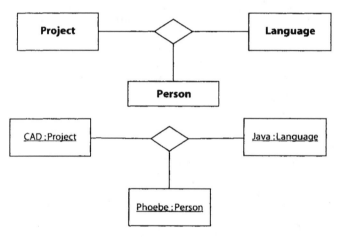

Figure 47.12 Ternary associations.

47.5.2 Identifying Associations Between Objects

The next step in OMT is to identify any (and all) associations between two or more classes. This is done by looking for references between two classes. OMT suggests that a good place to look for these relationships is to examine the problem description for verbs or verb phrases between known objects. In particular, it identifies the following types of relationship:

- physical location (next to, part of, contained in)
- directed actions (drives)
- communication (talks to)
- ownership (has, part of)
- satisfaction of some condition (works for, married to, manages)

Again, OMT exhorts you to identify all possible relationships and not to worry at this point about getting it right. If you have used a method such as OOA or CRC you may already have some knowledge about the relationships between the classes in the domain. If you have not used a method, then consider which classes are likely to need to work with which other classes (e.g. the accounts clerk may need to work with the salaries clerk). This process is simplified if you have performed a use case analysis.

Once you have a set of candidate associations, OMT provides a detailed set of criteria to help in refining them:

- *Is the association between eliminated classes?* If one of the classes involved in the association has been eliminated then the association should be eliminated.

- *Are any of the associations irrelevant or implementation associations?* Eliminate any associations that are outside the scope of the application domain (including implementation-related associations).

- *Are any associations transient?* An association should be a structural property of the application's domain. For example, *interacts with customer* is a temporary association in a hotel booking system.

- *Are any of the associations ternary?* Although the OMT and UML notations allow ternary associations, they are not encouraged. You should decompose these associations into binary ones (they are easier to implement, maintain and understand!).

- *Are any of the associations derivable?* OMT suggests that you should remove any associations that can be derived from other associations. However, you should be wary of removing such associations, as they may be critical to understanding the domain relationships. That is, if two existing associations can replace an association, only do so if the semantic meaning of the two associations can be combined to provide the same semantic meaning as the one to be removed. For example, a *GrandparentsOf* relationship can be replaced by two *ParentOf* relationships.

Having removed inappropriate associations, you can now consider the semantics of the associations you have left:

- *Are any of the associations misnamed?* Associations should reflect what they represent. They should be named after their use or the relationship they indicate.

- *Add role names where appropriate.* Role names describe the role that a class plays in the associations from the point of view of the other class.

- *Are there any qualified associations?* That is, are there any associations that require a qualifier to identify a unique object?

- *Specify multiplicity on the associations.* That is, indicate how may objects are involved in the association. By default all associations are 1 to 1 associations. Where no multiplicity is specified, check that they really are 1 to 1 links.

- *Are there any missing associations?* Check that all reasonable associations are present. You may need to do this in consultation with the domain expert.

47.5.3 Identifying Associations in the Online ATM System

To identify the associations we refer back to the use cases and determine which classes need to work with which other classes in order to achieve the use case. For example, consider the "check balance" use case. This use case has four steps:

1. Typing in the account number followed by the PIN
2. Requesting the current balance of the account
3. Receiving the balance
4. Logging off

The whole of this use case relates to the customer. We are therefore considering the classes Customer and Account and their relationship. In this situation a customer *has an* account. Thus there is an association between the Customer and Account classes which can be labelled as *has*. In addition, a customer can only have one account and we will assume that an account is associated with just one customer. If this process is applied to all the use cases we can obtain the set of associations illustrated in Figure 47.13.

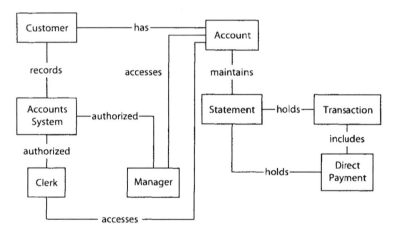

Figure 47.13 Basic class associations.

You may note that this diagram has introduced a new class: Accounts System. This is because it was necessary to define the relationship between a Clerk and Customers. It did not make sense to associate these classes together, as customers do not have clerks, nor do clerks have specific customers. Instead, a class was added to represent the overall system. This allows the concept of authorization to be introduced to show that a particular clerk can be authorized to use the system.

We are now ready to refine the associations. We can do this by considering the questions identified earlier. For example, one of the questions asks "are any of the associations transient?". In Figure 47.13 at least one of the associations may be transient. This is the association between the Clerk and the Account classes as well as the Manager and the Account classes. These associations are labelled accesses. However, this is a temporary association as a clerk does not permanently reference each and every customer account. Therefore this association should be removed. Having removed any inappropriate associations we are now in a position to refine the remaining associations.

The next set of questions identified by the OMT for refining associations relate to the semantics of the associations, such as checking the naming of associations or adding names where appropriate. For example, does a Statement hold a Transaction? Does it record a Transaction? What role does a Transaction play in a Statement and vice versa? There is no single answer to any of these questions. Finally, we must identify the multiplicity of the associations. Figure 47.14 illustrates the result of these refinements.

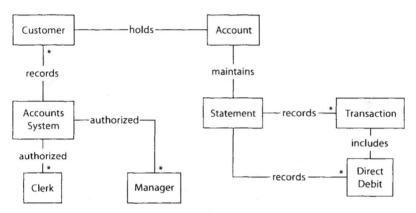

Figure 47.14 The associations after refinement.

47.6 Identifying Attributes

47.6.1 Representing Attributes

An attribute is a data item defined by a class. They can be associated with a class (e.g. a static or class variable) or with instances (e.g. an instance variable). They are not variables *per se* but may well be implemented as such in the actual system. An attribute has a name and a type specified in the following format:

```
name: type = initialValue
```

The name and type are strings that are ultimately language-dependent. The initial value is a string representing an expression in the target language.

You can hide the attribute compartment from view to reduce the detail shown in a diagram. If you omit a compartment, it says nothing about that part of the class definition. However, if you leave the compartment blank there are no definitions for that part of the class. Additional language dependent and user-defined information can also be included in each compartment in a textual format. The intention of such additions is to clarify any element of the design in a similar manner to a comment in source code.

Figure 47.15 illustrates two classes: Car and File. The Car class possesses three attributes: these are name, age and fuel, which are string, integer and string types, respectively.

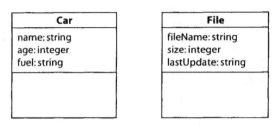

Figure 47.15 Classes with attributes and operations.

You can also indicate the intended scope of attributes in the class definition. The absence of any symbol in front of an attribute indicates that the element is public for that class. The significance of this depends on the language. The symbols currently supported are shown in Figure 47.16. You can combine symbols to indicate, for example, that an attribute is a class-side public value (such as +$defaultSize).

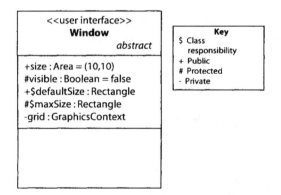

Figure 47.16 Class with additional annotations.

A derived value can be represented by a slash ("/") before the name of the derived attribute (see Figure 47.17). Such an attribute requires an additional textual constraint defining how it is generated; you indicate this by a textual annotation below the class between curly brackets ({ }).

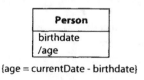

Figure 47.17 Derived values.

47.6.2 Identifying Attributes of Objects

OMT suggests that attributes correspond to nouns followed by possessive phrases, such as "the colour of the car" or "the position of the cursor" in the problem statement. The authors of OMT do admit that attributes are less likely to be fully described in the problem statement and that you must draw on your knowledge of the application domain and the real world to find them. If you have used a method such as OOA or CRC, you may already have identified the key attributes. Luckily, attributes can (usually) be easily added to objects as and when they are identified; it is rare that the addition of a new attribute causes the structure of the system to become unstable.

An important point to note is that you should only be trying to identify application domain attributes. This means that attributes that are needed during the implementation of the system should not be included at this stage. However, link attributes (which might appear to be implementation attributes) should be identified at this stage as they have an impact on the system's structure. A link attribute is a property of the link between two objects, rather than a property of an individual object. For example, the many to many association between Stockholder and Company has a link attribute of "number of shares".

Having identified the set of candidate attributes for each object, you should then challenge these attributes using the following criteria:

- *Should the attribute be an object?* Earlier we said that a telephone call should not be an object. However, if you are constructing a telephone call billing system, then perhaps it *should* be an object. You need to think carefully about the domain when deciding whether something is an attribute or an object. Do not worry about getting it wrong; you can come back to it later and refine the model.

- *Is an attribute really a name?* Names are often selectors used to identify a unique object from a set of objects. In such situations, a name should really be a qualifier.

- *Is an attribute an identifier?* Here, identifier means a computer-based identifier and is an implementation issue and not part of the application domain. For example, `objectId` is an identifier that is probably not in the application's domain.

- *Is an attribute really a link attribute?* Link attributes are often mistaken for object attributes. Link attributes are most easily identified when it becomes difficult to identify to which of two (or more) classes the attribute should belong. In such situations, it is an attribute of the link between the two classes.

- *Does the attribute represent an internal state of the object which is not visible outside the object?* If it does, remove the attribute. It is an internal implementation issue and not part of the domain problem.

- *Does the attribute represent fine detail?* If the attribute represents some aspect of the object that is relatively low-level, then omit it. It does not help with the overall understanding of the domain and increases the complexity of the object model.

- *Are any of the attributes unlike the others in their class?* Such discordant attributes may be misplaced (this may indicate that one class should actually be two or more) or the attribute may not be part of the current application (although it may be part of the overall domain).

47.6.3 Identifying Attributes in the Online ATM System

We are now ready to start identifying the attributes of the objects represented by the classes we have been defining. This can be done by returning to the use case analysis to see what information is provided or required. However, you will also have to rely on additional domain information. For example, nowhere in the descriptions of the online ATM system have we seen a reference to a customer's name. However, it is reasonable to assume that every customer will have a name (even if it is a business customer and the name is the name of a business). Table 47.2 illustrates the attributes identified for the classes we are defining.

Table 47.2 Attributes identified for classes.

Name	Customer	Account	Statement	Transaction
Attributes	name address account no. PIN	balance	period	date amount type
Name	**Direct Debit**	**Clerk**	**Manager**	**Accounts system**
Attributes	date amount recipient	name department	name department security code	customers

In Table 47.2 we have introduced a number of attributes which may not have been obvious from our previous analysis of the online ATM system. These become important when the responsibilities of the classes were considered. For example, a direct debit object must record when the debit occurred, how much was involved and to whom the payment was made. In turn, it was necessary to record the names of clerks or managers and their departments to identify them uniquely. For managers an additional security code was identified as a way of indicating that they had access to the "set Balance" operation. Note that the Account system class has no attributes. This is not a problem at the moment, as we introduced it to give meaning to the associations. However, we will need to come back to this class, as it may be an implementation class rather than a design class.

Having identified the attributes we must now analyze their validity. In this case we do not need to remove or alter any of the attributes identified.

47.7 Identifying Inheritance

47.7.1 Representing Inheritance

A solid line drawn from the subclass to the superclass with a large (unfilled) triangular arrowhead at the superclass end (see Figure 47.18) indicates inheritance of one class by a subclass. For compactness, you can use a tree structure to show multiple subclasses inheriting from a single superclass.

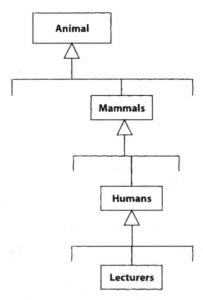

Figure 47.18 Inheritance hierarchy.

You can also model multiple inheritance, as languages such as the Common Lisp Object System (CLOS) and C++ support it. Multiple inheritance is represented by inheritance lines from a single subclass to two or more superclasses, as in Figure 47.19. In this figure, the class *Motor Powered Water Vehicle* inherits from both *Motor Powered* and *Water Vehicle*.

47.7.2 Organizing and Simplifying Object Classes Using Inheritance

You can refine your classes using inheritance in both directions. That is, you can group common aspects of existing classes into a superclass, or you can specialize an existing class into a number of subclasses that serve specific purposes. Again, if you have used an analysis method such as OOA you may already have done some of this.

Notice that you are not doing this with a view to implementing the generated class hierarchy; rather, you are trying to understand the commonalties in the domain.

Identifying potential superclasses is easier than identifying specialized subclasses. To find potential superclasses, you should examine the existing classes looking for common attributes, operations or associations. Any common patterns you find may indicate the potential for a superclass. If you find common features you should define the superclass with an appropriate name (i.e. one that encompasses the generic roles of the classes that inherit from it). Then move the attributes, associations and operations that are common up into this superclass.

Do not try to force unrelated classes to become subclasses of a superclass just because they happen to have similar attributes (or associations or operations). When

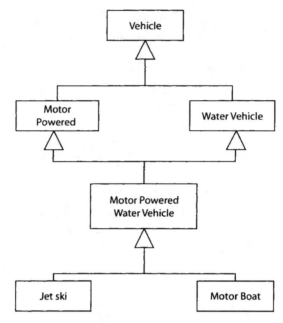

Figure 47.19 Multiple inheritance.

you group a set of classes together under a superclass, try to ensure that the grouping makes sense in the application domain. For example, grouping the classes car, truck and bus under a superclass vehicle makes sense. However, adding the class student, just because they all share the attribute *registrationNumber*, does not make sense!

Identifying specializations can be more difficult. However, if you find a class playing a number of specific roles then specialization may be appropriate. Notice that you should be wary of specialization, as you do not want to over-specialize the classes in your object model. You may be talking about separate instances of the same class, rather than subclasses.

47.7.3 Identifying Inheritance in the Online ATM System

We are now ready to identify any inheritance in the simple online ATM system. If we examine the classes illustrated in Figure 47.8 and Table 47.2 it quickly becomes clear that there are two situations in which common attributes and associations would suggest that inheritance may be used. These are in the classes Clerk and Manager and in the classes Transaction and Direct Debit.

There are two ways in which we may exploit inheritance. The first is to define a generic abstract class (for example, Employee) and allow the appropriate classes to inherit from this class. The other is to say that one class is a specialization of another existing domain class. These two options are presented in Figure 47.20 for the Clerk and Manager classes.

Which of these approaches is adopted depends on which is the more meaningful in the context of the application. Figure 47.20(b) implies that managers are actually a special type of clerk – which may not be meaningful. In this case we will adopt the approach illustrated in Figure 47.20(a).

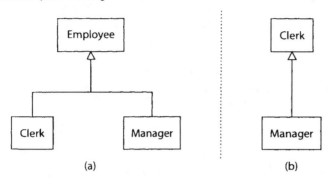

Figure 47.20 Alternative inheritance.

For the Transaction and Direct Debit classes we will adopt the style of approach indicated in Figure 47.20(b). This is because it does make sense to say that a direct debit is a type of Transaction This results in the object model illustrated in Figure 47.21.

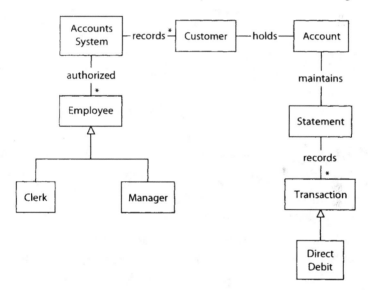

Figure 47.21 The final object model.

The remaining steps in this step of the OMT process involve checking the design and iterating and refining it. The resulting classes are then grouped into packages. In this case the system will be placed in a single package due to its simplicity.

47.8 Composites

A class may define a pattern of objects and links that exist whenever it is instantiated. Such a class is called a composite, and its class diagram contains an object diagram. You may think of it as an extended form of aggregation where the relationships among the parts are valid only within the composite. A composite is a kind of *pattern* or *template* that represents a conceptual clustering for a given purpose. Composition is shown by drawing a class box around the embedded components (see Figure 47.22) which are prototypical objects and links. That is, a composite defines a context in which references to classes and associations, defined elsewhere, can be used.

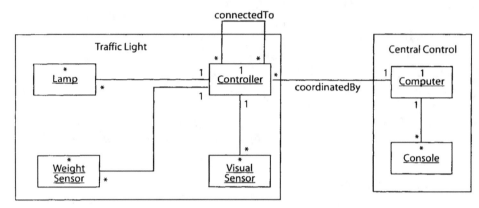

Figure 47.22 Composite classes.

47.9 Testing Access Paths

This step involves checking that paths in the model make sense, are sufficient and are necessary. OMT suggests that you trace access paths through the object model to see if they yield sensible results. You may wish to consider the following issues:

- Where a unique value is expected, is there a path yielding a unique result?
- For multiplicity, is there a way to pick out a unique value when needed?
- Are there any useful (domain-specific or application-specific) questions that cannot be answered?

47.10 Iterating and Refining the Model

Object design is still more of an art than a science and (unless the problem is trivial) the first version of the object model is probably not correct (or complete). Object-oriented design is far more iterative in nature than some other design methods and it therefore acknowledges that you need to repeat the above process a number of times to get a reasonable object model. Indeed some changes are initiated by the development of the dynamic model and the functional model that you have not even considered yet. However, you can ask yourself the following questions about the object model:

- Are there any missing objects (does one class play two roles)?
- Are there any unnecessary classes (such a class may possess no attributes)?
- Are there any missing associations (such as a missing access path for some opera-tion)?
- Are there any unnecessary associations (such as those that are not used by any-thing)?
- Are all attributes in the correct class?
- Are all associations in the correct place?

Cross-referencing the object model with the use case model may help answer some of the above questions.

47.11 Grouping Classes into Packages

The final step associated directly with the object model is to group classes into packages. You should identify packages by looking for classes that work together. Do not base the packages purely on system functionality, as this is likely to change and result in inappropriate packaging. OMT suggests that you ensure that a package can be fitted onto a single drawing surface (be that paper or the screen) as this aids comprehensibility. In addition, packages can be hierarchical and can be a very useful way of partitioning the design of the system amongst a number of designers.

47.11.1 Representing Packages

Packages group associated modelling elements such as classes in the object model (or subsystems in component diagrams). They are drawn as tabbed folders.

Figure 47.23 illustrates five packages called *Clients, Business Model, Persistent Store, Bank* and *Network*. In this diagram, the contents of *Clients, Persistent Store, Bank* and *Network* have been suppressed (by convention, the package names are in the body) and only *Business Model* is shown in detail (with its name in the top tab). *Business Model* possesses two classes, Customer and Account, and a nested package, *Bank*. The broken lines illustrate dependencies between the packages. For example, the package *Clients* directly depends on the packages *Business Model* and *Network* (i.e. at least one element in the *Clients* package relies on at least one element in the other two packages).

A class may belong to exactly one package but make reference to classes in other packages. Such references have the following format:

```
packageName :: className
Business Model :: Customer
```

Packages allow you to structure models hierarchically; they organize the model and control its overall complexity. Indeed you may use a package to enable top-down

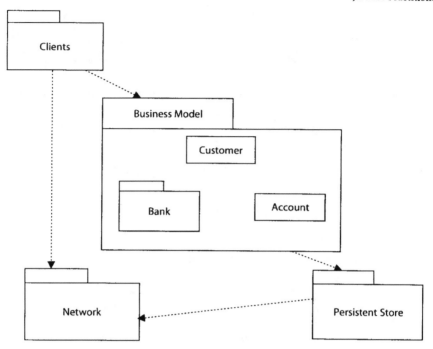

Figure 47.23 Packages with dependencies.

design of a system (rather than the bottom-up design typical of many object-oriented design methods) by allowing designers to specify high-level system functionality in terms of packages which are "filled out" as and when appropriate.

47.12 Reference

For information on the CRC technique see:

Wirfs-Brock, R., Wilkerson, B. and Wiener, L. (1990). *Designing Object-Oriented Software*. Prentice Hall, Englewood Cliffs NJ.

48 *The Analysis Phase: Dynamic Modelling*

48.1 Introduction

The dynamic model describes the behaviour of the application and the objects which comprise that application. The UML sequence, collaboration and state diagrams described in this chapter are the main components of the dynamic model. If you read any documentation on OMT you will find that it uses the term "event trace" to mean a sequence diagram and "event flow" to mean a collaboration diagram (in UML terms). Here we adopt the UML terminology, as we believe this will be the form generally used in the future.

The aim of dynamic model analysis is to identify the important events that occur and their effects on the state of the objects. OMT recommends that you perform the following steps in the construction of a dynamic model:

- Prepare scenarios of typical interaction sequences.
- Identify events between objects.
- Prepare a sequence diagram and collaboration diagram for each scenario.
- Build a state diagram.
- Match events between objects to verify consistency.

48.2 Identifying Scenarios

Scenarios illustrate the major interactions between the system and external actors on that system (whether human or otherwise). These scenarios are essentially the use cases in the use case model, if this has been performed. If not, you must consider the different ways in which the system will be used and determine the likely interactions. The scenarios can be written down as sequences of steps that describe one path through the systems. You should first prepare scenarios for normal system interaction and then for exceptional system interaction.

48.3 Identification of Events

The scenarios essentially document external events between the system and the actors. These events should trigger internal events between the objects in the system.

You should trace these events through the system, noting the objects involved and the types of events. Having obtained sets of events, you should group events that have the same effect (even if they have different parameters). For example, an event to close a file has the same effect, whichever file is being closed.

48.4 Preparation of Sequence and Collaboration Diagrams

48.4.1 Sequence Diagrams

A *scenario* shows a particular series of interactions among objects in a single execution of a system. That is, it is a history of how the system behaves between one start state and a single termination state. This differs from an *envisionment*, which describes all system behaviours from all start states to all end states. Envisionments thus contain all possible histories (although they may also contain paths which the system is never intended to take).

Scenarios can be presented in two different ways: Sequence Diagrams and Collaboration Diagrams. Both these diagrams present the same information, although they stress different aspects of this information. For example, sequence diagrams stress the timing aspects of the interactions between the objects, whereas collaboration diagrams stress the structure between these objects (which helps in understanding the requirements of the underlying software structure).

Figure 48.1 illustrates the basic structure of a sequence diagram. The objects involved in the exchange of messages are represented as vertical lines (which are labelled with the object's name). Caller, Phone Line and Callee are all objects involved in the scenario of dialling the Emergency services. The horizontal arrows indicate an event or message sent from one object to another. The arrow indicates the direction in which the event or message is sent, that is, the receiver is indicated by the

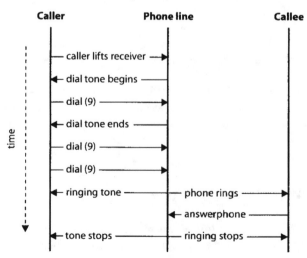

Figure 48.1 A sequence diagram.

head of the arrow. Normally return values are not shown on these diagrams. However, if they are significant you can illustrate them by annotated return events.

Time proceeds vertically down the diagram, as indicated by the broken line arrow, and can be made more explicit by additional timing marks. These timing marks indicate how long the gap between messages should be or how long a message or event should take to get from the sender to the receiver.

A variation of the basic sequence diagram (called a focus-of-control diagram) illustrates which object has the thread of control at any one time. A fatter line shows this during the period when the object has control (see Figure 48.2). Notice that the bar representing the object C only starts when it is created and terminates when it is destroyed.

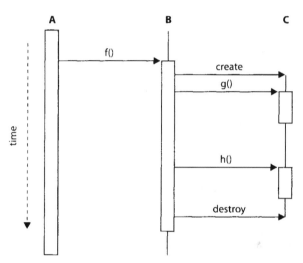

Figure 48.2 Sequence diagram with focus-of-control regions.

48.4.2 Collaboration Diagrams

As stated above, collaboration diagrams illustrate the sequence of messages between objects based around the object structure (rather than the temporal aspects of sequence diagrams). A collaboration diagram is formed from the objects involved in the collaboration, the links (permanent or temporary) between the objects and the messages (numbered in sequence) that are exchanged between the objects. An example collaboration diagram is presented in Figure 48.3.

The label *new* before the object name (e.g. the Line object in Figure 48.3) indicates objects that are created during the collaboration. Links between objects are annotated to indicate their type, permanent or temporary, existing for this particular collaboration. These annotations are placed in boxes on the ends of the links and can have the following values:

A   Association (or permanent) link
F   Object field (the target object is part of the source object)

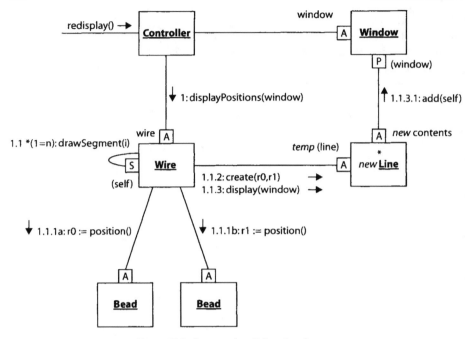

Figure 48.3 An example collaboration diagram.

G Global variable

L Local variable

P Procedure parameter

S Self (`this` in Java) reference

You can add role names to distinguish links (e.g. self, wire and window in Figure 48.3). Role names in brackets indicate a temporary link, i.e. one that is not an association.

Labels next to the links indicate the messages that are sent along links. One or more messages can be sent along a link in either or both directions. The format of the messages is defined by the following (some of which are optional):

1 . *A comma-separated list of sequence numbers in brackets, e.g. [seqno, seqno]* which indicate messages from other threads of control that must occur before the current message. This element is only needed with concurrency.

2. *A list of sequence elements separated by full stops, ".",* which represent the nested procedural calling sequence of the message in the overall transaction. Each element has the following parts:

 – A letter (or name) indicating a concurrent thread. All letters at the same level of nesting represent threads that execute concurrently, i.e. 1.2a and 1.2b are concurrent. If there is no letter, it usually indicates the main sequence.

 – An integer showing the sequential position of the current message within its thread. For example, message 2.1.4 is part of the procedure invoked by message 2.1 and follows message 2.1.3 within that procedure.

- An iteration indicator (*), optionally followed by an iteration expression in parentheses, which indicates that several messages of the same form are sent either sequentially (to a single target) or concurrently (to the elements of a set). If there is an iteration expression, it shows the values that the iterator assumes, such as "(i=1..n)"; otherwise, the details of the iteration must be specified in text or simply deferred to the code.
- A conditional indicator (?), optionally followed by a Boolean expression in parentheses. The iteration and conditional indicators are mutually exclusive.
3. *A return value name followed by an assignment sign (":="),* which indicates that the procedure returns a value designated by the given name. The use of the same name elsewhere in the diagram designates the same value. If no return value is specified, then the procedure operates by side effects.
4. *The name of the message,* which is an event or operation name. It is unnecessary to specify the class of an operation, since this is implicit in the target object.
5. *The argument list of the message,* which is made up of expressions defined in terms of input values of the nesting procedure, local return values of other procedures and attribute values of the object sending the message.

You may show argument values and return values for messages graphically using small data flow tokens near a message. Each token is a small circle, with an arrow showing the direction of the data flow, labelled with the name of the argument or result.

48.5 Constructing Sequence and Collaboration Diagrams

48.5.1 Generating Sequence and Collaboration Diagrams

Sequence diagrams should be generated before collaboration diagrams. This approach is easier, as sequence diagrams tend to deal with the sequential ordering of the events from one object to another, whereas a collaboration diagram may involve a number of objects.

48.5.2 Sequence and Collaboration Diagrams for the Online ATM System

As suggested above, we will start by producing a sequence diagram for the online ATM system. We shall use the results of the use case analysis as the basis of the scenarios and the events. To illustrate this we will consider the "Check Balance" use case. The basic steps for this use case are presented below:

1. Typing in the account number
2. Typing in the PIN
3. Requesting the current balance of the account (this may be on screen or a printout)
4. Receiving the balance

The users' actions will be used as the initiating events. These events must be sent somewhere, and the most logical place for them to be received is the Account System object. This is illustrated in Figure 48.4. Having identified these events, it is then necessary to identify the events triggered by these initial events and the receiving object. In this case the identification of subsequent events is fairly straightforward. For example, if the user inputs the account number, this number needs to be checked against those account numbers currently on the system. Checking each Customer object until the correct Customer object is identified does this. In Figure 48.4 this is indicated by the iteration symbol "*". This process is repeated until the complete sequence diagram is generated. Note that in order to return the current balance the Customer object sends events to the Account object.

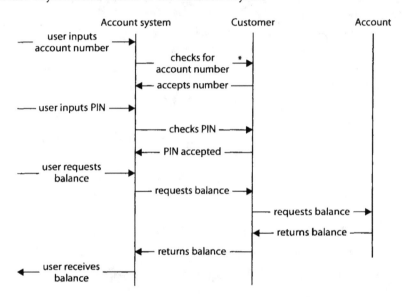

Figure 48.4 Sequence diagram for checking a balance.

Sequence diagrams should be produced for all use cases and for each scenario defined by the use case. Once this has been done, collaboration diagrams can be generated.

As noted above, a collaboration diagram represents a sequence of events that are based around the object's structure. Thus Figure 48.5 illustrates the associations between the Account system and the Customer and Account objects. In this case the links are annotated to indicate that they represent associations rather than any other type of link. Figure 48.5 illustrates the collaboration diagram resulting from the user requesting a balance. This is achieved by examining the associated sequence diagram. This gives us the objects and the events involved, as well as any return values.

As can be seen from the figure, a requestBalance() event will be sent to the Customer object. This event will return a value that will be represented by variable balance. In turn the Customer object sends another event (also called requestBalance) to the Account object. It is this object that actually returns the current balance.

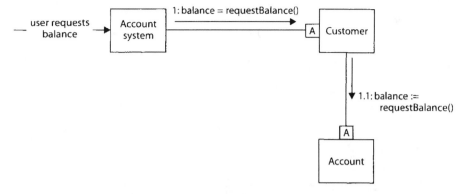

Figure 48.5 Part of the request balance collaboration diagram.

This collaboration diagram is very simple and would normally represent the whole of the associated sequence diagram. Such collaboration diagrams would be produced for all sequence diagrams. This is left as an exercise for the reader.

48.6 State Machine Diagrams

Scenarios are used to help understand how the objects within the system collaborate, whereas state diagrams illustrate how these objects behave internally. State diagrams relate events to state transitions and states. The transitions change the state of the system and are triggered by events. The notation used to document state diagrams is based on *statecharts*, developed by Harel (Harel *et al.*, 1987; Harel, 1988).

Statecharts are a variant of the finite state machine formalism, which reduces the apparent complexity of a graphical representation of a finite state machine. This is accomplished through the addition of a simple graphical representation of certain common patterns of finite state machine usage. As a result, a complex sub-graph in a "basic" finite state machine is replaced by a single graphical construct.

Statecharts are referred to as state diagrams in UML. Each state diagram has a start point at which the state is entered and may have an exit point at which the state is terminated. The state may also contain concurrency and synchronization of concurrent activities.

Figure 48.6 illustrates a typical state diagram. This state diagram describes a simplified remote control locking system. The chart indicates that the system first checks the identification code of the hand-held transmitter. If it is the same as that held in the memory, it allows the car to be locked or unlocked. When the car is locked, the windows are also closed and the car is alarmed.

A state diagram consists of a start point, events, a set of transitions, a set of variables, a set of states and a set of exit points.

48.6.1 Start Points

A start point is the point at which the state diagram is initialized. In the figure, there are four start points indicated (Start, lock, close and unlock). The Start

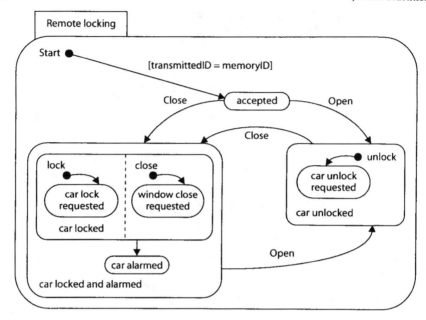

Figure 48.6 An example state diagram.

start point is the initial entry point for the whole diagram, while the other start points are for substate diagrams.

Any preconditions required by the state diagram can be specified on the transition from the start point (for example, the `transmittedID` must be the same as the `memoryID`). It is the initial transition from which all other transitions emanate. This transition is automatically taken when the state diagram is executed. Notice that the initial `Start` point is not equivalent to a state.

48.6.2 Events

Events are one-way asynchronous transmissions of information from one object to another. The general format of an event is as follows:

```
event:Name (paramet:er:t:ype, ...)
```

Of course many events do not have any associated parameters.

48.6.3 A Set of Transitions

These are the statements which move the system from one state to another. In a state diagram, each transition is formed of four (optional) parts:

1. An event (e.g. `lock`).
2. A condition (e.g. `[transmittedid = memoryID]`)
3. The initiated event (e.g. `^EngineManagementUnit.locked`)
4. An operation (e.g. `/setDoorToLock`)

The event is what triggers the transition; however, the transition only occurs if the condition is met. If the event occurs and the conditions are met, then the associated operation is performed. An operation is a segment of code (equivalent to a statement or program or method) which causes the system state to be altered. Some transitions can also trigger an event which should be sent to a specified object. The above example sends an event *locked* to the *EngineManagementUnit*. The process of sending a global event is a special case of sending an event to a specified object. The syntax of an event is as follows:

```
event(arguments)  [condition]
^t:arget.sendEvent(arguments)
/operation(arguments)
```

48.6.4 A Set of State Variables

These are variables referred to in a state diagram, for example, memoryID. They have the following format:

```
name: type = value
```

48.6.5 A Set of States

A state represents a period of time during which an object is waiting for an event to occur. It is an abstraction of the attribute values and links of an object. A state is drawn as a rounded box containing the (optional) name of the state. A state may often be composed of other states (the combination of which represents the higher level state). A state has duration; that is, it occupies an interval of time.

A state box can contain two additional sections: a list of state variables and a list of triggered operations (see Figure 48.7).

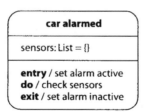

Figure 48.7 State box with state variables and triggered operations.

An operation can be of the following types:

- *entry* operations are executed when the state is entered. They are the same as specifying an operation on a transition. They are useful if all transitions into a state perform the same operation (rather than specifying the same operation on each transition). Such operations are considered to be instantaneous.

- *exit* operations are executed when the state is exited. They are less common than entry actions and indicate an operation performed before any transition from the state.
- *do* operations are executed while the state is active. They start on entry to the state and terminate when the state is exited.
- *events* can trigger operations while within a particular state. For example, the event *help* could trigger the *help* operation while in the state *active*.

Each operation is separated from its type by a forward slash ("/"). The ordering of operations is:

1. Operations on incoming transitions
2. Entry operations
3. Do operations
4. Exit operations
5. Operations on outgoing transitions

State diagrams allow a state to be a single state variable or a set of substates. This allows for complex hierarchical models to be developed gradually as a series of nested behaviour patterns. This means that a state can be a state diagram in its own right. For example, *car alarmed* is a single state and *car locked* is another state diagram. Notice that the transition from *car alarmed* to *accepted* jumps from an inner state to an outer state.

The broken line down the middle of the *car locked* state indicates that the two halves of that state run concurrently. That is, the car is locked as the windows are closed.

A special type of state, called a history state, represents a state which must be remembered and used the next time the (outer) state is entered. The symbol for a history state is an H in a circle.

48.6.6 A Set of Exit Points

Exit points specify the result of the state diagram. They also terminate the execution of the state diagram.

48.6.7 Building a State Diagram

You should construct a state diagram for each object class with non-trivial dynamic behaviour. Every sequence diagram (and thus collaboration diagram) corresponds to a path through a state diagram. Each branch in control flow is represented by a state with more than one exit transition. The procedure for producing state diagrams, as described by the OMT method, is summarized below by the following algorithm:

1. Pick a class.
2. Pick one sequence diagram involving that class.
3. Follow the events for the class; the gaps between the events are states. Give each state a name (if it is meaningful to do so).

4. Draw a set of states and the events that link them based on the sequence diagrams.
5. Find loops (repeated sequences of states) within the diagram.
6. Choose another sequence diagram for the class and produce the states and events for that diagram. Merge these states and events into the first diagram. That is, find the states and events which are the same and find where they diverge. Now add the new events and states.
7. Repeat Step 6 for all sequence diagrams involving this class.
8. Repeat from Step 1 for all classes.

After considering all normal events, add boundary cases and special cases. Also consider events which occur at awkward times including error events.

You should now consider any conditions on the transitions between states and any events that are triggered off by these transitions. Notice that we still have not really considered the system's operations.

Matching Events Between Objects

Having produced the state diagrams, you should now check for completeness and consistency across the whole system. Every event should have a sender and a receiver, all states should have a predecessor and a successor (even if they are start points or exit points) and every use case should have at least one state diagram which explains its effect on the system's behaviour. You should also make sure that events that are the same on different statecharts have the same name.

48.6.8 An Example State Diagram

In this section we follow the guidelines presented above. Therefore we select a class, in this case the class Customer. We then pick a sequence diagram and identify the required states and transitions. For example, if we select the check balance sequence diagram then we can see that that:

1. The customer must be in a state that allows the user to check the balance. We shall call this state "registered".
2. Although there is a lot of interaction with the customer object, none of that inter-action changes the state of that customer (although the state registered may be expended to represent states such as "Account No Accepted", "PIN Accepted" and "Balancd Provided". See Figure 48.8 for an example of this).
3. Part of the "check balance sequence diagram" results in the Customer object sending an event to the Account object. This must therefore be reflected in the state diagram.

Figure 48.9 illustrates the state of the state diagram at this point. As can be seen, it captures the information identified above, but does not take into account any other events or states implied by any other sequence diagrams – this is quite normal.

We are now ready to consider another sequence diagram. Essentially we need to repeat the above steps, attempting to identify any duplicate states or transitions. The results should then be merged with the evolving state chart. The result for the Customer object is illustrated in Figure 48.10. As you can see this is a far more

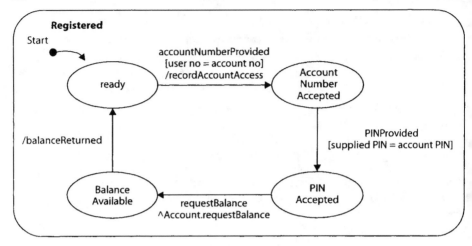

Figure 48.8 A state diagram for the "Registered" state.

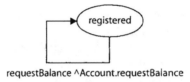

Figure 48.9 A partial state diagram.

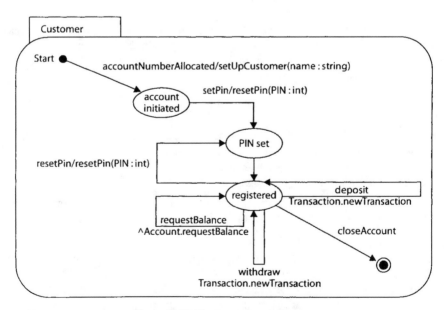

Figure 48.10 The customer state diagram.

complex state diagram and has introduced a number of states indicated by sequence diagrams derived from use cases with alternative courses (such as being overdrawn).

As a comparison we present below the statechart for the Accounts System itself (see Figure 48.11). This statechart indicates the states that the overall system can be in. These states are primarily derived from the use case analysis. For example, a user logs on to and off the system. Additional states were identified from the analysis of the object model. This shows that at some point it is necessary to obtain the employees and customers associated with the Accounts System (i.e. they are objects referenced by the Accounts System object but which are likely to be persistent – i.e. held in a database or on file). It is therefore necessary to identify the acquisition of this data as a specific system state (how the data is actually stored will be considered later in the design process). Also note that once a user is logged on there are three events which do not cause a change of state and thus return the user to the logged on state.

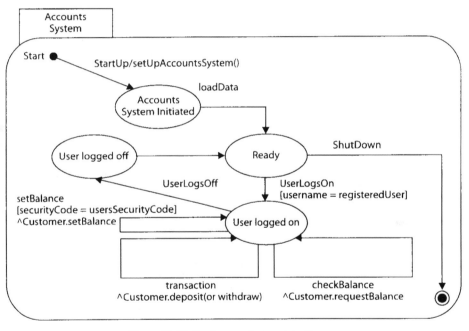

Figure 48.11 The Accounts System state diagram.

48.7 References

Harel, D. (1988). On visual formalisms. *Communications of the ACM*, **31**(5), 514–30.
Harel, D. *et al.* (1987). On the formal semantics of Statecharts. *Proceedings of the 2nd IEEE Symposium on Logic in Computer Science*, pp. 54–64.

49 *Functional Modelling and Operations*

49.1 Introduction

A functional model explains how the operations in the object model and the actions or activities of the dynamic model are achieved. It can also represent constraints among the values of the model. That is, the functional model represents the algorithmic or computational elements of the application analysis – the "how" rather than the "where" (object model) or "when" (the dynamic model). The UML does not possess any notation for representing functional models and this reflects the lack of emphasis placed on algorithmic analysis by many object-oriented design methods. The original OMT advocated the use of data flow diagrams (DFDs) as being a suitable representation for functional models. A DFD possesses inputs, outputs, data stores, processes and data flows. These will be discussed briefly below. However, in line with others, I have found DFDs difficult to use and have often resorted to using pseudo-code (with additional annotations to support the navigation of object models). However, a variety of notations can be, and are, used, including free text decision tables and formal methods. You should choose a representation which best suits the type of application you are building as well as the needs and experience of your organisation. For help in identifying the appropriate approach to use, see Chapter 8 of Blaha and Premerlani (1998).

In the remainder of this chapter we introduce DFDs for functional modelling and how they may be constructed, we consider pseudo-code enhanced with object navigation notation (Blaha and Premerlani, 1998) and examine a pseudo-code-based functional model of the online ATM system. We then consider the association of operations to classes.

49.1.1 DFD for Functional Modelling

The functional model in OMT describes how values are computed. The original version of OMT used data flow diagrams (DFDs) to represent these functional models. A DFD possesses inputs and outputs, data stores, processes and data flows (see Figure 49.1).

- *Data stores* are passive objects that store data for later use. They merely respond to requests to store and access data. The Icon Definitions label between two parallel bars indicates a data store.

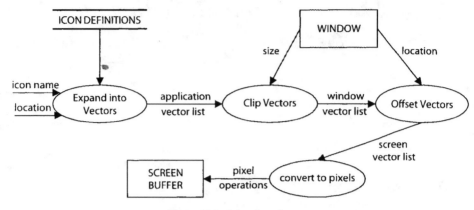

Figure 49.1 A data flow diagram.

- *Processes* possess a fixed number of inputs and outputs that are labelled with their type or name. Processes may be nested and of arbitrary complexity. Eventually, they reference atomic operations. A process is drawn as an ellipse.
- *Data flows* are indicated by an arrow labelled with the type of data. They may split or converge. The tail of the arrow indicates the source and the head of the arrow the sink for the data.
- *Actors* (drawn as rectangles) act as the eventual sources and sinks of the whole data flow. For example, the `screen buffer` is the eventual sink for the data flow in Figure 49.1.

OMT advises that you should construct the functional model after the object and dynamic models. The steps in this phase defined by OMT are:

- Identify input and output values.
- Build data flow diagrams showing functional dependencies.
- Describe functions.
- Identify constraints.
- Specify optimization criteria.

Identifying Input and Output Values

Input and output values are parameters of events between the system and the outside world. You should reference the use case diagram to see whether the actors should provide information to the system or expect a response from the system.

Build Data Flow Diagrams

The data flow diagrams are constructed by producing a diagram which groups inputs, processes those values and generates outputs. You should then break down each non-trivial process (at a lower level) into smaller steps. This process is repeated until only atomic operations remain. The result is a hierarchical model containing data flow diagrams which implement (higher level) processes.

Objects can also store data for later use. These objects can be identified in a DFD because they receive values that do not result in immediate outputs but are used at some future time.

Describing Functions

Once the DFD for a particular function has been defined, you should write a description of that function. This description can be in the form of natural language, pseudocode, mathematical equations, decision tables or any other suitable form. The function description places the DFD (which indicates how data is processed) into context.

Identifying Constraints

Constraints are functional dependencies between objects. They may be pre-conditions or post-conditions on a function or a relationship (for example, `birthDate < currentDate`). They may exist between two instances or between different instances at different times. Either way, they need to be documented.

Specifying Optimization Criteria

Specify any data values which should be maximized (for example, process as many orders in an hour as possible), minimized (for example, ensure that system response is < 2 milliseconds) or otherwise optimized.

49.2 Pseudocode with the Object Navigation Notation

It is necessary to augment basic pseudocode, as it is primarily procedural in nature. This is a problem, because the intent of an object-oriented analysis and design is to identify the objects, the data they hold as well as what they do. Therefore it is necessary to think in terms of objects, object interactions and what objects provide. It is all too easy with procedural pseudocode to end up designing the implementation of the objects (remember: this is only the analysis phase).

The pseudocode used during the construction of the functional can be based on any syntax that is readily and widely understood by those involved in the analysis, design and the eventual implementation of the system. However, in order to provide some standard for the remainder of this chapter we shall consider a basic set of conventions commonly used by many pseudo-code (informed) languages:

- *Conditionality.* Follows the basic structure of an `if` statement in Java.
- *Iteration over a collection of objects.* This is a simplification of the approach used in Java. In this case the `for` loop directly references the collection, binding the loop variable to each element in the collection each time the loop is evaluated. For example:

```
for each element in a collection
   statement(s)
end for each
```

- *Iteration through a fixed loop.* This is essentially the `for` loop of many programming languages. For example:

```
for count := min to max increment by inc
   statement(s)
end for
```

Note that the range and increment values are made explicit.

- *Method signature.* This is the name of the function being defined. It is comprised of the class name, the name of the method, any arguments and a return type. For example:

```
class name :: method name (arguments) returns domain
```

If a method has no arguments the brackets can be omitted. A method that does not return a value need not include the `returns` clause.

Note that the returned element is a domain and not a type. A domain differs from a type in that it is an application-specific concept, whereas a type is an implementation detail. For example, the days of the week may be a domain, but might be implemented as integers in a particular system. From the point of view of an implementation the domain "Week Days" is more meaningful than a return type `int`!

- *Method invocation.* This is denoted by a #. It is placed between the object (or class) and the method name. For example:

```
object name # method name (arguments)
```

This notation may appear somewhat awkward, but does help to distinguish between method calls (particularly for methods with no parameters) and other types of reference (such as references to attributes).

- *Local variables.* These should be avoided if at all possible, as they tend to indicate implementation rather than design. Their definition is implicit when they are used.

- *Implicit method argument.* The reference to `this` is available within a pseudo-code method. As in Java, this pseudo-variable refers to the object executing the method.

- *Dot notation.* The dot notation is used to access attributes of classes, objects or links. Depending on the attribute referenced, the result can be an object, a class or a set of objects or classes. The notation used is:

```
Receiver.attribute
```

If the attributes is prefixed by a "~" then it indicates a reverse traversal of an association.

- *Qualified associations.* The value to be used by the qualified association can be specified in square brackets after the association role name. The notation is:

```
Receiver.role [qualifier = value]
```

This is illustrated in Figure 49.2.

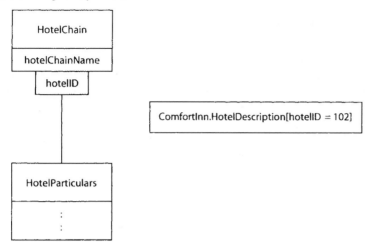

Figure 49.2 A qualified association.

- *Specialization/generalization.* This is indicated by two class names separated by a colon. No difference is made between specialization and generalization – it is the context that distinguishes which is being used. Figure 49.3 illustrates this.

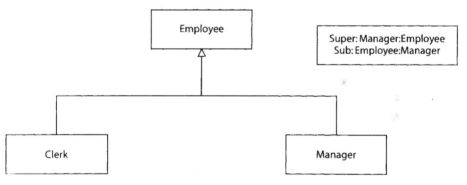

Figure 49.3 Specialization/generalization in pseudocode.

- *Filtering.* It is possible to specify that a subset of a collection of objects should be selected based on some filter. Specifying the filter in square brackets following the collection of objects does this. For example:

```
collection [filter]
freeRooms [from = 20-5-98 AND TO = 31-5-98]
```

In the second example above, each element in the list of free rooms is expected to provide the "from" and "to" values to be used in the filter.

- *Accessing the link/association.* The link between to objects can be referenced directly using the "@" symbol. Remember that when it comes to the implementation the link may be a reference or it may be an object in its own right.

49.3 The Online ATM System Functional Model

We will only consider the pseudocode definition for one method in the functional model. This is because this is the easiest process for many who have experience of designing for procedural languages. We shall examine the definition of the checkBalance method. To do this we must define a number of other methods. These are presented below:

```
Account System :: findAccount (accountNumber) returns
    Customer
  for each customer in this.customers
    if customer#isAccount(account Number) then
      result := customer
    end if
  end for each
  return result

Customer :: checkPIN (PIN) returns true or false
  if this.PIN equals PIN then
    return true
  else
    return false
  end if

Customer :: requestBalance returns money
  return this.account#requestBalance

Account System :: checkBalance (accountNumber, PIN)
    returns money
  Customer := findAccount(accountNumber)
  if customer#checkPIN(PIN) then
    return customer#requestBalance
  else
    ERROR
  endif
```

In a real functional model, these methods would be presented within the scope of each class rather than in the form of a listing as presented here.

To define the above pseudocode methods we started by returning to the sequence and collaboration diagrams. This indicated that additional methods would be required. These would need to identify the correct account, confirm the PIN number and obtain the balance. To define these methods it was necessary to refer to the object model in order to obtain the system's structure. Note that at this point it was also necessary to introduce a new operation (method) isAccount() on the Customer class. This illustrates the iterative nature of the design process – it would now be necessary to amend the object model to include this new operation.

Having defined these three methods we are now in a position to define the `checkBalance` method in terms of these methods.

49.4 Adding Operations

It is only at this point that the operations in the analysis models are considered. Note how this differs from the procedural approach, in which the operations to be performed would be considered first of all. The object model (but related to functions, actions and events in the functional and dynamic models) summarizes the operations.

49.4.1 Representing Operations

An operation has a name and may take one or more parameters and return a value. It is specified in the following format:

```
name (parameter : type = defaultValue, ...):
resultType
```

The constituent parts are language-dependent strings.

You can hide the operation compartment (as well as the attribute compartment) from view to reduce the detail shown in a diagram. If you omit a compartment, it says nothing about that part of the class definition. However, if you leave the compartment blank, there are no definitions for that part of the class. Additional language-dependent and user-defined information can also be included in each compartment in a textual format. The intention of such additions is to clarify any element of the design in a similar manner to a comment in source code.

Figure 49.4 illustrates two classes: `Car` and `File`. The `Car` class possesses three attributes (`name`, `age` and `fuel` are string, integer and string types, respectively) and four operations (`start`, `lock` and `brake` take no parameters; `accelerate` takes a single parameter, `to`, which is an integer that represents the new speed).

You can also indicate the intended scope of operations (and attributes) in the class definition. The absence of any symbol in front of an attribute or operation indicates

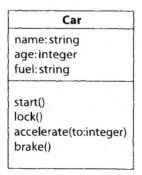
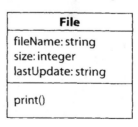

Figure 49.4 Attributes in a class.

that the element is public for that class. The significance of this depends on the language. In Java it means that the operation is visible in all packages. The symbols currently supported are shown in Figure 49.5. You can combine symbols to indicate, for example, that an operation is a class-side public method (such as +$new()).

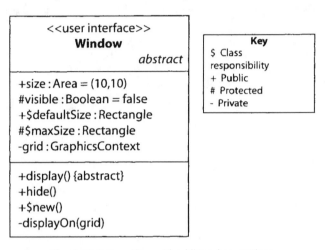

Figure 49.5 Operations with additional annotations.

49.4.2 Identifying Operations

To identify the operations to be added to the object model we must examine the dynamic and functional models. Thus we should look for:

- operations implied by events
- operations implied by state actions and activities
- operations from functions
- application or domain operations
- simplifying operations

Each of these will be considered in more detail below.

49.4.3 Operations Implied by Events

All the events in the object model correspond to operations (although a single operation may handle multiple events and vice versa). OMT suggests that during analysis "events are best represented as labels on state transitions and should not be explicitly listed in the object model". However, if you find it clearer to list the operations corresponding to the events in the object model, then do so.

49.4.4 Operations Implied by State Actions and Activities

The actions and activities in the state diagrams correspond to operations. These can be listed in the corresponding classes in the object model.

Operations from Functions

Each function corresponds to one or more operations. The functions should be organized into operations on objects. This is not as straightforward as it might at first seem, since we have not yet associated the functions with objects.

49.4.5 Domain Operations

There may be additional domain operations that are not immediately obvious from the problem description. These should be identified from additional domain knowledge and noted. For example, although a cash dispenser (ATM) system does not allow you to open and close accounts, such operations are appropriate within the domain and may be important for understanding the domain or for aspects of the application which have yet to come to light.

49.4.6 Simplifying Operations

Examine the object model for operations that are essentially the same. Replace these operations with a generic one. Notice that earlier steps may well have generated the same operation but with different names. Check each object's operations to see if they are intended to do the same thing even if they have very different names. Adjust the other models as appropriate.

49.5 Identifying Operations for the Online ATM System

To identify the operations in the online ATM system we can consider each of the points noted above.

49.5.1 Operations Implied by Events

There are a number of events (which are not considered elsewhere, e.g. in the functional model) which imply operations. For example, the closeAccount event identified in the last chapter is certainly an operation on a Customer but one which may not have generated a functional model (because it is not a functional entity – it merely changes the state of the associated object).

49.5.2 Operations Implied by State Actions and Activities

It is quite possible that these will have been explored in the online ATM system functional model. However, if they have not they should be registered as operations. For example, the actions identified in the "registered" substate diagram may not have been included; however, they will be operations on the customer object. In particular, actions such as recordAccountAccess need to be registered as operations.

49.5.3 Operations from Functions

This is where the majority of the operations for the online ATM system come from. All the functionality in the functional model should be recorded as operations on the appropriate class. This will have be easier if you have used the pseudo-code representation for the functional models rather than the data flow diagrams. Earlier in this chapter only a very few of the elements of the functional model were presented; however in the fully functional model of the online ATM there are 20 different functions defined.

49.5.4 Application or Domain Operations

In the case of the on-line ATM only a few application operations have been identified. These are operations such as being logged on to and off the system, which were not explicitly identified by the use case analysis but which are essential to the safe operating of the system.

49.5.5 Simplifying Operations

A couple of simplifying operations have been identified for the online ATM. These are operations such as newTransaction which are used in a similar manner to a constructor in Java (indeed in the implementation they will probably be replaced by Java constructors).

49.5.6 The Operations

The full set of operations produced by the analysis phase for each of the classes is presented in Table 49.1. You should add these operations to your evolving data dictionary and to your object model. In addition, you should identify the parameters they accept and the values they return, as well as their visibility. You should also identify which operations are class-side (or static) operations and which are instance operations. In the following we use "$" to indicate a class-side operation, "+" to indicate a public operation and "−" to indicate a private operation (in line with the UML).

Note that many of the above operations come from the complete analysis of the online ATM, which has not been presented here due to lack of space. However, it is hoped that enough of the analysis has been presented to allow you to obtain a feeling for how the process progresses. You should consult a variety of object-oriented design books as well as practising the design process yourself.

We should now return to our data dictionary and add the above operations. Note that we should examine the classes in the data dictionary to see if there are any attributes implied by the operations which are not present in the appropriate class. Having done this we should update the object model and examine the dynamic model to ensure that it is complete, repeating all analysis steps as appropriate.

Table 49.1 Operations produced by the analysis phase.

Customer	Account
+checkAccountNo(accountNumber : int) : boolean	+requestBalance() : double
+checkPIN(PIN : int) : boolean	+addTransaction(trans : Transaction)
+requestBalance() : double	+setBlanace(newBalance : double)
+closeAccount()	
$setUpCustomer(name : String, accountNumber : int, PIN : int, initialBalance : double)	
+resetPIN(PIN : int)	
+deposit(trans : Transaction)	
+withdraw(trans : Transaction)	
+printStatement()	
+setBalance(amount : double)	
-recordAccountAccess()	

Transaction	Direct Debit
+$newTransaction(type: String, amount : double)	+recordRecipient(name : String)

Statement	AccountSystem
+addTransaction(trans : Transaction)	+logon()
print()	+logoff()
	+checkBalance(accountNumber : int, PIN : int) : double
	-findAccount(accountNumber : int) : Customer
	+transaction(accountNumber : int, type : String, amount : int)

Employee	Clerk	Manager
+checkUser(name : String) : boolean		+checkSecurityCode(code : int) : boolean

50 *The Design and Implementation Phases*

50.1 Introduction

This chapter considers the final two phases in the OMT design process. These are the design and implementation phases. You may note that the last few chapters have been dedicated to the analysis phase, whereas the design and implementation phases are presented in a single chapter. This reflects the emphasis that OMT places on the analysis phase and the relative lack of support that it provides for the remainder of the design process.

We first present the design phase and then the implementation phase.

50.2 Design Phase

The OMT analysis phase identifies what *needs* to be done, not *how* it is done. The OMT design phase takes the models produced by the analysis and considers how the requirements can be *achieved*. This is done in two stages called the System Design stage and the Object Design stage. The system design stage considers the high-level design decisions where as the object design stage considers increasingly detailed design issues. These two stages are presented below.

Before we continue, a brief aside is necessary. As with the whole of the analysis phase the following material is presented in a sequential manner. This is primarily due to the constraints of a two-dimensional static medium, such as that found in a book. In reality it is unlikely that you will proceed in such a sequential manner from one phase to another and from one stage to another for all but the simplest of systems. For large real-world systems, the separation of one stage from another (as well as the separation of analysis from design) is rarely feasible. Indeed, in such systems it is much more normal for there to be interaction between the various steps in OMT. For example, a common approach is to consider only top-level classes in the analysis phase, moving these forward to the design phase and possibly into the implementation phase. At this point, enough is now known about those classes that they can be broken down into lower level classes which can be analyzed, designed and implemented etc. Of course, even this is rather more sequential than is the case in reality. You should bear this in mind when reading this chapter.

50.2.1 System Design Stage

This stage is primarily concerned with the identification of the overall architecture of the system. It is from this architecture that the structure of the actual design will be hung. That is, the subsystem architecture provides the context within which the more detailed design decisions, made during the object design, will be performed.

The subsystem decomposition defines an architecture which can be used as the basis by which the detailed design can be partitioned among a number of designers, thus allowing different designers to work independently on different subsystems. This is because it specifies the goals, strategies and policies within which each section of the system must be designed.

The steps used to generate this architecture are:

1. Organizing the system into subsystems
2. Identifying concurrency inherent in the problem
3. Allocating subsystems to processors and tasks
4. Choosing an approach for management of data stores
5. Handling access to global resources
6. Choosing the implementation of control in software
7. Handling boundary conditions
8. Setting trade-offs between competing priorities

Of course not all these steps are important for all applications. For example, a batch-oriented purely serial process probably cannot have much concurrency imposed on it. Equally, the precise ordering of these steps will vary according to the domain, type of application and problem being solved. You should there attempt to use this list in the most appropriate manner for your particular situation.

Breaking the System into Subsystems

Most systems comprise a number of subsystems. For example, a payroll system might possess a file subsystem, a calculation subsystem and a printing subsystem. A subsystem is not an object or a function, but a package of classes, associations, operations, events and constraints that are interrelated and that have a reasonably well-defined and (hopefully) small interface with other subsystems. The package notation in the UML can be used to represent subsystems.

A subsystem (or package) is usually characterized by the common (or associated) set of services that it provides. For example, the file package would provide a set of services to do with creating, deleting, opening, reading and writing files. The use case model may be useful in identifying such common services.

Each package therefore provides a well-defined interface to the remainder of the system which allows other packages to use its facilities. Such an interface also allows the internals of the package to be defined independently of the rest of the system (i.e. it encapsulates the package). In addition, there should be little or no interaction between objects within the package and objects in another package (except via the specified interfaces).

In simple systems it is quite possible that there will be only a single tier to the package hierarchy. However, for most real-world systems it is likely that the packages will be hierarchical. You therefore need to identify sub-packages and the most appropriate architectures for these packages.

Packages can be involved in client–server or peer-to-peer relationships with other packages. Client–server relationships are easiest to implement and maintain, as one package responds to requests from another package and returns results. In peer-to-peer relationships both packages must be capable of responding to requests from the other. This can result in unforeseen circularities.

The above description implies that the identification of these packages is straightforward and that you should be able to do it in a methodological manner. However, for complex systems it is unlikely that the most appropriate architecture for every package will be immediately obvious. You therefore need to consider different alternative architectures and evaluate these alternatives against some criteria. One process identified to help with the generation of the architectures is outlined below:

- *Generate candidate architectures.* This is best done by a number of different people with different backgrounds, all of whom need to analyze the goals of the system as well as the results of the analysis phase in detail. I have found that brainstorming sessions can be a particularly effective way of coming up with different potential architectures.

- *Propose decision criteria and assign weights to them.* Considering the needs of various actors against the advantages and disadvantages of each candidate architecture can identify the criteria. The following criteria are often used: cost, ease of use, development effort, deployment effort, performance, reliability, extensibility, integrity and security. Having identified your criteria you must now assign weightings to each one to indicate the importance of these criteria in the final application. In particular you should indicate whether the criteria are essential or desirable. Any essential criteria must be met by any feasible architecture.

- *Quantify the compliance of the architectures against the decision criteria.* That is, assess the architectures against the criteria you have identified. This can be done by assigning a number (for example between 10 and 0) and then multiplying the assigned value by the weight to obtain an indication of how well that architecture matches that criterion. Note that at best these figures are indicative and should not be treated as absolute. Indeed, the best way to assign the numbers is relative to each other, rather then producing an absolute scale.

- *Compare scores for each candidate architecture.* You will now have some absolute values indicating how closely each architecture matches the criteria specified. However, these are really only tentative indicators of which architecture should be selected, and the absolute totals should not be relied upon as the sole selector. You now need to perform sensitivity analysis to develop confidence in the results. You should reassess the effects of different criteria, compare one architecture with another etc. You also need to take into account additional factors such as your organization's experience in a particular architecture.

Later in this chapter we illustrate this process for the simple online ATM we have been exploring over the last few chapters.

Identifying Concurrency

Concurrency can be very important for improving the efficiency of a system. However, to take full advantage of concurrency the system must be designed around the concurrency inherent in the application. You can do this by examining the dynamic model for objects that receive events at the same time or perform any state transitions (and associated actions) without interacting. Such transitions are concurrent and can be placed in separate execution threads without affecting the operation of the system.

Allocating Subsystems to Processors and Tasks

Each concurrent package should be allocated to an independent process or processor. The system designer must therefore:

- estimate performance needs and the resources needed to satisfy them
- choose hardware or software implementations for packages
- allocate packages to processors to satisfy performance needs and minimize interprocessor communication
- determine the connectivity of the physical units that implement the packages

You can use a UML deployment diagram to illustrate the results of this step.

Deployment Diagrams

A deployment diagram illustrates how the system will be physically distributed onto hardware. A simple single-user PC-based system will have a trivial deployment diagram. However, with the advent of Java, applets and the Java database interface JDBC, as well as facilities for enterprise development (such as the Java Message API and Java Transaction Service as well as the Java Naming Directory Interface), all three tiers in a "Web-deployed" client–server system may need to be designed. The deployment diagram for such a system might resemble that in Figure 50.1.

The elements in Figure 50.1 are called nodes. They represent processors (PCs and Server) and devices (Printer and Fax). A node is thus a resource in the real world upon which we can distribute and execute elements of the (logical) design model. A node is drawn as a three-dimensional rectangular solid with no shadows. The <<device>> stereotype designation of the Fax and Printer indicates that these nodes are not processors, that is, they do not have any processing ability (from the point of view of the model being constructed). You can also show how many nodes are likely to be involved in the system. Thus the Order Entry PC is of order * (0 or more), but there is exactly one server, printer, fax etc. Finally, the diagram also shows the roles of the associations between nodes and their stereotype. For example, the *Receiving* association on one PC uses a type of ISDN connection (which has yet to be specified).

Managing Data Stores

You must identify appropriate data stores for both internal and external data. This involves identifying the complexity of the data, the size of the data, the type of access to the data (single or multiple users), access times and portability. Having considered

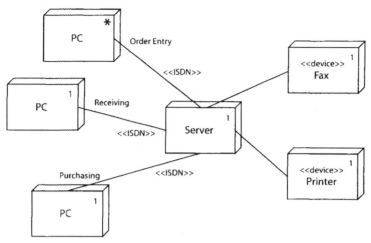

Figure 50.1 A deployment diagram.

these issues, you can make decisions about whether data can be held in internal memory or on secondary storage devices, and whether it should be held in flat file, relational or object database systems. Such considerations are not specific to object-oriented systems and so are not considered in detail here. The following issues should be considered when selecting an appropriate approach to data storage:

- *Data persistence.* Does data need to be persistent? If so, then files, serialization or a database must be considered.

- *Purchase cost.* If your systems requires a database system then it is likely that this will increase the cost of the system. It may also involve licensing agreements in order that you can redistribute the DBMS to your users' systems.

- *Lifecycle cost.* This reflects costs such as purchase, development, deployment, operating and maintenance costs. For example, files have no purchase cost but may have high development and maintenance costs. A database system, by contrast, may have a high purchase cost but lower development and maintenance costs.

- *Amount of data.* The more data you have the more carefully you need to think about how it should be stored, access times etc.

- *Performance.* In-memory storage will provide the fastest data access, while files are likely to provide the poorest performance for all but the smallest amounts of data. Note that techniques such as serialization make life easy for the programmer but provide poor performance.

- *Extensibility.* How easy will it be to extend your application in the future given the method of data storage selected?

- *Concurrent access.* If you need to take concurrent access into account you may need to consider the use of a database system.

- *Crash recovery.* If this is important, you need to think about how you will recover from a system crash (for example by providing backup files or by using the crash recovery facilities of a database system).

- *Distribution.* Will the data need to be distributed among a number of sites? If so, careful thought needs to be given to this issue. Some database systems provide facilities for replicating data across multiple sites.

Handling Access to Global Resources

The system designer must identify what global resources are required and how access to them can be controlled. Global resources include processors, disk drives, disk space and workstations, as well as files, classes and databases.

Choosing the Implementation of Control in Software

The choice of the internal control mechanism used by the system is mediated by the facilities provided by the implementation language. For example, Ada supports concurrent tasks but Visual Basic does not. Smalltalk and Java support lightweight processes and can be said to mimic concurrent systems. The choices available for implementation of control are:

- *Procedure-oriented systems.* Such a system represents a procedure-calling mechanism in which the flow of control is passed from one procedure or method to another when the first calls the second. This type of control tends to be favoured for applications that lack a substantial user interface (or for parts of an application that are remote from the user interface).
- *Event-driven systems.* This is the approach taken by the dynamic model of the analysis phase. Essentially, operations are triggered by events that are received by objects. Many window-based interfaces operate in this manner. This type of control tends to be used for applications that require a polished user interface (and is the control used by Java's GUI facilities and for JavaBeans).
- *Concurrent systems.* In these the system exists in several processes that execute at the same time. Some synchronization between the processes may take place at certain times, but for the majority of the time they are completely separate. This approach tends to be used across applications (for example in client–server architectures) rather than within a single application.

Handling Boundary Conditions

There are three primary boundary situations that the designer should consider:

- Initialization involves setting the system into an appropriate, clean, steady state.
- Termination involves ensuring that the system shuts down in an appropriate manner.
- Failure involves dealing cleanly with unplanned termination of the system.

Setting Trade-Offs Between Competing Resources

In any design, there are various trade-offs to be made (for example the trade-off between speed of access and data storage is a common one in database systems). The larger the number of indexes used, the faster data retrieval can be; however; the indexes must be stored along with the data. Such design trade-offs must be made with regard to the system as a whole (including non-software issues), as sub-optimal decisions are made if they are left to designers concentrating on a single package.

Specifying Default Policies for the Object Design

Some of the issues that should be considered include:

- *Associations.* Choose a basic approach to designing associations that should only be deviated from for specific and justifiable reasons.
- *Null values.* Ensure that common values are used to indicate a null value. For example, in Java the null value of an integer instance variable is 0, while that for a reference variable (one containing an object) is the special value *null.*
- *Role names.* What a role name is converted into in the design is open to interpretation. Specify the approach to be taken.
- *Attribute names.* Specify any conventions to be used with attribute names.
- *Derived data.* Specify a policy for computing derived data (for example when needed or cached in advance). This policy can specify the conditions for either a lazy or future approach.

50.2.2 The Online ATM System Design

In this section we consider the system design of the online ATM. Not all of the issues identified above are relevant to this system, particularly as we are actually designing a prototype system rather than a fully operational system. For this reason, a number of issues are not considered, for example deploying the system onto distributed hardware.

Organizing the System into Subsystems.

As the online ATM system is relatively straightforward there is really only one subsystem, the ATM system. However, we will separate the GUI from the body of the main system. This is because the GUI part of the system will represent a substantial implementation in its own right. In reality there might also be a storage package to handle the maintenance of customer and employee records. However, we will ignore this issue for our example. Given that we have identified these two packages we need to decide how they interact. The basic options are client–server and peer-to-peer.

Table 50.1 presents an evaluation of the two candidate architectures based on some of the criteria presented earlier. Although the absolute values are not significant, the relative positions of the two architectures are. As we do not need a peer-to-peer relationship and client–server packages are easier to implement, we shall select a client–server architecture. Thus the subsystem diagram for the online ATM is that illustrated in Figure 50.2.

Identifying Concurrency

In a real online ATM concurrent access would be an issue. However, in this simple prototype we do not consider concurrency.

Table 50.1 Evaluating rival architectures

Criteria	Weight	Client–server	Peer-to-peer
Ease of use	10	5	5
Development effort	10	10	5
Performance	5	10	10
Integrity	10	10	7
Security	10	5	5
Total score		350	270

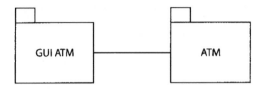

Figure 50.2 The subsystem architecture.

Allocating Subsystems to Processors

Again for the simple prototype we will assume that the whole system is running on a single processor within a single process.

Managing Data Stores

We can consider each of the issues identified above for data storage:

- *Data peristence*. Transient data does need to be persistent. If a deposit is made into a customer's account, this needs to be recorded so that that money is available at a later date.
- *Purchase cost*. As this is a prototype system this is a significant issue. We therefore wish to keep the purchase cost to a minimum. For a real system a budget for purchasing a suitable data storage system might well be available.
- *Life cycle cost*. Again, as this is a prototype system we are not concerned with life cycle cost. For a real-world system such as that of an online ATM, it would be a significant consideration.

The remaining issues can all be treated in the same manner as the life cycle cost. That is, for our prototype system they are not an issue, but for a real-world system, they would all require careful analysis.

The conclusion we can make from this is that flat ASCII text files are probably sufficient for our current needs.

Handling Access to Global Resources.

The only global resource in our prototype online ATM is the ATM system itself. In this system only one user can be logged on at a time. Thus the resource is only available when no user is logged on.

Choosing the Implementation of Control.

The primary choices available are procedure calling, event-driven or concurrent. We have already dismissed concurrency, leaving us with procedure calling and event-driven. As we intend to implement the system in Java, it is a good idea to consider any constraints imposed on us by the language. By default a Java GUI exploits an event-driven control mechanism, as exemplified by the delegation event model of the JDK 1.1 specification of Java. However, once the appropriate event listener calls a method on a particular object, a method-calling (for this read procedure-calling) form of control is instigated. Therefore in our online ATM system we are likely to employ both the event-driven mechanism (for the user interface package) and a method-calling mechanism (for the main ATM package).

Boundary Conditions

We shall consider two boundary conditions for the online ATM as, for a prototype, we are not concerned with a failure condition. For the initialization condition, the system must load information on its customers and users from a file. If no file is available default test data will be used.

For the termination condition, the system must save up-to-date data on its customers and users. Before doing this it should make a backup of any existing data files.

The data files should exist in the same directory as the class files of the online ATM and should be called `customers.data` and `users.data`.

Default Policies for the Object Design.

For the object design these guidelines are provided:

- *Associations.* These will be treated as references from one object to another unless an association is expected to possess data or operations. In this latter case the association will be treated as a link object.
- *Null values.* All variables should be initialized to their appropriate (Java) null value. Note that instance variables are automatically initialized; however, local variables are not.
- *Role names.* These will be treated as the names of instance variables in the appropriate objects that hold the associated reference.
- *Attribute and operation names.* Standard Java conventions will be used for these.

50.2.3 Object Design Stage

The object design essentially takes the models produced by the analysis phase and fleshes them out ready for the implementation. Thus the objects identified during the analysis act as skeletons for the design.

The designer must now consider how the analysis objects (partitioned into packages) should be implemented. They must express the operations in terms of algorithms that can be implemented, and the associations as appropriate references from one object to another (taking into account the type of facilities provided by the target language). You may need to introduce new classes to deal with aspects that are important for the design (and, ultimately, the implementation), but are not significant for the analysis.

The designer performs the following steps during the object design:

1. Combine the three models to obtain operations on the classes.
2. Design algorithms to implement operations.
3. Optimize access paths to data.
4. Implement control for external interactions.
5. Adjust class structure to increase inheritance.
6. Design associations.
7. Determine object representation.
8. Package classes and associations into modules.

Combining the Models

If the implied operations from the dynamic and functional models have not been added to the object model, you should add them now. In doing this you may need to identify new classes, associations or attributes – this is quite normal, and as long it is done in a principled manner should not pose a significant problem.

Designing Algorithms

You must express each of the DFDs or pseudocode methods in the functional model as a programmable algorithm that indicates how it performs the function. The DFD or pseudocode method should have stated what was required; the algorithm says in detail how it does it. For example, the pseudocode method might have stated that some data needed to be sorted; it is only now that a definition of that sorting routine is required. A bubble sort algorithm or an insertion sort may be used. It is up to the designer to determine the requirements of this algorithm and select the most appropriate. The algorithm designer must:

- Choose algorithms that minimize the cost of implementing operations.
- Select data structures appropriate to the algorithms.
- Define new internal classes and operations as necessary.
- Assign responsibility for operations to appropriate classes.

Notice that any algorithms defined in pseudocode during the analysis phase were intended to explain the required functionality. It is therefore necessary at this stage to consider which algorithms are required in the implementation.

Optimizing the Design

The analysis model only described the application and its requirements and did not attempt to take into account efficient access to information or processing. You must consider the following issues:

- adding redundant associations to minimize access cost and maximize convenience

- rearranging the computation for greater efficiency
- saving derived attributes to avoid recalculation of complicated expressions

You may also wish to start to identify attributes which were not part of the analysis model but which will be needed for the implementation. Do not go as far as specifying implementation detail attributes (these should be left to the implementation phase).

Implementing Control

During the system design, an approach for handling the internal control of the system must have been identified. That approach is fleshed out here. This includes determining how to implement the selected approach and identifying any constraints this choice imposes on the design.

Adjusting Class Structure

As the design progresses, the class hierarchy is likely to change, evolve and become refined. It is quite common to produce a design and then rearrange it in the light of commonalties that were hidden at an earlier stage. You should:

- rearrange and adjust classes and operations to increase inheritance
- abstract common behaviour out of groups of classes
- use delegation to share behaviour when inheritance is semantically invalid

Designing Associations

Associations are an important aspect of the analysis object model. However, they are conceptual relationships and not implementation-oriented relationships. You need to consider how the associations can be implemented in a given language. The choices made for representing associations may be made globally for the whole system, locally to a package, or on an association by association basis. The criteria used for determining how associations should be represented in the design are based on how are they traversed. If they are traversed in only one direction, then a pointer representation may be sufficient. However, if they are bi-directional an intermediate object may best represent the association.

Determining Object Representation

In most situations, it is relatively straightforward to identify how to represent an object if you are using an object-oriented programming language such as Java. However, even when using a language such as Java there are some cases in which you must consider whether to use a system primitive or an object. For example, Java has the basic types `int` and `char`, but it also has classes `Integer` and `Character`.

Packaging Classes

The system is decomposed into logical packages in the system design. However, different languages provide different facilities for the physical packaging of a system. For example, Java provides packages whereas Smalltalk does not.

50.2.4 The Online ATM Object Design

This section summarizes the process by which the design of the online ATM is fleshed out ready for implementation. As even the prototype online ATM is a significant piece of work, space precludes the elaboration of every detail of the design process (this could be a large part of a dedicated object-oriented design book). However, it is hoped that you will at least gain an appreciation of the process.

Combine the Three Analysis Models

The complete object model produced from this combination of models is presented in Figure 50.3. A number of the "setup" operations identified during the analysis phase have been omitted. This is because they will be provided by Java constructors and so are not listed as operations/methods. Of course it is very important that they are documented. These constructors have therefore been added to the data dictionary entry for the class and described in the associated class description. Note

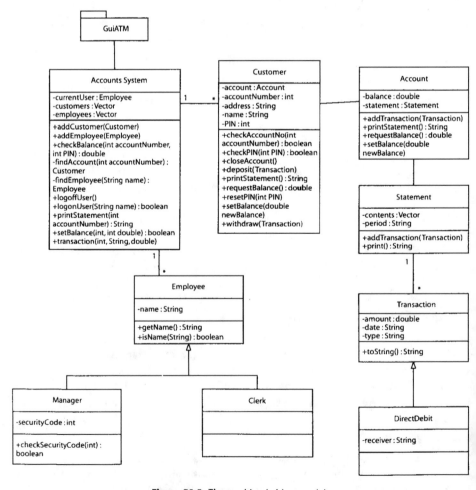

Figure 50.3 The combined object model.

this implies that the descriptions of the classes and the data dictionary have been evolving with the design.

You might also note from Figure 50.3 that we have identified the visibility of all variables and methods. We have also determined the types of variables as well as the parameters and return values of the methods. In addition, we have taken into account how the multiplicity of the links to the customer and employee objects will be handled. In this case we have decided to use Vectors as they represent growable collections of objects. Note that we have started to take into account the facilities provided by our target language. It is natural to do this at this stage.

Designing Algorithms

In general, for the online ATM this involves examining the pseudocode definitions in the functional model and expanding any references to undefined functions (such as "sort the list") or to methods provided by other objects which were not examined in the functional model. Note that, at this stage, we are still considering the algorithms and not the actual implementation.

In the online ATM the place where this step is most obvious is in the ATM-GUI package. It is only at this stage that consideration is given to the generation of panels, the display of panels and the definition of event listeners. Part of the structure of the GUI is illustrated in Figure 50.4 with the algorithmic definition of the action-Performed(ActionEvent) method for the MainPanelController illustrated in Figure 50.5. Note that the ATM object is a convenience object which will contain the public static void main() method and will instantiated the GuiAtm object (thus triggering off the application).

Optimizing the Design

As this is a prototype online ATM, no attempt was made to optimize the design for performance etc. Clarity was considered more important.

Implementing Control

Given the decision made in the system design to allow the GUI to use an event-driven mechanism and the ATM to use a method-calling mechanism, it is necessary to determine how these two control mechanisms interact. We shall adopt an approach based on the Model–View–Controller model and treat the GUI as the View and Controller elements and the Accounts System as the Model. Thus the model is unaware of what is calling its methods, while the GUI is not expected to do anything other than call the appropriate methods on the account system object and display the result.

Adjusting the Class Structure

If we examine the classes in the online ATM there are only a few places in which additional inheritance could be employed. For example, an abstract class Person could be defined. This class could define that a person has a name and methods to get and test the name of a person. This class could then be the parent class of customer and employee. The only other area in which the structure of the system could be

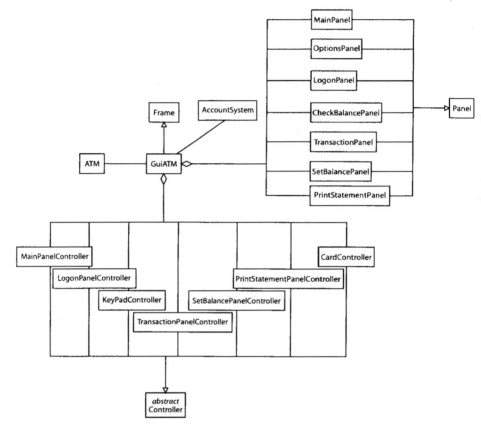

Figure 50.4 The objects in the GUI of the online ATM.

```
MainPanelController :: actionPerformed(ActionEvent e)
return void
  if balance action then
    atm#showCheckBalancePanel();
  else if action is transaction then
    atm#showTransactionPanel();
  else if action is logon then
    atm#showLogonPanel();
  else if action is logoff then
    atm#logoff();
  else if action is set balance then
    atm#showSetBalancePanel();
  else if action is print statement then
    atm#showPrintStatementPanel();
  endif
```

Figure 50.5 The action performed method of the MainPanelController.

modified is the GUI. In here the controllers could be made inner classes of the main GUI class, thus simplifying the access of date and methods. However, for the simple online ATM we will make no changes, as we wish to adopt clarity as our overriding design principle.

Designing associations

In the online ATM, all link associations will be implemented by references as no link variables or methods have been identified. The inheritance associations will be implemented by the "extends" inheritance mechanism in Java.

Determining Object Representation.

In the online ATM the object instantiation mechanism in Java will be used to create instances. Primitive types will be used where possible as they are more efficient than their object counterparts. Otherwise everything else will be an object.

50.3 Implementation Phase

50.3.1 Implementing an Object Design

OMT states that implementation is "an extension of the design process" and that "writing code should be straightforward, almost mechanical, because all the difficult decisions should already have been made".

However, implementation still tends to pose unexpected design problems which you must solve. These decisions should be subject to, and determined by, the processes described above. Because of this, OMT places a limited amount of emphasis on the implementation phase, concentrating instead on stylistic points.

You should treat the implementation of an object-oriented system in just the same way as you would treat the implementation of any software system. This means that it should be subject to, and controlled by, the same processes as any other implementation. In addition it should be subjected to similar testing. This is where the use cases may come back into play. They can help to identify suitable test scenarios.

50.3.2 Implementation of the Online ATM

Many implementation issues have not been covered, such as the use of the classes `Date` and `DateFormat` to provide the string representing the date of a transaction. We also need to identify which classes require a `toString()` method so that an appropriate string representation of an object can be provided.

50.4 Summary

OMT concentrates the majority of its guidance on the analysis phase; the design and implementation phases are far less well supported. It is, however, one of the most widely used object-oriented design methods and is likely to have a very large influence on any method developed by Booch, Rumbaugh and Jacobson to support the UML. It is hoped that the last few chapters have provided you with an appreciation of object-oriented design. You are now ready to delve further into this huge subject!

Part 5

The Future

51 *The Future for Java*

51.1 Introduction

It is always difficult to predict the future of the computer industry. Had I been writing in 1994, I would not have predicted the emergence of a new object-oriented language which could well come to dominate the object-oriented programming market. This chapter is therefore divided into a number of sections. The first considers the developments which are likely to occur to the Java language and the Java environment. The next section considers the influence and effect of the Internet and the World Wide Web. The following section considers Java's role as an educational tool (rather than as an industrial-strength development language) and the final section predicts a little of what might happen over the next five years.

51.2 The Java Language

This section considers the likely (immediate) developments in the Java language. At present Java is developing at such a pace that, since I began using Java, I have already had to rewrite significant parts of applications three times in order to use the latest facilities. This has happened with the move from JDK 1.0.2 to 1.1. Most recently it has happened with the introduction of the Swing set of components in JDK 1.2. This section thus only attempts to predict what will happen in the very near future to Java.

51.2.1 Language Developments

Fundamental changes to the Java language are likely to be held to a minimum. This is because nobody wants to rewrite their applications just because they have obtained the latest release of the JDK (or other vendors' compilers and virtual machines). However, there is scope for new features to be added to the language without affecting existing programs. This is because there are some reserved words which are not yet used (for example generic, const, future and volatile are not currently used). They could provide a number of extensions. Some language additions are likely, such as more powerful packaging and package versioning (initial version control has already been added to JDK 1.2). These are relatively easy to add and could be straightforward to use. However, the Java language aims to be (relatively) simple and clean, so more complex structures such as templates are unlikely to be added in the short term. Other omissions from Java, such as enumerated types that possess an explicit order, may also be added.

Language Standardization

Java is likely to stabilize in the very near future, even given the above discussion. Indeed, work is already under way to produce an ISO standard for Java. In 1995, ISO/IEC JTC 1 launched a program whereby an organisation could act as a submitter of a Publicly Available Specification (PAS) to enable the rapid approval of international standards.

In March 1997, Sun applied to JTC 1 to become a recognized PAS submitter for Java. Although there were some initial problems, Sun has now been accepted as a PAS submitter for Java (and the APIs which are currently stable) as the initial Java standard. Such a standard would be extremely important for establishing Java as a business-critical application language, as it would take it out of the control of a single firm. It would also help deter those few organizations who are attempting to produce their own versions of Java (and thus reduce its ability to be "write once, run anywhere"). Information on the JTC 1 can be found on the Web via ANSI (at `http://www.ansi.org/`).

GUI Developments

Once a Java standard is in place, it will be more difficult to change the language. It is therefore likely that new features will be added in the form of class libraries (such as the AWT and JDBC) or via the Java Beans mechanism. However, a new feature in JDK 1.2, the Java extensions architecture, also makes third-party extensions easier to add on and include in the environment (so expect to see more of these).

Existing class libraries will be refined and extended. This has already been illustrated by developments in the AWT between versions 1.0, 1.0.2 and 1.1 of the JDK. This process was continued with Swing and JDK 1.2.

As anyone who has tried to use the AWT knows, its facilities were rather limited and many development environments provide superior GUI-building components. In response, Sun developed (along with Netscape and IBM) the Java Foundation Classes (JFC), which of course include the Swing set of GUI components. These classes were intended to be a comprehensive set of tools for defining the look and feel of Java applications and applets. Developments such as Swing will continue in Java (indeed, the JFC as it stands is merely the first incarnation; it is expected to develop and grow). The result is that the developer should have a much more powerful set of GUI component tools.

New APIs

If one examines the range of APIs available for Java just from Sun it is staggering. However, further class libraries are likely to be provided as and when needs are identified. For example, the Media APIs provide a whole host of facilities for 3D, Animation and Telephony which were previously unheard of. Similarly, the development of the security API is likely to continue.

At present, the JDBC provides an interface between Java and relational databases (via the ODBC interface). This will be extended to support object databases, allowing Java to work with both industry-standard relational databases and object databases.

Native Code Interface

The native code interface may yet undergo change, as it has already done between versions 1.1 and 1.2 as well as previous releases of the JDK. Such changes may lead to modification of any Java-to-native interfaces and possibly to recompilation of the native source code. Such changes will aim to improve the performance of the Java-to-native code interface.

51.2.2 Technology Issues

There are a number of technology-based issues which will affect Java's popularity in the coming years. These are less related to Java itself and more to the way in which software is, and will be, developed. The majority of software today is developed for use on PCs running either Windows 95/98, Windows NT or Windows 3.x. Therefore Java needs to be able to interact easily and simply with these environments. For example, explicit support for OLE and dynamically linked libraries is a must. This is beginning to happen with the recent release of a JavaBeans bridge to ActiveX.

Object sharing and notification must be made significantly easier. This is being addressed to some extent by the Java Naming and Directory Interface (JNDI). CORBA, while providing a possible infrastructure for such object sharing, results in large cumbersome ORBs (see Ben-Natan (1995) for a summary of the CORBA standard and Orfali *et al.* (1995) for an excellent compendium of distributed object technology, including OLE, OpenDoc and CORBA). Simpler and easier to use solutions which suit the requirements of less technically complex systems are needed, such as a database server which is accessed by a small number of interacting Java clients.

Improved support for deploying applications is also required. Although the JAR facility allows you to deploy the .class files as a single tar file over the Web, this is not really an acceptable format in which to release commercial application software to end users. Some way of packaging the required .class files is required.

Java needs analysis tools like QAC for C and C++. These tools analyze a software system to identify whether any known faults, poor style or weaknesses exist in the language. Such tools tend only to appear once experience has been gained with a language (and the poor style, bugs or weaknesses become known). It will therefore be some time before these tools are available for Java. However, the need for such tools is probably greater now than at any time in the future, due to the relative lack of experience available in the language.

Improved debugging tools (compared with the jdb) are required. These are already available in development tools such as Microsoft's J++ and Symantec's VisualCafé. However, it would be extremely useful if Sun were to make such a debugger available with its JDK.

Since JDK 1.1.6 Sun has also bundled a Just-In-Time (or JIT) interpreter with the JDK. This run-time provides greatly enhanced performance (compared with the standard Java Virtual Machine). In addition, Sun is also producing the "HotSpot" Virtual Machine. This technology has, claims Sun, the potential to enable Java to run as fast as compiled C++. It will thus eliminate the trade-off between performance and portability. If this new technology can supply such performance, then it will surely propel Java into the forefront as the language of choice for full-scale deployed applications.

Even if the HotSpot technology is as good as predicated, there will still need to be support for native compilers. There are many applications which cannot accept the performance overhead imposed by the Java run-time interpreter (or any interpreter, including JIT). Such applications need to be able to compile Java into a directly executable format. They are unlikely to be used with the Web and will therefore not be concerned with the implications that this has for portability (of the executable). A number of companies already supply such compilers, as discussed earlier in this book, and this trend is likely to grow.

51.3 The Web and Objects

The World Wide Web is one of the phenomena of the last few years. It has revolutionized the way we think about computers and computing. The Web has already evolved significantly from the days when most information available on the Web was in the form of static Web pages. They were useful for providing information, but were fairly limited in their ability to do much more. Java, of course, allows Web pages to possess some dynamic element, and already Java is moving away from the animated cartoon character applet and into the domain of Web interfaces to legacy and other enterprise applications. This trend is likely to continue, and the Web will become more and more commercial (in its content).

Java, of course, has already guaranteed that object technology will play an important role in the development of such applications. Java is in many ways just another object-oriented language, which, like Smalltalk, is not compiled into an executable but into byte codes which are then "executed" by an interpreter (or virtual machine). Any Java applet is an object or set of objects which communicate with each other via message-passing. These applets should be capable of communicating, relatively easily, with a distributed object system. Indeed developments are already under way to link Java applets to CORBA-compliant ORBs and to OLE/COM.

To simplify this sort of task, special object-oriented Web site development tools have been (and are being) developed. It is also likely that many of the existing object-oriented CASE tools will provide Web additions so that they too can be used for Web development.

However, which language will dominate, and which type of distributed system will be adopted, are two different questions. Java will certainly be the dominant Web language, although there is no great reason why Java should be any better as a Web language than Smalltalk or any other interpreted object-oriented language such as Objective-C or Eiffel, other than the fact that Java got there first and has the backing of both Netscape and Sun.

The question of which distributed object technology will be adopted is more complex. OMG would certainly like CORBA to be adopted as the accepted standard, while Microsoft would prefer their own OLE/COM infrastructure standard. An open question is what will Netscape do? It is probable that Netscape will do both. Sun has already linked Java with CORBA and Sun and Netscape are closely linked, but a great deal of the world uses Microsoft products.

51.4 Object-Oriented Databases and the Web

Web developments are not only based around a variety of different data types, they also require the ability to navigate easily around data in a domain model. Many object-oriented database vendors (as well as many users) are coming to the conclusion that object-oriented databases are ideal for supporting an HTTP server. By storing the Web site within the object-oriented database the process of exchanging data with the database and modifying the Web pages is simplified.

This trend is likely to increase significantly in the future. Other object-oriented database suppliers are already adding Java interfaces or making their systems Web-compliant. The Web is also likely to act as the motivating force which will force many organizations to adopt object-oriented (as opposed to relational) database technology.

51.5 JavaStation, JavaOS and HotJava Views

Sun Microsystems have not just produced a portable language which can be used for building standalone applications or Web-based applets. They have also produced microprocessors which are optimized for the Java language, used these to produce Network Computers (NCs) called JavaStations, developed a JavaOS operating system for use with these (and other) computers and implemented a Web-top environment called HotJava Views.

The development of each of the above is significant and means that Java and object technology will continue to be adopted at an astonishing rate. Enterprises that would not have considered moving to a new-fangled language will find that they do so naturally as part of moving to a network-oriented culture. The multi-layered approach of Sun (providing environments and operating systems which can run on various hardware platforms as well as hardware) enables organizations to migrate to the new technology as and when they need to and can afford to. The enabling technologies, all of which exploit or support Java, are considered briefly below.

51.5.1 JavaChips

Sun will initially provide three Java processors as part of the JavaChips family. These three processors are to be called picoJava, microJava and UltraJava.

The picoJava chip provides direct Java byte code execution. Which gives an excellent cost-to-performance ratio for Java applications. It is already available and is intended to be used in NCs, PDAs and low-cost/low-power consumer appliances (such as smart phones). This is ironic, as this was where the Oak language (Java's original incarnation) originally came in.

The microJava chip (which is expected to be available at the end of 1998) builds on the picoJava specification by adding application-specific I/O, memory, communications and control functions. It is intended for use in low-cost network appliances as well as NCs and PDAs.

The UltraJava chip represents the high end of the market. It is intended as a high-performance Java processor providing support for VIS (Visual Instruction Set) technology. The intended markets for this chip include NC, 3D graphics and imaging applications, and entertainment systems.

From this range of JavaChips, you can see that Sun intends to provide microprocessors for all types of situations, allowing Java to become the language of choice for a huge range of applications.

51.5.2 JavaStation

The JavaStation is an NC which is intended for use with Java applications. It is a thin client (it provides limited local processing power, no local storage – although local hard disks are likely to be included to improve performance – and limited memory) which is designed to work seamlessly with the Internet and intranets, thus reducing the administrative load on network administrators.

JavaStations were primarily conceived as meeting the needs of task-specific users. These are users who tend to spend their entire day using a single application (or a small group of related applications). Such users include data entry clerks, airline reservations clerks and bank tellers. Sun estimates that 50% of enterprise computing users fall into this category. At present such users tend to use low-end, superseded PCs (such as 386 and 486 machines) or IBM 3270 class terminals. Such users are likely to need to upgrade their systems in the near future as enterprise applications are moved to the intranet.

Sun intends the initial cost of a JavaStation to be much less than the cost of upgrading to a Pentium-based PC. Indeed, Sun has indicated its intent to target this market by providing a 3270 terminal emulator for JavaStations and by providing an easy to use, Web-top environment, which simplifies the use of local and remote applications. This environment is called HotJava Views. In addition, JavaStations will be able to access legacy Windows-based applications.

It is worth noting that the hype surrounding JavaStations has been huge over the last year or so (1997–1998), but that the reality of a JavaStation on millions of office (and potentially home) desks is a long way from being realized. That is not to say the JavaStations won't be very successful, but as yet they have still to prove themselves. However, their primary rival, the NetPC (a low-end, low-cost PC which is preconfigured for the Internet), appears to have died a death at this stage; JavaStations may still inherit the Internet.

51.5.3 JavaOS

The JavaOS operating system has been developed by Sun to take advantage of both the features of the Java language and to make the Internet or intranet available as simply and as easily as possible on a range of computers (including the JavaStation). JavaOS is a small and efficient operating system that can execute Java applications directly and provides inherent support for networking. At present, it has been ported to the SPARC processor, the x86 family of processors and the StrongARM processor. It is currently being licensed by hardware and software companies who are actively porting it to other processors. It will therefore be possible to install JavaOS on a range of computers, thus providing a Java-enabled environment on existing equipment. The intention is that users can migrate to dedicated JavaStations by first migrating their environment and then their hardware. It also means that PC, NCs etc. can all be used in the same way, using the same software, transparently, on a network.

JavaOS has an architecture consisting of various components:

- The *JavaOS Microkernel* handles booting, interrupt handling, multiple threads, traps, DMA, executing multiple applets etc.
- The *Java Virtual Machine*, like the JVM provided with the JDK, executes Java byte codes. This version of the JVM extends the memory model to optimize memory usage and accommodate low-memory conditions.
- The *JavaOS device drivers* (all written in Java) allow access to system devices.
- *JavaOS Graphics* handles all common graphic operations such as drawing lines and filling boxes.
- *JavaOS Windowing System* deals with displaying windows and user interface components such as buttons and menus. Together, the JavaOS Graphics and Windowing Systems directly support the Java AWT facilities.
- *JavaOS network classes* provide support for TCP/IP, UDP and ICMP protocols. They also provide facilities that support network addresses and eliminate client administration.

JavaOS, including the HotJava environment, requires 4 Mbyte of disk space (or ROM) and 4 Mbyte of memory. JavaOS and HotJava use less than 2.5 Mbyte, leaving more than 1.5 Mbyte to handle caching of pages, images or applications.

51.5.4 HotJava Views

HotJava Views is a Web-top environment for NCs and PCs which allows applications to be viewed via a common interface, no matter where they are located, or where they run. HotJava Views 1.0 provides an email client, a calendar, name directory access and Web-browsing capabilities. It also supports Java applications.

You can use HotJava Views within the JavaOS environment or on any system that supports the Java Virtual Machine. You can, therefore, use the same Web-top on a JavaStation and a Pentium PC.

One of HotJava Views's most radical features is that it can save the state of the users' environment when they exit. This means that the next time they log on, they can resume from where they left off (even if they were in the middle of running an application). As HotJava Views saves this state information remotely, users can log on to any NC machine and obtain their own Web-top. This is akin to logging on to a PC in another office and finding your own hard disk and environment setting appear!

HotJava 1.0 runs solely on top of JavaOS; however, HotJava Views 2.0 will be fully platform-independent and will run on servers that contain the Java Virtual Machine.

51.6 Java as a Training Language

Far too many people believe that it is possible to move from a procedural development language, such as C, to an object-oriented language just by reading a book on C++. The result is that they develop C programs but maintain their data in objects. I have been involved in discussions with developers who have claimed that object technology is a waste of time because they did not accrue the benefits claimed. When pressed, it is almost always the case that they failed to invest in appropriate training for their staff. This was their mistake.

The transition to object technology is not an easy one. Indeed it becomes harder the greater the level of experience of those trying to make the change. This does not necessarily have anything to do with their ability to adapt to new ideas; rather, I believe it is to do with the fact that they have a very firm grasp of one paradigm, whereas less experienced software developers have a poorer grasp of, for example, the procedural paradigm.

The first object-oriented development attempted by an organization must include a suitable training budget. This budget needs to be seen as an investment in the future, rather than a cost of the actual project involved. In addition, it should not be seen as a language programming exercise. The best approach is to view it as a training in the philosophy and techniques of object technology. The aim of such training is not necessarily to educate those involved in the use of the tools (such as object-oriented CASE tools and the object-oriented language to be used). Such an approach allows the staff involved to explore the concepts rather than worrying about a particular syntax and how it differs from what they are used to.

Of course, educating software developers in abstract concepts is of limited use; therefore such training courses should reinforce what is being taught with practical experience of a pure object-oriented language such as Java. After all, you cannot write anything in Java without using objects and passing messages. In addition, it is easier to spot conceptual problems in Java (as evidenced by students attempting to write the main program or worrying about procedures rather than objects).

I believe that Java will have a concrete future as an educator as well as a practical object-oriented development language. Indeed, it may have a greater influence as an educational language that allows organizations to migrate to object technologies in as painless a manner as possible.

51.7 Object Technology: the Next Five Years

What will happen to object technology over the next five years? This is both an interesting and a difficult question. Object technology is certainly gaining an ever increasing share of the market for commercially developed systems, however there is still a great deal of resistance to it in many quarters. This resistance is sometimes due to ignorance and sometimes due to bigotry. In either case it requires someone to champion its cause in the affected organizations. However the Web is here, and despite the hype, is likely to be a major factor during the next ten years. Indeed e-commerce is a growing force in the market place and is forcing companies to take Java, object orientation and the web seriously.

Thanks mostly to Java, object technology is seen as the developer's Web technology. This therefore means that much of the development in object technology will be Web-driven (we have already considered some of its effects above). This will probably continue to grow and may have both a positive effect and a detrimental effect. The positive effect will be that many new and existing companies will adopt object technology, many other companies will move to support their requirements and many new companies will be created. Over time, many of these companies will close down again only to be replaced by other small companies. It is within these companies that many of the most innovative ideas will probably be generated (consider Netscape as an example). This will be a very creative and dynamic time.

However, there are two possible results. One is that object technology becomes so successful that one or two very big companies consider it a part of their core business and move into the market with such force that they come to dominate. I have always believed that monopolies (or virtual monopolies) are a bad idea and certainly tend to be bad for any industry. The other concern is that object technology becomes so tightly linked to the Web in people's minds that the technology providers ignore other aspects of the computer world and focus solely on the Web (which I believe would be a mistake). Such a close binding might have a short-term benefit, but let us hope that when the Web bubble bursts or when the next great new thing comes along, object technology is not left behind with the Web and ignored. It is worth noting that Java has already outgrown the Web as a tool with the introduction of initiatives such as EmbeddedJava and PersonalJava. In both cases this is pushing Java into new and innovative markets. For example, think of a situation where your house recognizes you as you walk up to the door, just because of the ring you are wearing – fancy maybe, but may be not. At the 1998 JavaOne conference delegates were provided with a Java ring which was used to uniquely identify them. This ring contained a Java Virtual Machine and Java applications. The delegates could use it to specify the exact makeup of their coffee merely by inserting the ring into the ring reader. It could also be used to identify them for conference details, seminars etc. Java thus opens up a whole new field for modern computers (and object technology with it).

51.9 References

Ben-Natan, R. (1995). *CORBA: A Guide to Common Object Request Broker Architecture.* McGraw-Hill, New York.

Orfali, R., Harkey, D. and Edwards, J. (1995). *The Essential Distributed Objects Survival Guide.* John Wiley, New York.

Appendices

Appendix A *Java 1.1.* Core API Packages*

The JDK provides many packages (JDK 1.1 had 26 packages) and others are being developed (such as the 2D, 3D and Media packages). You must prefix the names of the packages in Table A.1 with `java`.

Table A.1 The Java 1.1 Core API packages

Package name	Contents
`applet`	Applet-related classes
`awt`	Platform-independent windowing classes
`awt.datatransfer`	Support for cut and paste-style operations
`awt.event`	Delegation event model classes
`awt.image`	Image manipulation classes
`awt.peer`	Native windowing facilities classes
`beans`	Beans facilities for developers
`io`	Input and output classes
`lang`	Basic Java classes
`lang.reflect`	Java reflection classes
`math`	`BigDecimal` and `BigInteger` classes
`net`	Java networking facilities
`rmi`	Remote method invocation classes
`rmi.dgc`	Distributed garbage collection
`rmi.registry`	Facilities for mapping names to remote objects
`rmi.server`	Facilities for the server side of RMI
`security`	Java Security for signed applets
`security.acl`	Access control list
`security.interfaces`	Digital Signature Algorithm interface specifications
`sql`	JDBC SOL interface classes
`text`	Internationalization facilities
`util`	General utility classes
`util.zip`	Java archive (JAR) support classes

For further information on these packages, see books such as Chan and Lee (1996) and Gosling and Yellin (1996a,b). Note that Appendices B–H relate to the packages as specified in the JDK 1.1 standard. Appendix I relates to the new packages in the beta release of JDK 1.2.

Chan, P. and Lee, R. (1996). *The Java Class Libraries: An Annotated Reference.* Addison-Wesley, Reading, MA.

Gosling, J. and Yellin, F. (1996a). *The Java Application Programming Interface, Vol. 1: Core Packages.* Addison-Wesley, Reading, MA.

Gosling, J. and Yellin, F. (1996b). *The Java Application Programming Interface, Vol. 2: Window Toolkit and Applets.* Addison-Wesley, Reading, MA.

Appendix B *The java.lang Package*

B.1 Introduction

The java.lang package contains the classes and interfaces which are the basis of the Java environment (as distinct from the Java language). For example, the class Object (the root of all classes) is defined in this package.

This package is automatically imported into every Java program (whether it is an application or an applet). The facilities provided by this package are, therefore, always available. Notice that the errors and exceptions generated directly by the Java Virtual Machine are defined in this package.

Figure B.1 shows the classes and interfaces defined in this package and the relationships between them. A solid line indicates inheritance; a dashed line indicates an implementation; a rectangle indicates a class; and an oval indicates an interface.

B.2 The Classes

The Object class is the root of the class hierarchy. Every class has Object as a superclass. All objects, including arrays, implement the methods of this class.

Boolean The wrapper for the primitive type boolean. It provides methods for working with boolean values and converting boolean values to strings and vice versa.

Character The wrapper for char values. It provides methods for manipulating and converting chars (e.g. from upper case to lower case).

Class Instances represent classes and interfaces in a running Java application. Objects are constructed automatically by the Java Virtual Machine and by calls to the defineClass method in the class loader.

ClassLoader An abstract class, of which subclasses extend the manner in which the Java Virtual Machine dynamically loads classes. The defineclass method converts an array of bytes into an instance of Class.

Compiler Support and related services for Java-to-native-code compilers.

Math Many standard mathematical operations such as tan and cos. To promote portability, the algorithms that implement the mathematical operations must match the output of algorithms available from the network library(netlib) package "Freely Distributable Math Library".

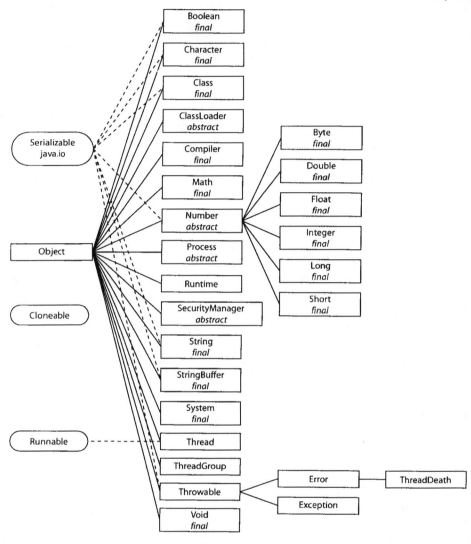

Figure B.1 The java.lang package.

Number An abstract class, which is the superclass of Byte, Double, Float, Integer, Long and Short. Subclasses must provide methods to convert the represented numeric value to byte, double, float, int, long and short.

    Byte The wrapper class for byte values.

    Double The wrapper class for double values.

    Float The wrapper class for float values.

    Integer The wrapper class for int values.

    Long The wrapper class for long values.

    Short The wrapper class for short values.

Process Allows native operating system programs to be run via the exec command (or one of its variants).

Run time Environment and system-related functions such as garbage collection, tracing and library loading.

SecurityManager An abstract class that allows applications to implement their own security policy.

String Character strings which cannot be changed.

StringBuffer Sequences of characters which can be altered. The primary methods used with this class are insert and append.

System A variety of utility methods such as standard input, standard output, and error output streams; access to externally defined properties; and a way of loading files, libraries and interfaces to the Run time class.

Thread Lightweight processes, called threads. A Java program can have multiple, potentially interacting, threads.

ThreadGroup An instance represents a group of threads that can be treated as a single entity.

Throwable The root of all error or exception classes.

    Error Indicator of a serious problem in a program (programs are not expected to catch errors).

        ThreadDeath Although a subclass of Error, it is not really an error condition; it is generated when a thread terminates. You should only need to catch an instance of ThreadDeath if the program performs housekeeping (or similar) activities when a thread terminates.

    Exception The root class of all exception classes in Java.

Void An uninstantiable placeholder that references the primitive Java type void.

B.3 The Interfaces

Serializable Defines the common protocol for objects which can be saved to a file (defined in the java.io package, but implemented by many classes in this package).

Cloneable Indicates that the implementing object can be cloned (i.e. you can copy this object field by field).

Runnable Defines the common protocol for objects which expect to be run in their own thread.

Appendix C *The* `java.util` *Package*

C.1 Introduction

This package provides a variety of utility classes such as `Date` and `Random`, as well as the `Vector` and `HashTable` growable data structures (see Figure C.1). Note that in Java 2 this package also includes the `Collections` classes.

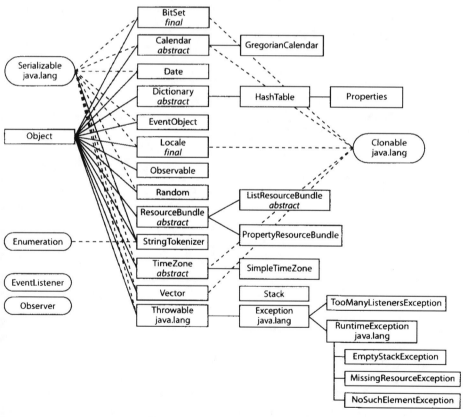

Figure C.1 The `java.util` package.

635

C.2 The Classes

Bitset A growable index of bits (boolean values) which provides logical operators such as or and xor, as well as operations to set and reset bits in the set.

Calendar Provides conversion functions between date objects and integer fields representing dates. Subclasses interpret a date according to the rules of a specific calendar system, for example GregorianCalendar.

Date Represents a particular date and time.

Dictionary An abstract superclass of classes which associate a key with a value (see Hashtable).

EventObject The root for all event objects (for example AWTEvnt).

GregorianCalendar Implements the Gregorian calendar, with AD and BC dates.

Hashtable Implements a traditional hash table.

Locale Represents a region (geographical, political or cultural).

ResourceBundle Contains locale-specific objects which programs can load. The program code can be largely independent of the user's locale; most, if not all, of the locale-specific information is in the resource bundles.

ListResourceBundle An abstract subclass of ResourceBundle which handles resources in a list-oriented manner.

PropertyResourceBundle An abstract subclass of ResourceBundle which handles resources using a set of static strings from a property file.

Observable An abstract superclass of classes that can have observers associated with them and respond to the setChanged and notifyObservers methods.

Properties Instances represent system (and user) properties, such as user name.

Random An instance generates a stream of pseudo-random numbers.

TimeZone Instances represent time zones, such as GMT.

SimpleTimeZone Defines a time zone for use with the GregorianCalendar class.

Stack A basic stack type class, of which instances are growable.

StringTokenizer Instances of this class allow a string to be broken down into tokens identified by delimiters (i.e. space, period etc.).

Vector Implements a growable array of objects.

C.3 The Interfaces

Enumeration Instances which implement this interface generate a series of elements. Successive calls to the nextElement method return successive elements of the series.

EventListener The root of all event listeners.

Observer The common protocol for all classes which wish to take part in an observer–observable dependency relationship.

C.4 The Exceptions

`EmptyStackException` Raised by the stack class when asked to return a value from an empty stack.

`MissingResourceException` Indicates that a resource is missing.

`NoSuchElementException` Raised by a class implementing the `Enumeration` interface when the `nextElement` is sent and there are no remaining elements in the series.

`TooManyListenersException` Thrown when only one listener may be registered on a particular event listener source, and more than one such registration is attempted.

Appendix D *The* `java.io` *Package*

D.1 Introduction

The `java.io` package provides the basic input/output facilities for the Java environment. Primarily, this input/output is built around the use of data streams. For example, to read data from a file a stream is associated with that file and then the data in read from the stream. In general, higher level streams build on lower level streams; thus a data input stream will build on a lower level input stream. The classes defined in this package are illustrated in Figures D.1 and D.2.

D.2 The Classes

`BufferedinputStream, BufferedOutputStream` An input or output stream that does not necessarily make calls to the underlying system for each byte. The data is read or written into a buffer and subsequent accesses use the data in the buffer.

`BufferedReader, BufferedWriter` Read text from (or writes it to) a character stream, buffering characters so as to provide for efficient access to characters, arrays and lines.

`ByteArrayInputStream, ByteArrayOutputStream` Allow an application to create an input (output) stream in which the bytes are supplied by the contents of a byte array.

`CharArrayReader, CharArrayWriter` Instances provide a buffer that can be used as a character input (output) stream.

`DataInputStream, DataOutputStream` Allow an application to read primitive Java data types from an underlying input (output) stream in a machine-independent way.

`File` Instances represent the name of a file or directory on the host file system. Methods allow various file manipulation operations (e.g. deleting or renaming the file; checking permissions and that the file exists).

`FileDescriptor` Instances serve as an opaque handle to the underlying machine-specific structure representing an open file or an open socket. Applications should not create their own file descriptors.

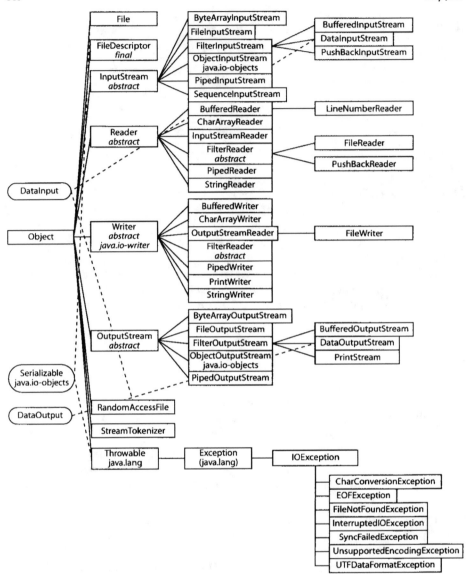

Figure D.1 The `java.io` package.

FileInputStream, FileOutputStream An input (output) stream designed to read data from (write data to) a file.

FileReader, FileWriter Convenience classes for reading (writing) character files.

FilterInputStream, FilterOutputstream Instances allow some filtering of the data being read (written). These streams sit on top of an underlying input (output) stream.

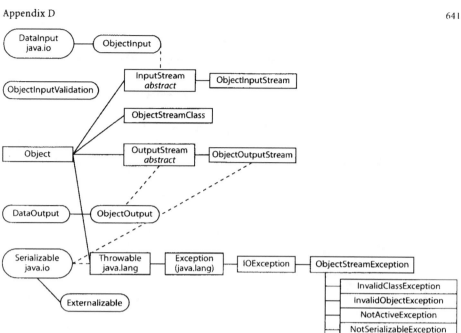

Figure D.2 The object-related `java.io` classes and interfaces.

`FilterReader, FilterWriter` Abstract class for reading (writing) filtered character streams.

`InputStream` Abstract root class of all input streams.

`InputStreamReader` A bridge between byte streams and character streams. It reads bytes and translates them into characters according to a specified character encoding.

`LineNumberReader` A buffered character input stream that keeps track of line numbers (a line is terminated by any one of a line feed, a carriage return, or a carriage return followed immediately by a linefeed).

`ObjectInputStream` Deserializes primitive data and objects previously written using an `ObjectOutputStream`.

`ObjectOutputStream` Serializes primitive data and objects to a file. The information can be restored using an `ObjectInputStream`.

`ObjectStreamClass` Describes a class that can be serialized to a stream. It contains the name and the `serialVersionUID` of the class.

`OutputStream` The abstract root class of all output streams.

`OutputStreamWriter` Instances of this class convert characters to bytes and write them out to a more basic data stream.

`PipedInputStream, PipedOutputstream` Instances provide the source of a communications pipe between two threads (a producer–consumer relationship).

`PipedReader, PipedWriter` Provides a character-based pipe.

`PrintStream` An output stream filter that provides convenient methods for printing types other than bytes and arrays of bytes.

`PrintWriter` Instances print formatted representations of objects to a text output stream.

`PushbackInputStream` An input stream filter that provides a one-byte buffer which allows an application to "unread" the last character that it read. The next time that a read is performed on the input stream filter, the "unread" character is re-read.

`PushbackReader` As for `PushbackInputStream`, except that it is focused on characters rather than bytes.

`RandomAccessFile` An interface to a random access file.

`Reader` The abstract superclass for character readers.

`SequenceInputStream` Instances allow a number of streams to be joined together in sequence and treated as a single stream.

`StreamTokenizer` Allows a stream to be separated into tokens (delimited by a specific character such as a space or a period).

`StringReader, stringwriter` Instances treat a string (as opposed to a file or other data source) as the source (sink) of the stream.

`Writer` The abstract superclass for character writers.

D.3 The Interfaces

`DataInput, DataOutput` Implemented by streams that can read (write) primitive Java data types from (to) a stream in a machine-independent manner.

`Externalizable` Allows a class to specify the methods to be used to write the object's contents to a stream and read them back.

`FilenameFilter` Instances of classes that implement this interface filter filenames.

`ObjectInput, Objectoutput` Extends the `DataInput` (`DataOutput`) interface to include reading (writing) objects.

`ObjectInputValidation` Callback interface that allows validation of objects within a graph (used in serialization).

`Serializable` The protocol that enables an object to be serialized.

D.4 The Exceptions

`CharConversionException` Root class for character conversion exceptions.

`EOFException` End of file.

`FileNotFoundException` The specified file does not exist.

`IOException` Root class of all IO exceptions.

`InterruptedIOException` During either input or output an interrupt occurred.

`InvalidClassException` The serialization run-time detects a problem with a class.

`InvalidObjectException` A deserialized object cannot be made valid.

`NotActiveException` Serialization or deserialization is not active.

`NotSerializableException` The data being written or read is not a serializable object.

`ObjectStreamException` Root class of all object stream exceptions.

`OptionalDataException` There is primitive data in the stream and an object is expected. The length field of the exception indicates the number of bytes that are available in the current block.

`StreamCorruptedException` A stream header is invalid or control information in the stream is not found or is invalid.

`SyncFailedException` A synchronization process has failed.

`UTFDataFormatException` A malformed UTF-8 string has been read in a data input stream or by a class that implements the data input interface.

`UnsupportedEncodingException` The character encoding being used is not supported.

`WriteAbortedException` Thrown when reading a stream terminated by an exception that occurred while the stream was being written.

Appendix E *The* `java.awt` *Package*

E.1 Introduction

The `java.awt` package contains the majority of classes used to create graphical user interfaces (GUIs) and for drawing graphics and images (see Figures E.1 and E.2).

The four other packages associated with the AWT are `java.awt.event` (see Appendix F), `java.awt.image` (see Appendix G), `java.awt.datatransfer` and `java.awt.peer`.

E.2 The Classes

`AWTEvent` The root class for all AWT events.

`AWTEventMulticaster` Implements efficient multi-cast event dispatching for AWT events.

`BorderLayout` A layout manager which can lay components out within a container at five different locations.

`Button` A button component.

`Canvas` A generic component whose subclasses provide the required functionality (i.e. drawing some graphic components).

`CardLayout` A layout manager for a container that contains several "cards". Only one card is visible at a time, allowing you to flip through the cards.

`Checkbox` A graphical component which comprises a label, a toggle and a state.

`CheckboxGroup` An object which associates a set of checkboxes in a radio button-style relationship.

`CheckboxMenuItem` A checkbox that represents a choice in a menu.

`Choice` A button which presents a number of selections.

`Color` RGB colours (e.g. `Color.red` gives the RGB code for red).

`Component` A generic component which acts as the root of all graphic components (e.g. `Button`, `Label`).

`Container` Instances can hold one or more graphic components.

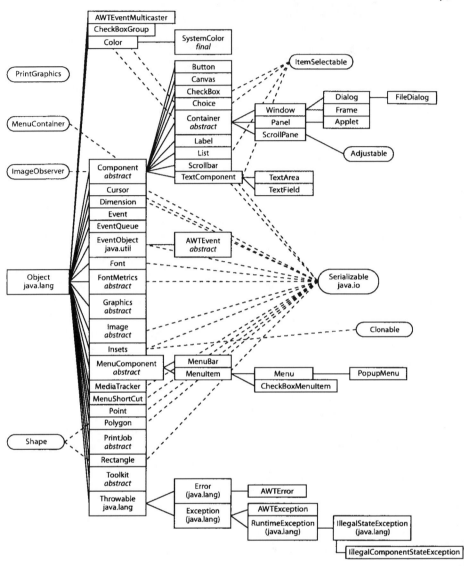

Figure E.1 The `java.awt` package.

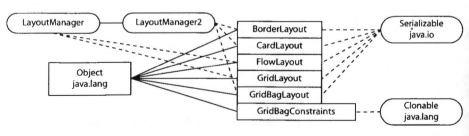

Figure E.2 The layout managers.

Cursor Encapsulates the bitmap representation of the mouse cursor (e.g. crosshair, arrow, hand).

Dialog Instances are simple windows that receive data from a user. They can be modal or non-modal.

Dimension Instances represent a particular dimension in 2D (e.g. a width and a height).

Event A platform-independent class that encapsulates events from the local GUI platform.

EventQueue A platform-independent class that queues events, both from the underlying peer classes and from trusted application classes. There is only one event queue for the system.

FileDialog Defines a file selection dialog appropriate for the current platform, thus removing the need for the user to write a different dialog for each platform. It is a modal dialog.

FlowLayout Arranges components in rows from left to right.

Font Instances represent fonts.

FontMetrics Instances represent font metrics.

Frame A top-level window with a title and zero or more components and containers.

Graphics An abstract class that represents a graphics context onto which graphic elements can be drawn. These elements are then rendered onto the displayed window.

GridBagConstraints Instances specify constraints for components laid out using the GridBagLayout manager.

GridBagLayout A flexible layout manager that aligns components vertically and horizontally, without requiring that the components be the same size. The actual layout is controlled by an associated GridBagConstraints instance.

GridLayout A layout manager that arranges components according to a 2D grid (the size of which is determined when the manager is constructed). Components are placed in equal-sized locations within the grid.

Image An abstract class that is the root of platform-dependent classes used to represent a set of pixel values.

Insets Used to lay out containers.

Label Used to construct textual labels for display within a window.

List Facilities for single (and multiple) selection lists.

MediaTracker Instances manage the loading of images (for example, in the background).

Menu Defines an object on a menu bar.

MenuBar A platform-dependent representation of a menu bar.

MenuComponent The abstract superclass of all components of a menu.

MenuItem An object which can be used as an option on a menu.

MenuShortcut Instances represent keyboard shortcuts for menu items.

Panel A generic container class for components and other containers.

Point Instances represent x and y coordinates in a 2D space.

Polygon Instances represent a series of x and y locations.

PopupMenu A dynamically generated and displayed menu which can pop up at a specific point within a window.

PrintJob An abstract class which initiates and executes a print job. It provides access to a print graphics object which renders to an appropriate print device.

Rectangle Instances represent a rectangle as an x and y point (top left-hand corner), a width and a height.

ScrollPane Can be used with a canvas to provide a scrollable region

Scrollbar Allow a variable's value to be modified within a range.

SystemColor Encapsulates symbolic colours representing the colour of GUI objects on a system.

TextArea A direct subclass of TextComponent that provides a graphical component for displaying and editing multiple lines of text.

TextComponent A generic class that provides a component which allows editable text.

TextField Manages the display (and editing) of a single line of text.

Toolkit An AWT toolkit that binds the abstract AWT classes to a particular native toolkit implementation.

Window A top-level window with no borders and no menu bar. It could be used to implement a pop-up menu.

E.3 The Interfaces

Adjustable The protocol for classes which implement an numeric value contained within a bounded range of values.

ItemSelectable The protocol for objects which contain a set of items of which zero or more can be selected.

LayoutManager The protocol for classes that lay out containers.

LayoutManager2 A protocol for classes that lay out containers based on a layout constraints object. It extends the LayoutManager interface and is intended primarily for tool builders.

MenuContainer The protocol for classes that can contain menus.

PrintGraphics The protocol for classes that can print from a graphics context.

Shape The common protocol for objects that represent some form of geometric shape.

E.4 The Exceptions

AWTException indicates that an AWT exception has occurred.

`IllegalComponentStateException` An AWT component is not in an appropriate state for the requested operation.

E.5 The Errors

`AWTError` A fatal problem from which the AWT cannot recover.

Appendix F
The `java.awt.event` Package

F.1 Introduction

This package defines the classes and interfaces which comprise the delegation event model (see Figure F.1).

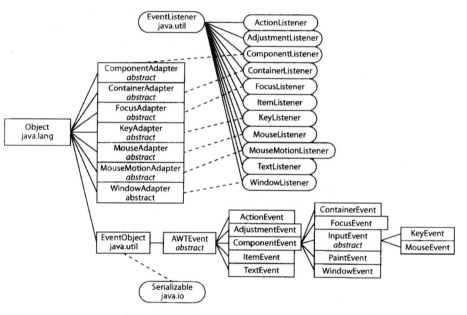

Figure F.1 The `java.awt.event` package.

F.2 The Classes

`ActionEvent` indicates that an action type event has occurred.

`AdjustmentEvent` Indicates that an adjustment event has occurred.

`ComponentAdapter` The adapter which receives component events.

`ComponentEvent` The root event class for all component-level events.

`ContainerAdapter` The adapter which receives container events.

`ContainerEvent` Indicates that a container event has occurred.

`FocusAdapter` The adapter which receives focus events.

`FocusEvent` The component-level focus event.

`InputEvent` Indicates that an input event has occurred.

`ItemEvent` Generated when an item is selected, deselected, expanded or contracted.

`KeyAdapter` The adapter which receives keyboard events.

`KeyEvent` The component-level keyboard event.

`MouseAdapter` The adapter which receives mouse events.

`MouseEvent` Indicates that a mouse event, such as a button being pressed or released, has occurred.

`MouseMotionAdapter` The adapter which receives mouse motion events.

`PaintEvent` The component-level paint event. This event is not designed to be used with the Event Listener model; programs should continue to override paint and update methods in order to render themselves properly.

`TextEvent` The text event emitted by a `TextComponent`.

`WindowAdapter` The adapter which receives window events.

`WindowEvent` The window-level event.

F.3 The Interfaces

`ActionListener` The protocol for receiving action events.

`AdjustmentListener` The protocol for receiving adjustment events.

`ComponentListener` The protocol for receiving component events.

`ContainerListener` The protocol for receiving container events.

`FocusListener` The protocol for receiving focus events.

`ItemListener` The protocol for receiving item events.

`KeyListener` The protocol for receiving keyboard events.

`MouseListener` The protocol for receiving mouse events.

`MouseMotionListener` The protocol for receiving mouse motion events.

`TextListener` The protocol for receiving text events.

`WindowListener` The protocol for receiving window events.

Appendix G
The `java.awt.image` Package

G.1 Introduction

This package defines the classes and interfaces used to create, modify and manipulate images (see Figure G.1).

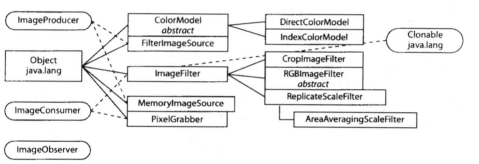

Figure G.1 The `java.awt.image` package.

G.2 The Classes

`AreaAveragingScaleFilter` An `ImageFilter` class for scaling images using a simple area averaging algorithm that produces smoother results than the nearest-neighbour algorithm.

`ColorModel` An abstract class that encapsulates the methods for translating from pixel values to alphabetic red, green and blue colour components for an image.

`CropImageFilter` An `ImageFilter` class for cropping images.

`DirectColorModel` A `ColorModel` class that specifies a translation from pixel values to alphabetic red, green and blue colour components for pixels which have the colour components embedded directly in the bits of the pixel.

`FilteredImageSource` This class is an implementation of the `Image-Producer` interface. It takes an image and a filter object and uses them to produce image data for a new filtered version of the original image.

`ImageFilter` A filter for the set of interface methods that are used to deliver data from an `ImageProducer` to an `ImageConsumer`.

653

IndexColorModel A ColorModel class that specifies a translation from pixel values to alphabetic red, green and blue colour components which represent indices into a fixed colour map.

MemoryImageSource An implementation of the ImageProducer interface which uses an array to produce pixel values.

PixelGrabber An implementation of the ImageConsumer which can be attached to an Image or ImageProducer object to retrieve a subset of the pixels in that image.

RGBImageFilter An abstract class that provides an easy way to create an ImageFilter which modifies the pixels of an image in the default RGB ColorModel.

ReplicateScaleFilter An ImageFilter class for scaling images using the simplest algorithm.

G.3 The Interfaces

ImageConsumer The protocol for objects which express an interest in image data through an ImageProducer interface.

ImageObserver An asynchronous update interface for receiving notification of image information as an Image is constructed.

ImageProducer The protocol for objects that can produce the image data for an Image.

Appendix H *Java Keywords*

H.1 Keywords

There are 45 keywords and 3 literals (true, false and null) in Java:

abstract	boolean	break	byte
case	catch	char	class
continue	default	do	double
else	extends	false	final
finally	float	for	if
implements	import	instanceof	int
interface	long	native	new
null	package	private	protected
public	return	short	static
super	switch	synchronized	this
throw	throws	transient	true
try	void	volatile	while

Notice that goto and const are also reserved, but they currently have no meaning.

H.2 Java Comments

There are three types of comment in Java:

//	Single line comments
/* */	C-style comments (rarely used in Java)
/** */	javadoc-style comments (used to document classes, instance and class variables, and methods)

Appendix I Java 1.2/Java 2 Core API Packages

JDK 1.2/Java 2 has added many new packages to the Java platform. The additional packages on top of those provided with JDK 1.1 are presented in Tables I.1 and I.2. This brings the number of packages to 63. Once again you must prefix the names of the packages in Table A.1 with `java`.

Table I.1 The Java 1.2 core API packages

Package name	Contents
awt.accessibility	This is part of the JFC and allows support for disabled users
awt.color	Provides improved support for platform-independent colour
awt.dnd	Support drag and drop style operations
awt.font	Provides improved support for platform-independent fonts
awt.geom	Implements various graphical facilities, including the Java2D API
awt.im	Input method support
awt.print	Improved support for printing
javax.swingx	The Swing API
javax.swingx.basic	Provides a basic look and feel implementation
javax.swingx.beaninfo	BeanInfo class for Swing components for use with JavaBeans
javax.swingx.border	Provides various border facilities
javax.swingx.event	Extensions to the event package specifically for Swing
javax.swingx.jlf	Implements Java look and feel
javax.swingx.motif	Implements Motif look and feel
javax.swingx.multi	Implements the Multi look and feel
javax.swingx.plaf	Implements support for different look and feels
javax.swingx.table	Provides the Swing table facilities
javax.swingx.target	An extension of the event handling mechanism using triggers and targets
javax.swingx.text	Improved text support including RTF and HTML
javax.swingx.tree	Support classes for creating trees
javax.swingx.undo	Provides for undo facilities in Swing
beans.beancontext	Addition support for JavaBeans
lang.ref	Support for references to objects

Table I.1 *(continued)*

Package name	Contents
`rmi.activation`	Additional support for RMI (activation of remote objects)
`security.cert`	Support for certification of applets
`security.spec`	Additional security support for keys
`util.jar`	Java archive (JAR) support classes
`util.mime`	MIME support classes

The remaining packages in JDK 1.2 (Table I.2) support the Java IDL API. These packages are all of the form `org.omg` (and thus are not prefixed by `java`).

Table I.2 JDK 1.2 packages supporting the Java IDL API

`org.omg.CORBA`	Core CORBA package
`org.omg.CORBA.ContainedPackage`	Auxiliary helper package
`org.omg.CORBA.ContainerPackage`	Auxiliary helper package
`org.omg.CORBA.InterfaceDefPackage`	Auxiliary helper package
`org.omg.CORBA.ORBPackage`	Auxiliary helper package
`org.omg.CORBA.TypeCodePackage`	Auxiliary helper package
`org.omg.CORBA.portable`	Auxiliary helper package
`org.omg.CosNaming`	Specifies the naming service for Java IDL
`org.omg.CosNaming.NamingContextPackage`	Auxiliary classes which support the naming service package

Note that at the time of writing the JDK 1.2 was in its beta4 release and thus changes could still be made between this release and the final JDK 1.2 release. In particular, the Swing components of the JFC have been the subject of many changes and the Swing 1.0.2 release (the current Swing release at time of writing) and the JDK 1.2/Java 2 release possess significant differences. Thus the exact composition of the packages may change.

Index